DATE DUE

BRODART, CO.

Cat. No. 23-221-003

HANDBOOK OF THE ECONOMICS OF EDUCATION
VOLUME 2

HANDBOOKS
IN
ECONOMICS

26

Series Editors

KENNETH J. ARROW
MICHAEL D. INTRILIGATOR

AMSTERDAM · BOSTON · HEIDELBERG · LONDON
NEW YORK · OXFORD · PARIS · SAN DIEGO
SAN FRANCISCO · SINGAPORE · SYDNEY · TOKYO

ELSEVIER

HANDBOOK OF THE ECONOMICS OF EDUCATION

VOLUME 2

Edited by

ERIC A. HANUSHEK
Hoover Institution, Stanford University, CA

and

FINIS WELCH
Welch Consulting, Bryan, TX

AMSTERDAM · BOSTON · HEIDELBERG · LONDON
NEW YORK · OXFORD · PARIS · SAN DIEGO
SAN FRANCISCO · SINGAPORE · SYDNEY · TOKYO

ELSEVIER

11355949
KSG - PED 101

North-Holland is an imprint of Elsevier
Radarweg 29, PO Box 211, 1000 AE Amsterdam, The Netherlands
The Boulevard, Langford Lane, Kidlington, Oxford OX5 1GB, UK

First edition 2006

Library of Congress Cataloging-in-Publication Data
A catalog record for this book is available from the Library of Congress

British Library Cataloguing in Publication Data
A catalogue record for this book is available from the British Library

ISBN-13: 978-0-444-52819-3
ISBN-10: 0-444-52819-9

ISSN: 0169-7218 (Handbooks in Economics series)
ISSN: 1574-0692 (Handbook of the Economics of Education series)

For information on all North-Holland publications
visit our website at books.elsevier.com

Printed and bound in The Netherlands

06 07 08 09 10   10 9 8 7 6 5 4 3 2 1

INTRODUCTION TO THE SERIES

The aim of the *Handbooks in Economics* series is to produce Handbooks for various branches of economics, each of which is a definitive source, reference, and teaching supplement for use by professional researchers and advanced graduate students. Each Handbook provides self-contained surveys of the current state of a branch of economics in the form of chapters prepared by leading specialists on various aspects of this branch of economics. These surveys summarize not only received results but also newer developments, from recent journal articles and discussion papers. Some original material is also included, but the main goal is to provide comprehensive and accessible surveys. The Handbooks are intended to provide not only useful reference volumes for professional collections but also possible supplementary readings for advanced courses for graduate students in economics.

KENNETH J. ARROW and MICHAEL D. INTRILIGATOR

CONTENTS OF THE HANDBOOK

CONTENTS OF VOLUME 2

Chapter 15
Drinking from the Fountain of Knowledge: Student Incentive to Study and
Learn – Externalities, Information Problems and Peer Pressure
JOHN BISHOP   909

Chapter 16
Schools, Teachers, and Education Outcomes in Developing Countries

Chapter 17
Has School Desegregation Improved Academic and Economic Outcomes for
Blacks?

Chapter 23
Public Intervention in Post-Secondary Education
THOMAS J. KANE

Chapter 24
US Higher Education Finance
MICHAEL S. McPHERSON AND MORTON OWEN SCHAPIRO

PREFACE

There are many ways to date the development of the economics of education. In the 17th Century, Sir William Petty began writing about the valuation of lives in terms of the productive skills of individuals – a precursor of human capital considerations. Adam Smith followed a century later with direct consideration of the organization and finance of education. Yet, the more natural dating is much more recent with the development and legitimization of the study of human capital lead by Gary Becker, Jacob Mincer, and T.W. Schultz. These initial forays have, however, been followed by a torrent of recent work.

The initial human capital contributions focused largely on differential wages of individuals as they related to skills. And, the most natural way to identify differential skills was the amount of schooling by individuals. The continuing power of this early work is seen easily by the myriad of analyses that simply note that they ran a "Mincer earnings function" – with no need to explain or to cite the original source.

The field has developed and expanded in a number of directions for the past half century. The work on the impacts of schooling on observable outcomes – labor market returns, health, and more – has grown. Increasingly detailed and sophisticated analyses have pushed the questions asked and the interpretations of existing work. For example, how does the social return to education relate to the private return? Does the growth of nations relate to schooling?

The economics of education has also reached back in the direction of understanding what goes on in schools. What factors influence the quality and outcomes of schools? How does institutional structure influence outcomes? How does finance interact with the level and distribution of outcomes?

While each of these questions entered the discussion early in the modern history of the economics of education, the recent explosion of work has introduced new developments and new approaches in each of these areas. Indeed, the standards of analysis have changed dramatically as the various subfields have developed.

Part of the explosion is undoubtedly related to the new availability of relevant data. Many countries have developed regularly available large surveys of households along with a variety of "outcome" measures. Extensive panel data sets on labor market outcomes have grown in the U.S. and increasingly in other countries. Administrative data on school operations are increasingly accessible to researchers. These sources of data are being cleverly exploited to build new knowledge about the economics of education.

The heavy influence of governments in educational policy has also contributed. Governments at all levels enter into many supply decisions – and they frequently look for analyses and evaluations that will guide their decisions.

These conditions have induced a complementary growth in the number of researchers working in the economics of education. The upsurge in Ph.D. theses related to education issues is remarkable. Similarly, while the field was once very skewed to work in the U.S. – again related to the availability of U.S. data, this is no longer the case.

One implication of this growth is that the field is rapidly developing and changing. The chapters in these volumes were designed to cover the broad range of existing research and to suggest productive lines of development. They do that. But even the relatively short production lags in these volumes imply that a number of new and exciting works are only hinted at in the chapters. In short, there is much more work to be done as this field unfolds.

A variety of factors went into the selection of authors of these chapters. Quite clearly, a fundamental requirement was that the authors had to be leaders in the intellectual development of the various topics. But, beyond that, authors were selected because they had a point of view, one designed to provoke thought and new work.

The ideas put forward here are likely to be challenged in further work. And, some may not survive such challenges. The idea is not to write the final word on any of these topics, because each is the source of lively current debate. The idea instead is to provide an intermediate assessment of dynamic research areas in order to push the research further. Perhaps the success will be judged by the intensity of future challenges to thinking in each of the areas.

The development of *Handbook* chapters is not an easy task. Blending existing work into a picture that at once categorizes the current position and simultaneously pushes research forward takes skill, insight, and simply a lot of hard work. We wish to thank each of the authors for conscientiously confronting the enormity of their assigned tasks.

The effort was also aided by the editorial and production team that has developed in the *Handbook* series, not the least of which includes the general editors of Kenneth Arrow and Michael Intriligator. It also includes Valerie Teng and the others at Elsevier. We also wish to thank the Bush School of Government and Public Service at Texas A&M. They generously hosted a conference where early versions of these papers were presented.

Eric A. Hanushek
Finis Welch
July 2006

Chapter 13

USING WAGES TO INFER SCHOOL QUALITY

ROBERT SPEAKMAN

Welch Consulting

FINIS WELCH

Unicon Research Corporation,

Welch Consulting

Contents

Handbook of the Economics of Education, Volume 2
Edited by Eric A. Hanushek and Finis Welch
© 2006 Elsevier B.V.   All rights reserved
DOI: 10.1016/S1574-0692(06)02013-7

Abstract

This chapter examines the literature that attempts to measure the relationship between labor earnings and the average quality of a state's elementary and secondary schools where school quality is approximated by statewide average characteristics like the teacher–pupil ratio. We present evidence of a number of problems which are difficult, and in our view insurmountable. In short; we argue that the Hedonic approach to inferring school quality is totally unproductive. Even so, we include an annotated bibliography of the various papers that have addressed this topic.

The main problems we discuss include: (1) interstate differences in wages are not consistent with a simple school quality–wage relation; we cannot assume a simple national labor market with factor price equalization throughout; (2) interstate migration is differentially selective between state origin and destination pairs and across school completion levels; (3) there need not be a direct relation between the quality of schooling and the wage increments from added schooling; (4) using a single residence state or geographic division for school quality evaluation appears insufficient to resolve the ambiguous link between school quality and wages.

In addition, (5) the large majority of empirical studies of school quality represent schools by using characteristics of elementary and secondary schools although a major part of the measured incremental value of schooling refers to wage gains from attending college; (6) the Census-based studies that assume schools are attended in birth states can be wide of the mark; and finally, (7) it is unclear whether the positive correlations between wages and either school expenditures or teachers' wages found in much of this literature is indicative of a causal relationship or whether it captures other economic phenomena that supersede the relationship being suggested.

Keywords

school quality, wages, returns to education

JEL classification: J31

Introduction

If there is a consensus regarding the quality of colleges and universities, it is probably closely related to the average SAT scores of entering freshmen and, perhaps, to the reputation of the their faculties. Although it may be that the general public tends to judge the quality of elementary and secondary schools similarly, that is, by the quantity of the inputs such as numbers of teachers per pupil and by the quality of the inputs such as the test scores of peers, we economists are presumably more sophisticated. We would argue for value-added measures especially given the widespread belief that the technology of education is essentially a mystery. The issue, of course, is which measures of value added should we use? Some have adopted achievement tests as a simple expedient, but even though the criticisms of using wages or income are endless, in a world of poor alternatives, it is our opinion that wages are superior to other potential choices. This chapter reviews the literature that explores the relation between wages and characteristics of schools. As such, it is a rather unpleasant piece; it points to many problems that have been largely ignored with the implication that any relation between the wage–productivity of school resources and the estimates provided by the literature may be coincidental.[1] To dispel any notion that we advocate test scores as an alternative to wages, we begin by illustrating that test scores are so poorly related to income that it is hard to imagine that if we were to use school characteristics to predict test scores, we would have unraveled the mysteries of school quality.

Let's begin with the thought experiment of measuring an individual's educational accomplishments. The completion level is suggestive, but think of all it omits. Among those who attended the same schools at the same time and completed the same number of grades there will be differences that depend on school and home resources, paths chosen, levels of effort, endowments and the randomness of teacher assignment. School standards will also have an effect since lower standards permit greater diversity. Among those who attend the same schools at different times, in addition to the sources of differentials just mentioned, there will be differences in school standards and emphasis as well as in one's own expectations and the expectations of parents and peers. Now, add the complexity of large heterogeneous school districts along with differences among districts and it seems, a priori, that the level of schooling, i.e., the number of grades completed, may carry little information of, for example, wage potential. We mention this because, believe it or not, the nominal level of an individual's schooling is at least as good a predictor of his or her salary as is test measured achievement.

If you examine the wage literature, you will be hard pressed to find a large number of cases where the standard deviation of (log) wage or annual earnings residuals from individuals matched on gender, age, race or ethnicity, and school completion is less

---

[1] One exception is the excellent criticism of much of this work by Heckman, Layne-Farrar and Todd (1996) which focuses primarily on the Card and Krueger (1992a, 1992b) papers. See also Speakman and Welch (1995).

than 0.25. A simple way of interpreting the differences in wages that are predicted by a logarithmic standard deviation of 0.25 is to calculate the average difference that one expects to observe between two individuals selected at random and, in this case, the expectation is roughly 36 percent. That is, on average, the higher wage will exceed the lower wage by 36 percent. This difference is less than the average difference that we find between high school and college graduates today, but it exceeds the college wage premium of the mid- to late-1970s. The point is simply that, for other things – age, sex, race – equal, there is a lot of wage diversity among individuals with the same level of school completion. If the level of one's schooling measures the quality of the school attended, it is at best a noisy measure. This said, Table 1 summarizes comparisons between the ability of the level of individual school completion and the AFQT (the Armed Forces Qualifying Test) to predict wages.

The data are from the NLSY79 and follow the sample selections and variable definitions used by Johnson and Neal (1996). The top panel of the table lists partial correlations between individual wages and the AFQT score in the first column and the level of school completion in the second column. Neither for men nor for women does the AFQT "explain" a higher fraction of the residual wage variation, after age and race is regressed out, than does the level of school completion. The lower panel in Table 1 lists the wage gradients on the AFQT test score from a regression of (log) wages on the AFQT score, age, race and the level of schooling. The coefficients are scaled to indicate the logarithmic wage increase that is estimated to be associated with a one standard deviation increase in the test score. For comparison, the note to the table indicates that

Table 1
AFQT scores and highest grade completed in wage predictors from NLSY79

Other controls	Partial R^2	
	AFQT	Schooling
Men		
Age and race	0.110	0.123
Add schooling	0.034	–
Add AFQT	–	0.048
Women		
Age and race	0.146	0.183
Add schooling	0.036	–
Add AFQT	–	0.078
Linear gradients for AFQT score conditional on schooling		
(AFQT scaled to unit standard deviation)		
Men	0.101 (std. error 0.015)	
Women	0.125 (std. error 0.018)	

Note. Calculations are based on a replication of Johnson and Neal (1996). At the center of a normal distribution, a one-standard deviation increase in AFQT score will increase the percentile score by 38.3 points.

at the center of a normal distribution, a one standard deviation increase (from one-half of a standard deviation below the mean to one-half above) will contain 38.3 percent of the population. The point is that, holding the level of school completion constant, a one-percentile increase in the score is predicted to increase wages by only about one-third of a percent;[2] which is the same thing, if your score exceeds by a whopping 10 percentile points that of a classmate who is the same age, sex, race and grade completion level, then you can *expect* to earn an amazing 3 percent more than him or her!

This chapter is arranged in two parts. After a brief outline of the literature, Part I addresses problems associated with a major branch of the literature that attempts to assess the statewide average quality of elementary and secondary schools using income data from the U.S. Censuses of Population and Housing. Among the working populations whose incomes are studied, the Census provides information neither of the state where an individual attended school nor whether the schools attended were private or public. Most of the Census-based studies use state of birth to approximate the state where the individual attended school while Welch (1966) uses state of residence for farm families. In addition to not knowing where the individuals attended school, the other problems considered involve the market determination of wages where, for example, increased school quality may lower wages, the vagaries of selective interstate migration, the problem of deducing the effects of elementary and secondary schooling from populations where nontrivial proportions attend college and inferences regarding the quality of colleges are not and cannot be addressed, and so forth. Part II is more structured. It is a summary of the literature.

The summary of the literature is not critical. Rather, after identifying each study, it describes the source of the earning data, the population studied, the source of the school data, and the school variables used to attempt to infer quality. Next, the empirical model is outlined along with a description of variables other than the school ones. Finally, the author's conclusions are reported. We have restricted attention to published studies that examine earnings for those educated, often inferred by place of birth, in the US. In reviewing our outline, please note that if there is a consensus it is that wages are positively correlated with either school's expenditures, which are dominated by teacher costs, or teacher salaries per se. We note this relation out of a concern that it may be spurious in the sense that in the cross-section, wages for one group may be positively correlated with the wages of others for reasons that supercede the causality of teacher to student.[3]

---

[2] For men, the calculation is $0.101/0.383 = 0.26$, and for women it is $0.125/0.383 = 0.33$.

[3] There are large interstate differences in wages and costs-of-living. The current differentials appear to have persisted throughout the range of the available data; wages are low in Mississippi, South Carolina and Arkansas and they are high in Pennsylvania, New Jersey and New York. Most wage earning adults reside in the state of their birth, so if – across states – we compare wages today with teacher salaries or educational expenditures in earlier periods, we expect positive covariances. A few papers, notably, Card and Krueger (1992a) and Heckman, Layne-Farrar and Todd (1996), adjust teachers salaries for area wide differences in wages, but the large majority of the papers ignore this confounding influence.

Part I. Problems

The summary of the literature in Part II includes studies that examine wage and individual characteristics taken from a wide variety of sources: the U.S. Decennial Censuses (1960–1990), various releases of the original cohort files of the National Longitudinal Surveys of Young Men and Young Women (NLS-YM and NLS-YW), the NBER–Thorndike data, the Panel Survey of Income Dynamics (PSID), the National Longitudinal Survey of Youth 1979 (NLSY79), High School and Beyond (HSB), the National Longitudinal Study of the High School Class of 1972 (NLS72), Project Talent, the Postcensal Survey of Professional and Technical Manpower (conducted in 1962), and a Minnesota Twin Registry survey.

Several of these sources – NLS-YM, NLS-YW, NLSY79, HSB and NLS72 – provide school characteristics from the high schools or districts attended by the respondents. Available information that has been utilized includes district level expenditures per pupil in average daily attendance (both adjusted and unadjusted for cost-of-living differences), teachers per pupil, counselors per pupil, the starting pay of teachers with a bachelor's degree, school enrollment, library books per student, the percent of teachers with a master's degree, and the curriculum available.

The remainder of the earnings data sources are combined with school characteristic data from alternative sources. Most have relied upon the information contained in the *Biennial Survey of Education*[4] and the *Digest of Education Statistics*[5] matched to the state of birth (most Census studies) or state of residence at age 12 (all PSID studies) or the city where attended high school (some NBER–Thorndike studies[6]) to the earnings data. The *Biennial Survey* reports statewide averages of expenditures, teacher salaries, pupils enrolled and pupils in average daily attendance, term lengths, and other variables in even-numbered school years from 1918 to 1958 for public elementary and secondary

---

[4] U.S. Department of Health, Education, and Welfare, Office of Education: the *Biennial Survey of Education in the United States*, Washington, DC, 1918–1958. In the earlier years, the *Survey* was published by the U.S. Department of the Interior (1918–1936) and the Federal Security Agency (1938–1948) and, in the first several years it was published by the Bureau of Education (part of the Department of the Interior).

[5] U.S. Department of Health, Education, and Welfare, Education Division, National Center for Education Statistics: the *Digest of Education Statistics*, Washington, DC, 1962–2002. Publications through 1974 were titled the *Digest of Educational Statistics* and were published by the following organizations within the U.S. Office of Education: Division of Educational Statistics (1962–1964), Bureau of Educational Research and Development (1965), the National Center for Educational Statistics (1966–1973), and the National Center of Education Statistics (1974).

[6] We would include two studies by Wachtel (1975, 1976) and one by Link and Ratledge (1976) in this category. These authors cite the *Biennial Survey* and appear to use city level data published for large city school systems matched to the high school attended in the NBER–Thorndike survey.

schools.[7] Data is reported separately by race for white and black schools in 18 states[8] with segregated school systems from 1918 until the *Brown v. Board of Education* decision in 1954. The *Digest of Education Statistics* continued where the *Biennial Surveys* left off and has been published annually since 1962.[9]

While almost all of the studies we summarize focus exclusively on elementary and high school characteristics, there are a handful that examine characteristics of the college attended such as expenditures per full-time equivalent student, faculty salaries, and faculty per full-time equivalent student. This information has been gleaned from publications by the U.S. Office of Education, the Integrated Postsecondary Education Data System (IPEDS), Barron's Guides and CASPAR data. In addition, some have attempted to use rankings of colleges such as those produced by Gourman (1967), Carter (1966), Astin (1965) and Cass and Birnbaum (1964) as a proxy for college quality.[10]

Although it is clear that data is available for many inputs that might enter into the production of education, most of the studies documented examine primarily expenditures per pupil or teacher salaries, a major component of total expenditures. We find this peculiar given that the production function for education is essentially a mystery and the ways schools spend money is likely to be as important as the amount spent. Equally important if the purpose of the analysis is to inform public policy, a recommendation either to spend more or to spend less does not appear to be especially informative.

In the remainder of this part we address empirical and theoretical problems that require consideration before proceeding to estimating the wage–school quality relation. Since, with few exceptions, the papers that we review proceed as though there is a simple direct relation, we begin by describing the relation to be expected in a market with well-specified prices of labor attributes where problems of selective ability and migration, fallible assumptions, regional differences in costs-of-living, etc. can be ignored.

Wage variation

Figure 1 is illustrative. The comparison is between products of two schools where school quality is higher in one than in the other. In each case the wage increases with the level of schooling but the increase is faster for students of the higher-quality school where,

---

[7] We would include two studies by Wachtel (1975, 1976) and one by Link and Ratledge (1976) in this category. These authors cite the *Biennial Survey* and appear to use city level data published for city school systems matched to the high school attended in the NBER–Thorndike survey.

[8] They are Alabama, Arkansas, Delaware, District of Columbia, Florida, Georgia, Kentucky, Louisiana, Maryland, Mississippi, Missouri, North Carolina, Oklahoma, South Carolina, Tennessee, Texas, Virginia and West Virginia.

[9] Except for combined editions that were issued in 1977–1978, 1983–1984 and 1985–1986.

[10] Gourman (1967), *The Gourman Report*. Carter (1966), *An Assessment of Quality in Graduate Education*. Astin (1965), *Who Goes Where to College*. Cass and Birnbaum (1964), *Comparative Guide to American Colleges*.

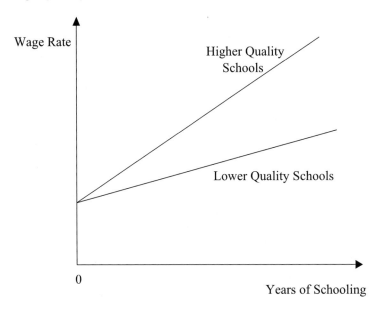

Figure 1. Illustrative wage–schooling profiles contrasting students from lower- and higher-quality schools.

by assumption, a year of schooling resulted in greater learning (more education). Note, however, that as the wage profiles are projected to zero schooling, they converge because at zero schooling there can be no school quality differential.

The point of the figure is that if the students from the two schools were matched on levels of schooling, the wage difference between the two will increase with the level of schooling.

Table 2 uses data from the 1980 and 1990 U.S. Censuses to examine dispersion in weekly wages of men employed full time, by level of schooling. The purpose is to compare what is to what we might hope to expect if school quality was the primary source of wage differentials among individuals matched on age and schooling.

The calculations summarized in Table 2 are standard deviations of regression coefficients. There are separate regressions for each of the indicated schooling levels and age intervals. The regressions include indicators for state-of-birth and state-of-residence and a wage is predicted for each state-of-birth, as though the individuals considered in the prediction also resided in that state. The table includes results of regressions where the wage is expressed both in logarithmic and arithmetic terms.

Beginning with the 1980 Census, where schooling levels were reported in terms of years (or grades) completed, we see that contrary to the simple expectation that wages diverge as the level of schooling increases through the grade completion levels, 1–12, the converse is true; the interstate wage differentials narrow.

Table 2
Differences between states in age-adjusted weekly wages of representative individuals

Years of school completed	Standard deviations of wages					
	Logarithmic			Arithmetic		
	Ages 30–39	Ages 40–49	Ages 50–59	Ages 30–39	Ages 40–49	Ages 50–59
1980 Census						
1	0.69	0.49	0.47	$189	$102	$108
2	0.39	0.39	0.37	83	113	91
3	0.46	0.34	0.28	83	80	62
4	0.41	0.30	0.26	83	70	70
5	0.38	0.22	0.19	58	62	40
6	0.18	0.14	0.14	45	33	34
7	0.15	0.13	0.12	39	38	31
8	0.09	0.10	0.10	22	27	27
9	0.10	0.12	0.11	27	34	32
10	0.10	0.11	0.11	29	35	32
11	0.11	0.11	0.09	31	35	28
12	0.08	0.09	0.08	28	30	28
13	0.09	0.10	0.10	30	36	38
14	0.08	0.11	0.10	29	41	37
15	0.08	0.11	0.11	29	43	42
16	0.07	0.09	0.08	28	41	40
17	0.07	0.11	0.13	29	52	61
18	0.09	0.10	0.13	38	49	59
19	0.11	0.15	0.16	42	72	73
20	0.10	0.10	0.12	43	51	56
1990 Census						
1–4 years	0.29	0.40	0.25	$68	$140	$128
5–8 years	0.14	0.12	0.11	48	48	44
9 years	0.10	0.13	0.11	38	52	48
10 years	0.12	0.12	0.12	47	53	58
11 years	0.10	0.13	0.13	43	69	61
12 years, no degree	0.11	0.10	0.13	47	53	60
High school degree[a]	0.10	0.10	0.10	47	57	54
Some college	0.11	0.11	0.11	58	65	69
AA, vocational	0.12	0.12	0.14	65	73	78
AA, academic	0.10	0.11	0.14	53	70	87
Bachelor's degree	0.11	0.12	0.12	70	88	97
Master's degree	0.13	0.13	0.14	91	106	115
Professional degree	0.13	0.11	0.13	111	115	136
Doctorate degree	0.20	0.11	0.15	148	102	127

[a]Or equivalent.

The "theory", such as it is, is that the divergence will occur arithmetically with no prediction for logarithmic divergence, but the arithmetic *convergence* that we see also appears to hold for the logarithmic differentials as well.

The second panel of Table 2, for the 1990 Census, reveals similar patterns so it appears state differences in wages are affected by factors in addition to the possible effects of differences in school quality.

Migration and schooling

Welch (1966, 1970) shows that among farm operator families, differences between states in the relative wages of more highly educated farmers are sensitive to differences in average levels of schooling. On balance, in those states where college educated farmers were abundant, the relative wage of college trained farmers is lower. Although the evidence is for wages in 1960 and for farmers where an assumption of interstate migration to equate wages might be questionable, it, together with the data summarized in Table 2, raises a question as to whether in modeling the wage–school quality relations we want to think of the US as a single-national labor market or as a conglomeration of related but somewhat independent markets.

To maintain a national labor market, labor must be mobile. Table 3, from the 1990 Census, provides interstate mobility summaries by schooling level. For practical purposes the relation is monotone; the higher the level of schooling, the higher the probability that an individual will not reside in the state of his birth. Among white men

Table 3

State of birth and state of residence among white men ages 30–59, 1990 Census

	Not living in state of birth	Living in state of birth
Schooling		
1–4 years	27.3	72.7
5–8 years	27.3	72.7
9 years	28.4	71.6
10 years	29.2	70.8
11 years	29.8	70.2
12 years, no degree	32.3	67.7
High school graduate	30.2	69.8
College, no degree	41.2	58.8
AA, vocational	37.8	62.2
AA, academic	42.5	47.5
Bachelors	49.0	51.0
Masters	55.6	44.4
Professional	51.8	48.2
Doctorate	71.8	28.2

30–59 years old, 72.7 percent of those who completed only 1–4 grades reside in the state of their birth. In contrast, only 28.2 percent of the men with doctorate degrees live in the state where they were born.

The interstate mobility of college graduates may be sufficient for us to assume that the market for college graduates is national and that systematic differences in wages among individuals with different training experiences, i.e., those attending different schools as an example, refer to differences in their productivities. Even so, inferences in school quality are drawn from calculations of the way that *additional* schooling enhances income. For this purpose, factor–price equality at one end of the schooling spectrum is not sufficient for the inference of a national market.

Wages and school quality

Suppose that aggregate output is a function of the stock of school-trained labor, which we refer to as aggregate education E, and a numeraire input X.

$$Y = f(E, X), \tag{1}$$

where education is the sum, over schooling levels s, of the education of those who completed s grades and no more, i.e.,

$$E = \sum_s E(s) = \sum_s N(s)e(Q_s, s) \tag{2}$$

with $N(s)$ being the number who completed s grades and $e(Q_s, s)$ measures their average school acquired job skills. This average $e(Q_s, s)$ depends both on school quality, at s, and the level of schooling.

There is a technological issue regarding the nature of the relation, $e(Q_s, s)$. In much of the literature there is an implicit assumption that it is multiplicative, i.e.,

$$e = Q_s h(s). \tag{3a}$$

In this form, if the quality of schools in one place is twice that of another then regardless of the level of schooling, so long as students from the two places are matched on schooling, those from the superior school system will have twice as much "education" as students from the inferior system. In this form, $h(s)$ is the effective units of "schooling" for one at s, in Mincer's (1974) famous specification, $h(s)$ is a simple exponential, i.e., $e = Q \exp(s)$.

The alternative specification used by Card and Krueger (1992a) is exponential in both s and Q. It is

$$e = \exp\{s(a_0 + a_1 Q_s)\} \tag{3b}$$

so that for fixed quality differentials between school systems, the logarithmic educational differential increases with the level of schooling.

In what follows we use the simpler, (3a), specification. The analysis with (3b) is left as an exercise for the reader. In this form, the marginal product of a representative individual with schooling s is

$$\frac{\partial Y}{\partial N(s)} = Q_s h(s) f_1 \tag{4}$$

with wages expressed relative to the numeraire as

$$w(s) = Q_s h(s) \frac{f_1}{f_2}. \tag{4'}$$

In this form the ratio f_1/f_2 is the unit price of education so that the wage is the quantity of education times its unit price.

Now assume that school quality is uniform over s and consider the effect of an increase in quality.

$$\frac{\partial w(s)}{\partial Q} = h(s) \frac{f_1}{f_2} + Q h(s) \frac{\partial (f_1/f_2)}{\partial E} \frac{\partial E}{\partial Q}. \tag{5}$$

Notice that the second term on the right-hand side of Equation (5) is the effect of increasing school quality on the stock of education and, therefore, on its price. Since, holding the distribution of school completion constant, an increase in school quality will increase the stock of education, the effect must be to lower its price. Note also that if the labor market was truly national, we could ignore the second term on the right-hand side of Equation (5) since an increase in the quality of schools in the areas typically studied in the literature would not have an appreciable effect on the aggregate stock of education.

$$\frac{\partial (f_1/f_2)}{\partial E} = (f_2 f_{11} - f_1 f_{12}) f_2^{-2} \tag{6}$$

which, if $f(\cdot, \cdot)$ is linear homogeneous, becomes

$$\frac{\partial (f_1/f_2)}{\partial E} = -\frac{f_1}{f_2} \frac{1}{E} \frac{1}{\sigma}, \tag{6'}$$

where σ is the elasticity of substitution between E and X in f, i.e., $\sigma = f_1 f_2/(y f_{12})$, $y = E f_1 + X f_2$ and $E f_{11} + X f_{12} = 0$.

Because $\frac{\partial (f_1/f_2)}{\partial Q} = \frac{\partial (f_1/f_2)}{\partial E} \frac{\partial E}{\partial Q}$ it follows that

$$\frac{\partial (f_1/f_2)}{\partial Q} = \frac{f_1}{f_2} \left(-\frac{1}{\sigma} \right) \frac{1}{E} \frac{\partial E}{\partial Q} \tag{6''}$$

and with uniform Q, $E = Q \sum_s N(s) h(s)$. It is obvious that holding the distribution of schooling constant that $\frac{Q}{E} \frac{\partial E}{\partial Q} \equiv 1$.

Thus from Equations (5) and (6''),

$$\frac{Q}{\partial Q} \frac{\partial w(s)}{\partial Q} = w(s) \left(1 - \frac{1}{\sigma} \right) \tag{7}$$

and

$$\frac{\partial \ln w(s)}{\partial \ln Q} = \frac{\sigma - 1}{\sigma}. \tag{7'}$$

In the two-factor case the elasticity of substitution is (the negative of) the demand elasticity and we are reminded that if demand is inelastic, $\sigma < 1$, holding other things constant, an increase in quality of schooling will *lower* wages. More, if demand is of unit elasticity, $\sigma = 1$, there is *no* relation between school quality and wages. We point this out to amplify our main point thus far that since the data do not appear to be consistent with exogenous labor factor prices, empirical investigations of the wage–school quality relation ought to consider the endogeneity of wages.

Wages by birth and residence states

In an attempt to recognize the potential endogeneity of wages, Card and Krueger (1992a) modeled them as dependent both on the state-of-birth (and the characteristics of public elementary and secondary schools in that state) and the geographic division of current residence. The 50 US states are arranged into nine Census divisions. With the exception of the Pacific Division which includes Alaska, Hawaii along with California, Oregon and Washington, the divisions consist of geographically adjacent states. The division of residence is intended to represent the labor market so by comparing people who were born in and presumably attended schools in different states who reside and work in the same labor market, the problem of resolving the endogeneity of wages is assumed to be resolved.

We are frankly attracted by the approach but, as is true of any empirical assumption, the proof is not conjectural. To pursue the validity of the assumption that issues of wage determination could be resolved by pairing birth and residence data, we selected a sample of white men aged 30–59 who had reportedly graduated from high school and did not report having completed any post-high school education. To be included in our sample an individual must reside in one of the 10 states where the largest numbers of interstate migrants reside and must have been born in one of the 10 states that supply the largest numbers of interstate migrants.

The idea is to examine average wage rankings across birth states to see whether they are invariant with respect to residence. Put simply, suppose the schools in New York are superior to those in Texas. If so, we might reasonably expect that high school graduates from New York would earn more than high school graduates from Texas as long as their productivity is evaluated the same way, that is, in the same market.

The results of our comparisons are displayed in Table 4. The age-adjusted wage rates in Table 4 are reported in logarithms. To simplify the comparison – the reported wages are relative to a fixed weight index of the average wage of residents who were born in one of the four states that provide the largest number of interstate migrants. The reference states are New York, Pennsylvania, Illinois and Ohio. The reference wage

Table 4

Log wage differential of high school graduates in selected states of residence between those born in indicated states and a fixed weight average wage for those born in four reference states

Residence	Birth state									
	CA	IL	MA	MI	MO	NJ	NY	OH	PA	TX
Ages 30–39										
CA	2.3	−2.0	7.9	0.6	−3.1	6.2	5.1	−3.7	−3.5	−4.4
FL	−5.6	−4.2	1.1	1.0	−4.9	4.2	3.7	−3.4	−0.4	0.5
IL	−0.8	−2.2	25.4	12.1	−13.2	−14.6	−2.7	2.2	3.7	−8.1
MI	13.7	−10.1	−30.6	−0.7	−8.2	6.4	−3.7	7.7	6.2	−16.3
NJ	−16.3	4.2	0.5	−0.8	13.1	−2.9	4.3	−7.7	−3.4	−4.4
NY	−0.9	6.1	−1.6	−0.2	28.2	14.1	5.7	−2.2	−10.2	−0.5
NC	−14.6	−9.7	−8.9	3.7	0.2	6.2	5.0	−0.1	−1.0	−7.0
OH	6.3	−8.2	−7.9	5.6	−7.8	−0.7	−0.5	1.3	4.8	−8.3
PA	−11.1	−10.2	1.5	21.2	−21.3	15.0	0.8	3.6	2.7	7.8
TX	−13.8	−4.4	4.0	−7.9	−7.6	−2.4	2.5	−7.0	3.8	−8.5
Ages 40–49										
CA	0.5	3.5	1.5	2.5	−5.2	0.3	0.5	−7.6	2.2	−7.4
FL	−6.7	1.8	−2.7	1.1	8.2	−0.8	0.1	−9.6	5.2	0.1
IL	−10.1	−9.9	3.4	−11.1	−5.4	10.2	1.0	1.4	3.7	−7.7
MI	19.5	−21.5	2.9	−4.3	−4.7	−3.9	1.3	5.6	7.5	13.8
NJ	−26.6	−13.4	−6.5	−29.0	24.9	−1.8	11.4	−8.8	−1.9	15.8
NY	10.0	−22.8	25.8	31.9	12.0	6.2	10.5	−5.4	2.7	9.8
NC	−20.8	22.8	−2.5	17.2	−42.8	0.2	−8.0	1.1	−3.4	28.5
OH	7.6	−3.7	19.1	3.0	12.0	0.0	−0.7	−0.3	3.4	3.2
PA	−38.6	16.8	−1.3	8.1	13.8	2.4	−3.0	−3.4	−3.8	3.1
TX	−17.4	2.6	−0.4	−6.5	−0.5	10.5	−2.9	−8.0	7.7	−13.4
Ages 50–59										
CA	−3.7	3.4	2.8	2.5	−7.0	0.5	3.6	−5.5	−3.4	−13.1
FL	−5.8	−3.8	−5.6	−2.7	2.0	−1.6	−0.5	−4.0	5.7	−10.9
IL	−0.4	−19.2	−66.2	−7.8	−12.6	25.1	11.1	1.0	−4.5	−19.1
MI	−29.7	−11.6	−12.9	−7.5	−2.1	57.9	7.4	−2.4	−1.6	−1.9
NJ	26.4	−9.7	13.0	23.2	30.0	−3.9	10.8	−9.5	−2.9	15.2
NY	49.2	15.0	−3.2	−1.5	−20.8	8.9	0.4	−17.1	1.7	−10.2
NC	56.9	1.1	−6.9	−10.9	−12.9	5.7	3.8	4.7	−9.1	27.4
OH	31.0	11.1	−13.9	−7.4	−22.8	−2.8	2.7	−10.8	−3.3	15.6
PA	6.7	18.8	20.2	−23.3	25.0	−11.4	−3.9	1.0	−6.7	−45.5
TX	−13.4	−4.6	−7.0	−18.8	1.7	−18.6	6.2	−16.3	5.0	−9.7

Notes. The 10 residence states are those with the largest number of residents who were born outside the state. The 10 birth states are those originating the largest numbers of interstate migrants. Wages are age adjusted via regression to the mid-point of the indicated age interval. New York, Pennsylvania, Illinois and Ohio are the only four states that individually provide at least five percent of the US interstate migrant population. Log wages for each residence/birth state pair are deflated using a fixed weight average of the age adjusted wages of high school graduates living in the indicated residence states and born in the four reference states. Weights are the proportion of interstate migrants, living in the selected residence states, ages 30–59 from each of the four birth states.

index is calculated separately for each of the 10 residence states shown. For example, among the residents of California who were born in one of the four reference states, we compute an average age-adjusted wage, first by averaging the wage within the birth state and then averaging over the four reference states. Moving down the rows of Table 4, we next calculate a reference wage for residents of Florida, then Illinois, and so forth. In each case the birth-state averages for the four reference states are combined using the same fixed weights.

The numbers in Table 4 are the logarithmic differences between the average age-adjusted wage for indicated birth state and the corresponding average for the reference states. Ideally, if the controls work, then aside from sampling error, if one reads down a column of Table 4 to hold birth state constant, but across states of residence (the rows), the numbers should remain constant.

We do not report sampling errors for these numbers because they are small relative to the variability we observe. The high school graduates born in California earn 13.7 percent more than the reference wage in Michigan, but 16.3 percent less than it in New Jersey. Those born in Massachusetts are even more extreme. In Illinois they earn a 25.4 percent premium but they suffer a 30.6 percent penalty in Michigan! These comparisons are drawn from the aged 30–39 panel of Table 4. The more extreme cases are in the panel for ages 50–59 where, for example, the California advantage in North Carolina is 56.9 percent alongside a disadvantage of 29.7 percent in Michigan.

The purpose of Table 4 is to see whether we can comfortably infer school quality by controlling for residence state. To see where this takes us, let's compare the wages of high school graduates who were born in California to those born in Illinois among men 30–39. If they reside in California, Illinois, Michigan or Ohio then the California born earn more than those from Illinois so we can infer that California schools are "better" than schools in Illinois. However, the inference from the California versus Illinois birth comparisons for residents of Florida, New Jersey, New York, North Carolina, Pennsylvania or Texas is the opposite; schools in Illinois are better than in California.

The California–Illinois comparison involves the first two birth states in the first of the three panels of Table 4. Among the three panels are a total of 135 pair-wise comparisons. The inconsistency noted for the California–Illinois comparison is typical.

The role of college in valuing elementary and secondary school inputs

Invariably, the empirical wage–school quality literature attempts to compare the incremental value of an additional year of schooling to school characteristics. In the majority of cases school characteristics refer to only public elementary and secondary schools but the wage information includes those who have attended college. The fact of college attendance is troublesome because the continuation rate into college as well as performance in college is undoubtedly affected by the quality of the preparation which presumably interacts with student abilities and family backgrounds. Even so, it may seem strange to infer quality of elementary and secondary schools from wages of those who have attended college.

To illustrate what is at issue, consider the following example:

Average weekly wages by school completion – an illustration

Attended elementary and secondary in	Completed		
	8 grades	High school	College
Region A	$225	$315	$474
Region B	$225	$315	$410

Although we know that those represented in the first row of the illustration attended elementary and secondary school in Region A, we know nothing about the college(s) they subsequently attended. Similarly, we know nothing about the colleges of those from Region B. Which region has the better elementary and secondary schools? Would a sane person seriously venture a guess? On the one hand, students from Region A gained more from attending college than those from Region B, so schools in Region A must be better than those from Region B. On the other hand, high school completion in Region B is valued equally with Region A, but college is less valuable. Clearly the students from Region B are less able but the schools are better! We suspect that none of us would be comfortable drawing either conclusion. Consider a simple regression of wages on school completion of the form

$$y = a + bs(\ell) + u \qquad (8)$$

with y being the income or wage or its logarithm and $s(\ell)$ being the school years associated with level ℓ. In this case the calculated gradient, $\hat{b}$, is a measure of the incremental value of a year of schooling and, despite the illustration, is typically viewed in the literature as being positively related to the quality of the schools attended.

The regression calculation is $\hat{b} = \sum_{i,\ell} y_{i\ell}(s_{i\ell} - \bar{s}) / \sum_{i,\ell}(s_{i\ell} - \bar{s})^2$ which simplifies to $\hat{b} = \sum_{\ell} N_{\ell} y_{\ell}(s_{\ell} - \bar{s}) / \sum_{\ell} N_{\ell}(s_{\ell} - s)^2$, where N_{ℓ} is the number of observations at level ℓ and y_{ℓ} is the mean of y at ℓ and $\bar{s}$ is the population mean of s.

Now consider the differences between the adjacent values of y_{ℓ}, normalized by the school year differences between them:

$$\begin{cases} \tilde{y}_1 = \frac{y_1 - y_0}{s_1 - s_0}, \\ \tilde{y}_2 = \frac{y_2 - y_1}{s_2 - s_1}, \\ \tilde{y}_N = \frac{y_N - y_{N-1}}{s_N - s_{N-1}}. \end{cases} \qquad (9)$$

Each value in this series measures the average incremental value of a year of schooling over the completion interval that is indicated. Since $\hat{b}$ measures an average increment over the full span, s_0 to s_N, it must be an average of the components in Equation (9).

Although we do not provide the derivation, readers are invited to verify that

$$\hat{b} \equiv \sum_{j=1}^{N} \omega_j \tilde{y}_j,$$ (10)

where $\omega_j = (s_j - s_{j-1}) \sum_{i=j}^{N} N_i (s_i - \bar{s})/\Delta$ with $\Delta = \sum_{\ell=0}^{N} N_\ell (s_\ell - \bar{s})^2$. Moreover, $\omega_j > 0$ and $\sum_{j=1}^{N} \omega_j = 1$ so that the average in (10) is a simple one. Notice that the weights depend exclusively on the distribution of completion levels.

Table 5 provides the national average (age-adjusted) log wage differentials associated with an additional year of schooling from the 1980 Census. These differentials, in Table 5a, are presented only for reference to show that wage growth is not uniform across the various levels. For example, there is a clear "sheepskin" effect with completion of high school (the 12–11 grade differential) adding 10.7 percent to weekly wages and with completion of college (the 16–15 differential) adding 19.9 percent. Since the regression method of averaging depends on the schooling distribution, it follows that if regressions were run on identical wage increments to those listed in Table 5a, the calculated averages will vary with differences in distributions of completion levels.

Table 5b reports the aggregated weights associated with college attendance. In the top panel there is a line separating the differentials that involve post-secondary attendance

Table 5a
National average (log) weekly wage differences, age adjusted for adjacent levels of schooling (1980 Census)

Grades	Wage difference	Grades	Wage difference	Grades	Wage difference	Grades	Wage difference
1–0	0.1567	6–5	0.0697	11–10	0.0432	16–15	0.1987
2–1	0.0368	7–6	0.0611	12–11	0.1005	17–16	0.0236
3–2	−0.0510	8–7	0.0747	13–12	0.0722	18–17	0.0613
4–3	0.0957	9–8	0.0698	14–13	0.0501	19–18	−0.0232
5–4	−0.0085	10–9	0.0488	15–14	0.0370	20–19	0.1253

Note. Linear regressions of wages on years of school completed produce a single gradient that is a weighted average of differences such as these. The weights depend on the distributions of school years completed.

Table 5b
The fraction of the weights assigned to post-secondary gradients for selected state-of-birth, state-of-residence pairs

Birth	Residence		
	California	New York	Texas
California	0.793	0.856	0.715
New York	0.854	0.736	0.834
Texas	0.565	0.837	0.518

from those that do not. The lower panel reports the aggregated regression weights [defined in Equation (10)] that are associated with college-based wage differentials. Recall from Table 2 that interstate migration is educationally selective. That, in part, accounts for the amazingly high off diagonal fractions in the panel.

It should be noted that the three states in Table 5b are selected only for illustrative purposes. They were *not* selected because the weights that are associated with college attendance are high.

The difference between the state of birth and the state of school attendance

We end our recitation of problems with a simple comparison.

Table 6 lists the 50 US states and the District of Columbia. Beside each state there are two numbers. The first is the fraction of students who were born in the indicated state that are attending public school in that state. The denominator for this calculation is the number of students born in the indicated state regardless of where they were attending school in 1990. The second number refers to all students attending public school in the indicated state so that the proportion shown is the percentage of those who were born in the state. For clarity, DC is a good example.

For the District of Columbia, only 23.9 percent of the students born there attend public schools in the district, but 67.9 percent of those attending public schools in the district were born there.

The first of the two columns is relevant to the assumption in the Census-based studies regarding the location of schools attended. While it seems valid for the majority, there is a nontrivial margin of error.

Summary and conclusions

To summarize this part of our chapter:

(1) Interstate differences in wages are not consistent with a simple school quality–wage relation; we cannot assume a simple national labor market with factor price equalization throughout;

(2) interstate migration is selective vis-à-vis school completion;

(3) there need not be a direct relation between the quality of schooling and the wage increments from added schooling; and

(4) using a single residence state or geographic division for school quality evaluation appears insufficient to resolve the ambiguous link between school quality and wages. Inferences regarding relative quality vary immensely depending on the site of the evaluation. Quite possibly, the ability selectiveness of interstate migration depends both on origin and destination.

Moreover,

(5) the large majority of empirical studies of school quality represent schools by using characteristics of elementary and secondary schools although a major part of

Table 6

Public school attendance among those enrolled in kindergarten, elementary and secondary schools (1990 Census)

State	Percentage of those		State		
	Born in state who are attending public schools in state	Residing in state who are attending public schools and were born in state	State	Born in state who are attending public schools in state	Residing in state who are attending public schools and were born in state
AL	76.8	75.5	MT	67.0	69.1
AK	57.1	56.8	NE	65.8	70.5
AZ	70.9	61.3	NV	61.4	46.6
AR	73.6	71.0	NH	64.6	55.3
CA	76.6	76.5	NJ	67.9	67.4
CO	64.8	63.9	NM	69.0	66.3
CT	71.0	69.4	NY	68.9	77.2
DE	57.9	58.3	NC	79.2	75.1
DC	23.9	67.9	ND	63.4	77.4
FL	70.9	57.0	OH	73.8	77.0
GA	77.0	71.1	OK	73.1	70.7
HI	56.9	66.4	OR	69.6	66.2
ID	66.1	66.4	PA	71.2	72.9
IL	69.0	74.8	RI	64.6	68.8
IN	74.6	76.3	SC	76.5	72.7
IA	71.0	76.8	SD	67.1	72.0
KS	68.1	66.4	TN	73.2	73.5
KY	72.4	75.4	TX	80.4	78.9
LA	70.0	75.9	UT	74.8	79.0
ME	80.5	71.8	VT	73.3	65.9
MD	69.3	59.1	VA	71.1	65.2
MA	70.3	75.6	WA	72.6	64.4
MI	77.6	79.1	WV	69.9	76.2
MN	76.4	75.9	WI	74.1	72.6
MS	71.4	73.6	WY	56.5	58.6
MO	67.9	69.6			

the measured incremental value of schooling refers to wage gains from attending college; and finally,

(6) the Census-based studies that assume schools are attended in birth states can be wide of the mark. According to the 1990 Census, among school-aged children attending elementary and secondary schools who were born in the District of Columbia, only 23.9 percent attend public schools in the district. The corresponding numbers for Wyoming, Hawaii and Alaska are 56.5 percent, 56.9 percent and 57.1 percent, respectively. At the opposite extreme there is Georgia (77.0 percent), Michigan (77.6 percent), North Carolina (79.2 percent) and Texas (80.4 percent).

Part II. A summary of studies examining the effect of school quality on earnings

The following abbreviations are adopted throughout this summary: teacher/pupil (T/P) or pupil/teacher (P/T) ratio, school quality measures (Q), years of schooling or a transform (S), family characteristics (F), individual characteristics (X), and average daily attendance (ADA).

A. Decennial Census data matched to the *Biennial Survey of Education* and the *Digest of Education Statistics*

1. Welch (1966)

a. *Data*
Earnings source: 1960 Census from four sources: (1) State Reports, Series D, (2) the 1 in 1000 sample, (3) the matched sample for farm operator families of the 1960 Sample of the Survey of Agriculture and the Census of Population, and (4) the subject report "Whites with Hispanic surnames".
Earnings sample: Rural farm males, ages 25 or more with earned income in 1959, who had not attended college, and who were not residing in Alaska, Hawaii or RI. Twelve "states" are dropped in Stage 2 due to insufficient school system data. ("States" are defined separately for the segregated Southern states.)
Quality source: *Biennial Survey*, 1955–1956.
Quality variables: Teacher/Pupil ratio (T/P ratio), teacher wages (no adjustment mentioned), enrollment, and expenditures per pupil ($/pupil; no adjustment mentioned) for rural counties.

b. *Model*
(1) $\hat{y}_{ij} - \hat{y}_{0j} = B_i C_j,$
(2) $C_j = Q\alpha_2 A N^{\alpha_1} (Q \sum B_i N_i)^{\alpha_2 - 1} K^{\alpha_3}.$
The variable $\hat{y}_{0j}$ is the predicted earnings of a noneducated worker living in state j and $\hat{y}_{ij}$ is the predicted earnings of a worker with i years of schooling living in state j. C_j is the return to one unit of schooling and B_i is the number of units of schooling possessed.
   In practice, estimation proceeds in two stages. In the first stage, (the log of) the return to schooling is regressed on state (j) and years of schooling (i) indicators. In stage two, the estimates of (the log of) C_j are regressed on Q, K (nonlabor inputs), N (people) and education (the term in parentheses, which includes college attendees; B_i is estimated in Stage 1). Also included in Stage 2 is an indicator for nonwhite "states" and indicators for the Pacific and Southern regions.

c. *Stated findings*
The T/P ratio and teacher wages are highly correlated with $/pupil reflecting a tradeoff between the two.

The effect of teachers' wages is consistently positive across specifications.

The coefficient on T/P ratio is negatively signed and seems to capture school size as rural schools with higher T/P ratios are typically smaller and have teachers with widely diverse teaching loads.

The most important determinants of school quality are teacher salaries and the size of the secondary school.

2. Rizzuto and Wachtel (1980)

a. *Data*
Earnings source: 1960 and 1970 Censuses.

Earnings sample: Excludes: those under age 14 or over age 65, females, those missing state-of-birth, those with mother tongue other than English or Spanish, nonwhites other than black, NILF, self-employed, and those not born in the 50 states or DC.

Quality source: *Biennial Survey*, 1909–1910, 1919–1920, . . . , 1959–1960.

Quality variables: $/pupil in elementary school (extrapolated from measures that include elementary and high school combined; adjusted for price levels using the index for local and state government expenditures). Also examines P/T ratio, teachers' wages (CPI adjusted), term length, and various components of expenditures.

b. *Model*
$y = X\beta + \delta S + \theta Q + \varepsilon.$

Estimated separately by census year and race.

y – (the log of) 1959 and 1969 annual earnings.

S – years of schooling.

X – experience, experience squared, ln(weeks worked), urban residence.

Q – ln($/pupil).

c. *Stated findings*
The returns to Q are positive and significant for whites and blacks in both census years; they are generally higher for blacks, higher in 1960, and higher than the returns to S.

The marginal social rate of return to Q ranges between 5 percent and 18 percent (depending on race, census year and schooling).

Expenditure measures perform better than the other quality measures.

3. Nechyba (1990)

a. *Data*
Earnings source: 1950–1980 Census summary tables. Data collected for whites and blacks at the state-level for the 25–34, 35–44, 45–54 and 55–64 age cohorts.

Quality source: *Biennial Survey* as well as data extracted from published and unpublished research.

Quality variable: Expenditures on teacher salary per pupil (expressed as a ratio of black to white expenditures).

b. *Model*

$y = X\beta + \delta S + \theta Q + \varepsilon.$

   y – median annual earnings.

   S – median education.

   X – percent in urban residence, fraction of cotton picked manually in the last 5 and 10 years (Cotton5, Cotton10), and the number of discrimination charges filed with the EEOC relative to the black labor force (AA).

Observations are at the state level. All variables except AA and COTTON are ratios of the values for blacks relative to that for whites.

c. *Stated findings*

Q has a positive and significant effect on earnings.

   Almost half of the closing gap in earnings ratios between whites and blacks is attributable to changes in the relative school quality between blacks and whites.

4. Card and Krueger (1992a)

a. *Data*

Earnings source: 1980 Census.

Earnings sample: White males born in the 48 states or DC between 1920 and 1949 and living in the 50 states or DC. Those with imputed values for age, race, sex, education, weeks worked, or earnings are excluded as are those reporting no weeks worked. Those with annual income less than $101 or with weekly wages less than $36 or more than $2,500 are also excluded.

Quality source: *Biennial Survey* and *Digest of Education* (many years).

Quality variables: P/T ratio, term length, and teacher wage (normalized by state average wages and divided by the national average in the year). Other measures examined include: percent male teachers, teacher experience, teacher education, private school attendance, and the difference in the P/T ratio between Catholic and public schools.

b. *Model*

   (1) $y = X_1\beta_1 + S\Delta\delta_1 + S\Gamma\delta_2 + \varepsilon,$

   (2) $\delta_1 = X_2\beta_2 + Q\theta + \upsilon.$

Stage 1 regressions are run separately for each 10-year birth cohort. Stage 2 regressions are weighted by the inverse variance of the dependent variable.

   y – (the log of) 1979 weekly wages.

   S – years of schooling truncated at the 2nd percentile for the cohort in the state where born. Δ and Γ represent state-of-birth and region-of-residence indicators.

X_1 – experience, experience squared, marital status, SMSA status, state-of-birth and state-of-residence indicators.

X_2 – cohort indicators and (in their preferred specification) state-of-birth indicators.

Extensions:

1. Adds median education, (log) per capita income of parents' generation, percent of high school graduates and percent of college graduates in the Stage 2 regressions.
2. A reduced-form model that includes Q and excludes S in Stage 1 (all cohorts combined, without cohort indicators).

c. *Stated findings*

The coefficients on the quality measures are, in general, correctly signed and statistically significant.

The inclusion of family background, labor supply factors (the education distribution of the labor force), and additional quality measures do not change the conclusions from the basic model.

The state-of-birth intercepts are negatively correlated with Q and S is positively correlated with Q. The positive correlation with S more than offsets the negative correlation with the state-of-birth intercepts so that there is no evidence of a negative effect of school quality in the lower tail of the earnings distribution.

Estimates of the impact of Q on Y from the reduced-form models are 30–40 percent larger than in the two-stage models.

5. Card and Krueger (1992b)

a. *Data*

Earnings source: 1960–1980 Censuses.

Earnings sample: White and black males born in 18 Southern states (including DC), living in the metro areas of nine Northern states. See Card and Krueger (1992a) for exclusions based on imputations and wages.

Quality source: *Biennial Survey*, 1920–1954 and Southern Education Reporting Services publications for the 1955–1966 data.

Quality variables: P/T ratio, term length, and teachers' wages.

b. *Model*

(1) $y = X\beta + S\Delta\delta + \varepsilon$,

(2) $\delta = X_2\beta_2 + \theta Q + \upsilon$.

Stage 1 is run separately by race, Census year and 10-year birth cohort. The Stage 2 regressions are weighted by the inverse variance of the dependent variable. Card and Krueger (1992a) also estimate a reduced-form model that includes Q directly in Stage 1 and excludes S.

y – (the log of) weekly wages.

S – years of schooling, Δ represents state-of-birth indicators.

X_1 – experience, experience squared, state-of-residence and state-of-birth indicators.

X_2 – race by cohort indicators, race by census year indicators, and state-of-birth indicators.

c. *Stated findings*
The primary model includes only the P/T ratio, which has a positive and significant effect on earnings.

When teacher salaries and term length are added, the coefficient on teacher salaries is consistently positive and significant under various specifications, but the coefficients on P/T ratio and term length change signs depending upon the specification.

School quality changes explain 50–80 percent of the change in the relative black/white return to education between the 1910 and 1940 birth cohorts.

6. Heckman, Layne-Farrar and Todd (1996)

a. *Data*
Earnings source: 1970–1990 Censuses.
Earnings sample: Parallels the Card and Krueger (1992a) sample restrictions with adjustments made for each Census year given real dollar amounts and the variables available.
Quality source: *Biennial Survey, Digest of Education*, and state reports.
Quality variables: P/T ratio, term length, and teachers' wages (normalized by regional average wage). Variables are adjusted given the timing of desegregation.

b. *Model*
 (1) $y = X_1\beta_1 + S\Delta\delta_1 + S\Gamma\delta_2 + \varepsilon,$
 (2) $\delta_1 = X_2\beta_2 + Q\theta + \upsilon.$
See Card and Krueger (1992a) for a description of the variables.
Extensions:
 1. Examines the effect of Q on the state-of-birth intercepts.
 2. Examines sheepskin effects by adding interactions between some college and college graduate by state-of-birth indicators and by region-of-residence indicators.
 3. Adds region-of-residence by region-of-birth indicators in Stage 1.
 4. Adds region-of-residence by Q interactions and migration distance in Stage 2.

c. *Stated findings*
Correlations within region of residence (ROR) between region of birth (ROB) average wages and ROB averages of the quality measures are weak and inconsistent. However, rankings of ROB average wages within ROR show some consistency across ROR, especially for those with four or more years of college. This supports the existence of early environmental factors, but not school quality measures.

The correlation between state-of-birth (SOB) intercepts from Stage 1 and Q is negative. Examining only the effect of Q on S will overstate the total impact of Q on earnings.

Sheepskin effects are important, i.e. there are discrete jumps in the return to education for those with some college and those with 4 or more years of college.

ROB by ROR indicators (in Stage 1) are significant and reduce the impact of Q on earnings. This suggests that selective migration is an important issue. "Because of this ... interaction, ... no unique quality effect on returns to education can be defined independently of the market in which it is used".

When ROB by ROR interactions and sheepskin effects are included in Stage 1, "the only support for an effect of school quality on earnings is through the return to college education".

Allowing the effect of Q to vary by ROR and adding migration distance in the second stage weakens (and sometimes reverses) the impact of Q and reveals that the effects of Q vary across regions, with the exception of teacher salary, which is positive, significant, and not statistically different across regions.

Q is positively correlated with the percentage of college graduates, is weakly correlated with the percent of high school graduates, and is negatively correlated with high school dropout rates.

B. The National Longitudinal Survey of Young Men/Young Women (NLS-YM/YW)[11]

1. Link and Ratledge (1975a)

a. *Data*

Earnings source: NLS-YM conducted in 1967.
Earnings sample: Males ages 15–25 out of school at least one year with positive earnings.
Quality source: NLS-YM.
Quality variable: $/pupil in ADA in 1968 in the district where attended high school.

b. *Model*

$y = X\beta + \delta S + \theta Q + F\pi + A\varphi + \varepsilon.$

Model run separately for whites and blacks and then run with both groups combined including a race indicator.

y – 1967 annual earnings.
S – years of schooling.
X – experience [minimum of (age-education-6) and (age-16)], hours worked, marital status, occupational knowledge test.
F – Duncan index of father's occupation and whether had access to newspapers, magazines or a library card at age 14.
A – IQ.

---

[11] Link, Ratledge and Lewis (1980) examine the NLS-YM and the PSID.

c. *Stated findings*

The coefficient on Q is positive and significant in all models and the internal rate of return associated with additional expenditures is higher for blacks than whites.

The coefficient on "black" in the total population regression is not significant.

2. Link and Ratledge (1975b)

a. *Data*

Earnings source: NLS-YM conducted in 1968.
Earnings sample: Males ages 16–26 out of school at least one year.
Quality source: NLS-YM.
Quality variable: $/pupil in ADA in 1968 in the district where attended high school.

b. *Model*

$y = X\beta + \delta S + \theta Q + F\pi + A\varphi + \varepsilon.$

Model estimated separately for whites and blacks.

y – (the log of) 1968 annual earnings.
S – years of schooling.
X – experience [minimum of (age-16) and (age-S-5)], experience squared, urban residence (integers from 1 to 6), the log of hours worked last year.
F – residence at age 14 (integers from 1 to 6 representing urbanness).
A – IQ.
Q – ln($/pupil).

c. *Stated findings*

This study parallels Johnson and Stafford (1973) using district-level expenditure data and reports similar findings.

The coefficient on Q is positive and significant for both whites and blacks and the return-to-quality is higher for blacks than for whites.

The omission of A from the equation causes the return-to-education to be overstated by 15 percent and the return-to-quality to be overstated by 10 percent.

3. Parnes and Kohen (1975)

a. *Data*

Earnings source: NLS-YM conducted in 1968.
Earnings sample: Males ages 14–24 in 1966 with at least 8 years of schooling, not currently enrolled, and currently employed.
Quality source: NLS-YM.
Quality variables: An index constructed by the authors that includes the availability of library facilities, P/T ratio, counselors/100 students, and starting teacher's salary. (Construction not described by authors.)

b. *Model*

$y = X\beta + \delta S + \theta Q + F\pi + A\varphi + \varepsilon.$

Model estimated separately for blacks and whites.

   y – 1968 hourly earnings.

   X – experience, health, South, SMSA, an occupational knowledge test (with three components).

   S – years of schooling.

   F – a constructed index based on father's education, mother's education, father's occupation, education of oldest older sibling; and availability of reading materials in the home.

   A – IQ.

c. *Stated findings*

The coefficient on Q is positive but not significant for blacks and is negative and not significant for whites. However, the occupational knowledge test, the primary focus of their study, has a positive and significant effect on earnings.

This study also examines the determinants of the occupational knowledge test, including Q (counselors per 100 pupils in the high school) which has a negative effect (higher quality leads to lower test scores) in three of the four specifications and the coefficient on Q is never statistically significant.

4. Link, Ratledge and Lewis (1976)

a. *Data*

Earnings source: NLS-YM conducted in 1969.

Earnings sample: Males ages 17–27 out of school at least one year.

Quality source: NLS-YM.

Quality variable: $/pupil in ADA in 1968 in the district where attended high school.

b. *Model*

$y = X\beta + \eta SQ + \gamma S * Exp + \varepsilon.$

Model estimated separately for blacks and whites.

   y – (the log of) 1969 annual earnings.

   S – years of schooling.

   X – ln(weeks worked), experience [minimum of (age-education-5) and (age-16)], and experience squared.

   Q – ln($/pupil).

c. *Stated findings*

This study examines the "vintage effect" of Q (the changing relative quality of education for blacks and whites over time) on black/white wage ratios.

The schooling by quality interaction is positive and statistically significant for both blacks and whites (evidence of a vintage effect), where as the schooling by experience interaction is not statistically significant (no evidence of a life cycle effect).

5. Jud and Walker (1977)

a. *Data*
Earnings source: NLS-YM conducted in 1970.
Earnings sample: Males ages 18–28 out of school at least one year with positive earn-
    ings.
Quality source: NLS-YM.
Quality variable: $/pupil in ADA in 1968 in the district where attended high school.

b. *Model*
    (1) $A = X_1\beta_1 + Q\theta_1 + F_1\pi_1 + \varepsilon_1,$
    (2) $S = X_1\beta_2 + Q\theta_2 + F_1\pi_2 + A\varphi_2 + \varepsilon_2,$
    (3) $y = X_2\beta_3 + S\delta_3 + Q\theta_3 + F_2\pi_3 + A\varphi_3 + \varepsilon_3.$
    y – 1970 annual earnings.
    S – years of schooling.
    X_1 – race.
    X_2 – race, experience, experience squared, a vocational tech indicator, marital status,
        ability to work indicator, hours/week, South, and SMSA.
    F_1 – Duncan's index of father's occupation, size of community at age 14 (1 =
        farm, ..., 6 = 100,000+), father's education, mother's education.
    F_2 – Duncan index of father's occupation.
    A – IQ.

c. *Stated findings*
The coefficient on Q is a statistically significant and positive determinant of ability, but
not of schooling or earnings directly; this suggests that the impact of Q is transmitted
through a sequential process.

6. Link, Ratledge and Lewis (1980)

a. *Data*
Earnings source 1: NLS-YM conducted in 1971 [updated from Link, Ratledge and
    Lewis (1976)].
Earnings sample 1: Males ages 19–29 who worked at least 30 weeks, at least 30 hours
    per week, had positive wages, and were not in school.
Earnings source 2: PSID 1968–1972. Designed to match Akin and Garfinkel (1980),
    male household heads, ages 30–55 excluding self-employed and those with no earn-
    ings. Several data handling errors committed by Akin and Garfinkel (AG) are cor-
    rected.
Quality source: NLS-YM and the *Biennial Survey* for 1930, 1940, 1950, 1960.
Quality variables: $/pupil in 1968 in the district where attended high school
    (NLS-YM). $/pupil (*Biennial Survey*) was matched to the PSID based on state of
    residence at age 12 (linearly interpolated) to replicate AG.

b. *Model*

(AG) $y = X\beta_1 + \delta_2 S + \gamma_1 S * Exp + \theta_1 Q + \eta_1 SQ + \varepsilon_1,$

(LRL–A) $y = X\beta_2 + \gamma_2 S * Exp + \eta_2 SQ + \varepsilon_2,$

(LRL–B) $y = X\beta_3 + \delta_3 S + \gamma_3 S * Exp + \eta_3 SQ + \varepsilon_3.$

Regressions are run separately for blacks and whites.

NLS-YM:

y – (the log of) 1971 hourly wage race.

X – experience [minimum of (age-S-5) and (age-16)], experience squared.

F – father's education.

A – IQ.

Q – ln($/pupil).

PSID: See AG (1980).

c. *Stated findings*

This study examines the "vintage effect" of Q on earnings for blacks and whites in response to AG and its findings run counter to those of AG (1980).

Using the NLS-YM, the returns to Q are positive and significant in all models (except the AG equation for blacks where they may or may not be jointly significant) and the elasticities range between 0.13 and 0.23 and are, in general, slightly higher for blacks. The returns to schooling are comparable for young blacks and whites, but unfavorable for older blacks relative to older whites.

Using the PSID, the returns to Q are also positive and significant in all models (jointly in the AG model) and the elasticity estimates range from 0.14 to 0.32. Returns to schooling are favorable for younger blacks and unfavorable for older blacks relative to whites of the same ages.

7. Tremblay (1986)

a. *Data*

Earnings source: NLS-YM conducted in 1976.

Earnings sample: Males ages 24–34 working full-time (35–40 hrs/week) and not enrolled in 1976. Wages are adjusted for regional (South, non-South, metro, nonmetro) cost-of-living differences.

Quality source: NLS-YM? (Source not mentioned.)

Quality variables: $/pupil in primary and secondary school and $/pupil in 1970–1971 at the most recently attended college. ($/pupil amounts are adjusted for regional cost-of-living differences and time using the CPI deflator.)

b. *Model*

$y = X\beta + \delta S + \theta_{PS}(Q_{PS} \times S_{PS}) + \theta_c(Q_C \times S_C) + \varepsilon.$

Regressions run separately for the South and the non-South.

y – (the log of the) hourly wage rate.

S – years of schooling, S_{PS} is years of primary and secondary education, S_C is years of college.

X – seniority at current job, age, race, marital status, union, SMSA, industry (11 values), occupation (10 values), and whether participated in an occupational training program.

A – IQ.

Q – ln($/pupil).

c. *Stated findings*
The coefficients on Q (both pre-college and college) are positive in both the South and the non-South regressions, but are only significant in the South.

Estimated elasticities are higher in the South and for primary and secondary expenditures than for college expenditures.

8. Altonji and Dunn (1996)

a. *Data*
Earnings source: NLS-YM and NLS-YW. Utilizes all surveys through 1981 for the YM and through 1988 for the YW.

Earnings sample: Males ages 14–24 in 1966 and females ages 14–24 in 1967 who were at least 24 years old at the time of the survey, not enrolled (and did not return to school that year), with wages above $1.5/hour in 1982–1984 dollars and with valid school quality data.

Quality source: NLS-YM and NLS-YW.

Quality variables: P/T ratio, starting wages of teachers with a B.S., $/pupil, and a composite measure constructed by the NLS. Also examines enrollment, percent disadvantaged, and percent dropping out.

b. *Model*
$$y = X\beta + S\delta + SZ\gamma + Q\theta + SQ\eta + F\pi + \varepsilon.$$

The model is also estimated including $(A \times S)$ and using differences in residence at age 14 as an instrument for differences in Q. All variables except Q are interacted with gender.

y – (the log of) hourly earnings.

S – years of schooling minus 12 (cubic).

X – year indicators, experience (quartic), female, South, SMSA.

Z – mother's education, father's education.

F – two specifications: (1) family indicators or (2) number of siblings, black, and two parents in household at age 14.

A – IQ (model run with and without).

c. *Stated findings*
While the level effects (Q not interacted with S) are all correctly signed and significant (except P/T ratio), the coefficients on the interactions of Q with S are generally (6 of

8 estimates) perversely signed.

Adding an indicator for each family increases the coefficients on the quality variables.

Adding ability and an ability by schooling interaction has very little effect on the quality estimates.

The coefficients on Q are identified by movers within family in the specification with family indicators. IV estimates using city size as an instrument result in correctly signed level and interaction estimates, except for the P/T ratio by S interaction.

"We find that teachers' salaries, expenditures per pupil, and a composite index of school quality indicators have a substantial positive effect on the wages of high school graduates.".

9. Betts (2001)

a. *Data*

Earnings source: NLS-YW, includes all surveys between 1966 and 1991 (ages 14–24 in 1967).

Earnings sample: Black and white women ages 18 or more and not in school.

Quality source: NLS-YW from the 1968 survey.

Quality variables: $/pupil, P/T ratio, starting wages of teachers with a B.S., and library books per student. (Dollar amounts are adjusted by survey administrators for cost-of-living differences between cities.)

b. *Model*

$y = X\beta + Q\delta + F\gamma + \varepsilon.$

Models run separately for blacks and whites. Also examines a model with age interacted with Q.

  y – (the log of) hourly wages.

  X – age, age squared, marital status, number of children, year indicators, and an inverse Mills ratio (from a probit model of labor force status).

  F – whether educated in a large city (25k+), whether educated in the South, census region where educated, father's education, mother's education, Duncan index of family head, and number of siblings in 1968.

The model does not include years of schooling.

c. *Stated findings*

Elasticities are higher for black women than for white women. P/T ratios and books/pupil are significant in both regressions, although correctly signed for blacks and perversely signed for whites.

When outliers are omitted, all four measures are significant for blacks, with no meaningful changes in the results for whites.

The effects of Q generally weaken with age.

C. The National Bureau of Economic Research – Thorndike and Hagen data (NBER–TH) matched to the Biennial Survey and various college data sources

1. Wales (1973)

a. *Data*
Earnings source: NBER–TH.
Earnings sample: No restrictions mentioned.
Quality source: *The Gourman Report*.
Quality variables: The Gourman ranking (averaged across departments) was divided into quintiles and matched to the undergraduate and graduate institution attended.

b. *Model*
$y = X\beta + \eta SQ + F\pi + A\varphi + \varepsilon.$

   y – 1969 monthly earnings.
   X – whether a college teacher, whether other teacher, religion indicators, age and marital status.
   S – indicators for some college, bachelor's, some graduate training, master's degree, and Ph.d. interacted with quintiles of the undergraduate and graduate Gourman index (two separate indexes). Only significant interactions are included.
   F – indicators for quintiles of a composite hobbies index, family income, pre-1943 schooling, math ability, father's education, and other characteristics.
   A – indicators for quintiles of a "mathematical factor" taken from a factor analysis of 17 ability tests.

c. *Stated findings*
This study examines the effect of college quality on earnings.
   Quality is a positive and significant determinant of earnings at both the graduate and undergraduate levels.
   This may capture increases in marginal productivity, screening by firms, or omitted ability variables.
   The quality of undergraduate training is positively (but weakly) correlated with graduate training.

2. Solmon (1975)

a. *Data*
Earnings source: NBER–TH.
Earnings sample: Respondents with at least some college.
Quality source: Various sources including Cass and Birnbaum's *Comparative Guide of American Colleges*, Astin's *Who Goes Where to College*, *The Gourman Report*, Carter's *An Assessment of Quality in Graduate Education*, etc. Quality variables are matched to the most recently attended college.

Quality variables: Quality of instruction includes average faculty salary; expenditures on instruction, research and library facilities per full-time equivalent student; T/P ratio; income and expenditures per pupil; and the Gourman index (overall and academic). Quality for students includes SAT scores, Astin's intellectualism index and Astin's selectivity index.

b. *Model*

$$y = X\beta + \delta S + \theta Q + A\varphi + \varepsilon.$$

y – (the log of) 1969 annual earnings.

S – years of schooling.

X – experience, experience squared.

A – IQ.

Extensions examine data by schooling levels, 1955 earnings, and include general occupation categories.

c. *Stated findings*

This study examines the effects of college quality on earnings.

Each quality variable is significant when examined in isolation. When entered simultaneously, faculty salary and peer effects (SAT verbal score) appear to be the most important components of college quality.

The impact of Q increases with experience.

Extra schooling has a greater impact for those from lower quality undergraduate institutions.

The return to graduate school quality is higher for those who attended higher quality undergraduate institutions.

The coefficients on Q change only slightly when family background variables are included.

3. Wachtel (1975)

a. *Data*

Earnings source: NBER–TH.

Earnings sample: Excludes those who are airplane pilots, are unmarried, are in poor health, attended private or parochial schools, have earnings less than $4,000 or more than $75,000 (in 1958$) in 1955 or less than $5,000 or more than $75,000 in 1969 and those for whom school expenditure data could not be matched.

Quality source: *Biennial Survey*, district-level elementary and high school expenditures per pupil for 1936–1938. *The Gourman Report*, Office of Education data for college expenditures, National Research Council (NRC) data for the high school attended.

Quality variables: Primarily examines $/pupil for pre-college education, but also examines P/T ratio, teachers' wages, teachers' wages relative to state median income, enrollment per building, term length, and expenditures on texts and other instructional expenses. College quality measures include the Gourman index and $/student at the college attended. The NRC data (matched for a sub-sample and using data from the actual high school attended) includes size of graduating class, percent of teacher's with a graduate degree, and percent of high school graduates with Ph.d.'s.

b. *Model*

(1) $A = Q\theta_1 + F_1\pi_1 + \varepsilon_1,$

(2) $S = X_1\beta_2 + Q\theta_2 + F_1\pi_2 + A\varphi_2 + \varepsilon_2,$

(3) $y = X_2\beta_3 + S\delta_3 + Q\theta_3 + F_2\pi_3 + A\varphi_3 + \varepsilon_3.$

y – (the log of) annual earnings in 1969 (also examines 1955 earnings).

S – years of schooling.

X_1 – age.

X_2 – experience and ln(hours worked per week).

F_1 – number of siblings, mother's education and father's education.

F_2 – father's education.

A – a composite of various test scores (ability).

Extensions: including median income where grew up, examining the impact of Q by city size and ability, including college quality (expenditures and Gourman index), including 1955 earnings in the 1969 earnings equation, and a fuller model with occupation, religion, and additional family variables.

c. *Stated findings*

This study examines the effects of both college and pre-college school quality on earnings.

The effect of $/pupil is positive, but insignificant, in (2) and positive and significant in (1) and (3). The rate-of-return to school spending is 12.6 percent.

All nonexpenditure quality variables are significant in the earnings equation, except for the P/T ratio.

Q has a larger impact in large cities and for those with lower values of A.

Pre-college expenditures are positively correlated with college quality and both pre-college quality and college quality have positive and significant effects on earnings.

Q has a smaller impact on earnings earlier in the career. Q and the rate of growth of earnings are positively correlated.

The coefficients on all three variables in the NRC data (school-level information) are positive and statistically significant.

4. Link and Ratledge (1976)

a. *Data*

Earnings source: NBER–TH.

Earnings sample: Excludes airline pilots, those in poor health, farm proprietors, if single, graduates of nonpublic high schools, and those with earnings less than $75,000 or more than $5,000 in 1969.

Quality source: *Biennial Survey*, 1936–1938.

Quality variable: $/pupil at the district and state levels.

b. *Model*
$$y = X\beta + \delta S + \theta Q + A\varphi + \varepsilon.$$
   y – (the log of) 1969 annual earnings.
   S – years of schooling.
   X – experience.
   A – IQ.

c. *Stated findings*
This study is done in response to Akin and Kniesner's (1976) claim that it is unclear whether district-level or state-level data on Q contains less measurement error.

Both state-level and district-level expenditures have positive and significant effects on earnings.

The estimates using the district-level expenditures are higher with larger t-statistics than those using state-level expenditures. This is consistent with larger measurement error in the state-level data.

5. Wachtel (1976)

a. *Data*
Earnings source: NBER–TH.
Earnings sample: Excludes airplane pilots, those with no earnings or earnings less than $75,000, those in poor health, those without schooling variables, and private school attendees.
Quality source: *Biennial Survey*, 1936–1938 for pre-college measures and Office of Education data for post-secondary measures.
Quality variables: $/pupil (elementary and high school) in the district attended (1958$, adjusted using the deflator for state and local government purchases) and $/pupil in 1962–1963 at the college attended (1958$) for both undergraduate and graduate training.

b. *Model*
$$y = X\beta + \delta S + \theta Q + F\pi + A\varphi + \varepsilon.$$
   Estimates run by level of schooling (12, 13–15, 16, 16+) and for all levels combined.
   y – (the log of) 1969 annual earnings. (Also examines 1955 annual earnings.)
   S – years of schooling (where levels can vary) and indicators for 12+ and 16+ years completed included in regressions with all levels combined.
   X – experience, experience squared.
   F – father's education.
   A – an ability test score.
   Q – pre-college, college and graduate expenditures.

c. *Stated findings*

This study examines the effects of pre-college, college and post-college school quality on earnings.

Pre-college, college and graduate spending all have positive and significant effects on earnings. The rates of return are 10–15 percent for pre-college expenditures, 10–19 percent for college expenditures, and 14 percent for graduate school expenditures.

D. The Panel Survey of Income Dynamics (PSID) matched to the *Biennial Survey of Education*

1. Morgan and Sirageldin (1968)

a. *Data*

Earnings source: PSID. Described as a national sample of 1,525 family heads interviewed in 1965. (Source never explicitly referenced by authors.)

Earnings sample: Household heads with positive earnings in 1964 that attended school between 1910 and 1963 and had information for where grew up. Self-employed workers and those owning farms are excluded. This study includes both males and females and whites and minorities.

Quality source: *Biennial Survey* (1929–1930, 1939–1940 and 1949–1950). They also examine the Cass and Birnbaum college ranking for college quality. Not stated how college measures are mapped to workers.

Quality variable: $/pupil in ADA averaged across the three decades above and deflated for price changes (deflator not described by authors).

b. *Model*

(1) $y = X\beta + \delta S + \varepsilon$,

(2) $\hat{\bar{\varepsilon}} = \alpha + \theta Q + \upsilon$.

The authors estimate Stage 1 and then regress the average state residuals on Q in Stage 2.

y – 1964 hourly earnings.

X – age, race, sex, and whether grew up on a farm.

S – years of schooling.

$\hat{\bar{\varepsilon}}$ – the average residual for each state, computed from individual's residuals in Stage 1.

c. *Stated findings*

The coefficient on Q is positive and statistically significant with a rate-of-return of over 15 percent.

Findings could be due to omitted family variables.

There is also a positive correlation between college quality and earnings.

2. Johnson and Stafford (1973)

a. *Data*
Earnings source: PSID. (Described as Survey Research Center data, 1968 Survey.)
Earnings sample: Excludes African-Americans, females, retirees, farmers, self-employed, those NILF, and those with no earnings in 1964.
Quality source: *Biennial Survey*, 1957–1958. Utilizes data for 1929–1930, 1939–1940 and 1949–1950.
Quality variables: $/pupil in ADA for elementary students (derived from the value for elementary and high school combined), deflated using the price deflator for state and local government expenditures.

b. *Model*
$y = X\beta + \delta S + \theta Q + F\pi + \varepsilon.$
   y – (the log of) 1964 hourly earnings.
   X – experience (age-educ-7), experience squared, whether urban residence.
   S – years of schooling.
   F – whether grew up in an urban area.
   Q – ln($/pupil).

c. *Stated findings*
The coefficient on Q is positive and statistically significant with an elasticity of 0.198 and rates-of-return between 11 percent and 21 percent.
   The return to years of schooling doesn't change when Q is added to the model.
   The returns to school quality are higher than the returns to schooling.
   Quality is also positively correlated with the amount of schooling attained.

3. Akin and Garfinkel (1977)

a. *Data*
Earnings source: PSID conducted in 1972 (includes 1968–1972 data).
Earnings sample: Male household heads ages 30–55 in 1972 that are not self-employed and that have earnings. Per capita income (PCY) by state is taken from the 1930–1960 Censuses. All monetary values (y, Q and PCY) are deflated over time and by state.
Quality sources: *Biennial Survey* for 1930, 1940, 1950 and 1960.
Quality variable: $/pupil (by race where available). Off census years are linearly interpolated and workers are assigned the value for the state where they lived when age 12.

b. *Model*
   (1) $A = Q\theta_1 + F_1\pi_1 + \varepsilon_1,$
   (2) $V = X_1\beta_1 + Q\theta_2 + F_1\pi_2 + A\varphi_2 + \varepsilon_2,$

(3) $S = X_1\beta_3 + Q\theta_3 + F_2\pi_3 + A\varphi_3 + V\gamma_3 + \varepsilon_3,$
(4) $y = X_2\beta_4 + S\delta_4 + Q\theta_4 + F_3\pi_4 + A\varphi_4 + V\gamma_4 + \tau_4 S * Exp + \varepsilon_4.$

All models are run separately for whites and blacks. Earnings models are run with and without PCY. Also examines the impact of using different deflators on earnings and adding the variables city size and area wage.

- y – (the log of) the average hourly wage rate from 1968–1972 (also examines average annual earnings).
- S – years of schooling.
- X_1 – age.
- X_2 – experience (age-S-6), experience squared.
- F_1 – father's income, father's education, whether middle income, whether upper income, number of siblings, whether father owned or operated a farm.
- F_2 – F_1 and whether grew up in a city.
- F_3 – F_2 excluding number of siblings.
- A – an achievement orientation index score.
- V – a test of verbal ability.
- Q – ln($/pupil).

c. *Stated findings*

$/pupil has a positive and significant effect in (2)–(4) and a positive, but insignificant effect in (1).

Including PCY reduces the impact of Q, becoming insignificant in all equations, except for the black earnings equation.

4. Akin and Garfinkel (1980)

a. *Data*

Earnings source: PSID conducted in 1972 (includes 1968–1972 data).
Earnings sample: Male household heads ages 30–55 that are not self-employed and that have positive earnings. All monetary values (y, Q) are deflated over time and by state.
Quality sources: *Biennial Survey* for 1930, 1940, 1950 and 1960.
Quality variable: $/pupil (by race where available). Off census years are linearly interpolated and workers are assigned the value for the state where they lived when age 12.

b. *Model*

(AG) $y = X\beta_1 + \delta_1 S + \gamma_1 S * Exp + \theta_1 Q + \eta_1 SQ + F\pi_1 + A\varphi_1 + \varepsilon_1,$
(LRL) $y = X\beta_2 + \gamma_2 S * Exp + \eta_2 SQ + F\pi_2 + A\varphi_2 + \varepsilon_2.$

Regressions are run separately for whites and blacks.

- y – (the log of) the average hourly wage rate, 1968–1972.
- S – years of schooling.
- X – experience [minimum of (age-S-5) and (age-16)], experience squared.

    F – father's income; grew up poor, middle class, or rich; father's education; grew up
       on farm.
    A – IQ (from a sentence completion test); achievement motivational index.

c. *Stated findings*
This article examines the "vintage effect" of Q (the change in the quality of black
schools relative to white schools) on black/white wage ratios in response to Link, Ratledge and Lewis (1976).

    The coefficients on Q in (AG) and SQ in (LRL) are positive and significant in both
models; however, the SQ interaction coefficients are negative and insignificant in the
(AG) equation. The negative interaction term is not large enough to offset the positive
levels effect for all practical levels of schooling.

E. The National Longitudinal Survey of Youth 1997 (NLSY79)[12]

1. Betts (1995)

a. *Data*
Earnings source: NLSY79 conducted in 1990 (includes observations from 1979 through
    1990).
Earnings sample: Includes white males ages 17 or more with positive earnings, who
    attended public high school, living in the 50 states or DC, and that have nonmissing
    values for wage, race and sex. The military sub-sample is excluded. (This study also
    examines various subpopulations.)
Quality source: NLSY79. (Data is for the most recently attended HS if 17 or older in
    1979, matched by school to those under 17 in 1979 where possible.)
Quality variables: T/P ratio, starting teachers' wages for those with a B.S. (relative to
    per capita earnings in the state), and percent of teachers with a graduate degree.

b. *Model*
$y = X\beta + \delta S + \Gamma S + \theta Q + \eta SQ + \varepsilon.$
    y – (the log of) weekly wages (also examined hourly and annual with similar results,
       not reported).
    S – years of schooling; Γ represents nine region-of-residence indicators.
    X – experience (quartic), SMSA, marital status, region-of-residence and year indi-
       cators.

---

[12] Betts (1996) uses both the NLSY79 and the U.S. Census.

c. *Stated findings*

When school indicators are included (with Q omitted), they are jointly significant; schools matter.

However, the quality measures are not significant in the intercepts (not interacted with other variables) or when interacted with years of schooling.

These results are robust within various sub-samples of the population, in reduced-form estimates (without years of schooling), and when additional quality measures are included.

When state-level measures (from the *Biennial Survey*) are included, the coefficient on the T/P ratio is positive and significant and the coefficient on teachers' wages is positive and insignificant.

2. Betts (1996)

a. *Data*

Earnings source 1: 1970 and 1980 Census.

Earnings sample 1: Same as in Card and Krueger (1992a) except that the age restrictions vary across calculations. The 1970 Census restrictions parallel the 1980 Census restrictions with real wage adjustments calculated using the CPI.

Earnings source 2: NLSY79.

Earnings sample 2: Same as Betts (1995).

Quality source: *Biennial Survey*, *Digest of Education* and the NLSY79.

Quality variables: T/P ratio, teachers' wages relative to teachers' wages in the census region, and percent of teachers with a graduate degree (from the NLSY79). T/P ratio (attendance based), T/P ratio (enrollment based), term length, and relative teacher's salary (from the *Biennial Survey* and the *Digest of Education*).

b. *Model*

(1) $y = X_1 \beta_1 + \varepsilon,$

(2) $\lambda = X_2 \beta_2 + \theta Q + \eta QS + S \Gamma \delta + v.$

Stage 1 is run for white males ages 40–55 using the 1980 Census. Stage 2 is run using the NLSY79 sample with the coefficients on the occupation indicators (λ's) from Stage 1 matched to the NLSY79 respondents given their occupation. The second stage regression weights observations by the square root of the sampling variance of the occupation coefficients.

y – (the log of) 1979 weekly wages.

S – years of schooling. Γ represents region of residence indicators.

X_1 – age, age squared, marital status, SMSA, 503 occupational indicators.

X_2 – experience (quartic), marital status, SMSA, and census region.

Q – T/P ratio, relative teacher salary, percent of teachers with a graduate degree.

Extensions:

1. Estimates Stage 1 for each occupation including age, marital status, and SMSA in X_1. The age coefficients are then substituted for the occupational indicators in Stage 2.
2. Stage 2 is estimated substituting the Duncan socioeconomic index for each respondent's occupation (λ) in Stage 2.

Betts also re-estimates the Card–Krueger model using their main specification and the 1980 Census data with the age range extended to 20–59 so as to overlap the ages of respondents in the NLSY79. In Stage 2 of their procedure, Betts includes age (in five-year cohort bands, 20–24, 25–29, ...) by Q interactions and tests whether the coefficients are significantly different for younger workers. Extensions to this model examine the 1970 Census alongside the 1980 Census and tests for differences in the return to education within cohorts between these two years.

c. *Stated findings*
Most of the studies that fail to find that school spending has a significant impact on earnings examine younger workers; those that find that school spending has a significant impact on earnings examine samples that include older workers. If the impact of school spending only manifests itself later in the work career, this would explain the discrepancy in findings.

School inputs are not statistically significant predictors of mid-career earnings estimated by occupational differentials; they are not statistically significant predictors of the age-earnings profile within workers' chosen occupations; and they are not strongly related to a workers' occupational status (Duncan index).

Using Census data and the Card–Krueger model, the effects of school quality are not weaker for younger workers.

"... age dependence [of the impact of school inputs] is not the main explanation for the divergent results in the literature on the link between school resources and earnings".

3. Griffin and Ganderton (1996)

a. *Data*
Earnings source: NLSY79 conducted in 1990.
Earnings sample: Excluded if hours per week less than 20; no earnings; hourly wages less than \$2; not white, black or Hispanic; or missing Q, F or A.
Quality source: NLSY79.
Quality variable: A composite is constructed which includes the number of library books, T/P ratio, counselor/pupil ratio, dropout and attendance rates, and the characteristics and salaries of teachers. (Construction not described by the authors.)

b. *Model*
$$y = X\beta + \delta S + \theta Q + \pi F + \varphi A + \varepsilon.$$
Model estimated separately for each race and for all races combined.
y – (the log of) hourly wages.

S – years of schooling.

X – experience, experience squared, marital status, urban and regional indicators.

F – father's and mother's education, whether single parent family, number of siblings, reading composite (newspapers, magazines, library card).

A – AFQT score adjusted for age and then for differences in Q and F.

c. *Stated findings*

Q does not have a significant, direct effect on earnings. However, in other regressions they show that "school quality is an important determinant of ability, and ability is an important determinant of earnings". Therefore, Q matters through its impact on A.

4. Strayer (2002)

a. *Data*

Earnings source: NLSY79. (Includes data from 1979 to 1994.)

Earnings sample: Excludes the military sub-sample, high school dropouts, and those enrolled in school.

Quality source: NLSY79 for high school characteristics and uses IPEDS for college characteristics (only used to identify two and four year colleges).

Quality variables: percent of teachers with a graduate degree, P/T ratio, availability of technical programs, and availability of agricultural programs.

b. *Model*

  (MNL) $p = f(X, Q, F, A)$,

  (OLS) $y = X\beta + \delta S + \theta Q + \varepsilon$.

  (MNL) estimates the probability of attending no college, a 2-year college, or a 4-year college using a multinomial logit and (OLS) estimates separate wage equations using OLS for those with no college, those with 2 years of college and those with 4 years of college.

  MNL:

  X – sex, race, marital status, 2-year college tuition, 4-year college tuition, year indicators.

  F – family income, mother's education, father's education, number of siblings, and whether foreign born.

  A – AFQT percentile score.

  Q – quality variables plus attendance rate and dropout rate of high school.

  OLS:

  y – (the log of) hourly wages.

  S – highest grade completed.

  X – race, sex, marital status, region (4 values), SMSA, PT/FT, union, experience (quartic), year and industry indicators, and the selection parameters from (MNL).

  Q – quality variables plus the P/T ratio squared.

c. *Stated findings*

Q has a positive and significant effect on the probability of college attendance and on the type of college attended. College choice affects post-school earnings.

The direct effect of Q on earnings is positive but insignificant.

"The results suggest that high school quality influences earnings by affecting college choice behavior, while the direct effect of school quality on earnings is less evident".

F. High School and Beyond (HSB)[13]

1. Grogger (1996a)

a. *Data*

Earnings source: HSB. Earnings in 1986 (seniors), 1988 (sophomores) and 1991 (sophomores).

Earnings sample: The senior sample is restricted to full-time workers with positive earnings in 1986 and hourly wages between \$1 and \$100 per hour. The sophomore sample is restricted to those with monthly earnings between \$500 and \$6,000 and with at least nine months of employment. Those with values of \$/pupil that seem too low (less than \$200/pupil) are also excluded.

Quality source: HSB and NCES.

Quality variable: \$/pupil in 1980 and 1982 in the district attended (HSB). State-level \$/pupil in 1979–1980 (NCES).

b. *Model*

$y = X\beta + Q\theta + F\pi + \varepsilon.$

Regressions run separately for seniors and sophomores and for each year for sophomores.

> y – (the log of) hourly wages (seniors) and (the log of) monthly wages (sophomores).
>
> X – race, census division where school located, school type (urban, suburban, or rural), whether school had an alternative-curriculum, whether school is predominantly Hispanic.
>
> F – lived with father, number of siblings, father's education, family income.
>
> Q – ln(\$/pupil).

Years of schooling and experience are excluded from the model.

---

[13] Grogger (1996b) uses HSB as well as the National Longitudinal Survey of the High School Class of 1972 (NLS72).

c. *Stated findings*

Regressions including district-level expenditures are, in general, positive but insignificant. Estimates using state-level expenditures are generally higher, but still not significant.

IV estimates (using the other year's district-level $/pupil and, separately, state-level $/pupil) are higher than the OLS estimates and are significant in some of the comparisons. This indicates that measurement error may weaken estimates that use district-level expenditures.

State-of-birth indicators in regressions that include district-level estimates are jointly significant. Omitted state effects are important and may bias state-level and state-instrumented estimates.

"School spending matters, but it matters too little".

2. Grogger (1996b)

a. *Data*

Earnings source: HSB (senior cohort) and NLS72. Uses 1986 wages for HSB and 1979
  wages for NLS72.
Earnings sample: In the original survey and the follow-up, full-time, not enrolled,
  and with hourly wages between $1 and $100 (in 1986$). There are no high school
  dropouts in these samples.
Quality source: NLS72 and HSB (data collected from school administrators' offices).
Quality variables: P/T ratio, term length, whether 30 percent of teachers have a graduate degree, school size and percent black.

b. *Model*

$$y = X\beta + \delta S + \theta Q + \pi F + \varphi A + \varepsilon.$$

Regressions run separately for NLS72 and HSB samples.
y – (the log of) hourly earnings.
S – indicators for high school degree, college degree and graduate degree.
X – experience, experience squared, race, region and urban.
F – family income.
A – test scores and grades.

c. *Stated findings*

The coefficients on P/T ratio and term length are insignificant whereas teacher education (NLS72 only), school size and percent black are significant. The effects of school size are small.

School indicators are jointly significant and greatly increase the explanatory power of the model (with Q omitted). Including school indicators reduces the black/white wage differential by 17% in the 1979 data, but increase it by 38% in the 1986 data.

Schools matter, but school characteristics do not explain these effects.

3. Rivkin (2000)

a. *Data*

Earnings source: HSB (sophomore cohort).

Earnings sample: Includes black men and women from public schools in large, urban districts with at least five nonblack students. Excludes those with no earnings.

Quality source: HSB.

Quality variables: P/T ratio and a value added measure constructed from an auxiliary regression of a 12th grade test score on the 10th grade test score, individual and family characteristics and school indicators. The school indicators are the value added measure.

b. *Model*

$y = X\beta + \theta Q + F\pi + A\varphi + \varepsilon.$

Model estimated with and without A.

y – (the log of) 1991 monthly earnings.

X – gender, public in-state tuition and unemployment rate in the year of graduation.

F – parental education, family income, and whether school located in the South.

A – a composite of reading and math scores in the 10th grade.

Q – percent of students who are Hispanic, percent of students who are white, P/T ratio, value added measure.

c. *Stated findings*

The P/T ratio and the school average value added measures are positive and significant in models both with A and without A included.

In regressions that examine determinants of schooling level completed, the coefficient on the value added measure was positive and significant and the coefficient on the P/T ratio was positive but insignificant.

Q had a smaller impact in districts where desegregation was involuntary.

G. Miscellaneous data sources (two or fewer studies using a particular source): The Postcensal Survey of Professionals (1962), 1968 Urban Problems Survey, Project Talent, and Minnesota Twin Registry Data

1. Link (1973)

a. *Data*

Earnings source: Postcensal Survey of Professional and Technical Manpower conducted in 1962 (of persons included in the 1960 Census).

Earnings sample: Currently employed, male chemical engineers with some college training. Professors are excluded.

Quality source: Engineers' Council for Professional Development and Astin's selectivity index.

Quality variables: Whether the chemical engineering program or the engineering department is accredited and Astin's selectivity index.

b. *Model*

$$y = X\beta + \delta S + \theta Q + F\pi + A\varphi + \varepsilon.$$

y – 1961 annual earnings (excludes consulting earnings).

X – age, marital status, employer type (government, private, self-employed), region, whether received formal training, years in present field, and whether published.

S – indicators for 12–15 years, 16 years with no degree, bachelor's degree, some graduate study (omitted category), master's degree, and Ph.d.

F – type of residence when a youth, father's occupation, and size of high school graduating class (results not reported).

A – Astin's intellectualism index.

c. *Stated findings*

This study examines the effects of college quality on earnings.

The coefficient on Q is positive and statistically significant when A is excluded from the model.

However, when Astin's intellectualism index ("a proxy for student ability and motivation") and Q are simultaneously included in the model, A is positive and significant whereas the coefficient on Q is positive and insignificant. Higher earnings are primarily due to ability differences and not school quality differences.

2. Link (1975)

a. *Data*

Earnings source: Postcensal Survey of Professional and Technical Manpower conducted in 1962 (of persons included in the 1960 Census).

Earnings sample: Male electrical engineers with some graduate schooling, excluding professors.

Quality source: Allan M. Carter's index (of faculty rankings) of the quality of graduate education in the U.S. categorized into five groups (distinguished and strong, good, adequate, marginal with no Ph.d. program, and not rated).

b. *Model*

$$y = X\beta + \delta S + \theta Q + F\pi + A\varphi + \varepsilon.$$

y – 1961 annual earnings.

X – marital status, employer type (private, government, self), employment status (with job, but not at work), region of residence (4 values), whether published, whether any formal training, years in field, years with firm, age, whether published.

S – indicators for master's degree and Ph.d.
F – father's occupation and residence as a youth.
A – Astin's intellectualism index (3 categories).

c. *Stated findings*
This study examines the effects of college quality on earnings.

The two highest quintile categories of Q are individually statistically significant and all quintiles of φ are jointly significant.

The effects of higher quality diminish with age.

The typical estimates of the return-to-schooling are overstated by 25–33 percent when Q is omitted.

3. Morgenstern (1973)

a. *Data*
Earnings source: 1968 Urban Problems Survey conducted by the SRC. Survey conducted in 15 largely northern cities and two suburbs.
Earnings sample: Excludes self-employed, NILF, and nonrespondents.
Quality source: Source not mentioned, but data is matched by state and decade, suggesting the *Biennial Survey*.
Quality variables: \$/pupil (deflated by the national average for the year). In unreported results, also examines P/T ratio and teacher salaries.

b. *Model*
$$(1) \quad y = X\beta_1 + \delta S + \theta_1 Q + F_1\pi_1 + \varepsilon_1 \quad \text{(direct effect)},$$
$$(2) \quad S = X\beta_2 + \theta_2 Q + F_2\pi_2 + \varepsilon_2 \quad \text{(indirect effect)},$$
$$(3) \quad y = X\beta_2 + \theta_3 Q + F_2\pi_3 + \varepsilon_3 \quad \text{(reduced form)}.$$
Regressions are run separately for blacks and whites.
y – hourly wage rates.
X – indicators for gender, experience, and whether living in the South.
S – indicators for 0–7, 8–11, 13–15 and 16+ years of schooling.
F_1 – whether father had low education.
F_2 – F_1 and Duncan index of father's occupation.

c. *Stated findings*
In Stage 1, the coefficient on Q is significant for blacks (10 percent rate of return), but not for whites.

In Stage 2, the coefficient on Q is positively correlated and significant for whites and blacks and the impact is larger for blacks.

In Stage 3, the coefficient on Q is positive and significant and has a larger impact on whites' earnings.

"...this study ... finds that, especially for blacks, the quality of education is economically important".

4. Ribich and Murphy (1975)

a. *Data*

Earnings source: Project Talent (interview of 9th grade males in 1959 with a follow-up in 1968).

Earnings sample: Males attending public schools that are not on active military duty and that answered the education and occupation questions. If still in school, they answered the degree plan and course of study questions. Includes several extensions on sub-populations.

Quality source: Project Talent.

Quality variable: \$/pupil in the system (elementary and high school) where educated in the 9th grade.

b. *Model*

(1) $A = X\beta_1 + \theta_1 Q + F\pi_1 + \varepsilon_1,$

(2) $S = X\beta_2 + \theta_2 Q + F\pi_2 + A\varphi_2 + \varepsilon_2,$

(3) $y = X\beta_3 + \delta_3 S + \theta_3 Q + F\pi_3 + A\varphi_3 + \varepsilon_3.$

y – final adjusted lifetime earnings (predicted from 1967 annual earnings).

X – race, South.

S – years of schooling (completed or expected, depending on enrollment status).

F – socioeconomic index (contained in the data) and average socioeconomic index of 9th graders in the same school.

A – TAFQT (similar to AFQT).

c. *Stated findings*

Although the coefficient on Q is insignificant in (1) and (3), it is positive and significant in (2). Therefore, "the chief effect of spending differences on lifetime income is found to work through this school continuation link".

The rate-of-return to increased educational spending (Q), however, is negative.

5. Behrman, Rosenzweig and Taubman (1996)

a. *Data*

Earnings source: Minnesota Twin Registry survey conducted in 1994.

Earnings sample: MZ and DZ female twins with earnings data (the authors use the last available, real wage). Data includes the names of colleges attended by the respondents.

Quality source: CASPAR and Barron's Guides to 2- and 4-year colleges.

Quality variables: \$/student, full-time equivalent enrolled students, students/faculty, whether grants Ph.d.'s, whether public or private, and mean salaries of full professors. Specifications also include an indicator for absent faculty salary along with all other college characteristics (results not reported by the authors).

b. *Model*

$$y = X\beta + S\delta + Q\theta + \varepsilon.$$

Model estimated for (1) DZ twins, (2) within DZ twin pairs, (3) within MZ twin pairs, and (4) a BRT model using DZ and MZ twins. (Not clear what the BRT model is, but it has 179 variables.)

y – (the log of) full-time earnings.

S – years of schooling.

X – full-time experience.

c. *Stated findings*

Examines the effect of college quality on earnings.

Attendance at higher quality colleges leads to higher earnings. "The statistically-preferred estimates suggest that Ph.d.-granting, private universities with well-paid senior faculty and smaller enrollments produce students who have significantly higher earnings later in life.".

Those with higher individual and family endowments attend higher quality colleges.

References

Akin, J.S., Garfinkel, I. (1977). "School expenditures and the economic return to schooling". Journal of Human Resources 12 (4, Winter), 460–481.

Akin, J.S., Garfinkel, I. (1980). "The quality of education and cohort variation in black–white earnings differentials: Comment". American Economic Review 70 (1, March), 186–191.

Akin, J.S., Kniesner, T.J. (1976). "Proxies for observations on individuals sampled from a population". Journal of Human Resources 11 (3, Summer), 411–413.

Altonji, J.G., Dunn, T.A. (1996). "Using siblings to estimate the effect of school quality on wages". Review of Economics and Statistics 78 (4, November), 665–671.

Astin, A.W. (1965). Who Goes Where to College? Science Research Associates, Chicago.

Behrman, J.R., Rosenzweig, M.R., Taubman, P. (1996). "College choice and wages: Estimates using data on female twins". Review of Economics and Statistics 78 (4, November), 672–685.

Betts, J.R. (1995). "Does school quality matter? Evidence from the National Longitudinal Survey of youth". Review of Economics and Statistics 77 (2, May), 231–250.

Betts, J. (1996). "Do school resources matter only for older workers?". Review of Economics and Statistics 78 (4, November), 638–652.

Betts, J.R. (2001). "The impact of school resources on women's earnings and educational attainment: Findings from the National Longitudinal Survey of young women". Journal of Labor Economics 19 (3, July), 635–657.

Card, D., Krueger, A.B. (1992a). "Does school quality matter? Returns to education and the characteristics of public schools in the United States". Journal of Political Economy 100 (1, February), 1–40.

Card, D., Krueger, A.B. (1992b). "School quality and black–white relative earnings: A direct assessment". Quarterly Journal of Economics 107 (1, February), 151–200.

Carter, A.M. (1966). An Assessment of Quality in Graduate Education. American Council on Education, Washington, DC.

Cass, J., Birnbaum, M. (1964). Comparative Guide to American Colleges. Harper and Row, New York.

Gourman, J. (1967). The Gourman Report: Ratings of American Colleges. Continuing Education Institute, Phoenix.

Griffin, P., Ganderton, P.T. (1996). "Evidence on omitted variable bias in earnings equations [family effects]". Economics of Education Review 15 (2, April), 139–148.

Grogger, J. (1996a). "School expenditures and post-schooling earnings: Evidence from the high school and beyond". Review of Economics and Statistics 78 (4, November), 628–637.

Grogger, J. (1996b). "Does school quality explain the recent black/white wage trend?". Journal of Labor Economics 14 (2, April), 231–253.

Heckman, J., Layne-Farrar, A., Todd, P. (1996). "Human capital pricing equations with an application to estimating the effect of schooling quality on earnings". Review of Economics and Statistics 78 (4, November), 562–610.

Johnson, G.E., Stafford, F.P. (1973). "Social returns to quantity and quality of schooling". Journal of Human Resources 8 (2, Spring), 139–155.

Johnson, W.R., Neal, D.A. (1996). "The role of premarket factors in black–white wage differences". Journal of Political Economy 104 (5, October), 869–895.

Jud, G.D., Walker, J.L. (1977). "Discrimination by race and class and the impact of school quality". Social Science Quarterly 57 (4, March), 731–749.

Link, C.R. (1973). "The quantity and quality of education and their influence on earnings: The case of chemical engineers". Review of Economics and Statistics 55 (2, May), 241–247.

Link, C.R. (1975). "Graduate education, school quality, experience, student ability, and earnings". Journal of Business 48 (4, October), 477–491.

Link, C.R., Ratledge, E.C. (1975a). "The influence of the quantity and quality of education on black–white earnings differentials: Some new evidence". Review of Economics and Statistics 57 (3, August), 346–350.

Link, C.R., Ratledge, E.C. (1975b). "Social returns to quantity and quality of education: A further statement". Journal of Human Resources 10 (1, Winter), 78–89.

Link, C.R., Ratledge, E.C. (1976). "Proxies for observations on individuals sampled from a population: Replay". Journal of Human Resources 11 (3, Summer), 413–419.

Link, C., Ratledge, E., Lewis, K. (1976). "Black–white differences in returns to schooling: Some new evidence". American Economic Review 66 (March), 221–223.

Link, C., Ratledge, E., Lewis, K. (1980). "The quality of education and cohort variation in black–white earnings differentials: Reply". American Economic Review 70 (1, March), 196–203.

Mincer, J. (1974). Schooling, Experience, and Earnings. Columbia University Press, New York and London.

Morgan, J., Sirageldin, I. (1968). "A note on the quality dimension in education". Journal of Political Economy 76 (September/October), 1069–1077.

Morgenstern, R.D. (1973). "Direct and indirect effects on earnings of schooling and socio-economic background". Review of Economics and Statistics 55 (May), 225–233.

Nechyba, T.J. (1990). "The southern wage gap, human capital and the quality of education". Southern Economic Journal 57 (2, October), 308–322.

Parnes, H.S., Kohen, A.I. (1975). "Occupational information and labor market status: The case of young men". Journal of Human Resources 10 (Winter), 44–55.

Ribich, T.I., Murphy, J.L. (1975). "The economic returns to increased educational spending". Journal of Human Resources 10 (Winter), 56–77.

Rivkin, S.G. (2000). "School desegregation, academic attainment, and earnings". Journal of Human Resources 35 (2, Spring), 333–346.

Rizzuto, R., Wachtel, P. (1980). "Further evidence on the returns to school quality". Journal of Human Resources 15 (2, Spring), 240–254.

Solmon, L. (1975). "The definition and impact of college quality". Explorations in Economic Research 2 (Fall), 537–587.

Speakman, R., Welch, F. (1995). "Does school quality matter? A reassessment". Working paper.

Strayer, W. (2002). "The returns to school quality: College choice and earnings". Journal of Labor Economics 20 (3, July), 475–503.

Tremblay, C.H. (1986). "The impact of school and college expenditures on the wages of southern and non-southern workers". Journal of Labor Research 7 (2), 201–211.

Wachtel, P. (1975). "The effect of school quality on achievement, attainment levels, and lifetime earnings". Explorations in Economic Research 2 (Fall), 502–536.

Wachtel, P. (1976). "The effect of earnings of school and college investment expenditures". Review of Economics and Statistics 58 (August), 326–331.

Wales, T.J. (1973). "The effect of college quality on earnings: Results from the NBER–Thorndike data". Journal of Human Resources 8 (3, Summer), 306–317.

Welch, F. (1966). "Measurement of the quality of schooling". American Economic Review 56 (May), 379–392.

Welch, F. (1970). "Education in production". Journal of Political Economy 78 (1, January), 35–59.

Chapter 14

SCHOOL RESOURCES

ERIC A. HANUSHEK

Stanford University,
National Bureau of Economic Research

Contents

Handbook of the Economics of Education, Volume 2
Edited by Eric A. Hanushek and Finis Welch
© 2006 Elsevier B.V.   *All rights reserved*
DOI: 10.1016/S1574-0692(06)02014-9

Abstract

Although there is intense policy interest in improving educational outcomes around the world, there is much greater uncertainty about how to accomplish this. The primary governmental decisions often relate to the resources that are devoted to schooling, but the research indicates little consistent relationship between resources to schools and student achievement. Much of the research considers how resources affect student achievement as measured by standardized test scores. These scores are strongly related to individual incomes and to national economic performance, making them a good proxy for longer run economic impacts. But, the evidence – whether from aggregate school outcomes, econometric investigations, or a variety of experimental or quasiexperimental approaches – suggests that pure resource policies that do not change incentives are unlikely to be effective. Importantly, the results appear similar across both developed and developing countries.

Keywords

school resources, class size, achievement, experimental evidence, economic growth, incomes

Introduction

Perhaps no issue in the economics of education is as contentious as debates about the role and impact of school resources. Governments, legislatures, and at times courts routinely decide on the amount of money and resources to go to schools. Parents in part assess the quality of schools by the resources available. Taxpayers consider how resources relate to school performance and to other uses of those funds. As such, research into the effectiveness of various school resources and the efficiency of educational production are relevant to the policy debates, and many research results enter swiftly into the discussions. Yet, available research raises questions about the effectiveness of current spending.

This chapter considers the underlying approach to understanding the impact of resources and provides an overview of the current state of knowledge. Because of the interest in the topic and the recent dramatic expansions in the data available about schools, the field is rapidly expanding. Thus, the empirical results are soon dated, even if the general approach and conclusions remain viable.

The discussion is broad in its coverage – identifying research around the globe. But it is also narrow in its focus – emphasizing resource effects while leave details such as the impacts of teacher quality to other chapters. The chapter also attempts to link research and policy implications, since the attention given to the area is largely driven by its closeness to actual policy making.

1. Overview and motivation

A wide variety of policy discussions about schools revolve around the quality of schools. Most schooling around the world is publicly provided, and governments routinely and regularly make decisions about the support of schools. In that, they are frequently motivated by goals of student performance, but they cannot directly affect the level of outcomes. This leads to a concentration on items that can be directly controlled or affected by policy. Perhaps the most common focus is the level of resources provided to schools, although this clearly is just one part of the overall policy picture. Governmental policy can and does have considerable impact through the regulations on schools and the incentives that are set up by the funding, monitoring, and regulation of schools [see, for example, the international evidence in Wößmann (2001, 2003a, 2003b)].

Indeed, one major thrust of policy over recent years has been the concentration more directly on outcomes through the specification of objectives (or standards) for schools and through the assessment of student accomplishment of these objectives through a range of accountability systems.[1] The policies of individual US states, for example, were reinforced by federal policy to hold schools responsible for achievement results.

---

[1] See, for example, Hanushek and Raymond (2005) for the US or Burgess et al. (2005) for England.

Nonetheless, even when the focus is on student outcomes, the debates invariably return to questions about whether the resources provided to the schools are sufficient.

The discussion of resource usage in schools is closely related to questions about the efficiency of schools. It is quite natural to think of the level of resource usage as an index of school quality. By analogy to a profit maximizing firm, if schools are effectively maximizing outcomes and are producing efficiently, then the resources into schools will be an index of the outcomes. Moreover, more inputs to the firm can be expected to raise the level of outputs. The key element in this analogy is that the market competition forces the for-profit firm to efficient production.

The situation with government provision of schools and without direct competition changes the perspective dramatically. The presumption of efficient provision is suspect when government produces the services. And, if the resource use is inefficient, the relationship between added resources and outcomes is unclear. This simple observation motivates a direct investigation of the relationship between outcomes and inputs to schools.

Much of the policy discussion throughout the world concentrates on schooling inputs, a seemingly natural focus. And, with the longstanding importance that has been attached to schooling, considerable change has occurred in the levels of common inputs. Class sizes have fallen, qualifications of teachers have risen, and expenditures have increased. Unfortunately, little evidence exists to suggest that any significant changes in student outcomes have accompanied this growth in resources devoted to schools. Because many find the limited relationship between school inputs and student outcomes surprising and hard to believe, this chapter delves into the evidence available on this score in some detail.

2. Measurement of outcomes

Economists have devoted considerable attention to understanding how human capital affects a variety of economic outcomes. The underlying notion is that individuals make investment decisions in themselves through schooling and other routes. The accumulated skills that are relevant for the labor market from these investments over time represent an important component of the human capital of an individual. The investments made to improve skills then return future economic benefits in much the same way that a firm's investment in a set of machines (physical capital) returns future production and income. In the case of public education, parents and public officials act as trustees for their children in setting many aspects of the investment paths.

In looking at human capital and its implications for future outcomes, economists are frequently agnostic about where these skills come from or how they are produced. Although we return to that below, it is commonly presumed that formal schooling is one of several important contributors to the skills of an individual and to human capital. It is not the only factor. Parents, individual abilities, and friends undoubtedly contribute.

Schools nonetheless have a special place because they are most directly affected by public policies. For this reason, we frequently emphasize the role of schools.

The human capital perspective immediately makes it evident that the real issues are ones of long-run outcomes. Future incomes of individuals are related to their past investments. It is not their income while in school or their income in their first job. Instead, it is their income over the course of their working life.

The distribution of income in the economy similarly involves both the mixture of people in the economy and the pattern of their incomes over their lifetime. Specifically, most measures of how income and well-being vary in the population do not take into account the fact that some of the low-income people have low incomes only because they are just beginning a career. Their lifetime income is likely to be much larger as they age, gain experience, and move up in their firms and career. What is important is that any noticeable effects of the current quality of schooling on the distribution of skills and income will only be realized years in the future, when those currently in school become a significant part of the labor force. In other words, most workers in the economy were educated years and even decades in the past – and they are the ones that have the most impact on current levels of productivity and growth, if for no reason other than that they represent the larger share of active workers.

Much of the early and continuing development of empirical work on human capital concentrates on the role of school attainment, that is, the quantity of schooling. The revolution in the United States during the twentieth century was universal schooling. This has spread around the world, encompassing both developed and developing countries. Quantity of schooling is easily measured, and data on years attained, both over time and across individuals, are readily available.

Today, however, policy concerns in most corners of the world revolve much more around issues of quality than issues of quantity.

Most economists tend to emphasize labor market outcomes when thinking about differences in individual skills (as with the basic human capital models). For most schooling discussions, however, direct analysis of labor market outcomes is not practical, because these outcomes are only observed years after the schooling takes place. This fact makes it difficult to relate schooling experiences or other background factors to outcomes.

The widely adopted alternative considers, at least conceptually, a two step analytical procedure. The first step involves considering how schools and other influences on students relate to proxy measures of individual skills, of which measures of cognitive skills are the most readily available and most common object of analysis. The second step, rarely done within the same analysis, considers how the proxy relates to labor market outcomes. In fact, the second step has been infrequently considered at all and has largely been just assumed.

This initial discussion fills in the relationship between standardized tests of cognitive skills and later outcomes. While this step is also difficult, because it generally requires fairly long panel observations, there is now a reasonable amount of evidence that has accumulated.

Two other observations help in the interpretation of these results. First, many general discussions of schools consider a range of outcomes that include cognitive skills but also a variety of other factors such as creativity, teamwork, political knowledge, and the like.[2] Concentration on cognitive skills is not meant to deny other potential outcomes, although the limited analysis of other things makes it difficult to say much about them. Second, while part of the subsequent discussion refers to differences in test scores as reflecting school quality, it is also clear that test score variations can come from a variety of nonschool factors including families, peers and neighborhoods. The reasoning in using the narrower language about school quality is simply that we generally believe (and have evidence) that school quality differences are directly related to test score differences.

2.1. Impacts of quality on individual incomes – developed countries

One of the challenges in understanding the impact of quality differences in human capital has been simply knowing how to measure quality. Much of the discussion of quality – in part related to new efforts to provide better accountability – has identified cognitive skills as the important dimension. And, while there is ongoing debate about the testing and measurement of these skills, most parents and policy makers alike accept the notion that cognitive skills are a key dimension of schooling outcomes. The question is whether this proxy for school quality – students' performance on standardized tests – is correlated with individuals' performance in the labor market and the economy's ability to grow. Until recently, little comprehensive data have been available to show any relationship between differences in cognitive skills and any related economic outcomes. Such data are now becoming available.

Beginning with Mincer (1970, 1974), economists have employed readily available census data to estimate what is now simply referred to as a "Mincer equation":

$$\ln(y_i) = a_0 + \rho S_i + a_1 Exp + a_2 Exp^2 + X_i \beta + \varepsilon_i, \tag{1}$$

where y_i is earnings, S_i is years of schooling, Exp_i is labor market (or potential) experience, X_i is a vector of other individual attributes and ε_i is an error term. The object of attention, ρ, is interpreted as the rate of return to a year of schooling, and this has been estimated for a very large number of countries around the world [see Psacharopoulos (1994)].[3]

---

[2] Indeed, much of the discussion of human capital and schooling makes a distinction between private and social returns to schooling. The social returns often include a broad set of factors that might have externalities such as the impact on crime, the functioning of democracy, and so forth. See Hanushek (2002).

[3] There has been some controversy over exactly how to estimate the rate of return to school attainment. The main issue has revolved around whether or not a causal interpretation can be given to ρ. The argument has been that higher-ability students are more likely to continue in schooling. Therefore, part of the higher earnings observed for those with additional schooling really reflects pay for added ability and not for the additional schooling. Early discussion of ability bias can be found in Griliches (1974). Economists have pursued

A variety of researchers, however, have investigated how quality enters, and they document that the earnings advantages to higher achievement on standardized tests are quite substantial. These results are derived from different specific approaches, but the basic underlying analysis involves estimating a standard "Mincer" earnings function and adding a measure of individual cognitive skills,

$$\ln(y_i) = a_0 + \rho S_i + \gamma T_i + a_1 Exp + a_2 Exp^2 + X_i \beta + \varepsilon_i, \qquad (2)$$

where T_i is the individual's measured cognitive skill and γ is the return to quality.

There is mounting evidence that quality measured by test scores is directly related to individual earnings, productivity, and economic growth. A variety of researchers documents that the earnings advantages to higher achievement on standardized tests are quite substantial.[4] While these analyses emphasize different aspects of individual earnings, they typically find that measured achievement has a clear impact on earnings after allowing for differences in the quantity of schooling, the experiences of workers, and other factors that might also influence earnings. In other words, higher quality as measured by tests similar to those currently being used in accountability systems around the country is closely related to individual productivity and earnings.

Three recent US studies provide direct and quite consistent estimates of the impact of test performance on earnings [Mulligan (1999), Murnane et al. (2000), Lazear (2003)]. These studies employ different nationally representative data sets that follow students after they leave schooling and enter the labor force. When scores are standardized, they suggest that one standard deviation increase in mathematics performance at the end of high schools translates into 12 percent higher annual earnings.

Murnane et al. (2000) provide evidence from the High School and Beyond and the National Longitudinal Survey of the High School Class of 1972. Their estimates suggest some variation with males obtaining a 15 percent increase and females a 10 percent increase per standard deviation of test performance. Lazear (2003), relying on a somewhat younger sample from NELS88, provides a single estimate of 12 percent. These estimates are also very close to those in Mulligan (1999), who finds 11 percent for the normalized AFQT score in the NLSY data. By way of comparison, estimates of the value of an additional year of school attainment are typically 7–10 percent.

a variety of analytical approaches for dealing with this. The approaches have included looking for circumstances where the amount of schooling is affected by things other than the student's valuation of continuing and considering the income differences among twins [see Card (1999)]. The various adjustments for ability differences typically make small differences on the estimates of the value of schooling, and Heckman and Vytlacil (2001) argue that it is not possible to separate the effects of ability and schooling.

[4] These results are derived from different specific approaches, but the basic underlying analysis involves estimating a standard "Mincer" earnings function and adding a measure of individual cognitive skills. This approach relates the logarithm of earnings to years of schooling, experience, and other factors that might yield individual earnings differences. The clearest analyses are found in the following references [which are analyzed in Hanushek (2002)]. See Bishop (1989, 1991), O'Neill (1990), Grogger and Eide (1993), Blackburn and Neumark (1993, 1995), Murnane, Willett and Levy (1995), Neal and Johnson (1996), Mulligan (1999), Murnane et al. (2000, 2001), Altonji and Pierret (2001) and Lazear (2003).

There are reasons to believe that these estimates provide a lower bound on the impact of higher achievement. First, these estimates are obtained fairly early in the work career (age from mid-twenties to early-thirties), and other analysis suggests that the impact of test performance becomes larger with experience.[5] Second, the labor market experiences that are observed begin the mid-1980s and extend into the mid-1990s, but other evidence suggests that the value of skills and of schooling has grown throughout and past that period. Third, future general improvements in productivity are likely to lead to larger returns to skill.[6]

A limited number of additional studies are available for developed countries outside of the United States. McIntosh and Vignoles (2001) study wages in the United Kingdom and find strong returns to both numeracy and literacy.[7] Finnie and Meng (2002) and Green and Riddell (2003) investigate returns to cognitive skills in Canada. Both suggest that literacy has a significant return, but Finnie and Meng (2002) find an insignificant return to numeracy. This latter finding stands at odds with most other analyses that have emphasized numeracy or math skills.

Another part of the return to school quality comes through continuation in school.[8] There is substantial US evidence that students who do better in school, either through grades or scores on standardized achievement tests, tend to go farther in school.[9]

---

[5] Altonji and Pierret (2001) find that the impact of achievement grows with experience, because the employer has a chance to observe the performance of workers.

[6] The earnings analyses typically compare workers of different ages at one point in time to obtain an estimate of how earnings will change for any individual. If, however, productivity improvements occur in the economy, these will tend to raise the earnings of individuals over time. Thus, the impact of improvements in student skills are likely to rise over the work life instead of being constant as portrayed here, at least if the technologies expand similar to the past with biases toward skilled labor.

[7] Because they look at discrete levels of skills, it is difficult to compare the quantitative magnitudes directly to the US work.

[8] Much of the work by economists on differences in worker skills has actually been directed at the issue of determining the average labor market returns to additional schooling. The argument has been that higher-ability students are more likely to continue in schooling. Therefore, part of the higher earnings observed for those with additional schooling really reflects pay for added ability and not for the additional schooling. Economists have pursued a variety of analytical approaches for dealing with this, including adjusting for measured cognitive test scores, but this work generally ignores issues of variation in school quality. The approaches have included looking for circumstances where the amount of schooling is affected by things other than the student's valuation of continuing and considering the income differences among twins [see Card (1999)]. The various adjustments for ability differences typically make small differences on the estimates of the value of schooling, and Heckman and Vytlacil (2001) argue that it is not possible to separate the effects of ability and schooling. The only explicit consideration of school quality typically investigates expenditure and resource differences across schools, but these are known to be poor measures of school quality differences [Hanushek (2002)].

[9] See, for example, Dugan (1976), Manski and Wise (1983). Rivkin (1995) finds that variations in test scores capture a considerable proportion of the systematic variation in high school completion and in college continuation, so that test score differences can fully explain black–white differences in schooling. Bishop (1991) and Hanushek, Rivkin and Taylor (1996), in considering the factors that influence school attainment, find that individual achievement scores are highly correlated with continued school attendance. Neal and

Murnane et al. (2000) separate the direct returns to measured skill from the indirect returns of more schooling and suggest that perhaps one-third to one-half of the full return to higher achievement comes from further schooling. Note also that the effect of quality improvements on school attainment incorporates concerns about drop out rates. Specifically, higher student achievement keeps students in school longer, which will lead among other things to higher graduation rates at all levels of schooling.[10]

The impact of test performance on individual earnings provides a simple summary of the primary economic rewards to an individual. This estimate combines the impacts on hourly wages and on employment/hours worked. It does not include any differences in fringe benefits or nonmonetary aspects of jobs. Nor does it make any allowance for aggregate changes in the labor market that might occur over time.

2.2. Impacts of quality on individual incomes – developing countries

Questions remain about whether the clear impacts of quality in the US and other developed countries generalize further, particularly developing countries. The literature on returns to cognitive skills in developing countries is restricted to a relatively limited number of countries: Ghana, Kenya, Morocco, Pakistan, South Africa and Tanzania. Moreover, a number of studies actually employ the same basic data, albeit with different analytical approaches, but come up with somewhat different results.

Table 1 provides a simple summary to the quantitative estimates available for developing countries. The summary of the evidence permits a tentative conclusion that the returns to quality may be even larger in developing countries than in developed countries. This of course would be consistent with the range of estimates for returns to quantity of schooling [e.g., Psacharopoulos (1994)], which are frequently interpreted as indicating diminishing marginal returns to schooling.

There are some reasons for caution in interpreting the precise magnitude of estimates. First, the estimates appear to be quite sensitive to the estimation methodology itself. Both within individual studies and across studies using the same basic data, the results are quite sensitive to the techniques employed in uncovering the fundamental parameter

---

Johnson (1996) in part use the impact of achievement differences of blacks and whites on school attainment to explain racial differences in incomes. Their point estimates of the impact of cognitive skills (AFQT) on earnings and school attendance appear to be roughly comparable to that found in Murnane et al. (2000). Behrman et al. (1998) find strong achievement effects on both continuation into college and quality of college; moreover, the effects are larger when proper account is taken of the various determinants of achievement. Hanushek and Pace (1995) find that college completion is significantly related to higher test scores at the end of high school.

[10] This work has not, however, investigated completely how achievement affects the ultimate outcomes of additional schooling. For example, if over time lower-achieving students tend increasingly to attend further schooling, these schools may be forced to offer more remedial courses, and the variation of what students know and can do at the end of school may expand commensurately.

Table 1

Summary of estimated returns to a standard deviation increase in cognitive skills

Country	Study	Estimated effect[a]	Notes
Ghana	Glewwe (1996)	0.21**–0.3** (government) 0.14–0.17 (private)	Alternative estimation approaches yield some differences; math effects shown generally more important than reading effects, and all hold even with Raven's test for ability
Ghana	Jolliffe (1998)	0.05–0.07*	Household income related to average math score with relatively small variation by estimation approach; effect from off-farm income with on-farm income unrelated to skills
Ghana	Vijverberg (1999)	?	Income estimates for math and reading with nonfarm self-employment; highly variable estimates (including both positive and negative effects) but effects not generally statistically significant
Kenya	Boissiere, Knight and Sabot (1985), Knight and Sabot (1998)	0.19**–0.22**	Total sample estimates: small variation by primary and secondary school leavers
Morocco	Angrist and Lavy (1997)	?	Cannot convert to standardized scores because use indexes of performance; French writing skills appear most important for earnings, but results depend on estimation approach
Pakistan	Alderman et al. (1996)	0.12–0.28*	Variation by alternative approaches and by controls for ability and health; larger and more significant without ability and health controls
Pakistan	Behrman, Ross and Sabot (2006)	0.25	Estimates of structural model with combined scores for cognitive skill; index significant at 0.01 level
South Africa	Moll (1998)	0.34**–0.48**	Depending on estimation method, varying impact of computation; comprehension (not shown) generally insignificant
Tanzania	Boissiere, Knight and Sabot (1985), Knight and Sabot (1998)	0.07–0.13*	Total sample estimates: smaller for primary than secondary school leavers

*Significant at 0.05 level.

**Significant at 0.01 level.

[a]Estimates indicate proportional increase in wages from a one standard deviation increase in measured test scores.

for cognitive skills.[11] Second, the evidence on variations within developing countries is not entirely clear. For example, Jolliffe (1998) finds little impact of skills on farm income, while Behrman, Ross and Sabot (2006) suggest an equivalence across sectors at least on theoretical grounds.

Nonetheless, the overall summary is that the available estimates of the impact of cognitive skills on outcomes suggest strong economic returns within developing countries. The substantial magnitude of the typical estimates indicates that quality concerns are very real for developing countries and that this aspect of schools simply cannot be ignored – a topic that comes up below.

2.3. Impacts of quality on economic growth

The relationship between measured labor force quality and economic growth is perhaps even more important than the impact of human capital and school quality on individual productivity and incomes. Economic growth determines how much improvement will occur in the overall standard of living of society. Moreover, the education of each individual has the possibility of making others better off (in addition to the individual benefits just discussed). Specifically, a more educated society may lead to higher rates of invention; may make everybody more productive through the ability of firms to introduce new and better production methods; and may lead to more rapid introduction of new technologies. These externalities provide extra reason for being concerned about the quality of schooling.

The current economic position of the United States, for example, is largely the result of its strong and steady growth over the twentieth century. Economists have developed a variety of models and ideas to explain differences in growth rates across countries – invariably featuring the importance of human capital.[12]

The empirical work supporting growth analyses has emphasized school attainment differences across countries. Again, this is natural because, while compiling comparable data on many things for different countries is difficult, assessing quantity of schooling is more straightforward. The typical study finds that quantity of schooling is highly related to economic growth rates. But, quantity of schooling is a very crude measure of the knowledge and cognitive skills of people – particularly in an international context.

Hanushek and Kimko (2000) go beyond simple quantity of schooling and delve into quality of schooling.[13] Kimko and I incorporate the information about international differences in mathematics and science knowledge that has been developed through testing over the past four decades. And we find a remarkable impact of differences in school quality on economic growth.

---

[11] The sensitivity to estimation approach is not always the case; see, for example, Jolliffe (1998). A critique and interpretation of the alternative approaches within a number of these studies can be found in Glewwe (2002).

[12] Barro and Sala-i-Martin (2003) review recent analyses and the range of factors that are included.

[13] Barro and Lee (2001) provide an analysis of qualitative differences that also includes literacy.

The international comparisons of quality come from piecing together results of a series of tests administered over the past four decades. In 1963 and 1964, the International Association for the Evaluation of Education al Achievement (IEA) administered the first of a series of mathematics tests to a voluntary group of countries. These initial tests suffered from a number of problems, but they did prove the feasibility of such testing and set in motion a process to expand and improve on the undertaking.[14]

Subsequent testing, sponsored by the IEA and others, has included both math and science and has expanded on the group of countries that have been tested. In each, the general model has been to develop a common assessment instrument for different age groups of students and to work at obtaining a representative group of students taking the tests. An easy summary of the participating countries and their test performance is found in Figure 1. This figure tracks performance aggregated across the age groups and subject area of the various tests and scaled to a common test mean of 50.[15] (The United States and the United Kingdom are the only countries to participate in all of the testing.)

There is some movement across time of country performance on the tests, but for the one country that can be checked – the United States – the pattern is consistent with other data. The National Assessment of Educational Progress (NAEP) in the United States is designed to follow performance of US students for different subjects and ages. NAEP performance over this period, shown in Figure 2, also exhibits a sizable dip in the seventies, a period of growth in the eighties, and a leveling off in the nineties.

Kimko's and my analysis of economic growth is very straightforward. We develop a consistent measure of labor force quality based on information about international differences in mathematics and science knowledge. We combine all of the available earlier test scores into a single composite measure of quality and consider statistical models that explain differences in growth rates across nations during the period 1960 to 1990.[16] The basic statistical models relate annual growth rates of GDP per capita (g_c) to our measure of labor force quality (T_c), the initial level of income (Y^0), the quantity of schooling (S_c), and a vector of other control variables (Z_c) which includes

---

[14] The problems included issues of developing an equivalent test across countries with different school structure, curricula and language; issues of selectivity of the tested populations; and issues of selectivity of the nations that participated. The first tests did not document or even address these issues in any depth.

[15] The details of the tests and aggregation can be found in Hanushek and Kimko (2000) and Hanushek and Kim (1995). Figure 1 excludes the earliest administration and runs through the Third International Mathematics and Science Study (TIMSS) administered in 1995. Other international tests have been given and are not included in the figure. First, reading and literacy tests have been given in 1991 and very recently. The difficulty of unbiased testing of reading across languages plus the much greater attention attached to math and science both in the literature on individual earnings and in the theoretical growth literature led to the decision not to include these test results in the empirical analysis. Second, the most recent follow-up to the 1995 TIMSS in math and science (given in 1999) plus the 2003 TIMSS and the PISA tests for 2000 and 2003 are excluded from the figure simply for presentational reasons.

[16] We exclude the recent TIMSS tests from 1995 through 2003 and the OECD's PISA tests because they were taken outside of the analytical period on economic growth. We combine the test measures over the 1965–1991 period into a single measure for each country. The underlying objective is to obtain a measure of quality for the labor force in the period during which growth is measured.

Figure 1. Performance on international mathematics and science examinations.

in different specifications the population growth rates, political measures, openness of the economies, and the like:

$$g_c = \alpha_0 + \eta T_c + \alpha_1 Y_c^0 + \alpha_2 S_c + Z_c \phi + v_c. \tag{3}$$

Most important, the impact of the quality of the labor force as measured by math and science scores (η) is extremely important. One standard deviation difference on test performance is related to 1 percent difference in annual growth rates of gross domestic product (GDP) per capita.[17] This quality effect, while possibly sounding small, is actually very large and significant. Because the added growth compounds, it leads to powerful effects on national income and on societal well-being.

One common concern in analysis such as this is that schooling might not be the actual cause of growth but, in fact, may just reflect other attributes of the economy that are beneficial to growth. For example, as seen in Figure 1, the East Asian countries consistently score very highly on the international tests, and they also had extraordinarily high growth over the 1960–1990 period. It may be that other aspects of these East Asian economies have driven their growth and that the statistical analysis of labor force quality simply is picking out these countries. But in fact, even if the East Asian countries are excluded from the analysis, a strong – albeit slightly smaller – relationship is still observed with test performance. This test of sensitivity of the results seems to reflect a basic importance of school quality, a factor that contributes also to the observed growth of East Asian countries.

Another concern might be that other factors that affect growth, such as efficient market organizations, are also associated with efficient and productive schools – so that, again, the test measures are really a proxy for other attributes of the country. In order to investigate this, we concentrate on immigrants to the United States who received their education in their home countries. We find that immigrants who were schooled in countries that have higher scores on the international math and science examinations earn more in the United States. This analysis makes allowance for any differences in school attainment, labor market experience, or being native English-language speakers. In other words, skill differences as measured by the international tests are clearly rewarded in the United States labor market, reinforcing the validity of the tests as a measure of individual skills and productivity.[18]

In sum, although cognitive test scores may not measure all of the various outcomes expected from schools, they do provide important information on quality as related to the labor market returns. Further, no other measure provides such a consistent and validated assessment of the quality of educational outcomes.

[17] The details of this work can be found in Hanushek and Kimko (2000) and Hanushek (2003b). Importantly, adding other factors potentially related to growth, including aspects of international trade, private and public investment, and political instability, leaves the effects of labor force quality unchanged.

[18] Finally, the observed relationships could simply reflect reverse causality, that is, that countries that are growing rapidly have the resources necessary to improve their schools and that better student performance is the result of growth, not the cause of growth. This in fact is closely related to the analysis below about the impact of resources on achievement, and thus the discussion is left until later.

3. Aggregate United States performance

Given that student assessments provide a measure of school outcomes, it is possible to begin the investigation of how school resources (and other factors) relate to student performance. It is instructive to begin with the simplest overall evidence that comes from aggregate scores and then to move to more detailed analytical studies.

The simplest and perhaps clearest demonstration of the resource story is found in the aggregate United States data over the past few decades. The United States, operating under a system that is largely decentralized to the fifty separate states, has pursued the conventionally advocated resource policies vigorously. Table 2 tracks the patterns of pupil–teacher ratios, teacher education and teacher experience. Between 1960 and 2000, pupil–teacher ratios fell by almost 40%. The proportion of teachers with a master's degree or more over doubled so that a majority of all US teachers today have at least a master's degree. Finally, median teacher experience – which is more driven by demographic cycles than active policy – increased significantly, almost doubling since its trough in 1970.

American teachers are heavily unionized, and the most common structure of teacher contracts identifies teacher education levels and teacher experience as the driving force behind salaries. Thus, as teacher inputs rise and as the numbers of students per teachers decline, expenditure per pupil rises. As seen in the bottom row of Table 2, real expenditures per pupil more than tripled over this period.[19] In fact, this period is not special in US schools. Over the entire 100 years of 1890–1990, real spending per pupil rose by at a remarkably steady pace of 3.5% per year [Hanushek and Rivkin (1997)]. Over this longer period, real per student expenditure in 1990 dollars goes from $164 in 1890 to $772 in 1940 to $4,622 in 1990 – roughly quintupling in each fifty-year period.[20]

Table 2
Public school resources in the United States, 1960–2000

	1960	1970	1980	1990	2000
Pupil–teacher ratio	25.8	22.3	18.7	17.2	16.0
Percent of teachers with master's degree or more	23.5	27.5	49.6	53.1	56.2[a]
Median years teacher experience	11	8	12	15	15[a]
Current expenditure/ADA (2000/2001)	$2,235	$3,782	$5,124	$6,867	$7,591

Source: US Department of Education (2002).
[a]Data pertain to 1995. The statistical data of the National Education Association on characteristics of teachers was discontinued.

[19] The calculation of real expenditures deflates by the Consumer Price Index. Use of a wage deflator (see the discussion of prices below) does not significantly change this picture.
[20] These calculations differ from those in Table 1 both in using a different deflator (GDP deflator in 1990 dollars) and in calculating spending per pupil on a membership rather than an attendance basis.

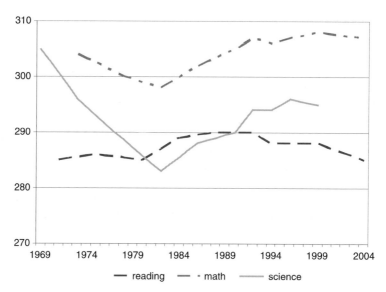

Figure 2. Trends in NAEP performance by subject, 17-year-olds.

The question remains, what was obtained for these spending increases? As mentioned above, since the early 1970s, a random sample of students in the US has been given tests at differing ages in various subjects under the auspices of the National Assessment of Educational Progress, or NAEP. These tests have been designed to provide a consistent measure of performance over time. Figure 2 gives performance data for the relevant period as the previously described input data.[21] In this figure the pattern of average performance by 17-year-olds is traced for reading, mathematics and science. The performance of students in math is slightly higher (less than 0.1 standard deviations) in 2004 than thirty years earlier when spending was dramatically lower. The performance in reading in 2004 is exactly where it was in 1971. The performance of students in science is significantly lower in 1999 (the latest observation) than it was in 1970. Writing performance (not shown) was first tested in 1984 and declined steadily until 1996 when testing was discontinued.[22]

The only other test that provides a national picture of US performance over a long period of time is the Scholastic Aptitude Test, or SAT. This college admissions test has the advantage of providing data going back to the 1960s but the disadvantage of being a

---

[21] The cumulative nature of the educational process implies that scores will reflect both current and past spending. A 17-year-old in 1970, for example, would have entered school in the late 1950s, implying that the resource growth in Table 2 that goes back to 1960 is relevant for comparison with the NAEP performance data.

[22] With writing, test reliability is an issue, and this led to suspension of the writing testing in NAEP.

voluntary test taken by a selective subset of the population.[23] Scores on this test actually plunged from the mid-1960s until the end of the 1970s, suggesting that the NAEP scores that begin in the 1970s may understate the magnitude of the performance problem.[24]

In simplest terms, input policies have been vigorously pursued over a long period of time, but there is no evidence that the added resources have improved student performance, at least for the most recent three decades when it has been possible to compare quantitative outcomes directly. This evidence suggests that the efficacy of further input-based policies depends crucially on improved use of resources compared to past history.

Three arguments are made, however, for why the simple comparison of expenditures and student performance might be misleading: (1) the characteristics of students may have changed such that they are more difficult (and expensive) to educate now than in the past; (2) other expansions of the requirements on schools have driven up costs but would not be expected to influence observed student performance; and (3) changing relative prices have increased schooling costs.

3.1. Changes in students

One simple explanation for why added resources yield no apparent performance improvement is that students are more poorly prepared or motivated for school over time, requiring added resources just to stay even. For example, there have been clear increases in the proportion of children living in single-parent families and, relatedly, in child poverty rates – both of which are hypothesized to lead to lower student achievement. Between 1970 and 1990, children living in poverty families rose from 15% to 20%, while children living with both parents declined from 85% to 73%. The percent of children not speaking English at home also rose from 9% in 1980 to 17% in 2000. But, there have also been other trends that appear to be positive forces on student achievement. Family sizes have fallen, and parental education levels have improved. Among all families with children, the percentage with three or more children fell from 36% to 20%. Moreover, over the same period, adults aged 25–29 with a high school or greater level of schooling went from 74% to 86% (up from 61% in 1960). Finally, enrollment in kindergarten and pre-school increased dramatically over the period.

It is difficult to know how to net out these opposing trends with any accuracy. Extensive research, beginning with the Coleman Report [Coleman et al. (1966)] and continuing through today [Hanushek (1997a)], has demonstrated that differences in families are very important for student achievement. Most of these studies have not focused

---

[23] NAEP samples are not tainted by selection. The school completion rate and the rate of attendance of private schools have been essentially constant over the period of the NAEP tests and testing involves a random sample of public school children.

[24] Analyses of the changes in SAT scores suggest that a portion of the decline in scores comes from increases in the rate of test taking but that the decline also has a real component of lesser average performance over time [Wirtz (1977), Congressional Budget Office (1986)].

their primary attention on families, however, and thus have not delved very far into the measurement and structure of any family influences.[25]

Changes in family inputs have occurred over time, making it possible that a portion of the increased school resources has gone to offset adverse factors. The evidence is nonetheless quite inconclusive about even the direction of any trend effects, let alone the magnitude. The only available quantitative estimates [Grissmer et al. (1994a)] indicate that changing family effects are unable to offset the large observed changes in pupil–teacher ratios and school resources and may have even worked in the opposite direction, making the performance of schools appear better than it was, but there are reasons to be skeptical about these results.[26]

3.2. Exogenous cost increases

The most discussed cost concern involves "special education", programs to deal with students who have various disabilities. The issue is that these programs are expensive but the recipients tend not to take standardized tests. Thus, even if special education programs are effective [Hanushek, Kain and Rivkin (2002)], the increased expenditures on special education will not show up in measured student performance.

Concerns about the education of children with both physical and mental disabilities were translated into federal law with the enactment of the Education for All Handicapped Children Act in 1975. This Act prescribed a series of diagnostics, counseling activities, and educational services to be provided for handicapped students. To implement this and subsequent laws and regulations, school systems expanded staff and programs, developing entirely new administrative structures in many cases to handle

[25] Grissmer et al. (1994b) attempts to sort out the various factors in a crude way. That analysis uses econometric techniques to estimate how various family factors influence children's achievement at a point in time. It then applies these cross-sectionally estimated regression coefficients as weights to the trended family background factors identified above. Their overall findings are that black students performed better over time than would be expected from the trends in black family factors. They attribute this better performance to improvements in schools. On the other hand, white students, who make up the vast majority, performed worse over time than would expected, leading presumably to the opposite conclusion that schools for the majority of students actually got worse over time.

[26] Skepticism comes from methodological problems. First, they do not observe or measure differences in schools but instead simply attribute unexplained residual differences in the predicted and observed trends to school factors. In reality any factor that affects achievement, that is unmeasured, and that has changed over their analysis period would be mixed with any school effects. Second, in estimating the cross-sectional models that provide the weights for the trending family factors, no direct measures of school inputs are included. In the standard analysis of misspecified econometric models, this omission will lead to biased estimates of the influence of family factors if school factors are correlated with the included family factors in the cross-sectional data that underlie their estimation. For example, better educated parents might systematically tend to place their children in better schools. In this simple example, a portion of the effects of schools will be incorrectly attributed to the education of parents, and this will lead to inappropriate weights for the trended family inputs. Third, one must believe either that the factors identified are the true causal influences or that they are stable proxies of the true factors, but there is doubt about this [cf. Mayer (1997)].

"special education". The general thrust of the educational services has been to provide regular classroom instruction where possible ("mainstreaming") along with specialized instruction to deal with specific needs. The result has been growth of students classified as the special education population even as the total student population fell. Between 1977 and 2004, the percentage of students classified as disabled increases from 8.3% to 13.8%. Moreover, the number of special education teachers increases much more rapidly than the number of children classified as disabled.

The magnitude of special education spending and its growth, however, are insufficient to reconcile the cost and performance dilemma. Using the best available estimate of the cost differential for special education – 2.3 times the cost of regular education [Chaikind, Danielson and Brauen (1993)], the growth in special education students between 1980 and 1990 can explain less than 20% of the expenditure growth [Hanushek and Rivkin (1997)]. In other words, while special education programs have undoubtedly influenced overall expenditures, they remain a relatively small portion of the total spending on schools.

Direct estimates of other exogenous programs and changes resulting from other academic aspects of schools such as language instruction for immigrants or nonacademic programs such as sports, art, or music are not readily available. Nonetheless, no evidence suggests that these can explain the magnitude of spending growth.

3.3. Changing prices

A series of well-known arguments emphasize the cost implications of differential technological change and productivity growth [Scitovsky and Scitovsky (1959), Baumol and Bowen (1965), Baumol (1967)]. The focus of this work is the cost disadvantage of a sector that experiences little apparent technological change while other sectors undergo regular productivity improvements. Because the rise in real wages – increases above general inflation – are roughly proportional to the average growth rate of labor productivity in all sectors, the technologically stagnant sector faces increased real labor costs. In other words, industries with rapid improvements in their ability to produce outputs can afford to pay more for workers and will bid up the wages of workers. It is often assumed that the nature of production prevents the stagnant sector from hiring fewer of the increasingly costly labor inputs, thus leading to increases in the price of output. The lack of substitutability of machines for workers can arise either because of some necessity (e.g., the need for four musicians in a horn quartet) or because the quantity of labor input is directly related to perceived quality (e.g., class sizes and the demand for teachers in schools).[27] These simple predictions of increasing costs in low

---

[27] Measurement issues abound. For example, while musical groups may be constrained to a relatively fixed mix of musicians, some believe the advent of recordings, radio, television, and now the Internet have led to a very large expansion of output for the same number of musicians. If defined solely in terms of concert performances, there may be little substitutability, but this does not hold if defined in terms of total music output.

productivity growth sectors, often termed simply "Baumol's disease", dominate explanations for cost growth in government services, the arts, many nonprofit activities, and other industries in which labor services are the most significant input factor. Part of this price increase in schools might simply reflect Baumol's disease. Schools rely heavily on college-trained workers, and the relative pay of college workers has risen dramatically since the mid-1970s [Murphy and Welch (1992), Hanushek et al. (1994)].

This argument cannot, however, change the conclusions on inputs and school outcomes. First, it is important to note that these arguments do not apply to the changes in real resources in Table 2 but only to the cost aggregation in the final line. Second, in terms of real spending, the arguments would imply that the cost deflator understates the change in input costs. But, if costs are deflated on a wage basis for recent periods (1967–1991), the results are quite ambiguous because schools were actually drawing from a lower point in the wage distribution over time [see Hanushek and Rivkin (1997) and Hanushek (1997b)]. Finally, as shown in Table 2, schools have actually substituted *more* of the expensive input (teachers) rather than less over time.

4. Aggregate international data

Most other countries of the world have not tracked student performance over any length of time, making analyses comparable to the United States discussion impossible. Nonetheless, international testing over the past four decades permits an overview of spending across countries. As discussed above, a series of international tests – given from 1963 through 2003 – provide some indication of national performance. (Only the US and UK participated in all tests.) The test performance across time, updated from Hanushek and Kimko (2000), were summarized in Figure 1.

The important feature of these is that cross-country performance bears little relationship to the patterns of expenditure across the countries. Figure 3 shows the comparison of scores on the PISA tests in 2003 and the spending of nations in purchasing power parity terms.[28] Countries are ranked in terms of the average score on the PISA tests, and the height of the bars indicates spending. Except for the developing countries, which both spend noticeably less than the others and perform noticeably poorer, there is little association between spending and performance. For all countries spending at least $1,500 per student, the correlation of spending and performance is 0.18. (At the low end of performance, there are also questions about the validity of the assessments. Scores in the developing countries are very far from the mean of the distribution for developed countries, the set for which the tests were developed.)

---

[28] The Programme for International Student Assessment (PISA) is conducted by the OECD and tests 15-year-olds in mathematics, science and reading. It has been conducted in 2000 and 2003. The scores in the figure are the average across the three subjects. The spending calculations come from Organisation for Economic Co-operation and Development (2003).

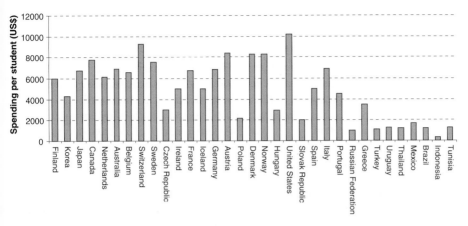

Figure 3. Expenditure per student at all levels (countries ranked by combined PISA 2003 scores).

International comparisons, of course, amplify the problems of possible contamination of the influence of factors other than schools that was considered previously in the case of the United States. As a preliminary attempt to deal with some of these issues, Hanushek and Kimko (2000) estimate models that relate spending, family backgrounds, and other characteristics of countries to student performance for the tests prior to 1995.[29] This estimation consistently indicates a statistically significant negative effect of added resources on performance after controlling for other influences.[30]

Gundlach, Wossmann and Gmelin (2001) consider changes in scores of a set of developed nations between 1970 and 1995 and their relationship to spending changes. They conclude that productivity of schools has fallen dramatically across these countries. Wößmann (2001, 2003b) also performs a related analysis that relies on just the 1995 performance information from the Third International Mathematics and Science Study (TIMSS). His analysis suggests that traditional resource measures bear little consistent relationship to differences in scores among the 39 nations participating in TIMSS for 13-year-olds.

Analysis of aggregate performance data is subject to a variety of problems. Any relationship between resources and student achievement – whether within a single country or across different countries – might be distorted by other influences on performance. Nonetheless, the variations in resources are huge, suggesting that any effect should be apparent in even crude comparisons. No significant effect of spending comes through in the aggregate, even when consideration of family background differences is introduced.

---

[29] The estimation includes average schooling of parents, population growth rates, school participation rates, and separate intercepts for each of the different tests. Several measures of school resources including spending as a proportion of GNP, current expenditures per student, and class size in elementary and secondary schools were also included.

[30] This can also be thought of as an additional causality test in the growth models, because growing countries that spend more on schools to not see higher achievement – the concern with reverse causality.

5. Econometric approach

The aggregate story is supported by an extensive body of direct evidence coming from detailed econometric analyses of student achievement. This evidence has been motivated by a monumental governmental study of US achievement that was conducted in the mid-1960s. The "Coleman Report" [Coleman et al. (1966)] presented evidence that was widely interpreted as saying that schools did not matter. The most important factor in achievement was the family, followed by peers in school. This study led to a great amount of research – research that has supported part of the conclusions of the Coleman study but, more importantly, has clarified the interpretation.

This initial study led to much follow on work of both an empirical and a conceptual variety. This genre is often labeled "education production function" analysis and has pursued a wide variety of specialized analyses. Various conceptual discussions and reviews currently exist, and the focus here is understanding the results and their interpretation.[31]

The framework of analysis of educational performance considers a general production function such as:

$$O_{it} = f\left(F_i^{(t)}, P_i^{(t)}, S_i^{(t)}, A_i\right) + v_{it},\tag{4}$$

where O_{it} – performance of student i at time t, $F_i^{(t)}$ – family inputs cumulative to time t, $P_i^{(t)}$ – cumulative peer inputs, $S_i^{(t)}$ – cumulative school inputs, A_i – innate ability, and a stochastic term v_{it}.

This general structure has motivated an extensive series of empirical studies. The typical empirical study collects information about student performance and about the various educational inputs and then attempts to estimate the characteristics of the production function using econometric techniques.

Two aspects of this formulation are important to point out. First, a variety of influences outside of schools enter into the production of achievement. Second, the production process for achievement is cumulative, building on a series of inputs over time. Both of these are important in the specification and interpretation of educational production functions.

The relevance of many factors outside schools highlights the necessity of going beyond simple comparisons of student performance across schools. Most of the attention in analytical studies has focused on the measurement of school attributes. This focus seems natural from a policy point of view. It also reflects the common use of administrative data in estimating production functions, because administrative data are frequently short of many measures of family background. Nonetheless, this lack of attention to other inputs is unfortunate. First, increasing attention has been given to

---

[31] Conceptual discussions can be found in Hanushek (1979) and Todd and Wolpin (2003). Prior reviews of different strands of work along with more detailed considerations of the range of studies can be found in Hanushek (1986, 2003a) and Betts (1996).

potential policies related to families – such as preschool and daycare programs, after school programs, parent education and the like. Second, because families frequently exert preferences for the schools that their children will attend, incomplete measurement of external influences on performance raise intense issues of selection bias and preclude simple statements about causal influences of schools. Such an observation of course does not seem very profound, but, as discussed below, many empirical studies give little attention to nonschool influences in addressing the impact of school factors. Moreover, public policy debates surprisingly frequently rely on simple accounting of performance across schools. For example, much of the current movement toward increased school accountability often relies on just aggregate student scores for a school.[32] Just the level of student performance is not a reliable indicator of the quality of schools students are attending.

The cumulative nature of achievement, where the learning in any time period builds on prior learning, implies that any analysis must take into account the time path of inputs. This places heavy demands on measurement and data collection, because historical information is frequently difficult to obtain.

The cumulative nature of the production process has been a prime motivation for considering a value-added formulation. At least in a linear version of Equation (4), it is possible to look at the growth in contemporaneous performance over some period of time, instead of the level of performance, and relate that to the flow of specific inputs. The general value-added formulation can be written as

$$O_{it} - O_{it^*} = f^*\left(F_i^{(t-t^*)}, P_i^{(t-t^*)}, S_i^{(t-t^*)}\right) + \upsilon_{it} - \upsilon_{it^*}, \tag{5}$$

where outcome changes over the period $(t - t^*)$ are related to inputs over the same period. Note that this formulation dramatically lessens the data requirements and eliminates anything that appears as a fixed effect in the level of achievement [Equation (5)].

This formulation presumes that innate abilities are constant and thus fall out of achievement growth. With more information on variations over time, it is also possible to allow for ability differences in growth [Rivkin, Hanushek and Kain (2005)]. Alternative formulations have prior achievement, O_{it^*}, on the right-hand side, allowing for coefficient different than one [Hanushek (1979)]. This latter approach has the advantages of allowing for different scales of measurement in achievement during different years and introducing the possibility that growth in performance differs by starting point. It has the disadvantages of introducing measurement error on the right-hand side and of complicating the error structure, particularly in models relying on more than a single year of an individual's achievement growth.

---

[32] With the increasing popularity of publishing average performance of students in different schools, the interpretation of scores becomes more important. In fact, without consideration of the various inputs that go beyond just schools, alternative accountability systems can have perverse effects [cf. Hanushek and Raymond (2001)]. The integration of the underlying theoretical and empirical analysis of the determination of achievement with accountability and incentive systems is an important but underdeveloped area of investigation.

When this formulation is generalized by moving lagged achievement to the right-hand side, the coefficient on lagged achievement indicates the persistence of any prior input effects. The estimation becomes problematic if one is including fixed effects for individual students, since this implies biases from the endogeneity of prior achievement. In this case, it is necessary to use an instrumental variables approach. The statistical problems in estimation using the difference form of Equation (5) depend directly on how far the coefficient on lagged achievement is from one.

In any event, a key element in the consideration of estimation results is the likelihood that they are biased because of the estimation approach, model specification, or available samples of observations. These issues, along with a variety of approaches for dealing with them, are discussed below.

6. United States econometric evidence

With the exception of the Coleman Report, the subsequent analysis seldom has relied on data collected specifically for the study of the educational process. Instead, it has tended to be opportunistic, employing available data to gain insights into school operations. The focus of much of this work has been the effect of varying resources on student achievement. This focus flows from the underlying perspective of production functions; from its obvious relevance for policy; and from the prevalence of relevant resource data in the administrative records that are frequently used.

The summary of production in United States schools here begins with all of the separate estimates of the effects of resources on student performance, and then concentrates on a more refined set of estimates.[33] The underlying work includes all published analyses prior to 1995 that include one of the resource measures described below, that have some measure of family inputs in addition to schools, and that provides the sign and statistical significance of the resource relationship with a measurable student outcome. The 89 individual publications that appeared before 1995 and that form the basis for this analysis contain 376 separate production function estimates. While a large number of analyses were produced as a more or less immediate reaction to the Coleman Report, half of the available estimates have been published since 1985. Of course, a number of subsequent analyses have also appeared since 1995. While not formally assessed, it is

---

[33] Individual publications included in the following summary typically contain more than one set of estimates, distinguished by different measures of student performance, by different grade levels, and frequently by entirely different sampling designs. If, however, a publication includes estimates of alternative specifications employing the same sample and performance measures, only one of the alternative estimates is included. As a general rule, the tabulated results reflect the estimates that are emphasized by the authors of the underlying papers. In some cases, this rule did not lead to a clear choice, at which time the tabulation emphasized statistically significant results among the alternatives preferred by the original author. An alternative approach, followed by Betts (1996), aggregates all of the separate estimates of a common parameter that are presented in each individual paper. Still another approach, followed by Krueger (2002, 2003), aggregates all estimates in a given publication into a single estimate, regardless of the underlying parameter that is being estimated.

clear that including them would not significantly change any of the results reported here, given their mixed results and the large number of prior estimates. No attempt has been made to catalog the newer general analyses, because they have not yielded markedly different results. Individual studies of note will, however, be separately discussed.

Understanding the character of the underlying analyses is important for the subsequent interpretation. Three-quarters of the estimates rely on student performance (O_{it}) measured by standardized tests, while the remainder uses a variety of different measures including such things as continuation in school, dropout behavior, and subsequent labor market earnings. Not surprisingly, test score performance measures are more frequently employed for studying education in primary schools, while a vast majority of the analyses of other outcomes relate to secondary schools. The level of aggregation of the school input measures is also an issue considered in detail below. One-quarter of the estimates consider performance in individual classrooms, while 10% focus on school inputs only at the level of the state. Moreover, fully one-quarter of the estimates employing nontest measures rely solely on interstate variations in school inputs.[34]

Table 3 presents the overall summary of basic results about the key resources that form the basis for most overall policy discussions.[35] The standard hypothesis driving

Table 3

Percentage distribution of estimated effect of key resources on student performance, based on 376 studies

Resources	Number of estimates	Statistically significant		Statistically insignificant
		Positive	Negative	
Real classroom resources				
Teacher–pupil ratio	276	14%	14%	72%
Teacher education	170	9	5	86
Teacher experience	206	29	5	66
Financial aggregates				
Teacher salary	118	20	7	73
Expenditure per pupil	163	27	7	66
Other				
Facilities	91	9	5	86
Administration	75	12	5	83

Source: Hanushek (1997a), revised.

---

[34] A more complete description of the universe of studies that are reviewed can be found in Hanushek (1997a).

[35] A more complete description of the studies can be found in Hanushek (1997a), which updates the analysis in Hanushek (1986). The tabulations here correct some miscoding of effects in these original publications. They also omit the estimates from Card and Krueger (1992b). In reviewing all of the studies and estimates, it was discovered that the results of that paper were based on models that did not include any measures of family background differences and thus could not be interpreted as identifying any resource parameter. As a minimal quality criterion, tabulated estimates must come from statistical models that include some measure of family background, since omission will almost certainly lead to biased resource estimates.

policy initiatives is that each of these resources should have a positive effect on student performance.[36] In terms of real classroom resources, only 9% of the estimates considering the level of teachers' education and 14% of the estimates investigating teacher–pupil ratios find positive and statistically significant effects on student performance.[37] These relatively small numbers of statistically significant positive results are balanced by another set finding statistically significant negative results – reaching 14% in the case of teacher–pupil ratios.[38] A higher proportion of estimated effects of teacher experience are positive and statistically significant: 29%. Importantly, however, 71% still indicate either worsening performance with experience or less confidence in any positive effect. And, because more experienced teachers can frequently choose their school and/or students, a portion of the positive effects could actually reflect reverse causation [Greenberg and McCall (1974), Murnane (1981), Hanushek, Kain and Rivkin (2004b) and Hanushek et al. (2005)]. In sum, the vast number of estimated real resource effects gives little confidence that just adding more of any of the specific resources to schools will lead to a boost in student achievement. Moreover, this statement does not even get into whether or not any effects are 'large'. Given the small confidence in just getting noticeable improvements, it seems somewhat unimportant to investigate the size of any estimated effects.

The financial aggregates provide a similar picture. There is very weak support for the notion that simply providing higher teacher salaries or greater overall spending will lead to improved student performance. Per pupil expenditure has received the most attention, but only 27% of the estimated coefficients are positive and statistically significant. In fact, 7% even suggest some confidence in the fact that spending more would harm student achievement. In reality, as discussed below, analyses involving per pupil expenditure tend to be the lowest quality, and there is substantial reason to believe that even these results overstate the true effect of added expenditure.

The studies that include measures of facilities or administration fail to show much of significance. These factors are generally, however, quite poorly measured – thus complicating the interpretation.

Finally, this review does not concentrate on specific measures of teachers, since that is covered in the chapter on teacher quality in this volume. It is true that measures of teacher test scores and their impact on student performance are more consistently related

---

[36] It is possible that the level and shape of the salary schedule with respect to experience are set to attract and retain an optimal supply of teachers and that the year-to-year changes in salaries do not reflect short run productivity differences. This possibility would introduce some ambiguity about expectations of estimates of experience and salary effects.

[37] The individual studies tend to measure each of these inputs in different ways. With teacher–pupil ratio, for example, some measure actual class size, while the majority measure teacher–pupil ratio. In all cases, estimated signs are reversed if the measure involves pupil–teacher ratios or class size instead of teacher–pupil ratio.

[38] While a large portion of the studies merely note that the estimated coefficient is statistically insignificant without giving the direction of the estimated effect, those statistically insignificant studies reporting the sign of estimated coefficients are split fairly evenly between positive and negative.

to student outcomes than the factors identified previously.[39] But, they are generally not paid for directly or indirectly and thus are not directly related to resources. Thus, the general character of the evidence and implications of these analyses are left for the chapter on teacher quality.

6.1. Study quality

The tabulated analyses of educational performance clearly differ in quality and their potential for yielding biased results. Two elements of quality, both related to model specification and estimation, are particularly important. First, education policy in the United States is made chiefly by the separate 50 states, and the resulting variations in spending, regulations, graduation requirements, testing, labor laws, and teacher certification and hiring policies are large. These important differences – which are also the locus of most current policy debates – imply that any estimates of student performance across states must include descriptions of the policy environment of schools or else they will be subject to standard omitted variables bias. The misspecification bias of models that ignore variations in state education policy (and other potential state differences) will be exacerbated by aggregation of the estimation sample. Second, as noted, education is a cumulative process, but a majority of analyses are purely cross-sectional with only contemporaneous measures of inputs. In other words, when looking at performance at the end of secondary schooling, many analyses include just measures of the current teachers and school resources and ignore the dozen or more prior years of inputs. Obviously, current school inputs will tend to be a very imperfect measure of the resources that went into producing ending achievement. This mismeasurement is strongest for any children who changed schools over their career (a sizable majority in the United States) but also holds for students who do not move because of the heterogeneity of teachers within individual schools [see Hanushek, Kain and Rivkin (2004a), Rivkin, Hanushek and Kain (2005)].[40] Even if contemporaneous measures were reasonable proxies for the stream of cumulative inputs, uncertainty about the interpretation and policy implications would remain. But there is little reason to believe that they are good proxies.

While judgments about study quality often have a subjective element, it is possible to make straightforward distinctions based on violations of these two problems. We begin with the issue of measuring the policy environment. States differ dramatically in their policies, and ignoring any policies that have a direct impact will bias the statistical results if important policies tend to be correlated with the resource usage across states. While the direction of any bias depends on the magnitude and sign of correlation, under

---

[39] Of the 41 studies with measures of teacher test scores, 41 percent are positive and statistically significant, while 10 percent are negative and statistically significant.

[40] A third argument on quality is made in Krueger (2002). He argues that summaries of econometric results should be weighted by publication counts, i.e., a published study that provides separate estimates on resource effects in grades 3, 6 and 9 should received the same weight as a study that provides a single estimate for grade 3. He provides no theoretical or empirical justification for this weighting, and it is not employed here.

quite general circumstances, the severity will increase with the level of aggregation of the school inputs. That is, any bias will tend to be more severe if estimation is conducted at the state level rather than if conducted at the classroom level [Hanushek, Rivkin and Taylor (1996)].[41]

Table 4 provides insight into the pattern and importance of the specific omitted variables bias resulting from lack of information about key educational policy differences. This table considers two input measures: teacher–pupil ratio and expenditure per pupil. These inputs, on top of being important for policy, are included in a sufficient number of analyses at various levels of aggregation that they can point to the potential misspecification biases. As discussed previously, the overall percentage of all estimates of teacher–pupil ratios that are statistically significant and positive is evenly balanced by those that are statistically significant and negative. But this is not true for estimates relying upon samples drawn entirely within a single state, where the overall policy environment is constant and thus where any bias from omitting overall state policies is

Table 4

Percentage distribution of estimated effect of teacher–pupil ratio and expenditure per pupil by state sampling scheme and aggregation

Level of aggregation of resources	Number of estimates	Statistically significant		Statistically insignificant
		Positive	Negative	
A. *Teacher–pupil ratio*				
Total	276	14%	14%	72%
Single state samples[a]	157	11	18	71
Multiple state samples[b]	119	18	8	74
Disaggregated within states[c]	109	14	8	78
State level aggregation[d]	10	60	0	40
B. *Expenditure per pupil*				
Total	163	27%	7%	66%
Single state samples[a]	89	20	11	69
Multiple state samples[b]	74	35	1	64
Disaggregated within states[c]	46	17	0	83
State level aggregation[d]	28	64	4	32

Source: Hanushek (1997a), revised.

[a]Estimates from samples drawn within single states.

[b]Estimates from samples drawn across multiple states.

[c]Resource measures at level of classroom, school, district, or county, allowing for variation within each state.

[d]Resource measures aggregated to state level with no variation within each state.

[41] The discussion of aggregation is part of a broader debate trying to reconcile the findings of Card and Krueger (1992a) with those presented here. For a fuller discussion, see Burtless (1996). Of particular relevance is Heckman, Layne-Farrar and Todd (1996a, 1996b), which raises other issues with the Card and Krueger estimation. Specifically, their key identifying assumption of no selective migration is violated. Similarly, assumptions about homogeneity of effects across schooling categories are found not to hold.

minimized or eliminated. For single state estimates, the statistically significant effects are disproportionately negative. Yet, as the samples are drawn across states, the relative proportion positive and statistically significant rises. For those aggregated to the state level where the expected bias is largest, almost two-thirds of the estimates are positive and statistically significant. The pattern of results also holds for estimates of the effects of expenditure differences (which are more likely to come from highly aggregate analyses involving multiple states).[42]

This pattern of results is consistent with expectations from considering specification biases when favorable state policies tend to be positively correlated with resource usage. The initial assessment of effects indicated little reason to be confident about overall resource policies. This refinement on quality indicates that a number of the significant effects may further be artifacts of the sampling and methodology.

The second problem, improper consideration of the cumulative nature of the educational process, is a different variant of model specification. Relating the level of performance at any point in time just to the current resources is likely to be very misleading. The standard approach for dealing with this is the estimation of value-added models where attention is restricted to the growth of achievement over a limited period of time (where the flow of resources is also observed). By concentrating on achievement gains over, say, a single grade, it is possible to control for initial achievement differences, which will be determined by earlier resources and other educational inputs. In other words, fixed but unmeasured factors are eliminated.

Table 5 displays the results of estimates that consider value-added models for individual students. The top panel shows all such results, while the bottom panel follows the earlier discussion by concentrating just on estimates within an individual state. With the most refined investigation of quality, the number of analyses gets quite small and selective. In these, however, there is no support for systematic improvements through increasing teacher–pupil ratios and hiring teachers with more graduate education. The effects of teacher experience are largely unaffected from those for the universe of estimates.

The highest quality estimates indicate that the prior overall results about the effects of school inputs were not simply an artifact of study quality. If anything, the total set of high quality estimates paints a stronger picture. Therefore, a more careful set of econometric analyses confirms the basic picture presented in the aggregate data.

---

[42] Expenditure studies virtually never include include direct analysis at performance across different classrooms or schools, since expenditure data are typically available only at the district level. Thus, they begin at a more aggregated level than many studies of real resources. An alternative explanation of the stronger estimates with aggregation is that the disaggregated studies are subject to considerable errors-in-measurement of the resource variables. The analysis in Hanushek, Rivkin and Taylor (1996), however, suggests that measurement error is not the driving force behind the pattern of results.

Table 5
Percentage distribution of estimated influences on student performance, based on value-added models of individual student performance

Resources	Number of estimates	Statistically significant		Statistically insignificant
		Positive	Negative	
A. *All studies*				
Teacher–pupil ratio	78	12%	8%	80%
Teacher education	40	0	10	90
Teacher experience	61	36	2	62
B. *Studies within a single state*				
Teacher–pupil ratio	23	4%	13%	83%
Teacher education	33	0	9	91
Teacher experience	36	39	3	58

Source: Hanushek (1997a), revised.

6.2. Overall econometric specification

A key issue in considering the results of the educational production function analyses is whether they provide the necessary guidance for policy purposes. Specifically, while they show a pattern of association, is it reasonable to infer that they identify causal relationships?

The issue is particularly important when put into the context of educational policy. Resource allocations are determined by a complicated series of political and behavioral choices by schools and parents. The character of these choices could influence the estimates of the effectiveness of resources. Consider, for example, the result of systematically assigning school resources in a compensatory manner. If low achieving kids are given extra resources – say smaller classes, special remedial instruction, improved technology, and the like – there is an obvious identification problem. Issues of this kind suggest both care in interpretation of results and the possible necessity of alternative approaches.

Before continuing, however, it is important to be more precise about the nature and potential importance of these considerations. Funding responsibility for schools in the United States tends on average to be roughly equally divided between states and localities with the federal government contributing only about 7% of overall spending. Huge variation in funding levels and formulae nonetheless exists across states. In most state funding of schools in the United States, the distribution of expenditure does not depend on the actual performance of individual students, but instead (inversely) on the wealth and income of the community. In models of achievement that include the relevant family background terms (such as education, income, or wealth), this distribution of state resources would simply increase the correlations among the exogenous variables but would not suggest any obvious simultaneity problems for the achievement models. In fact, while the compensatory nature of funding often motivates some concerns, even this correlation of background and resources is not clear. Much of the funding debate in the United States has revolved around a concern that wealthier communities and parents can afford to spend more for schools, and in fact almost all state financing formula are designed to offset this tendency at least partially. Thus, the actual correlations of resources and family backgrounds often are not very high.[43]

At the individual student level, correlations with aggregate district resources through either formula allocations or community decisions are not a major cause of concern. The individual classroom allocations may, however, be a concern. For example, within a school, low achievers may be placed in smaller classes, suggesting the possibility of simultaneity bias. Any such problems should be largely ameliorated by value-added models, which consider the student's prior achievement directly. The only concern then becomes allocations made on the basis of unmeasured achievement influences that are unrelated to prior achievement.

Particularly in the area of class size analysis, a variety of approaches do go further in attempting to identify causal effects, and the results are quite varied. Hoxby (2000) used detrended variations in the size of birth cohorts to identify exogenous changes in class size in small Connecticut towns. Changes in cohort sizes, coupled with the lumpiness of classes in small school districts, can provide variations in class size that are unrelated to other factors.[44] Other estimates have also explicitly considered exogenous factors affecting class size within the context of instrumental variables estimators for the effects of class size [Akerhielm (1995), Boozer and Rouse (2001)]. Unfortunately, identification of truly exogenous determinants of class size, or resource allocations more generally, is sufficiently rare that other compromises in the data and modeling are frequently required. These coincidental compromises jeopardize the ability to obtain clean estimates of resource effects and may limit the generalizability of any findings. Rivkin, Hanushek and Kain (2005), employing an approach similar in spirit to that used by Hoxby, make use of exogenous variations in class sizes within Texas schools across multiple cohorts of varying sizes.[45] They find some small class size effects, but the effects vary significantly across grades and specifications.

---

[43] The distribution of state funds varies across the states, but one fairly common pattern is that major portions of state funds are distributed inversely to the property wealth of the community. Because community wealth includes the value of commercial and industrial property within a community, the correlation of community wealth with the incomes of local residents tends to be low and sometimes even negative.

[44] While pertaining directly to the international evidence below, in a related approach Angrist and Lavy (1999) note that Maimonides' Rule requires that Israeli classes cannot exceed forty students, so that, again, the lumpiness of classrooms may lead to large changes in class size when the numbers of students in a school approaches multiples of forty (and the preferred class size is greater than forty). They formulate a regression discontinuity approach to identify the effects of class size, but many of their estimates also use class size variation other than that generated by the discontinuities. Similarly, Case and Deaton (1999) concentrate on the impact of white decision making on black schools in South Africa (where endogeneity from compensatory policies is arguably less important). They conclude that smaller classes have an impact on student outcomes in that setting.

[45] The nature of this analysis is discussed further in the chapter on teacher quality.

These alternative approaches yield inconsistent results both in terms of class size effects and in terms of the effects of alternative methodologies. The results in each of these analyses tend to be quite sensitive to estimation procedures and to model specification. Further, they are inconsistent in terms of statistical significance, grade pattern, and magnitude of any effects. As a group, the results are more likely to be statistically significant with the expected sign than those presented previously for all estimates, but the typical estimate (for statistically significant estimates) tends to be very small in magnitude.

The inconsistency of the limited existing set of analyses should not, however, detract from the importance of the issue. Continued close attention to the nature of the statistical models and the estimation approach is warranted, and the area of attention is a fruitful one for future research efforts.

7. International econometric evidence

The evidence for countries other than the United States is potentially important for a variety of reasons. Other countries have varying institutional structures, so different findings could help to identify the importance of organization and overall incentives. Moreover, other countries frequently have much different levels of resources and exhibit larger variance in resource usage, offering the prospect of understanding better the importance of pure resource differences. For example, one explanation of the lack of relationship between resources and performance in the United States is its schools there are generally operating in an area of severe diminishing marginal productivity, placing most observations on the "flat of the curve". Thus, by observing schools at very different levels of resources, it would be possible to distinguish between technological aspects of the production relationship and other possible interpretations of the evidence such as imprecise incentives for students and teachers.

While the international evidence has been more limited, this situation is likely to be reversed profitably in the future. A key problem has been less available performance data for different countries, but this lack of information is being corrected as many other countries introduce regular student assessment. As student outcome data become more plentiful – allowing investigation of value added by teachers in schools in different environments, international evidence can be expected to grow in importance.

7.1. Developing countries

Existing analyses in less developed countries have shown a similar inconsistency of estimated resource effects as that found in the United States. While these estimates typically come from special purpose analyses and are frequently not published in refereed journals, they do provide insights into resource use at very different levels of support. Table 6 provides evidence on resource effects from estimates completed by 1990.[46] Two

---

[46] This compilation of results from Hanushek (1995) incorporates information from Fuller (1985), Harbison and Hanushek (1992), and a variety of studies during the 1980s.

Table 6

Percentage distribution of estimated expenditure parameter coefficients from 96 educational production function estimates: developing countries

Input	Number of estimates	Statistically significant		Statistically insignificant
		Positive	Negative	
Teacher–pupil ratio	30	27%	27%	46%
Teacher education	63	56	3	41
Teacher experience	46	35	4	61
Teacher salary	13	31	15	54
Expenditure/Pupil	12	50	0	50
Facilities	34	65	9	26

Source: Hanushek (1995).

facets of these data compared to the previous United States data stand out: (1) in general, a minority of the available estimates suggests much confidence that the identified resources positively influence student performance; and (2) there is generally somewhat stronger support for these resource policies than that existing in United States analyses. Thus, the data hint that the importance of resources may vary with the level of resources, a natural presumption. Nonetheless, the evidence is not conclusive that pure resource policies can be expected to have a significant effect on student outcomes.

The major concern with the work on developing countries is study quality. Virtually no research in developing countries has had longitudinal data on individuals.[47] Further, the data collected are often limited considerably by the survey and sampling procedures. These issues imply real concerns about any causal interpretation of the estimated relationships.

7.2. Developed countries

The evidence on developed countries outside of the United States is more difficult to compile. The review by Vignoles et al. (2000) points to a small number of analyses outside of the US and shows some variation them similar to that already reported among estimates elsewhere. And, new articles continue to appear [e.g., Dustmann, Rajah and van Soest (2003)].

One set of consistent estimates for the TIMSS data is presented in Hanushek and Luque (2003). They employ the data on variations in scores across schools within individual countries. The 17 countries with complete data for 9-year-olds and the 33 countries with complete data for 13-year-olds are weighted toward more developed countries but do include poor countries. As shown in Table 7, they find little evidence that any

---

[47] An exception is the work on Brazil in Harbison and Hanushek (1992), where a subsample of students was followed over time.

Table 7
Distribution of estimated production function parameters across countries and age groups, by sign and statistical significance (10% level).
Dependent variable: classroom average TIMSS mathematics score

	Age 9 population					Age 13 population				
	Negative		Positive		Number of countries	Negative		Positive		Number of countries
	Significant	Not significant	Not significant	Significant		Significant	Not significant	Not significant	Significant	
Class size	**3**	11	2	0	17	**2**	8	6	17	33
Teacher with at least a bachelor's degree	0	3	12	**0**	15	2	11	12	**2**	32
Teacher with special training	0	7	4	**1**	12	0	12	11	**2**	25
Teacher experience	0	7	6	**4**	17	3	9	17	**4**	33

Note: Bold indicates the number of statistically significant results with the expected sign of the effect. Because these estimates rely on actual class size, the expected sign is negative (and not reversed as for teacher–pupil ratios in the prior tables).
Source: Hanushek and Luque (2003).

of the standard resource measures for schools are related to differences in mathematics scores within countries, although a majority of the class size results for the youngest age group do have the expected negative sign. Note, however, that these estimates are all cross-sectional in nature and subject to a variety of concerns about specification.

An extension of the estimation considers the possibility of compensatory allocation of students to varying class sizes. Specifically, estimation for rural schools with a single classroom – where compensatory placement is not feasible – yields little change in the overall results.[48] The lack of significant resource effects when corrected for selection does differ from the findings of Angrist and Lavy (1999) and of Case and Deaton (1999), which find more significant resource effects in Israel and South Africa. It is nevertheless inconsistent with the overall findings of Wößmann and West (2006), who use within school variations to identify the impacts of class size.

Moreover, there is no evidence in this consistent work that there are different effects of resources by income level of the country or by level of the resources. Thus, contrary to the conclusions of Heyneman and Loxley (1983), schools do not appear relatively more important for poorer countries.

Wößmann (2001, 2003b) looks at cross national differences in TIMSS math and science scores and concludes that the institutional structure matters importantly for achievement. By pooling the individual student test scores across countries and estimating models that include both school and national characteristics, he finds suggestive evidence that the amount of competition from private schools and the amount of decentralization of decision making to individuals schools have significant beneficial impacts, while union strength is detrimental and standard differences in resources across countries are not clearly related to student performance. The limited number of national observations for institutions nevertheless leaves some uncertainty about the estimates and calls for replication in other samples that permit, say, variations within individual countries in the key institutional features.

8. Project STAR and experimental data[49]

A different form of evidence – that from random assignment experiment – has recently been widely circulated in the debates about class size reduction. In assessing resource effects, concern about selection frequently remains, even in the instrumental approaches. Following the example of medicine, one large scale experimental investigation in the State of Tennessee in the mid-1980s (Project STAR) pursued the effectiveness of class size reductions. Random-assignment experiments in principle have considerable appeal. The underlying idea is that we can obtain valid evidence about the impact of a

---

[48] An additional check analyzes whether smaller classes in a given grade seem to be allocated on compensatory or elitist grounds and finds countries split on this. The impact of such considerations on the estimated effects is nonetheless minimal.

[49] For a more extensive discussion of Project STAR, see Hanushek (1999a, 1999b).

given well-defined treatment by randomly assigning subjects to treatment and control groups, eliminating the possible contaminating effects of other factors and permitting conceptually cleaner analysis of the outcomes of interest across these groups. With observations derived from natural variations in individual selection, one must be able to distinguish between the treatment and other differences that might directly affect the observed outcomes and that might be related to whether or not they receive the treatment. Randomization seeks to eliminate any relationship between selection into a treatment program and other factors that might affect outcomes. [See, however, the caution provided in Todd and Wolpin (2003).]

Project STAR was designed to begin with kindergarten students and to follow them for four years. Three treatments were initially included: small classes (13–17 students); regular classes (22–25 students); and regular classes (22–25 students) with a teacher's aide. Schools were solicited for participation, with the stipulation that any school participating must be large enough to have at least one class in each treatment group. The initial sample included 6,324 kindergarten students, split between 1,900 in small classes and 4,424 in regular classes. (After the first year, the two separate regular class treatments were effectively combined, because there were no perceived differences in student performance. The result about the ineffectiveness of classroom aides has received virtually no attention.) The initial sample included 79 schools, although this subsequently fell to 75. The initial 326 teachers grew slightly to reflect the increased sample size in subsequent grades, although of course most teachers are new to the experiment at each new grade.

The results of the Project STAR experiment have been widely publicized. The simplest summary is that: (1) students in small classes perform better than those in regular classes or regular classes with aides starting in kindergarten; (2) the kindergarten performance advantage of small classes widens a small amount in first grade but then either remains quantitatively the same (reading) or narrows (math) by third grade; and (3) taking each grade separately, the difference in performance between small and regular classes is statistically significant.

This summary reflects the typical reporting, focusing on the differences in performance at each grade and concluding that small classes are better than large [e.g., Finn and Achilles (1990), Mosteller (1995)]. But, it ignores the fact that under the common conceptual discussions one would expect the differences in performance to become wider through the grades because they continue to get more resources (smaller classes) and that should keep adding an advantage. This issue was first raised by Prais (1996), who framed the discussion in terms of the value-added. As Krueger (1999) demonstrates, the small class advantage is almost exclusively obtained in the first year of being in a small class – suggesting that the advantages of small classes are not generalizable to any other grades.

Importantly, this pattern of effects is at odds with the normal rhetoric about smaller classes permitting more individualized instruction, allowing improved class room interactions, cutting down on disruptions, and the like. If these were the important changes, small classes should confer continuing benefits in any grades where they are employed.

Instead, the results appear more consistent with socialization or introduction into the behavior of the classroom – one time effects that imply more general class size reduction policies across different grades will not be effective – or with simple problems in the randomization and implementation of the experiment.

The actual gains in performance from the experimental reduction in class size were relatively small (less than 0.2 standard deviations of test performance), especially when the gains are compared to the magnitude of the class size reduction (around 8 students per class). Thus, even if Project STAR is taken at face value, it has relatively limited policy implications.

The importance of the methodology does deserve emphasis. Because of questions about effectiveness and causality in the analysis of schools, further use of random assignment experimentation would have high value. As Todd and Wolpin (2003) point out, random assignment experiments do not answer all of the policy questions. Nonetheless, it would seem natural to develop a range of experiments that could begin to provide information about what kinds of generalizations can be made.

Project STAR also teaches the difficulty in conducting true random assignment experiments. First, many people resist experiments, largely on ethical grounds. While seemingly less important than similar issues in medical research where experimentation is well established, this issue remains important. Second, it is difficult to ensure that the implementation of experiments matches the conceptual ideal.[50] Interestingly, experimentation appears to be more common in developing countries than in developed countries [e.g., see Kremer (2003)].

---

[50] While the experimental approach has great appeal, the actual implementation in the case of Project STAR introduces considerable uncertainty into these estimates [Hanushek (1999b)]. The uncertainty arises most importantly from questions about the quality of the randomization over time. In each year of the experiment, there was sizable attrition from the prior year's treatment groups, and these students were replaced with new students. Of the initial experimental group starting in kindergarten, 48% remained in the experiment for the entire four years. No information, such as pretest scores before entry to the experiment, is available to assess the quality of student randomization for the initial experimental sample or for the subsequent additions to it. Throughout the four years of the experiment there was substantial and nonrandom treatment group crossover (about 10% of the small class treatment group in grades 1–3). There is also substantial, nonrandom test taking over the years of the experiment, exceeding 10% on some tests. Most important, the results depend fundamentally on the assignment of teachers. While the teachers were to be randomly assigned to treatment groups, there is little description of how this was done. Nor is it easy to provide any reliable analysis of the teacher assignment, because only a few descriptors of teachers are found in the data and because there is little reason to believe that they adequately measure differences in teacher quality. The net result of each of these effects is difficult to ascertain, but there is prima facie evidence that the total impact is to overstate the impact of reduced class size [Hanushek (1999b)]. Hoxby (2000) further points out that because teachers and administrators knew they were participating in an experiment that could have significant implications for future resources, their behavior in the experiment could be affected.

9. Interpreting the resource evidence

A wide range of analyses indicate that overall resource policies have not led to discernible improvements in student performance. It is important to understand what is and is not implied by this conclusion. First, it does not mean that money and resources *never* matter. There clearly are situations where small classes or added resources have an impact. It is just that no good description of when and where these situations occur is available, so that broad resource policies such as those legislated from central governments may hit some good uses but also hit bad uses that generally lead to offsetting outcomes. Second, this statement does not mean that money and resources *cannot* matter. Instead, as described below, altered sets of incentives could dramatically improve the use of resources.

The evidence on resources is remarkably consistent across countries, both developed and developing. Had there been distinctly different results for some subsets of countries, issues of what kinds of generalizations were possible would naturally arise. Such conflicts do not appear particularly important, although there are some obvious qualifications. When considering countries that do not have a fully functioning education system even at the primary level, there clearly is some minimal level of resources for the definition of a school.[51] Nonetheless, even in the poorest areas of the world, it is difficult to identify a minimum threshold of resources where there are clear impacts on student outcomes. More refined policies that go beyond simply adding resources with no concomitant sets of policies and incentives still have high payoffs in areas with undeveloped school systems.

There is a tendency by researchers and policy makers to take a single study and to generalize broadly from it. By finding an analysis that suggests a significant relationship between a specific resource and student performance, they conclude that, while other resource usage might not be productive, the usage that is identified would be. If this is so, it leads to a number of important questions. Why is that schools have failed to employ such a policy? Is it just that they don't have the information that the researcher has? That of course seems unlikely since schools in fact constantly experiment with a variety of approaches and resource patterns. Alternatively, it seems more likely that schools have limited incentives to seek out and to employ programs that consistently relate to student achievement. It also appears, as discussed below, that much of the research employed in active policy debates has not adequately identified the causal structure and thus cannot be generalized in useful ways.

It is just this tendency to overgeneralize from limited evidence that lies behind the search for multiple sources of evidence on the effectiveness of different resource usage. That broader body of evidence provides little support for the input policies that continue to be the most common approach to decision making.

---

[51] As an example, in their study of the rural Northeast of Brazil, Harbison and Hanushek (1992) find that some of the "schools" lack an permanent physical structure, lack textbooks, and have teachers with a fourth grade education. In this situation, modest resources can in fact have readily discernible effects.

10. Implications for research

The recent rapid expansion of research into the economics of education in general and the determination of school performance in particular is clearly warranted by the value of the undertaking. Education remains one of the largest expenditures on government budgets around the world. Thus, information that could improve the efficiency of resource usage could have enormous impacts.

The review of existing data and studies demonstrates quite conclusively that the conclusions about the general inefficiency of resource usage are unlikely to be overturned by new data, by new methodologies, or the like. On the other hand, much remains to be learned about when and where resources are most productively used.

There appears to be enormous value in analyzing the implications and outcomes of alternative incentive structures. The observed inefficiency represented by the inconsistent relationship between resources and outcomes almost certainly reflects the nature of current incentives within education. But recognizing the importance of incentives, particularly ones related to student outcomes, is quite different from knowing exactly what to do to improve the situation.

A wide variety of altered incentives currently are being instituted in schools, ranging from varying use of choice to bonus pay schemes for teachers to overall school accountability plans with different rewards and sanctions. Consideration of the consequences of these plans offers an opportunity to investigate who schools, teachers, and students respond to varying incentives.

Focusing on such alternative analyses also highlights one of the key elements for future work. It is common within educational policy discussions to hear that "plan X worked where it was first tried but it could not be brought to scale". This shorthand discussion refers to the frequent observation that promising looking ideas cannot be transported to other places with the same success. The best way to think of this is that much of the research that moves into policy has not adequately identified the underlying causal structure. Considerable progress has recently been made in understanding alternative approaches to investigating causal relations, and pushing this work forward in terms of schooling outcomes is an obvious high-priority item.

References

Akerhielm, K. (1995). "Does class size matter?". Economics of Education Review 14 (3, September), 229–241.

Alderman, H., Behrman, J.R., Ross, D.R., Sabot, R. (1996). "The returns to endogenous human capital in Pakistan's rural wage labor market". Oxford Bulletin of Economics and Statistics 58, 29–55.

Altonji, J.G., Pierret, C.R. (2001). "Employer learning and statistical discrimination". Quarterly Journal of Economics 116 (1, February), 313–350.

Angrist, J.D., Lavy, V. (1997). "The effect of a change in language of instruction on the returns to schooling in Morocco". Journal of Labor Economics 15, S48–S76.

Angrist, J.D., Lavy, V. (1999). "Using Maimondides' rule to estimate the effect of class size on scholastic achievement". Quarterly Journal of Economics 114 (2, May), 533–575.

Barro, R.J., Lee, J.-W. (2001). "International data on educational attainment: Updates and implications". Oxford Economic Papers 53 (3, July), 541–563.

Barro, R.J., Sala-i-Martin, X. (2003). Economic Growth, second ed. MIT Press, Cambridge, MA.

Baumol, W.J. (1967). "Macroeconomics of unbalanced growth: The anatomy of urban crisis". American Economic Review 57 (3, June), 415–426.

Baumol, W.J., Bowen, W.G. (1965). "On the performing arts: The anatomy of their economic problems". American Economic Review 55 (May), 495–502.

Behrman, J.R., Kletzer, L.G., McPherson, M.S., Schapiro, M.O. (1998). "The microeconomics of college choice, careers, and wages: Measuring the impact of higher education". Annals of the American Academy of Political and Social Science 559 (September), 12–23.

Behrman, J.R., Ross, D., Sabot, R. (2006). "Improving the quality versus increasing the quantity of schooling: Estimates of rates of return from rural Pakistan", in preparation.

Betts, J.R. (1996). "Is there a link between school inputs and earnings? Fresh scrutiny of an old literature". In: Burtless, G. (Ed.), Does Money Matter? The Effect of School Resources on Student Achievement and Adult Success. Brookings Institution Press, Washington, DC, pp. 141–191.

Bishop, J. (1989). "Is the test score decline responsible for the productivity growth decline?". American Economic Review 79 (1), 178–197.

Bishop, J. (1991). "Achievement, test scores, and relative wages". In: Kosters, M.H. (Ed.), Workers and Their Wages. AEI Press, Washington, DC, pp. 146–186.

Blackburn, M.L., Neumark, D. (1993). "Omitted-ability bias and the increase in the return to schooling". Journal of Labor Economics 11 (3, July), 521–544.

Blackburn, M.L., Neumark, D. (1995). "Are OLS estimates of the return to schooling biased downward? Another look". Review of Economics and Statistics 77 (2, May), 217–230.

Boissiere, M.X., Knight, J.B., Sabot, R.H. (1985). "Earnings, schooling, ability, and cognitive skills". American Economic Review 75 (5), 1016–1030.

Boozer, M.A., Rouse, C. (2001). "Intraschool variation in class size: Patterns and implications". Journal of Urban Economics 50 (1, July), 163–189.

Burgess, S., Propper, C., Slater, H., Wilson, D. (2005). "Who wins and who loses from school accountability? The distribution of educational gain in English secondary schools". Working Paper No. 05/128. Centre for Market and Public Organisation, University of Bristol (July).

Burtless, G. (Ed.) (1996). Does Money Matter? The Effect of School Resources on Student Achievement and Adult Success. Brookings Institution Press, Washington, DC.

Card, D. (1999). "Causal effect of education on earnings". In: Ashenfelter, O., Card, D. (Eds.), Handbook of Labor Economics. North-Holland, Amsterdam, pp. 1801–1863.

Card, D., Krueger, A.B. (1992a). "Does school quality matter? Returns to education and the characteristics of public schools in the United States". Journal of Political Economy 100 (1, February), 1–40.

Card, D., Krueger, A.B. (1992b). "School quality and black–white relative earnings: A direct assessment". Quarterly Journal of Economics 107 (1, February), 151–200.

Case, A., Deaton, A. (1999). "School inputs and educational outcomes in South Africa". Quarterly Journal of Economics 114 (3, August), 1047–1084.

Chaikind, S., Danielson, L.C., Brauen, M.L. (1993). "What do we know about the costs of special education? A selected review". Journal of Special Education 26 (4), 344–370.

Coleman, J.S., Campbell, E.Q., Hobson, C.J., McPartland, J., Mood, A.M., Weinfeld, F.D., York, R.L. (1966). Equality of Educational Opportunity. U.S. Government Printing Office, Washington, DC.

Congressional Budget Office (1986). Trends in Educational Achievement. Congressional Budget Office, Washington, DC.

Dugan, D.J. (1976). "Scholastic achievement: Its determinants and effects in the education industry". In: Froomkin, J.T., Jamison, D.T., Radner, R. (Eds.), Education as an Industry. Ballinger, Cambridge, MA, pp. 53–83.

Dustmann, C., Rajah, N., van Soest, A. (2003). "Class size, education, and wages". Economic Journal 113 (485, February), F99–F120.

Finn, J.D., Achilles, C.M. (1990). "Answers and questions about class size: A statewide experiment". American Educational Research Journal 27 (3, Fall), 557–577.

Finnie, R., Meng, R. (2002). "Minorities, cognitive skills, and incomes of Canadians". Canadian Public Policy 28, 257–273.

Fuller, B. (1985). Raising School Quality in Developing Countries: What Investments Boost Learning. The World Bank, Washington, DC.

Glewwe, P. (1996). "The relevance of standard estimates of rates of return to schooling for educational policy: A critical assessment". Journal of Development Economics 51, 267–290.

Glewwe, P. (2002). "Schools and skills in developing countries: Education policies and socioeconomic outcomes". Journal of Economic Literature 40 (2, June), 436–482.

Green, D.A., Riddell, W.C. (2003). "Literacy and earnings: An investigation of the interaction of cognitive and unobserved skills in earnings generation". Labour Economics 10, 165–184.

Greenberg, D., McCall, J. (1974). "Teacher mobility and allocation". Journal of Human Resources 9 (4, Fall), 480–502.

Griliches, Z. (1974). "Errors in variables and other unobservables". Econometrica 42 (6, November), 971–998.

Grissmer, D.W., Kirby, S.N., Berends, M., Williamson, S. (1994a). Student Achievement and the Changing American Family. RAND Corporation, Santa Monica, CA.

Grissmer, D.W., Kirby, S.N., Berends, M., Williamson, S. (1994b). Student Achievement and the Changing Family. RAND Corporation, Santa Monica, CA.

Grogger, J.T., Eide, E. (1993). "Changes in college skills and the rise in the college wage premium". Journal of Human Resources 30 (2, Spring), 280–310.

Gundlach, E., Wossmann, L., Gmelin, J. (2001). "The decline of schooling productivity in OECD countries". Economic Journal 111 (May), C135–C147.

Hanushek, E.A. (1979). "Conceptual and empirical issues in the estimation of educational production functions". Journal of Human Resources 14 (3, Summer), 351–388.

Hanushek, E.A. (1986). "The economics of schooling: Production and efficiency in public schools". Journal of Economic Literature 24 (3, September), 1141–1177.

Hanushek, E.A. (1995). "Interpreting recent research on schooling in developing countries". World Bank Research Observer 10 (2, August), 227–246.

Hanushek, E.A. (1997a). "Assessing the effects of school resources on student performance: An update". Educational Evaluation and Policy Analysis 19 (2, Summer), 141–164.

Hanushek, E.A. (1997b). "The productivity collapse in schools". In: Fowler Jr., W.J. (Ed.), Developments in School Finance 1996. National Center for Education Statistics, Washington, DC, pp. 185–195.

Hanushek, E.A. (1999a). "The evidence on class size". In: Mayer, S.E., Peterson, P.E. (Eds.), Earning and Learning: How Schools Matter. Brookings Institution Press, Washington, DC, pp. 131–168.

Hanushek, E.A. (1999b). "Some findings from an independent investigation of the Tennessee STAR experiment and from other investigations of class size effects". Educational Evaluation and Policy Analysis 21 (2, Summer), 143–163.

Hanushek, E.A. (2002). "Publicly provided education". In: Auerbach, A.J., Feldstein, M. (Eds.), Handbook of Public Economics. Elsevier, Amsterdam, pp. 2045–2141.

Hanushek, E.A. (2003a). "The failure of input-based schooling policies". Economic Journal 113 (485, February), F64–F98.

Hanushek, E.A. (2003b). "The importance of school quality". In: Peterson, P.E. (Ed.), Our Schools and Our Future: Are We Still at Risk?. Hoover Institution Press, Stanford, CA, pp. 141–173.

Hanushek, E.A., Kain, J.F., O'Brien, D.M., Rivkin, S.G. (2005). "The market for teacher quality". Working Paper 11154. National Bureau of Economic Research (February).

Hanushek, E.A., Kain, J.F., Rivkin, S.G. (2002). "Inferring program effects for specialized populations: Does special education raise achievement for students with disabilities?". Review of Economics and Statistics 84 (4, November), 584–599.

Hanushek, E.A., Kain, J.F., Rivkin, S.G. (2004a). "Disruption versus Tiebout improvement: The costs and benefits of switching schools". Journal of Public Economics 88 (9–10), 1721–1746.

Hanushek, E.A., Kain, J.F., Rivkin, S.G. (2004b). "Why public schools lose teachers". Journal of Human Resources 39 (2), 326–354.

Hanushek, E.A., Kim, D. (1995). "Schooling, labor force quality, and economic growth". Working Paper 5399. National Bureau of Economic Research (December).

Hanushek, E.A., Kimko, D.D. (2000). "Schooling, labor force quality, and the growth of nations". American Economic Review 90 (5, December), 1184–1208.

Hanushek, E.A., Luque, J.A. (2003). "Efficiency and equity in schools around the world". Economics of Education Review 22 (5, August), 481–502.

Hanushek, E.A., Pace, R.R. (1995). "Who chooses to teach (and why)?". Economics of Education Review 14 (2, June), 101–117.

Hanushek, E.A., Raymond, M.E. (2001). "The confusing world of educational accountability". National Tax Journal 54 (2, June), 365–384.

Hanushek, E.A., Raymond, M.E. (2005). "Does school accountability lead to improved student performance?". Journal of Policy Analysis and Management 24 (2, Spring), 297–327.

Hanushek, E.A., Rivkin, S.G. (1997). "Understanding the twentieth-century growth in U.S. school spending". Journal of Human Resources 32 (1, Winter), 35–68.

Hanushek, E.A., Rivkin, S.G., Taylor, L.L. (1996). "Aggregation and the estimated effects of school resources". Review of Economics and Statistics 78 (4, November), 611–627.

Hanushek, E.A. with others (1994). Making Schools Work: Improving Performance and Controlling Costs. Brookings Institution Press, Washington, DC.

Harbison, R.W., Hanushek, E.A. (1992). Educational Performance of the Poor: Lessons From Rural Northeast Brazil. Oxford University Press, New York.

Heckman, J.J., Layne-Farrar, A., Todd, P. (1996a). "Does measured school quality really matter? An examination of the earnings–quality relationship". In: Burtless, G. (Ed.), Does Money Matter? The Effect of School Resources on Student Achievement and Adult Success. Brookings Institution Press, Washington, DC, pp. 192–289.

Heckman, J.J., Layne-Farrar, A., Todd, P. (1996b). "Human capital pricing equations with an application to estimating the effect of schooling quality on earnings". Review of Economics and Statistics 78 (4, November), 562–610.

Heckman, J.J., Vytlacil, E. (2001). "Identifying the role of cognitive ability in explaining the level of and change in the return to schooling". Review of Economics and Statistics 83 (1, February), 1–12.

Heyneman, S.P., Loxley, W. (1983). "The effect of primary school quality on academic achievement across twenty-nine high and low income countries". American Journal of Sociology 88 (May), 1162–1194.

Hoxby, C.M. (2000). "The effects of class size on student achievement: New evidence from population variation". Quarterly Journal of Economics 115 (3, November), 1239–1285.

Jolliffe, D. (1998). "Skills, schooling, and household income in Ghana". World Bank Economic Review 12, 81–104.

Knight, J.B., Sabot, R.H. (1998). Education, Productivity, and Inequality. Oxford University Press, New York.

Kremer, M. (2003). "Randomized evaluations of educational programs in developing countries: Some lessons". American Economic Review 93 (2, May), 102–104.

Krueger, A.B. (1999). "Experimental estimates of education production functions". Quarterly Journal of Economics 114 (2, May), 497–532.

Krueger, A.B. (2002). "Understanding the magnitude and effect of class size on student achievement". In: Mishel, L., Rothstein, R. (Eds.), The Class Size Debate. Economic Policy Institute, Washington, DC, pp. 7–35.

Krueger, A.B. (2003). "Economic considerations and class size". Economic Journal 113 (485, February), F34–F63.

Lazear, E.P. (2003). "Teacher incentives". Swedish Economic Policy Review 10 (3), 179–214.

Manski, C.F., Wise, D.A. (1983). College Choice in America. Harvard University Press, Cambridge.

Mayer, S.E. (1997). What Money Can't Buy: Family Income and Children's Life Chances. Harvard University Press, Cambridge, MA.

McIntosh, S., Vignoles, A. (2001). "Measuring and assessing the impact of basic skills on labor market outcomes". Oxford Economic Papers 53, 453–481.

Mincer, J. (1970). "The distribution of labor incomes: A survey with special reference to the human capital approach". Journal of Economic Literature 8 (1, March), 1–26.

Mincer, J. (1974). Schooling Experience and Earnings. NBER, New York.

Moll, P.G. (1998). "Primary schooling, cognitive skills, and wage in South Africa". Economica 65, 263–284.

Mosteller, F. (1995). "The Tennessee study of class size in the early school grades". The Future of Children 5 (2, Summer/Fall), 113–127.

Mulligan, C.B. (1999). "Galton versus the human capital approach to inheritance". Journal of Political Economy 107 (6, December), S184–S224. Part 2.

Murnane, R.J. (1981). "Teacher mobility revisited". Journal of Human Resources 16 (1, Winter), 3–19.

Murnane, R.J., Willett, J.B., Braatz, M.J., Duhaldeborde, Y. (2001). "Do different dimensions of male high school students' skills predict labor market success a decade later? Evidence from the NLSY". Economics of Education Review 20 (4, August), 311–320.

Murnane, R.J., Willett, J.B., Duhaldeborde, Y., Tyler, J.H. (2000). "How important are the cognitive skills of teenagers in predicting subsequent earnings?". Journal of Policy Analysis and Management 19 (4, Fall), 547–568.

Murnane, R.J., Willett, J.B., Levy, F. (1995). "The growing importance of cognitive skills in wage determination". Review of Economics and Statistics 77 (2, May), 251–266.

Murphy, K.M., Welch, F. (1992). "The structure of wages". Quarterly Journal of Economics 107 (1, February), 285–326.

Neal, D.A., Johnson, W.R. (1996). "The role of pre-market factors in black–white differences". Journal of Political Economy 104 (5, October), 869–895.

O'Neill, J. (1990). "The role of human capital in earnings differences between black and white men". Journal of Economic Perspectives 4 (4, Fall), 25–46.

Organisation for Economic Co-operation and Development (2003). Education at a Glance: OECD Indicators 2003. Organisation for Economic Co-operation and Development, Paris, France.

Prais, S.J. (1996). "Class-size and learning: the Tennessee experiment – what follows?". Oxford Review of Education 22 (4), 399–414.

Psacharopoulos, G. (1994). "Returns to investment in education: A global update". World Development 22, 1325–1344.

Rivkin, S.G. (1995). "Black/white differences in schooling and employment". Journal of Human Resources 30 (4, Fall), 826–852.

Rivkin, S.G., Hanushek, E.A., Kain, J.F. (2005). "Teachers, schools, and academic achievement". Econometrica 73 (2, March), 417–458.

Scitovsky, T., Scitovsky, A. (1959). "What price economic progress?". Yale Law Review 49 (Autumn), 95–110.

Todd, P.E., Wolpin, K.I. (2003). "On the specification and estimation of the production function for cognitive achievement". Economic Journal 113 (485, February), F3–F33.

U.S. Department of Education (2002). Digest of Education Statistics, 2001. National Center for Education Statistics, Washington, DC.

Vignoles, A., Levacic, R., Walker, J., Machin, S., Reynolds, D. (2000). "The relationship between resource allocation and pupil attainment: A review". DP 02. Centre for the Economics of Education, London School of Economics and Political Science (November).

Vijverberg, W.P.M. (1999). "The impact of schooling and cognitive skills on income from non-farm self-employment". In: Glewwe, P. (Ed.), The Economics of School Quality Investments in Developing Countries: An Empirical Study of Ghana. St. Martin's Press (with University of Oxford), New York.

Wirtz, W. (1977). On Further Examination: Report of the Advisory Panel and the Scholastic Aptitude Test Score Decline. College Entrance Examination Board, New York.

Wößmann, L. (2001). "Why students in some countries do better". Education Matters 1 (2, Summer), 67–74.

Wößmann, L. (2003a). "Central exit exams and student achievement: International evidence". In: Peterson, P.E., West, M.R. (Eds.), No Child Left Behind? The Politics and Practice of School Accountability. Brookings Institution Press, Washington, DC, pp. 292–323.

Wößmann, L. (2003b). "Schooling resources, educational institutions, and student performance: The international evidence". Oxford Bulletin of Economics and Statistics 65 (2), 117–170.

Wößmann, L., West, M.R. (2006). "Class-size effects in school systems around the world: Evidence from between-grade variation in TIMSS". European Economic Review 50 (3), 695–736.

Chapter 15

DRINKING FROM THE FOUNTAIN OF KNOWLEDGE: STUDENT INCENTIVE TO STUDY AND LEARN – EXTERNALITIES, INFORMATION PROBLEMS AND PEER PRESSURE

JOHN BISHOP

Cornell University

Contents

Handbook of the Economics of Education, Volume 2
Edited by Eric A. Hanushek and Finis Welch
© 2006 Elsevier B.V.   *All rights reserved*
DOI: 10.1016/S1574-0692(06)02015-0

Abstract

Students face four decision margins: (a) How many years to spend in school, (b) What to study, (c) How much effort to devote to learning per year and (d) Whether to disrupt or assist the learning of classmates. The thousands of studies that have applied human capital theory to the first two questions are reviewed elsewhere in this volume and the Handbook series. This chapter reviews an emerging economic literature on the effects of and determinants of student effort and cooperativeness and how putting student motivation and behavior at center of one's theoretical framework changes one's view of how schools operate and how they might be made more effective. In this new framework students have a dual role. They are both (a) investors/consumers who choose which goals (outputs) to focus on and how much effort to put into each goal and (b) workers getting instruction and guidance from their first-line supervisors, the teachers. A simple model is presented in which the behavior of students, teachers and administrators depends on the incentives facing them and the actions of the other actors in the system. The incentives, in turn, depend upon the cost and reliability of the information (signals) that is generated about the various inputs and outputs of the system. Our review of empirical research support many of the predictions of the model.

Student effort, engagement and discipline vary a lot within schools, across schools and across nations and have significant effects on learning. Higher extrinsic rewards for learning are associated the taking of more rigorous courses, teachers setting higher standards and more time devoted to homework. Taking more rigorous courses and studying harder increase student achievement. Post-World War II trends in study effort and course rigor, for example, are positively correlated with achievement trends.

Even though, greater rigor and higher standards improve learning, parents and students prefer easy teachers. They pressure tough teachers to lower standards and sign up for courses taught by easy graders. Curriculum-based external exit examinations (CBEEES) improve the signaling of academic achievement to colleges and the labor market and this increases extrinsic rewards for learning. Cross-section studies suggest that CBEEES result in greater focus on academics, more tutoring of lagging students, and higher levels of achievement. Minimum competency examinations (MCE) do not have significant effects on learning or dropout rates but they do appear to have positive effects on the reputation of high school graduates. As a result, students from MCE states earn significantly more than students from states without MCEs and the effect lasts at least eight years.

Students who attend schools with studious well-behaved classmates learn more. Disruptive students generate negative production externalities and cooperative hardworking students create positive production externalities. Peer effects are also generated by the norms of student peer cultures that encourage disruptive students and harass nerds. In addition learning is poorly signaled to employers and colleges. Thus, market signals and the norms of student peer culture do not internalize the externalities that are pervasive in school settings and as a result students typically devote less effort to studying than the taxpayers who fund schools would wish.

Keywords

academic achievement, signaling achievement, student motivation, student engagement, homework, high school exit exams, student accountability, human capital theory, peer culture, peer effects, student norms, educational standards, peer learning externalities, payoffs to academic achievement, academic climate, nerd harassment, secondary education, K-12 education, PISA (Program for International Student Assessment)

JEL classification: I20, I21, I28, H42, H72, J24

The theory of human capital provides a unified explanation of why students invest in education, how much and what type of education and training they choose and how these investments determine an individual's future productivity and earnings. This very fruitful theory has been the stimulus for thousands of studies assessing student incentives to stay in school, the returns to years of schooling, to field of study, to type of school attended, school quality and to employer training, the sources of variation in these returns and who chooses to get different amounts and types of schooling and training [Freeman (1986), Card (1999), other papers written for this Handbook volume].

Human capital theory, however, has seldom been applied to studying the educational process itself or the internal workings of schools. Economists have instead employed a production function paradigm. Conventionally, test scores measuring academic achievement are the outputs, school administrators are the managers, teachers the labor input and students are goods in process. But a research program that treats students as the object of the actions of teachers and administrators has inherent limitations. Learning requires active participation of the learner. Students or parents choose the difficulty level – honors, regular college prep or remedial – of courses. If typical classes have twenty-five students, the students are spending at least 25 times as many hours trying to learn (or possibly choosing not to try) as teachers are spending teaching. They decide whether to skip school, how much effort to devote to each course and whether to help or obstruct the learning of others in the class. On any given day in 1900 twenty-eight percent of enrolled students were absent from school. By 1997–1998 absenteeism had dropped to 7 percent, but in some states it reaches 15 percent [NCES (2001), Tables 38, 41, 43]. Studies of time use in classrooms have found that American students actively engage in a learning activity for only about half the time they are scheduled to be in school. A study of schools in Chicago found that public schools with high-achieving students averaged about 75 percent of class time for actual instruction. For schools with low-achieving students, the average was 51 percent of class time [Frederick (1977)]. Overall, Frederick, Walberg and Rasher (1979) estimated 46 percent of the potential learning time is lost due to absence, lateness, inattention, classroom disruptions or teachers being off task.

Time devoted to homework also varies a great deal. In 1998, 21 percent of high school seniors reported doing 10 or more hours of homework per week, while another 23 percent reported not being assigned homework or not doing the homework assigned [NCES (2002), p. 41]. Studies have found that learning has a strong relationship with time on task [Wiley (1976)], time devoted to homework [Cooper (1989), Betts (1996)] and the share of homework that is completed. Differentials in time committed to learning are likely to be an important reason for variations in achievement across students, across schools and across nations.

Just as important as the time devoted to learning is the student's engagement in the process. John Goodlad (1983) study of American high schools described: "*a general picture of considerable passivity among students...* (p. 113)". Asked "How often does your mind wander" during class, 23 percent of a large sample of American middle school and high school students said "usually" or "always", while 33 percent said "seldom" or "never" [Educational Excellence Alliance (2002)].[1] Sixty-two percent of 10th graders agreed with the statement, "I don't like to do any more school work than I have to" [Longitudinal Survey of American Youth, LSAY (1988), Q. AA37N].

A second problem with the education production function literature is its failure to deal with the fact that academic achievement (as assessed by math, science and reading tests) is just one of the many goals that schools are expected to serve. Many studies use math test scores as the sole measure of output even though elementary students spend less than a quarter of their time doing math and high school students spend only 14 percent of their time in math classes. Nonacademic courses account for 35 percent of credits earned in American high schools. For 2000 graduates, personal use courses accounted for 11.1 percent of total credits, art and music for 7.8 percent and vocational education for 16.2 percent of total credits earned [NCES (2003a), Table 139]. In multivariate models predicting earnings, credits taken in occupational specialties have significantly more positive effects on wages and earnings (both immediately and eight years after graduation) than academic credits [conditional on school attendance and years of schooling, Bishop and Mane (2004)]. Nonacademic goals – vocational training, developing artistic talent, discouraging drug use, learning teamwork, providing opportunities for physical exercise, developing respect and tolerance for others and community entertainment (e.g., band, cheer leading and interscholastic sports), etc. – are very important in the eyes of students and the community.

These two observations suggest that students play a dual role in schools. They are (1) investors/consumers who choose which goals (outputs) to focus on and how much effort to put into each goal and (2) workers getting instruction and guidance from their first-line supervisors, the teachers. Teachers also have a great deal of discretion over how much emphasis they place on various aspects of their subject and how they handle discipline and character development. Students must cooperate with the teacher and each other if educational goals are to be achieved. In practice this means that classroom goals are often negotiated between teacher and students [Sizer (1984), Powell, Farrar and Cohen (1985)]. The behavior of each of the system's actors (teachers, administrators, school board, parents, students and the leaders of student crowds) depends on the incentives facing them. The incentives, in turn, depend upon the cost and reliability of the information (signals) that are generated about the various outputs and inputs of the system.

This chapter focuses on the incentives faced by students, the effects of incentives on student behavior and the character and quality of the information about performance that generates these incentives. Similar issues arise in modeling the behavior of teachers and school administrators. I point out the similarities as the analysis develops, but the

---

[1] The Educational Excellence Alliance is a consortium of schools and school districts that have administered the ED-Excel survey of student peer culture and received reports comparing their students' responses to the responses at other comparable schools. A total of about 325 schools and 110,000 students have participated in the study [Bishop et al. (2003)].

focus is on student incentives, student norms and student behavior. This review has five sections.

The first section of the chapter presents evidence that student effort accounts for an important share of the variance across individuals and nations in student achievement. The second section of the chapter outlines a simple model of how students decide how much effort to put into their studies and how their decisions interact with public support for greater spending on education. It also reviews evidence on the effects of extrinsic rewards for learning on student effort, school quality and achievement. The third section of the chapter reviews the empirical literature on the effects of improved signaling of student achievement at the end of high school on the rewards for learning, on student effort, teacher's standards and student achievement. The fourth section of the chapter reviews studies of the effects of raising the standards for getting good grades, promotion to the next grade or a diploma. The final section of the chapter examines how externalities generated by peer effects and grading on a curve influence student peer culture and norms about study effort. I then discuss two economic models of student peer groups and pressures – Akerlof and Kranton's 'identity' model and a model in which norms are signaled by the behavior of a crowd's leaders and enforced by threats of harassment and social exclusion.

1. Student effort influences learning

Not surprisingly students who do not pay attention in class and/or frequently skip school are poorer readers and less competent mathematicians than students who attend regularly and pay attention. In the Programme for International Student Assessment (PISA) study [OECD (2003a)], the 3.1 percent of American 15-year-olds who had skipped five or more classes in the past two weeks scored slightly more than a standard deviation lower [approximately four grade-level equivalents (GLE)] on the PISA reading literacy assessment than the 55 percent of students who said they were attending regularly. Data for 25 other countries on class skipping and the reading deficit of those who skip 5 or more classes is presented in columns (4) and (5) of Table 1.[2] The reading deficit of students who skip a lot of classes is 79 points on average (about three-quarters of a standard deviation) in the other nations that participated in PISA-2000.

PISA also found that student achievement was correlated with the disciplinary climate of the student's classroom. Column 6 of the table presents the mean value of

---

[2] PISA assesses the cumulative educational experiences of all students at age 15 regardless of the grade levels or type of institution they are attending. The students complete a 20–30 minute background questionnaire and a 90-minute assessment consisting of a mix of multiple choice, short answer, and extended response questions. It's most recent report [OECD (2003a)] presents data on 222,948 students from 43 nations accounting for one-third of the world's population. Great care is taken to insure that the schools and students who are assessed are representative of the all 15-year-old students in the nation.

PISA's standardized index of a positive disciplinary climate.[3] Column (7) presents the difference between the reading scores of students who reported few disruptions in their classes (top quartile of the index) and the scores of students who reported many disruptions (bottom quartile of the index). The reading differential between students in classrooms with low and high levels of disruption varies a good deal across countries. It is over 90 points for Hungary and Japan and under 10 points in Brazil, Finland and Mexico. For the United States the differential is 31 points (about 1.2 grade-level equivalents).

While these positive associations are consistent with the hypothesis that student effort and discipline improve achievement, the bivariate relationships presented in Table 1 exaggerate the magnitude of any causal relationship. PISA has looked at the effect of disciplinary climate on achievement while controlling for many potentially confounding variables: student background, school SES, student–teacher ratios, teacher qualifications and student use of school resources (library, computers, Internet and science labs). They found that the "students are disciplined" index was a highly significant (t statistics above 5.7) predictor of reading, mathematics and science achievement. Numerous other studies also find that indicators of student effort such as absenteeism, paying attention, completing homework assignments and hours doing homework have significant effects on learning in multivariate models controlling for prior achievement and family background [e.g., Cooper (1989), Betts (1996), Bishop et al. (2003)]. Their importance in any given study will depend on how well effort and discipline are measured, whether complementary inputs such as quality instruction are being provided and the sensitivity of the achievement indicator to student effort levels.

Do variations in student effort and discipline across countries account for some of the large differences in average achievement levels? Lets look at the data in Table 1 columns (1)–(4) and (6) on how student effort and engagement varies across nations. Column 1 reports the proportion of 15–19-year-olds enrolled in school. On this indicator the United States lags behind most of Western Europe, the Czech Republic, Korea and Hungary. Column (2) presents a proxy for student engagement – the percent of students who say they "often feel bored" in school. Sixty-one percent of American students say they are often bored. The OECD average is 48 percent. Lack of engagement seems to be a pretty universal problem. Column (3) reports the percentage of schools in a nation that have absenteeism rates exceeding 5 percent. Here there are big differences across nations. Absenteeism is above five percent for 60 percent of American schools, 76 percent of Australian schools and 80 percent of New Zealand schools but only 5 percent of Japanese and Korean schools. Class skipping was also much lower in Japan and Korea and student discipline was better as well [see columns (4) and (6)]. Possibly this

---

[3] Students were asked the frequency in their language arts class of: "the teacher has to wait a long time for the students to <quieten down>; students cannot work well; students don't listen to what the teacher says; students don't start working for a long time after the lesson begins; there is noise and disorder; and, at the start of class, more than five minutes are spent doing nothing". The response alternatives were 'never', 'some lessons', 'most lessons' and 'every lesson'.

Table 1

Effort, discipline and achievement of secondary school students

	Share 15–19 in school in 2001	I often feel bored	Percent schools with absenteeism	Percent who skipped 1 or more class	Reading deficit of students who skipped	Disciplinary climate	Reading difference between top and bottom quartile	TIMSS end of HS	TIMSS end of HS	PISA age 15 (native-born students)	
										Reading	Math
	(percent)	(% agree)	(above 5 %)	(in last 2 weeks)	(5 or more classes)	(student rept.)	(on disc. climate)	(math)	(science)		
	(1)	(2)	(3)	(4)	(5)	(6)	(7)	(8)	(9)	(10)	(11)
Australia	81.1	60	76	43	46	−0.09	47	522	527	532	536
Austria	76.9	49	46	37	61	0.19	41	518	520	515	523
Belgium	91.0	46	35	28	108	−0.12	10	–	–	522	536
Brazil	74.6	30	–	53	52	−0.34	−18	–	–	398	337
Canada	75.0	58	59	47	60	−0.14	25	519	532	538	536
Chile	67.8	–	–	47	79	−0.32	35	–	–	411	384
Czech Rep.	87.8	47	81	53	76	0.14	55	466	487	501	504
Denmark	82.9	41	41	49	37	−0.20	27	547	509	504	520
Finland	85.3	60	–	43	42	−0.16	9	–	–	548	537
France	86.6	32	28	34	100	−0.05	16	523	487	512	523
Germany	89.4	49	37	26	67	0.10	48	495	497	507	510
Hungary	79.0	29	45	33	64	0.23	93	483	471	482	489
Iceland	79.2	30	12	37	46	−0.08	23	534	549	509	516
Italy	72.2	54	–	56	99	−0.24	79	476	475	489	459
Japan	–	32	5	10	na	0.49	92	–	–	525	559
Korea	79.3	46	5	20	35	0.20	47	–	–	525	547
Mexico	41.0	28	–	32	70	0.17	4	–	–	427	391
NZ	73.0	60	80	44	92	−0.15	24	522	529	538	543
Norway	85.3	58	31	35	78	−0.36	18	528	544	510	503
Portugal	73.3	24	44	16	72	−0.05	39	–	–	472	456

Table 1
(Continued)

	Share 15–19 in school in 2001	I often feel bored	Percent schools with absenteeism	Percent who skipped 1 or more class	Reading deficit of students who skipped	Disciplinary climate	Reading difference between top and bottom quartile	TIMSS end of HS (math)	TIMSS end of HS (science)	PISA age 15 (native-born students)	
										Reading	Math
	(percent)	(% agree)	(above 5 %)	(in last 2 weeks)	(5 or more classes)	(student rept.)	(on disc. climate)	(math)	(science)		
	(1)	(2)	(3)	(4)	(5)	(6)	(7)	(8)	(9)	(10)	(11)
Russia	70.8	27	–	34	34	0.45	40	471	481	463	480
Spain	80.1	66	26	33	71	–0.17	30	–	–	494	478
Sweden	86.4	58	45	38	33	–0.19	35	552	559	523	517
Switzerland	83.3	38	13	32	56	0.30	28	540	523	514	548
UK	74.7	54	78	35	71	0.02	45	–	–	528	534
United States	77.6	61	60	38	112	0.03	31	461	480	511	500
OECD Avg.	77.7	48	44	33	79	0.00	39	–	–	503	500

Sources:

Enrollment rate [column (1)] – *Education at a Glance* [OECD (2003b), p. 258];

Bored in class [column (2)] – *Education at a Glance* [OECD (2002), p. 330];

School means of absenteeism [column (3)] – *Education at a Glance* [OECD (2000), p. 241];

Class skipping and reading deficit [columns (4) and (5)] – *Literacy Skills for the World of Tomorrow: Further Results from PISA 2000* [OECD (2003a), p. 290];

Student reported disciplinary climate and it's association with reading achievement [columns (6) and (7)] – *Literacy Skills for the World of Tomorrow: Further Results from PISA 2000* [OECD (2003a), p. 372];

TIMSS Scores at end of secondary school for all students [columns (8) and (9)] – *Pursuing Excellence*, Gonzales (2000), p. 92;

PISA reading and math for 15-year-old students who were born in the country to at least one parent from the country [columns (10) and (11)] – *Literacy Skills for the World of Tomorrow: Further Results from PISA 2000* [OECD (2003a), p. 351].

is the explanation for the remarkably high achievement levels of students in East Asia: students are more disciplined in class and study harder.

To test this hypothesis, an effort/discipline scale combining the PISA student discipline index [column (6)] and the school skipping data in column (4) was created and then included in models predicting PISA literacy scales for native-born students. The achievement of native-born students is analyzed in order to eliminate variation in rates of immigration as a confounding variable. The base line model has two variables: GDP per capita (to capture national wealth, the socio-economic background of parents and the efficiency of the nation's institutions) and a dummy variable for East Asia intended to capture cultural differences between East and West that produce the remarkable work ethic of Asian students. This dummy variable has always been a significant predictor of mathematics and science achievement in my previous work. Table 2 presents the results. The effort/discipline index is a significant predictor of national mean achievement levels in mathematics and science. A one-standard deviation (measured in the sample of 42 nations) improvement in both components of the index predicts a 14 point (about 0.50 GLE) higher level of science achievement and a 20 point (a 0.80 GLE) higher level in mathematics. When the effort/discipline index is added to the model, the Asian dummy becomes insignificant. Apparently differentials in student effort and discipline do account for some of the differences between nations in academic achievement and contribute to the outstanding achievement levels of East Asian nations.

Table 2

Student effort and academic achievement (Program for International Student Assessment 2000 data)

Native of the country	Effort index	Log GDP/Pop 1995	East Asia	Adj R^2 RMSE	Number of observations
Mathematics – 15-year-olds	20.8***	87.6***	26.8	0.746	41
	(7.5)	(8.2)	(19.0)	33.9	
		86.3***	52.8***	0.702	41
		(8.9)	(17.9)	36.7	
Science – 15-year-olds	14.0**	70.6***	26.9	0.720	41
	(6.4)	(7.0)	(16.2)	29.0	
		69.8***	44.3***	0.721	41
		(7.3)	(14.8)	29.7	
Combined reading literacy – 15-year-olds	4.5	76.8***	20.8	0.794	41
	(5.6)	(6.1)	(14.2)	25.3	
		76.5***	26.5**	0.796	41
		(6.1)	(12.1)	25.2	

Source: OECD (2003a).

**Significant at the 5% level on a two tail test.

***Significant at the 1% level on a two tail test.

We now turn to a discussion of policy options for inducing students to try harder. We begin with a simple model that elucidates some of the key issues.

2. A model of student learning

2.1. The model of student effort

The student's decision about effort in school can be simply represented by three equations: a learning function, a rewards for learning function and a costs of student effort function.

The learning function

Learning is a change that takes place in a person. It occurs when an individual who is *ready and able* to learn, is offered an *opportunity* to learn and makes the *effort* to learn. All three elements are essential. Learning readiness and ability – indexed by A_i – depends on prior learning, intelligence and family background. A_i is exogenous (i.e. determined outside the model). The part of the learning equation controlled by individual students is effort (E_i).

While, in principle, every literate individual with access to a library has the opportunity to learn, schools and teachers have, in practice, a great deal of influence on what youngsters learn and at what pace. Educators determine what courses are required, the topics covered, teaching methods, homework and paper assignments and classroom expectations. In the model opportunity to learn is operationalized as IX^m or school quality. X^m is per pupil expenditure on school inputs and policies that foster academic achievement for the school 'm'. I is an exogenous efficiency parameter for these school inputs/policies. While facilitating academic learning is the primary purpose of American schools, other goals compete for school resources and administrative attention. Consequently, X^m is not the same thing as per pupil expenditure.

The fourth input in the individual's learning function is the effort and cooperativeness of the other students at the school. Empirical studies of peer effects and social interactions have generated persuasive evidence that individuals are influenced by the norms and behavior of co-workers and close associates. Education value-added production function studies consistently find that the socio-economic status of the other students in a school influences learning gains. Until recently it was not clear, however, whether this finding reflected a causal relationship or was instead a selection effect caused by parents with strong preferences for education choosing to move to high SES communities. Recent studies based on data free from such bias show that causal peer effects do exist. Randomly assigned college roommates have been shown to influence each other's academic performance [Zimmerman (1999), Sacerdote (2000)]. An elegant study by Hoxby (2000) has shown that boys and girls learn more when girls account for a larger share of the students in a grade. Angrist and Lang's (2002) study of Brookline schools found that increasing the number of Boston Metco students in a classroom did not affect the learning of white students but had significant negative effects on learning of black 3rd graders who were Brookline residents. Hanushek, Kain and Rivkin's (2002) analysis of Texas data found that high ability black students learned more in years in which their grade had a higher proportion of nonblack students. Using experimental data from Project Star, Boozer and Cacciola (2001) have demonstrated that the students who were taught in small classes during their first years in school had positive spillover effects on their classmates in regular third and fourth grade classrooms once the experiment was completed. Using panel evidence from administrative data, Betts and Zau (2002) found that "changes in the average achievement at the school have independent large effects on student learning". These effects were substantially larger than the effects of class size and teacher credentials, education and experience.

These studies are strong evidence that peer effects are real. But before peer spillover effects can be manipulated to further learning, we must understand exactly how they are generated. The SES, skin color and gender of classmates probably do not directly influence learning. Rather the observed spillover effects are probably generated by the norms and behavior of classmates. Some students help their classmates learn, others disrupt their learning. Some honor academic engagement, others make fun of kids who are friendly with teachers. The norms and behavior patterns of young women are more supportive of academic learning than the norms and behavior patterns of young men. This is probably the reason for Hoxby's gender composition findings.

There are two distinct ways that peers influence a student's learning. First, their behavior influences how much classroom time is devoted to maintaining discipline and to other distractions, how much is learned from classroom discussions and projects that students work on together, how rapidly teachers move through the curriculum and how many students require one-on-one assistance. These influences are production externalities and are represented in our model by including average effort levels of other students as one of the inputs in the individual's learning production function. Lazear has demonstrated that when students are heterogeneous with respect to disruptive behavior, it is optimal for more disruptive students to be placed in smaller classes [Lazear (2001)].

The second mechanism by which peers influence learning outcomes is the effect of their norms and teasing and harassment behavior on the individual's own effort level. A discussion of these influences is postponed to Section 5.

To keep the model simple, years attending K-12 schools are assumed to be predetermined. The learning that occurs during that period is described by the simple equation

Human capital at the end of secondary school $= L = AE^\alpha (E^m)^\rho (IX^m)^\beta$,

$$\alpha + \rho + \beta < 1, \tag{1}$$

where

E – effort of the individual student – an index of the time and psychic energy that the ith pupil devotes to learning (years spent in K-12 school are taken as predetermined);

E^m – mean effort of all other students at school m – an index of the time and psychic energy that the other pupils at school m annually devote to learning;

X^m – expenditure on school inputs and policies that foster academic achievement at school m. This is not equivalent to spending per pupil because school budgets contain items serving other purposes – e.g., sports, art, music, occupational skills, etc.;

I – an exogenous efficiency parameter for school inputs that foster academic achievement;

α – elasticity of the ith student's human capital (L) with respect to her effort;

ρ – elasticity of the ith student's human capital (L) with respect to the effort of all other students in the school; ρ is also referred to as the effort externality multiplier;

β – elasticity of the ith student's human capital (L) with respect to $(I X^m)$.

Note that the 'i' superscript has been suppressed throughout. While the choice of a Cobb–Douglas function is more specific than is necessary to reach the conclusions of the model, the main intuition and results of the model can readily be followed in this specific functional form.[4] It implies that:

(a) School quality and student effort interact positively. An improvement in teacher quality enhances the effect of greater student effort and vice versa.

(b) Effort by one student interacts positively with the effort of classmates (e.g., one student can disrupt the learning of an entire class).

(c) A 20 percent increase in effort by all students (E and E^m) and school quality (X^m) increases human capital (L) by less than 20 percent.

The private rewards for achievement function

The model assumes that young people have high rates of time preference, so the present discounted value of future payoffs is heavily influenced by the signals of L that are available to colleges and employers immediately after high school.[5] An individual's

---

[4] The main necessary features of a more general model are that there is complementarity between individual student effort, school disciplinary climate and resource input in educational production and that certain institutional features enhance the productivity of resource usage [Bishop and Woessmann (2004)].

[5] Observing how a worker performs on the job should allow employers to develop more accurate opinions about L over time. There are, however, job and firm specific match components to job performance that may cloud an employer's ability to evaluate general human capital. Nevertheless, the difficulties of signaling L at the end of high school become less important to job placement and wages as the worker gains labor market experience. But they nevertheless have very large effects on the choice of college, field of study and early entry into desirable occupations that have lasting effects on earnings even when better information on L later becomes available. These early outcomes are particularly salient to students and parents and influence their expectations about the long run consequences of learning in high school [Rosenbaum (2001)]. Their lack of knowledge about the true long term consequences may lead them to focus on manipulating the signals – SAT-1, class rank and GPA – that they know influence immediate outcomes and to neglect developing a really good education [Bishop (1990)].

productivity depends on L, a latent variable that is not visible to college admissions officers and employers. When a student leaves high school, colleges and employers have four indicators they can use to predict L: (1) aptitude and family background (A), (2) achievement relative to others at the school such as class rank or GPA ($L - L^m$), (3) a pass/fail dummy variable for a minimum competency exam (MCE) and (4) a vector of scores on curriculum-based external exit exams (CBEEEs). Students are pooled across schools.[6] L is positively correlated with both A and ($L - L^m$) and even more strongly correlated with scores on CBEEEs when they have been taken.

Present discounted value of intrinsic and extrinsic (both pecuniary and nonpecuniary) rewards for achievement, Π, is

$$\Pi = (j + w)L + \theta\left(L - L^m\right) + \sigma A, \tag{2}$$

where

j – the present discounted value of the intrinsic nonpecuniary benefits, joy, of learning received by the ith student and her parents. Note that these benefits are assumed to occur regardless of whether the learning is signaled to others or honored publicly;

w – the impact of absolute levels of achievement (human capital) at the end of secondary school on the present discounted value of lifetime after-tax earnings and other extrinsic rewards for learning for person i. It includes the effects of secondary school learning on wage rates conditional on years of schooling and on the years and quality of post-secondary schooling obtained. It also includes the benefits that parents derive from the economic success of their children and the honor and prestige given to those who are signaled to be high achievers. The magnitude of these benefits increase when L is more reliably signaled to colleges and employers [Becker and Rosen (1992)]. Curriculum-based external examinations increase w, the payoff to absolute achievement, and tend to reduce θ, the payoff to one's relative position (rank) in the secondary school's graduating class, and σ, the payoff to IQ and family background. The introduction of an MCE has a similar but smaller effects on w, θ and σ;

$L - L^m$ – achievement of the ith student relative to the representative student's achievement (L^m). Rank in class and grades awarded on a curve are examples of signals of achievement that describe the student's achievement relative to others in the school;

---

[6] Pooling occurs when employers do not know which school a student has graduated from or when schools have not developed reliable reputations that employers and colleges can use to improve their prediction of L [Betts and Costrell (2001)]. If grading standards of schools and of courses within schools were known, it might be feasible to handicap class rank and course grades so as to construct a good measure of L. Constructing such estimates for 100s of schools and tens of thousands of courses would be extremely costly. Some employers and colleges use subjective judgments to handicap GPAs and class rank, but these judgments are unreliable and infrequently updated [Bishop (1999b)].

θ – the impact of achievement relative to the school mean (e.g., effects of class rank and grades assigned on a curve) on social status in the community, admission to preferred colleges and lifetime income;

σ – the impact of A_i (i.e., early IQ, early achievement and family background) on the present discounted value of lifetime earnings; σ will be large and w and θ small if access to college depends solely on family background and IQ test scores obtained prior to entering secondary school. The SAT is not a pure IQ test, but relative to curriculum based exams it is at the aptitude end of the spectrum. Consequently, substituting curriculum-based exams for the SAT in university admissions decisions would lower σ and raise w. Since A is assumed exogenous, changes in σ do not affect student incentives to study or community incentives to invest in schools.

Choosing learning effort

Students compare expected benefits to expected costs.

Benefits of effort for student i

$$= B = (j + w + \theta)\big[AE^\alpha (E^m)^\rho (IX^m)^\beta\big] - \theta\big[A^m (E^m)^{\alpha+\rho} (IX^m)^\beta\big], \qquad (3)$$

where $L^m = A^m (E^m)^{\alpha+\rho} (IX^m)^\beta \approx$ human capital at graduation of the representative student at school m; A^m is the ability of this representative student.

Studying generates costs – psychic energy, loss of free time and boredom – that are assumed to be an increasing function of the time and energy devoted to schoolwork:

Costs of student effort $= C = C_0 E^\mu$, $\qquad (4)$

where $\mu > 1$ because the marginal costs of effort rise as effort increases.

Determining student effort

To study the determinants of student effort, we define a net benefits of study effort equation, $B - C$, and obtain it's maximum by differentiating with respect to E, assuming X^m and E^m fixed,

$$\max(B - C) = (j + w + \theta)\big[AE^\alpha (E^m)^\rho (IX^m)^\beta\big] - C_0 E^\mu. \qquad (5)$$

The derivative of (5) with respect to E for each student is

$$\frac{\partial(B - C)}{\partial E} = \alpha(j + w + \theta)\big[AE^{\alpha-1} (E^m)^\rho (IX^m)^\beta\big] - \mu C_0 E^{\mu-1} = 0, \qquad (6)$$

$$E = \left\{\left[\frac{\alpha}{\mu C_0}\right][j + w + \theta]\big[A^m (E^m)^\rho (IX^m)^\beta\big]\right\}^{1/(\mu-\alpha)}, \qquad (7)$$

and

$$\ln E = \left(\frac{1}{\mu - \alpha}\right)\left[\ln \alpha - \ln \mu C_0 + \ln(j + w + \theta)\right.$$
$$\left. + \ln A + \rho \ln E^m + \beta \ln(I X^m)\right]. \tag{8}$$

The policy implications of Equations (7) and (8) are straightforward. To induce students to study longer and harder, educators, employers and parents must either:

- Lower the opportunity costs of studying ($\downarrow \mu C_0$), e.g., by requiring that homework be completed before television or a video game is turned on or establishing homework clubs after school.
- Increase the effectiveness of study time ($\uparrow \alpha$), e.g., by providing a quiet place to study, learning aids (such as encyclopedias, computers and the Internet) and tutoring/assistance if needed.
- Improve the quality of one's peers ($\uparrow E^m$), e.g., by moving to a higher income community or getting your child into honors courses or a school or program for the 'gifted'.
- Improve the quality of instruction ($\uparrow I X^m$), e.g., by developing excellent courses and curricula, hiring gifted teachers, providing excellent professional development and holding them accountable.
- Increase intrinsic rewards for learning ($\uparrow j$), e.g., by hiring more interesting teachers, making content more engaging, allowing students to select the course they take and instilling a love of learning in children.
- Increase extrinsic rewards for learning $\uparrow (w + \theta)$, e.g., by awarding merit scholarships and greater social prestige to high achievers, persuading employers to offer bigger wage increments immediately after high school for skills and for college completion and persuading colleges to become more selective and admit students into competitive programs on the basis of learning during high school (L), not ability (A), family background or ability to pay tuition.

2.2. Model of government effort

To determine the government's choice of the level of spending X^m, we have to look at the benefits and costs of the government (G). The government's benefits B_G are given by

$$B_G = P(j^m + w^m)L^m = P(j^m + w^m)A^m(E^m)^{\alpha + \rho}(I X^m)^{\beta}. \tag{9}$$

Assuming for simplicity no external benefits of education, the average intrinsic rewards for learning for students at school m (j^m) and the average extrinsic rewards (w^m) for L are equivalent for the individual student and for the general public. Note, however, that the rewards for learning generated by a student's high rank relative to other students at the school, θ, that motivate some students to excel are not found in the community's payoff function. Note further that the mean community benefits, $(j^m + w^m)L$, of learning are weighted by the parameter P which reflects the priority government gives to the quality of a school's academic program. P characterizes the political power of supporters of high academic standards in the governance of schools relative to the political power of those whose objectives lie elsewhere.

The government's cost C_G is defined as expenditure per pupil on the academic goals of school

$$C_G = X^m. \tag{10}$$

Note that X^m is the choice variable under the control of the government. It chooses X^m in order to maximize its net benefits ($B_G - C_G$), given students' effort and the institutional setting. After reorganizing the first-order condition for a maximum, we have the following equation for government effort.

$$X^m = \left\{\beta P\left[j^m + w^m\right]\left[A^m\left(E^m\right)^{a+\rho}I^\beta\right]\right\}^{1/(1-\beta)}. \tag{11}$$

An examination of Equation (11) characterizing government effort reveals that public investments in the quality and quantity of academic instruction (X^m) are driven by many of the same forces – intrinsic and extrinsic rewards for learning, school efficiency (I), the elasticity of learning with respect to inputs – as student decisions to study hard [Bishop and Woessmann (2004)]. E^m on the right-hand side of (11) is implying that diligence and engagement on the part of students tends to induce taxpayers to fund schools more generously. Note also that X^m is on the right-hand side of the student effort equation implying that politically powerful parents who obtain generous funding of the school's academic program find that the students attending their local school will become more engaged and diligent. These positive feedbacks mean that policy multipliers for the equilibrium of this system are quite large [Bishop and Woessmann (2004)]. As a result, decentralized governance and funding is likely to result in Matthew effects. Schools with politically powerful parents and able students who believe rewards for learning are large will significantly outperform schools with politically weak parents and disadvantaged students who dislike academics. If a society with a decentralized education system wants to equalize achievement outcomes across schools, it must establish compensatory systems of financing, teacher assignment and/or student assignment.

One important exception to the generalization that X^m and E are driven by the same forces is the absence of θ, *the payoff to class rank*, in the equation for school quality investments. If selective colleges admit students solely on the basis of class rank [i.e., θ is large and $(j + w) = 0$], some students will be motivated to try to do better than their classmates, but parents will see no benefit to introducing more rigorous courses and hiring more qualified teachers.

2.3. Evidence that extrinsic rewards matter

What evidence is there for the claim that student effort responds to extrinsic rewards? When students are asked why they study, 79 percent say "I need the grades to get into college" and 58 percent say "Help me get a good job" [Educational Exellence Alliance, EEA (2002)]. Generous merit scholarship programs provide a natural experiment for evaluating the effects of pecuniary incentives. Studies have found that the $3000+ Hope Scholarship for Georgia high school graduates with averages of B or better increased SAT scores, GPAs and college attendance rates relative to other states in the South [Henry and Rubenstein (2002), Dynarski (2000), Cromwell, Mustard and Sridhar (2003)]. When the payoff to college rises, college attendance rates rise. When payoffs fall, attendance falls [Freeman (1975, 1976,1986), Bishop (1977, 1990)]. Preparations for college during high school appear to be similarly responsive? College–high school pay differentials in the regional labor market surrounding a high school had significant effects on the academic orientation of students' courses and their likelihood of going to college [Bishop (1991)].

For students planning on college, the key determinants of the extrinsic rewards for study $(w + \theta)$ are how important high school learning is for getting into and completing college and the payoff to getting a college degree. For those not planning to go to college, better jobs are the relevant pecuniary inducement for study. During the last fifty years, these indicators of the payoff to effort and learning in high school have tended to rise and fall together. Let us review their history and then compare that history to trends in the academic focus of schools, student effort and achievement.

Wage premium for college. The college wage premium for 25–34 year old men and women rose during the 1950s, stabilized during the 1960s, then fell precipitously during the early 1970s, stabilized again for 5 years at a low level and then climbed rapidly during the 1980s and more slowly during the 1990s [Census Bureau (1974), NCES (2003b), Table 16.1].

College selectivity. During the 1930s social class was the primary determinant of who went to college. College entrants in 1929 were on average at the 55th percentile of ability among high school graduates. Those who did not enter college were at the 44th percentile on average; a gap of only 11 points. The percentile gap between college entrants and high school graduates not going to college rose to 15 points in 1934, 20 points in 1946, 19 points in 1950, 22 points in 1957, 28 points in 1960 Project Talent data [Taubman and Wales (1972)]. The trend toward growing academic selectivity of college enrollment reversed during the 1960s and early 1970s. Many two-year colleges with open admissions policies were founded and males attended college in record numbers to postpone being drafted. The class rank gap between those who attend college and those who do not fell to 21 points in 1972. During the late 1970s the relationship grew stronger (reaching 24.7 points in 1980) [Bishop (1991)].

Wage payoff for academic achievement. In the United States, reading and math skills have historically not had large effects on the wage rates of young workers who have not gone to college. Even so, the payoffs to these skills appeared to decline during late 1960s and early 1970s. The threat of litigation brought under the 1971 Griggs interpretation of Title 7 of the Civil Rights Act of 1965 induced many employers to stop using tests assessing reading and mathematics to help in the selection of new employees [Friedman and Belvin (1982)]. As a result, during the 1970s young high school graduates who had learned English, science and mathematics thoroughly typically did not earn appreciably more than the high school graduates who had done poorly in these subjects [Bishop (1989)]. Individuals who have strong mathematics skills and good grades in high school are better employees [Department of Labor (1970), Ghiselli (1973), Hunter, Crosson and Friedman (1985), Hartigan and Wigdor (1989), Bishop (1992)]. Over time employers learn which employees are the most competent by observing job performance and greater productivity is eventually recognized and rewarded though it often takes a decade or so [Hauser and Daymont (1977), Taubman and Wales (1975), Bishop (1992), Farber and Gibbons (1996), Grubb (1993), Bishop (1989), Altonji and Pierret (1998)].

The environment changed during the 1980s and 1990s due to the spread of personal computers and the rapid growth of professional-technical and managerial jobs. The Supreme Court's Wards Cove decision made it easier to defend using reading and mathematics tests as part of a selection process and some employers reintroduced basic skills tests into their selection procedures for clerical and factory jobs. As a result, the labor market rewards for mathematical ability of young workers rose. Murnane, Willett and Levy (1995) found that the effect of a one standard deviation increase in mathematics skill on the wage rates of 24 year old men rose from $0.46 per hour in 1978 to $1.15 per hour in 1986. The wage payoff for young women rose from $1.15 per hour to 1.42 per hour in 1986.

The Bishop–Woesmann model predicts that the rise during the 1980s and 1990s in the payoff to college and to mathematics achievement should have stimulated schools to set higher standards and induced students to study harder. Many states increased the number of mathematics and science courses required for graduation and established minimum competency tests for graduation. Students are taking more rigorous courses. Between 1982 and 2000 the share of students taking Geometry rose by 31 percentage points, Algebra II by 28 percentage points, Chemistry by 30 points and Physics by 16 points [NCES (2003a), p. 164]. The number of students taking AP calculus quintupled. Homework assigned and completed increased. Hofferth and Sandberg (2000) report that 9–12 year old students in the US averaged 3 hours and 41 minutes of homework per week in 1997, a 9 percent increase since 1981. The percentage of 13 year olds reporting they either had no homework or did not do it fell from 33 percent in 1982 to 9 percent in 1990. The percentage of 17 year olds reporting they did at least one hour of homework each day rose from 32.5 percent in 1978 to 66 percent in 1990.

As predicted, achievement improved. NAEP reading scores in 1999 were two grade level equivalents (GLEs) higher than in 1980 for African-American and Hispanic 17-year-olds. For whites the gain on the reading tests was only 0.2 GLEs. NAEP math scores were up one grade level equivalent (GLE) since 1982 for whites, two GLEs for African-Americans and 1.6 GLEs for Hispanics. SAT scores were flat in verbal and up by 24 points in math. NAEP science scores rose 1.3 GLEs for whites, 1.9 GLEs for African-Americans and 2.7 GLEs for Hispanics [NCES (2002)].

These positive trends contrast with the trends of the previous decade – the late 1960s and the 1970s when college selectivity and payoffs to learning and college attendance were declining. During the 1970s the summed math and verbal SAT-1 declined

50 points. Scores of Iowa 12th graders on the Iowa Test of Educational Development which had risen steadily during the 1940s, 1950s and the first half of the 1960s, declined by more than a grade level equivalent after 1966 [Bishop (1989)].

There may, however, be other explanations for the post 1966 test score decline and the rebound during the 1980s and 1990s. Graduation requirements and teacher expectations appear to have followed the same cycle. While the Bishop–Woesmann theory explains these changes in teacher expectations and school policies as responses to shifts in economic payoffs, others might argue the causes lie elsewhere. As a result, the examination of aggregate time series data for just one country can never be conclusive evidence for the changing economic payoffs hypothesis. Other data need to be examined. The quality and reliability of signals of academic achievement can have big effects on extrinsic rewards for learning, w and θ. We turn now to a review of evidence on how mechanisms for signaling student achievement influence academic achievement (L), public investment in student learning (X^m) and student effort (E, E^m).

3. The effects of better signaling of academic achievement

In most European and Asian nations externally set high school exit exams assessing the secondary school curriculum determine university admission and access to preferred fields of study. Grades on these exams are requested on job applications and typically included on resumes. Consequently, curriculum-based external exit exam systems (CBEEES) like the Baccalaureate in France and the GCSE and A levels in England and Wales have profound effects on student incentives to study. What are the critical features of a CBEEES? How are they different from the minimum competency exams minimum competency exams (MCE) that so many American states have established? We begin by noting the features that MCEs and CBEEES have in common. They:

1. *Produce signals of accomplishment that have real consequences for the student.* MCEs are tests that must be passed to get a high school diploma. For CBEEES the nature and the magnitude of the rewards vary. In Canada CBEEE grades are averaged with teacher assessments to generate final grades for specific courses. In Europe and East Asia exam results influence hiring decisions of employers and access to popular lines of study in university that are oversubscribed. CBEEES sometimes make one eligible for a more prestigious diploma or confer rights to enroll in higher level post-secondary institutions.

2. *Define achievement relative to an external standard, not relative to other students in the classroom or the school.* Fair comparisons of achievement across schools and across students taught by different teachers are now possible.[7] Costrell's

---

[7] When grading standards vary across high schools, across classrooms within the school and over time, employers and universities are not able to place applicants for jobs or admission on a common scale. Students must be pooled together so schools and teachers have an incentive to help their students compete for jobs and colleges by inflating grades.

(1994, 1997) and Bett's (1998) analysis of the optimal setting of educational standards when students from schools with different grading standards are pooled concluded that centralized standard setting (state or national achievement exams) with a local option to set even higher standards results in higher standards, higher achievement and higher social welfare than decentralized standard setting (i.e., teacher grading or school defined graduation requirements).

3. *Are controlled by the education authority that establishes the curriculum for and funds K-12 education.* When a national or provincial ministry of education sponsors an external exam, it is more likely to be aligned with the national or provincial curriculum. It is, consequently, more likely to be used for school accountability; not just as an instrument of student accountability. Curriculum reform is facilitated because coordinated changes in instruction and exams are feasible. Tests established and mandated by other organizations serve the interests of other masters. America's most influential high stakes exams – the SAT-I and the ACT – serve the needs of colleges to sort students by aptitude *not* the needs of high schools to reward students who have learned what schools are trying to teach.

4. *Cover the vast majority of students.* Exams for a set of elite schools or advanced courses influence standards at the top but may have limited effects on the rest of the students.

Curriculum-based external exit exam systems are distinguished from MCEs by the following additional features. CBEEES:

5. *Assess a major portion of what students are expected to know or be able to do.* Studying to prepare for an exam (whether set by one's own teacher or by a ministry of education) should result in the student learning important material and developing valued skills. Some exit exams do a better job of achieving this goal than others. Dimensions of achievement that cannot be reliably assessed by external means should be evaluated by teachers.

6. *Are collections of End-of-Course Exams (EOCE).* This requires that the Ministry of Education forge an agreement on minimum content standards for each subject that will have an exit exam. Since they assess the content of specific sequences of courses, alignment between instruction and assessment is maximized and teacher accountability is enhanced. This feature also aligns the interests of teachers, students and parents. Teachers become coaches helping their team do battle with the national or provincial exam. Students should be less likely to pressure teachers to lower standards.

7. *Signal multiple levels of achievement in the subject.* If only a pass–fail signal is generated by an exam, the standard will, for political reasons, have to be set low enough to allow almost everyone to pass. The achievement of most students will be so far above this level, the threat of failing the exam will not stimulate them to greater effort [Kang (1985), Becker and Rosen (1992), Costrell (1994), Betts and Costrell (2001)]. CBEEEs signal the student's achievement level in the subject, not just whether the student exceeds or falls below a specific cut point that all high school graduates are required to surpass. Consequently all students, not just

those at the bottom of the class, are given an incentive to study hard to do well on the exam [Becker and Rosen (1992)]. Consequently, EOCE are hypothesized to improve classroom culture more than a pass–fail minimum competency exam.

8. *Assess more difficult material.* Since CBEEES are supposed to measure and signal the full range of achievement in the subject, they contain more difficult questions and problems. This induces teachers to spend more time on cognitively demanding skills and topics. MCEs, by contrast, are designed to identify which students have failed to surpass a rather low minimum standard, so they do not to ask questions or set problems that students near that borderline are unlikely to be able to answer or solve.[8] This tends to result in too much class time being devoted to practicing low level skills.

The SAT-I and the ACT are not CBEEES because they are not curriculum-based, cover only a narrow slice of the high school curriculum and are not controlled by a Ministry of Education that funds education and sets the curriculum. As Harvard's admissions director put it shortly after the switch to the SAT-1, "Learning in itself has ceased to be the main factor [in college admissions]. The aptitude of the pupil is now the leading consideration" [Gummere (1943), p. 5]. If students are admitted to selective colleges on the basis of aptitude and IQ [i.e., σ is large in Equation (2)] not achievement [$(w + \theta)$ is small], student incentives to learn and community incentives to invest in school quality (IX^m) are weakened and all students arrive in college less well prepared [Bishop (1999c)]. Rick Harbaugh has shown that, if admissions decisions are centralized for all public institutions in a state, the central authority will choose to admit on the basis of knowledge and achievement (not aptitude) because this policy induces students to work harder in high school. Competition between colleges leads colleges "to put more emphasis on aptitude tests … and less emphasis on achievement tests and grades" [Harbaugh (2003), p. 1].

Curriculum-based external exit exam systems (CBEEES) increase w, the pecuniary rewards for absolute levels of academic achievement by improving the signals of the latent variable academic achievement made available to colleges and employers [Becker and Rosen (1992)]. This causes these institutions to give greater weight to achievement when they make admissions and hiring decisions. They also shift attention and rewards away from aptitude tests, measures of relative achievement such as rank in class and teacher grades, family connections, recommendations and interviews toward measures of absolute achievement (e.g. grades on the external exam). The student's rewards for achievement rise and the community benefits of increasing school quality rise even more,

$$\frac{\partial[P(j^m + w^m)]}{\partial(CBEEE)} > \frac{\partial(j^m + w^m)}{\partial(CBEEE)} > \frac{\partial(j + w + \theta)}{\partial(CBEEE)} > 0.$$

---

[8] In 1996 only 4 of the 17 states with MCEs targeted their graduation exams at a 10th grade proficiency level or higher. The tests can be taken multiple times. Eventual pass rates for the class of 1995 were quite high: 98% in Louisiana, Maryland, New York, North Carolina and Ohio; 96 % in Nevada and New Jersey, 91% in Texas and 83% in Georgia. American Federation of Teachers (1996), *Making Standards Matter.* American Federation of Teachers, Washington, DC, p. 30.

First, community benefits of school quality increase more than the student's private benefits because $\frac{\partial(\theta)}{\partial(CBEEE)} < 0$. Making better measures of L available reduces the weight attached to class rank and GPA in college and employer selection decisions. Secondly, the education system's sponsorship makes the CBEEE a highly-visible signal of the school's academic success and strengthens the hands of the local advocates for increased emphasis on the academic (as distinct from the artistic, athletic and vocational) goals of the school $\frac{\partial P}{\partial(CBEEE)} > 0$. Since organizations tend to get what they measure, it is very important that the Ministry use high-quality exams that challenge students and induce good teaching.

3.1. Does better signaling of achievement result in students learning more?

The hypothesis that curriculum-based external exit examination systems improve achievement has been tested by comparing nations and provinces that do and do not have such systems. Six different international data sets have been examined. In most studies of the effect of CBEEES national mean test scores (for an age group or a grade) are regressed on per capita gross domestic product deflated by a purchasing power parity price index, a dummy for East Asian nation and a dummy for CBEEES. Analyzing 1994–1995 Third International Math and Science Study (TIMSS) data, Bishop (1996, 1997) found that 13 year old students from countries with medium and high stakes CBEEE systems outperformed students from other countries at a comparable level of economic development by 1.3 US grade level equivalents (GLE) in science and by 1.0 GLE in mathematics. A similar analysis of International Assessment of Educational Progress data on achievement in 1991 of 13-year-olds in 15 nations found that students from countries with CBEEES outperformed their counterparts in countries without CBEEES by about 2 US grade level equivalents in math and about two-thirds of a GLE in science and geography. Analysis of data from the 1990–2001 International Association for the Evaluation of Educational Achievement's study of the reading literacy study of 14-year-olds in 24 countries found that students in countries with CBEEES were about 1.0 GLE ahead of students in nations that lacked a CBEEES [Bishop (1999a, 1999b)]. Analysis of data from both waves of TIMSS data collection also implies that CBEEES have highly significant effects (of about 1.5 GLEs) on the math and science achievement in 8th grade [Bishop (2003a)]. Analysis of PISA data presented in rows 1, 4 and 7 of Table 3 also yields large statistically significant estimated effects of CBEEES on reading, mathematics and science literacy of native-born students.

Two other studies [Wößmann (2000, 2002)] have conducted hierarchical analyses of the entire TIMSS and TIMSS-R micro data set and included a comprehensive set of controls for family background, teacher characteristics, school resources and policies at the individual and school level. In Wößmann's study the 8th graders in CBEEES nations were about 1.1 international grade level equivalents ahead in mathematics and about 0.8 international grade level equivalents ahead in science. He also found that learning gains between 7th and 8th grade were significantly larger in CBEEES nations.

Table 3
Academic achievement in nations with and without curriculum-based external exit examination systems (Program for International Student Assessment 2000 data)

	Effort index	Curriculum-based external exit exam	Log GDP/Pop 1995	East Asia	Share upper secondary students in CTE	Adj R^2 RMSE	Number of observations
Native born students							
Mathematics – 15-year-olds		39.9***	84.9***	36.6**		0.764	41
		(12.1)	(7.9)	(16.7)		32.7	
	19.6***	38.2***	86.2***	12.8		0.805	41
	(6.6)	(11.0)	(7.2)	(17.1)		29.7	
	21.9***	40.2***	95.4***			0.807	41
	(5.8)	(10.6)	(7.1)			29.6	
Science – 15-year-olds		32.4***	71.3***	29.7**		0.756	41
		(9.9)	(6.5)	(13.9)		27.1	
	12.9**	31.2***	72.1***	14.2		0.780	41
	(5.7)	(9.4)	(6.2)	(14.9)		25.7	
	15.4**	33.5***	71.4***			0.780	41
	(5.1)	(9.8)	(6.2)			25.7	
Combined reading		25.2***	76.6***	15.7		0.828	41
literacy – 15-year-olds		(8.8)	(5.6)	(11.9)		23.1	
	3.7	24.8**	76.9***	11.2		0.826	41
	(5.2)	(8.9)	(5.6)	(14.6)		23.3	
	5.7	26.7***	76.3***			0.827	41
	(4.6)	(8.6)	(5.6)			23.2	
School/College enroll. of		−5.7	13.1***	−1.1	0.18*	0.552	30
15–19-year-olds (percent)		(4.8)	(4.3)	(7.7)	(0.10)	10.3	
Expected FTE yrs of		−0.11	2.51***	0.27	0.020*	0.700	32
schooling: 5–65		(0.47)	(0.40)	(0.73)	(0.010)	1.10	
Upper-secondary		4.9	27.2***	14.3*	0.23*	0.725	26
graduation rate		(6.9)	(4.5)	(8.2)	(0.12)	11.7	

Sources: Data on PISA is from OECD (2003a), *Literacy Skills for the World of Tomorrow: Further Results From PISA 2000.* Upper-secondary graduation rates, enrollment rates and expected FTE years of schooling are from OECD (2000), Education at a Glance 2000. The full-time equivalent number counts part-time enrollment as 0.5 years.
*Significant at the 10% level on a two-tail test.
**Significant at the 5 % level on a two-tail test.
***Significant at the 1% level on a two-tail test.

Another five studies compare students living in different provinces/states in Germany, Canada and the United States. Wößmann found that the German Lander with centralized secondary school exit examinations had significantly higher scores on the PISA literacy assessments. Students attending school in Canadian provinces with CBEEES were a statistically significant one-half of a US grade level equivalent ahead in math and science of comparable students living in provinces without CBEEES [Bishop (1997, 1999a)]. In 1990 New York State's Regents exam system was the only example of a curriculum-based external exit exam system in the United States. Graham and Husted's (1993) analysis of 1991 SAT test scores in the 37 states with reasonably large test taking populations found that New York State students did much better than students of the same race and social background in other states. Bishop, Moriarty and Mane (2000) and Bishop and Mane (2001) confirmed Graham and Husted's SAT findings and also found that 1992 NAEP math scores of New York 8th graders were significantly higher than in other demographically similar states. Analyzing NELS-88 data Bishop et al. (2001) found that learned about a half a GLE more between 8th grade and 12th grade than comparable students in other states. By the middle of the 1990s another state, North Carolina, had established a CBEEES. Controlling for ethnicity, social background and other standard's based reform policies, 8th graders in New York and North Carolina in 1996–1998 were about one-half of a GLE ahead of comparable students in other states in reading, math and science. State minimum competency exams had much smaller nonsignificant effects on achievement [Bishop et al. (2001)].

3.2.   Does better signaling of achievement change teaching and student attitudes?

What is the primary mechanism by which CBEEES increase student achievement? Do they induce school districts to hire more qualified teachers, to devote more time to teaching core subjects, to assign more homework, etc.? The impacts of CBEEES on school policies and instructional practices have been studied in the TIMSS data, in the Canadian IAEP data and in PISA data. CBEEES are not associated with higher teacher–pupil ratios nor greater spending on K-12 education. They are, however, associated with higher minimum standards for entry into the teaching profession, higher teacher salaries, a greater likelihood of having teachers specialize in teaching one subject in middle school and a greater likelihood of hiring teachers who have majored in the subject they will teach. Teacher satisfaction with their job appeared to be lower, possibly because of the increased pressure for accountability that results from the existence of good signals of individual student achievement. Schools in CBEEES jurisdictions devote more hours to math and science instruction and build and equip better science labs [Bishop (1997, 1999b)].

Fears that CBEEES have caused the quality of instruction to deteriorate appear to be unfounded. Students in CBEEES jurisdictions were less likely to say that memorization is the way to learn the subject and more likely to do experiments in science class. Apparently, teachers subject to the subtle pressure of an external exam four years in the future adopted strategies that are conventionally viewed as "best practice", not strategies designed to maximize scores on multiple-choice tests. Quizzes and tests were more common, but in other respects CBEEES jurisdictions were no different on a variety of indicators of pedagogy. Students were more likely to get tutoring assistance from teachers after school. They were just as likely to enjoy the subject and they were more likely to believe that science is useful in every day life. Canadian students did more homework and talked with their parents more about schoolwork [Bishop (1999b)].

Was attending more regularly and better discipline the mechanism by which CBEEES increased student achievement? Apparently not, the student effort and discipline index was not significantly higher in nations with CBEEES. When the effort/discipline index was added to the model, the coefficient on CBEEES hardly changed (contrast rows 1 and 2 in each panel of Table 3). On the other hand, students in CBEEES jurisdictions did more homework, got more tutoring and were tested more frequently. Possibly teachers responded to the external exam by assigning more homework and scheduling more students for tutoring. Many researchers have described classrooms as regulated by implicit treaties between students and the teacher [Sizer (1984), Powell, Farrar and Cohen (1985)]. External exams may allow teachers to require a higher standard of work from students but claim they are being forced to become tougher by the necessity to prepare them to pass the graduation exam. More research on the mechanisms by which examination systems influence classroom interactions and student achievement is clearly needed.

3.3. Does better signaling of achievement influence school attendance and labor market success?

What effects do high stakes curriculum-based external exit exam systems have on high school enrollment rates and college attendance? This question was addressed by analyzing OECD data on school enrollment rates of 15–19-year-olds, upper-secondary graduation rates and years spent in school (summed net-enrollment rates of people from age 5–65) [OECD (2000), Table C1.1]. Regressions predicting these variables are presented in rows 10, 11 and 12 of Table 3. CBEEES had no significant effect on any of these indicators. The statistically significant predictors were per capita GDP and the share of upper-secondary students in pre-vocational and career-technical educational programs [Bishop and Mane (2004)]. Analyses of US state cross-section data have also found that CBEEES (i.e., a dummy for New York State) and MCEs had no significant effect on aggregate enrollment rates or graduation rates in the early 1990s. The total number Carnegie units required to graduate, however, is negatively related to enrollment rates and graduation rates [Bishop et al. (2001), Lillard and DeCicca (2001)].

Longitudinal NELS-88 data sets allow a more refined look at the distributional effects of CBEEES and MCEs on high school completion. Students with low or average GPAs in 8th grade were significantly more likely to get their diploma late or to get a GED when they were from New York or a state with an MCE. The proportion of 8th graders who eventually got either a regular diploma or a GED was no different in New York but significantly lower for low GPA students from other MCE states [Bishop et al. (2001)]. As in Europe, fast paced instruction and high standards for getting an academic diploma results in some students taking longer to get the diploma and other students switching over to less demanding programs of study.

There is only one study of the effects of MCEs and CBEEES on college attendance in the United States. When eighth graders in 1988 were followed up in the fall of 1994, those who lived in New York or a state with an MCE were significantly more likely to be in college than students who attended school in other states [Bishop et al. (2001)].

Economic theory predicts that raising graduation standards will improve the average quality of high school graduates and raise their mean wage and earnings [Betts and Costrell (2001)]. Analysis of HSB and NELS-88 data support this prediction. Controlling on high school completion, college attendance and local labor market characteristics, students from states with MCEs earned significantly more – *9 percent more* in the calendar year following graduation – than students from states without MCEs. [Bishop et al. (2001)].

4. Setting higher standards for course grades and promotion to the next grade

Do higher expectations and tougher grading standards induce students to work harder and learn more? Sociologists and psychologists have been studying this issue for decades. Those taking more rigorous courses get lower grades but learn a good deal more [Gamoran and Barends (1987)]. Kulik and Kulik's (1984) meta analysis of the educational literature found that students chosen to skip a grade or to take an accelerated curriculum score 75 percent of a standard deviation higher on tests a few years later than matched students who were not accelerated. Repeating a grade effectively lowers learning goals and reduces the retained child's achievement a few years later by about 30 percent of a standard deviation [Holmes (1989)].

The goal setting literature is also relevant. Wood, Mento and Locke's (1987) meta-analysis of experimental studies of the effect of goal difficulty on various kinds of achievement concluded that on highly complex tasks like school and college course work, specific hard goals raised achievement by 47 percent of a standard deviation relative to students instructed simply to "do your best". Achievement goes up, but so does the probability of failing to reach the goal. In most studies more than two-thirds of those in the "hard goal" condition failed to achieve their goal [Locke (1968), pp. 163–165]. Will effort be sustained in the face of repeated failure?

In the laboratory and field settings used by psychologists, subjects have generally accepted the goal set for them by the researcher. Stedry (1960) found, however, that when subjects who had already set their own goals were assigned even higher goals by the study director, they rejected the assigned goal and achievement did not rise. Will students accept the goals that teachers set for the class? Can, for example, teachers induce students to set higher learning goals by raising the learning target that students must achieve to get an A or a B grade? Betts (2001), Betts and Grogger (2003) and Figlio and Lucas (2001) have addressed this question. Grading standards were measured by comparing student test scores to the grades teachers award. Schools and teachers that gave better grades than predicted were classified as having low grading standards. Worse grades than predicted classified the teacher as a tough grader. In multivariate models controlling for characteristics of students and teachers, students in the tough grading standards schools/classrooms had significantly larger test score gains. Aware that these results could be generated by unmeasured variations in teacher quality and grading on a curve, a series of robustness tests were conducted that tend to support the causal interpretation of the finding.

Figlio and Lucas have particularly rich data so their tests are the most convincing. They have four years of longitudinal data and are able to match pupils to individual teachers for whom they have good measures of grading standards. Controlling for classroom composition and school and student fixed effects, they find that one year gains are about 20 percent greater in math and one-third greater in reading for students assigned to teachers who are tough graders. They also found that parents spent 60 percent more time helping their child with homework when the child's teacher was a tough grader. This was probably one of the mechanisms by which students in the high standards classes learned more.

These parents did "not perceive tougher teachers to be better teachers" [Figlio and Lucas (2001), p. 20]. Difficult homework assignments intrude on parents' time and often put the family under stress, so parents complain. This is one of the reasons why 30 percent of American teachers feel pressured "to reduce the difficulty and amount of work you assign" and "to give higher grades than students' work deserves" [Hart (1995)]. When the only signal of student achievement is teacher grades, parents typically prefer high grades not high standards. Teachers who work in systems with external exams are aware of this. When a proposal was put forward in Ireland to drop the nation's system of external assessments and have teachers assess students for certification purposes, the union representing Ireland's secondary school teachers reacted as follows:

> Major strengths of the Irish educational system have been:
> (i) The pastoral contribution of teachers in relation to their pupils
> (ii) the perception of the teacher by the pupil as an advocate in terms of nationally certified examinations rather than as a judge.
> The introduction of school-based assessment by the pupil's own teacher for certification purposes would undermine those two roles, to the detriment of all concerned....
> The role of the teacher as judge rather than advocate may lead to legal accountability in terms of marks awarded for certification purposes. This would automatically result in a distancing between the teacher, the pupil and the parent. It also opens the door to possible distortion of the results in response to either parental pressure or to pressure emanating from competition among local schools for pupils. [Association of Secondary Teachers of Ireland (1990), p. 1.]

Note how the Irish teachers union feared that switching entirely to internal assessment would result in teachers being pressured to lower standards. If they are right, school choice does not inevitably lead to higher standards and better teaching. Higher standards will result only if student achievement is externally assessed, the results of these assessments are published and students benefit from attending schools that set high standards.

Gresham's law of course selection. American high schools offer courses in core subjects at vastly different levels of rigor and allow students to choose their level. A good grade requires less work in the lower level classes so a Gresham's law of course selection tends to prevail in which easy courses displace rigorous courses. Admissions officers at elite colleges have reacted by telling prospective students to take rigorous courses and are factoring course rigor into their deliberations. But most students do not aspire to attend elite colleges. Community colleges admit just about everyone and send students into noncredit remedial classes if they do poorly on placement exams given to arriving students. State universities seldom formally consider course rigor in their formula driven admissions process.

Asian and European schools also allow students to choose lower standards options. But the option chosen is well signaled to others by the name or type of secondary school or program. There is considerable prestige and honor attached to pursuing a high standards option, so competition for admission to the most demanding programs is often fierce, particularly in Asia. Once the school or program is selected, European students are typically formed into classes that take almost all subjects together. The class often remains intact for a couple of years and friendships tend to develop within this class. Students who are not able to keep up with the fast paced curriculum are asked to repeat the grade or to transfer to an easier school or an easier line of study. When I asked a Dutch student who, despite long hours of study had been required to repeat a grade, why she had studied so hard, she responded, *"I wanted to stay with my class!"*. Apparently, trying to keep up academically (i.e. accepting the academic goals of the school) is viewed positively by peers because it is an expression of commitment to the group. Indeed Dutch teachers and students tell me it is common for some of the better students to help struggling students pass the courses they are having difficulty with.

While the threat of retention appears to have the intended incentive effects in Belgium, France, Netherlands and Germany, the institutional features that make it such a powerful incentive – the intimate class that takes all its courses together and stays intact multiple years – are absent in large American comprehensive high schools. Failing a course only means it must be repeated during the summer or next year. It does not push you out of your clique, so the incentive effects of the threat of retention are likely to be weaker in the US than in Europe. Furthermore, retention is very costly because keeping a student in school for an extra year costs around $7,000. Compulsory summer school and after school programs appear to be a better and less costly alternative [Jacob (2002), Roderick et al. (1999), Roderick, Engel and Nagaoka (2003)]. This is a policy issue that needs a great deal more research.

5. Peer norms about studying and academic engagement

Kenneth Arrow has said that "norms of social behavior, including ethical and moral codes, ... are reactions of society to compensate for market failure" [Arrow (1971)]. At most schools, students have developed strong independent sub-cultures that make highly prescriptive demands on group members – no squealing on classmates, for example. Since disruptive students prevent classmates from learning, the "internalize the externalities" explanation of social norms predicts peers will enforce a norm against class disruptions. When secondary school students were asked, however, 60 percent of them disagreed with the proposition that "it was annoying when other students talk or joke around in class". Why do so many students give silent support to disruptive students? Why also does:

> The adolescent peer culture in America demeans academic success and scorns students who try to do well in school ... less than 5 percent of all students are members of a high-achieving crowd that defines itself mainly on the basis of academic excellence ... Of all the crowds the 'brains' were the least happy with who they are – nearly half wished they were in a different crowd [Steinberg, Brown and Dornbusch (1996), p. 145].

Are there other externalities at work here that can explain the peer culture's toleration of disruptive students and it's dislike of nerds. The beginnings of an answer can be found by looking very closely at (3), the expression for the benefits of learning. Let's ask: 'How large a benefit do I derive from others studying harder?'. This can be calculated by taking the derivative of (3) with respect to E^m holding E and X^m constant,

My benefit from effort by classmates

$$= \frac{\partial B^i}{\partial E^m} = \frac{\{(j+w)\rho L^i - \theta\alpha L^m + \theta\rho(L^i - L^m)\}}{E^m}. \tag{12}$$

When we ask "what is the effect of my study effort on aggregated learning payoffs of other students at the school", we get an even simpler expression:

Others payoff with respect to my effort

$$= \Psi = \frac{E^m}{L^m}\frac{\partial B^m}{\partial E^i} = \frac{E^m}{L^m}\frac{\partial B^m}{\partial E^m}\frac{\partial E^m}{\partial E^i} = (j^m + w^m)\rho - \theta\alpha. \tag{13}$$

Note that both of these expressions are negative when $\theta\alpha$ is large and ρ is sufficiently small.

Why are nerds unpopular and targeted for harassment? Equations (12) and (13) tell us that students are made worse off by the studying of others when (a) most of the rewards for learning arise from how one is ranked relative to other students in the class [θ is large relative to $(j+w)$], (b) the elasticity of learning with respect to others effort (ρ) is much smaller than α, the elasticity of learning with respect to own effort and (c) the student is a slow learner ($L^i < L^m$). When many of the extrinsic rewards for learning depend on rank in class or grades calculated on a curve, students may come to believe they have a common interest in persuading each other "not to study too much". Evidence for this comes from the EEA survey, where those who strongly agreed that "It is harder for me to get good grades, ... if others study hard" were three times more likely to have friends who "make fun of those who try to do well in school" than those who disagree. Thus the purpose of nerd harassment is not punishing high aptitude students for being smart, but discouraging study effort. Indeed, pressure against doing all your homework or volunteering comments during class will probably be stronger in low track classes than high track classes because the students in low track classes are more likely to have chosen an identity that rejects school [Akerlof and Kranton (2002)].

In Akerlof and Kranton's very interesting theory a student's primary motivation derives from his or her identity – jock, brain, burnout, party animal, etc. Associated with each identity is an ideal type – stereotypical physical attributes and behaviors that characterize the members of the crowd. "Individuals then gain or lose utility insofar as they belong to social categories with high or low social status and their attributes and behavior match the ideal of their category" [Akerlof and Kranton (2002), p. 1168]. Students with physical and social attributes that bring them close to the 'ideal' of a particular crowd tend to join that crowd. Once you join a crowd you try to live the ideal. Crowds tend toward homogeneity and socializing with members of lower status crowds is discouraged. "The quality of a school depends on how students fit in a school's social setting" (p. 1167). While they argue that the distribution of student identities (crowds) at a school and how they interact are more important determinants of learning than measurable school inputs, they do not put forward a set of policy prescriptions.

Akerlof and Kranton do not try to explain what determines the ideals and norms that characterize an identity, how new students learn the norms and are induced to conform to them and how norms evolve over time in response to changes in the environment and school policy. In three recent papers [Bishop et al. (2003, 2004), Bishop (2003b)] my colleagues and I have constructed a model that addresses these questions. Students entering middle school learn its norms by trying to copy the traits and behaviors of students who are respected and avoiding contact with those who are frequently harassed. Not conforming to the school's norms generates harassment and social exclusion.[9] Consequently, one can infer the norms by noting who gets harassed and who does not. Traits that in EEA data led to higher risks of being bullied and harassed were: being in a special education, being in gifted programs, taking accelerated courses in middle school, tutoring other students, enjoying school assignments, taking a theater course, saying

---

[9] Peer norms are enforced by encouraging 'wannabes', aspirants for admission to popular crowds, to harass those who visibly violate them. Fehr and Gachter (2000) found that allowing participants in a four-person public goods experiment to punish anonymous players who contributed little to the public investment, resulted in free riders being heavily punished and a big increase in contributions to the public investment. Many players devoted some of their money to punishing norm violators even though punishing others was costly for them. Harassing a student who has violated peer norms is close to costless in American secondary schools. If done in the service of defending school norms, harassing norm violator is rewarded by peers [Bishop et al. (2003)].

that rap–hip hop is not your favorite music and preferring musicals, heavy metal, country, or classical music. The relationship between harassment and academic effort was curvilinear; both nerds and slackers were harassed. To some degree these norms are, as Kenneth Arrow suggests, trying to internalize externalities. But why does music preference predict harassment? Why are student tutors victimized?

We propose that school wide norms also have a "We're cool, Honor us" function of legitimating the high status that the leading crowds claim for themselves. While norms tend to be passed from one generation to the next, the mass of students learn the norms by noting the example set by current members of the leading crowds. If leaders of popular crowds spend more time on and are particularly talented at sports, extracurricular activities, hanging out and partying, the theory predicts that peer culture will give high priority to extracurricular and social achievements. Academic norms will also reflect the interests of the leading crowds. If state government introduces a tough graduation exam and leaders of the popular crowd fear they may not be able to graduate if they do not study harder, study norms will rise. If a new generation of leaders of the popular crowd aspires to go to the highly competitive flagship state university rather than a local college with open door admissions, study effort norms will rise. The theory suggests, therefore, that peer norms are not immutable. They adjust to changes in graduation requirements, school policies and the labor market and they are influenced by the values and abilities of the students who become leaders of a crowd.

References

Akerlof, G., Kranton, R. (2002). "Identity and schooling: Some lessons for the economics of schooling". Journal of Economic Literature 41 (4, December).

Altonji, J., Pierret, C. (1998). "Employer learning and the signaling value of education". In: Ohashi, Tachibanaki, T. (Eds.), Internal Labour Markets: Incentives and Employment. McMillan Press, pp. 159–195.

American Federation of Teachers (1996). Making Standards Matter 1996.

Angrist, J.D., Lang, K. (2002). "How important are classroom peer effects? Evidence from Boston's Metco Program". Working Paper 9263. National Bureau of Economic Research, Cambridge, MA, 1–38.

Arrow, K. (1971). "Political and economic evaluation of social effects and externalities". In: Intriligator, M. (Ed.), Frontiers of Quantitative Economics. North-Holland, Amsterdam, pp. 3–25.

Association of Secondary Teachers of Ireland (1990). Flyer.

Becker, W., Rosen, S. (1992). "The learning effect of assessment and evaluation in high school". Economics of Education Review 11 (2), 107–118.

Betts, J. (1996). "The role of homework in improving school quality". Discussion Paper 96-16. Department of Economics, UCSD.

Betts, J. (1998). "The impact of educational standards on the level and distribution of earnings". American Economic Review 88 (1), 266–275.

Betts, J. (2001). "Do grading standards affect the incentive to learn?". Department of Economics, UC San Diego, pp. 1–36.

Betts, J., Costrell, R. (2001). "Incentives and equity under standards-based reform". In: Ravitch, D. (Ed.), Brookings Papers on Education Policy 2001. Brookings Institution Press, Washington, DC, pp. 9–74.

Betts, J.R., Grogger, J. (2003). "The impact of grading standards on student achievement, educational attainment, and entry-level earnings". Economics of Education Review 22 (4, August), 343–352.

Betts, J., Zau, A. (2002). "Peer groups and academic achievement: Panel evidence from administrative data". Public Policy Institute of California.

Bishop, J.H. (1977). "The effect of public policies on the demand for higher education". Journal of Human Resources XII (3, Summer).

Bishop, J.H. (1989). "Is the test score decline responsible for the productivity growth decline?". American Economic Review (March), 178–197.

Bishop, J.H. (1990). "Incentives to study: Why American high school students compare so poorly to their counterparts overseas". In: Crawford, D., Bassi, L. (Eds.), Research in Labor Economics, vol. 11. JAI Press, Greenwich, CT, pp. 17–51.

Bishop, J.H. (1991). "Achievement, test scores and relative wages". In: Kosters, M. (Ed.), Workers and Their Wages. The AEI Press, Washington, DC, pp. 146–181.

Bishop, J.H. (1992). "Impact of academic competencies on wages, unemployment and job performance". In: Carnegie–Rochester Conference Series on Public Policy, vol. 37, pp. 127–194.

Bishop, J.H. (1996). "The impact of curriculum-based external examinations on school priorities and student learning". International Journal of Education Research 23 (8).

Bishop, J.H. (1997). "The effect of national standards and curriculum-based external exams on student achievement". American Economic Review 87 (2, May), 260–264.

Bishop, J.H. (1999a). "Nerd harassment, incentives, school priorities and learning". In: Mayer, S., Peterson, P. (Eds.), Earning and Learning. Brookings Institution Press, Washington, DC.

Bishop, J.H. (1999b). "Are national exit examinations important for educational efficiency?". Swedish Economic Policy Review 6 (2, Fall), 349–401.

Bishop, J.H. (1999c). "Nerd harassment and grade inflation: Are college admissions policies partly responsible?". Center for Advanced Human Resources Discussion Paper 99-14. Cornell University.

Bishop, J.H. (2003a). "What is the appropriate role of student achievement standards". In: Kodrzycki, Y. (Ed.), Education in the 21st Century: Meeting the Challenge of a Changing World. Federal Reserve Bank of Boston, Boston, MA, pp. 249–278.

Bishop, J.H. (2003b). "An economic theory of nerd and slacker harassment and it's role in enforcing social norms in schools?". Center for Advanced Human Resources Discussion Paper 03-06. Cornell University.

Bishop, J., Bishop, M., Gelbwasser, L., Green, S., Zuckerman, A. (2003). "Nerds and freaks: A theory of student culture and norms". In: Ravitch, D. (Ed.), Brookings Papers on Education Policy 2003. Brookings Institution Press, Washington, DC, pp. 141–213.

Bishop, J., Bishop, M., Gelbwasser, L., Green, S., Zuckerman, A. (2004). "Nerds and slackers: The struggle for popularity in American secondary schools". Journal of School Health.

Bishop, J., Mane, F. (2001). "The impacts of minimum competency exam graduation requirements on high school graduation, college attendance and early labor market success". Labour Economics 8 (2, Spring), 203–222.

Bishop, J., Mane, F. (2004). "The impacts of career-technical education on high school completion and labor market success". Economics of Education Review.

Bishop, J., Mane, F., Bishop, M., Moriarty, J. (2001). "The role of end-of-course exams and minimum competency exams in standards-based reforms". In: Ravitch, D. (Ed.), Brookings Papers on Education Policy 2001. Brookings Institution Press, Washington, DC, pp. 267–346.

Bishop, J.H., Moriarty, J., Mane, F. (2000). "Diplomas for learning: Not seat time". Economics of Education Review 19 (3).

Bishop, J., Woessmann, L. (2004). "Institutional effects in a simple model of educational production". Education Economics 12 (1), 17–38.

Boozer, M., Cacciola, S.E. (2001). "Inside the 'black box' of Project Star: Estimation of peer effects using experimental data". Economic Growth Center Discussion Paper 832. Yale University.

Card, D. (1999). "The causal effects of education on earnings". In: Ashenfelter, O., Card, D. (Eds.), Handbook of Labor Economics, vol. 3. Elsevier, Amsterdam, pp. 1801–1863.

Census Bureau (1974). "Annual mean income, lifetime income and educational attainment of men, 1956–1972". Current Population Reports, Series P60-92. U.S. Government Printing Office, Washington, DC.

Cooper, H.M. (1989). Homework. Longman, White Plains, NY.

Costrell, R. (1994). "A simple model of educational standards". American Economic Review 84 (4), 956–971.

Costrell, R.M. (1997). "Can centralized educational standards raise welfare?". Journal of Public Economics 65, 271–293.

Cromwell, C., Mustard, D., Sridhar, D. (2003). "The enrollment effects of merit-based financial aid: Evidence from Georgia's HOPE scholarship". University of Georgia, Athens, GA, January, pp. 1–49.

Department of Labor (1970). "General aptitude test battery manual". Superintendent of Documents.

Dynarski, S. (2000). "Hope for whom? Financial aid for the middle class and it's impact on college attendance". National Tax Journal 53 (3, September), 629–661.

Educational Excellence Alliance, EEA (2002). EEA Survey, 2002.

Farber, H., Gibbons, R. (1996). "Learning and wage dynamics". Quarterly Journal of Economics, 1007–1047.

Fehr, E., Gachter, S. (2000). "Cooperation and punishment in public goods experiments". American Economic Review 90 (4, September), 980–994.

Figlio, D., Lucas, M. (2001). "Do high grading standards affect student performance". University of Florida, MO, 1–38.

Frederick, W.C. (1977). "The use of classroom time in high schools above or below the median reading score". Urban Education 11 (4, January), 459–464.

Frederick, W., Walberg, H., Rasher, S. (1979). "Time, teacher comments, and achievement in urban high schools". Journal of Educational Research 73 (2, November/December), 63–65.

Freeman, R. (1975). "Over investment in college training?". Journal of Human Resources 10 (Summer), 287–311.

Freeman, R. (1976). The Overeducated American. Academic Press, New York.

Freeman, R. (1986). "Demand for education". In: Ashenfelter, O., Layard, R. (Eds.), Handbook of Labor Economics, vol. 1. Elsevier, Amsterdam, pp. 357–386.

Friedman, T., Belvin, W. (1982). "Current use of tests for employment". In: Wigdor, A.K., Gardner, W.R. (Eds.), Ability Testing: Uses, Consequences, and Controversies, Part II: Documentation Section. National Academy Press, Washington, DC, pp. 999–1169.

Gamoran, A., Barends, M. (1987). "The effects of stratification in secondary schools: Synthesis of survey and ethnographic research". Review of Education Research 57, 415–435.

Ghiselli, E.E. (1973). "The validity of aptitude tests in personnel selection". Personnel Psychology 26, 461–477.

Gonzales, P. (2000). Pursuing excellence: Comparisons of international eighth-grade mathematics and science achievement from a U.S. perspective, 1995 and 1999. National Center for Educational Statistics Educational Resources Information Center, Washington, DC.

Goodlad, J. (1983). A Place Called School. McGraw-Hill, New York.

Graham, A., Husted, T. (1993). "Understanding state variation in SAT scores". Economics of Education 12 (3), 197–202.

Grubb, N. (1993). "The varied economic returns to postsecondary education: New evidence from the national longitudinal study of the class of 1972". Journal of Human Resources 28 (2, Spring), 365–382.

Gummere, R. (1943). "The independent school and the post war world". Independent School Bulletin 4 (April) [quoted in A. Powell (1995), Standards, Chapter 6].

Hanushek, E.A., Kain, J., Rivkin, S.G. (2002). New evidence about Brown v. Board of Education: The complex effects of school racial composition on achievement", Working Paper 8741. National Bureau of Economic Research, Cambridge, MA, 1–38.

Harbaugh, R. (2003). "Achievement vs. aptitude: The incentive-screening tradeoff in college admissions". Claremont Working Papers in Economics 2003-11.

Hart, P.D., Research Associates (1995). "Valuable news: A public opinion research report on the views of AFT teachers on professional issues". American Federation of Teachers, Washington, DC.

Hartigan, J., Wigdor, A. (Eds.) (1989). Fairness in Employment Testing. National Academy Press, Washington, DC.

Hauser, J.C., Daymont, T.M. (1977). "Schooling, ability and earnings: Cross-sectional evidence 8–14 years after high school". Sociology of Education 50 (July), 182–206.

Henry, G.T., Rubenstein, R. (2002). "Paying for grades: Impact of merit-based financial aid on educational quality". Journal of Policy Analysis and Management 21 (1), 93–109.

Hofferth, S., Sandberg, J.F. (2000). "Changes in American children's time 1981–1997". Center for the Ethnography of Everyday Life Working Paper 013-00, University of Michigan, Institute for Social Research, 1–47.

Holmes, C.T. (1989). "Grade level retention effects: A meta-analysis of research studies". In: Shepard, L., Smith, M.L. (Eds.), Flunking Grades. Falmer, New York, pp. 16–33.

Hoxby, C. (2000). "Peer effects in the classroom: Learning from gender and race variation". Working Paper 7867. National Bureau of Economic Research, Cambridge, MA.

Hunter, J.E., Crosson, J.J., Friedman, D.H. (1985). "The validity of the armed services vocational aptitude battery (ASVAB) for civilian and military job performance". Department of Defense, August.

Jacob, B. (2002). "Accountability, incentives and behavior". Working paper. NBER.

Kang, S. (1985). "A formal model of school reward systems". In: Bishop, J. (Ed.), Incentives, Learning and Employability. National Center for Research in Vocational Education, Columbus, OH.

Kulik, J., Kulik, C.L. (1984). "Effects of accelerated instruction on students". Review of Educational Research 54 (3, Fall), 409–425.

Lazear, E.P. (2001). "Educational production". Quarterly Journal of Economics 116 (3, August), 777–803.

Lillard, D., DeCicca, P. (2001). "Higher standards, more dropouts? Evidence within and across time". Economics of Education Review 20 (5), 459–473.

Locke, E. (1968). "Toward a theory of task motivation and incentives". Organizational Behavior and Human Performance 3, 157–189.

Longitudinal Survey of American Youth (1988). Data File User's Manual. Public Opinion Laboratory, Dekalb, IL.

Murnane, R., Willett, J., Levy, F. (1995). "The growing importance of cognitive skills in wage determination". Review of Economics and Statistics 77 (2, May), 251–266.

National Center for Education Statistics (2001). The Digest of Education Statistics, 2000. U.S. Department of Education, Washington, DC.

National Center for Education Statistics (2002). The Condition of Education 2000. U.S. Department of Education, Washington, DC.

National Center for Education Statistics (2003a). The Digest of Education Statistics, 2002. U.S. Department of Education, Washington, DC.

National Center for Education Statistics (2003b). The Condition of Education 2002. U.S. Department of Education, Washington, DC.

Organization of Economic Co-operation and Development (2000). Education at a Glance 2000. Organization for Economic Co-operation and Development, Paris, France.

Organization of Economic Co-operation and Development (2002). Education at a Glance 2002. Organization for Economic Co-operation and Development, Paris, France.

Organization of Economic Co-operation and Development (2003a). Literacy Skills for the World of Tomorrow: Further Results from PISA 2000. Organization for Economic Co-operation and Development, Paris, France.

Organization of Economic Co-operation and Development (2003b). Education at a Glance 2003. Organization for Economic Co-operation and Development, Paris, France.

Powell, A., Farrar, E., Cohen, D. (1985). The Shopping Mall High School. Houghton Mifflin, New York.

Roderick, M., Bryk, A.S., Jacob, B.A., Easton, J.Q., Allensworth, E. (1999). "Ending social promotion: Results from the first two years". http://www.consortium-chicago.org/publications/p0g04.html. Consortium on Chicago School Research, December 1999.

Roderick, M., Engel, M., Nagaoka, J. (2003). "Ending social promotion: Results from summer bridge". http://www.consortium-chicago.org/publications/p59.html. Consortium on Chicago School Research.

Rosenbaum, J. (2001). Beyond College for All: Career Paths for the Forgotten Half. Russell Sage Foundation, New York.

Sacerdote, B. (2000). "Peer effects with random assignment: Results for Dartmouth roommates". Dartmouth College.

Sizer, T.R. (1984). Horace's Compromise: The Dilemma of the American High School. Houghton Mifflin, Boston, MA.

Stedry, A.C. (1960). Budget Control and Cost Behavior. Prentice Hall, Englewood Cliffs, NJ.

Steinberg, L., Brown, B., Dornbusch, S. (1996). Beyond the Classroom. Simon and Schuster, New York, 1–223.

Taubman, P., Wales, T. (1972). "Mental ability and higher educational attainment in the 20th century". National Bureau of Economic Research Occasional Paper 118.

Taubman, P., Wales, T. (1975). "Education as an investment and a screening device". In: Juster, F.T. (Ed.), Education Income and Human Behavior. McGraw-Hill, New York, pp. 95–122.

Wiley, D.E. (1976). "Another hour, another day: Quantity of schooling, a potent path for policy". In: Sewell, W.H., Hauser, R.M., Featherman, D.L. (Eds.), Schooling Achievement in American Society. Academic Press, New York.

Wood, R.E., Mento, A., Locke, E. (1987). "Task complexity as a moderator of goal effects: A meta analysis". Journal of Applied Psychology 72 (3), 416–425.

Wößmann, L. (2000). "Schooling resources, educational institutions, and student performance: The international evidence". Kiel Working Paper No. 983. Kiel Institute of World Economics, Germany (May). http://www.uni-kiel.de/ifw/pub/kap/2000/kap983.htm.

Wößmann, L. (2002). "How central exams affect educational achievement: International evidence from TIMSS and TIMSS-repeat". Paper presented at conference on: Taking Account of Accountability: Assessing Politics and Policy. Kennedy School, June 2002.

Zimmerman, D. (1999). "Peer effects on academic outcomes: Evidence from a natural experiment". NBER.

Chapter 16

SCHOOLS, TEACHERS, AND EDUCATION OUTCOMES IN DEVELOPING COUNTRIES

PAUL GLEWWE

University of Minnesota

MICHAEL KREMER

Harvard University,

Brookings Institution,

Center for Global Development,

NBER

Contents

Handbook of the Economics of Education, Volume 2
Edited by Eric A. Hanushek and Finis Welch
© 2006 Elsevier B.V. All rights reserved
DOI: 10.1016/S1574-0692(06)02016-2

Abstract

About 80% of the world's children live in developing countries. Their well-being as adults depends heavily on the education they receive. School enrollment rates have increased dramatically in developing counties since 1960, but many children still leave school at a young age and often learn little while in school. This chapter reviews recent research on the impact of education and other policies on the quantity and quality of education obtained by children in developing countries. The policies considered include not only provision of basic inputs but also policies that change the way that schools are organized. While much has been learned about how to raise enrollment rates, less is known about how to increase learning. Randomized studies offer the most promise for understanding the impact of policies on learning.

Keywords

education, developing countries, school enrollment, learning, academic skills, quality of education, school finance, randomized evaluations, health and schooling, school reform

JEL classification: I21, J24, O12, O15

1. Introduction

Eight out of 10 of the world's children live in developing countries [World Bank (2003)]. For economists working on education, the study of developing countries offers both policy questions of fundamental importance and a rich set of experiences to examine.

The important policy questions stem from the potential role of education in improving the welfare of the 5 billion people living in developing countries. Many macroeconomists have emphasized the impact of education on economic growth [Lucas (1988), Barro (1991), Mankiw, Romer and Weil (1992)] (although some others have raised questions about the causal relationship between education and economic growth).[1] Among microeconomists, both an older literature using ordinary least squares (OLS) regressions [Psacharopoulos (1985, 1994)] and a newer literature using natural experiments and instrumental variable techniques [Duflo (2001)] estimate that both the private and social rates of return to education are high in developing countries. Education has also been found to play a crucial role in the adoption of new agricultural technologies in those countries [Foster and Rosenzweig (1996)]. Finally, education is also seen as a means to improve health and reduce fertility [Schultz (1997, 2002), Strauss and Thomas (1995)] and is seen as an intrinsic good in itself [Sen (1999), pp. 292–297]. Behrman (1999), Glewwe (2002) and Huffman (2001) provide recent reviews of the microeconomic literature on the impact of education on income and other outcomes in developing countries.

This support for education among economists is matched by equal or greater enthusiasm among development policymakers [UNDP (1990), World Bank (2001a)]. As discussed in Section 2, developing countries have massively expanded their education systems in the last 40 years.[2] One example demonstrating the focus policy makers have placed on education is that two of the eight Millennium Development Goals (MDGs) adopted at the United Nations Millennium Summit in September 2000 focus on education: first, for all children to complete primary school by 2015, and second, to achieve gender equality at all levels of education by 2015.

The rich set of experiences worth examining includes wide variation in input levels and education systems across developing countries and, in recent years, dramatic policy changes and reforms in many developing countries. In addition, in the last 10 years randomized evaluations of education policies (which are rare in developed countries) have been undertaken in several developing countries. All of this makes the study of education in developing countries a potentially fruitful area of research.

---

[1] Pritchett (1996) argues that it is difficult to find a relationship between education and growth. Others, such as Krueger and Lindahl (2001), argue otherwise. Bils and Klenow (2000) argue the evidence favors a dominant role for growth impacting schooling. See also Levine and Renalt (1992, Table 5) and Easterly (2001, pp. 71–85).

[2] Behind average figures on the remarkable expansion of schooling in developing countries lie educational miracles like Nepal, which increased primary enrollment from 10 percent in 1960 to 80 percent in 1990.

In view of the widespread consensus on the importance of education and the existence of several reviews on the impact of education on income and other outcomes, this chapter focuses not on those impacts but rather on issues pertaining to the provision of education: namely, how education programs and systems affect the quantity and quality of education obtained by children in developing countries.[3] This focus implies that we do not examine the impact on schooling of factors outside the education system such as economic crises [Frankenberg et al. (1999)], orphan status [Case, Paxson and Ableidinger (2003), Evans and Miguel (2004)], or early childhood nutritional status [Glewwe (2005)].

Despite the tremendous progress in expanding enrollment and increasing years of schooling since 1960, 113 million children of primary school age are still not enrolled in school [UNDP (2003)], 94 percent of whom live in developing countries [UNESCO (2002)]. In addition, the quality of schooling in developing countries is often very low. Grade repetition and leaving school at an early age are common, teachers are often absent from classrooms, and many children learn much less than the learning objectives set in the official curriculum [Lockheed and Verspoor (1991), Harbison and Hanushek (1992), Hanushek (1995), Glewwe (1999)]. Visitors from developed countries are often shocked at the conditions in many (but not all) schools in developing countries. Many schools lack the most basic equipment and school supplies – textbooks, blackboards, desks, benches, and sometimes even classrooms (in which case classes meet outside and are canceled when it rains). In rural areas of Vietnam's Northern Uplands region in 1998, 39 percent of primary school classrooms did not have blackboards. In India in 1987, more than 8 percent of schools did not have a building in which to meet [World Bank (1997a)].

Teacher quality and availability is also a common problem. In rural areas of Northeast Brazil in the early 1980s, 60 percent of primary school teachers had not even completed primary education [Harbison and Hanushek (1992)]. Shortages of teachers and school buildings can result in double shifts (which shorten the school day for individual pupils) or very large class sizes. In Vietnam, more than 90 percent of children in rural areas attend schools with two or more shifts, resulting in an average class time of only 3 hours and 10 minutes per day [Glewwe (2004)]. In districts with low literacy rates in the Indian State of Tamil Nadu, the average class size in primary school was 78 students [World Bank (1997a)]. Teachers often have weak incentives and little supervision, and their absenteeism runs high. Chaudhury et al. (2006) reports that when enumerators made surprise visits to primary schools in six developing countries, on average (across these countries) about 19 percent of teachers were absent. Beyond absence, many "present" teachers were found not to be actually teaching; for example, in India one quarter of government primary school teachers were absent from school, but only about half of

---

[3] Due to the dearth of rigorous research on post-secondary education in developing countries, we focus here on primary and secondary education. In addition, this chapter excludes the transition economies of Central and Eastern Europe, the Balkans, and the Commonwealth of Independent States (CIS); on labor markets and the impact of education on wages in those countries see Svejnar (1999).

the teachers were actually teaching in their classrooms when enumerators arrived at the schools.

The research discussed in this chapter suggests a number of conclusions, both substantive and methodological. First, additional children can be attracted to school at relatively low cost, either by reducing the cost of schooling and providing incentives for school attendance or by addressing basic health problems. Second, the evidence is mixed concerning the impact on learning of providing more educational inputs. Earlier surveys based on retrospective studies suggest that providing additional resources (given the existing education systems in developing countries) may have little impact on learning. More recent evidence from natural experiments and randomized evaluations paints a more mixed, but far from uniformly positive, picture. Third, education systems in developing countries are weak: education finance systems lead to budget distortions, incentives for teachers are weak or nonexistent, and curriculums are often inappropriate. Decentralization and school choice programs offer some promise, but their impact depends on the details of implementation. Finally, we offer methodological suggestions regarding the study of education in developing countries. In particular, we argue that there is scope for increasing the use of randomized evaluations in assessing the impact of education programs in developing countries.

With regard to education initiatives in developing countries more broadly, some observers emphasize that schools need more money while others emphasize the weaknesses of the schools systems and the need for reform. While these two views are often placed at odds with each other, we argue they are not mutually exclusive; in fact, both may be true. By definition, highly distorted systems are such that marginal products have not been equalized across all expenditure categories. Thus, in settings with highly distorted education systems some types of spending will have low marginal product while others will have high marginal product.

The remainder of this chapter is organized as follows. Section 2 provides a general context for the chapter by giving background on primary and secondary education in developing countries. Section 3 outlines an analytical framework that we will use in interpreting the studies discussed in this chapter. We then review selected empirical work: Section 4 examines the factors influencing the quantity of education obtained; Section 5 focuses on education quality by examining the determinants of skills obtained while in school; and Section 6 examines distortions in education systems, the political economy of education, and school reform initiatives. Finally, Section 7 reviews methodological lessons and provides recommendations for future research on education in developing countries.

2. Education in developing countries

Almost every chapter in this Handbook focuses on education issues in developed countries. There are many differences between the education systems of developed and developing countries, so this section provides basic information on education in developing countries. Section 2.1 discusses trends in the quantity of education provided, Section 2.2 discusses the persistent problems of school quality, and Section 2.3 provides background on the more general issues of education finance, school organization, and education management policies.

2.1. Trends in the quantity of education: enrollment, years of schooling and literacy

School enrollment rates and adults' years of schooling have increased dramatically in almost all developing countries since 1960 (the earliest year for which reliable data are available), but despite significant progress toward universal primary education and rapid increases in secondary school enrollment, there is still much room for improvement. In 2000, about 850 million adults (age 15 or older) in developing countries – 1 out of every 4 – were illiterate [UNESCO (2002)]. This is in part because a sizable percentage of the adult population in these countries never attended school. This subsection examines some basic data on the quantity of schooling attained in developing countries and discusses current patterns by income levels, geographic region, and gender. In particular, it examines statistics on gross and net enrollment rates, rates of completion of 4 years of schooling, average years of schooling of the adult population, and adult literacy rates.

The most cited and most widely available indicator of the education quantity is the *gross enrollment rate*, defined as the number of children enrolled in a particular level of education, regardless of age, as a percentage of the population in the age group associated with that level. The age range for primary school is usually 6–11 years. In 1960, primary school gross enrollment rates were 65 percent in low-income countries, 83 percent in middle-income countries, and over 100 percent in high-income countries (Table 1).[4] By 2000, enrollment rates had reached or exceeded 100 percent in both low- and middle-income countries and in all regions except Sub-Saharan Africa, where gross enrollment rates peaked at 80 percent in 1980 and then declined slightly.

Gross enrollment rates above 100 percent do *not* imply all school-age children are in school. First, grade repetition raises gross enrollment rates. For example, in a school system with 6 years of primary education, a 100 percent gross enrollment rate is consistent with 75 percent of children taking 8 years to complete primary school (because each child repeats two grades) and 25 percent of children never attending school. Second, gross enrollment rates are typically computed by comparing census data on the school-age population with Ministry of Education data on school enrollment, obtained from school principals reports. In many countries, principals and teachers have incentives to exaggerate the number of students enrolled [PROBE Team (1999)]. An example of this is from India; the official primary gross enrollment rate in 1993 was 104.5 percent, but

---

[4] This classification of countries is defined by per capita income in 1960. *Low-income countries* are those with a per capita income below $200 per year, *middle-income countries* are those with an income between $200 and $450, and *high-income countries* are those with an income greater than $450. These cutoff points, while arbitrary, yield about the same number of countries in each group.

Table 1
Primary school gross enrollment rates (percent of students of primary school age)

Area	1960	1970	1980	1990	2000
World	80	87	97	102	104
Country group					
Low-income	65	77	94	102	102
Middle-income	83	103	101	103	110
High-income	109	100	101	102	102
Region					
Sub-Saharan Africa	40	51	80	74	77
Middle East/North Africa	59	79	89	96	97
Latin America	91	107	105	106	127
South Asia	41	71	77	90	98
East Asia	87	90	111	120	111
East Europe/Former Soviet Union (FSU)	103	104	100	98	100
Organization for Economic Cooperation and Development (OECD)	109	100	102	103	102

Note. Countries with populations of less than 1 million are excluded.
Sources: UNESCO (2002), World Bank (2003).

household survey data for 1993 show a rate of 95.9 percent [World Bank (1997a)]. Both overreporting and grade repetition can cause reported gross enrollment rates to reach or exceed 100 percent even when many children never enroll in school.

An alternative measure of progress toward universal primary education is *net enrollment rates*, the number of children enrolled in a particular level of schooling *who are of the age associated with that level of schooling*, divided by all children of the age associated with that level of schooling. Net enrollment rates can never exceed 100 percent, and they remove the upward bias in gross enrollment rates cause by the enrollment of "overage" children in a given level (due to repetition or delayed enrollment). They do not, however, address overreporting in official data. Net enrollment rates are much lower than gross enrollment rates for low- and middle-income countries (Table 2). The lower net rates for low- and middle-income countries reflect higher repetition of grades in those countries (Table 2, column 3) and late school-starting age in many developing countries (Table 2, column 4).

Statistics on the percentage of children who have completed 4 years of schooling (Table 2, column 5) are the most appropriate for assessing whether universal primary education has been achieved. Although the gross enrollment rates in 2000 were over 100 percent in both low- and middle-income countries, universal completion of primary school has not been attained in either group of countries. In 1999 only 80 percent of children in low-income countries and 88 percent of children in middle-income countries had completed 4 years of primary school.

Over the past 40 years, enrollment has increased dramatically at both the primary and secondary levels. However, progress in secondary enrollment has slowed in the past two decades (Table 3). In both low- and middle-income countries the secondary gross

Table 2
Primary school enrollment, repetition, and grade 4 survival rates (percents)

Area	Gross enrollment 2000	Net enrollment 2000	Repetition 2000	On-time enrollment 2000	Grade 4 survival 1999
Country group					
Low-income	102	85	4	55	80
Middle-income	110	88	10	61	88
High-income	102	95	2[a]	73[b]	98[b]
Region					
Sub-Saharan Africa	77	56	13	30	76
Middle East/North Africa	97	84	8	64	96
Latin America	127	97	12	74	86
South Asia	98	83	5	–	55
East Asia	111	93	2	56	97
East Europe/FSU	100	88	1	67[a]	97[b]
OECD	102	97	2[a]	91[a]	99[b]

Note. Countries with populations of less than 1 million are excluded.
Source: UNESCO (2003).
[a]Data are based on between 25 percent and 50 percent of the total population of the country group or region.
[b]Data are based on between 10 percent and 25 percent of the total population of the country group or region.

Table 3
Secondary school gross enrollment rates (percent of students of secondary school age)

Area	1960	1970	1980	1990	2000
World	29	36	49	55	67
Country group					
Low-income	14	21	34	41	54
Middle-income	21	33	51	59	77
High-income	63	74	87	92	101
Region					
Sub-Saharan Africa	5	6	15	23	27
Middle East/North Africa	13	25	42	56	66
Latin America	14	28	42	49	86
South Asia	10	23	27	39	47
East Asia	20	24	44	48	67
East Europe/FSU	55	64	93	90	88
OECD	65	77	87	95	107

Note. Countries with populations of less than 1 million are excluded.
Sources: UNESCO (2003), World Bank (2003).

enrollment rate increased by about 150 percent from 1960 to 1980, while the increase from 1980 to 2000 was 59 percent in low-income countries and about 51 percent in middle-income countries. Another way to see this is to note that from 1970 to 1980 middle-income countries increased their secondary enrollment ratio from 33 percent to 51 percent in only one decade, while low-income countries took 20 years (1980 to 2000) to increase from 34 percent to 54 percent. Middle-income countries progress slowed down sharply in the 1980s, increasing by only eight percentage points (51 percent to 59 percent) in that decade, although the increase was stronger in the 1990s (from 59 percent to 77 percent).

Trends in secondary gross enrollment rates from 1960 to 2000 differ substantially by region. For example, secondary school rates in South Asia, Latin America and the Middle East and North Africa were similar in 1960 (10 percent, 14 percent and 13 percent, respectively), but by 2000 the rate in Latin America (86 percent) was much higher than in South Asia (47 percent) and the Middle East and North Africa (66 percent). Sub-Saharan Africa's performance over time has been slower than that of other regions. A final interesting comparison is between Latin America and East Asia. East Asia had a higher secondary enrollment rate than Latin America in 1960 (20 percent vs. 14 percent), but the rates in Latin American countries surged in the 1990s, so that the average rate in 2000 was 86 percent, compared to 67 percent in East Asia.

In low-, middle-, and high-income countries, average years of schooling increased by about 3 years between 1960 and 2000 (Table 4).[5] (See Pritchett, this volume, for further discussion of this issue.) If the 1.7-year increase in schooling from 1980 to 2000 in middle-income countries continues from 2000 to 2020, middle-income countries will reach a level of 7.6 years of education in 2020, slightly above the level of high-income countries in 1960. Thus middle-income countries are about 60 years behind high-income countries in the level of schooling of their adult population. Similarly, low-income countries are 10–20 years behind middle-income countries (their schooling level of 5.4 in 2000 was reached sometime between 1980 and 1990 in middle-income countries), or about 70–80 years behind high-income countries.

Literacy rates show similar trends (Table 5): low-income countries are about 30 years behind middle-income countries, which are about 60 years behind developed countries (assuming the literacy rate for middle-income countries will increase from 85 percent in 2000 to 95 percent in 2020). There are some notable regional differences in the trends for adult years of schooling and literacy rates. In 1960, Sub-Saharan Africa, the Middle East and North Africa, and South Asia were similar in their years of adult schooling (about 1.5) and literacy rates (between 24 percent and 33 percent). By 2000, the Middle East and North Africa region had an average of 5.4 years of education, while South

---

[5] The increase for low-income countries is 3.6, but this comparison is biased because data are not available for China in 1960 and 1970. When China is excluded in 2000, adult years of schooling is 4.5, which implies a change of 2.9 years.

Table 4
Average years of school of adults, age 15+

Area	1960	1970	1980	1990	2000
Country group					
Low-income	1.6[a]	2.2[a]	3.7	4.6	5.2
Middle-income	2.8	3.5	4.2	5.1	5.9
High-income	7.4	7.9	9.2	9.5	10.1
Region					
Sub-Saharan Africa	1.7	2.0	2.3	3.0	3.4
Middle East/North Africa	1.4	2.2	2.9	4.1	5.4
Latin America	3.2	3.7	4.4	5.3	6.0
South Asia	1.5	2.0	3.0	3.8	4.6
East Asia	2.5[b]	3.4[b]	4.6	5.6	6.2
East Europe/FSU	6.5[b]	7.6[b]	8.5[b]	9.0[b]	9.7[b]
OECD	7.3	7.8	9.1	9.5	10.1

Note. Countries with populations of less than 1 million are excluded.
Source: Barro and Lee (2001).
[a]Data are based on between 25 percent and 50 percent of the total population of the country group or region.
[b]Data are based on between 10 percent and 25 percent of the total population of the country group or region.

Table 5
Literacy rate among adults, age 15+

Area	1960	1970	1980	1990	2000
Country group					
Low-income	32[a]	44	54	63	70
Middle-income	62	68	75	80	85
High-income	95[a]	96[a]	97[a]	98[a]	98[a]
Region					
Sub-Saharan Africa	24[b]	41	54	67	77
Middle East/North Africa	33[b]	54	66	76	83
Latin America	67	84	90	93	95
South Asia	26	43	52	61	69
East Asia	54[b]	83	91	95	97
East Europe/FSU	93[b]	99	100	100	100
OECD	95	98	99[b]	100[b]	100[b]

Note. Countries with populations of less than 1 million are excluded.
Source: UNESCO (2003).
[a]Data are based on between 25 percent and 50 percent of the total population of the country group or region.
[b]Data are based on between 10 percent and 25 percent of the total population of the country group or region.

Asia had 4.6 years and Sub-Saharan Africa only 3.4 years. Yet in terms of literacy rates the ranking is different: in 2000 South Asia has a lower literacy rate than Sub-Saharan Africa. This apparent contradictory pattern most likely reflects greater inequality in the distribution of education in South Asia: 46 percent of adults 15 years and older in South Asia have no formal education, while 2 percent have completed some form of higher education; the analogous figures for Sub-Saharan Africa are 44 percent and 0.8 percent.

In many countries, gender disparities in access to education are significant. About 56 percent of the 113 million school-age children not in school are girls [UNESCO (2002)]. In low-income countries, primary gross enrollment rates are 107 percent for boys and 98 percent for girls; this gender gap is wider at the secondary level, 60 percent for boys and 47 percent for girls (Table 6). In middle-income countries, the primary-school enrollment gap between boys and girls is smaller (only 4 percentage points), and in secondary school girls have a slightly higher rate than boys. In high-income countries, there is almost no difference in primary enrollment rates, and girls have a slightly higher rate at the secondary level.

Major differences in gender gaps emerge across different regions of the world. In Latin America, East Asia, and Eastern Europe/Former Soviet Union and in the countries in the Organization for Economic Cooperation and Development (OECD), there is almost no gender gap at the primary level, although East Asian countries have a gender gap at the secondary level. In contrast, in Sub-Saharan Africa and Middle East/North Africa, gender gaps are sizable at both the primary and secondary levels. The largest gender gaps at both the primary and the secondary levels are in South Asia.

Table 6
Gender disparities in gross primary and secondary enrollment rates, 2000

Area	Primary		Secondary	
	Boys	Girls	Boys	Girls
Country group				
Low-income	107	98	60	47
Middle-income	112	108	77	78
High-income	102	101	100	102
Region				
Sub-Saharan Africa	83	71	29	24
Middle East/North Africa	101	92	71	61
Latin America	129	125	83	89
South Asia	107	90	53	39
East Asia	112	111	73	60
East Europe/FSU	100	99	88	89
OECD	102	102	106	108

Note. Countries with populations of less than 1 million are excluded.
Source: World Bank (2003).

2.2. *The quality of education: resources and academic achievement*

The focus thus far has been on *quantity* of education; however, the *quality* of education in many developing countries is low in the sense that children learn much less in school than the curriculum states they should learn [Lockheed and Verspoor (1991), Harbison and Hanushek (1992), Hanushek (1995), Glewwe (1999)]. This low quality is not entirely surprising because the rapid expansion of primary and secondary education in developing countries has strained those countries' financial and human resources.

Comparisons of education quality across countries require internationally comparable data on academic performance. The two main sources of such data are the TIMSS (Third International Mathematics and Science Study) and PIRLS (Progress in International Reading Literacy Study) projects administered by the International Association for the Evaluation of Educational Achievement (IAEEA) and the PISA (Programme for International Student Assessment) project managed by the OECD.[6] The TIMSS, PIRLS and PISA data are primarily from developed countries, but they include a few, mostly middle-income, developing countries.

The scores of students in grades 7 and 8 on the 1999 TIMSS mathematics test are shown in the first two columns of Table 7. The two developed countries, Japan and the United States, have scores of 579 and 502, respectively. South Korean students scored even higher (587), and Malaysian students also performed well (519). Scores were generally considerably lower in other developing countries, ranging from 275 in South Africa to 467 in Thailand. In fact, the gap between these developing countries and the developed countries is underestimated because of the low secondary school enrollment rates in those countries (ranging from 40 percent in Morocco to 85 percent in Chile). Assuming that more academically talented students are more likely to remain in school, the scores from those developing countries are for students of above average talent.

Reading results for grade 4 students in 2001 are shown in the last column of Table 7. All seven of the participating developing countries (Argentina, Belize, Colombia, Iran, Kuwait, Morocco and Turkey) have much lower performance than the three developed countries shown (France, the United Kingdom and the United States). The PISA tests in mathematics and reading, which were administered to 15-year-old students, tell a similar story (Table 8). South Korea outperforms all four developed countries in reading, and almost all in mathematics (the exception being Japan), but the other seven developing countries lagged far behind.[7] The percentage of students with very low reading skills was much higher in these seven countries than in the developed countries (ranging

---

[6] The first and second studies that were precursors to TIMSS were undertaken between 1964 and 1984; the results are not comparable with those of the TIMSS, and very few developing countries were included.

[7] The PISA was administered to 15-year-old students enrolled in any kind of educational institution (including vocational and technical education). Many developed countries participated in 2000 (including all OECD countries), as did three developing countries (Brazil, Mexico and South Korea). Six new developing countries (Argentina, Chile, Hong Kong, Indonesia, Peru and Thailand) participated in 2002.

Table 7
Mean mathematics and reading achievement, TIMSS and PIRLS studies

Country	Mathematics (TIMSS), 1999		Reading (PIRLS), 2001
	Grade 7	Grade 8	Grade 4
France	–	–	525
Japan	–	579	–
UK (England)	–	–	553
US	–	502	542
Argentina	–	–	420
Belize	–	–	327
Chile	–	392	–
Colombia	–	–	422
Indonesia	–	403	–
Iran	–	422	414
Jordan	–	428	–
Korea (South)	–	587	–
Kuwait	–	–	396
Malaysia	–	519	–
Morocco	337	–	350
Philippines	345	–	–
South Africa	–	275	–
Thailand	–	467	–
Tunisia	–	448	–
Turkey	–	429	449

Source: IAEEA (2000, 2003).

from 2.7 percent to 6.4 percent).[8] Again, the gap is probably underestimated because secondary school enrollment is well below 100 percent in almost all of these countries (except for South Korea).

A clear regional difference exists among the developing countries tested: two of the three East Asian countries (the exception being Indonesia) have test score means exceeding those of each of the five Latin American countries. Although Indonesia has lower scores than do most Latin American countries, one must bear in mind that in 2000 Indonesia's per capita income was about $730, while per capita incomes in five other Latin American countries ranged from $2,080 (Peru) to $7,690 (Argentina). This regional pattern, together with the small difference in adult years of schooling and adult literacy seen in the previous section, suggests that, if education played a role in East Asia's "economic miracle", it may have been as much due to the *quality* of education as to the quantity. [See Hanushek and Kimko (2000), for a detailed examination of this role of school quality.]

---

[8] In fact, the Brazil scores may be lower, because the 16 percent of Brazil's 15-year-old students, those who were in or below grade 6, were excluded from the assessment.

Table 8
Mathematics and reading achievement of 15-year-olds, PISA study

Country	Mathematics	Reading	
	Mean score	Mean score	Percent with very low skills
France	517	505	4.2
Japan	557	522	2.7
United Kingdom	529	523	3.6
United States	493	504	6.4
Argentina[a]	388	418	22.6
Brazil	334	396	23.3
Chile[a]	384	410	19.9
Indonesia[a]	367	371	31.1
Mexico	387	422	16.1
Peru[a]	292	327	54.1
South Korea	547	525	0.9
Thailand[a]	432	431	10.4

Note. Data are for the year 2000.
Source: OECD and UNESCO (2003).
[a]Data are for the year 2002.

Internationally comparable data are not available for very low-income countries, but the performance of students on achievement tests administered within many of these countries suggests that academic achievement is often very low. In Bangladesh, for example, Greaney, Khandker and Alam (1999) found that 58 percent of a sample of rural children age 11 and older failed to identify seven of eight presented letters, and 59 percent correctly answered only five or fewer of eight tasks requiring recognition of one- and two-digit numbers, writing one-digit numbers and recognizing basic geometric shapes. In Ghana, the mean score of grade 6 students on a very simple multiple-choice reading test was 25 percent, the score one would expect from random guessing [Glewwe (1999)]. In India, 36 percent of grade 6 students were unable to understand and correctly answer the following question: "The dog is black with a white spot on his back and one white leg. The color of the dog is mostly: (a) black, (b) brown, or (c) grey" [Lockheed and Verspoor (1991)].

In summary, primary and secondary school students in most (but not all) developing countries learn less than their counterparts in developed countries. Moreover, these gaps are significant: mathematics (TIMSS) score disparities are equivalent to about a 3-year education gap between developed and developing countries.[9] These large gaps could

[9] The 1995 TIMSS results show 30–40 point differences between seventh and eighth grade students in France, Japan and the United States, suggesting that the 100 point gaps commonly found between developed and developing countries are equivalent to about 3 years of education. Yet it is worth noting that when the

reflect differences in family characteristics, but they almost certainly also reflect low school quality in developing countries.

2.3. School finance and education systems

Government spending on education as a percentage of total gross domestic product (GDP) is similar across different groups of countries (Table 9). The percentages are larger in high-income countries than in low-income countries but not remarkably so. Neither are the differences dramatic across regions. Yet since school age children are a much larger percentage of the population in developing countries, educational resources

Table 9
Government expenditures on education (percentage terms)

Area	Expenditure as percent of GDP		Expenditures per student as percent of GDP per capita		Expenditures per tertiary student as a ratio of expenditures per student at lower levels	
	Primary	Secondary	Primary	Secondary	Primary	Secondary
Country group						
Low-income	1.0	1.1	7.0	16.7	33.6	13.6
Middle-income	1.8	1.4	13.3	15.5	5.0[a]	4.4[a]
High-income	1.4	1.9	18.8	21.5	1.8[a]	1.3
Region						
Sub-Saharan Africa	1.9[a]	1.2[a]	10.6	25.8	198.5[a]	81.1[a]
Middle East/North Africa	1.8[a]	1.4[a]	15.0	19.5	5.4	5.3
Latin America	1.6	1.6	12.2	14.3	4.3	4.0
South Asia	1.0	1.2	7.4	22.0	5.6[b]	3.3[b]
East Asia	0.9	0.8	6.6	11.8	12.5	6.5
East Europe/FSU	0.2[b]	2.3[b]	21.4[c]	19.1	2.0[b]	1.5
OECD	1.2[b]	2.1[b]	18.6	22.8	1.8[a]	1.5[a]

Note. Expenditures as a percent of GDP are for 2000.
Source: UNESCO (2003).
[a]Data are based on between 25 percent and 50 percent of the total population of the country group or region.
[b]Data are based on between 10 percent and 25 percent of the total population of the country group or region.
[c]Data are based on less than 10 percent of the total population of the country group or region.

mean scores of some developing countries on the TIMSS, PIRLS or PISA assessments are two or three standard deviations below the mean in developed countries it may be difficult to use those scores to measure precisely the gaps between those countries and developed countries, since the tests were not designed to measure outcomes precisely at the extremes of the distribution found in developed countries.

per child are typically lower in developing countries relative to GDP per capita. In low-income countries, spending per primary student is about 7 percent of per capita GDP, and this figure increases to 13.3 percent and 18.8 percent for middle- and high-income countries, respectively (Table 9, column 3). In contrast, spending per secondary student as a percent of per capita GDP is much more similar (ranging from 15.5 percent to 21.5 percent).

Table 10 presents expenditures per pupil in US dollars using two different methods, both revealing significant disparities due to large differences in per capita income. Using current exchange rates, middle-income countries outspend low-income countries by a ratio of 12–1 for primary education and about 8–1 for secondary education. Expenditures in high-income countries exceed those in low-income countries by a ratio of about 70–1 for primary education and about 50–1 for secondary education. Since expenditure on education is on nontraded goods and services (e.g., teacher salaries), a better method to obtain comparable figures across countries is to convert local currencies to purchasing power parity (PPP) dollars, which account for price differences in nontraded goods and services across countries. This reduces the gaps somewhat. In primary education, middle-income countries spend 4 times more, and high-income countries nearly 15 times more, than low-income countries. For secondary education, the analogous figures are 3 and 10.

Table 10
Government expenditures on education (in dollars)

Area	Expenditure per student			
	US dollars		PPP dollars	
	Primary	Secondary	Primary	Secondary
Country group				
Low-income	48	87	202	366
Middle-income	555[a]	660[a]	833[a]	1013
High-income	3263[a]	4279[a]	3059[c]	3915[c]
Region				
Sub-Saharan Africa	68[b]	171[b]	338[b]	638[b]
Middle East/North Africa	157[b]	316[a]	429[b]	809[a]
Latin America	364[b]	504[a]	588[b]	877[a]
South Asia	34	66	167	322
East Asia	66	101	214	347
East Europe/FSU	564[b]	555[b]	1401[b]	1250[b]
OECD	4310[b]	5655[a]	3760[b]	4933[a]

Note. Expenditures per student are for 1996.
Source: World Bank (2003).
[a]Data are based on between 25 percent and 50 percent of the total population of the country group or region.
[b]Data are based on between 10 percent and 25 percent of the total population of the country group or region.
[c]Data are based on less than 10 percent of the total population of the country group or region.

Teacher salaries are by far the largest component of government expenditures on education in developing countries. According to a study of 55 low-income countries, on average, teacher salaries and benefits account for 74 percent of government recurrent expenditures on education [Bruns, Mingat and Rakotomalala (2003)]. One reason for the high proportion of teacher salaries in education spending in developing countries is that low-income countries typically pay high teacher salaries, relative to GDP per capita, partly due to the scarcity of skilled workers in poor countries but also partly due to political economy factors. Countries respond to this high cost of teachers by maintaining large class sizes (Table 11, columns 1 and 2). Sub-Saharan Africa and South Asia have the highest pupil–teacher ratios. As a country develops, teachers' relative salaries decrease. [See Lakdawalla (2001) for an analysis of the evolution of teachers' salaries and class size in the United States over the twentieth century.]

Developing countries also respond to the scarcity of trained teachers by hiring more untrained teachers. Whereas almost all teachers in developed countries are trained, in low-income countries, only 90 percent of primary school teachers and 69 percent of secondary school teachers are trained (Table 11). The amount of training required for certification as a teacher varies, but requirements in poor countries are typically lower than in more affluent countries. The two regions with the smallest percentage of trained teachers at the primary level (data at the secondary level are less reliable) are Sub-Saharan Africa and South Asia, also the regions with the highest pupil–teacher ratios. These two regions simply have too few teachers to accommodate their rapid expansion

Table 11
Pupil–teacher ratios and percentage of teachers with training

Area	Pupil–teacher ratio		Percent trained teachers		Teacher salary as percent of per capita GDP
	Primary	Secondary	Primary	Secondary	
Country group					
Low-income	32	25	90	69[b]	
Middle-income	25	20	90	83[a]	
High-income	16	14	–	–	
Region					
Sub-Saharan Africa	43	24	69	78[b]	6.7
Middle East/North Africa	23	18	96	85[a]	
Latin America	26	19	87	77	1.4
South Asia	42	33	62[b]	–	
East Asia	22	19	96	71[b]	
East Europe/FSU	17	12	93[b]	–	
OECD	16	14	–	–	1.3

Note. Countries with populations of less than 1 million are excluded.
Source: UNESCO (2003).
[a]Data are based on between 25 percent and 50 percent of the total population of the country group or region.
[b]Data are based on between 10 percent and 25 percent of the total population of the country group or region.

in school enrollment. This is not surprising, since they also had the lowest years of schooling of the adult populations in 1990 and 2000 (Table 4).

Most countries spend more per tertiary (post-secondary) student than per primary and secondary students, but the gap is much larger in developing countries (Table 9, column 5). On average, governments in low-income countries spend 34 times more on a student in tertiary education than they spend on a student in primary education and 14 times more than on a student in secondary education. The analogous figures for high-income countries are 1.8 and 1.4. Since the poorest children rarely reach high levels of schooling, greater per student spending at higher (rather than lower) levels of education is likely to be regressive.

This low spending on primary and (to a lesser extent) secondary education in developing countries often implies that households bear much of the cost of that education. Thus parents, rather than the school or ministry of education, are responsible for providing many basic school inputs such as textbooks, chairs, and even the school building itself. Some of these costs are the collective responsibility of parents, but some are passed on to parents through official or unofficial school fees or by requiring parents to purchase uniforms and textbooks for their children. Data on such costs are not available for many countries, but a few examples are worth considering, although it is worth bearing in mind that they may not be representative. In Jamaica, government expenditures per primary school student are US$221 while private expenditures are $178 [Planning Institute of Jamaica (1992)]. In the Philippines, the analogous figures are $110 and $309 [Asian Development Bank (1999)], and for Vietnam they are $23 and $14 [World Bank (1997b)]. These figures include students who attend private schools.

Aside from differences in education finance, education systems in developing countries differ in other ways from those in developed countries. In many developing countries, school systems are highly centralized and teachers' unions are strong. Teachers often have weak incentives and little supervision, and absence rates are high (Table 12). A team of researchers who visited schools in India [PROBE Team (1999)] found some teachers who kept schools closed or nonfunctional for weeks or months at a time, drunken teachers, and a headmaster who expected the students to perform domestic chores and babysitting. Sexual abuse of female students by male teachers is a problem in several countries. To the extent that teachers do have incentives, these incentives are often focused on exam scores. Teachers often instruct by rote, sometimes copying from textbooks onto the blackboard and having students copy from the blackboard onto notebooks or slates.

The lack of teacher accountability in many developing countries may reflect the colonial legacy, the hierarchical nature of many developing societies, and the large gaps in education and social status between teachers and their pupils' families. In many countries, teachers offer, and pressure parents to pay for, "extra lessons" after school or on weekends to prepare students for important examinations [Bray (1999)]. In such situations, increased teaching effort at school could reduce the demand for extra lessons, and thus teacher income.

Table 12
Absence rates among teachers in developing countries

Country	Primary schools
Ecuador	14
India (average over 14 states)	25
Indonesia	19
Papua New Guinea	15
Peru	11
Zambia	17
Uganda	27

Notes. The absence rate is the percentage of staff who are supposed to be present but are not on the day of an unannounced visit. It includes staff whose absence is "excused".
Sources: Chaudhury et al. (2006), Habyarimana et al. (2004) and NRI and World Bank (2003).

Another unusual characteristic of many developing countries is that students are taught in a language that is not their mother tongue. This primarily reflects the fact that almost all developing countries were once colonies of developed countries, and their school systems still embody many elements of the systems developed under colonial rule. Many Sub-Saharan African countries use English or French as their national language, and most of India's 1 billion inhabits are not native speakers of either of the two official national languages (Hindi and English).

Given the heterogeneity in educational background, school quality, and language within many developing countries, designing a single curriculum appropriate for all students is difficult for any country. Yet most developing countries have a single centrally set curriculum, often geared to the needs of relatively elite students, which leaves many other students behind. This contributes to the poor performance of a significant percentage of students on national examinations and to high dropout and repetition rates. For example, in Tanzania between 1997 and 2001, only 22 percent of the students who attempted were able to pass the primary education final examination, and only 28 percent of those who attempted passed the certificate of secondary education exam [Tanzania Media Monitoring (2002)].

In response to the high cost and low quality of some centralized school systems, alternative, locally controlled systems have been established in some countries. These include nonformal education (NFEs) centers in India and the EDUCO schools in El Salvador. NFEs in India hire locally and pay a tiny fraction of regular salaries. Most teachers are not officially qualified. EDUCO schools in El Salvador allow local education committees to monitor teacher performance, hire and fire teachers, and manage school equipment and maintenance [Jimenez and Sawada (1999)].

The potential for competition among schools and for Tiebout sorting in developing countries is limited, since substantial proportions of the populations in developing countries reside in rural areas – 68 percent in low-income countries, 50 percent in middle-income countries [World Bank (2002)]. Rural areas are often characterized by low residential mobility, land markets subject to major transaction costs, and limited transportation networks. Nonetheless, some rural areas have sufficiently dense populations to allow for significant competition between schools. For example, one out of every four households in a rural area of Kenya sends their child to a school that is not the closest to their house [Miguel and Gugerty (2005)]. Among middle school students in Ghana, at least 26 percent of those living at home do not attend the closest middle school [Glewwe and Jacoby (1994)].

Policies toward private schools in developing countries vary widely, from outright prohibition (Cuba, Sri Lanka) to heavy subsidization (Chile). Consequently, in some countries (Algeria, Mongolia, Tanzania), less than 1 percent of primary school students are enrolled in private schools. In other countries (Chile, Pakistan, Zimbabwe), nearly one half or more are enrolled in private primary schools.

In summary, in recent years, education systems in developing countries have rapidly expanded from a very low base, but there is still room for improvement in enrollment rates (especially net enrollment rates). In general, school quality in developing countries is low (in the sense that students in these schools do not learn as much as their counterparts in more developed countries), and per-pupil expenditures are often quite low as compared to high- or middle-income countries, even after adjusting for price differences. Finally, although schools in developing countries vary from country to country, many of these education systems are highly centralized and have weak teacher incentives.

3. Methodological issues

A substantial and rapidly growing literature attempts to estimate the causal relationships underlying education outcomes in developing countries, and to formulate policy recommendations based on those estimates. To evaluate this body of literature, a methodological framework is needed to clarify the different types of causal relationships that one might try to estimate and to judge the credibility of the estimation methods used. This section provides such a general framework and discusses its implications for estimation. Section 3.1 outlines the framework that will be used to interpret the research discussed in later sections. Section 3.2 discusses estimation using retrospective data, and Section 3.3 discusses estimation using randomized trials and natural experiments.

3.1. Behavioral models and causal relationships

To understand the impact of education policies on years of schooling and skills learned, a useful assumption for economists is that each household (in particular, the parents of the child) maximizes, subject to constraints, a (life-cycle) utility function. The main arguments in the utility function are consumption of goods and services (including leisure) at different points in time, and each child's years of schooling and learning. The constraints faced are the production function for learning, the impacts of years of schooling and of skills obtained on the future labor incomes of children, a life-cycle budget constraint, and perhaps some credit constraints or an agricultural production function (for which child labor is one possible input), or both. The production function for learning is a structural relationship that can be depicted as:

$$A = a(S, \mathbf{Q}, \mathbf{C}, \mathbf{H}, \mathbf{I}), \tag{1}$$

where A is skills learned (*achievement*), S is years of schooling, $\mathbf{Q}$ is a vector of school and teacher characteristics (*quality*), $\mathbf{C}$ is a vector of child characteristics (including "innate ability"), $\mathbf{H}$ is a vector of household characteristics and $\mathbf{I}$ is a vector of educational inputs under the control of parents, such as children's daily attendance and purchases of textbooks and other school supplies. Although children may acquire different skills in school, which suggests that (1) should have multiple outputs and A should be a vector, for the purposes of this chapter little is lost, and some simplicity is gained, by treating A as a scalar.

Assume that all elements in the vectors $\mathbf{C}$ and $\mathbf{H}$ are exogenous. Examples of such variables are parental education and children's genetic endowments of "ability". Some child characteristics affecting education outcomes (such as child health) could be endogenous; such variables can be treated as elements of $\mathbf{I}$, all of which are endogenous.[10] Another important set of variables to introduce in this framework is prices related to schooling, denoted by the vector $\mathbf{P}$. These prices can include school fees, prices for school supplies purchased by parents, and even wages paid for child labor. $\mathbf{P}$ does not appear in Equation (1) because it has no direct effect on learning; its effect works through decisions made for the endogenous variables S and $\mathbf{I}$.

In the simplest scenario, assume that only one school is available to each household and that parents can do nothing to change the characteristics of that school. Thus all variables in $\mathbf{Q}$ and $\mathbf{P}$ are exogenous to the household. Parents choose S and $\mathbf{I}$ (subject to the above-mentioned constraints) to maximize household utility, which implies that years of schooling S and educational inputs $\mathbf{I}$ can be expressed as general functions of the four vectors of exogenous variables, where $\mathbf{H}$ includes not only the household variables in (1) but also household variables with indirect effects (such as credit constraints and parental tastes for schooling),

$$S = f(\mathbf{Q}, \mathbf{C}, \mathbf{H}, \mathbf{P}), \tag{2}$$

$$I = g(\mathbf{Q}, \mathbf{C}, \mathbf{H}, \mathbf{P}). \tag{3}$$

Inserting (2) and (3) into (1) gives the reduced form equation for A

$$A = h(\mathbf{Q}, \mathbf{C}, \mathbf{H}, \mathbf{P}). \tag{4}$$

---

[10] For a similar exposition that focuses on the role of child health, see Glewwe (2005).

This reduced form equation is a causal relationship, but it is not a production function because it reflects household preferences and includes prices among its arguments.

The more realistic assumption that households can choose from more than one school implies that $\mathbf{Q}$ and $\mathbf{P}$ are endogenous even if they are fixed for any given school. In this scenario, households maximize utility with respect to each schooling choice, and then choose the school that leads to the highest utility. Conditional on choosing that school, they choose S and $\mathbf{I}$, as in the case where there is only one school from which to choose.

Policymakers are primarily concerned with the impact of education policies on years of schooling S, and eventual academic achievement A. For example, reducing class size can be seen as a change in one element of $\mathbf{Q}$, and changing tuition fees can be seen as altering one component of $\mathbf{P}$. Equations (2) and (4) show how such changes would affect S and A. Assuming the cost of such changes is not difficult to calculate, the benefits in terms of increases in S and A can be compared to those costs. Of course, the costs should include costs borne by households from the policy change, so changes in $\mathbf{I}$, as expressed in Equation (3), and in household leisure must be included in the overall cost figure.

Consider a change in one element of $\mathbf{Q}$, call it Q_i. Equation (1) shows how changes in Q_i affect A when all other explanatory variable are held constant, and thus provides the *partial* derivative of A with respect to Q_i. In contrast, Equation (4) provides the *total* derivative of A with respect to Q_i because it allows for changes in S and $\mathbf{I}$ in response to the change in Q_i. Parents may respond to better teaching by increasing their provision of educational inputs such as textbooks. (Alternatively, if they consider better teaching a substitute for those inputs, they may decrease those inputs.) For example, Das and others suggest that household educational expenditures and governmental nonsalary cash grants to schools are substitutes, and that households cut back on expenditures when the government provides grants to schools [Das et al. (2004)]. In general, the partial and total derivatives could be quite different, and researchers should (but often do not) always clarify which relationship they are estimating. One possible reason (but not the only one) why different studies obtain different estimates of the factors that affect learning is that they are estimating different relationships.

When examining the impact of policies on academic skills A, should policymakers look at Equation (1), or Equation (4)? Equation (4) is of interest because it shows what will actually happen to A after a change in one or more element in $\mathbf{Q}$ or $\mathbf{P}$. In contrast, Equation (1) will not show this because it does not account for changes in S and $\mathbf{I}$ in response to changes in $\mathbf{Q}$ and $\mathbf{P}$. Although the total derivative obtained from Equation (4) is of clear interest to policymakers, the partial derivative from (1) is also of interest because it may better capture overall welfare effects. Intuitively, if parents respond to an increase in Q_i by (for example) reducing purchases of inputs $\mathbf{I}$, they will be able to raise household welfare by purchasing more of some consumer good. The reduced form impact (total derivative) reflects the drop in A due to the reduction in $\mathbf{I}$, but it does not account for the increase in household welfare from the increased purchase of consumer goods. In contrast, the structural impact measured in Equation (1) ignores both effects. Since these two effects have opposing effects on household welfare, they tend to cancel each other out, so the overall welfare effect is reasonably approximated by the change in A measured in Equation (1). This is explained more formally in Glewwe et al. (2004).

Results from randomized evaluations provide reduced form estimates of the impacts of changes in **P** and **Q**, and these reduced form parameters are total derivatives that reflect both the partial derivatives and agents' optimizing responses. For example, suppose school quality increases in some way. One possible response of parents is to reduce the time they spend helping their children with schoolwork. An education production function would not include this response, but a reduced form estimate (e.g., by a randomized trial) would include both responses. Thus, if a researcher conducting a randomized trial wants to measure welfare, he or she should measure not only the program impact on the outcome variable, but also its impact on all other inputs. By combining these data with price data, a measure of the program's impact on welfare could be obtained.

This framework can be extended to examine policies that do not directly change **P** and **Q** but instead change the way schools are organized such as decentralization, promoting competition by removing restrictions on private schools, or developing incentive schemes that link teacher pay to student performance. In principle, these types of policies affect schooling outcomes by changing what happens in the classroom. For example, increased competition may change the behavior of teachers, and these behaviors can be included as components of the vector **Q**. Formally, education policies, denoted by **EP**, may interact with local community characteristics, denoted by **L**, to determine the quality of a school and even the prices of educational inputs in some cases (e.g., policies that allow communities to set school fees):

$$\mathbf{Q} = q(\mathbf{L}, \mathbf{EP}), \tag{5}$$

$$\mathbf{P} = p(\mathbf{L}, \mathbf{EP}). \tag{6}$$

Estimating Equations (5) and (6) would require very detailed data on what happens in schools such as the many dimensions of teacher behavior. An alternative is to substitute (5) and (6) into (2) and (4) to obtain the reduced form relationships:

$$S = j(\mathbf{C}, \mathbf{H}, \mathbf{L}, \mathbf{EP}), \tag{7}$$

$$A = k(\mathbf{C}, \mathbf{H}, \mathbf{L}, \mathbf{EP}). \tag{8}$$

Knowledge of these functions would directly link education policies to the main outcomes of interest to policymakers.

The methodological framework presented in this subsection, while simple, is a useful guide for evaluating empirical work on education in developing countries. Yet it does have two limitations. First, it assumes a unitary household model and thus abstracts from bargaining among household members regarding education decisions. Indeed, common sense suggests that education decisions can be affected by household bargaining both between men and women and between parents and children. For example, Miguel and Kremer (2003) find that child social networks are as important as, or more important than, adult social networks in influencing take-up of school-based deworming programs. The framework presented above could be adapted to situations where adults disagree or children disagree with adults. In particular, the reduced form demands in Equations (2)–(4), (7) and (8) can be supplemented with **C** and **H** variables that reflect the relative power of different household members such as individual wealth or income sources.

A second limitation of the methodological framework is that it abstracts from the general equilibrium effects of education policies. Changes in education inputs or education policy may eventually change the supply of educated adults and thus change the returns to education and thereby the demand for education. These relatively long-run impacts are, for the most part, ignored in the rest of this chapter.

3.2. Estimation using retrospective data

Most empirical studies of the determinants of years of schooling and learning in both developed and developing countries are *retrospective studies*, based on data generated by ordinary (nonexperimental) variation across schools and households. This subsection discusses the feasibility of using such data to estimate the relationships of interest discussed above, especially Equations (1), (2), (4), (7) and (8). As we will see, there are formidable estimation problems even for this relatively simple scenario, and prospects dim further when more complicated scenarios are considered.

Consider estimation of Equation (2), the (reduced form) determinants of years of schooling (S). For simplicity, assume that school quality (**Q**) and prices (**P**) are exogenous, the policies of interest can be adequately described by changes in the elements of **Q** and **P**, and there is only one school from which to choose (a relatively remote rural area, for example). Since **C** and **H** are also considered to be exogenous, OLS estimates of (2) will provide unbiased estimates of the causal parameters associated with each variable as long as one has (retrospective) data on S and on *all* the elements in the vectors **Q**, **C**, **H** and **P**. In practice, it is neither necessary nor possible to have data on all elements in these four vectors. Data are not needed for any unobserved elements that are unlikely to be correlated with the variables in the four vectors for which one has data, so all such elements can be combined to form the error term in the regression equation.

Unfortunately, if any of these unobserved elements that are part of the error term are correlated with the variables for which one does have data, that correlation will lead to omitted variable bias in OLS estimates of the relationship being estimated. Such omitted variable bias is very likely: no retrospective data set will have data on all the elements in the vectors **Q**, **C**, **H** and **P**, and it is very common for many of the unobserved elements to be correlated with some of the variables that are observed. Examples of variables that are almost impossible to observe (with the vectors they pertain to) are: the child's innate ability (**C**) and motivation (**C**), parents' willingness (**H**) and capacity (**H**) to help their children with schoolwork, teachers' interpersonal skills (**Q**) and motivation (**Q**), and the management skills of school principals (**Q**). When such data are missing from estimates of Equation (2), OLS parameter estimates are likely to be biased because these variables are likely to be correlated with some of the observed variables in the regression. For example, schools that are "high quality" are likely to be high quality in many dimensions, both observed and unobserved. This will produce positive correlation between the error term and the observed school and teacher quality variables, leading to overestimation of the impact of observed school variables. Another example is parental tastes for their children's education, which is rarely observed and is likely to be positively correlated with parental education, leading to overestimation of the impact of parental education. When this type of bias occurs, it affects the estimated parameters not only for the observed variables that are correlated with the error term but also for the observed variables that are uncorrelated with the error term.

Researchers sometimes try to measure variables that they think are the most important omitted variables. For example, they may use an IQ test as a measure of innate ability or use parental schooling to indicate parents' ability to assist their children, but even here there are problems. It is not clear that innate ability can be measured: any test that claims to do so (in the sense of measuring a genetic endowment) almost always reflects environmental factors [American Psychological Association (1995)]. One may be able to address this problem by using data on twins [e.g., Behrman, Rosenzweig and Taubman (1994)], but such data from developing countries are very rare.

Measurement error in observed explanatory variables is another very difficult estimation problem. Anyone who has seen how household or school survey data are collected in developing countries understands that even the best surveys contain a substantial amount of error. Data on school characteristics (including fees and prices of educational inputs) may be inaccurate or out of date. Indeed, they are often averages across grades and across classes within grades and thus do not match the experience of any particular child attending the school. Child and household variables can also be measured with a substantial amount of error in developing countries, including data on the age of the child, the distance to the nearest school, the education of the parents, and household resources (e.g., land owned). Random measurement error typically leads to underestimation of the true underlying impacts, while nonrandom measurement error could lead to biases in either direction.

Even when parents cannot alter school quality, quality could be correlated with the error term if governments provide better schools to areas with unobserved education problems [Pitt, Rosenzweig and Gibbons (1993)]. On the other hand, governments are just as likely (and some observers would argue much more likely) to provide more school inputs in areas that already have good education outcomes, since these areas may have disproportionate political influence in both autocratic and democratic systems, may pay more taxes, and may put higher weight on education than other areas when choosing how to spend the resources they receive from the central government [World Bank (2001a)]. Whatever the direction, correcting for this "endogenous program placement" bias is difficult.

One approach toward addressing the problems of omitted variables, measurement error, and endogenous program placement is instrumental variables. Unfortunately, it is often difficult to find plausible instruments – that is, variables correlated with the observed variables that are not orthogonal to the error term but uncorrelated with the error term. Some examples of this will be discussed in Section 4.

Now consider estimation of Equations (1) and (4), the structural and reduced form determinants of learning, respectively. All of the above problems apply to these equations as well, and there is another problem: attrition bias. Communities with high-quality schools will keep children in school longer, leading to a student population with lower average innate ability (more "low ability" children stay in school). This will lead to underestimation of the impact of observed school quality on learning if no variable accurately measures innate ability.

Further complications arise for Equations (1), (2) and (4) when allowing for endogeneity of school quality (and prices) in the sense that parents can choose from among more than one school, although they have no influence on the quality of any given school. Parents in remote rural areas may have little choice, so that all school characteristics are exogenous – but this is doubtful. First, parents may send their children to live with relatives (allowing them to attend a nonlocal school) or to a boarding school. About 19 percent of secondary students in rural Peru live away from their families [Gertler and Glewwe (1990)], and the same holds for 27 percent of middle school students in Ghana [Glewwe and Jacoby (1994)]. Second, families with stronger tastes for educated children may migrate to areas with better schools, a common occurrence in the United States.

When parents can alter school quality through school choice, selection bias is possible if unobserved characteristics of children and households that affect test scores and years of schooling are correlated with unobserved factors that determine school choice. If data are available on some of the school choices, including schools not chosen, standard selection correction methods can be used [Heckman (1979), see also Pagan and Ullah (1999), Chapter 8]. In particular, exclusion restrictions can be used to identify the generated selection correction term, namely the characteristics of the schools not chosen. In practice, however, modeling school choice in a tractable way may be difficult when many schooling options exist.

A final approach to consider is to abandon attempts to estimate Equations (1), (2) and (4) because of the impossibility of collecting all the price and school characteristic variables in **P** and **Q** and instead estimate Equations (7) and (8). An example of this, which will be examined in Section 6, is from Nicaragua, where some schools follow the "old" education policies and others follow the policies of the EDUCO program. In this case, all one needs is a dummy variable indicating which schools are EDUCO schools. This approach may be attractive if data on education policies and local characteristics, **EP** and **L**, are of lower dimension and therefore easier to collect than data on **P** and **Q**.

While this approach appears promising, it can still suffer from omitted variable bias if unobserved child, household, or community characteristics are correlated with the **EP** variables. In practice, retrospective estimates of Equations (7) and (8) face many problems. First, in many programs, procedures that are supposed to be followed as part of a particular education policy are often not followed. Second, it is quite possible for unobserved child, household and community variables to be correlated with the new education policies, since the location of the programs may be affected by household actions (omitted variable bias) or government choices (endogenous program placement).

In summary, uncritical application of simple OLS regressions using retrospective data can lead to biased estimates of the impact of the determinants of learning and years of schooling. Some problems underestimate the impacts, others overestimate them, and some could go either way. These difficulties are so daunting that some economists doubt that they can be overcome [Hanushek (1995)]. One response to these problems is to turn to randomized trials and natural experiments. Next, we review estimation issues that arise using these approaches.

3.3. Natural experiments and randomized trials

Suppose Equations (1)–(4), (7) and (8) could not be estimated using retrospective data, due to the problems raised above. An alternative approach is to exploit natural experiments generated by idiosyncratic details of policies that create instrumental variables for program participation that are plausibly uncorrelated with the error term for schooling outcomes [on natural experiments, see Campbell (1969), Meyer (1995), Rosenzweig and Wolpin (2000)]. Randomized trials are a third approach. Such trials are very common in medicine and are increasingly common in labor economics [Heckman, Lalonde and Smith (1999), Manski and Garfinkel (1992), and the special issue of the *Journal of Labor Economics*, 1993].

A few clarifications are in order regarding the use of randomized evaluations to estimate program effects. First, a distinction can be made about what exactly the evaluation is attempting to estimate. Randomized evaluations can be used to estimate the effect of a treatment on either the entire population subject to the randomization or on a subset defined by predetermined characteristics. In contrast, instrumental variable techniques estimate local average treatment effects, which are the effects on the population whose participation in the treatment was strongly influenced by the instrumental variable [Imbens and Angrist (1994), Heckman, Ichimura and Todd (1997), Heckman et al. (1998), Heckman, Lalonde and Smith (1999)]. In some settings, for example where enrollment is 100 percent, this distinction does not exist. In general, studies should clarify which type of treatment effect they are attempting to estimate. Second, randomized evaluations estimate partial equilibrium treatment effects, which may differ from general equilibrium treatment effects [Heckman, Lochner and Taber (1998)]. If some educational programs were implemented on a large scale, the programs might affect the functioning of the school system and thus have a different impact.

The basic idea of randomized evaluations of any kind is to compare two groups of observations that have no systematic differences other than one group received the treatment and the other did not. The simplest method is to sample a population of interest and randomly divide the sample into treatment and comparison groups. Under certain assumptions, discussed below, differences in the variables of interest across the two groups are unbiased estimates of the (reduced form) effect of the treatment.

Randomized trials and natural experiments typically do not estimate an education production function, that is Equation (1), but they can provide reduced form estimates (total derivatives) of the impacts of changes in C, H, P and Q on S, I and A, as in Equations (2)–(4) or Equations (7) and (8).[11] To the extent that some inputs provided by other actors, in particular the variables in I in Equation (1), can be adjusted over different time horizons, the total derivative measured by these studies may be different in the short and the long run. For example, if treatment schools are provided with abundant supplies of a particular input, parents may reduce their efforts to supply these inputs. However, parents may not immediately throw out existing inputs such as parent-provided textbooks, and hence the stock of these inputs may decline only gradually over time. These studies can examine the reduced form impact of the program at various time horizons, and it can also measure the inputs provided by parents, but it does not directly measure the (partial derivative) impact of public provision of textbooks, holding parental provision constant.

Randomized trials can avoid, or reduce, some of the problems that arise with estimates based on retrospective data (discussed in Section 3.2). In particular, random assignment of observations into treatment and control groups implies that both observed and unobserved characteristics of those observations are uncorrelated in expectation with treatment status. Another problem that randomized studies should resolve is measurement error: in any well-managed study, treatment status should be measured without error.

Yet randomized evaluations do not address all of the statistical issues associated with retrospective analysis. Problems of selection and attrition bias remain, and randomized evaluations may generate new problems to the extent that people change their behavior because they know they are taking part in an evaluation. As we discuss in Section 7, a number of techniques can be used to address these issues. However, rather than discuss these issues in the abstract, first we review some examples.

4. Factors influencing the quantity of education attained

The MDGs adopted in 2000 call for universal primary education by 2015, yet there is little consensus on how best to achieve this goal or on how much it would cost. One view holds that attracting additional children to school will be difficult, since most children not in school in developing countries are earning income that their families need. Another view is that the potential contribution of children of primary-school age to family income is very small, which implies that modest incentives or improvements in school quality Q could significantly increase enrollment. Neither is there agreement on the role

---

[11] Technically speaking, Equations (2)–(4) show the relationship for all possible values of the variables in the vectors C, H, P and Q, while a series of randomized trials can at most show a finite number of points on the "surface" of these relationships. The same point applies to Equations (7) and (8).

of school fees (elements of **P**). Some observers see fees as crucial for ensuring account-ability in schools and as only a slight barrier to school enrollment; others contend that reducing school fees would greatly increase enrollment.

This section reviews the recent evidence on these issues. Section 4.1 discusses two general measurement problems that often arise when examining issues concerning the quantity of schooling in developing countries. Section 4.2 considers the tradeoff be-tween investing in the construction of additional schools (making schools more accessi-ble to students by increasing capacity and reducing distance) and investing in improving the quality of existing schools (making them more attractive). Section 4.3 examines the impact of reducing the cost of school or even compensating students for school at-tendance (changes in **P**), either implicitly (e.g., offering school meals) or explicitly. Because poor health may also limit school participation, Section 4.4 reviews recent work on school-based health programs [see Glewwe (2005), for a review of recent work on the impact of health and nutrition in early childhood on education outcomes]. We then discuss lessons from this work concerning the differential sensitivity of girls' and boys' schooling decisions (Section 4.5) and the cost-effectiveness of various inter-ventions to increase school participation (Section 4.6). As we will see throughout this section, the evidence suggests that there are several promising avenues to increase the quantity of education attained by children.

Several of the studies discussed in this section examine both quantity of schooling and determinants of students' academic performance; in those cases we consider the findings with respect to the quantity of schooling in this section and report the findings on academic performance in the next section. Similarly, since grade repetition primarily reflects academic performance it will also be addressed in Section 5.

4.1. Two measurement issues

This subsection discusses two measurement issues that often arise in research on the quantity of schooling in developing countries. First, defining what "quantity" should be measured can be difficult. Second, difficulties often arise when attempting to match the current and historical data on school and individual characteristics that are needed to investigate the factors affecting the quantity of schooling.

Measuring current school participation

The framework presented in Section 3 defined the quantity of schooling (S) as years of completed schooling, but in practice sometimes researchers look at the determinants of completed schooling and sometimes at measures of current schooling such as the com-pletion of a given level of schooling or the decision to drop out or continue to the next grade, both of which are incomplete measures of eventual years of schooling completed. One issue is whether educational inputs and education policies that increase the prob-ability of staying in school or completing a given level of schooling will also increase years of schooling eventually completed, rather than simply creating intertemporal substitution in the timing of education.

Another issue is that in developing countries many pupils attend school erratically and the line between a "frequently absent pupil" and a "dropout" is often unclear. Attendance rates can vary dramatically among individuals. Thus large differences in the quantity of schooling would be overlooked by considering only years of schooling. One attractive way to incorporate wide variation in attendance when measuring the quantity of schooling is to focus on a more comprehensive measure of schooling often called "participation". For any child, *participation* is defined as the proportion of days that he or she is present in school for a given number of days that the school is open [e.g., Miguel and Kremer (2003, 2004)]. This can be applied to a child's schooling over one or more years, or just for a few days for which reliable data are available. Participation differs from attendance in that it includes all children in the appropriate age range while *attendance* is usually defined only for children officially enrolled in school. Throughout the rest of this chapter, we use the terms *quantity of schooling* and *school participation* interchangeably. Both can be thought of as total time in school, which is imperfectly measured by years of schooling.

Classroom attendance registers are often very inaccurate in developing countries. One solution is to organize independent data collection in which unannounced observers visit schools a few days a year to record which children are actually in class.

Examining determinants of completed schooling

The other general measurement issue is that any individual's completed years of schooling (or some other measure of completed time in school) is known only many years after he or she first enrolled in school, which implies that data on years of schooling must be collected several years after data are collected on household and school characteristics. Thus cross-sectional data sets covering a relatively young population will include many children still in school, for whom the years of completed schooling variable is (right) censored. Alternatively, if cross-sectional data are collected from an older cohort for whom years of completed schooling is known, examining the impact of school characteristics on educational attainment requires historical data on school and household characteristics data. For example, consider a student who began school at age 6, left at age 16, and is surveyed at age 18: the relevant school characteristic data refer to a time period from 2 to 12 years before the time of the survey. Finding historical data on school quality in developing countries is often quite challenging, and matching it to individual students who attended those schools during those years is more difficult still. One common approach is to collect current school quality data and assume school characteristics have changed very little in the past 5 to 10 years, but, if this assumption is incorrect, the consequent measurement error could introduce serious biases into any econometric estimates.

4.2. Building additional schools versus improving the quality of existing schools

Many students in developing countries must travel long distances to attend school, so one policy option is to construct new schools in communities that have none. However, an inherent tradeoff exists between investing in the construction of new schools and investing in improvements in the quality of existing schools, which would make these schools more attractive to students. For example, the PROBE report [PROBE Team (1999)], based on in-depth surveys in five Indian states, argues that a key factor in low school participation is the low quality (unmotivated teacher incentives, weak curriculums, inadequate physical facilities) of available schools.

Several retrospective studies examine the impact of both distance to school (often measured by travel time) and school quality on the quantity of schooling. A number of concerns, particularly omitted variable biases, provide reason for caution in interpreting the results of these retrospective studies. We first present several retrospective studies, and some caveats which should be applied in interpreting their results. We then present results from natural experiments and randomized evaluations which likely offer more credible evidence on the relative impacts of distance to school and school quality.

A retrospective study in Ghana by Glewwe and Jacoby (1994) presents evidence on the impact of distance and school quality on the years of schooling of individuals aged 11–20, using data collected in 1988–1989 on household, school and teacher characteristics.[12] To estimate the impact of school characteristics and other factors on years of schooling attained, an ordered probit specification was used that allows for right censoring. According to the study findings, years of schooling was reasonably responsive to school quality. The estimates indicate that years of completed schooling could increase by 2–2.5 years by raising average teacher experience (from 2 years to 10 years), repairing leaking roofs, reducing travel time (from 2 hours to a few minutes), or providing blackboards to schools without them. Since repairing roofs and providing blackboards is much less expensive than building new schools, these results suggest that repairing classrooms in Ghana is a more cost-effective means of increasing the quantity of schooling than building new schools to reduce travel time.

Although the results from the Ghana study appear plausible, the estimates could be biased for a number of reasons. The data had 18 school and teacher variables, but schools can differ in many more ways, which raises the problem of omitted variable bias. Measurement error in these variables is also a potential problem, either because the assumption that they change little over time is false or because errors were made in collecting the data. Finally, no attempt was made to avoid bias due to endogenous program placement.

---

[12] Lavy (1996) used the same data to study the impact of secondary school characteristics (particularly distance) on primary school attainment. He found that the secondary school distance variables had significantly negative impacts. The school quality variables were almost always insignificant, perhaps because they were aggregated up to 33 regions, which reduced their variation and introduced random measurement error.

In a retrospective study in Tanzania, Bommier and Lambert (2000) found that distance to school had a significantly negative effect on years of schooling, while the quality of Swahili teaching had a positive effect. However, the authors note some problems with measurement error in these variables. For example, many households reported implausible distances to the nearest primary schools, sometimes more than 100 kilometers. Moreover, since school characteristics were averaged over responses given by households, there could be systematic bias. For example, parents may "justify" a decision to allow a child to drop out of school by claiming that the local school was of low quality (in the Ghana study school quality variables were collected from schools, not households). Finally, given that there are only four school quality variables, there are serious concerns of omitted variable bias.

Using retrospective data from India, Drèze and Kingdon (2001) found that several school quality variables had statistically significant effects on years of primary school attained: both provision of a mid-day meal and "waterproof" classrooms had no effect on boys but strong positive effects on girls; teacher absences due to nonteaching duties had a negative effect on boys but no effect on girls; a parent–teacher cooperation index had a positive effect on both sexes; and class size had a negative effect on both sexes. Though plausible, these results should be interpreted very cautiously. Omitted variable biases are likely. Indeed, the authors suggest that the strong and significant effect of "waterproof" classrooms could also be interpreted as representing the general state of the school building. They also suggest that the (unobserved) motivation of school principals, parents, or both may be the real reason for both higher quality of schooling and the associated higher quantity of schooling.

Another strand in the literature looks at "natural experiments". Case and Deaton (1999) examined education outcomes in South Africa using data collected in 1993, when government funding for schools was highly centralized and blacks (people of African descent) had virtually no political representation of any kind. The authors argue that blacks did not control the funds provided to their children's schools and that tight migration controls limited their ability to migrate to areas with better schools. They show that pupil–teacher ratios varied widely across black schools, and argue that this variation, combined with migration barriers and black South Africans' lack of control over their schools, generates a kind of natural experiment.

Case and Deaton's estimates indicate that raising school resources (as measured by student–teacher ratios) increases years of completed schooling and enrollment rates for blacks but not for whites. Since blacks had much larger class sizes than whites, this is consistent with the idea that there are diminishing returns to reductions in class size. They estimate large effects from reducing class size at black schools: decreasing the student–teacher ratio from 40 to 20 (the approximate means in black and white schools, respectively) increases grade attainment by 1.5–2.5 years.

Several issues raise concerns about the interpretation of these results. A key point is that, even if blacks could not influence class size in their children's schools, someone, presumably some government officials, made decisions that influenced class sizes in South Africa's black schools. If these decisions were influenced by education outcomes in those schools, or were merely correlated with such outcomes for some reason other than the causal impact of class size, they could yield biased estimates of the impact of class size (and, more generally, school resources) on those outcomes. This is the problem of endogenous program placement discussed in Section 3. Another issue is that the children tested were not a random sample of household members, and data on student–teacher ratios from the Ministry of Education are not highly correlated – an R^2 coefficient of 0.15 – with the authors' community data for that variable.

In another natural experiment, Duflo (2001) took advantage of a rapid school expansion program in Indonesia to estimate the impact of building schools on years of schooling attained (as well as on subsequent wages, which is beyond the scope of this chapter). In 1973, the Indonesian government decided to use a portion of its oil revenues to build more schools. The allocation rule for the schools was known (more schools were built in places with low initial enrollment rates), and cohorts participating in the program are easily identified (children 12 years or older when the program started did not participate in the program). Duflo found that the school construction policy was effective in increasing the quantity of education and calculates that each school built for every 1,000 children led to an average increase of 0.12 years of education. Trends across regions were parallel before the program and shifted clearly for the first cohort exposed to the program, which raises confidence in the identification assumption.

Chin (2002) also takes a natural experiment approach to estimate the impact of placing additional teachers in Indian schools, an investment in school quality. "Operation Blackboard", a recent major policy initiative in India, addressed low primary school enrollment rates by mandating the provision of a second teacher to all primary schools with a single teacher. Chin (2002) evaluated the second teacher placement program and found that the program helped girls but had no effect on boys: girls' primary school completion increased by 3–4 percentage points, and the girls' literacy rate increased by 2–3 percentage points. Identification is again based on the fact that cohorts participating in the program are easily identified (only children attending primary school after 1987 were exposed).

A third strand of literature is based on randomized evaluations. As discussed in Section 4.5, Banerjee et al. (2000) find that provision of additional teachers (usually female) in Indian nonformal education centers increased school participation by girls. A number of randomized evaluations recently done in Kenya (most of them discussed in Section 5) found that programs designed to improve school quality, for example, by providing inputs like textbooks, had no detectable effect on school participation, and limited effects on test scores [see, for example, Glewwe, Kremer and Moulin (2006)]. Programs that reduced the cost of schooling or provided incentives to attend school had a much greater impact on school participation, as discussed below.

4.3. Reducing the cost of education

In many developing countries, parents face significant private costs of education for school fees and required inputs such as uniforms. For example, in Kenya parents have historically been required to purchase uniforms that cost about $6 – a substantial expense in a country with a per capita income of $340. One simple way to increase the quantity of schooling would be to remove financial barriers by reducing the cost of school or paying students to attend. However, the desirability of school fees is much debated. Proponents argue that fees are necessary to finance inputs, that they increase parental participation in school governance, and that the price elasticity of demand for schooling is low [Jimenez and Lockheed (1995)]. Opponents argue that school fees prevent many students from attending school and cite dramatic estimates from Sub-Saharan Africa: when free schooling was introduced in Uganda in 1997, primary school enrollment reportedly doubled from 2.6 million to 5.2 million children [UNICEF (1999)]; when primary school fees were eliminated in Tanzania in 2002, an estimated 1.5 million students (primarily girls) began attending primary school almost immediately [Coalition for Health and Education Rights (2002)]; and when Kenyan President Mwai Kibaki eliminated primary school fees in late 2002, a massive influx of new students reportedly overwhelmed school systems in certain districts [Lacey (2003)]. While there can be little doubt that eliminating school fees generated a large enrollment response, the magnitudes cited in these accounts should be taken with a grain of salt. The data on which they are based are often unclear, and free schooling is sometimes announced simultaneously with other policy initiatives and often accompanied by programs that replace school fees with per-pupil grants from the central government, which create incentives for schools to over report enrollment.

Several recent randomized evaluations examine the impact of reducing costs on the quantity of schooling. Kremer, Moulin and Namunyu (2002) conducted a randomized trial in rural Kenya to evaluate a program in which a nongovernmental organization (NGO), Internationaal Christelijk Steunfonds Africa (ICS), provided uniforms and textbooks and built classrooms for 7 schools randomly selected from a pool of 14 poorly performing schools. Dropout rates fell considerably in the 7 schools selected for participation, and after 5 years pupils in those schools had completed about 15 percent more years of schooling. In addition, many students from nearby schools transferred into program schools, raising class size by 50 percent. This suggests that students and parents were willing to trade off much larger class sizes for the benefit of free uniforms, textbooks, and improved classrooms. The authors argue that the main reason for the increase in years of schooling is most likely the financial benefit of free uniforms. A randomized trial of textbook provision in Kenya, discussed in the next subsection, showed almost no impact of textbooks on the quantity of schooling, and while the new classroom construction may have had an impact, the first new classrooms were not built until the second year of the program, while dropout rates fell dramatically in the first year. Anticipation of later classroom construction may have influenced these results, but the authors doubt it, because effects were present for students in the upper grades who would have finished school by the time the classrooms were built.

Several programs have gone beyond simply reducing school fees; they actually pay students to attend school, in the form of either cash grants or school meals. Perhaps the best known randomized evaluation is the PROGRESA program in Mexico, which was designed to increase school enrollment and academic performance by paying cash grants to mothers conditional on their children's school attendance and participation in preventative health measures (nutrition supplementation, health care visits, and health education programs). The program was launched in 1998; of 506 communities, half were randomly selected to participate. Schultz (2004) finds a 3.4 percent increase in enrollment, on average, for all students in grades 1–8. The largest increase, 14.8 percent, was among girls who had completed grade 6. Using a difference-in-difference estimator, Schultz finds that PROGRESA increases educational attainment for the poor by 0.66 years, with a particularly large impact on the enrollment in the transition year to junior secondary school (20 percent for girls and 10 percent for boys). In part because these evaluations clearly documented the program's success, PROGRESA was subsequently expanded to urban communities and, with support from the World Bank, similar programs are being implemented in several neighboring Latin American countries (e.g., the PRAF program in Honduras).[13] Schultz (2004) estimates that if the current neighboring urban wage differentials approximate what PROGRESA program beneficiaries can expect to earn from their schooling in terms of future percentage increases in ages, the internal rate of return to the educational grants provided by PROGRESA is 8 percent per year in real terms (adjusted for inflation).

Conditional transfers such as those awarded through the PROGRESA program leave open one potential problem: in some contexts, the people administering the program may not enforce the conditionality [Sen (2002)]. Linden and Shastry (2005) provide evidence that teachers mis-represented student attendance in response to a program which provided grain to students who regularly attended school. In these circumstances, school meals may provide a stronger incentive to attend school, because children must go to school to receive the rations. Government-subsidized school meals have been provided in India, Bangladesh, Brazil, Swaziland and Jamaica to increase both enrollment and attendance [World Food Programme (2002)]. Proponents of school meals also claim that school meals can increase both the quantity of schooling and academic performance by improving child nutrition. Others argue that families may reduce resource allocation to children who receive school meals. However, school meals would nonetheless serve as an incentive for families to send children to school. Moreover, Jacoby (2002) presents evidence from the Philippines that parents do not reduce food provided at home in response to school feeding programs [see also Long (1991), Powell, Grantham-McGregor and Elston (1983)]. The Drèze and Kingdon (2001) study discussed in Section 4.2 examined, among other variables, the impact of providing mid-day meals, which increased years in primary school for girls but not for boys.

Vermeersch and Kremer (2004) conducted a randomized evaluation of the impact of school meals on participation in Kenyan pre-schools, and found that school participation was 30 percent greater in the 25 Kenyan pre-schools where a free breakfast was

---

[13] Morley and Coady (2003) review and evaluate several Conditional Transfer for Education programs (CTEs) that have been implemented in developing countries, including PROGRESA, and conclude that CTEs are effective instruments for reducing poverty and increasing school enrollments.

introduced than in the 25 comparison schools. There was some evidence that the provision of meals cut into instruction time. In schools where the teacher was relatively well trained prior to the program, the meals program led to higher test scores (0.4 of a standard deviation) on academic tests. There were no effects on tests of general cognitive skills, implying the school meals program did not improve children's nutritional status and that the academic test score increases were likely due to more time spent in school.

4.4. School-based health programs

Poor health may also limit school participation: for example, intestinal helminths (e.g., hookworm, roundworm, whipworm and schistosomiasis) affect a quarter of the world's population, and are particularly prevalent among school-age children. Miguel and Kremer (2004) used randomized methods to evaluate a program of twice-yearly school-based mass treatment with inexpensive deworming drugs in Kenya (where the prevalence of intestinal worms among children is very high). They found that child health and school participation (as defined in Section 4.1) improved not only for treated students but also for untreated students at treatment schools (22 percent of pupils in treatment schools did not receive deworming medicine) and untreated students at nearby nontreatment schools due to reduced disease transmission. The authors used two approaches to address identification issues that arise in the presence of these disease-reduction externalities. First, randomization at school level allows them to estimate the overall effect of deworming on a school even if there are treatment externalities among pupils within treatment schools. (The authors use nonexperimental means to decompose the overall effect on treatment schools into a direct effect and a within-school externality effect.) Second, cross-school externalities – the impact of deworming for pupils in schools located near treatment schools – are identified using exogenous variation in the local density of treatment school pupils generated by the school-level randomization. The authors find that absenteeism in treatment schools was 25 percent (7 percentage points) lower than in comparison schools. This reflects both the direct effect of deworming and any within-school externalities. Including the cross-school externalities, they find that deworming increased schooling by 0.15 years per pupil treated: decomposed into an effect of the treatment on the students treated and a spillover effect, school participation on average increased by 7.5 percent among pupils in treatment schools and by 2 percent among pupils in comparison schools.

Bleakley (2002) provides retrospective estimates of the effects of deworming from the United States. He finds that areas in the US South with higher hookworm infection levels prior to the 1910–1920 Rockefeller Sanitary Commission deworming campaign experienced greater increases in school attendance after the intervention, and estimates that each case of hookworm reduced the number of children attending school by 0.23 [similar to the estimates of Miguel and Kremer (2004)]. Although it is difficult to fully rule out omitted variable bias using a nonexperimental approach, an important strength of Bleakley's work is that the Rockefeller campaign was introduced throughout a large geographic area, and thus the estimates are not subject to the biases faced by medical studies that randomize treatment at the individual level.

Bobonis, Miguel and Sharma (2004) find evidence from a randomized evaluation conducted in India that health programs can raise pre-school attendance in urban areas. While in the Kenyan sample 92 percent of surveyed primary school pupils had at least one helminth infection [Miguel and Kremer (2004)], in this sample of Indian pre-schoolers "only" 30 percent were found to have worm infections but 69 percent of children were found to have moderate to severe anemia. The program therefore provided both iron supplementation and deworming medicine to these preschool students. After five months of treatment, the authors found large weight gains and a 5.8 percent reduction in absenteeism among 4–6 year olds (but not for younger children).

These findings that school health programs can increase the quantity of schooling raise the question of how best to implement such programs in developing countries. One view is that reliance on external financing of medicine is not sustainable and instead advocates health education, water and sanitation improvements, or financing the provision of medicine through local cost sharing. Kremer and Miguel (2003) analyzed several deworming interventions, including numerous "sustainable" approaches such as cost sharing, health education, verbal commitments (a mobilization technique), and improvements in sanitation (all but the sanitation efforts were examined with randomized evaluations). Overall, their results suggest that there may be no alternative to continued subsidies for deworming. The "sustainable" public health strategies of health education, community mobilization, and cost recovery were ineffective, while provision of free deworming drugs led to high drug take-up and large reductions in the incidence of serious worm infections. A related paper [Miguel and Kremer (2003)] examines data on social networks to explore the effects of variation in social contacts' program exposure on individuals' adoption decisions. The authors found that children with (randomly) more social links to early treatment schools are themselves significantly less likely to take deworming drugs (perhaps because they learn that the drugs work for only a few months and seek to free ride on others' use of the drugs).

4.5. Gender and school participation

There is some evidence that the elasticity of demand for schooling may be higher for girls than for boys, so that even policies and programs that do not specifically target girls may result in greater increases in school participation for girls than for boys. Many of the studies described above support this hypothesis: Chin (2002), regarding placement of additional teachers in schools; Drèze and Kingdon (2001), on the provision of midday meals; and both Schultz (2004) and Morley and Coady (2003), in their evaluations of PROGRESA.

Section 4.3 discussed several types of programs that reduced households' cost of schooling for both boys and girls, but an alternative is to implement programs that specifically target girls. For example, research in several countries suggests that one way to increase girls' school enrollment may be to hire female teachers [World Bank

(2001b), Herz et al. (1991), Rugh (2000)]. However, it is very difficult to assess causality without conducting a randomized evaluation since in regions that are more open toward women's education, more women will obtain the education needed to become teachers.

Banerjee et al. (2000) used a randomized evaluation to examine the impact of a program in India that attempted to raise school quality by hiring additional teachers, especially female teachers. An Indian NGO, Seva Mandir, runs nonformal schools that teach basic numeracy and literacy skills to children who do not attend formal schools and, in the medium term, attempts to "mainstream" these children into the regular school system. These schools are plagued by high teacher and child absenteeism, so the NGO decided to evaluate the impact of hiring a second teacher (where possible, a woman) in the hope of increasing the number of days the school was open, increasing student attendance, improving performance through individualized attention to students, and making school more attractive to girls. The program reduced the number of days a school was closed (one-teacher schools were closed 44 percent of the time, whereas two-teacher schools were closed 39 percent of the time), and girls' attendance increased by 50 percent. However, the program had no significant effect on the attendance of boys. One possible interpretation is that more girls are at the margin of choosing between some schooling and no schooling and that they would have been attracted to school by additional teachers independent of the teachers' gender. Another interpretation is that girls were attracted by hiring female teachers. Some weak support for the latter hypothesis is provided by the fact that the effect on girls' enrollment was smaller when the original teacher was female. This is consistent with the possibility that the presence of at least one female teacher is important in providing a role model for girls but that the addition of a second female teacher has a comparatively minor role-model effect. There is no clear evidence of the program impacting test scores either positively or negatively.

Research on girls' scholarship programs is limited but suggests that scholarships can have major impacts on girls' enrollment rates. Research on a small fellowship program in Pakistan that subsidized girls' primary education in private schools was shown to be successful in urban areas but a failure in rural areas [Kim, Alderman and Orazem (1999), Alderman, Kim and Orazem (2003)].[14] A national scholarship program for girls in rural Bangladesh increased girls' enrollment rates even after controlling for other measurable influences [World Bank (2001b)]. Because with economic development enrollment of girls usually rises (and the gender gap between boys' and girls' enrollments narrows), it is potentially very problematic to draw conclusions from before and after comparisons of girls' enrollment rates. This difficulty highlights the need for randomized evaluations of such programs.

---

[14] The authors note several reasons for the relative success of the program in urban schools in contrast to rural schools. First, the latent demand for girls' schooling was higher in the urban areas. Second, urban parents were able to pay more than rural parents. Third, urban schools could take advantage of economies of scale to reduce costs per pupil. Finally, urban schools found it much easier than rural schools to attract good teachers (especially female teachers).

Kremer, Miguel and Thornton (2004) conducted a randomized evaluation of the Girl's Scholarship Program (GSP), introduced in rural Kenya in late 2001 to enhance girls' education. Out of a set of 128 schools, half were randomly chosen as schools eligible for the program. The program consisted of a merit-based scholarship awarded to girls in two districts of Western Kenya who scored in the top 15 percent on tests administered by the Kenyan government. One portion of the scholarship was paid directly to the school for school fees, the other portion to the family for school supplies and uniforms. Girls eligible for the scholarship had significantly higher school attendance rates (as well as significantly higher test scores, average gains of 0.12–0.19 standard deviations). Schools offering the scholarship also had significantly higher teacher attendance after the program was introduced, and there is evidence of positive program externalities on boys (who were ineligible for the awards) as well as on girls with low pre-test scores (who were unlikely to win awards).

4.6. Summary

The studies discussed in this chapter provide mixed evidence on the extent to which school participation responds to school quality but suggest that it is fairly responsive to incentives.

Anecdotal evidence from East Africa, as well as randomized studies in Kenya and Mexico, shows sizable impacts on school participation from reducing the cost of schooling (including subsidies conditional on school attendance). Randomized studies in Kenya and India demonstrate that school health programs can also increase the quantity of schooling. Finally, several retrospective and randomized studies provide evidence that girls' school attendance is particularly elastic.

Many of the studies based on natural experiments and randomized evaluations are limited in that a central policy concern for developing countries is the *relative cost-effectiveness* of various interventions to increase school participation. Evaluations of cost-effectiveness require knowledge of a program's costs as well as its impact, and comparability across studies requires some common environment. Comparing the impact of PROGRESA's cash transfers and school meals in Kenya is difficult, since it is unclear whether the resulting differences are associated with the type of program or the larger environment. Policymakers are usually left with an unappealing choice between retrospective studies, which allow comparisons of different factors affecting school participation but may yield biased estimates, and randomized evaluations, which yield credible estimates but only for a single program.

One exception to our general inability to compare cost-effectiveness of credible estimates is the recent set of studies conducted in Kenya. Because the Kenyan programs discussed in this section were conducted in similar environments, cost-effectiveness estimates from these randomized evaluations can be readily compared [see Poverty Action Lab (2005)]. Deworming was found to be extraordinarily cost-effective at only $3.50 per additional year of schooling [Miguel and Kremer (2004)]. In contrast, even under optimistic assumptions, provision of free uniforms would cost $99 per additional year of school participation induced [Kremer, Moulin and Namunyu (2002)]. The school meals program, which targeted pre-schoolers rather than primary school age children, cost $36 per additional year of schooling induced [Vermeersch and Kremer (2004)]. This suggests that school health programs may be one cost-effective way of increasing school participation, and the Bobonis and others results for India suggest that this conclusion may be relevant in low-income countries outside Sub-Saharan Africa. More research on school-based health programs in developing countries is needed to confirm this.

5. Empirical results on quality: Factors affecting skills obtained in school

Increases in the quantity of education in developing countries could be jeopardized by weaknesses in the quality of education. The success since 1960 in expanding the quantity of education in most developing countries (see Section 2) has shifted attention to education quality, especially as measured by student performance on academic tests. This section examines recent research that attempts to identify the impact of school and teacher characteristics (Q) on learning in primary and secondary schools in developing countries. The first subsection reviews retrospective studies, and the second subsection examines "natural experiments" and randomized trials. The final subsection concludes.

5.1. Retrospective studies

Many researchers, both economists and other social scientists, have used retrospective data to investigate the impact of school and teacher characteristics on learning. Hanushek's (1995) review of the evidence up to the mid-1990s draws the pessimistic conclusion that there is little empirical evidence that commonly used educational inputs raise students' test scores in developing countries. To support this claim, he presents evidence from 96 studies, summarizing the findings for six educational inputs: teacher–pupil ratio, teacher's education, teacher's experience, teacher's salary, expenditure per pupil, and physical facilities (Table 13). Based on the results in Table 13, Hanushek concludes that, except for physical facilities, measured resources are not systematically related to student performance. Kremer (1995) points out that an alternative interpretation of the studies in Table 13 is that almost all of the school inputs in the table raise test scores (the exception being the teacher–pupil ratio) because the probability is very small that several studies will find a statistically positive coefficient when the real coefficient is zero or negative. Even so, Kremer notes that improvements in student performance may be modest for some inputs and thus may not be worth the costs.

A third and perhaps most reasonable interpretation is that the simultaneous presence of so many significantly positive and negative coefficients suggests that either the studies do not measure the same parameter or the estimates are biased. This would be the case, for example, if there were omitted variable bias in many of these estimates, with some of the estimates having a positive omitted variable bias and some having a negative omitted variable bias. Drawing any definite conclusions from these data is difficult

Table 13

Summary of 96 studies on the estimated effects of resources on education in developing countries

Input	Number of studies	Statistically significant		Statistically insignificant
		Positive	Negative	
Teacher–pupil ratio	30	8	8	14
Teacher's education	63	35	2	26
Teacher's experience	46	16	2	28
Teacher's salary	13	4	2	7
Expenditure per pupil	12	6	0	6
Facilities	34	22	3	9

Source: Hanushek (1995).

without knowing more precisely what the parameters represent (including whether they are structural production functions or reduced form relationships) and what biases may be present in the estimates.

Since the mid-1990s, the most significant recent retrospective studies of the determinants of learning in developing countries are: the research of Ghanaian middle schools by Glewwe and Jacoby (1994); the study of Jamaican primary schools by Glewwe et al. (1995); the investigation of grade 8 students in India by Kingdon (1996); and the paper on Philippines primary schools by Tan, Lane and Coustere (1997).[15] We first review the results of these retrospective studies and then provide a summary of critiques and concerns over why the results of these and other retrospective studies need to be interpreted very cautiously. In the following subsections we will then review evidence from natural experiments and randomized evaluations which allow for more credible estimation of factors impacting school quality.

The study by Glewwe and Jacoby (1994) on Ghana discussed in Section 4 also examined student achievement in 1988–1989, using scores on reading (English) and mathematics in Ghanaian middle schools (grades 7–10). Eighteen school and teacher variables were examined, but most estimated effects were small and statistically insignificant. The only statistically significant teacher variable was teaching experience, but its effect was indirect: it raised children's grade attainment, which increased both reading and mathematics test scores. In contrast, school facilities had larger impacts. The estimated impact (direct plus indirect) of repairing leaking classrooms was an increase of 2.0 standard deviations in reading scores and 2.2 in math scores; this impact

---

[15] A very recent study by Bedi and Marshall (2002) presents regressions on the factors that determine reading (Spanish) and mathematics scores of Honduran primary school students, but the impacts of the teacher and school variables on the scores of second grade students are so different from the impacts on fourth grade students that the authors conclude that they "are unable to identify clear-cut, policy-relevant variables that influence educational achievement" (p. 147) despite very large samples of more than 7,000 second grade students and more than 5,000 fourth grade students.

seems to operate by reducing school closings due to rain. Blackboards also had large estimated impacts (direct plus indirect), raising reading scores by 1.9 standard deviations and mathematics scores by 1.8. Adding a library led to smaller increases, 0.3 standard deviations for reading scores and 1.2 for mathematics scores.

A study by Glewwe et al. (1995) used Jamaican data collected in 1990 to examine the performance of primary school students in reading (English) and mathematics. More than 40 school and teacher characteristics were examined, including pedagogical processes and management structure. Most variables had statistically insignificant effects. The school variables with significantly positive impacts were administration of eye examinations (reading only), teacher training within the past 3 years (mathematics), routine academic testing of students (reading and mathematics), and the use of textbooks in class (reading). Class time devoted to written assignments had a significantly negative impact in both subjects. The size of these estimated impacts (in standard deviations of the test score variable) were lower than those for Ghana. The largest impact is a change from never using textbooks in instruction to using them in almost every lesson, which raises reading scores by 1.6 standard deviations. The smallest is from teacher training: a school in which all teachers were trained is estimated to have mathematics scores 0.7 standard deviations higher than an otherwise identical school with untrained teachers.

Kingdon's (1996) study of India is based on data collected in 1991. Tests in reading (Hindi and English) and mathematics were given to students in "class 8" (grade 8). Kingdon examined five teacher variables (years of general education, years of teacher training, marks received on official teacher exams, years of teaching experience and salary) and three school variables (class size, hours per week of academic instruction and an index of 17 physical characteristics). The teacher variables with significant effects were teacher exam marks, which had significantly positive impacts on both mathematics and reading scores, and teachers' years of education, which had a significantly positive impact on reading scores. Two of the three school variables, the physical characteristics index and time in academic instruction, had significantly positive effects on both reading and mathematics scores. Class size was not significantly correlated with mathematics scores, and was correlated *positively* and significantly with reading scores. The impact of the teacher's exam marks is not robust to attempts to control for selection into schools (an issue further discussed below). These impacts are not particularly large. An additional year of teacher's education raises reading scores by 0.13 standard deviations. Going from zero to all 17 physical facilities (which would be quite costly since this includes toilets, computers, and musical instruments) increases mathematics scores by 0.7 standard deviations and reading scores by 1.0 standard deviations. Adding another hour per week of instructional time raises mathematics and reading scores by only 0.04 and 0.02 standard deviations, respectively.

Tan, Lane and Coustere (1997), using data from 1990 and 1991, investigate the impact of school and teacher variables on the mathematics and reading scores of 2,293 first graders in the Philippines. The five teacher variables examined were academic qualifications (master's degree or not), abstract reasoning ability, scores on subject-based tests, years of teaching experience, and the teacher's attitude toward "innovation in learn-ing". The eight school variables included whether the classroom had sufficient furniture (as judged by the teacher), the pupil–teacher ratio, the value of pedagogical materi-als received from a government program (PRODED), the availability of textbooks and workbooks per pupil, and four variables on the attitudes and practices of the school head. Of the teacher variables, the score on the subject knowledge test in reading had a positive impact on students' reading scores: a one standard deviation increase in the teacher's score raised student learning by 0.12 standard deviations. The same is true for mathematics scores: a one standard deviation increase in the teacher's score raised student learning by 0.10 standard deviations. Turning to school characteristics, the im-pact of textbooks was unstable for both subjects, in some cases significantly negative. More plausibly, the workbook–pupil ratio had significantly positive coefficients for both subjects, so that providing a workbook for each student in schools that have none in-creases math and reading scores by 0.22 and 0.21 standard deviations, respectively. The only other school variable significant at the 5 percent level was the lack of adequate furniture, which was associated with a drop of −0.32 standard deviations in math and −0.29 standard deviations in reading.

In all four studies, most school and teacher variables were not significantly different from zero, although this could reflect both low sample sizes (163 students in Ghana and 355 in Jamaica) and high correlation among many of these variables.[16] While each study did find that one or more teacher variables had statistically significant impacts, they differed widely across the studies. Similarly, three of the four studies find significant impacts of physical inputs (the exception being the Jamaica study), but again the specific inputs vary across the different studies. Part of this variation could reflect differences in the variables available in the data, and part could reflect large socioeconomic differences across countries (e.g., Jamaica has a much higher income than Ghana and India) but, whatever the reason for this variation, the conclusion is that there are no general results regarding which teacher and school variables raise learning in developing countries.

The summary of the results in the previous paragraphs assumes that the estimated impacts of these four retrospective studies are accurate, but the discussion in Section 3 provides many reasons to worry about biases in such estimates. One potential source of bias is that unobserved components of a child's innate ability and motivation, as well as parents' motivation, may be positively correlated with school quality because high-ability children tend to enroll in higher-quality schools [see Glewwe (2002), for a simple behavioral model that demonstrates this point]. This leads to upwardly biased estimates of the impact of school quality variables. The Ghana and India studies used data from an "intelligence" test, the Raven's Coloured Progressive Matrices test, to con-trol for innate ability. The Ghana study concedes that this test measures not only innate

---

[16] Although the sample size in the India study was larger, with 902 students, students are concentrated in 30 schools, which limits variation in school characteristics. The Philippines study has by far the largest sample, with 2,293 students in 110 schools.

ability (however defined) but also reflects environmental influences, including time in school. It used a simple "family fixed effects" procedure to extract what is probably a cleaner estimate of innate ability from the Raven's test, but this method relies on several simplistic assumptions. The India study used the Raven's test score directly, without any refinement, and the Jamaica and Philippines studies had no variables to control for child innate ability. One of the four studies, the one on India, attempted to control for child motivation as a factor distinct from innate ability. Regarding parents' motivation and ability to help their children, none of these studies goes beyond the common practice of using mother's and father's years of education. Three of the four studies (the exception being the Philippines study) use standard selectivity correction methods (primarily to account for choices among different types of schools). Although this may reduce bias caused by a variety of unobserved variables, including innate ability, these methods may be sensitive to functional form assumptions. They may also yield misleading results if factors assumed to influence choice of school such as distance from school interact with factors that can affect learning such as child ability or household income.

Another potential problem is bias due to omitted school and teacher quality variables. If unobserved school and teacher variables are positively correlated with observed school and teacher variables, the estimated impacts on the observed variables will tend to be biased upward. At first glance, all four studies seem to minimize this problem by including large numbers of school and teacher variables. The original Ghana study used 18 school variables [Glewwe and Jacoby (1992)], and the Jamaica study had 42, including variables on pedagogical techniques and "school organization, climate and control". The India study used data on about 24 variables, although 17 were aggregated into a single index, and the Philippines study used 13 variables. Yet some variables, such as teacher motivation, are inherently difficult to measure and thus are not used in any of these studies (unless the variable on teacher "attitude toward innovation in teaching" used in the Philippine study reflects teacher motivation). Thus, the large number of school variables used does not necessarily avoid bias due to omitted school and teacher characteristics.

A third potential problem is sample selection bias. In many developing countries, some children never attend school, grade repetition is common, and a substantial fraction of children drop out of school after only a few years. As explained in Section 3, if weak students are less likely to drop out of high quality schools, the impact of school quality could be underestimated (unless student ability is adequately measured). Biases can also arise due to the choices parents make regarding the schools their children attend and actions parents may take to change those schools, since this may also cause child and household variables to be correlated with unobserved components of school quality. Each of these studies attempted to address at least some of these problems. Although the sample size in the India study was larger, with 902 students, students are concentrated in 30 schools, which limits variation in school characteristics. The Philippines study has by far the largest sample: 2,293 students in 110 schools. The India study appeals to the Ghana study for evidence that selection of students (in terms of "survival" to higher grades) does not matter. It does address selection into public and private schools but without explaining how the selection term is identified. The efforts to deal with selection bias are better in the Ghana and Jamaica studies. Both explain the identification strategy (the identifying variables are characteristics of the school not chosen), and the Ghana study accounts for sample selection effects due to delayed enrollment and dropping out (using a similar identification strategy). In both cases, controlling for sample selection has little impact on the results, but this is not the case in the India study. While bias due to school selection is small in two of the three studies, results from more countries are needed before concluding that this problem is not serious.

A fourth potentially serious problem is measurement error in the regressors. Only one of the four studies, the Philippines study, addresses this issue; the other three do not mention it. The Philippines study found evidence of measurement error in the textbook and workbook variables and used, as instruments, textbooks and workbooks in other subjects. A potential downside of this approach is that books in one subject could affect the scores in other subjects, violating the exclusion restrictions. Measurement error in other school and teacher variables is assumed to be unimportant. Yet a plausible case can be made that measurement error is a serious problem: most such errors are probably random, so that the true effects are likely to be underestimated. This may explain why in each study most of the teacher and school variables were insignificant.

A final potential problem is that school and teacher characteristics could be correlated with the error term in estimates of Equations (1), (4) or (8) if governments build schools or allocate resources to schools based on unobserved community characteristics. This is the problem of endogenous program placement, discussed in Section 3. None of these four retrospective studies explicitly addresses this issue, although, arguably, the selection correction methods for school choice decisions may reduce such biases.

This review of conventional studies leads to several conclusions. First, many studies suffer from multiple estimation problems. Second, recent studies have made some progress, but many problems remain. In particular, they use more sophisticated econometric methods, or show an awareness of many of the potential estimation problems, but they have not overcome all of them. Third, three problems are difficult to resolve in conventional studies that attempt to estimate the impact of school characteristics on student achievement: omitted school characteristics, unobserved characteristics of children and their households, and measurement error in school variables. Regarding the first problem, although the Ghana, Jamaica, India and Philippines studies included large numbers of school characteristic variables in their regressions, other important, but hard to observe, characteristics such as teacher motivation may be highly correlated with the variables that are observed. This will lead to biased estimates. Some results seem counterintuitive; for example, the most important single school characteristic in the Ghana study was leaking roofs. Perhaps the underlying relationship is that more motivated teachers, principals, and parents were more likely to keep the building in good repair. The inability to observe certain child and household characteristics such as the child's innate ability and parental tastes for education also leaves lingering doubts. Finally, it is likely that school variables are measured with a large amount of error – examples have been presented for Tanzania (distance to schools) and the Philippines (books per pupil).

Random measurement error could explain why these variables are often statistically insignificant.

In the past few years, two new approaches have been used to investigate how school characteristics affect student achievement, natural experiments and randomized evaluations.

5.2. Natural experiments

In this subsection we examine studies that use "natural" variation in a school characteristic that is plausibly uncorrelated with other determinants of child learning to assess the impact of school quality on performance.[17]

Before asking which characteristics of schools affect learning, the first question is "Do schools affect learning at all?" Gould, Lavy and Paserman (2004) shed light on this question using data on Ethiopian Jews brought to Israel on an overnight airlift ("Operation Solomon") in 1991. Gould and his coauthors argue that sorting the refugees into absorption centers and initial schooling environment was random and can be considered exogenous to both family background and parental decisions. According to the authors, this creates a natural experiment that can be used to study the impact of primary school environments on secondary school outcomes. They find that attending an elementary school with a good mathematics program (as measured by grade 4 and 5 standardized test scores prior to the arrival of the Ethiopian emigrants) reduced students' probability of dropping out of high school from 10 percent to 4.9 percent and increased passing rates on high school matriculation exams by 26 percent. The authors note that attending elementary schools with good verbal programs (also measured by grades 4 and 5 standardized test scores) did not improve most high school outcomes. They conjecture that this was because the Ethiopian students were learning Hebrew in separate classes with inexperienced teachers. It is important to note that although the authors control for observed community characteristics, it is difficult to isolate the effect of the quality of elementary school from other potentially unobservable characteristics of the students and parents in the community.

Since teachers account for the bulk of school spending, understanding the impact of class size on learning is critical. The Case and Deaton (1999) analysis of South Africa, discussed above, also examined test scores. They found that decreasing the student–teacher ratio from 40 to 20 raises students' reading test scores (conditional on years of school attendance) by an amount equivalent to the impact of two additional years of schooling. In contrast, there was no significant impact on mathematics scores. However, in interpreting the results of this study one must keep in mind the caveats discussed above in Section 4.2.

---

[17] See Rosenzweig and Wolpin (2000) for a thorough discussion of "natural" natural experiments, i.e., natural experiments whose parameters of interest are identified by date of birth, twin births, gender of newborn child or siblings and weather. The issues raised in that paper also apply to "less natural" experiments, and most of the natural experiments discussed here are of the "less natural" type.

A recent study of class size based on a natural experiment is that of Angrist and Lavy (1999), who examine the impact of class size on student academic performance in Israel. A rule proposed by Moses Maimonides, a twelfth century Talmudic scholar, stipulates that class size should not exceed 40 students, and a form of this rule is used in Israel today. The limits on class size determined by this rule lead to actual class sizes that vary nonmonotonically with total enrollment in a given grade, providing an unusually credible instrumental variable to get around the problem that class size may be correlated with unobserved determinates of student learning. The authors use data from the early 1990s on a national test for Israeli third, fourth and fifth graders. Most of the data, and the analysis, are at the classroom level. For each grade, the sample is approximately 2,000 classrooms from about 1,000 schools.

The only explanatory variables used by Angrist and Lavy are class size, the percentage of disadvantaged students in the school (averaged over all grades), and total enrollment for the grade. Maimonides' rule generates a zigzag relationship between class size and total school enrollment. In grades with an enrollment of 40 or less, class size will equal total enrollment. When total enrollment hits 41, the class must be split into two, so that class size falls abruptly – class size is half of total enrollment for grades with 41–80 students. When total enrollment hits 81 a third teacher must be hired, and class size falls again. This zigzag relationship between total enrollment and class size allows the authors to create an instrument for class size that is not highly correlated with total enrollment, so they can include total enrollment and its square as additional regressors.[18]

A potential problem with the estimation strategy is that some parents may know how Maimonides' rule is applied, and those with high tastes for child education may transfer their children out of schools where that rule leads to large classes. This could cause correlation between unobserved parental tastes for child education and the instrumental variable used to predict class size. The authors argue that this bias should be small since most Israeli parents would not want to transfer their child into another school or switch the child from a secular to a religious school to take advantage of smaller class sizes. Angrist and Lavy find a significantly negative impact of class size on the reading and mathematics scores of fifth graders. The estimated effects of a one standard deviation decrease in class size (a reduction of 6.5 pupils) are increases in reading scores of 0.2–0.5 standard deviations and in mathematics, scores of 0.1–0.3 standard deviations (the range reflects differences in the sample and in the other covariates). The effects on fourth graders are less precisely estimated. Sometimes they are significantly negative for reading scores, but for mathematics scores the effects are all insignificant. For third graders, all estimated impacts are insignificant; the authors suggest that this may reflect difficulty in measuring a presumably cumulative effect at lower grades. They also point

---

[18] Some estimates are restricted to students in schools whose total enrollments are either slightly above or slightly below these "break points". This smaller sample is known as the discontinuity sample, and the results are similar to those for the full sample.

out that testing conditions for the third graders were different from those for fourth and fifth graders.

A final recent paper on education that could be interpreted as a natural experiment on school inputs is by the same authors, also on Israel, Angrist and Lavy (2002). The authors investigate whether providing computers for pedagogical use in classrooms, *computer-aided instruction* (CAI), increased learning in reading (Hebrew) and mathematics among fourth and eighth graders in Israel. The data are from about 200 schools in 1996, 2 years after the introduction of a program that gave Israeli schools funds to purchase computers. The full data include 4,779 fourth graders for math (but only 3,689 for Hebrew) and about 3,200 eighth graders for both subjects.

The authors first present OLS and 2SLS results that are not based on any natural experiment. The OLS results are mostly insignificant, although for some specifications the use of computers appears to have a negative impact on grade 8 math scores. The 2SLS estimates use funding from the Tomorrow-98 program, begun in 1994, under which two thirds of the schools received funding for computers. This instrument had explanatory power for use of computers only for fourth grade students, so 2SLS estimates could not be done for grade 8. The results for fourth grade students show small reductions in the reading and math scores from the use of computers, but only the math score effects are statistically significant (and only for some specifications).

The use of funding from the Tomorrow-98 program as an instrument may be problematic, because local communities (towns) had to apply to the program to receive funding, and those that did apply were required to submit a priority ranking for the schools in their community. Thus, if schools that performed poorly were given higher priority, and other regressors in the second stage estimates do not account for all of this poor performance, this instrument will be correlated with the error term in the second stage equation. The authors present evidence that this is not the case, but they also devise an estimation method that uses information on how the ranking affected the probability of receiving program funding. The assumption behind this method is that the ranking variable can be used in two ways. It is assumed that any correlation between the ranking variable and the error term in the second regression is adequately controlled for by including a quadratic specification of that variable in the second stage equation, while the relation between the ranking variable and receipt of funds from the Tomorrow-98 program is sufficiently nonlinear and irregular that the prediction of receipt of funding based on the ranking variable is not completely collinear with the quadratic specification of that variable (and thus can serve as an instrument for use of computers). The validity of this method is debatable since it essentially achieves identification using functional form assumptions. The paper shows that the same results are found with this estimator; there is no evidence that computers improve learning, and in one specification they appear to reduce learning.

Angrist and Lavy (1997) study the effect of changing the language of instruction on test scores and returns to schooling in Morocco.[19] To reaffirm independence from

---

[19] A recent paper on Tanzania and Kenya by Miguel (2003) provides one example of how public schools affect the cohesiveness of a nation. Miguel finds that nation-building policies (including the adoption of

colonial rule and promote nationalism, the language of instruction of Moroccan sixth graders was switched from French to Arabic in 1983. The authors use the sharp change in the language of instruction as a natural experiment to identify the relation between language skills and earnings. They find that the Arabization program reduced returns to secondary education by 20 percent and that the main mechanism was a significant decline in French writing skills. However, the results of this study should be interpreted with caution since the evaluation was done soon after the change, so the results may partially reflect a temporary process of adjustment as workplaces were caught with older cohorts educated in one system and younger cohorts educated in another. Moreover, teachers may have had trouble adjusting to the change in language.

5.3. Randomized evaluations

Jamison et al. (1981) conducted a randomized trial in Nicaragua in which 48 first-grade classrooms received radio mathematics instruction, 20 received mathematics work-books, and 20 served as a comparison group. After 1 year, on mathematics tests the radio students scored more than one standard deviation higher, and the workbook students about a third of a standard deviation higher, than students in the control group. Both differences were highly statistically significant.

Three of the Kenya studies discussed in Section 4 also examine student academic achievement. As noted in Section 4, a package of assistance including uniforms, text-books, and school construction led to a tremendous increase in class size as students were attracted from neighboring schools and dropout rates fell. There is no evidence that the combination package of increased class size and more nonteacher inputs led to a change in test scores. These data are consistent with several hypotheses. One hypothesis is that textbooks have a strong positive impact on learning, but this was offset because of the increase in class size. Another is that neither textbooks nor class size had much impact on test scores. However, as seen below, provision of textbooks in the same area of Kenya had very little effect on test scores, suggesting that the change in class size brought about by this program also had little effect.

Glewwe, Kremer and Moulin (2006) find no evidence that provision of official Kenyan government textbooks increased scores for the typical student. However, they do find evidence that textbooks led to higher test scores for the subset of students who scored well on a pretest. The authors note that English, the medium of instruction in Kenyan schools and the language in which textbooks were written, was the third language for most pupils, and cite evidence that many pupils had difficulty reading the books. As discussed further below, there is reason to think that the Kenyan curriculum is not appropriate for the typical student in rural areas.

Swahili as a national language) have allowed ethnically diverse areas in Tanzania to achieve considerably better local public good outcomes, including primary school funding, than their counterparts in Kenya.

The third Kenya study discussed in Section 4, Miguel and Kremer (2004), examined the impact of deworming medicine not only on the quantity of schooling but also on test scores. A priori, the impact on learning may be small because this intervention raised attendance rates by about 5 percentage points for 2 years, which implies attending school only 20 additional days over 2 years. Moreover, the impact on learning per day in school may also be small because very few cases of severe infection were reported. Indeed, the authors find that the deworming treatment had no effect at all on students' test scores after 2 years.

A third Kenyan study, not discussed above, is Glewwe et al. (2004). It examined flip charts: large poster-sized charts with instructional material that can be mounted on walls or placed on easels. This intervention, which was not examined in Section 4 because it did not evaluate the impact of flip charts on any indicators of the quantity of schooling, covered 178 primary schools, half of them randomly selected to receive flip charts covering science, mathematics, geography and health. Despite a large sample size and 2 years of follow-up data, the estimated impact of flip charts on student test scores is very close to zero and completely insignificant. In contrast, several conventional OLS estimates, which may suffer from many of the problems described in Section 3.2, show impacts as large as 0.2 standard deviations, 5–10 times larger than the estimates based on randomized trials.

A remedial education program in urban India, focused on improving the learning environment in public schools, appears to have increased test scores at a low cost. Banerjee et al. (2004) conducted a randomized evaluation of a 2-year remedial education program in Mumbai and Vadodara, India. The remedial education program is run by a collaboration between a local NGO and the Indian government, and hires (at a yearly cost of only US$5 per child) young women from the community to teach basic literacy and numeracy skills to children who reach grade 3 or 4 without mastery of some basic competencies. On average, the program increased test scores by 0.14 standard deviations in the first year and 0.28 in the second year. The gains were largest for children at the bottom of the distribution, which is unusual for educational programs. Results were similar in both grade levels and in two different cities. The authors note that this program would be several times more cost-effective than hiring new teachers. The success of this program suggests that students were being poorly served by the existing education system.

Finally, Banerjee et al. (2004) recently conducted a randomized evaluation of a computer-assisted learning (CAL) program in India and found much more positive results than those from the computer-assisted learning program in Israel [Angrist and Lavy (2002)]. The idea of using computers in schools seems particularly promising in areas where both the number of qualified teachers and the quality of employed teachers is notoriously poor. The Indian CAL program took advantage of a donation by the state government of four computers to each municipal primary school in Vadodara and gave each child in the fourth standard (grade) 2 hours of shared computer time to play educational games that reinforced mathematical concepts (ranging from standard 1 to standard 3 levels). The program was found to be quite effective, with average mathematics score increases of 0.36 standard deviations in the first year and 0.51 standard deviations in the second year. The program was equally effective across student ability levels.

5.4. Summary

Policymakers are keen to know the likely impacts on student academic achievement of various policy interventions, but retrospective studies offer only limited guidance. Even the best retrospective studies suffer from serious estimation problems, the most serious being omitted variable bias with respect to school and teacher characteristics, unobserved child and household characteristics that are correlated with observed school and teacher variables, and measurement error in school and teacher data. This has turned attention in recent years to many studies based on natural experiments and randomized trials.

Evidence from recent natural experiments in middle-income countries suggests that increases in school resources (as measured by the student–teacher ratio) raise academic achievement on reading tests (but not math tests) among black students in South Africa. Studies using Israeli data indicate that reducing class size raises reading scores and (less often) math scores and that providing computers has no effect on academic performance.

Finally recent randomized trials offer evidence from some relatively poor developing countries. In Nicaragua, workbooks and radio instruction had significant impacts on pupils' math scores, and the impact of radio education was particularly high. (Ironically, radio education was never implemented in Nicaragua after this study demonstrated its effectiveness.) Provision of textbooks in Kenya had a little effect on academic tests; the only effect of textbooks was among the better students (most likely because the textbooks were too difficult for many students). Evidence from Kenya also suggests little impact on test scores of reductions in class size, flip charts and deworming medicine, although school meals were found to have positive impacts on test scores as long as teachers were well trained. A remedial education program in urban India, focused on improving the learning environment in public schools, appears to have increased test scores at a low cost. Finally, a computer-assisted learning program in India suggests that such programs have potential in developing countries. The findings on radio education in Nicaragua and computer instruction in India suggest that technologies that help substitute for weak teachers may be particularly helpful.

While these natural experiments and randomized trials are beginning to build a database of results that are less likely to suffer from the estimation problems that plague retrospective studies, a much larger set of results is needed before general conclusions can be drawn for policymakers. However, one interpretation of these results is that in many developing countries, the most effective means of improving school quality may be through addressing the problem of weak teaching. The remedial education program in urban India, the radio mathematics program in Nicaragua, and the computer instruction program in India all provided inputs which addressed the problem of weak teaching, whereas programs which provided inputs that were dependent on use by the teachers themselves (such as the flipcharts and, to some extent, the textbook program in Kenya) were less effective.

Below we discuss the problem of incentives and education systems more broadly.

6. Education systems, the political economy of education, and reform initiatives

The studies reviewed in Sections 4 and 5 considered education policies that consisted primarily of direct changes in educational inputs available in the classroom such as textbooks, blackboards and other physical supplies, new schools and repairs of existing ones, and more and better trained teachers. In terms of the analytical framework presented in Section 3, these policies directly change the characteristics of schools ($\mathbf{Q}$), the prices of educational inputs ($\mathbf{P}$), or both. Thus the studies discussed in Section 4 were attempts to estimate Equation (2) and the studies in Section 5 were attempts to estimate Equations (1), (4), or both. Yet many education policies do not directly attempt to change the classroom environment but instead change the fundamental institutional arrangements in the education system such as incentives for teachers and financing arrangements. These changes should affect what happens in the classroom and, through this, learning. The impacts of such policies on the quantity and the quality of schooling are depicted in Equations (7) and (8) in Section 3.

6.1. Institutional issues and problems

Education systems in developing countries face many challenges. In some cases, resources intended for education are diverted for other purposes. Teachers may be paid but nonetheless are absent from their classrooms, and while funds may be budgeted for inputs such as textbooks those textbooks may never reach the students. Second, financing distortions may imply the funds spent on education are often allocated inefficiently. For example, spending on salaries relative to nonsalary inputs is inefficiently high, and many local communities are not in control of their own budget and thus cannot reallocate resources to fit local needs. Third, the curriculum used in many schools is inappropriate for the typical child due to an elite orientation of many curricula.

In examining the education finance system, it cannot be assumed that resources are being used, and personnel deployed, in accordance with official budgets. Reinikka and Svensson (2004) examine a program launched in Uganda in 1991 that provided a per-student grant to cover schools' nonwage expenditures, using district education offices as distribution channels. The 250 schools surveyed over a 5-year period (1991–1995) received on average only 13 percent of the grants, based on the authors' comparison of the disbursed flows from the central government and the schools' records of resources received. It is not clear whether the funds were stolen, used for other purposes within or outside the education system, or simply not disbursed. Reinikka and Svensson argue that they were probably used to finance the local political machinery. The extent to which such diversion of education funds occurs in other developing countries is unknown. The program was new at the time of the original study, and Reinikka and Svensson find considerable improvement after the introduction of improved budgetary procedures and steps to publicize the program to local schools.

Most educational spending is on teacher salaries. Teachers are usually in a strong position to ensure that these funds reach them, but this does not necessarily mean that teachers are in the classroom. A recent study by Chaudhury et al. (2006) reports survey results in which enumerators made surprise visits to primary schools in Bangladesh, Ecuador, India, Indonesia, Peru, and Uganda and recorded whether teachers were present (Table 12). Averaging across the countries, about 19 percent of teachers were absent. The authors found that absence is not typically concentrated among a small number of frequently absent providers, but seems rather to be fairly widespread.

Absence rates across Indian states varied from 15 percent in Maharashtra to 42 percent in Jharkhand. Both cross-country [Chaudhury et al. (2006)] and cross-state within India [Kremer et al. (2006)] analyses suggest absence rates are generally higher in poorer regions: doubling national- or state-level per-capita income (PPP-adjusted) is associated with absence rates that are 5.8 percentage points lower. Proxies for salary levels and intensity of community monitoring are not robust predictors of absence. Higher-ranking and more powerful providers, such as headmasters, are absent more often than lower-ranking ones. The relationship between absence and contractual terms for teachers seems more complicated than often hypothesized. Community managed schools and schools managed by the central ministry have similar absence rates. Contract teachers' absence rates are typically similar to those of regular civil servants, and sometimes considerably higher. In India, where the authors examined absence rates in private schools, the study found that they were similar to those in public schools, but considerably lower than those of public schools in the same village. However, private school teachers and contract teachers are often paid much less than civil servants, which will enter into any judgment about the cost effectiveness of these teachers.

While high absence rates in some developing countries may reflect a variety of factors, including the prevalence of infectious diseases such as malaria and AIDS, these unavoidable absences are unlikely to account for all absences. Glewwe, Ilias and Kremer (2004) found that in a region of Kenya with 20 percent teacher absenteeism, staff at a nonprofit organization working in the same area had absence rates of only 6.3 percent.

A second basic institutional problem is that even when the allocated funds are spent on education, they may be used inefficiently. Pritchett and Filmer (1999) argue that policymakers do not choose inputs solely to maximize the production of educational outputs but also try to provide rents to teachers. The authors argue that several studies have found that the marginal product per dollar of inputs not directly valued by teachers (such as textbooks and infrastructure) are 10–100 times higher than that of inputs valued by teachers such as salaries and class size [World Bank (1996), Harbison and Hanushek (1992)]. They conduct a meta-analysis of educational studies [taken from Fuller and Clarke (1994)], showing that nonteacher inputs have a much higher probability of being statistically significant and of the expected sign than inputs they argue are more likely to appear directly in teacher's utility functions. Though suggestive, the underlying studies may suffer from many of the biases discussed in Section 3. One could easily imagine that coefficients on individual nonteacher inputs are picking up a much broader set of omitted inputs. Another caveat is that, in the absence of direct evidence, it is not clear that teachers care more about class size than infrastructure or textbooks – they may also like having electricity and school buildings that do not leak.

A third issue is that in many developing countries, educational systems are oriented towards elites. As we discussed in Section 2, per-pupil expenditures in most developing countries are much higher for tertiary (post-secondary) students than for primary and secondary students. Another manifestation of this elite orientation is that in many developing countries there is a mismatch between the curriculum and the typical student. Many educational systems in developing countries are highly centralized (certainly compared to the educational system in the US), and to the extent that policymakers are often members of elite groups, it is not surprising that the chosen curricula are often much more suitable for advanced students than for the typical student. For example, Glewwe, Kremer and Moulin (2006) provide evidence from Kenya that increasing availability of official textbooks raised test scores for the top two quintiles of students (as measured by initial academic achievement) but had no effect on either test scores or dropout and repetition rates of average and below average students. Indeed, the authors found that the typical median student in grades 3, 4 and 5 could not read the English textbooks designed for those grades. When curricula are set too far beyond the level of the average student, too many students fall behind, and lose the ability to follow. The results of the evaluation of a remedial education program in India (as discussed in Section 5) suggest that the school system is not taking advantage of opportunities to serve students at the bottom of the distribution there, either [Banerjee et al. (2004)]. The remedial education program was found to have substantial positive impacts on test scores – gains which were largest for children at the bottom of the distribution. There is likely much more heterogeneity in a variety of factors – including student school attendance, teacher absence, educational backgrounds, etc. – among students in less developed countries than there is among students in developed countries. This heterogeneity implies it is difficult to devise a single curriculum suitable for the entire population.

Recognition of the institutional weaknesses of education systems in developing countries has led both policymakers and researchers to shift their focus to policy reforms that attempt to reduce distortions and inefficiencies in the institutional arrangements of education systems. Reform initiatives range from policies that preserve current education governance structures but seek to strengthen links between teachers' pay and students' performance, to decentralizing budget authority so that local communities have more power to manage their resources, to introducing vouchers and other methods to increase school choice. Now, we turn to empirical evidence on each of these reforms.

6.2. Teacher incentives

According to advocates of incentive pay for teachers, teachers in many developed and developing countries face weak incentives, with pay determined almost entirely by educational attainment, training, and experience instead of by performance. In some developing countries, incentives are extremely weak, with no effective sanctions for behavior that would invite disciplinary action in developed countries. Some observers see linking teachers' pay to students' performance as a way to increase teacher effort.

In developed countries, opponents of teacher incentives based on students' test scores argue that, since teachers' tasks are multidimensional and only some aspects are measured by test scores, linking compensation to test scores could cause teaches to sacrifice promoting curiosity and creative thinking in order to teach the skills tested on standardized exams [Holmstrom and Milgrom (1991), Hannaway (1992)]. Another concern is that linking pay to individual teachers' performance could undermine cooperation among teachers. Education experts are therefore generally less sympathetic to individual-based incentives than to school-based incentives, which they feel are more conducive to cooperation among teachers.

The extremely weak teacher-supervision systems in many developing countries raises both the potential benefits and costs of teacher incentives. On one hand, it could be argued that teachers in many developing countries are already teaching to the test, that the first-order problem is to get teachers to show up to work, and hence that teacher incentives are particularly appropriate for developing countries. On the other hand, developing countries with weak systems of teacher accountability may be more prone to attempts by teachers to game incentive systems. In particular, teachers could try to force weak students to drop out so as to avoid bringing down average scores, or they could make it difficult for weak students to enroll in the first place. Empirical evidence on the effectiveness of monetary teacher incentives is scarce, particularly in developing countries. Nevertheless, two recent studies from Israel and Kenya provide some initial, and intriguing, evidence. The first study, by Lavy (2002), evaluates a program in Israel that offered teachers monetary incentives based on their students' achievements in three dimensions: the average number of credits per student, the proportion of students receiving a matriculation certificate (required for college admission), and the school dropout rate. Awards were given at the school level, so that all teachers in a school shared the same award. The program was implemented in 62 nonrandomly selected secondary schools starting in 1995. The incentives took the form of awards on a rank order tournament: only the top three schools, ranked by relative improvement, received a prize.

Lavy's identification strategy is based on the program's selection criteria, which limited participation to schools that were the only school of their kind in a community (religious girls' and boys' Jewish schools, secular Jewish schools, and Arab schools). He compares the results of program schools with control group schools where there are more than one kind of school in the same community. Using a fixed effects estimation procedure, Lavy finds that, after 2 years, the program had a positive and significant effect on two of the three student outcomes evaluated: average credits were 0.7 units higher and the proportion of students sitting for the matriculation exam increased by 2.1 percent. He then interacts the treatment dummy with mother's education and finds that the program mainly affected weaker students.

The findings from Israel are consistent both with the conjecture that incentive pay affects teacher effort and the claim that incentive pay causes teachers to teach more strictly to the test. To distinguish between these two hypotheses not only the effect of the program on test scores must be considered, but also the channels through which this effect occurs. Glewwe, Ilias and Kremer (2004) do this, examining a randomized evaluation of the impact of a teacher incentives program in Kenya on both teacher behavior and test scores. They consider a model in which teachers can invest both in efforts to promote long-run learning and in short-run manipulation of test scores. Data were collected on many types of teacher effort – attendance, homework assignment, pedagogical techniques, and holding extra exam-preparation sessions – and on scores after the end of the program.

The teacher incentive program in Kenya offered teachers prizes based on their schools' average scores on district-wide exams. The program penalized teachers for dropouts by assigning low scores to students who did not take the exam. During the two years the program was in place, student scores increased significantly in treatment schools (0.14 standard deviations above the control group). However, analysis of the Kenyan data suggests that this improvement did not necessarily occur through the channels intended. Teacher attendance and student dropout and repetition rates did not improve, and no changes were found in either homework assignment or pedagogy. Instead, teachers were more likely to conduct test-preparation sessions outside of normal class hours. Data from the year after the program ended show no lasting test score gains, which suggests that the teachers' effort was concentrated in improving short-run outcomes, rather than stimulating long-run learning. The test-score effect was strongest for subject tests on geography, history, and Christian religion, arguably the subjects involving the most memorization. Also consistent with this hypothesis, the program had no impact on dropout rates, but exam participation rose (presumably because teachers wanted to avoid penalties for no-shows at exams).

6.3. Decentralization and local community participation

In response to the failures of centralized school systems, many observers advocate decentralization and community participation [World Bank (2004)]. Local communities arguably have the best knowledge about the needs of their children, strong incentives to monitor the performance of teachers and headmasters, and a comparative advantage in conducting this monitoring. Decentralization reforms are increasingly being adopted. At this point, however, rigorous empirical evidence on their impact is scarce.

The EDUCO program in El Salvador is often cited as an example of the benefits of decentralization. Under the program, school committees are responsible for contracting and removing teachers and closely monitoring their performance and for equipping and maintaining the schools. All of their resources come from the central government and international organizations. An evaluation by Jimenez and Sawada (1999) finds that the program successfully expanded education in poor rural areas (its main objective) and also reduced student absences by 3–4 days in a 4-week period. No effect was found on student achievement. However, credibly identifying the impact of the EDUCO program is very difficult because the program was not implemented in any randomized way. The authors use standard selection correction techniques, and the selection correction term is identified primarily by functional form assumptions. The only variables in the selection equation excluded from the equations of interest are district dummies variables, and the theoretical justification for this exclusion restriction is unclear. Overall, the results are intriguing and intuitively plausible, but more research is needed before making policy recommendations.

Reinikka and Svensson (2003) examine the effect of local community empowerment through an information campaign on delivery of nonwage funds from the central government to schools in Uganda. Using a survey similar to Reinikka and Svensson (2003), the authors calculate that the percentage of the funds from the central government that actually reached the schools increased from 20 percent in 1995 to 80 percent in 2001. The authors argue that the improvement was mainly the result of better monitoring of local officials' handling of resources by the schools, stimulated by an information campaign launched by the government after the results of the 1991–1995 survey came out. Under the campaign, data on monthly capitation grant transfers to districts was published in major newspapers and broadcast on the radio. Exploiting differential access to newspapers across schools, the authors argue that schools with access to newspapers increased their funding on average by 12 percentage points more than schools with no access to newspapers, despite the fact that the two groups had similar funding levels in 1995. Monitoring from the center of the districts was also strengthened. While the fixed effects control for time-independent determinants of funding, this identification strategy cannot rule out the possibility that other features of schools, correlated with newspaper access, could have had an effect on funding in the later period but not earlier. For example, economic development was uneven across Uganda during this period and could have been correlated with newspaper access. It is unclear what caused the large reported increase in funds reaching schools: the authors argue this information campaign was successful through a "bottom-up" approach, but it is unclear whether this or more of a "top down" approach deserves more emphasis, since Uganda had an authoritarian leadership that was strongly committed to reform, and since international donors also played an important role in Uganda at the time in promoting both the original grant program and the survey designed to determine whether funds were reaching schools. The grant program was also relatively new at the time of the original survey, and part of the increase in funds reaching schools may reflect implementation over time.

Overall, more work on the impacts of informational campaigns would be useful. Partly in response to a desire among policymakers to improve the accountability of social services, several ongoing randomized evaluations being led by researchers at the Poverty Action Lab at MIT are studying the impact of information on the quality of education services. In rural Uttar Pradesh, India, Abhijit Banerjee and others are evaluating various strategies designed to empower villages to demand better quality education; one strategy is to provide villagers with information such as the names of local (village) officials responsible for education, the funds available for education, and the number of children in the village who are unable to read. In Sierra Leone, Rachel Glennerster and Edward Miguel are examining how providing communities with information about how many textbooks the communities are meant to receive from the government influences the actual number of government-provided textbooks these communities receive.

Miguel and Gugerty (2005) suggest that the impact of decentralization can vary with the local environment. In Kenya local school committees must raise funds to build schools and provide nonwage inputs, and they do so through school fees and local fundraisers called *harambees*. Miguel and Gugerty argue that communities with high ethnic diversity have major difficulties overcoming free-rider problems in collective action, such as imposing and enforcing sanctions, and therefore have less local school funding and lower quality school facilities than homogeneous ones. Using data on 100 rural primary schools, the authors find that moving from complete ethnic homogeneity to average school-level ethnic diversity is associated with a drop in funding of 20 percent of average local funding.

Kremer, Moulin and Namunyu (2002) examine Kenya's mix of centralized and decentralized control over different aspects of education. They argue that the system creates incentives for misallocation and then test for empirical evidence of misallocation. At independence Kenya adopted an education finance system in which local communities were responsible for raising the resources to build schools, while the central government assigned teachers to schools and paid their salaries once the schools were built. Local communities had to provide nonteacher inputs such as textbooks and chalk, which they typically did by levying school fees. The system blended substantial centralization with elements of local control and school choice. The authors argue that the system suited the interests of the ruling coalition at independence, which drew support from some of the country's more educationally advanced and politically organized regions. The system allocated resources disproportionately to these regions, since they were best placed to build schools. At the same time, it retained central control over teachers, thus avoiding the possibility that local hiring would lead to discrimination against outsiders (which would have hurt the constituents of the ruling coalition). However, the education finance system created an interlocking set of distortions. Local communities had strong incentives to build new schools, because once they had built one, the central government provided the teachers, which absorbed more than 90 percent of the present discounted cost of operating the school. Thus, many small schools, with small classes, were built close together. In the districts studied in the paper, the median distance between primary schools was 1.5 kilometers, and Kenya's average pupil–teacher ratio of 28 in 1998 is much lower than the average of 43 for Sub-Saharan Africa in 2000 (Table 11). The system led to excessive spending on teachers relative to nonteacher inputs. For example, a Ministry of Education survey showed that, on average, 17 primary-school pupils in Kenya shared one textbook.

The education system also created incentives for schools to set high fees and other attendance requirements, which kept many children out of school. Typically, increasing enrollment did not bring any more resources from the central government, because a new teacher was assigned only when class size surpassed 55, and most classes were substantially smaller, at least in the upper grades, given the large number of schools that had been constructed. Setting fees that lead marginal students to drop out eases teacher workload and could potentially help increase the school's average score on the national exams, the main criterion used to judge schools and headmasters.

Empirical evidence of distortions in education systems is provided by the evaluation of an NGO program. In 1994, the NGO selected 14 poor schools and divided them randomly into treatment and comparison groups. For the next 5 years, treatment schools were provided with uniforms, textbooks, and new classrooms. The free uniforms represented a substantial reduction in the cost of schooling. The program schools attracted a large influx of pupils from neighboring schools, increasing average class size by 8.9 students. The combination of larger classes, more nonteacher inputs, and lower schooling costs led to a large expansion in the quantity of education, and no apparent reduction in quality. Students in the seven treatment schools remained enrolled an average of 0.5 years longer and advanced an average of 0.3 grades further than their counterparts in the seven comparison schools. There is no evidence that the combination of larger class sizes and more nonteacher inputs led to different test scores among students originally enrolled in treatment schools than among those originally enrolled in comparison schools. The revealed preferences of the households that transferred their children from other schools into the treatment schools suggest that they were willing to accept an increase in class size of at least 8.9 students in exchange for lower costs and extra nonteacher inputs. The inefficiencies of the current education system are apparent from the fact that the Kenyan government could have financed this package of textbooks, classroom construction, and uniforms using the savings that could be generated from much, much smaller increases in class size than those associated with the program. Overall, this evidence suggests that the details of decentralization are critical. The results do not imply that decentralization is ineffective but suggest that inefficiencies arose in Kenya from a mismatch between decision-making power and financial responsibilities. Local communities had authority to start new schools while covering only a fraction of the cost.

6.4. Vouchers and school choice programs

Perhaps the most fundamental policy reforms are voucher and school choice programs, which provide government funds that students can use to enroll in either public or private schools. A number of studies published in the 1980s and 1990s argue that private schools are much more efficient than public ones. However, the econometric difficulties surrounding such comparisons are formidable.[20] Vouchers have been implemented

---

[20] The studies typically regress children's test scores, and in some cases school expenditures per pupil, on a private–public dummy variable and attempt to correct for selection bias using observed variation in child characteristics and a selection term from prior estimation of the choice between public and private schools. Cox and Jimenez (1991) find that private secondary schools in Colombia and Tanzania have robust advantage

in two Latin American countries, Chile and Colombia, on a much larger scale than voucher programs in the United States.

Angrist et al. (2002) examine the effects on education outcomes of Colombia's voucher program, which offered vouchers to attend private secondary schools to more than 125,000 students from poor urban neighborhoods. In most communities, the demand for vouchers exceeded the supply, so voucher eligibility was determined by a lottery, generating a natural experiment. Data were collected from 1,600 applicants for the vouchers (primarily from Bogota) three years after they had started high school. The sample was stratified so that half those sampled were lottery winners and half were lottery losers. Angrist and his coauthors find that lottery winners were between 15 percent and 20 percent more likely to be in private schools, 10 percent more likely to complete eighth grade, and scored 0.2 standard deviations higher on standardized tests, equivalent to a full grade level. A number of channels could account for the impact of the vouchers. First, lottery winners were more likely to have attended participating private schools, and these schools may be better than public schools. Second, vouchers allowed some pupils who would have attended private schools anyway to attend more expensive schools. Finally, because voucher recipients who failed a grade risked losing vouchers, lottery winners had an incentive to devote more effort to school, and the schools they attended had an incentive not to fail them. The authors also find that vouchers affected noneducation outcomes: winners spent less time working in the labor market than losers and were less likely to marry or cohabit as teenagers. Analysis of the economic returns to the additional schooling attained by winners after 3 years of participating in the program suggests that the benefits likely greatly exceeded the $24 per winner additional cost to the government of supplying vouchers instead of public school places.

Work by Angrist, Bettinger and Kremer (2004) suggests that the vouchers not only had significant effects on the short-run outcomes of their recipients, but that their impact persisted over time. Using administrative records on registration and test scores on a centralized college entrance examination, the authors find the lottery program increased secondary school completion rates by 15–20 percent. Correcting for the greater percentage of lottery winners taking college admissions tests, the program increased test scores by two-tenths of a standard deviation in the distribution of potential test scores. Boys, who have lower scores than girls in this population, show larger test score gains, especially in math.

The analysis of school vouchers in Colombia by Angrist et al. (2002), discussed above, is based on random assignment, and therefore addresses many omitted variable bias concerns. It is important to note that their estimates capture the overall effect of

---

over public schools in test scores and unit costs. However, their results may be sensitive to their identification strategy, which relies on the exclusion restriction that family background and the child's ability do not enter into the test score regression. Using a similar method, and therefore subject to the same caveats, Kingdon (1996) finds that private unaided schools in India have a ratio of cost over test score that is only about half of the corresponding ratios for public schools and private-aided schools.

the voucher program, rather than simply the effect of moving pupils from public to private schools. Because voucher recipients who failed a grade risked losing the vouchers, lottery winners also had increased incentives to devote more effort to school, and the private schools they attended had an incentive not to fail them.

While Angrist et al. (2002) examine the effect of vouchers on participants in voucher programs, such programs may also affect children who do not participate and instead stay in public schools. If more advantaged public school students switch to private schools, and if these students generate positive externalities for their public school peers, the students who remain in public schools might be hurt by vouchers. However, competition from private schools might improve public schools, as argued by Hoxby (2000). The overall effect is therefore an empirical question.

Hsieh and Urquiola (2002) address this question by looking at Chile, which in 1981 began a nationwide school voucher program that gave a fixed per student voucher payment to any participating school, public or private. The main features of the program remain in today's school system; the 20-year program has substantially changed the education market in Chile. When the program started, 22 percent of all students were in private schools; by 1990 this number had risen to 41 percent. These numbers hide a wide cross-sectional variation on the change in private enrollment, however, with highly urbanized, educated, and densely populated areas experiencing a much larger expansion of private schooling. Using fixed effects, Hsieh and Urquiola (2002) argue that higher private enrollment rates negatively affect the relative test scores, repetition rates, and socio-economic status of students in public schools. They also find that higher private enrollment rates did not affect the average outcomes of municipalities. They interpret these results as evidence that the program merely increased sorting rather than adding value to education. However, their identification is problematic, because their fixed effect estimation does not control for time-varying unobserved characteristics and idiosyncratic shocks to schools and municipalities that may be related to private enrollment trends. In particular, it is plausible that people in areas experiencing negative shocks to public schools turned to private schools in response. This would produce the correlations found by Hsieh and Urquiola.

More research is needed to provide a firmer assessment of the impact of voucher programs on nonparticipants. One way to shed light on this would be through randomization evaluations at the level of local communities, which could allow estimation of the total program effect.

Another strand of the literature examines the political economy of school choice. School systems not only teach students skills but also shape their preferences and ideology. In theory, in a public school system, the median voter determines the ideology taught. Under a voucher system, parents might choose to educate their children in schools with an ideology similar to their own, leading to potentially conflict-generating ideological and cultural segregation [Kremer and Sarychev (2000)]. These issues may be particularly important in countries with ethnic diversity.

One reform that may be worth considering is allowing increased choice within the public school system and allocating resources to public schools based on enrollment.

This would create some competition among schools for students and is also likely to be more equitable than current school finance systems which often allocate not budgets, but teacher slots, in proportion to the number of pupils. Since more experienced and better qualified teachers are likely to wind up in better-off areas, allocating teacher slots on a per pupil basis provides more funding for students in richer regions.

6.5. Summary

Many education systems in developing countries are subject to major distortions. The evidence presented in this section suggests that schools in these countries face significant challenges: distortions in educational budgets often lead to inefficient allocation and spending of funds; weak teacher incentives lead to problems such as high rates of teacher absenteeism; and curriculums are often focused excessively on the strongest students and are not well matched with the typical student, especially considering the high rates of teacher and student absenteeism.

Numerous school reform initiatives have been proposed, ranging from programs designed to strengthen links between teacher pay and performance, to reforms to decentralize budget authority, to voucher and school choice programs. Although the evidence is scarce on teacher incentive programs in developing countries, results from Israel suggest that teacher incentives positively and significantly affected student education outcomes (and mainly for weaker students). Results from Kenya suggest that teacher incentives increased teachers' efforts on short-run outcomes (test scores) but not on stimulating long-run learning (through changes in teacher attendance, student dropout rates, or pedagogy). Decentralization programs appear promising, but the results of decentralization policies appear to be very heavily dependent on the details of implementation. Finally, a school choice program in Colombia yielded dramatic benefits for participants, but evidence from voucher programs in Chile as well as numerous developed countries suggests that more research is needed to gauge the generalizability of such program impacts.

7. Conclusions and directions for future research

This section summarizes some of what research has taught us about education in developing countries and then discusses ways that research can help shed light on some of the open questions. In particular it discusses the potential of randomized evaluations to improve knowledge about education in developing countries.

7.1. Conclusions regarding the determinants of education outcomes in developing countries

Despite rapid progress in expanding school enrollment since 1960, many children are still not in school, the quality of education is often low in developing countries, and many education systems are dysfunctional.

As discussed in Section 4, a number of techniques can be used to expand school participation fairly easily. To what extent investing in school quality attracts children to school, however, is unclear. Programs that reduce the cost of schooling or provide attendance incentives (either implicitly through school meals, or explicitly) have sizable impacts on school participation. Randomized evaluations of school-based health programs suggest that, in some situations, these programs can be an extraordinarily cost-effective means of increasing the quantity of schooling attained in developing countries.

Evidence concerning the impact of additional educational inputs is more mixed. In general, retrospective studies suggest that educational inputs have limited impact on improving the quality of schooling in developing countries. However, since even the best retrospective studies suffer from serious estimation problems, attention has turned in recent years to studies based on natural experiments and randomized trials, both of which paint more mixed pictures of the impact of educational inputs. Evidence from recent natural experiments in middle-income countries suggests that reducing class size can raise academic achievement but that providing computers has little effect. Recent randomized trials conducted in low-income countries provide a more mixed picture.

The evidence suggests that the most effective forms of spending are likely to be those that respond to inefficiencies in schooling systems. Providing textbooks written with atypical students in mind will benefit only atypical students, whereas remedial education may be extremely effective in an environment in which many students fall behind and are no longer able to follow teachers' lessons. Providing radio mathematics education or computer-based education may be effective when teachers attend irregularly.

Schools in developing countries face significant institutional problems: distortions in education budgets often result in inefficient allocation and spending of funds; weak teacher incentives lead to problems such as high rates of teacher absenteeism; and, given the difficulties faced by these school systems, curriculums are often inappropriately matched with the level of the typical student. Yet reform initiatives can easily have unintended consequences. The details of these programs are critical for their incentive effects. Governance reforms and allowing school choice appear to hold more promise than simply providing monetary incentives to teachers based on test scores, but much more empirical evidence is needed on the impact of these reforms as well.

As noted in the Introduction, sometimes a false dichotomy is constructed regarding education initiatives in developing countries. Some observers argue that these schools need more money; others emphasize the weaknesses of the school systems and the need for reform. These two views are not, however, mutually exclusive; in fact, both may be true. In settings with highly distorted education systems, some types of spending will have low marginal product while others will have high marginal product. Hence, carefully targeted spending can be extremely productive in such settings.

7.2. Methodological conclusions

We have learned some things about education, but much remains to be learned. This section presents some methodological lessons for future research, drawing on the examples discussed in this chapter.[21]

1. *Estimates from randomized evaluations can be quite different from those drawn from retrospective evaluations*

As seen in the studies of textbooks and flip charts in Kenya, estimates from prospective randomized evaluations can often be quite different from estimated effects in a retrospective framework, suggesting that omitted variable bias is a serious concern [Glewwe et al. (2004)]. Similar disparities between retrospective and prospective randomized estimates arise in studies of the impact of deworming in Kenya [Miguel and Kremer (2004)] and the impact of social networks on take-up of deworming drugs [Miguel and Kremer (2004)]. This is consistent with the findings of Glazerman, Levy and Meyers (2002), who assessed both prospective (experimental) and retrospective (nonexperimental) methods in studies of welfare, job training, and employment service programs in the United States, synthesizing the results of 12 design replication studies. They found that retrospective estimators often produce results dramatically different from randomized evaluations, that the estimated bias is often large, and that they were unable to identify any strategy that could consistently remove bias and still answer a well-defined question.[22] We are not aware of any systematic review of similar studies in developing countries. Future research along these lines would be valuable, since comparative studies can be used to assess the size and prevalence of biases in retrospective estimates. However, when the comparison group for the retrospective portions of these comparative studies is selected ex post, the evaluator may be able to pick from a variety of plausible comparison groups, some of which may have results that match experimental estimates and some of which may not. To address these concerns, future researchers should conduct retrospective evaluations before the results of randomized evaluations are released or conduct blind retrospective evaluations without knowledge of the results of randomized evaluations or other retrospective studies.

2. *Publication bias appears to be substantial with retrospective studies. Randomized evaluations can help address publication bias problems, particularly if institutions are put in place to compile the study results systematically*

There is a natural tendency for positive results to receive a large amount of publicity: agencies that implement programs seek publicity for their successful projects, and

---

[21] This section draws upon the discussion in Duflo and Kremer (2005).

[22] A recent study by Buddlemeyer and Skofias (2003) is not included in the analysis of Glazerman, Levy and Meyers (2002). Buddlemeyer and Skofias use randomized evaluation results as a benchmark to examine the performance of regression discontinuity design (a type of natural experiment) for evaluating the impact of the PROGRESA program on child health and school attendance. In this case, they found the performance of regression discontinuity design to be good.

academics are much more interested in publishing and more able to publish positive results than modest or insignificant results. However, many programs are failures, and publication bias will be substantial if positive results are much more likely to be published. In particular, if comparison groups are defined ex post, as in retrospective studies, researchers who obtain negative results using one potential comparison group may simply try other comparison groups instead. There is evidence of strong publication bias [DeLong and Lang (1992)]. Instrumental variable estimates may be particularly subject to such bias because such estimates tend to have larger standard errors. Ashenfelter, Harmon and Oosterbeek (2000) show strong evidence of publication bias of instrumental variables estimates of the returns to education: on average, estimates with larger standard errors also tend to be larger. This accounts for most of the often-cited result that instrumental estimates of the returns to education are higher than ordinary least squares estimates.

Randomized evaluations are likely less subject to publication bias because they require committing considerable resources in advance to a particular comparison group: once the evaluation is done the results are usually documented and published even if the results suggest quite modest effects or even no effects at all.

However, it is also important to put institutions in place to ensure that negative results are disseminated. Such a system is in place for medical trial results, and creating a similar system for documenting evaluations of social programs would help alleviate the problem of publication bias. For example, donors could require programs to submit the results of their evaluations to a database. Such a database would ideally be readily searchable and would contain numerous types of information that could be useful in interpreting the results (e.g., estimates, sample size, region and time, type of project, cost, cost-benefit analysis, caveats). Over time, such a database could become a basic reference for organizations and governments as they seek project funding.

3. *Randomized evaluations are feasible and can be conducted successfully, although they are labor-intensive. Nongovernmental organizations are well suited to conduct randomized evaluations but will require outside technical assistance and financing*

As is clear from the examples discussed in this chapter, a number of randomized evaluations have been conducted successfully in developing countries. Randomized evaluations are labor-intensive and costly, but no more so than other data collection activities. As the example of the initial PROGRESA program indicates, governments can sometimes conduct randomized evaluations successfully. However, political constraints often make it difficult for governments to randomize their programs, especially as governments are expected to serve their entire populations. For example, "Opportunidades", the urban version of PROGRESA, did not start with a randomized evaluation because of opposition to delaying access to the program for any randomly chosen control group.

Nongovernmental organizations in developing countries may be very well placed to conduct randomized evaluations. Unlike governments, NGOs are not expected to serve entire populations. Also unlike governments, financial and administrative constraints often lead NGOs to phase in programs over time, and randomization will often be the fairest way to of determining the phase-in order. In contrast to developed countries, where NGOs typically do not have sufficient resources to conduct large programs that could serve as a model for public policy, this is not the case in developing countries. Since many NGOs exist and they frequently seek out new projects, NGOs willing to conduct randomized evaluations can often be found. For example, the set of recent studies conducted in Kenya have been carried out through a collaboration with the Kenyan NGO Internationaal Christelijk Steunfonds (ICS) Africa. ICS was keenly interested in using randomized evaluations to see the impact of its programs as well in sharing credible evaluation results with other stakeholders and policymakers. A second example is the collaboration between the Indian NGO Pratham and researchers from the Massachusetts Institute of Technology that led to the evaluations of the remedial education [Banerjee et al. (2000)] and computer-assisted learning programs [Banerjee et al. (2004)]. However, while NGOs are well placed to conduct randomized evaluations, expecting them to finance the research is less reasonable, as the results are global public goods. The evaluations of the ICS deworming programs were made possible by financial support from the World Bank, the Partnership for Child Development, the U.S. National Institutes of Health, and the MacArthur Foundation. In the case of the Indian educational programs, Pratham found a corporate sponsor, India's second-largest bank, ICICI Bank, which was keenly interested in evaluating the impact of the program and helped finance part of the evaluation.

4. *Costs can be reduced and comparability enhanced by conducting a series of evaluations in the same area*

Once evaluation staffs are trained, they can work on multiple projects. Since data collection is the most costly element of these evaluations, cross-cutting the sample can also dramatically reduce costs. For example, many of the programs to increase school participation and learning were implemented in the same area, by the same organization. The teacher incentives [Glewwe, Ilias and Kremer (2004)] and textbook [Glewwe, Kremer and Moulin (2006)] programs were evaluated in the same 100 schools: one group had textbooks only, one had textbooks and incentives, one had incentives only, and one had neither. The effect of the incentive program should thus be interpreted as the effect of an incentive program conditional on half the schools having extra textbooks. Likewise, a computer-assisted learning program was implemented in Vadodara, India, in the same set of schools where the remedial education study was conducted. This approach must consider potential interactions between programs (which can be estimated if the sample is large enough), and may be inappropriate if one program makes the schools atypical. Finally, as discussed in Section 4, another advantage is that conducting a series of studies in the same area (such as the set of studies recently conducted in Kenya) enhances comparability by allowing researchers to compare the cost-effectiveness estimates of different interventions in the same setting.

5. *Randomized evaluations have limitations, but many of those limitations also apply to nonrandomized studies*

Sample selection bias, attrition bias, and spillover effects can affect both randomized and retrospective evaluations. When conducting randomized evaluations, correcting for these limitations is often easier than when conducting retrospective studies.

Sample selection problems could arise if factors other than random assignment influence program allocation. For example, parents may attempt to move their children from a class (or a school) without the program to a class with the program. Conversely, individuals allocated to a treatment group may not receive the treatment (for example, because they decide not to take up the program). Even if randomized methods have been employed and the intended allocation of the program was random, the actual allocation may not be. This problem can be addressed through intention to treat methods or by using random assignment as an instrumental variable for actual assignment. It is much harder to address in retrospective studies, since it is often difficult to find factors that plausibly affect exposure to the program that would not affect education outcomes through other channels.

A second issue affecting both randomized and retrospective evaluations is differential attrition in the treatment and the comparison groups: program participants may be less likely to move or otherwise drop out of the sample than nonparticipants. However, at a minimum, randomized evaluations can use statistical techniques to bound the potential bias and can attempt to track down individuals who drop out of the sample (e.g., administer tests to students who have dropped out of school), which is often not possible with retrospective evaluations.

Third, programs may create spillover effects on untreated people. These spillovers may be physical, as found for the Kenyan deworming program. Deworming interferes with disease transmission and thus makes children in treatment schools (and in schools near treatment schools) less likely to have worms even if they were not themselves given the medicine. Spillovers may also operate through prices. Vermeersch and Kremer (2004) found that provision of meals in some schools leads other schools to reduce school fees. Finally, there might also be learning and imitation effects [Duflo and Saez (2004), Miguel and Kremer (2004)]. If such spillovers are global (e.g., due to changes in world prices), identification of total program impacts will be difficult with any methodology. However, if such spillovers are local, randomization at the group level can allow estimation of the total program effect within groups and can generate sufficient variation in local treatment density to measure spillovers across groups. For example, the solution in the case of the deworming study was to choose the *school* (rather than the pupils within a school) as the unit of randomization and to look at the number of treatment and comparison schools within neighborhoods. Of course, this requires a larger sample size.

One limitation of randomized evaluations is that the evaluation itself may cause the treatment group to change its behavior (the Hawthorne effect) or the comparison group to change its behavior (the John Henry effect). The Hawthorne and John Henry effects are specific concerns for randomized evaluations, but similar effects can occur in other settings. For example, the provision of inputs could temporarily increase morale among students and teachers, which could improve performance. While this would create problems for randomized evaluations, it would also create problems for fixed-effect or difference-in-difference estimates.

A final issue is that the program may generate behavioral responses that would not occur if the program were generalized. For example, children may switch into a school receiving additional inputs. This may affect the original pupils by increasing class size (if class size affects the outcome of interest). This would not be part of a reduced form effect because a nationwide adoption of the policy would not have this effect.

In summary, while randomized evaluation is not a bulletproof strategy, the potential sources of bias are well known and can often be corrected. This stands in contrast to biases of most other types of studies, where the bias due to the nonrandom treatment assignments often cannot be signed or estimated.

A challenge for the future is to integrate randomized evaluations with theory to shed light on issues of more general interest. In particular, evaluating various school reform initiatives is likely to shed light on more general issues of incentive and political economy.

Acknowledgements

We would like to thank Patricia Cortes, Hai-Anh Hoang Dang, Lynn Johnson, Muthoni Ngatia, Courtney Umberger, Heidi Williams, and Meng Zhao for outstanding research assistance. Some of the material in this chapter draws on Glewwe (2002), Kremer (2003) and Duflo and Kremer (2005). We thank Rachel Glennerster, Eric Hanushek and Kathleen Lynch for comments.

References

Alderman, H., Kim, J., Orazem, P. (2003). "Design, evaluation, and sustainability of private schools for the poor: The Pakistan urban and rural fellowship school experiments". Economics of Education Review 22, 265–274.

American Psychological Association (1995). Intelligence: Knowns and Unknowns. American Psychological Association, Washington, DC.

Angrist, J., Bettinger, E., Bloom, E., King, E., Kremer, M. (2002). "Vouchers for private schooling in Colombia: Evidence from a randomized natural experiment". American Economic Review 92 (5), 1535–1558.

Angrist, J., Bettinger, E., Kremer, M. (2004). "Long-term consequences of secondary school vouchers: Evidence from administrative records in Colombia". Working Paper 79. BREAD (Bureau for Research in Economic Analysis of Development).

Angrist, J., Lavy, V. (1997). "The effect of a change in the language of instruction on the return to schooling in Morocco". Journal of Labor Economics 15 (1), S48–S76.

Angrist, J., Lavy, V. (1999). "Using Maimonides' rule to estimate the effect of class size on children's academic achievement". Quarterly Journal of Economics 114 (2), 533–576.

Angrist, J., Lavy, V. (2002). "New evidence on classroom computers and pupil learning". The Economic Journal 112 (482), 735–786.

Ashenfelter, O., Harmon, C., Oosterbeek, H. (2000). "A review of estimates of schooling/earnings relationship, with tests for publication bias". Working Paper 7457. NBER.

Asian Development Bank (1999). "Education costs and financing in the Philippines". Technical Background Paper 2 for the 1998 Philippines Education Sector Study. Asian Development Bank, Manila.

Banerjee, A., Cole, S., Duflo, E., Linden, L. (2004). "Remedying education: Evidence from two randomized experiments in India". Mimeo. MIT.

Banerjee, A., Jacob, S., Kremer, M., Lanjouw, J., Lanjouw, P. (2000). "Promoting school participation in rural Rajasthan: Results from some prospective trials". Mimeo. MIT.

Barro, R. (1991). "Economic growth in a cross-section of countries". Quarterly Journal of Economics 106 (2), 407–443.

Barro, R., Lee, J.-W. (2001). "International data on educational attainment: Updates and implications". Oxford Economic Papers 53 (3), 541–563.

Bedi, A.S., Marshall, J.H. (2002). "Primary school attendance in Honduras". Journal of Development Economics 69 (1), 129–153.

Behrman, J. (1999). "Labor markets in developing countries". In: Ashenfelter, O., Card, D. (Eds.), Handbook of Labor Economics, vol. 3B. Elsevier, Amsterdam.

Behrman, J., Rosenzweig, M., Taubman, P. (1994). "Endowments and the allocation of schooling in the family and in the marriage market: The twins experiment". Journal of Political Economy 102 (6), 1131–1174.

Bils, M., Klenow, P. (2000). "Does schooling cause growth?". American Economic Review 90 (5), 1160–1183.

Bleakley, H. (2002). "Disease and development: Evidence from hookworm eradication in the American south". Mimeo. MIT.

Bobonis, G., Miguel, E., Sharma, C. (2004). "Iron deficiency anemia and school participation". Mimeo. University of California, Berkeley.

Bommier, A., Lambert, S. (2000). "Education demand and age at school enrollment in Tanzania". Journal of Human Resources 35 (1), 177–203.

Bray, M. (1999). The Shadow Education System: Private Tutoring and Its Implications for Planners. International Institute for Educational Planning, Paris.

Bruns, B., Mingat, A., Rakotomalala, R. (2003). Achieving Universal Primary Education by 2015: A Chance for Every Child. The World Bank, Washington, DC.

Buddlemeyer, H., Skofias, E. (2003). "An evaluation on the performance of regression discontinuity design on PROGRESA". Discussion Paper 827. Institute for Study of Labor.

Campbell, D.T. (1969). "Reforms as experiments". American Psychologist 24, 407–429.

Case, A., Deaton, A. (1999). "School inputs and educational outcomes in South Africa". Quarterly Journal of Economics 114 (3), 1047–1085.

Case, A., Paxson, C., Ableidinger, J. (2003). "The education of African orphans". Mimeo. Princeton University.

Chaudhury, N., Hammer, J., Kremer, M., Muraldhiran, K., Rogers, H. (2006). "Missing in action: Teacher and health worker absence in developing countries". Journal of Economic Perspectives 20 (1), 91–116.

Chin, A. (2002). "The returns to school quality when school quality is very low: Evidence from operation blackboard in India". Mimeo. University of Houston.

Coalition for Health and Education Rights (2002). "User fees: The right to education and health denied". CHER, New York.

Cox, D., Jimenez, E. (1991). "The relative effectiveness of private and public schools: Evidence from two developing countries". Journal of Development Economics 34, 99–121.

Das, J., Dercon, S., Habyarimana, J., Krishnan, P. (2004). "When can school inputs improve test scores?". Policy Research Working Paper 3217. World Bank, Washington, DC.

DeLong, J.B., Lang, K. (1992). "Are all economic hypotheses false?". Journal of Political Economy 100 (6), 1257–1272.

Drèze, J., Kingdon, G. (2001). "School participation in rural India". Review of Development Economics 5 (1), 1–33.

Duflo, E. (2001). "Schooling and labor market consequences of school construction in Indonesia: Evidence from an unusual policy experiment". American Economic Review 91 (4), 795–814.

Duflo, E., Kremer, M. (2005). "Use of randomization in the evaluation of development effectiveness". In: Pitman, G., Feinstein, O., Ingram, G. (Eds.), Evaluating Development Effectiveness. Transaction Publishers, New Brunswick, NJ.

Duflo, E., Saez, E. (2004). "The role of information and social interactions in retirement plan decisions: Evidence from a randomized experiment". Quarterly Journal of Economics 118, 815–842.

Easterly, W. (2001). The Elusive Quest for Growth: Economists' Adventures and Misadventures in the Tropics. MIT Press, Cambridge, MA.

Evans, D., Miguel, E. (2004). "Orphans and schooling in Africa: A longitudinal analysis". Working Paper 056. Harvard Center for International Development.

Foster, A.D., Rosenzweig, M.R. (1996). "Learning by doing and learning from others: Human capital and technical change in agriculture". Journal of Political Economy 103 (6), 1176–1209.

Frankenberg, E., Beegle, K., Thomas, D., Suriastini, W. (1999). "Health, education, and the economic crisis in Indonesia". Unpublished manuscript.

Fuller, B., Clarke, P. (1994). "Raising school effects while ignoring culture? Local conditions and the influence of classroom tools, rules, and pedagogy". Review of Educational Research 64 (1), 119–157.

Gertler, P., Glewwe, P. (1990). "The willingness to pay for education in developing countries: Evidence from rural Peru". Journal of Public Economics 42, 251–275.

Glazerman, S., Levy, D., Meyers, D. (2002). "Nonexperimental replications of social experiments: A systematic review". Interim report/Discussion paper. Mathematica Policy Research, Inc.

Glewwe, P. (1999). The Economics of School Quality Investments in Developing Countries. St. Martin's Press, New York.

Glewwe, P. (2002). "Schools and skills in developing countries: Education policies and socioeconomic outcomes". Journal of Economic Literature 40 (2), 436–482.

Glewwe, P. (2004). "An investigation of the determinants of school progress and academic achievement in Vietnam". In: Glewwe, P., Dollar, D., Agrawal, N. (Eds.), Economic Growth, Poverty, and Household Welfare in Vietnam. The World Bank, Washington, DC.

Glewwe, P. (2005). "The impact of child health and nutrition on education in developing countries: Theory, econometric issues and recent empirical evidence". Food and Nutritional Bulletin 26 (2), S235–S250.

Glewwe, P., Grosh, M., Jacoby, H., Lockheed, M. (1995). "An eclectic approach to estimating the determinants of achievement in Jamaican primary education". World Bank Economic Review 9 (2), 231–258.

Glewwe, P., Jacoby, H. (1992). "Estimating the determinants of cognitive achievement in low-income countries: The case of Ghana". Living Standards Measurement Study Working Paper 91. The World Bank, Washington, DC.

Glewwe, P., Jacoby, H. (1994). "Student achievement and schooling choice in low-income countries: Evidence from Ghana". Journal of Human Resources 29 (3), 843–864.

Glewwe, P., Ilias, N., Kremer, M., (2004). "Teacher incentives". Mimeo. Harvard University.

Glewwe, P., Kremer, M., Moulin, S. (2006). "Textbooks and test scores: Evidence from a randomized evaluation in Kenya". Mimeo. University of Minnesota and Harvard University.

Glewwe, P., Kremer, M., Moulin, S., Zitzewitz, E. (2004). "Retrospective vs. prospective analyses of school inputs: The case of flip charts in Kenya". Journal of Development Economics 74, 251–268.

Gould, E., Lavy, V., Paserman, D. (2004). "Immigrating to opportunity: The effect of school quality using a natural experiment on Ethiopians in Israel". Quarterly Journal of Economics 119 (2), 489–526.

Greaney, V., Khandker, S.R., Alam, M. (1999). Bangladesh: Assessing Basic Learning Skills. University Press, Dhaka, Bangladesh.

Habyarimana, J., Das, J., Dercon, S., Krishnan, P. (2004). Sense and Absence: Absenteeism and Learning in Zambian Schools. The World Bank, Washington DC.

Hannaway, J. (1992). "Higher order thinking, job design, and incentives: An analysis and proposal". American Education Research Journal 29 (1), 3–21.

Hanushek, E. (1995). "Interpreting recent research on schooling in developing countries". World Bank Research Observer 10 (2), 227–246.

Hanushek, E., Kimko, D. (2000). "Schooling, labor force quality, and the growth of nations". American Economic Review 90 (5), 1184–1208.

Harbison, R., Hanushek, E. (1992). Educational Performance of the Poor: Lessons from Rural Northeast Brazil. Oxford University Press.

Heckman, J. (1979). "Sample selection bias as a specification error". Econometrica 47 (1), 153–160.

Heckman, J., Ichimura, H., Smith, J., Todd, P. (1998). "Characterizing selection bias using experimental data". Econometrica 66 (5), 1017–1098.

Heckman, J., Ichimura, H., Todd, P. (1997). "Matching as an econometric evaluation estimator: Evidence from evaluating a job training program". Review of Economic Studies 64 (4), 605–654.

Heckman, J., Lalonde, R., Smith, J. (1999). In: Ashenfelter, O., Card, D. (Eds.), Handbook of Labor Economics, vol. 3B. Elsevier, Amsterdam.

Heckman, J., Lochner, L., Taber, C. (1998). "General equilibrium treatment effects: A study of tuition policy". Working Paper 6426. NBER.

Herz, B., Subbarao, K., Habib, M., Raney, L. (1991). "Letting girls learn: Promising approaches in primary and secondary education". Discussion Paper 133. The World Bank.

Holmstrom, B., Milgrom, P. (1991). "Multi-task principal-agent analysis: Incentive contracts, asset ownership, and job design". Journal of Law, Economics, and Organization 7, 24–52.

Hoxby, C. (2000). "Does competition among public schools benefit students and taxpayers?". American Economic Review 90 (5), 1209–1238.

Hsieh, C., Urquiola, M. (2002). "When schools compete, how do they compete?". Mimeo. Princeton University.

Huffman, W. (2001). In: Gardner, B., Rausser, G. (Eds.), Handbook of Agricultural Economics, vol. 1A. Elsevier, Amsterdam.

IAEEA (2000). "TIMSS 1999: International Mathematics Report". International Study Center, Boston College.

IAEEA (2003). "PIRLS 2001 International Mathematics Report". International Study Center, Boston College.

Imbens, G., Angrist, J. (1994). "Identification and estimation of local average treatment effects". Econometrica 62 (2), 467–475.

Jacoby, H. (2002). "Is there an intrahousehold flypaper effect? Evidence from a school feeding program". Economic Journal 112 (476), 196–221.

Jamison, D., Searle, B., Galda, K., Stephen, H. (1981). "Improving elementary mathematics education in Nicaragua: An experimental study of the impact of textbooks and radio on achievement". Journal of Educational Psychology 73 (4), 556–567.

Jimenez, E., Lockheed, M. (1995). "Public and private secondary education in developing countries". Discussion Paper 309. The World Bank, Washington, DC.

Jimenez, E., Sawada, Y. (1999). "Do community-managed schools work? An evaluation of El Salvador's EDUCO Program". World Bank Economic Review 13 (3), 415–441.

Kim, J., Alderman, H., Orazem, P. (1999). "Can private school subsidies increase enrollment for the poor? The Quetta Urban Fellowship Program". World Bank Economic Review 13 (3).

Kingdon, G. (1996). "The quality and efficiency of public and private schools: A case study of urban India". Oxford Bulletin of Economics and Statistics 58 (1), 55–80.

Kremer, M. (1995). "Research on schooling: What we know and what we don't – A comment on Hanushek". World Bank Research Observer 10 (2), 247–254.

Kremer, M. (2003). "Randomized evaluations of educational programs in developing countries: Some lessons". American Economic Review Papers and Proceedings 93 (2), 102–115.

Kremer, M., Miguel, E. (2003). "The illusion of sustainability". Mimeo. Harvard University.

Kremer, M., Miguel, E., Thornton, R. (2004). "Incentives to learn". Mimeo. Harvard University.

Kremer, M., Moulin, S., Namunyu, R. (2002). "Unbalanced decentralization". Mimeo. Harvard University.

Kremer, M., Muraldhiran, K., Chaudhury, N., Hammer, J., Rogers, F.H. (2006). "Teacher absence in India: A snapshot". Journal of the European Economic Association, in press.

Kremer, M., Sarychev, A. (2000). "Why do governments operate schools?". Mimeo. Harvard University.

Krueger, A.B., Lindahl, M. (2001). "Education for growth: Why and for whom?". Working Paper 7591. NBER.

Lacey, M. (2003). "Primary schools in Kenya, fees abolished, are filled to overflowing". The New York Times (7 January), A8.

Lakdawalla, D. (2001). "The declining relative quality of teachers". Working Paper 8263. NBER.

Lavy, V. (1996). "School supply constraints and children's educational outcomes in rural Ghana". Journal of Development Economics 51 (2), 291–314.

Lavy, V. (2002). "Evaluating the effect of teachers' performance incentives on pupils' achievements". Journal of Political Economy 110 (6), 1286–1318.

Levine, R., Renalt, D. (1992). "A sensitivity analysis of cross-country growth regressions". American Economic Review 82 (4), 942–963.

Linden, L., Shastry, K. (2005). "Grain inflation: Misrepresenting student attendance in response to a school meals program". Mimeo. Harvard University.

Lockheed, M., Verspoor, A. (1991). Improving Primary Education in Developing Countries. Oxford University Press, New York.

Long, S.K. (1991). "Do the school nutrition programs supplement household food expenditures?". The Journal of Human Resources 26, 654–678.

Lucas, R. (1988). "On the mechanics of economic development". Journal of Monetary Economics 22, 3–42.

Mankiw, N.G., Romer, D., Weil, D. (1992). "A contribution to the empirics of economic growth". Quarterly Journal of Economics 107 (2), 407–437.

Manski, C., Garfinkel, I. (Eds.) (1992). Evaluating Welfare and Training Programs. Harvard University Press.

Meyer, B. (1995). "Natural and quasi-experiments in economics". Journal of Business and Economics Statistics 3 (2), 151–168.

Miguel, E. (2003). "Tribe or nation? Nation-building and public goods in Kenya versus Tanzania". Mimeo. University of California, Berkeley.

Miguel, E., Gugerty, M.K. (2005). "Ethnic diversity, social sanctions, and public goods in Kenya". Journal of Public Economics 89 (11/12), 2325–2368.

Miguel, E., Kremer, M. (2003). "Social networks and learning about health in Kenya". Mimeo. Harvard University.

Miguel, E., Kremer, M. (2004). "Worms: Identifying impacts on education and health in the presence of treatment externalities". Econometrica 72 (1), 159–217.

Morley, S., Coady, D. (2003). From Social Assistance to Social Development: Education Subsidies in Developing Countries. Institute for International Economics, Washington, DC.

OECD, UNESCO (2003). "Literacy skills for the world of tomorrow: Further results from PISA 2000". OECD, Paris.

Pagan, A., Ullah, A. (1999). Nonparametric Econometrics. Cambridge University Press, Cambridge, UK.

Pitt, M.M., Rosenzweig, M.R., Gibbons, D.M. (1993). "The determinants and consequences of the placement of government programs in Indonesia". World Bank Economic Review 7 (3), 319–348.

Planning Institute of Jamaica (1992). "Jamaica survey of living conditions: Analytical review, 1990". Kingston.

Poverty Action Lab (2005). "Fighting poverty: What works?". Bulletin 1.

Powell, C., Grantham-McGregor, S., Elston, M. (1983). "An evaluation of giving the Jamaican government school meal to a class of children". Human Nutrition: Clinical Nutrition 37 (C), 381–388.

Pritchett, L. (1996). "Where has all the education gone?". World Bank Policy Research Working Paper 1581.

Pritchett, L., Filmer, D. (1999). "What education production functions really show: A positive theory of education expenditures". Economics of Education Review 18, 223–239.

PROBE Team (1999). Public Report on Basic Education in India. Oxford University Press, New Delhi.

Psacharopoulos, G. (1985). "Returns to education: A further international update and implications". Journal of Human Resources 20 (4), 583–604.

Psacharopoulos, G. (1994). "Returns to investment in education: A global update". World Development 22, 1325–1344.

Reinikka, R., Svensson, J. (2003). "The power of information: Evidence from a campaign to reduce capture". Mimeo. The World Bank.

Reinikka, R., Svensson, J. (2004). "Local capture: Evidence from a central government transfer program in Uganda". Quarterly Journal of Economics 119 (2), 679–705.

Rosenzweig, M., Wolpin, K. (2000). "Natural 'natural experiments' in economics". Journal of Economic Literature 38, 827–874.

Rugh, A. (2000). Starting Now: Strategies for Helping Girls Complete Primary. Academy for Educational Development, Washington, DC. SAGE Project.

Schultz, T.P. (1997). "Demand for children in low-income countries". In: Rosenzweig, M., Stark, O. (Eds.), Handbook of Population and Family Economics. North-Holland, Amsterdam.

Schultz, T.P. (2002). "Why governments should invest more to educate girls". World Development 30, 207–225.

Schultz, T.P. (2004). "School subsidies for the poor: Evaluating the Mexican PROGRESA Poverty Program". Journal of Development Economics 74 (1), 199–250.

Sen, A. (1999). Development as Freedom. Knopf, New York.

Sen, A. (2002). "The Pratichi report". Pratichi India Trust.

Strauss, J., Thomas, D. (1995). "Human resources". In: Behrman, J., Srinivasan, T.N. (Eds.), Handbook of Development Economics, vol. 3. North-Holland, Amsterdam.

Svejnar, J. (1999). "Labor markets in the transitional central and east European economics". In: Ashenfelter, O., Card, D. (Eds.), Handbook of Labor Economics, vol. 3B. Elsevier, Amsterdam.

Tan, J.-P., Lane, J., Coustere, P. (1997). "Putting inputs to work in elementary schools: What can be done in the Philippines?". Economic Development and Cultural Change 45 (4), 857–879.

Tanzania Media Monitoring (2002). Weekly Newsletter from World Bank Country Office, Dar Es Salaam, Sept. 30–Oct. 6, 2002.

UNDP (1990). "Human development report". United Nations Development Programme, New York.

UNDP (2003). "Human development report". United Nations Development Programme, New York.

UNESCO (2002). Education for All: Is the World on Track? UNESCO Publishing, Paris.

UNESCO (2003). UNESCO Institute of Statistics Electronic Database: http://www.uis.unesco.org/ev.php?URL_ID=5187&URL_DO=DO_TOPIC&URL_SECTION=201.

UNICEF (1999). The State of the World's Children. UNICEF Publishing, Paris.

Vermeersch, C., Kremer, M. (2004). "School meals, educational attainment, and school competition: Evidence from a randomized evaluation". World Bank Policy Research Working Paper WPS3523.

World Bank (1996). "India: Primary education achievement and challenges". Report 15756-IN. The World Bank Washington, DC.

World Bank (1997a). Primary Education in India. The World Bank, Washington, DC.

World Bank (1997b). Vietnam: Education Financing. The World Bank, Washington, DC.

World Bank (2001a). World Development Report 2000/2001: Attacking Poverty. The World Bank, Washington, DC.

World Bank (2001b). Engendering Development: World Bank Policy Research Report. The World Bank and Oxford University Press.

World Bank (2002). World Development Indicators 2002. The World Bank, Washington, DC.

World Bank (2003). World Development Indicators 2003. The World Bank, Washington, DC.

World Bank (2004). World Development Report 2004: Making Services Work for Poor People. The World Bank, Washington, DC.

World Food Programme (2002). "Global school feeding report 2002". World Food Programme School Feeding Support Unit, Rome.

Chapter 17

HAS SCHOOL DESEGREGATION IMPROVED ACADEMIC AND ECONOMIC OUTCOMES FOR BLACKS?

STEVEN RIVKIN

Amherst College

FINIS WELCH

Unicon Research Corporation

Contents

Handbook of the Economics of Education, Volume 2
Edited by Eric A. Hanushek and Finis Welch
© 2006 Elsevier B.V.   *All rights reserved*
DOI: 10.1016/S1574-0692(06)02017-4

Abstract

A half a century has passed since the landmark decision Brown v. Board of Education (1954) overturned the doctrine of separate but equal in the realm of public education. This chapter attempts to summarize what we know about the impact of *Brown* on enrollment patterns and academic and economic outcomes for blacks. There can be little doubt that the decisions in *Brown* and several subsequent cases dramatically altered public education in the US. From 1968 to 1980 there is an almost 67 percent increase in the average percentage of blacks' schoolmates who are white in the US as a whole and a whopping 130 percent increase in the south despite the efforts of many whites to avoid the newly integrated schools. The discontinuous nature of the white enrollment changes following the implementation of desegregation programs provides strong evidence of a causal link between desegregation and white enrollment declines. Not surprisingly, programs that require student participation and urban areas with larger numbers of alternative school districts appear to evoke a larger enrollment response. This responsiveness along with other factors that determine the choices of neighborhoods and schools complicate efforts to identify desegregation program and racial composition effects on academic, social, and labor market outcomes. The evidence on school demographic composition indicates that expanded inter-racial contact improves both academic and labor market outcomes for blacks. There is less evidence on desegregation program effects, and existing evidence is mixed. In recent years demographic changes across the nation have reduced the average share of blacks' classmates who are white despite the fact that segregation of blacks from whites has declined in all regions since 1980 except in the south, where the increase has been small. Importantly, it is the sorting of families among communities rather than districts' allocations of students among schools that limit the extent of inter-racial contact in the schools.

Keywords

residential segregation, school segregation, school desegregation, white flight, peer racial composition effects, treatment effects, education policy, school quality, school integration, desegregation court decisions and policies

JEL classification: I21, I28, J15

The following two paragraphs come from the majority opinion in the case of Plessy v. Ferguson (1896):

> The object of the [Fourteenth] amendment was undoubtedly to enforce the absolute equality of the two races before the law, but in the nature of things it could not have been intended to abolish distinctions based on color, or to enforce social, as distinguished from political equality, or a commingling of the two races upon terms unsatisfactory to either. Laws permitting, and even requiring, that separation in places where they are liable to be brought into contact do not necessarily imply the inferiority of either race to the other, and have been generally, if not universally, recognized as within the competency of the state legislatures in the exercise of their police power.
>
> The most common instance of this is connected with the establishment of separate schools for white and colored children, which has been held to be a valid exercise of the legislative power even by courts of States where the political rights of the colored race have been longest and most earnestly enforced.

A half a century has passed since the landmark decision Brown v. Board of Education (1954) overturned the doctrine of separate but equal in the realm of public education. This and subsequent decisions engendered arguably the most far-reaching social experiment in the history of the United States, not only eliminating de jure segregation but compelling districts to work actively to end racial isolation in the schools. By radically altering the structure of public education, this decision had a profound effect on the social fabric of the nation.

From 1968 to 1980 there is an almost 67 percent (14 percentage point) increase in the average percentage of blacks' schoolmates who are white in the US as a whole and a whopping 130 percent (23 percentage point) increase in the south despite the efforts of many whites to avoid the newly integrated schools. The 1980 school enrollment patterns contrast sharply with the racial isolation described in the 1966 legislatively mandated report *The Equality of Education Opportunity* [Coleman et al. (1966)]. Although the average percentage of blacks' classmates who are white has declined in recent years, it remains far above 1968 levels in the US as a whole and in the south.

This recent decline has prompted many to bemoan the resegregation of America's schools [cf. Symonds (2004)]. It is a concern bolstered by evidence of a decline in the proportion of blacks attending schools with majority white enrollment during the 1980s [Orfield and Monfort (1992)]. However, a more comprehensive look at the evidence strongly refutes this view. The segregation of blacks from whites in the public schools (i.e., the extent to which black and white public school students have different attendance patterns) has declined in all regions since 1980 except in the south, where the increase has been small. Moreover, in recent years residential segregation has also declined in all regions following the rapid suburbanization of earlier decades. There has been a change in the demographic composition of school age children in the US, driven by immigration and declining birth rates among the endogenous Anglo population. Though the substantial reduction in the white enrollment share has altered the composition of most classrooms, this is not resegregation.

Unfortunately, our understanding of the impact of school desegregation on academic, social and economic outcomes for blacks remains far less certain than its effects on school enrollment patterns. Despite the magnitude of the unfolding changes, no large-scale data collection effort was undertaken to investigate program effects. Although the legal and ethical justifications for the elimination of de jure segregation supercede any cost benefit analysis, that is not justification for the failure to engage in comprehensive study of the numerous interventions associated with school desegregation.

This is not to say that we have learned nothing about the impact of *Brown*. There have been a variety of studies on the effects on academic, social and economic outcomes. They range from small, random assignment experiments to observational studies using survey and administrative data. Although methodological concerns raise some questions about the findings, the bulk of the evidence supports the belief that blacks benefit from attending less racially isolated schools.

This chapter attempts to summarize what we know about the impact of *Brown* on enrollment patterns and academic and economic outcomes for blacks. Section 1 describes the landmark court cases that established the legal environment governing the allocation of students among schools. Section 2 presents the main types of plans used to desegregate schools. Section 3 documents changes over time in school enrollment patterns, focusing both on the ways in which districts allocate students among schools and the distribution of students among districts. Sections 4 and 5 discuss the evidence on white flight and effects of school desegregation and racial composition on academic and economic outcomes. In the final section we consider implications for policy in the context of the current legal environment and discuss areas for future research.

1. Landmark court cases

Although public elementary and secondary education has a long history of state sovereignty over most aspects of the financing and provision of public schooling, school segregation provides a clear exception to state control. Beginning with the decision in *Brown*, states lost the power to separate blacks and whites into two entirely separate school systems, a power affirmed by the 1896 ruling in *Plessy v. Ferguson*. Some southern states resisted desegregation, and federal troops were sent in to enforce the law. Moreover, it soon became apparent that *Brown* alone was not enough to compel schools to integrate. Additional litigation was necessary to get desegregation under way on a large scale, and even today there remains great variation in the intensity of district desegregation efforts.

As Table 1 shows, there have been a number of supreme court decisions following *Brown* that have shaped the rules governing the allocation of students into schools. The early post-*Brown* decisions expanded the powers of those seeking to desegregate the schools and substantially broadened the arrangements classified as illegal. However, the

Table 1

Landmark school desegregation court cases

Year	Case	Decision	Implication
1896	Plessy v. Ferguson	Separate but equal constitutional	Legalized de jure segregation
1954	Brown v. Board of Education of Topeka, KS, 347 U.S. 483	Outlawed de jure segregation	Led to freedom of choice plans in some southern districts
1968	Green v. Board of Education of New Kent County, VA, 391 U.S. 430	Ended use of freedom of choice plans; decreed other methods be used	Led to debate over choice of desegregation technique required to achieve desegregation
1971	Swann v. Charlotte Mecklenburg (NC) Board of Education, 402 U.S. 1	Stated racially identifiable schools must cease to exist and sanctioned the use of district wide busing	Led to implementation of large scale involuntary plans throughout the South
1973	Keyes v. School District No. 1, Denver, CO, 413 U.S. 189	Official action leading to de facto segregation must be viewed in the same manner as de jure segregation; extended remedy to Hispanics	Led to increased desegregation activity outside of South
1974	Milliken v. Bradley, 418 U.S. 717	Detroit school district denied an interdistrict remedy; limited the inclusion of a suburban district in a metropolitan remedy to cases in which the suburban district had engaged in segregative practices that had interdistrict effects	Though there were a small number of interdistrict remedies, this case set very stringent conditions that were difficult to meet
1975	Morgan v. Kerrigan, 401 F. Supp. 216 (D. Mass.)	Sanctioned magnets as a component of a desegregation plan	Court later decided that a magnet plan could substitute for involuntary techniques
1991	Board of Education of Oklahoma v. Dowell	Formerly segregated districts can be released from court ordered busing once they have taken all "practicable" steps to eliminate the legacy of segregation; moreover, school districts are not responsible for remedying local conditions including segregated housing	Made it easier for districts to be released from desegregation orders or declared unitary
1995	Missouri v. Jenkins	Minority student achievement below the national average is not enough to require the continued enforcement of a desegregation plan	Limited responsibilities to do what is practicable for remedying the vestiges of past discrimination
1996	Sheff v. O'Neill (Connecticut Supreme Court)	Found that racial and ethnic isolation in Hartford, CT school district violated the state constitution's protection against segregation and denied students their constitutionally guaranteed rights to an education	Required state officials to desegregate the schools

Sources: Welch and Light (1987) for decisions up to 1975 and Weiler (1998) for decisions subsequent to 1975.

1974 ruling in *Milliken v. Bradley* made it difficult to seek a remedy for segregation across districts, and the 1975 ruling in *Morgan v. Kerrigan* sanctioning magnet schools as a valid desegregation method weakened the ability of the courts to mandate the implementation of coercive desegregation plans. Finally, the 1991 and 1995 decisions that require districts merely to take all *practical steps* to end the legacy of segregation (*Board of Education of Oklahoma v. Dowell*) and not to hold districts responsible for low achievement (*Missouri v. Jenkins*) reveal a movement away from mandatory desegregation as a primary means to increase school quality, at least at the federal level.

The recent Connecticut State Supreme Court ruling Sheff v. O'Neill (1996) that requires Connecticut officials to desegregate the schools may signal a shift of the desegregation battle to state courts, similar to the legal battle over school finance equity. If this comes to pass, the standards for desegregation will vary by state, just as do those for funding inequality.

2. School desegregation techniques

Districts have used a number of techniques to desegregate schools. Choice of program type has depended upon many factors including the legal precedents in effect, severity of segregation, residential housing patterns, availability of alternative public schools and the extent of community resistance. Circumstances have sometimes necessitated the use of more than one technique, while in other cases a simpler construct has been adequate.

Desegregation techniques can be classified as voluntary or involuntary depending upon whether students are permitted to choose the school they will attend; the distinction does not reflect whether or not the courts required desegregation. Welch and Light (1987) divide plans into six categories, three voluntary and three nonvoluntary. The voluntary techniques include open enrollment, magnet and other transfer programs, while the involuntary plans include neighborhood attendance zones, rezoning, and pairing and clustering.

Open enrollment. Students are free to attend almost any school in the district. If demand exceeds capacity, students in the school's own attendance zone typically receive priority. Importantly, there is no requirement that attendance at a school outside of the neighborhood reduce segregation.

Magnet schools. Magnets offer a particular type of learning environment or curriculum. For example, magnets may focus on the arts, college preparation, accelerated learning, math and science, vocational skills or other fields. Some magnets are open to all students while others give priority to students in particular attendance zones. If they are part of a school desegregation plan, magnets typically use racial guidelines in the admissions process.

Other voluntary transfers. This category encompasses a number of programs including majority to minority and one-way transfers. The former permits students to transfer from schools in which they were in the majority to schools in which they are in the minority or in some cases less of a majority, while the latter permits minority students attending predominantly minority schools to transfer to designated receiver schools that may be in a different district.

Neighborhood attendance zones. Students must attend the neighborhood school. Southern districts that had previously required some students to travel substantial distances to school often used this method to end de jure segregation.

Rezoning. Any change in attendance zones that does not involve pairing and clustering. Rezoning may be contiguous or noncontiguous. Contiguous rezoning plans alter the boundaries between adjacent schools, while noncontiguous rezoning reassigns students to a school that does not share a boundary with their current school. Junior and senior high schools may be rezoned by changing elementary school feeder patterns rather than by changing attendance boundaries.

Pairing and clustering. This technique reassigns students among a pair or cluster of schools, often by restructuring grades. For example, an elementary school in a predominantly white neighborhood may be combined with one in a predominantly black neighborhood. Rather than each school offering grades kindergarten through five to neighborhood students, one school would offer the first three grades and the other would offer grades three through five to students from both neighborhoods.

3. Trends in school enrollment patterns: 1968–2000

This section uses Office of Civil Rights Public Elementary and Secondary School Enrollment Data to describe school enrollment patterns for the years 1968, 1980, 1988 and 2000. Three inter-related pieces of information characterize school enrollment patterns, and we document changes over time in all three: demographic composition, segregation and inter-racial contact. By segregation, we refer to the extent to which students are mixed conditional on the overall demographic shares of the district, state or other geographic entity; by inter-racial contact we refer to the share of schoolmates who are white. Notice that overall demographic composition and degree of segregation jointly determine the level of inter-racial contact. It is also important to recognize that the distribution of students among districts is a result of both residential choice and the decision to opt out for private schooling and limits the potential effectiveness of district desegregation programs. Therefore we also describe trends over time in the allocation of students among districts.

Virtually all major studies of segregation and enrollment patterns use the Office of Civil Rights school enrollment survey.[1] The office collects biennial data on school enrollment from a sample of US public elementary and secondary schools. The data provide enrollment counts for Blacks, Hispanics, Native Americans, Asians and Whites.

---

[1] See Welch and Light (1987) for a comprehensive description of the data.

Table 2

Racial composition of public elementary and secondary schools, by region and the United States as a whole: 1968, 1980, 1988 and 2000 (percentages)

| Region | Percent | | | | | | | | | | | |
| | White | | | | Black | | | | Other* | | | |
	1968	1980	1988	2000	1968	1980	1988	2000	1968	1980	1988	2000
Northeast	84.4	78.3	75.8	67.5	11.5	13.6	12.4	15.3	4.1	8.1	11.8	17.2
North Central	87.9	83.8	83.6	76.6	10.6	12.5	11.4	14.7	1.5	3.7	5.0	8.7
South	70.1	65.9	63.7	56.3	25.3	25.4	25.3	26.4	4.6	8.7	11.0	17.3
West	78.2	67.1	62.6	50.2	6.3	6.7	5.7	6.5	15.5	26.2	31.7	43.3
National	79.9	73.3	70.7	61.4	14.8	16.1	15.2	17.1	5.3	10.6	14.1	21.5

*Residual category including Hispanic, Asian and Native American.

We use the 1968, 1980, 1988 and 2000 surveys and appropriate sampling weights to produce national and regional trends in enrollment, segregation and inter-racial contact.[2]

We focus exclusively on the enrollment patterns of non-Hispanic blacks and whites. Growing numbers of Asian and Hispanic students surely complicate the meaning of racial segregation, and their increasing presence in many school districts has likely had a large impact. Nevertheless, the nation's integration policies have focused on the segregation of blacks, and this section documents the effectiveness of these efforts.

We begin with a brief description of demographic trends prior to examining changes over time in school enrollment patterns. Table 2 shows the demographic composition of public schools by region. Between 1968 and 1988 the decline in white enrollment nationally as a percentage of the total was roughly offset by increases for Hispanics and Asians, while between 1988 and 2000 the continued decline in the white enrollment share was offset by increases in both the black (15.2–17.1%) and the Hispanic and Asian (14.1–21.5%) enrollment shares.

There are regional differences and similarities in both the magnitude and timing of demographic change. The decline in the white enrollment share was smaller in the north central region than in the rest of the country, particularly prior to 1988. On the other hand, all regions experienced their largest white enrollment share decline following 1988, driven in part by the very high rate of migration into the US from Asian, Latin American and West Indian countries.

Virtually all large urban districts witnessed dramatic decreases in the white enrollment share between 1968 and 2000. By 2000 the white enrollment share fell to 10 percent or less in Los Angeles, Chicago, Detroit, Oakland, the District of Columbia and

---

[2] It is important to note that the 1968 and 1980 samples were drawn from the universe of districts with enrollments of at least 300 students. Small districts received weights of zero, but since only a tiny percentage of students attended such districts their omission has virtually no impact on the regional and national projections.

New Orleans and to between 10 and 20 percent in a large number of other cities including Boston, New York, Philadelphia, Memphis and San Francisco. White enrollment remained much higher in the county wide southern districts, though they also experienced substantial declines during this period.

Although demographic changes tempered the effectiveness of desegregation efforts to raise black/white contact in the schools, Table 3 documents the substantial increase following 1968 in the exposure of black pupils to white schoolmates. The table reports national and regional trends over time using both the exposure index (average percentage of blacks' schoolmates who are white)[3] and more detailed information about changes across the distribution.

Nationally exposure to whites increased by more than 50 percent between 1968 and 1980, rising from 22.3 percent to 36.2 percent. Between 1980 and 1988 exposure remained relatively stable prior to declining by 5 percentage points between 1988 and 2000. The most striking changes occurred at the bottom of the distribution, as the share of blacks in schools with white enrollment below 5 percent fell by more than 50 percent following 1968. In sum, the decline in segregation between 1968 and 1988 swamped the loss of whites on a national level, while following 1988 the demographic changes reduced exposure to whites.

The bottom panels reveal regional differences in the timing of school enrollment changes. The region with the highest average exposure to whites in 1968, the northeast, had already become the region with the lowest average exposure to whites by 1980, while the south went from being the region with the lowest exposure to the region with the highest exposure during this same period. Trend differences in the share of blacks with few or no white schoolmates are particularly striking. In 1968 almost three fourths of students in the south have 5 percent or less white schoolmates; that number fell to one fifth in 1980 and remained below one quarter in 2000. In contrast, 35 percent of students in the northeast had 5 percent or less white schoolmates in 1968, and that number increased to 45 percent in 1980 before falling slightly in subsequent years. The other regions fell in between the south and northeast, though exposure to whites in the north central and west regions continued to increase during the 1980s.

The contrast between changes in overall demographic composition and the average exposure to whites provides clear evidence of a decline in segregation, and we now document changes in both school and district segregation. Following Taeuber and James (1982), analogues of Lorenz curves are used to describe segregation across the entire spectrum of schools. These segregation curves provide information on the entire distribution of white enrollment shares including the numbers of blacks attending schools with no whites or majority white enrollment and are not sensitive to changes in overall demographic composition that do not affect proportional allocation of whites among blacks.

---

[3] The average percentage of blacks schoolmates who are white, also known as the exposure index, equals $\sum_{i=1}^{n} B_i * PW_i / B$, where B_i equals the number of blacks in school i, PW_i equals the proportion of white students in school i, and B equals the number of black students in the region or nation.

Table 3
Percentage of blacks' schoolmates who are white by region: 1968–2000

Percent of schoolmates who are white	Distribution of black students enrollment (percentage)			
	1968	1980	1988	2000
United States				
0–5	61.6	29.5	28.2	31.3
6–25	7.8	13.8	14.6	19.2
26–75	16.7	43.8	44.4	40.1
76–95	12.0	11.7	11.7	8.7
96–100	1.9	1.2	1.1	0.7
All schools	100.0	100.0	100.0	100.0
Average percent white	22.3	36.2	36.2	31.1
Northeast				
0–5	35.9	45.3	43.3	44.4
6–25	16.8	13.3	14.6	18.9
26–75	28.6	29.4	29.8	26.6
76–95	15.3	9.3	10.0	8.6
96–100	3.4	2.6	2.3	1.5
All schools	100.0	100.0	100.0	100.0
Average percent white	33.7	27.8	26.9	24.9
North Central				
0–5	56.0	40.0	37.2	39.6
6–25	11.4	14.0	14.7	18.0
26–75	19.6	32.6	32.5	29.3
76–95	10.7	11.4	13.5	11.7
96–100	2.3	2.0	1.9	1.4
All schools	100.0	100.0	100.0	100.0
Average percentage white	23.3	30.9	32.1	29.1
South				
0–5	73.6	20.9	21.7	26.3
6–25	2.7	13.7	14.0	18.2
26–75	10.7	52.2	52.0	47.2
76–95	11.7	12.6	11.6	8.0
96–100	1.3	0.6	0.6	0.3
All schools	100.0	100.0	100.0	100.0
Average percent white	17.9	40.8	40.1	33.7
West				
0–5	44.8	29.8	23.9	22.2
6–25	16.2	14.8	18.3	28.5
26–75	27.2	43.5	46.4	42.2
76–95	10.6	11.5	11.0	7.0
96–100	1.1	0.5	0.3	0.1
All schools	100.0	100.0	100.0	100.0
Average percent white	26.7	34.6	36.0	30.7

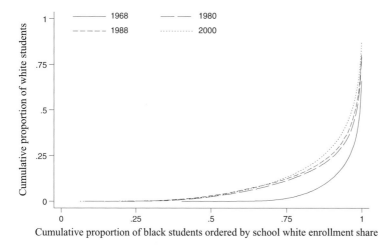

Figure 1. National school segregation curves: 1968, 1980, 1988 and 2000.

We also report the dissimilarity index as a summary measure of school segregation. This index is constructed conditional on the demographic composition of the nation, region, or some other grouping of schools, and it measures the degree to which the distribution of students among schools deviates from a distribution in which all schools have identical enrollment shares. The dissimilarity index varies from zero to one, with a value of one indicating complete segregation and a value of zero indicating complete integration. The magnitude of the index reflects the share of blacks (or whites) that would have to switch schools to achieve complete integration.[4]

Figure 1 presents school segregation curves for the nation as a whole. The 1968 curve traces the horizontal axis until the cumulative percentage of blacks equals 40.1 percent, meaning that 40.1 percent of blacks attended schools with no white students. The slope of the curve equals 1 at the 88th percentile for blacks, indicating that 88 percent of blacks attended schools in which white enrollment fell below the white share of total public school enrollment, which equaled 80 percent in 1968.[5] The cumulative percentage of whites equals 63.5 percent at the point where the cumulative percentage of blacks equals 100 percent, meaning that 36.5 percent of the white students had no black schoolmates in 1968. The remaining curves lie closer and closer to the 45 degree line, implying that segregation was declining over time. Interestingly, the largest decline occurred during the 1970s and second largest during the 1990s: the dissimilarity index fell from

---

[4] Formally, the dissimilarity index measuring school segregation between blacks and whites is defined as $\sum t_s |p_s - p|/2Tp(1 - p)$, where the subscript "$s$" indicates school, t_s is total enrollment in school s, p_s is the black share of enrollment in school s, p is the black enrollment share in the nation (or region) and T is total enrollment in the nation (or region).

[5] More generally, the slope equals $1/x$ at the percentile of the black distribution where the percentage of their schoolmates who were white equals $1/x$ times the percentage of all students who were white.

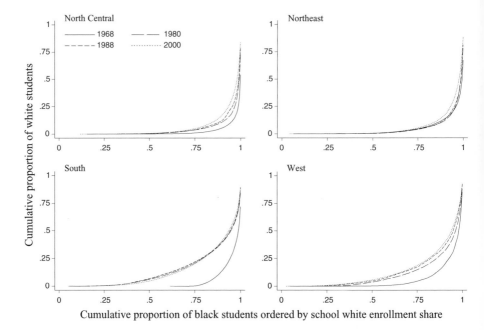

Figure 2.   School segregation curves by region: 1968, 1980, 1988 and 2000.

81.2 to 71.0 between 1968 and 1980, remained almost constant during the 1980s and fell to 66.7 between 1988 and 2000.

Figure 2 depicts substantial differences by region in the desegregation experience that match up with the observed differences in the changes in inter-racial contact. The south made by far the most headway against segregation during the 1970s but experienced little subsequent change throughout the distribution, while the desegregation gains in the north central region were smaller but steadier. The west also experienced a substantial segregation decline during the 1970s and additional gains during the 1980s and 1990s. Consistent with the decline in exposure to whites, the northeast experienced virtually no change in segregation through 1988 and a modest decline during the 1990s.

The curves in Figures 1 and 2 use school level data and reflect the influences of both the allocation of students among districts and school district attendance policies. It is important to recognize that the distribution of students among districts limits district efforts to increase inter-racial contact, providing an upper bound on the overall deseg-regation that would be possible even if all districts were completely integrated.

Figure 3 presents district segregation curves for the four regions that isolate changes in the distribution of students among districts by ignoring all within district segregation. In each region there was substantial segregation at the district level throughout the time period. Each region experienced some degree of additional segregation by district dur-ing the active desegregation period of the 1970s, but they differ in the extent to which

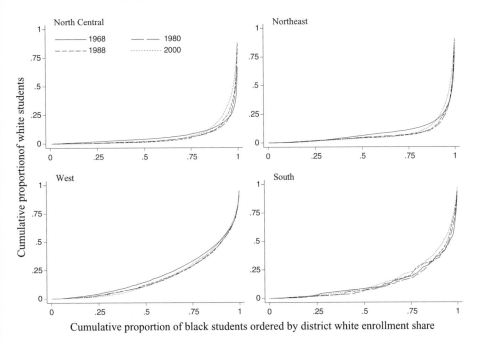

Figure 3. District segregation curves by region: 1968, 1980, 1988 and 2000.

Table 4
School and district dissimilarity indexes by region: 1968–2000

School districts	School				District			
	1968	1980	1988	2000	1968	1980	1988	2000
Northeast	76.9	78.8	78.5	76.0	70.9	76.7	76.7	74.0
North Central	85.7	80.1	78.9	76.4	74.5	77.4	76.9	74.5
South	80.1	57.3	57.1	58.8	44.2	48.9	49.9	49.2
West	81.4	70.6	66.9	64.3	65.7	66.5	63.4	59.6
National	81.2	71.0	70.4	68.7	63.8	66.2	66.2	63.7

segregation lessened in the subsequent decades. The south in particular was notable for its lack of progress following 1980.

As the school and district level dissimilarity indexes reported in Table 4 show, the remaining segregation in 2000 resulted primarily from the allocation of students among districts. Even if all schools had achieved complete integration without changing the distribution of students among districts, the school level dissimilarity index would have declined from only 76 to 74 in the northeast, 76.5 to 74.5 in the north central, 58.8 to 49.2 in the south, and 64.3 to 63.7 in the west. Clotfelter (1999) documents a

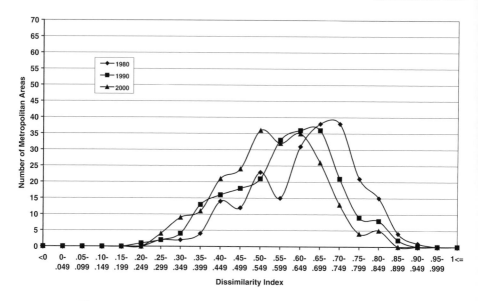

Figure 4. Distribution of dissimilarity index for blacks: 1980, 1990 and 2000.

similar degree of segregation using metropolitan area rather than district as the unit of analysis.

Although school districts are geographically defined, a change in the allocation of students among districts is not driven solely by housing. Rather changes in both housing patterns and private school attendance affect the distribution of students among public school districts. Moreover, residential movements within districts also affect the degree of segregation for given attendance policies. Unfortunately the Office of Civil Rights data provide no information on housing and private schooling. We conclude this section with information drawn from other sources.

The extent of residential segregation in the US has been well documented by Massey and Denton (1993). A particularly striking pattern is the degree of segregation within metropolitan areas that remained even among blacks and whites with similar incomes [Massey and Denton (1993)]. Recent evidence suggests, however, that black/white residential segregation in metropolitan areas declined during the 1980s and 1990s. Figure 4, taken from Iceland and Weinberg (2002), documents changes in the degree to which blacks and whites live in different census tracts within a metropolitan area for the 220 metropolitan areas that were at least 3 percent black or had at least 20,000 blacks in 1980. The figure reveals substantial black/white housing segregation in many metropolitan areas. Nevertheless, the median dissimilarity index declined from 0.75 in 1980 to 0.65 in 2000, and similar drops occurred at both the 25th (0.68 to 0.57) and 75th percentiles (0.81 to 0.73) of the distribution.

Table 5 shows that black and white private school enrollment patterns also exhibit quite a bit of variation across regions of the country. Because of changes in cohort size

Table 5

Percentage of elementary school students grades 1–4 enrolled in private school, by race and region: 1960–2000

	Year				
	1960	1970	1980	1990	2000
Blacks					
North East	5.7	6.3	11.1	11.2	10.2
North Central	4.4	4.5	8.1	7.0	7.7
South	1.8	2.1	3.7	3.1	4.4
West	4.4	5.1	9.5	8.8	8.7
US	2.9	3.5	6.4	5.7	6.3
Whites					
North East	25.3	19.4	16.7	15.3	15.2
North Central	20.4	14.9	14.0	13.6	15.1
South	8.2	7.5	10.5	10.0	12.8
West	10.3	8.0	10.5	10.0	12.8
US	16.4	12.6	12.6	11.8	13.4

and substantial differences in private school enrollment for elementary, junior high, and high school levels, this table reports enrollment patterns for grades 1–4 based on U.S. Census data. Very similar patterns hold for other grade levels.

In 1960 private school enrollment was much higher in the northeast and north central regions than either the south or west and not surprisingly much higher for whites than blacks. Over time there has been convergence by both region and race, some of which is consistent with white flight from desegregated public schools. Between 1960 and 1980 the 17 percentage point northeast/south gap in white private school enrollment declined to 6 percentage points, in part because private school enrollment in the south increased by 40 percent during the 1970s.

4. Desegregation and residential shifts

Table 6 describes major studies of enrollment shifts in response to school desegregation, beginning with Coleman, Kelley and Moore (1975). Although the exact methods varied, the predominant approach was to compare enrollment changes around the time of program implementation with those several years before and several years after, allowing for differential effects by a number of factors.

The pattern of findings up to 1985 provides no consensus on the magnitude or persistence of white flight from school desegregation. Although most studies reported sizable enrollment changes surrounding program implementation, these changes were often not related to program characteristics in the expected ways. In addition, the finding of little or no long-lasting effect reported by Wilson (1985) contradicted the earlier studies and

Table 6
Summary of selected research on white flight

Article	Data	Method	Findings
Coleman, Kelley and Moore (1975)	1968–1973 OCR surveys	Related contemporaneous annual changes in white enrollment to annual change in segregation	Plans reduced segregation but increased the white enrollment decline
Clotfelter (1976)	Mississippi Department of Education and HEW	Compared change in white private school enrollment with county racial composition	A higher nonwhite student population share increased growth of private school enrollment for whites
Taeuber and Wilson (1978)	Louisiana Department of Education and U.S. Census housing survey	Cohort comparisons of enrollment changes	No lasting desegregation effect on rate of white enrollment decline; schools not often cited as a primary reason for moving
Rossell (1978)	1968–1975 OCR surveys	Related contemporaneous annual changes in white enrollment to proportion of students reassigned, by type of plan (court ordered or voluntary)	Significant implementation year decline in white enrollment, but small or nonexistent longer term effects
Armor (1978)	1968–1976 OCR surveys and U.S. Census data	Compared white enrollment following plan adoption with projected district enrollment	Enrollment fell relative to its projection, dropping sharply following plan implementation and continuing to fall thereafter
Farley, Richards and Wurdock (1980)	1968–1976 OCR surveys	Used more flexible functional form than Coleman, Kelley and Moore (1975)	Confirmed findings of large contemporaneous white enrollment decline following plan implementation
Wilson (1985)	1968–1976 OCR surveys	Autoregressive model that related white enrollment changes with changes in exposure to blacks, conditioning on plan type	Enrollment response was short-lived and did not depend upon the attributes of the desegregation program
Welch and Light (1987)	1968–1982 OCR surveys augmented by district data	Related change in white enrollment to change in the index of racial dissimilarity by timing and type of desegregation plan and district characteristics	White enrollment dropped below trend when desegregation programs were introduced, and the effect appeared to persist. Effect magnitudes varied with plan type and district characteristics
Rivkin (1994)	1968–1988 OCR surveys	Related change in white enrollment to change in the Gini index of racial segregation	White enrollment declined substantially in virtually all large central city districts regardless of the scope of desegregation efforts

Table 6
(*Continued*)

Article	Data	Method	Findings
Reber (2003)	1968–1984 OCR surveys augmented by district and common core survey for the years 1987–1998	Used panel data models to estimate the dynamic effects of desegregation plans on white enrollment	Desegregation plans had a significant effect on white enrollment, and the type of program and number of nearby school districts were important predictors of white response
Lutz (2004)	1987–2001 common core surveys, school district data book, and information on desegregation plans and dismissal of desegregation orders	Used panel data models to estimate the dynamic effects of dismissal of desegregation orders on white enrollment	Dismissal of desegregation orders moderately reduced black exposure to whites and did not reverse white flight in the short term

raised doubts about the importance of white flight. However, problems with Wilson's analysis documented by Welch (1985) weakened the contradictory evidence.

Nevertheless, the failure to identify a pattern of enrollment responses that were consistent with expectations about the effects of transition costs and desegregation program characteristics meant that important questions remained unanswered. Welch and Light (1987) set out to resolve these issues through an analysis of 125 large districts. They compiled sixteen years of data on enrollments and desegregation program status and examined in detailed the changes in white enrollment surrounding the implementation of 116 major plans during the period of study.

The following two tables taken from Welch and Light (1987) contain their main findings on the changes in white enrollment surrounding the implementation of desegregation plans. The first reports average changes in white enrollment and segregation (as measured by the dissimilarity index) by timing of the plan (pre- and post-Swann) and plan type, while the second further divides the plans by region and district urban status. Note that both tables mix plans that had relatively small desegregation effects with those that brought about major changes.

The top panel of Table 7 [Table 19 in Welch and Light (1987)] reveals that the dissimilarity index fell an average of 0.217 during implementation, by roughly one third that amount in the years more than one year before, and by only a very small amount in the year before and years after. White enrollment also declined much more in the year of implementation, though in contrast to the change in segregation the average enrollment decline picked up in the year prior to implementation and remained above the pre-plan level in the year following implementation. The higher enrollment losses in the years following implementation are consistent with national enrollment data showing that losses were greater during the late 1970s than in earlier periods. But the fact that enrollment losses are much greater during implementation provides strong evidence of

Table 7
Average change in dissimilarity index and average annual percent change in white enrollment before, during and after plan implementation by plan type and implementation date

Number	Type	Before		During	After	
		More than one year	One year		One year	More than one year
116	All					
	Index	−0.066	−0.023	−0.217	−0.010	−0.010
	Enrollment	−2.51	−3.76	−6.27	−4.58	−2.85
Pre-Swann (1970 or earlier)						
3	Pair/Cluster					
	Index	−0.013	−0.036	−0.189	0.045	0.015
	Enrollment	−3.55	−2.17	−4.94	−9.35	−3.84
12	Rezone/Pair/Cluster					
	Index	−0.072	−0.025	−0.430	−0.024	0.026
	Enrollment	1.55	3.08	−2.20	−1.23	−1.76
17	Rezone					
	Index	0.001	−0.036	−0.247	−0.014	−0.047
	Enrollment	−0.118	0.795	−2.59	−1.53	−1.97
Post-Swann (1971 or later)						
14	Pair/Cluster					
	Index	−0.051	−0.025	−0.209	−0.007	0.025
	Enrollment	−3.00	−4.32	−7.75	−5.48	−3.76
23	Rezone/Pair/Cluster					
	Index	−0.098	−0.019	−0.250	−0.007	−0.021
	Enrollment	−3.05	−6.68	−11.7	−7.29	−3.58
6	Pair/Cluster/Magnets					
	Index	−0.026	−0.017	−0.165	−0.015	−0.032
	Enrollment	−4.05	−6.29	−12.7	−7.85	−3.33
17	Rezone					
	Index	−0.062	−0.038	−0.178	−0.004	0.014
	Enrollment	−1.06	−2.86	−4.20	−2.87	−2.09
5	Rezone/Magnets					
	Index	−0.130	−0.016	−0.143	−0.014	−0.022
	Enrollment	−2.98	−2.13	−3.50	−3.39	0.368
13	Major voluntary					
	Index	−0.081	−0.007	−0.111	−0.019	−0.019
	Enrollment	−3.90	−6.72	−5.13	−6.09	−3.25
3	Other voluntary					
	Index	−0.012	0.000	−0.038	−0.032	0.005
	Enrollment	−3.86	−10.2	−7.42	−7.11	−4.75

Source: Welch and Light (1987), Table 19.

the existence of an enrollment response to segregation, just as the timing of the changes in the dissimilarity index document desegregation's substantial effect on district attendance patterns.

The remainder of Table 7 partitions plans on the basis of timing and plan type. Not surprisingly, the most comprehensive plans led to larger declines in segregation. Both before and after the Swann (1970) decision stating that racially identifiable schools must cease to exist and sanctioning the use of district wide busing, plans that combined rezoning with pairing and clustering produced the largest decline in the dissimilarity index. A second clear pattern emerging in the post-Swann period is that plans using pairing and clustering produced larger average changes in enrollment (prior to Swann there is no obvious pattern in enrollment changes, likely because this was a period of trend reversal in total white enrollment that varied geographically).

The finding that pairing and clustering leads to greater departures from trend than rezoning, magnets, and other voluntary plans reflects qualitative differences among the desegregation techniques. Not only is pairing and clustering mandatory, but it typically requires that students travel greater distances than under rezoning, the other mandatory program type. All in all, it is not surprising that the mandatory plan type that is most disruptive for students produces the largest average changes in both segregation and white enrollment.

Table 8 [Table 21 in Welch and Light (1987)] further divides plans on the basis of region and district urban status in order to allow for different responses in the south and in county wide districts. County wide districts are particularly interesting, because the

Table 8

Average change in dissimilarity index and average annual percent change in white enrollment before, during and after plan implementation by plan type and implementation date

Number	Type	Before		During	After	
		More than one year	One year		One year	More than one year
Countywide southern districts; pre-Swann						
10	Rezone/Pair/Cluster					
	Index	−0.088	−0.034	−0.442	−0.037	0.050
	Enrollment	2.04	3.04	−2.50	−0.835	−1.55
11	Rezone					
	Index	−0.002	−0.043	−0.248	−0.008	−0.050
	Enrollment	4.30	2.00	−0.787	−0.199	−0.898
Countywide southern districts; post-Swann						
5	Rezone/Pair/Cluster					
	Index	−0.122	−0.034	−0.373	0.003	0.005
	Enrollment	−0.113	−2.56	−7.86	−4.47	−1.94
4	Rezone					
	Index	−0.061	−0.028	−0.356	0.020	0.087
	Enrollment	−0.073	−4.62	−5.45	−0.970	−1.38

Table 8
(*Continued*)

Number	Type	Before		During	After	
		More than one year	One year		One year	More than one year
Large urban southern districts; post-Swann						
4	Rezone/Pair/Cluster					
	Index	−0.047	−0.015	−0.147	−0.012	0.034
	Enrollment	−5.48	−10.6	−20.4	−11.6	−5.33
Large urban nonsouthern districts; post-Swann						
3	Pair/Cluster					
	Index	−0.004	−0.045	−0.148	−0.014	−0.009
	Enrollment	−8.27	−6.25	−13.2	−9.74	−6.54
6	Rezone/Pair/Cluster					
	Index	−0.085	−0.019	−0.222	−0.013	−0.103
	Enrollment	−4.40	−9.83	−10.7	−7.53	−4.51
4	Pair/Cluster/Magnets					
	Index	−0.042	−0.030	−0.173	−0.014	−0.025
	Enrollment	−4.69	−8.66	−14.3	−8.50	−3.20
7	Major voluntary					
	Index	−0.035	−0.002	−0.132	−0.017	−0.035
	Enrollment	−3.67	−7.39	−5.47	−7.05	−3.99
Medium urban nonsouthern districts; post-Swann						
4	Rezone/Pair/Cluster					
	Index	−0.107	−0.019	−0.211	0.011	0.005
	Enrollment	−2.96	−6.39	−10.2	−5.91	−3.05
4	Rezone					
	Index	−0.087	−0.030	−0.174	−0.005	−0.041
	Enrollment	−1.70	−3.32	−4.41	−4.18	−2.33
4	Major voluntary					
	Index	−0.139	−0.023	−0.087	−0.016	0.011
	Enrollment	−3.02	−5.20	−4.01	−5.07	−2.98
3	Pair/Cluster					
	Index	−0.054	−0.010	−0.097	0.002	0.006
	Enrollment	−2.33	−3.54	−5.48	−3.53	−4.24
Small urban nonsouthern districts; post-Swann						
3	Rezone					
	Index	−0.050	−0.033	−0.016	−0.015	−0.002
	Enrollment	−2.60	−3.32	−3.68	−2.79	−2.63

Source: Welch and Light (1987), Table 21.

districts typically include suburban areas where white students are concentrated. These geographically larger districts tend to raise both the cost of moving out of the district in terms of the additional commute time to work and average distance students must be bused to achieve a given amount of desegregation. Consequently it is unclear a priori whether county wide districts should experience a larger white enrollment response to desegregation plan implementation, though families in these districts do have an unambiguously greater incentive to switch to a private school if one is available. In fact the table shows that departures from trends in white enrollment tended to be smaller for the countywide districts than for the urban southern and nonsouthern districts despite the fact that the countywide districts experienced much larger average reductions in segregation.

The discontinuous nature of the white enrollment changes following the implementation of desegregation programs provides strong evidence of a causal link between desegregation and white enrollment declines. Nonetheless, the possibility remains that other factors could produce a similar pattern. As an alternative to the approach used by Welch and Light (1987), Reber (2003) uses differences in the timing of implementation for the same set of school districts to estimate white enrollment changes around the time of implementation. The panel data method essentially compares changes in school districts around the time of implementation to the national average white enrollment changes over corresponding years. Her results confirm the findings in Welch and Light (1987). Moreover, she finds that white flight appeared to increase with the number of districts in a metropolitan area, supporting the notion that the higher relocation costs of geographically larger districts more than offset larger increases in school commute times in terms of the incentive to switch districts.

An additional dimension over which the effects of desegregation programs could vary is the initial share of white enrollment, and Clotfelter (1976) finds evidence that white flight is an increasing function of the nonwhite share of the student population. Yet because the design of desegregation programs and other factors that affect residential relocation are almost certainly related to the nonwhite enrollment share, these findings are susceptible to omitted variables bias.

Importantly, desegregation induced enrollment declines may appear quite large at the time of program implementation but may have very little impact over the long term given the widespread suburban migration. The evidence in Rivkin (1994) suggests that desegregation programs may not have been a primary contributor to white enrollment loss over the longer term. Between 1968 and 1988, the distribution of white enrollment loss in the 10 large urban districts that experienced the largest decline in segregation is quite similar to the distribution for the ten large urban districts that experienced the smallest decline in segregation. This holds despite the fact that the ten nonintegrating districts began with much lower white enrollment shares and thus lower potential losses. It appears that as the time horizon increased the deviations from trend caused by the implementation of a desegregation plan diminished in importance relative to persistent long-term influences.

The ubiquitous white enrollment decline in large urban districts across the country also imposes a severe limit on district efforts to expand inter-racial contact. Even if whites in the 2000s were to respond much more favorably to expanded desegregation programs than did whites in the 1970s, the low white enrollment share in virtually all large districts precludes sizable increases in exposure to whites. As the district and school level segregation curves and measures highlighted in the previous section, it is the sorting of families among communities rather than district attendance policies that limit the extent of inter-racial contact in the schools as long as the Milliken (1974) finding that there can be no inter-district relief without an inter-district violation remains the law of the land.

Moreover, given recent Supreme Court decisions lowering barriers to the dismissal of desegregation orders, a contraction of desegregation efforts is much more likely than an expansion. Lutz (2004) finds that the dismissal of court ordered plans appeared to cause a modest reduction in black exposure to whites and no immediate white enrollment response. This preliminary evidence suggests that the dismissal of desegregation orders is unlikely to produce radical changes, though longer term effects may differ and the responses in the affected districts may not be representative of all districts with court ordered plans currently in place.

5. Racial composition and desegregation program outcome effects

Despite the movement of large numbers of whites out of central city school districts, school desegregation succeeded in dramatically increasing black exposure to whites. Moreover, many programs reallocated students among schools, exposing blacks and whites to different teachers, facilities and other factors thought to affect school quality. Supporters of desegregation expected these changes to improve the quality of education for blacks and reduce the racial gap in school quality and future economic and social outcomes.

There are also reasons to believe that student or school efforts to neutralize desegregation, longer commute distances and other adverse side effects might limit or even eliminate the benefits of school desegregation. Clotfelter, Ladd and Vigdor (2005) find evidence of substantial within school segregation in North Carolina junior high and high schools but not in elementary schools. Clotfelter (2002) also finds some racial differences in the distributions of blacks and whites across extra-curricular activities, although these activities do provide a vehicle for inter-racial contact. Such resegregation within schools not only reduces inter-racial contact, it may also lessen the improvement in teacher and school quality actually experienced by blacks bused to a nonneighborhood school.[6] Finally, evidence suggests that busing students out of their neighborhoods decreases parental participation [Edwards (1993), Leake and Faltz (1993)].

Consequently the question of whether desegregation benefited blacks must be answered empirically, and that answer likely depends on characteristics of both programs and students. This section describes existing research on racial composition and desegregation effects on achievement and other outcomes. It begins with a discussion of relevant methodological issues prior to summarizing the findings.

---

[6] Rivkin (2000) finds that busing and other desegregation programs appear to weaken the link between the quality of education experienced by blacks and nonblacks in the same school.

Methodological issues

School desegregation provides a prime example of the difficulty of isolating the causal effect of a social program. Consider the substantial improvement of blacks relative to whites on the National Assessment of Educational Progress (NAEP) during the 1970s and 1980s, a period in which the black/white mathematics and reading achievement gaps for thirteen year old children were cut by almost 50 percent. Although test changes and inadequacies of the sampling scheme may account for some of the decline, the evidence suggests substantial academic improvement for blacks coinciding with the desegregation of many large urban school districts.

However, other factors may also be responsible for this improvement, as this was a period of dramatic changes in schools, communities and families. In this vein, Armor (1992) argues that school desegregation accounted for little of the improvement based on the fact that the achievement of blacks in "segregated" districts (those less than 50% white) improved as much as the achievement of blacks in "desegregated" districts. Yet because many of the districts in the segregated category actually had desegregation plans in place and experienced sizable increases in black exposure to whites, the simple difference in differences comparison does not provide persuasive evidence. This example highlights the need to control for the influences of other changes and the importance of comprehensive information about schools and districts.

The endogeneity of school and neighborhood choice seriously complicates efforts to identify the causal effects of school racial composition and desegregation programs. Manski (1993), Moffitt (2001) and others consider these issues in the more general context of the estimation of peer effects; here we focus on those specific methods used in the study of racial composition and desegregation. Following a discussion of the impediments to the identification of causal effects of peer racial composition, we discuss briefly the relevance of empirical findings for current policy discussions.

Analyses of peer group influences typically divide peer measures into endogenous (behavioral) variables and exogenous or contextual variables. The first category refers to the contemporaneous and reciprocal influences of peer achievement on schoolmates, while the second refers to socio-demographic variables unaffected by the efforts of a student. Racial composition falls clearly in the latter category, making it unnecessary to consider the simultaneity issue that severely complicates efforts to identify effects of peer achievement. Nonetheless, the nonrandom grouping of students in districts and schools provides a formidable impediment to the identification of the relationship between academic, social and economic outcomes on the one hand and desegregation efforts and school racial composition on the other.

Equation (1) models outcome O for student i in grade G in school s as a function of family, desegregation program status, and peer influences:

$$O_{iGs} = X_{iGs}\beta + D_{Gs}\gamma + \overline{P}_{(-i)Gs}\lambda + D_G\overline{P}\theta + e_{iGs}, \qquad (1)$$

where D is an indicator variable for desegregation program status (or a vector of indictors for program type), $\overline{P}$ is peer quality measured by average characteristics of schoolmates (individual i is omitted from the calculation); X is a vector of family background variables; and e is the error term. Note that the effects of peer composition are permitted to vary by desegregation program status.

The identification of γ, λ and θ is complicated by the nonrandom sorting of children into schools and classrooms and the cumulative nature of schooling. Any correlation between $\bar{P}$ and D on the one hand and current or past unobserved factors that affect outcomes on the other leads to biased estimates of γ, λ or θ. Failure to account for the dynamic character of the learning process can also introduce bias and complicate the interpretation of the estimated effects.[7]

A number of different methods have been used to identify desegregation program and racial composition effects including random assignment experiments, ordinary least squares regression, value added models, and panel data techniques. Regardless of the approach, virtually all empirical work focuses on the identification of the "reduced form" relationship between outcomes and desegregation program status or peer racial composition, typically ignoring the precise structure of the underlying causal linkage. Peer racial composition may affect motivation, the quality of classroom interaction [cf. Lazear (2001)], teacher quality, or attitudes and expectations of teachers. Transportation of students to nonneighborhood schools certainly changes a number of components of the education experience, but it may also reduce parental participation, and the time cost of travel may adversely affect performance.

A separate issue from identification is the relevance of the results for education policy. Most desegregation programs were implemented around 1970, and much of the research on desegregation effects on achievement comes from that period. Not only have demographic changes and residential movements dramatically altered the composition of schools, school finance reform, shifts in student and teacher attitudes regarding race, expansion of school accountability systems, charter schools, and other public school reforms almost certainly affect the benefits of both expanded inter-racial contact and attendance at a nonneighborhood public school. The heterogeneity of both desegregation program types and the environments that form the context of racial interactions introduce additional variation into the likely effects of specific interventions.

The existing estimates of both desegregation and racial composition effects should be viewed most conservatively as capturing the effects of treatments on the treated. Care should be taking prior to drawing inferences about the likely effects of expansion or contraction of specific programs on students in different contexts. Nevertheless, the literature provides important information on the contribution of desegregation to black academic and economic progress, the likely benefits of program expansion and the potential harm from the dismissal of desegregation orders.

---

[7] Rivkin (2005) examines the identifying assumptions regarding the depreciation of knowledge for a number of education production function specifications.

Summary of results

The only social science evidence of harm from school segregation cited by the U.S. Supreme Court in *Brown* involved psychological studies of black children that related low self-esteem to segregated schooling.[8] Following the decision in *Brown* there have been numerous analyses of the effects of racial composition and desegregation on academic, social and labor market outcomes, and Table 9 summarizes a number of these.

The studies summarized in Table 9 provide mixed evidence on the effects of school desegregation programs and school racial composition. On the one hand, the random assignment experiments of the benefits of busing reveal little evidence that desegregation substantially increased black student achievement. On the other hand, observational studies generally support the hypothesis that desegregation and inter-racial contact are beneficial, particularly for longer term outcomes including school attainment and earnings. All in all, the diversity of research findings on effects of integration on black students remains largely unsettled. If there is a marginal consensus, it is that effects are probably small, but beneficial.

In a comprehensive summary of random assignment studies of school desegregation effects on reading and mathematics achievement in early grades, Cook (1984) concludes that meta-analyses of the results of a number of studies supports the view that the effects were quite small or even zero. There are a number of factors, however, that raise doubts about this interpretation of the evidence. First, the small sample sizes common in studies of single desegregation programs limit the power of the estimates, and this makes it very difficult to identify small but potentially important effects on test scores. Second, any heterogeneity in the effects of different types of desegregation programs implies that the estimates depend in part on the composition of programs included in the studies. Third, it may take a few years to work out the glitches of new programs.

Nevertheless, the contrast between the generally small estimated effects of desegregation on elementary school achievement in random assignment studies and the generally much larger effects on achievement and longer term outcomes in observational studies is striking. Beginning with the landmark legislatively mandated report, *Equality of Economic Opportunity* [Coleman et al. (1966)], the bulk of observational research finds that desegregation and inter-racial contact raised achievement, schooling, and earnings, and in some cases the estimated effects are quite large.

A number of alternative explanations could separately or together reconcile these disparate results. First is the aforementioned concern that the random assignment studies failed to uncover the true benefits of desegregation. Second is the possibility that contact with whites resulting from desegregation is less beneficial than contact resulting from residential integration, though Guryan (2004) finds that expanded interracial contact contributes to the positive desegregation effect on schooling. Third is the possibility that the benefits of desegregation and exposure to whites increase with age.

---

[8] Footnote 11 of *Brown* refers to the doll studies of Kenneth and Mamie Clark [Clark and Clark (1939)] that found that blacks in the segregated South tended to identify with white dolls and not black dolls.

Table 9
Selected research on effects of desegregation and racial composition on student outcomes

Article	Data	Method	Findings for black students
Coleman et al. (1966)	Survey	OLS	Higher percentage of black school-mates lowered achievement
Crain (1970)	1968 survey of blacks in northern metropolitan areas	Related incomes, education and occupational achievement of blacks to racial composition of high school	Found that exposure to whites raised income and occupational achievement by leading to greater interaction with whites
Cook (1984)		Summary of meta-analyses of random assignment studies of busing	Desegregation had at most a small effect on academic achievement
Armor (1992)	NAEP	Examine NAEP trends by school percentage white	School desegregation contributed little to the closing of the black/white achievement gap
Boozer, Krueger and Wolkon (1992)	National Survey of Black Americans	OLS and IV using year by state dummies as instruments	A higher proportion of high school schoolmates who were black was associated with fewer years of schooling, a less integrated work environment and lower wages
Grogger (1996)	NLS72 and High School and Beyond	OLS	A higher proportion of high school schoolmates who were black reduced wages, and the size of the effect increased between 1979 and 1986
Rivkin (2000)	High School and Beyond and OCR Surveys	OLS and IV using district exposure as instrument for school percent white	Finds little or no effect of exposure to whites on achievement, school attainment or earnings regardless of type of desegregation plan
Hoxby (2000)	Texas public school administrative data	OLS removing school specific enrollment trends	Higher black enrollment share lowered achievement, and the effect was larger in schools with a mid-range proportion black
Hanushek, Kain and Rivkin (2004)	Texas public school administrative data	Value added model with school by grade and school catchment area by year fixed effects	Higher black enrollment share lowers achievement, and peer average achievement accounts for little of the proportion black effect
Guryan (2004)	1970 and 1980 U.S. Census microdata	Difference in differences based on timing of desegregation program implementation	Desegregation accounted for roughly one half of the decline in the black high school dropout rate between 1970 and 1980
Angrist and Lang (2004)	Brookline public school administrative data	OLS and IV based upon Maimonides class size rule	Little or no evidence that urban, black and Hispanic students bused to a suburban district adversely affected achievement of nonblack or Hispanic suburban students

Again, the findings of positive effects on elementary school achievement in Hanushek, Kain and Rivkin (2004) and Hoxby (2000) contradict this view, as do the findings that neither desegregation nor increased exposure to whites benefits high school students and graduates [Rivkin (2000)]. The final explanation is that the observational studies fail to account for confounding factors and other sources of bias despite the use of a variety of empirical methods.

The early studies by Coleman et al. (1966) and Crain (1970) and later work by Grogger (1996) use observable characteristics alone to control for other determinants of achievement, schooling or earnings. Given the limited and often imprecise data that are available, this approach probably does not account for all confounding variables. In addition, both Crain (1970) and Boozer, Krueger and Wolkon (1992) rely on retrospective information on racial composition, raising the possibility of recall bias that could lead to overestimates of the benefits of exposure to whites if blacks who had more contact with whites later in life tended to systematically overestimate high school proportion white.

Two studies use instrumental variables to account for unobserved factors. Boozer, Krueger and Wolkon (1992) use state of birth by cohort fixed effects as instruments for school percent black. The IV results are quite imprecise but fairly similar to the OLS findings. Yet there is no strong reason to believe that the timing and scope of integration is the only or even the most important determinant of academic performance captured by these fixed effects. Rivkin (2000) uses district average exposure to whites as an instrument for school racial composition, thereby eliminating the effects of systematic sorting within districts. Although this does not alter the finding of no racial composition effect, these instruments do not account for between district differences in unobservable determinants of achievement.

Hanushek, Kain and Rivkin (2004) and Hoxby (2000) use panel data methods to investigate the effects of peer racial composition on achievement in Texas public elementary schools. Hoxby's use of de-trended between cohort differences in racial composition to identify the effects of peer racial composition eliminates school level confounding factors that evolve linearly over time, though the assumption that de-trended year-to-year differences in racial composition are orthogonal to all other determinants of achievement is likely to be violated. In addition, the large amount of student mobility introduces substantial year-to-year variation within cohorts, and the aggregate school data cannot distinguish between movers and stayers.

By comparison, Hanushek, Kain and Rivkin (2004) use a value added model with school by grade and school catchment area by year fixed effects. Although the fixed effects and included variables almost certainly account for the primary confounding factors, they also remove much of the variation in racial composition and raise the possibility that school switchers are driving the results. However, the pattern of findings reveals little or no evidence of mobility induced bias.

Finally, Guryan (2004) uses difference-in-difference and fixed effects methods and finds that desegregation explains roughly half of the decline in the black dropout rate during the 1970s. However, the lack of information on school or even district actually attended for a given year and heterogeneity of desegregation program type and timing raise questions about the validity of the approach, particularly given the high rate of school transfers among blacks.

A number of these studies also attempt to learn about the underlying sources of any effect on outcomes. Grogger (1996), Hanushek, Kain and Rivkin (2004) and Rivkin (2000) do find that effect magnitudes are largely insensitive to the inclusion of controls for school resources, and Hanushek, Kain and Rivkin (2004) provides evidence that peer average achievement does not account for a substantial portion of the racial composition effect.

It thus appears that racial composition does not serve as a proxy for school quality or peer achievement and that the observed racial composition and desegregation effects require alternative explanations. Some researchers, commentators, and community leaders argue that some blacks discourage others from excelling academically, but this view remains controversial.[9] A related literature focuses on cultural issues, including economic models that determine cultural behavior.[10] Others have suggested that teachers lower expectations for black students or that schools might adjust placement in academic tracks as the black concentration increases [see Ferguson (1998b)].

Finally, there is limited evidence of the effects of peer racial composition on whites owing in large part to the likely presence of white flight induced endogeneity bias. Angrist and Lang (2004) find that a program that provides opportunities for inner city children to attend school in affluent suburban districts does not adversely affect white students in the receiving districts. Instrumental variables estimates are noisy, and the fact that the suburban districts maintain strict controls over the number of incoming students and that all busing is voluntary makes it difficult to generalize beyond this limited type of intervention. In fact the finding in Hanushek, Kain and Rivkin (2004) that a higher black enrollment share reduces academic achievement for whites suggests that the costs to whites in terms of academic achievement are not generally zero.

6. Conclusion

Half a century has passed since the decision in Brown v. Board of Education profoundly altered public elementary and secondary education in the US. The persistent racial gaps in achievement, academic attainment, earnings, teen pregnancy, crime and poverty in combination with the extensive school segregation that remains has lead many to lament the failure of *Brown*. However, a closer look at the evidence reveals that Brown had a profound effect on the composition of schools and the academic experience of blacks

---

[9] Some early discussions, drawing on a number of perspectives and reaching different conclusions, can be found in Fordham and Ogbu (1986), Cook and Ludwig (1997), Steele and Aronson (1998), Ainsworth-Darnell and Downey (1998), Ferguson (1998a), McWhorter (2000) and Bishop et al. (2001).

[10] These include Austen-Smith and Fryer (2003), Fryer and Levitt (2003), Ogbu (2003) and Thernstrom and Thernstrom (2003).

and whites across the United States. In the absence of desegregation there would have been far less inter-racial contact in schools, and the weight of the evidence suggests that integration improved academic and labor market outcomes for blacks.

Yet given the level of residential segregation in the US today and recent Supreme Court decisions, desegregation programs are much more likely to contract than to expand. Perhaps most telling is the dwindling support for the view that schools must be integrated in order for blacks to receive a high quality education. This might connote implicit recognition of the limits of desegregation or a response to the continued racial gap in educational attainment. Regardless, arguments in support of charter schools, vouchers, accountability, and other reforms resonate in many predominantly black central city neighborhoods.

Nevertheless, the findings that racial isolation harmed blacks should not be dismissed as irrelevant to education policy today. The potential for widespread dismissal of desegregation orders and adoption of school reforms that increase segregation in many jurisdictions should evoke concern and a commitment to careful examination of future changes in school enrollment patterns and their effects on academic, social and labor market outcomes.

Acknowledgements

The project was funded in part by the H. Axel Schupf '57 Fund for Intellectual Life. We thank Maria Jones for excellent research assistance.

References

Ainsworth-Darnell, J.W., Downey, D.B. (1998). "Assessing the oppositional culture explanation for racial/ethnic differences in school performance". American Sociological Review 63, 536–553.

Angrist, J., Lang, K. (2004). "Does school integration generate peer effects? Evidence from Boston's Metco Program". The American Economic Review 94, 1613–1634.

Armor, D. (1978). "White flight, demographic transition, and the future of school desegregation". The RAND Paper Series 5931. Santa Monica, CA.

Armor, D. (1992). "Why is black educational achievement rising?". Public Interest 108, 65–80.

Austen-Smith, D., Fryer Jr., R.G. (2003). "The economics of 'acting white'". Working Paper 9904. National Bureau of Economic Research.

Bishop, J.H., Mane, F., Bishop, M., Moriarty, J. (2001). "The role of end-of-course exams and minimal competency exams in standards-based reforms". In: Ravitch, D. (Ed.), Brookings Papers on Education Policy 2001. Brookings Institution Press, Washington, DC, pp. 267–345.

Boozer, M.A., Krueger, A.B., Wolkon, S. (1992). "Race and school quality since Brown v. Board of Education". In: Baily, M.N., Winston, C. (Eds.), Brookings Papers on Economic Activity. Microeconomics. Brookings Institution Press, Washington, DC, pp. 269–338.

Brown v. Board of Education, 347 U.S. 483 (1954).

Clark, K., Clark, M. (1939). "The development of consciousness of self and the emergence of racial identity in Negro children". Journal of Social Psychology 10, 591–599.

Clotfelter, C.T. (1976). "School desegregation, 'tipping', and private school enrollment". Journal of Human Resources 22, 29–50.

Clotfelter, C.T. (1999). "Public school segregation". Land Economics 75, 487–504.

Clotfelter, C.T. (2002). "Interracial contact in high school activities". The Urban Review 34, 25–46.

Clotfelter, C.T., Ladd, H.F., Vigdor, J.L. (2005). "Who teaches whom? Race and the distribution of novice teachers". Economics of Education Review 24 (4), 377–392.

Coleman, J.S., Campbell, E.Q., Hobson, C.J., McPartland, J., Mood, A.M., Weinfeld, F.D., York, R.L. (1966). Equality of Educational Opportunity. U.S. Government Printing Office, Washington, DC.

Coleman, J.S., Kelley, S.D., Moore, J.A. (1975). "Trends in school integration, 1968–73". Urban Institute Paper 722-03-01. Washington, DC.

Cook, P.J., Ludwig, J. (1997). "Weighing the burden of 'acting white': Are there race differences in attitudes toward education?". Journal of Policy Analysis and Management 16, 256–278.

Cook, T.D. (1984). "What have black children gained academically from school desegregation? A review of the metaanalytic evidence". In: School Desegregation. National Institute of Education, Washington, DC.

Crain, R. (1970). "School integration and occupational achievement of Negroes". American Journal of Sociology 75, 593–606.

Edwards, P. (1993). "Before and after school desegregation: African American parents involvement in schools". Educational Policy 7, 340–369.

Farley, R., Richards, T., Wurdock, C. (1980). "School desegregation and white flight: An investigation of competing models and their discrepant findings". Sociology of Education 53, 123–139.

Ferguson, R.F. (1998a). "Comment [on Cook and Ludwig]". In: Jencks, C., Phillips, M. (Eds.), The Black–White Test Score Gap. Brookings Institution Press, Washington, DC, pp. 394–397.

Ferguson, R.F. (1998b). "Teachers' perceptions and expectations and the black–white test score gap". In: Jencks, C., Phillips, M. (Eds.), The Black–White Test Score Gap. Brookings Institution Press, Washington, DC, pp. 273–317.

Fordham, S., Ogbu, J. (1986). "Black students' school success: Coping with the burden of 'acting white'". The Urban Review 58, 54–84.

Fryer Jr., R.G., Levitt, S.D. (2003). "The causes and consequences of distinctively black names". Working Paper 9938. National Bureau of Economic Research.

Grogger, J.T. (1996). "Does school quality explain the recent black/white wage trend?". Journal of Labor Economics 14, 231–253.

Guryan, J. (2004). "Desegregation and black dropout rates". The American Economic Review 94, 919–943.

Hanushek, E., Kain, J., Rivkin, S. (2004). "New evidence about Brown v. Board of Education: The complex effects of school racial composition on achievement". Unpublished manuscript.

Hoxby, C. (2000). "Peer effects in the classroom: Learning from gender and race variation". Working Paper 7867. National Bureau of Economic Research.

Iceland, J., Weinberg, D.H. (2002). Racial and Ethnic Residential Segregation in the United States: 1980–2000. Census 2000 Special Reports. U.S. Bureau of the Census, Washington, DC.

Lazear, E.P. (2001). "Educational production". Quarterly Journal of Economics 116, 777–803.

Leake, D., Faltz, C. (1993). "Do we need to desegregate all of our black schools?". Educational Policy 7, 370–387.

Lutz, B. (2004). "Post Brown vs. the Board of Education: The effects of the end of court-ordered desegregation". Unpublished manuscript.

Manski, C.F. (1993). "Identification of endogenous social effects: The reflection problem". Review of Economic Studies 60, 531–542.

Massey, D., Denton, N. (1993). American Apartheid: Segregation and the Making of the Underclass. Harvard University Press, Cambridge, MA.

McWhorter, J.H. (2000). Losing the Race: Self-Sabotage in Black America. The Free Press, New York, NY.

Milliken v. Bradley, 418 U.S. 717 (1974).

Moffitt, R.A. (2001). "Policy interventions, low-level equilibria, and social interactions". In: Durlauf, S., Young, H.P. (Eds.), Social Dynamics. MIT Press, Cambridge, MA, pp. 45–82.

Ogbu, J.U. (2003). Black American Students in an Affluent Suburb: A Study of Academic Disengagement. Lawrence Erlbaum Associates, Mahwah, NJ.

Orfield, G., Monfort, F. (1992). Status of School Desegregation: The Next Generation. Report to the National School Boards Assoc. Harvard University Press, Cambridge, MA.

Plessy v. Ferguson, 163 U.S. 537 (1896).

Reber, S.J. (2003). "Court-ordered desegregation: Successes and failures integrating American schools since Brown". School of Public Policy and Social Research, UCLA.

Rivkin, S.G. (1994). "Residential segregation and school integration". Sociology of Education 67, 279–292.

Rivkin, S.G. (2000). "School desegregation, academic attainment, and earnings". Journal of Human Resources 35, 333–346.

Rivkin, S.G. (2005). "Cumulative nature of learning and specification bias in education research". Unpublished manuscript.

Rossell, C. (1978). The Unintended Impacts of Public Policy: School Desegregation and Resegregation. Institute of Political Science, Duke University.

Sheff v. O'Neill, 238 CT 1 (1996).

Steele, C.M., Aronson, J. (1998). "Stereotype threat and the test performance of academically successful African Americans". In: Jencks, C., Phillips, M. (Eds.), The Black–White Test Score Gap. Brookings Institution Press, Washington, DC, pp. 401–427.

Swann v. Charlotte-Mecklenburg Board of Education, 402 U.S. 1 (1970).

Symonds, W. (2004). "Brown v. Board of Education: A bittersweet birthday". Business Week (May 17).

Taeuber, K., James, D. (1982). "Racial segregation among public and private schools". Sociology of Education 55, 133–143.

Taeuber, K., Wilson, F. (1978). "The Demographic Impact of School Desegregation Policy". In: Kraft, M., Schneider, M. (Eds.), Population Policy Analysis. Lexington Books.

Thernstrom, S., Thernstrom, A. (2003). No Excuses: Closing the Racial Gap in Learning. Simon and Schuster, New York, NY.

Weiler, J. (1998). "Recent changes in school desegregation". ERIC/CUE Digest 133, 1–8.

Welch, F. (1985). "A reconsideration of the impact of school desegregation programs on public school enrollment of white students, 1968–1976". Sociology of Education 60, 215–221.

Welch, F., Light, A. (1987). New Evidence on School Desegregation. U.S. Commission on Civil Rights, Washington, DC.

Wilson, F. (1985). "The impact of school desegregation on white public school enrollment, 1968–1976". Sociology of Education 58, 137–153.

Chapter 18

TEACHER QUALITY

ERIC A. HANUSHEK

Stanford University,

National Bureau of Economic Research

and

University of Texas at Dallas

STEVEN G. RIVKIN

Amherst College,

National Bureau of Economic Research

and

University of Texas at Dallas

Contents

Handbook of the Economics of Education, Volume 2
Edited by Eric A. Hanushek and Finis Welch
© 2006 Elsevier B.V. *All rights reserved*
DOI: 10.1016/S1574-0692(06)02018-6

Abstract

Improving the quality of instruction is a central component to virtually all proposals to raise school quality. Unfortunately, policy recommendations often ignore existing evidence about teacher labor markets and the determinants of teacher effectiveness in the classroom. This chapter reviews research on teacher labor markets, the importance of teacher quality in the determination of student achievement, and the extent to which specific observable characteristics often related to hiring decisions and salary explain the variation in the quality of instruction. The evidence is applied to the comparison between policies that seek to raise quality by tightening the qualifications needed to enter teaching and policies that seek to raise quality by simultaneously loosening entry restrictions and introducing performance incentives for teachers and administrators.

Keywords

teacher salaries, incentives, teacher experience, teacher education, teacher test scores

JEL classification: H4, I2, J4

Introduction

Teachers are central to any consideration of schools, and a majority of education policy discussions focus directly or indirectly on the role of teachers. There is a *prima facie* case for the concentration on teachers, because they are the largest single budgetary element in schools. Moreover, parents, teachers, and administrators emphasize repeatedly the fundamental role that teachers play in the determination of school quality. Yet there remains little consensus among researchers on the characteristics of a good teacher, let alone on the importance of teachers in comparison to other determinants of academic performance.

This chapter considers research related to the quality of teachers. Like many other areas where quality is important but difficult to observe, much of the evidence is indirect. Consideration of quality variation in the education sector is complicated further by the dominance of public provision of education, constraints on market operations, and the importance of nonpecuniary factors in the teacher supply decision. With public provision, schools are not necessarily operating in an efficient manner and do not necessarily make hiring decisions based on expected performance.[1]

The relevant research follows three distinct lines that relate in varying ways to teacher quality. At the most aggregate level and possibly the most influential, a variety of studies have traced changes over time in the salaries of teachers relative to those in other occupations. This set of studies flows naturally into analyses of the importance of pay and nonpecuniary factors in determining the distribution of teachers among schools. A second line of research, following directly from the first, investigates the extent to which specific teacher characteristics account for differences in student achievement. Finally, the third line of research drops the parametric, input-based view of teacher quality and attempts to identify the total impact of teachers on student learning without the constraints imposed by relying on measurable characteristics.

Most of the evidence examines US schools, where data and analysis have been generally more plentiful. Relevant research on other countries is included and, where available, does not indicate qualitative differences in conclusions.

1. Aggregate salary trends

A starting point in the consideration of teacher quality is the evolution of teacher salaries over time in comparison to other workers.[2] Teacher salaries constitute equilibria in the teacher labor market, and both demand and supply side factors contribute to changes in relative teacher salaries. Importantly, even if the correlation between alternative employment opportunities and instructional quality is weak and school districts do not

---

[1] The issue of efficiency of public schools is the subject of Hanushek, this volume.

[2] More details on the time pattern of salaries in both the United States and the United Kingdom can be found in Dolton, this volume.

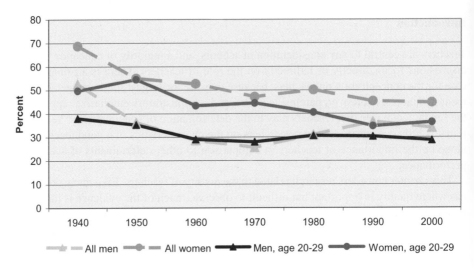

Figure 1. Percent college educated earning less than average teacher, by gender and age, 1940–2000.

systematically hire the best available teachers, any shift in supply would tend to move average quality in the same direction.

Figure 1 traces shows the proportion of 20–29 year old US college graduate non-teachers who earn less than the average 20–29 year old teacher by gender for the decennial censuses from 1940 to 2000.[3] Over this period the earnings of young female and male teachers both declined relative to those for other occupations. However, there are substantial gender differences in the time path of relative salaries. For males, relative salaries fell between 1940 and 1960 but remained roughly constant afterward. For females by comparison, relative salaries started out high – above the median for college educated females – but fell throughout the period. The changes are easiest to see for young teachers and college graduates, where the adjustment has been larger, but they also hold for teachers of all ages [see Hanushek and Rivkin (1997)]. In other words, growth in late career salaries has not offset the decline in salaries for younger teachers.

Discussions of the education industry cost structure and women's employment and earnings point to specific factors that have contributed to the decline in relative earnings of teachers and quite likely the quality of instruction as well. Perhaps most important

---

[3] Note that salaries for teachers include all earnings, regardless of source. Thus, any summer or school year earnings outside of teaching are included. No adjustments are made, however, for any differences in the length of the school day or in the days worked during the year. Nor is any calculation of employer paid fringe benefits made. A clear discussion of the importance of each of these along with interpretation of the overall salary differences can be found in Podgursky (2003). For the time series comparisons, these omitted elements of compensation are most relevant if there have been relative changes in the importance of them between teachers and nonteachers over time. We currently have little data on any such changes.

is the cost pressure placed on schools and other slow growth industries by productivity improvements elsewhere in the economy [see Baumol and Bowen (1965), Baumol (1967)]. In contrast to other industries, education has experienced little technological change, driving up the price of teachers in real terms [Lakdawalla (2001, 2002)]. Notice that real wages tend to rise even if districts do not absorb fully the increased price of skilled labor, in which case the relative quality of new teachers is likely to decline over time.

Because almost all teachers are college graduates and most elementary and secondary school teachers are women, any factors that affect the earnings of highly-skilled workers or women invariably affect the price of teacher quality. Many highlight the adverse impact of the recent expansion in job opportunities for women on the supply of teachers [Flyer and Rosen (1997), Corcoran, Evans and Schwab (2004b), Bacolod (2003), Hoxby and Leigh (2004)]. The aforementioned effects of productivity growth elsewhere in the economy and expansion of international trade in ways that favor skilled workers almost certainly amplify the adverse effects on the supply of teachers. On the other hand, the rapid rise in college enrollment and female employment almost certainly offset at least a portion of the negative effects on the supply of teachers. Nevertheless, as a whole these developments appear to have imposed severe cost pressures on schools, and schools appeared to have responded by raising salaries less than the full increase in the wage growth for college educated females.

The decline in the relative earnings of teachers has likely led to a fall in average teacher quality of incoming teachers over this period. But, as Ballou and Podgursky (1997) point out, the short term implications of a change in relative earnings are not clear cut, because salary affects both the supply of new teachers and retention of currently employed teachers.

The extent of any teacher quality decline remains unclear and depends in large part on the correlation between teaching skill and the skills rewarded in the nonteacher labor market. In a simple unidimensional skill framework in which nonpecuniary factors play no role, the substantial decline in relative salary would be expected to lead to a large fall in teacher quality. However, a more complex and realistic framework in which the skill set of teachers differs from that of other professionals suggests the possibility of a more muted response to the salary changes. For example, if teaching places greater emphasis on a set of communication and interpersonal relation skills than the general labor market, the salaries relative to all college graduates may not provide a particularly good index of teacher quality. These concerns about the congruence of skills in different sectors point to a priority area for further research. The discussion in the following sections offers some insights into possible separation of the various markets, but that evidence also remains indirect.

Another important determinant of the elasticity of teacher quality with respect to salary is the responsiveness of current and prospective teachers to salary changes. There is reason to believe that teachers may be less responsive than other professionals. Specifically, the "family friendly" nature of teacher employment (with, for example, hours and vacations coinciding with those of kids) or intrinsic rewards from teaching may have limited substitutes, making the decisions to enter or remain in teaching less sensitive to salary [see, for example, Scafidi, Sjoquist and Stinebrickner (2002)].

2. Distribution of teachers

One approach for disentangling the implications of the aggregate salary movements on quality has been to identify impacts on the distribution of observable teacher characteristics as proxies for quality. Investigations of salary effects on teacher characteristics take many forms and include both intertemporal evidence and cross-sectional evidence derived from different schooling systems and teacher labor markets.

A substantial body of research examines the effects of salary and nonpecuniary factors on the flows into and out of teaching and implicitly the supply of teachers with particular characteristics. This research, extended in a variety of dimensions, typically appears in two forms. The first analyzes the relationship between a specific teacher characteristic (TC) on the one hand and pay (P), benefits (B), or proxies for working conditions (WC) on the other. Examples include the determinants of the share of teachers with full certification, particular levels of experience, education, or teacher test scores,

$$TC = f(P, B, WC). \tag{1}$$

A second set of studies examines the determinants of teacher transitions, where transition probabilities are a function of the pecuniary and nonpecuniary factors described in equation (1), proxies for quality, and importantly the interactions of these two. Studies of shortages also fall into this category. Four types of teacher characteristics have received considerable attention: (1) experience; (2) measured achievement or skill; (3) specialty or subject area; and (4) credentials and teacher certification.

As is the case in other occupations, transition probabilities are quite high early in the career, decline with experience, and then increase as teachers move closer to retirement [e.g., Hanushek, Kain and Rivkin (2004)]. Evidence indicates that nonpecuniary characteristics likely related to working conditions have much stronger effects than pay on teacher transitions.[4] Moreover, it appears that opportunity costs in terms of foregone earnings in other occupations are much less important than the complementarity of family considerations and school working conditions [e.g., Scafidi, Sjoquist and Stinebrickner (2002), Podgursky, Monroe and Watson (2004)] in determining the probability of exiting teaching. This is consistent with the view that salary plays a larger role in the decision to become a teacher than the choice of schools or exit from teaching. Finally, studies of teacher exits find that salaries and outside opportunities have differing impacts on teachers depending on experience; see, for example, Murnane and Olsen

---

[4] Greenberg and McCall (1974), Murnane (1981), Hanushek, Kain and Rivkin (2004), Lankford, Loeb and Wyckoff (2002), Boyd et al. (2002, 2005) provide evidence on determinants of teacher transitions.

(1989, 1990), Dolton and Van der Klaauw (1995, 1999), Brewer (1996), Stinebrickner (1999, 2001a, 2001b), Gritz and Theobald (1996), Murnane et al. (1991), Scafidi, Sjoquist and Stinebrickner (2002).[5] It appears that district personnel policies also affect teacher flows [cf. Murnane (1981)]. Therefore this evidence captures the reduced form relationship between characteristics and transition probabilities, and inferences about supply responses rely upon specific assumptions about the demand side of the market.

Scores on licensing, college entrance, and other examinations provide objective skill measures, and a number of studies investigate the relationship between scores on a particular test on the one hand and salaries and other school or labor market characteristics on the other [Murnane et al. (1991), Hanushek and Pace (1995), Podgursky, Monroe and Watson (2004)]. The majority of this work considers entry into the teaching profession.

The change in the character of entering teachers over time has also been addressed [Bacolod (2003), Corcoran, Evans and Schwab (2004a, 2004b)]. The impact of salary changes and of changes in other occupational opportunities for women, discussed above, is clearly seen from data splicing together performance on standardized tests over time. Bacolod (2003) combines information from the various National Longitudinal Surveys (Young Men, Young Women and Youth). Corcoran, Evans and Schwab (2004a, 2004b) extend the samples of teachers to other data sets, thus expanding the periods that can be investigated, and also concentrate on individuals who actually enter teaching.

Bacolod (2003) shows that the standardized test scores of people entering teaching as opposed to other professions have fallen over time – dramatically in the case of females. Specifically, recent birth cohorts who score near the top of IQ or AFQT tests are much less likely to want to be teachers than those in earlier birth cohorts.[6] This drop is especially dramatic for women, but also holds for men and is consistent with the aggregate salary trends. Corcoran, Evans and Schwab (2004b) find that the relative fall in mean performance of female teachers, while significant, is much less than the fall at the top of the distribution.

The consideration of preparation has focused on the varying opportunity costs of teachers with different specialties. One of the first such studies considered how the uniform pay structure in teaching leads to shortages in specific areas, such as mathematics and science teachers who have better outside earnings opportunities [Kershaw and McKean (1962)]. That study highlighted the differential effects of policies and institutions on teachers with different characteristics. Following on Kershaw and McKean (1962), Rumberger (1987) examines how salaries affect the supply of science and math teachers.

Finally, considerable attention (although limited analysis) has been devoted to the possibility that school characteristics affect the ability of schools to hire fully credentialed teachers. In general this analysis simply reports gross correlations of lower

---

[5] Note that these conclusions are frequently implicit from an analysis of hazard functions for exiting teaching.

[6] This evidence splices together information from different surveys. By relying on relative performance measures, however, differences in tests are minimized.

proportions of uncertified teachers in central city and lower SES schools. Nonetheless, these casual observations almost surely do describe the reality – even if they do not fully identify the underlying impacts of individual, district, and state policy choices on the outcomes.

These studies provide information on the determinants of teacher transitions and the distributions teachers along a number of dimensions. The importance of the findings depends crucially on the relevance of the identified characteristics for determining student performance and other outcomes, i.e. the relationship with actual effectiveness in the classroom. This issue is the subject of the next section.

3. Teacher characteristics and student achievement

One general approach to understanding more about the extent to which specific teacher characteristics capture differences in instructional effectiveness is the estimation of the effects of specific characteristics on achievement and other student outcomes. We begin by describing the basic framework within which much of this research sits and then discuss the findings.

3.1. Basic structure

A large number of investigations of teacher quality focus on the effects of specific teacher characteristics on outcomes, controlling for student differences. These studies take a variety of forms. Here we provide an overview of the range of approaches that have been used. We critique the underlying modeling and interpretation in the subsequent sections.

A basic framework for the study of teacher effects begins with a model of achievement such as

$$O_g = f\big(F^{(g)}, P^{(g)}, C^{(g)}, T^{(g)}, S^{(g)}, \alpha\big), \tag{2}$$

where O_g is the outcome for a student in grade g; F, P, C, T and S represent vectors of family, peer, community, teacher and school inputs, respectively; α is ability; and the superscript g indicates all of the inputs are cumulative from birth through grade g. Simply put, student achievement at any point in time represents the cumulative outcome of a wide variety of inputs.

This model, which is frequently referred to as an educational production function, has been applied often. Its history is generally traced back to the "Coleman Report" [Coleman et al. (1966)], an early study conducted under the auspices of the United States government. Since 1966, over 400 such studies have been published in journals and books. Empirical research pursuing this type of analysis typically collects data on the relevant inputs into performance from either administrative records or surveys.

The numerous current and past factors that affect achievement at any point in time seriously complicate efforts to estimate the effects of specific characteristics. Perhaps most important is the extent to which any observed association between a school or teacher variable and student outcomes capture a causal relationship. For example, if children in higher income families attend schools with smaller classes on average than children in lower income families, the finding that smaller classes raise achievement may be driven in part by a failure to account fully for the direct effect of family income on student performance.

Teacher choice of schools can also complicate the estimation of teacher effects. As noted above, experienced teachers frequently have an option to move across districts and to choose the school within the district in which they are teaching, and they tend to take advantage of this [Greenberg and McCall (1974), Murnane (1981)]. Hanushek, Kain and Rivkin (2004) further show that teachers switching schools or districts tend to move systematically to places where student achievement is higher. This movement suggests the possibility of a simultaneous equations bias – that higher student achievement causes more experienced teachers or at least that causation runs both ways.

Another potential source of omitted variables bias is variation in state policy that might be correlated with the teacher characteristics. States, for example, determine the requirements to be a certified teacher, set the rules of collective bargaining on teacher contracts, and determine the financial structure including providing varying amounts of support for local schools depending upon their circumstances and tax base. States also specify the specific curriculum and outcome standards, establish testing requirements, and regulate a wide range of matters of educational process including various class size requirements, the rules for placement into special education classes, and disciplinary procedures. Because these policies vary widely across states, their omission could lead to bias coefficients in analyses that use data on a number of states. On the other hand, this concern is not relevant for cross-sectional analyses conducted within a single state where the policy environment is constant.[7]

More generally, value added models use prior achievement to mitigate problems of omitted variables bias. These models can take several forms depending upon assumptions regarding the depreciation of knowledge over time, and the most flexible form includes prior achievement in grade g^* as an additional explanatory variable:

$$O_g = f'\left(O_{g^*}, F^{(g)}, P^{(g)}, C^{(g)}, T^{(g)}, S^{(g)}, \alpha\right). \tag{3}$$

The precise estimation approach, and the resulting interpretation of any results, depends fundamentally on a series of assumptions about the structure of achievement and the underlying data generation process [see Hanushek (1979), Rivkin, Hanushek and Kain (2005), Todd and Wolpin (2003), Rivkin (2005)].

Though the use of such value added models mitigates problems resulting from the lack of historical information, it does not protect against the confounding influences of

---

[7] In some other estimation, say, related to overall spending or class sizes, aggregation of data becomes an additional issue, but this is relatively unimportant for the teacher characteristics considered here, because those analyses have uniformly been conducted at lower levels of aggregation (the school district down to the classroom). See Hanushek, Rivkin and Taylor (1996).

contemporaneous factors related to the variables of interest and not captured by prior achievement. Given the limitations of most data, available variables may not account for all relevant variables. This has led to the use of panel data methods, instrumental variables, and other approaches described below.

A remaining limitation of virtually all education production function studies is the use of a small number of observed characteristics to capture school and teacher quality. Although this parametric approach lends itself to standard regression techniques, it provides limited information on the variation in teacher quality, in part because most studies use administrative or survey data that typically contain a very limited set of characteristics. The most commonly available characteristics, teacher education and experience, are clearly important variables to consider, because they almost always enter into the determination of teacher pay. Yet, as described below, they explain little of the actual variation in teacher effectiveness, and even more detailed information about college quality, scores on standardized examinations or other information continues to leave much unexplained. Moreover, whenever separate surveys are designed to provide a richer set of characteristics, the specific items are seldom replicated in other surveys, thus providing little ability to ascertain the generalizability of any findings.

3.2. Evidence on measurable characteristics

Investigations of measurable teacher characteristics invariably begin with education and experience. In the United States and many other countries, these account for much of the salary variation within school districts. Because of their administrative use, these variables are frequently available for researchers. A smaller number of studies use other characteristics including teacher test scores, college quality, salary and teacher certification.

The empirical analyses take many forms. A vast majority investigate variable effects on student achievement as measured by some form of standardized test, while the others estimate effects on school attainment, future earnings and other outcomes. The studies cover a range of grade levels, types of schools, areas of the United States and other countries, and they produce a divergent set of results on the key variables of interest.

3.2.1. Teacher experience and education

As noted, the most frequently studied aspects of teachers include their education and experience levels, the items that generally enter into pay determination. The simplest summary of their impact on student achievement from available analyses comes from aggregating the results across studies. Table 1, taken from Hanushek (1997, 2003), describes the estimated parameters from studies through 1994 in the United States.[8]

---

[8] While more studies have appeared since then, they are small in numbers relative to the stock in 1994, and they show no discernibly different pattern of results from those in Table 1. For a description of the studies, a discussion of inclusion criteria, and the bibliography of included work, see Hanushek (1997).

Table 1
Percentage distribution of estimated effect of key teacher resources on student performance

Resources	Number of estimates	Statistically significant		Statistically insignificant
		Positive	Negative	
All estimates				
Teacher education	170	9%	5%	86%
Teacher experience	206	29	5	66
High-quality estimates[a]				
Teacher education	34	0	9	91
Teacher experience	37	41	3	56

Source: Hanushek (1997, 2003).
[a]High-quality estimates come from value-added estimation [equation (3)] where the sample is drawn for individual students from a single state.

Perhaps most remarkable is the finding that a master's degree has no systematic relationship to teacher quality as measured by student outcomes. This immediately raises a number of issues for policy, because advanced degrees invariably lead to higher teacher salaries and because advanced degrees are required for full certification in a number of states. Indeed, over half of current teachers in the US have a master's degree or more.

Teacher experience has a more positive relationship with student achievement, but still the overall picture is not that strong. While a majority of the studies finds a positive effect, only a minority of all estimates provides statistically significant results. Even the subset of studies that use a value added approach and information from a single state produce a highly variable set of results (see bottom panel in Table 1). If anything, the 37 value-added estimates within individual states suggest more strongly that experience has an impact, although still only 41% of the estimates are statistically significant. It is quite likely that a number of these studies lack the statistical power necessary to identify precisely the experience effects.

An important consideration in the case of experience is the possibility of a highly nonlinear relationship between the quality of instruction and experience. Murnane and Phillips (1981b) investigates the impact of experience with spline functions and find nonlinearities, although the actual estimates differ sharply across data samples. Rivkin, Hanushek and Kain (2005) also pursue a nonparametric investigation of experience and find that experience effects are concentrated in the first few years of teaching. Specifically, teachers in their first and, to a somewhat lesser extent, their second year tend to perform significantly worse in the classroom. Using a different estimation methodology, Hanushek et al. (2005) pinpoint the experience gains as arising during the first year of teaching, with essentially flat impacts of experience subsequently. Consequently, misspecification of the relationship between outcomes and experience likely contributed to the failure to find a systematic link between quality and experience.

Because of the high turnover rate early in the career, estimated returns to experience typically combine the acquisition of skills on the job with any nonrandom transitions out of teaching. Rivkin, Hanushek and Kain (2005) estimate experience coefficients identified by variation both across and within teachers with coefficients identified solely by within teacher changes in experience. The estimated experience effects are quite similar, indicating that the dominant effect is learning by doing in the first year in the classroom.

Similar investigations of teacher education and experience have been conducted in a wide range of developed and developing countries [Hanushek (2003)]. As a broad statement, the results are qualitatively similar except there is perhaps slightly stronger support for a positive impact of these in developing countries. At the same time, the additional support is slight with the majority of studies still not finding significant impacts. Moreover, these studies seldom provide truly adequate controls for the omitted variables problems discussed here.

3.2.2. Teacher salary

Instead of concentrating on the prior characteristics of teachers that enter into salary decisions, it is of course possible to analyze whether or not salary directly relates to student performance. Unfortunately such studies are frequently muddled. The majority of analyses relate the salary levels of teachers to the achievement of student. Yet, the salary level for any individual teacher is a composite of pay for specific characteristics (experience, education and other attributes as identified above) and, whenever the analysis crosses school districts, differences in the salary schedule. In other words, it has elements of movements along the salary schedule and shifts in the entire schedule.

The econometric evidence, presented in Table 2, again shows no strong evidence that salaries are a good measure of teacher quality. Overall, the studies show that salaries are more likely to be positively related to student achievement than negatively. Nonetheless, only a minority is statistically significant.

Many of the studies of teacher salaries are subject to the prior mentioned quality problems – lack of historical information and missing measures of state policy. The state policy concerns are especially important because states intervene in wage determination in a variety of ways that also are likely to influence school outcomes. The bottom portion of the table provides information on the more refined set of value-added, single state estimates. For this very small set of estimates, most are statistically insignificant. The estimates that are significant all come from a set of studies considering just single districts, so they provide estimates just about moves along the schedule and not what might happen with shifts in the entire schedule.

A series of other issues complicate efforts to identify the link between salaries outcomes. Perhaps most important is the possibility that nominal salaries in part reflect compensating differentials – for cost-of-living differences, for the desirability of partic-

Table 2
Percentage distribution of estimated effect of teacher salaries on student performance

Resources	Number of estimates	Statistically significant		Statistically insignificant
		Positive	Negative	
All estimates				
Teacher salary	118	20%	7%	73%
Teacher test scores	41	37	10	53
High-quality estimates[a]				
Teacher salary	17	18	0	82
Teacher test scores	9	22	11	67

Source: Hanushek (1997, 2003).
[a]High quality estimates come from value-added estimation [equation (3)] where the sample is drawn for individual students from a single state.

ular schools and their working conditions, or for such other things as urban crime.[9] Most of the studies considering compensating differentials do not directly relate job-related characteristics and salaries to student outcomes but simply show that salaries vary with such characteristics. [An exception is Loeb and Page (2000) who argue on the basis of state panel data that compensating differentials have masked the effects of salaries in many prior studies of educational outcomes.[10]]

A second vexing issue is the importance of both past and current salaries in the distribution of the current stock of teachers. Salary influences entry into the profession, choice of first job, and movements among jobs, but tenure, lack of transferability of experience credit, and other factors almost certainly reduce the sensitivity of teacher transitions to salary as experience rises. Because virtually all analyses of salary effects compare current salaries with the effectiveness of the existing stock of teachers, this stock/flow amalgamation raises questions about the findings. An exception is Hanushek et al. (2005) who use a sample of district switchers to identify the relationship between salary and the quality of instruction. They do not find that higher salaries attract significantly more effective teachers, though the very small number of district switchers leads to imprecise estimates.

[9] See, for example, Antos and Rosen (1975), Levinson (1988), Eberts and Stone (1985), Kenny (1980), Toder (1972), Hanushek and Luque (2000), Chambers and Fowler (1995), Fowler and Monk (2001) and Hanushek, Kain and Rivkin (2004).

[10] Their study, relying on interstate variations in school completion and teacher pay, faces an analytical tradeoff between using aggregate state data subject to potential missing policy information and providing some control for state amenity differences.

3.2.3. Teacher tests

One measured characteristic – teacher scores on achievement tests – has received considerable attention, because it has more frequently been significantly correlated with student outcomes than the other characteristics previously discussed. Table 2 displays the results of these studies. Several points are important. First, while the evidence is stronger than that for other explicit teacher characteristics, it is far from overwhelming. Second, the tests employed in these various analyses differ in focus and content, so the evidence mixes together a variety of things. At the very least, it is difficult to transfer this evidence to any policy discussions that call for testing teachers – because that would require a specific kind of test that may or may not relate to the evidence. Third, even when significant, teacher tests capture just a small portion of the overall variation in teacher effectiveness (see below).

The open research questions on both changes over time in the quality of instruction and the distribution among districts relate directly to the nature of tested knowledge and how it influences achievement. For example, Wayne and Youngs (2003) suggest that achievement does not uniformly matter but may relate to specific subjects (e.g., more important in secondary school mathematics instruction than in primary school reading). Additionally, as the investigations of time patterns cited suggest, the changes in teacher scores have not been uniform but instead have related more to the thickness of the upper tails of the distribution than to the mean. The existing research gives no hints of whether there is any nonlinear impact of knowledge in different ranges.

3.2.4. Teacher certification

The most pervasive policy action of states aimed at teacher quality is setting certification requirements. Although there is substantial variation across states in what is required for certification, the underlying theme is to set minimum requirements in an effort to ensure that no students are subjected to bad teaching. The problem is that, though certification requirements may prevent some poorly prepared teachers from entering the profession, they may also exclude others who would be quite effective in the classroom. Not only may some potentially good teachers be unable to pass the examinations, the certification requirements may discourage others from even attempting to enter the teaching profession; see, for example, Murnane et al. (1991). The nature of this tradeoff depends in large part on the objectives and skills of administrators who make teacher personnel decisions.[11]

The literature provides mixed evidence on the effects of certification on teacher quality. Extensive literature has been accumulating on the importance of teacher certification and credentials, although it has proved quite controversial. Much of the work is based on specifications that are susceptible to substantial biases from other determinants of

---

[11] We thank Dale Ballou for providing a clear description of this tradeoff.

achievement, though a few recent papers provide more persuasive empirical specifications. Wayne and Youngs (2003) document the limitations of most studies on certification while reviewing some of the components of certification. Elements of the debate over the effectiveness of teacher certification can be traced through National Commission on Teaching and America's Future (1996), Abell Foundation (2001), Walsh (2002), Goldhaber and Brewer (2000, 2001), Darling-Hammond, Berry and Thoreson (2001). Goldhaber and Brewer (2000) find, for example, that teachers with subject-matter certification in mathematics perform better than other teachers, while teachers with emergency certification perform no worse than teachers with standard certification, although Darling-Hammond, Berry and Thoreson (2001) dispute the interpretation. Jepsen and Rivkin (2002) find small certification effects on teacher value added to mathematics and reading achievement once the nonlinearities in the return to experience are adequately controlled.

Two elements of this line of research merit particular attention. First, most states require teachers to meet certification requirements either upon hiring or within a short period of time. The studies that investigate teacher certification rely upon observations of existing school systems, where the lack of a teaching certificate generally implies a special situation. For example, urban school systems with heavily disadvantaged populations frequently find it hard to attract sufficient numbers of fully certified teachers and thus resort to hiring noncertified teachers. A very different situation is the development of specialized recruitment programs that are designed to bring people into the teaching profession for short periods of time. For example, the Teach for America program actively recruits top graduates of some of the best undergraduate schools to teach in difficult urban schools for a two year period [Raymond, Fletcher and Luque (2001), Raymond and Fletcher (2002), Decker, Mayer and Glazerman (2004)]. In these cases, not having a teacher certificate is intertwined with having attended a high-quality college or university. The nature of these hires is seldom explicitly described, but it clearly complicates the interpretation of the estimated effects. None of the studies of certification is clear about the nature of the selection process and, thus, about the generalizations that can be drawn from the findings.

Second, teacher certification varies dramatically across states. Simply identifying whether or not a teacher is certified will mean very different things depending on the state. Moreover, a variety of states have gone into alternative entry systems, and many will award a teacher certificate based on different criteria from those entering through traditional training institutions. Thus, even within a state, a teaching certificate may not indicate the completion of a given set of requirements.

4. Outcome-based measures of quality

An alternative approach to the examination of teacher quality concentrates on pure outcome-based measures of teacher effectiveness. The general idea is to investigate "total teacher effects" by looking at differences in growth rates of student achievement across teachers. A good teacher would be one who consistently obtained high learning growth from students, while a poor teacher would be one who consistently produced low learning growth. In its simplest form, we could think of separating teacher effects from other inputs as in equation (4):

$$O_g - O_{g^*} = f''\left(F^{(g-g^*)}, P^{(g-g^*)}, C^{(g-g^*)}, T^{(g-g^*)}, S^{(g-g^*)}, \alpha\right) + t_j, \qquad (4)$$

where t_j is the influence of having teacher j [conditional upon the other inputs, $f''(\cdot)$].

Equation (4) obviously places some structure on the achievement process, but the approach is appealing for several reasons. First, it does not require the choice of specific teacher characteristics, a choice that data limitations often constrain. Second, and related, it does not require knowledge of how different characteristics might interact in producing achievement. (Most prior work on specific characteristics assumes that the different observed characteristics enter linearly and additively in determining classroom effectiveness.) Third, it gives a benchmark for the importance of variations in teacher quality against which any consideration of specific skills or types of policy interventions can be compared.

A variety of studies have pursued this general approach over the past four decades; see Hanushek (1971, 1992), Armor et al. (1976), Murnane (1975), Murnane and Phillips (1981a), Aaronson, Barrow and Sander (2003), Rockoff (2004), Rivkin, Hanushek and Kain (2005) and Hanushek et al. (2005). Careful consideration of such work reveals the difficulties that must be overcome in order to estimate the variation of overall teacher effects.[12]

The major threats to the semiparametric estimation of the variance of teacher quality result from the nonrandom sorting of families among schools, the nonrandom sorting of students among classrooms, and test measurement issues.[13] In addition to problems introduced by random measurement error, most achievement tests are not designed to provide valid rankings of the effectiveness of teachers with very different mixes of students in terms of academic preparation. For example, a test that concentrates on rudimentary material will do a poor job identifying differences in teacher quality among teachers whose students could answer the vast majority of questions on the basis of knowledge acquired prior to the current school year. Moreover, the average achievement gain could be higher for a poor teacher with initially low achieving students than for an excellent teacher with initially high achieving students if the test does not cover most of the material taught by the high-quality teacher.

Much of the early work was based on a single cross-section of teachers. In this framework, the observed student characteristics must control for all student heterogeneity. Moreover, the between teacher variance in achievement will conflate actual differences

---

[12] A similar study for developing countries (specifically Brazil) finds very consistent findings [Harbison and Hanushek (1992)].

[13] The discussion of measurement error in school accountability measures is related. Kane and Staiger (2002a, 2002b) point out that aggregate school measurement error will introduce variability in apparent school performance over time.

and measurement error requiring the estimation of the teacher fixed effect error variance.[14] In other words, the estimated teacher effect $(\hat{t})$ equals the true teacher effect (t) plus error.

The availability of multiple years of information for teachers permits the identification of the variance in teacher quality on the basis of the persistence of teacher fixed effects across years [Hanushek (1992), Hanushek et al. (2005)]. This eliminates the influences of random measurement error and year to year differences in student characteristics within classrooms. Specifically, if the measurement error in estimated teacher quality is uncorrelated across years, the expected value of the correlation of teacher by year fixed effects for years t_1 and t_2 is

$$E(r_{12}) = \frac{\text{var}(t)}{\text{var}(\hat{t})} \tag{5}$$

and the variance in true teacher quality (t) can be estimated directly (as long as it is constant across years).

Of course actual teacher effectiveness may change from year to year, and this approach classifies all nonpersistent outcomes as noise. This is particularly problematic in specifications that focus on within school and year variation. These estimated fixed effects are quite sensitive to teacher turnover, because turnover can dramatically change a teacher's place in the quality distribution in her school even when her effectiveness in the classroom is unchanged. Therefore, by focusing solely on the persistent quality differences [Equation (5)], some true systematic differences in teachers are masked by a varying comparison group and are treated as random noise. On the other hand, any persistent differences in classroom composition even within schools continue to bias the variance estimates.

Efforts to eliminate the confounding influences of student heterogeneity take a number of forms. Both Aaronson, Barrow and Sander (2003) and Hanushek et al. (2005) focus on within school variation in some specifications, eliminating both the actual variance in teacher quality between schools and any unobserved student, community, and school differences including the impacts of principals and other administrators. Controlling for differences in the quality of school administration is crucial given the important role attributed to principals and superintendents and the failure of observable characteristics to explain much of the variation in administrator quality.[15] This approach mitigates most of the problem introduced by the nonrandom sorting of students among schools, and the inclusion of observed student and peer characteristics further reduces the effects of confounding factors. Hanushek et al. (2005) also transform the test score gain measure such that teachers are measured on the basis of the performance of their students relative to other students at a similar place in the initial test score distribution.

---

[14] Aaronson, Barrow and Sander (2003) and Rockoff (2004) use different information from the teacher fixed effect regressions to construct estimates of the error component of the estimated between teacher variance.

[15] See Broad Foundation and Thomas B. Fordham Institute (2003) for a discussion of administrator credentials.

Using a very different approach, Rockoff (2004) simultaneously estimates both student and teacher fixed effects on the level of achievement. This controls for all time invariant student differences in the level of achievement but does not account for systematic changes as students progress through school. In particular, knowledge acquired in a given year likely affects achievement in subsequent years, raising serious questions about the validity of this approach.

Regardless of the approach, the direct estimates of the teacher quality variance remain subject to biases resulting from unobserved student differences across classrooms. In order to control fully for student heterogeneity and avoid problems introduced by measurement error, Rivkin, Hanushek and Kain (2005) aggregate across teachers in a grade, remove student and school by grade fixed effects, and focus on the link between teacher turnover and variation in student achievement. This approach produces a lower bound estimate of the variation in teacher quality that almost certainly underestimates the true variance by a substantial amount. Not only does it ignore all between school variation in teacher quality, but violations of the maintained assumptions (about the stability of teacher effects and about the distribution of teacher quality) and measurement error both attenuate the estimated variance.

The magnitude of estimated differences in teacher quality is impressive. Hanushek (1992) shows that teachers near the top of the quality distribution can get an entire year's worth of additional learning out of their students compared to those near the bottom.[16] That is, a good teacher will get a gain of 1.5 grade level equivalents while a bad teacher will get 0.5 year for a single academic year.

The more conservative lower bound estimators used by [Rivkin, Hanushek and Kain (2005)] also generate sizable estimates of the teacher quality variance: moving from an average teacher to one at the 85th percentile of teacher quality (i.e., moving up one standard deviation in teacher quality) increases student achievement gains by more than 4 percentile ranks in the given year. With their data, this is roughly equivalent to the effects of a ten student (approximately 50%) decrease in class size. As noted above, this method almost certainly understates the true variance in the quality of instruction. The within school estimators of the teacher quality variance reported in Hanushek et al. (2005) are roughly 50 percent larger. Importantly, the results for specifications that focus solely on within school differences do not differ markedly from those that also include teacher quality differences among schools, indicating that most of the variation in the quality of instruction occurs within schools.

The pattern of findings in the Project STAR study is also consistent with existence of substantial within school differences in teacher quality. Project STAR is the widely cited study of class size that involved random assignment of students to classes with varying numbers of students [Word et al. (1990)].[17] Average differences by class size

---

[16] These estimates consider value-added models with family and parental models. The sample includes only low-income minority students, whose average achievement in primary school is below the national average. The comparisons given compare teachers at the 5th percentile with those at the 95th percentile.

[17] Students were assigned to three separate treatment groups: regular-sized classes (22–25 students), regular-sized classes with an aide (22–25 students) and small classes (12–17).

were the focus of the experiment, but the student results actually differed widely by specific classroom. In only 40 out of 79 schools did the kindergarten performance in the small classroom exceed that in the regular classrooms (with and without aides). This is significantly greater than random (26 out of 79), but much smaller than might be expected to result from simple random test error given the large difference in class size among classrooms. The most straightforward interpretation of this heterogeneity is that variations in teacher quality are very important relative to the effects of smaller classes.[18]

These estimates of teacher quality can also be related to the popular argument that family background is overwhelmingly important and that schools cannot be expected to make up for bad preparation from home. This perspective emanates from work that treats schools as monolithic institutions or equates quality with expenditure. The existence of substantial within school variation in teacher quality documented in Rivkin, Hanushek and Kain (2005) points to the fact that high quality teachers can offset a substantial portion of disadvantage related to family economic and social circumstances.

The discussion to this point treats teacher quality as common to all students in a classroom, but evidence suggests that teachers may be more effective with some students than with others. Specifically, both Dee (2004) using the random assignment data from the Tennessee STAR experiment and Hanushek et al. (2005) find strong evidence that teachers are more effective with students whose race matches their own. Similar variations across student ability dimensions do not, however, show such variations – suggesting that a good teacher is generally good for all students.

5. Markets for teacher quality

Output-based quality measures can also be used to trace patterns of teacher movements by classroom effectiveness rather than by proxies for quality as is the case in the work discussed in Section 2. Hanushek et al. (2005) utilize the matched panel data for teachers and students for a single large metropolitan district in Texas to describe the distribution of teacher quality by transition status.

Figure 2 plots the distributions of estimated teacher fixed effects by transition status based just upon within school variations in teacher performance [Hanushek et al. (2005)]. Neither these distributions nor comparisons of average quality across transition categories indicate that the average quality of teachers who leave inner city schools either for other districts or for employment outside of the Texas public schools exceeds the average quality of those who remain. This contrasts sharply with the popular belief that inner city districts disproportionately lose their better teachers to other school districts or other occupations. The inner city districts do have higher teacher turnover, but this evidence suggests that it is not concentrated among higher-quality teachers.

---

[18] A discussion of the experiment and overall results can be found in Word et al. (1990). Hanushek (1999) analyzes the basic experimental results and identifies the variation across classrooms.

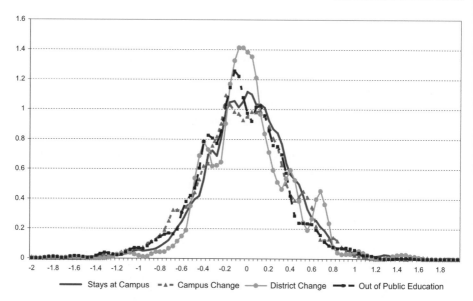

Figure 2. Kernal density estimates of teacher quality distribution: standardized average gains compared to other teachers at the same campus by teacher move status.

These data also permit an exploratory analysis of the market for quality and the competition across districts. Specifically, a number of the teachers in the large urban district decide to move to suburban districts. With the available data, the specifics of market interactions are not observed, only the results. It is not known where teachers applied for jobs or what districts were advertising for teachers. Nonetheless, if the simple assumption that higher salary and student demographic characteristics found to attract teachers deepens the applicant pool holds, the relationship between quality on the one hand and salary and school characteristics on the other provides information about district demand for quality. The preliminary results show little systematic evidence that districts prefer teachers who were more effective. Rather, the evidence suggests that higher salaries and lower minority enrollments enable districts to hire teachers with master's degrees, a characteristic with virtually no value in predicting quality. Importantly, this finding is consistent with both the inability to form an informative estimate of teacher effectiveness and with a lack of district focus on quality. Note, however, that the small sample size and use of estimates of teacher quality led to quite noisy estimates.

The possibility of obtaining outcome based quality measures from a wider range of local labor markets offers the prospect of understanding better the choices of teachers and of districts. It would, for example, be useful to investigate how the competitiveness of different areas in terms of alternative school districts affects the hiring patterns.

6. Policy connections

The research into teacher quality is scrutinized intensely because it has a direct relationship to current policy debates. Policy makers face conflicting suggestions about how to proceed. It is useful to relate the evidence on teacher quality to some of the central debates and to consider where the evidence is strong and weak.

Perhaps the key issue that pervades discussions is the tension between expanded state or even federal regulation of teacher labor markets versus decentralization of authority to schools and local education authorities. Another way to frame this discussion is as a debate over whether to tighten or to loosen licensing requirements for teachers.

The available evidence indicates clearly that legislating "good teachers" has been extraordinarily difficult. The idea behind most certification requirements is that they ensure that nobody gets a really terrible teacher. In other words, the general idea is that we can put a floor on quality. But doing this requires knowledge of characteristics that systematically affect performance. The prior evidence does not indicate that we can do this with any certainty.

Two caveats are, however, important. First, the existing research has not been very precise about the characteristics of certification requirements. The requirements in the US vary significantly by state, but the typical analysis has not investigated the components of certification in any detail. Second, and related, much of the attention to certification has centered on calls to expand current certification in significant ways. For example, certification for secondary school mathematics and science might require a college major in the subject (as opposed to a degree in mathematics education per se). Certification might also require advanced degrees in a combination of child psychology, pedagogy and the like. These details have not been adequately addressed in existing research.

Tightening up on requirements essentially makes it more costly to enter teaching, and thus one would expect it to the lower supply of teachers. This would imply that the cost of teachers of any given quality would rise. Nonetheless, virtually nothing is known about the magnitude or importance of such feedback effects on the teacher labor market.

The other side, loosening up, begins with the observation that existing evidence shows substantial variation in teacher quality, even among teachers with similar education and experience. This variation likely results from several factors: differences in teacher skill and effort; inadequate personnel practices (particularly the retention process but also the hiring process) in many schools and districts; and differences in the number and quality of teachers willing to work by subject and working conditions.

This policy position would allow more flexibility on who could enter the teaching profession but then would focus more on the overall incentive structure including retention, promotion, and pay decisions. The key ambiguities here center on the ability to identify teacher quality with sufficient precision to be useful in formulating policies and the ability to craft incentives that lead to higher quality.

Schools could utilize two basic methods for measuring teacher quality, one based on evaluations of overall effectiveness and the other based on statistical estimation of teacher value added. The former measure is clearly more comprehensive and nuanced, but it requires that administrators can both formulate a useful measure of teacher effectiveness and actually use that measure to rate teachers. There is evidence that principals can identify high-quality teachers in terms of value added to student learning. Early research on this by Murnane (1975) and Armor et al. (1976) showed that the normal evaluations of principals were highly correlated with the value added of teachers, even though the principal did not have the test and value added information available. This research has, nonetheless, not been replicated using different samples or different estimation approaches for finding the value added of teachers. In addition, the lack of success of merit pay programs suggests that it might be quite difficult for principals to actually apply these ratings in a high stakes environment.

In terms of the statistical evaluation approach, the State of Tennessee formalized the estimation of value added for teachers using annual state tests that linked pupil results with their teachers [Sanders and Horn (1994, 1995), Sanders, Saxton and Horn (1997)].[19] This approach, while mandated for the state, has not been directly linked to incentives for teachers in Tennessee, though other states have linked student performance with teacher compensation. Concerns have arisen about flaws in the structure of some state accountability systems, but little or no evidence exists regarding the impact of these systems on the quality of classroom instruction.

Most policy evaluations also take the existing training of teachers as given without considering alternatives.[20] For example, loosening up on the certification requirements for entry and relying more on subsequent evaluation of performance should, in theory, lead principals and school decision makers to pay more attention to teacher performance. This new role could well imply that they pay more attention to the pre-service and in-service training that teachers receive and this in turn could put pressure on education schools to alter their programs.

There remains limited evidence on the effect of incentive systems more generally on the quality of instruction. Some evidence has accumulated about merit pay plans, and this does not indicate that merit pay as applied to schools has been very effective [Cohen and Murnane (1986)]. There is reason to believe that these experiments are, however, too limited in the magnitude and character of the incentive scheme [cf. Hanushek et al.

---

[19] For a discussion of the specific approach along with an analysis of its sensitivity, see Ballou, Sanders and Wright (2004). The issues of error variance in teacher quality estimates are also relevant [Kane and Staiger (2002b)].

[20] There have been a variety of experiments in different states with alternative routes to teaching that do not involve traditional certification. The existing evidence on their success or failure is limited, but one program that has been carefully studied, the Teach for America program, shows generally positive results [see Raymond, Fletcher and Luque (2001), Decker, Mayer and Glazerman (2004)]. This program concentrates on getting graduates from very selective universities to commit to teaching for a limited amount of time and does not require the commitment to formal teacher training that normal certification requires.

(1994)]. Newer evidence from direct experiments provides stronger results with incentive pay comparing favorably to other school policies [Lavy (2002)]. For consideration of the available evidence on teacher merit pay, see Karnes and Black (1986), Cohen and Murnane (1985, 1986), Ballou and Podgursky (1993, 1997), Cohn (1996) and Brickley and Zimmerman (2001).[21]

Credible research into training versus selection issues as related to certification policies, merit pay, and so forth clearly requires longitudinal observations that link teachers, programs, and student performance. Until recently, there has been little possibility of such work, although recent developments of large, longitudinal databases from administrative records indicate that this may soon change.

7. Research agenda

The range of research needs and productive areas of inquiry can largely be seen by retracing the open questions of the previous sections. The most obvious complication to research arises from the fact that observed schooling situations represent the outcomes of several interrelated choices – those of parents, teachers, administrators and policymakers. This complexity makes it difficult to separate the various influences reliably. Thus, for example, judging variations in teacher quality require distinguishing teacher effects from elements of students and parents themselves.

Attention to these issues of selection, omitted variables bias, and causation was not a central element of the early work on teacher quality but has come to the forefront in recent research. As has developed in related work in public economics and in labor economics, there are a variety of ways of potentially disentangling the effects of various programs and elements. While this is not the place to go through these approaches, it is clear that refinement of research in these directions is an important part of any research agenda.[22]

Another area at the top of any agenda has to be developing a better understanding of how the market for teacher quality works. This research is clearly dependent upon developing reliable measures of teacher quality in a variety of different institutional circumstances. Suffice it to say that, even though a majority of discussion of teachers concentrates directly on teacher quality, most of the research about teacher markets lacks any direct investigation of teacher quality differences.

One area, however, warrants special attention. The discussion to this point has been virtually silent on the issue of cost. Policy decisions clearly require combining information about benefits with that about costs. Yet, almost nothing has been done to measure

---

[21] One important issue in the evaluation of merit pay schemes is the expectations for where results should show up. With an evaluation over a short period of time, the results would indicate whether a merit pay scheme affects the amount of additional effort that is induced from teachers. Over a longer period of time, however, evaluation would point to the impact on selection into teaching and retention of teachers.

[22] See also the related discussions in Hanushek, this volume, and Glewwe and Kremer, this volume.

the cost of teacher quality. For example, the costs of various training programs (pre-service and in-service) focused on improving teacher quality can be estimated, but they are never related to variations in teacher quality that are achieved. Similarly, discussions of salary policies tend not to be related to any measures of teacher quality. Attention to cost issues is a neglected area that sorely needs further work.

A second area of considerable neglect has been the interaction of teacher unions with teacher quality. Although it is widely believed that teacher unions create rigidities in hiring systems, little specific analysis identifies the magnitude or impact of these.[23] The discussion of retention and selection of teachers, for example, suggests that more focused policies might improve teacher quality, but these policies would appear to conflict with many union objectives and contract restrictions. Such an analysis, which necessarily gets into questions of political economy, is closely related to issues of policies related to incentives.

Along the same lines, much of the current policy discussion of accountability in schools and of choice in schools has a direct bearing on teacher quality concerns. Indeed, most people would see the potential effects of these policies as coming through their impacts on teacher quality. But, again, little is known about the potential interactions of these institutional structures and teacher quality.

Finally, recent advances in the economic analysis of contracting has obvious application to schools. The range of questions involving partial observability of performance, principal-agent problems, and the like are frequently motivated by suggestions of school reward structures [see, for example, Baker (1992, 2002), Lazear (1995)].

8. Conclusions

The growth in interest in questions of teacher quality is being met by an explosion of new data and analytical possibilities. This is married with increased interest in new strategies to separate true causal effects from associations due to selection and omitted variables. It seems reasonable then to presume that many of the open issues in the discussion here will soon be addressed if not resolved.

Acknowledgement

This research has been supported by a grant from the Packard Humanities Institute.

---

[23] One study finds that unions increase costs and lower productivity of schools, but it does not directly relate to issues of teacher quality [Hoxby (1996)].

References

Aaronson, D., Barrow, L., Sander, W. (2003). "Teachers and student achievement in the Chicago public high schools". WP 2002-28. Federal Reserve Bank of Chicago (June).

Abell Foundation (2001). Teacher Certification Reconsidered: Stumbling for Quality. Abell Foundation, Baltimore, MD.

Antos, J.R., Rosen, S. (1975). "Discrimination in the market for teachers". Journal of Econometrics 2 (May), 123–150.

Armor, D.J., Conry-Oseguera, P., Cox, M., King, N., McDonnell, L., Pascal, A., Pauly, E., Zellman, G. (1976). Analysis of the School Preferred Reading Program in Selected Los Angeles Minority Schools. RAND Corp., Santa Monica, CA.

Bacolod, M.P. (2003). "Do alternative opportunities matter? The role of female labor markets in the decline of teacher supply and teacher quality, 1940–1990". Department of Economics, University of California, Irvine (September).

Baker, G.P. (1992). "Incentive contracts and performance measurement". Journal of Political Economy 100 (3), 598–614.

Baker, G.P. (2002). "Distortion and risk in optimal incentive contracts". Journal of Human Resources 37 (4), 728–751.

Ballou, D., Podgursky, M. (1993). "Teachers' attitudes toward merit pay: Examining conventional wisdom". Industrial and Labor Relations Review 47 (1), 50–61.

Ballou, D., Podgursky, M. (1997). Teacher Pay and Teacher Quality. W.E. Upjohn Institute for Employment Research, Kalamazoo, MI.

Ballou, D., Sanders, W., Wright, P. (2004). "Controlling for student background in value-added assessment of teachers". Journal of Educational and Behavioral Statistics 29 (1), 37–65.

Baumol, W.J. (1967). "Macroeconomics of unbalanced growth: The anatomy of urban crisis". American Economic Review 57 (3), 415–426.

Baumol, W.J., Bowen, W.G. (1965). "On the performing arts: The anatomy of their economic problems". American Economic Review 55 (May), 495–502.

Boyd, D., Lankford, H., Loeb, S., Wyckoff, J. (2002). "Do high-stakes tests affect teachers' exit and transfer decisions? The case of the 4th grade test in New York State". Mimeo. Stanford Graduate School of Education.

Boyd, D., Lankford, H., Loeb, S., Wyckoff, J. (2005). "The draw of home: How teachers' preferences for proximity disadvantage urban schools". Journal of Policy Analysis and Management 24 (1), 113–132.

Brewer, D.J. (1996). "Career paths and quit decisions: Evidence from teaching". Journal of Labor Economics 14 (2), 313–339.

Brickley, J.A., Zimmerman, J.L. (2001). "Changing incentives in a multitask environment: Evidence from a top-tier business school". Journal of Corporate Finance 7, 367–396.

Broad Foundation and Thomas B. Fordham Institute (2003). Better Leaders for America's Schools: A Manifesto. Broad Foundation and Thomas B. Fordham Institute, Washington, DC.

Chambers, J., Fowler Jr., W.J. (1995). Public School Teacher Cost Differences Across the United States. National Center for Education Statistics, Washington, DC.

Cohen, D.K., Murnane, R.J. (1985). "The merits of merit pay". Public Interest 80 (Summer), 3–30.

Cohen, D.K., Murnane, R.J. (1986). "Merit pay and the evaluation problem: Understanding why most merit pay plans fail and a few survive". Harvard Educational Review 56 (1), 1–17.

Cohn, E. (1996). "Methods of teacher remuneration: Merit pay and career ladders". In: Becker, W.E., Baumol, W.J. (Eds.), Assessing Educational Practices: The Contribution of Economics. MIT Press, Cambridge, MA, pp. 209–238.

Coleman, J.S., Campbell, E.Q., Hobson, C.J., McPartland, J., Mood, A.M., Weinfeld, F.D., York, R.L. (1966). Equality of Educational Opportunity. U.S. Government Printing Office, Washington, DC.

Corcoran, S.P., Evans, W.N., Schwab, R.M. (2004a). "Changing labor-market opportunities for women and the quality of teachers, 1957–2000". American Economic Review 94 (2), 230–235.

Corcoran, S.P., Evans, W.N., Schwab, R.M. (2004b). "Women, the labor market, and the declining relative quality of teachers". Journal of Policy Analysis and Management 23 (3), 449–470.

Darling-Hammond, L., Berry, B., Thoreson, A. (2001). "Does teacher certification matter? Evaluating the evidence". Educational Evaluation and Policy Analysis 23 (1), 57–77.

Decker, P.T., Mayer, D.P., Glazerman, S. (2004). "The effects of teach for America on students: Findings from a national evaluation". Discussion Paper 1285-04. Institute for Research on Poverty, University of Wisconsin, Madison (July).

Dee, T.S. (2004). "Teachers, race, and student achievement in a randomized experiment". Review of Economics and Statistics 86 (1), 195–210.

Dolton, P.J., Van der Klaauw, W. (1995). "Leaving teaching in the UK: A duration analysis". The Economic Journal 105 (March), 431–444.

Dolton, P.J., Van der Klaauw, W. (1999). "The turnover of teachers: A competing risks explanation". Review of Economics and Statistics 81 (3), 543–552.

Eberts, R.W., Stone, J.A. (1985). "Wages, fringe benefits, and working conditions: An analysis of compensating differentials". Southern Economic Journal 52 (1), 74–79.

Flyer, F., Rosen, S. (1997). "The new economics of teachers and education". Journal of Labor Economics 15 (1), 104–139.

Fowler Jr., W.J., Monk, D.H. (2001). A Primer on Making Cost Adjustments in Education. National Center for Education Statistics, Washington, DC.

Goldhaber, D.D., Brewer, D.J. (2000). "Does teacher certification matter? High school teacher certification status and student achievement". Educational Evaluation and Policy Analysis 22 (2), 129–145.

Goldhaber, D.D., Brewer, D.J. (2001). "Evaluating the evidence on teacher certification: A rejoinder". Educational Evaluation and Policy Analysis 23 (1), 79–86.

Greenberg, D., McCall, J. (1974). "Teacher mobility and allocation". Journal of Human Resources 9 (4), 480–502.

Gritz, M.R., Theobald, N.D. (1996). "The effects of school district spending priorities on length of stay in teaching". Journal of Human Resources 31 (3), 477–512.

Hanushek, E.A. (1971). "Teacher characteristics and gains in student achievement: Estimation using micro data". American Economic Review 60 (2), 280–288.

Hanushek, E.A. (1979). "Conceptual and empirical issues in the estimation of educational production functions". Journal of Human Resources 14 (3), 351–388.

Hanushek, E.A. (1992). "The trade-off between child quantity and quality". Journal of Political Economy 100 (1), 84–117.

Hanushek, E.A. (1997). "Assessing the effects of school resources on student performance: An update". Educational Evaluation and Policy Analysis 19 (2), 141–164.

Hanushek, E.A. (1999). "Some findings from an independent investigation of the Tennessee STAR experiment and from other investigations of class size effects". Educational Evaluation and Policy Analysis 21 (2), 143–163.

Hanushek, E.A. (2003). "The failure of input-based schooling policies". Economic Journal 113 (485), F64–F98.

Hanushek, E.A., Kain, J.F., O'Brien, D.M., Rivkin, S.G. (2005). "The market for teacher quality". Working Paper 11154. National Bureau of Economic Research, Cambridge, MA (February).

Hanushek, E.A., Kain, J.F., Rivkin, S.G. (2004). "Why public schools lose teachers". Journal of Human Resources 39 (2), 326–354.

Hanushek, E.A., Luque, J.A. (2000). "Smaller classes, lower salaries? The effects of class size on teacher labor markets". In: Laine, S.W.M., Ward, J.G. (Eds.), Using what We Know: A Review of the Research on Implementing Class-Size Reduction Initiatives for State and Local Policymakers. North Central Regional Educational Laboratory, Oak Brook, IL, pp. 35–51.

Hanushek, E.A., Pace, R.R. (1995). "Who chooses to teach (and why)?". Economics of Education Review 14 (2), 101–117.

Hanushek, E.A., Rivkin, S.G. (1997). "Understanding the twentieth-century growth in U.S. school spending". Journal of Human Resources 32 (1), 35–68.

Hanushek, E.A., Rivkin, S.G., Taylor, L.L. (1996). "Aggregation and the estimated effects of school resources". Review of Economics and Statistics 78 (4), 611–627.

Hanushek, E.A., et al. (1994). Making Schools Work: Improving Performance and Controlling Costs. Brookings Institution Press, Washington, DC.

Harbison, R.W., Hanushek, E.A. (1992). Educational Performance of the Poor: Lessons from Rural Northeast Brazil. Oxford University Press, New York.

Hoxby, C.M. (1996). "How teachers' unions affect education production". Quarterly Journal of Economics 111 (3), 671–718.

Hoxby, C.M., Leigh, A. (2004). "Pulled away or pushed out? Explaining the decline of teacher aptitude in the United States". American Economic Review 94 (2), 236–240.

Jepsen, C., Rivkin, S.G. (2002). "What is the trade-off between smaller classes and teacher quality?". National Bureau of Economic Research.

Kane, T.J., Staiger, D.O. (2002a). "The promise and pitfalls of using imprecise school accountability measures". Journal of Economic Perspectives 16 (4), 91–114.

Kane, T.J., Staiger, D.O. (2002b). "Volatility in school test scores: Implications for test-based accountability systems". In: Ravitch, D. (Ed.), Brookings Papers on Education Policy 2002. Brookings Institution Press, Washington, DC, pp. 235–269.

Karnes, E.L., Black, D.D. (1986). Teacher Evaluation and Merit Pay: An Annotated Bibliography. Greenwood Press, New York.

Kenny, L.W. (1980). "Compensating differentials in teachers' salaries". Journal of Urban Economics 7 (March), 198–207.

Kershaw, J.A., McKean, R.N. (1962). Teacher Shortages and Salary Schedules. McGraw-Hill, New York.

Lakdawalla, D. (2001). "The declining quality of teachers". Working Paper 8263. National Bureau of Economic Research, Cambridge, MA (April).

Lakdawalla, D. (2002). "Quantity over quality". Education Next 2 (3), 67–72.

Lankford, H., Loeb, S., Wyckoff, J. (2002). "Teacher sorting and the plight of urban schools: A descriptive analysis". Educational Evaluation and Policy Analysis 24 (1), 37–62.

Lavy, V. (2002). "Evaluating the effect of teachers' group performance incentives on pupil achievement". Journal of Political Economy 110 (6, December), 1286–1317.

Lazear, E.P. (1995). Personnel Economics. MIT Press, Cambridge, MA.

Levinson, A.M. (1988). "Reexamining teacher preferences and compensating wages". Economics of Education Review 7 (3), 357–364.

Loeb, S., Page, M.E. (2000). "Examining the link between teacher wages and student outcomes: The importance of alternative labor market opportunities and non-pecuniary variation". Review of Economics and Statistics 82 (3), 393–408.

Murnane, R.J. (1975). Impact of School Resources on the Learning of Inner City Children. Ballinger, Cambridge, MA.

Murnane, R.J. (1981). "Teacher mobility revisited". Journal of Human Resources 16 (1), 3–19.

Murnane, R.J., Olsen, R. (1989). "The effects of salaries and opportunity costs on length of stay in teaching: Evidence from Michigan". Review of Economics and Statistics 71 (2), 347–352.

Murnane, R.J., Olsen, R. (1990). "The effects of salaries and opportunity costs on length of stay in teaching: Evidence from North Carolina". Journal of Human Resources 25 (1), 106–124.

Murnane, R.J., Phillips, B. (1981a). "What do effective teachers of inner-city children have in common?". Social Science Research 10 (1), 83–100.

Murnane, R.J., Phillips, B.R. (1981b). "Learning by doing, vintage, and selection: Three pieces of the puzzle relating teaching experience and teaching performance". Economics of Education Review 1 (4), 453–465.

Murnane, R.J., Singer, J.D., Willett, J.B., Kemple, J.J., Olsen, R.J. (1991). Who Will Teach? Policies that Matter. Harvard University Press, Cambridge, MA.

National Commission on Teaching and America's Future (1996). What Matters Most: Teaching for America's Future. NCTAF, New York.

Podgursky, M. (2003). "Fringe benefits". Education Next 3 (3), 71–76.

Podgursky, M., Monroe, R., Watson, D. (2004). "The academic quality of public school teachers: An analysis of entry and exit behavior". Economics of Education Review 23 (5), 507–518.

Raymond, M.E., Fletcher, S. (2002). "Teach for America". Education Next 2 (1), 62–68.

Raymond, M.E., Fletcher, S., Luque, J.A. (2001). Teach for America: An Evaluation of Teacher Differences and Student Outcomes in Houston, Texas. CREDO, Hoover Institution, Stanford, CA.

Rivkin, S.G. (2005). "Cumulative nature of learning and specification bias in education research". Mimeo. Department of Economics, Amherst College, Amherst, MA.

Rivkin, S.G., Hanushek, E.A., Kain, J.F. (2005). "Teachers, schools, and academic achievement". Econometrica 73 (2), 417–458.

Rockoff, J.E. (2004). "The impact of individual teachers on student achievement: Evidence from panel data". American Economic Review 94 (2), 247–252.

Rumberger, R.W. (1987). "The impact of salary differentials on teacher shortages and turnover: The case of mathematics and science teachers". Economics of Education Review 6 (4), 389–399.

Sanders, W.L., Horn, S.P. (1994). "The Tennessee value-added assessment system (TVAAS): Mixed-model methodology in educational assessment". Journal of Personnel Evaluation in Education 8, 299–311.

Sanders, W.L., Horn, S.P. (1995). "The Tennessee value-added assessment system (TVAA): Mixed model methodology in educational assessment". In: Shinkfield, A.J., Stufflebeam, D.L. (Eds.), Teacher Evaluation: Guide to Effective Practice. Kluwer Academic, Boston, pp. 337–376.

Sanders, W.L., Saxton, A.M., Horn, S.P. (1997). "The Tennessee value-added assessment system: A quantitive, outcomes-based approach to educational assessment". In: Grading Teachers, Grading Schools: Is Student Achievement a Valid Evaluation Measure? Corwin Press, Thousand Oaks, CA, pp. 137–162.

Scafidi, B., Sjoquist, D., Stinebrickner, T.R. (2002). "Where do teachers go?". Mimeo. Georgia State University (October).

Stinebrickner, T.R. (1999). "Estimation of a duration model in the presence of missing data". Review of Economics and Statistics 81 (3), 529–542.

Stinebrickner, T.R. (2001a). "Compensation policies and teacher decisions". International Economic Review 42 (3), 751–779.

Stinebrickner, T.R. (2001b). "A dynamic model of teacher labor supply". Journal of Labor Economics 19 (1), 196–230.

Todd, P.E., Wolpin, K.I. (2003). "On the specification and estimation of the production function for cognitive achievement". Economic Journal 113 (485).

Toder, E.J. (1972). "The supply of public school teachers to an urban metropolitan area: A possible source of discrimination in education". Review of Economics and Statistics 54 (4), 439–443.

Walsh, K. (2002). "Positive spin: The evidence for traditional teacher certification, reexamined". Education Next 2 (1), 79–84.

Wayne, A.J., Youngs, P. (2003). "Teacher characteristics and student achievement gains: A review". Review of Educational Research 73 (1), 89–122.

Word, E., Johnston, J., Bain, H.P., Fulton, B.D., Zaharies, J.B., Lintz, M.N., Achilles, C.M., Folger, J., Breda, C. (1990). Student/Teacher Achievement Ratio (STAR), Tennessee's K-3 Class Size Study: Final Summary Report, 1985–1990. Tennessee State Department of Education, Nashville, TN.

Chapter 19

TEACHER SUPPLY

PETER J. DOLTON

Department of Economics, Royal Holloway, University of London

and

Centre for Economic Performance, London School of Economics

Contents

Handbook of the Economics of Education, Volume 2
Edited by Eric A. Hanushek and Finis Welch
© 2006 Elsevier B.V. All rights reserved
DOI: 10.1016/S1574-0692(06)02019-8

Abstract

This chapter presents an overview of economic models of teacher supply and explains the modeling implications for both cross-section and time series econometric modeling. Specifically the literature on the determinants of teacher recruitment, turnover, mobility and re-entry into the profession are reviewed. It reviews the empirical evidence from the US, the UK on the labor supply of teachers and assesses the variation in teacher's real pay across in aggregate across 35 countries in the world. It also provides suggests for fruitful areas of future research.

Keywords

teachers, labor supply, occupational choice

JEL classification: J44, J45, J31, J33, I2

1. Introduction

In most countries in the world there is frequently a shortage of qualified teachers. Teacher shortages are not a new phenomenon. In 1967, 83 out of 91 countries, when surveyed [see IBE/UNESCO (1967)] said they were experiencing a shortage of secondary teachers. Since then, a vast literature in education policy from many different countries, has described the teacher supply problems and suggested policies to handle their own version of the shortage. Why does the supply of teachers cause a problem? Simply stated, in most countries in the world, the market for teachers is dominated by the government (or the federal state authorities) in the sense that the demand for teachers is a public sector demand and often the government will set teachers wages. In this context the root of the problem will be that the relative wages in teaching are too low to attract young people into the profession.

It is difficult to overstate the importance of teacher supply issues. Accordingly the problems have received high profile attention in the UK and the USA. In a major high level review of the problems in the US education system Darling-Hammond (2000) suggests that qualified teachers are not only a major determinant of student achievement but also one of the most inequitably distributed resources. She documents how poor children are exposed to lower quality teachers and poorer curricula. She describes a range of policy options to successfully recruit, prepare, retain and support a diverse, well-qualified teaching force. She comes down in favor of policies which increase teacher salaries, provide teachers with more support, renewed efforts on training and recruitment including more proactive recruitment, improved mentoring and induction for beginning teachers and designing schools to provide more support for teaching and learning.

The approach of this overview will be to first provide some empirical insight into the market for teachers by examining the supply of teachers and their salaries in the UK, USA and the rest of the world. We then provide an overview of the different theoretical and statistical models which have been used in the literature to investigate the supply of teachers. Sections 4 and 5 of the chapter provide an overview of the results which have been found from various countries about the factors which empirically influence the supply of teachers.

2. Empirical evidence on teacher supply and salaries

2.1. Measuring teacher supply

The measurement of teacher supply and most specifically the changes in teacher supply from year to year is problematic. The teacher supply function would theoretically be described by knowing how many teachers would be prepared to work at any given teacher wage on offer. Such a supply function, based on aggregating individual potential supply decisions, is difficult to recover. To clarify the different concepts we employ the terminology used in the UK. In the data which exists in several countries there are a variety of ways in which the change in teacher supply can be measured:

1. Changes in the pool of inactive teachers (PIT), i.e., those who have previously qualified as teachers but are currently not working as teachers.
2. Changes in the size of the pool of recoverable teachers (PRT) – who are those members of the PIT who can, in fact, be induced to re-enter teaching.
3. Changes in the stock of those teachers actually in service. This is the Zabalza, Turnbull and Williams (1979) definition and it relies on the idea that this stock is the number of people actually employed at the current salary on offer.
4. The number of new entrants into teaching.
5. The number of those leaving teaching.
6. The number of people enrolling and leaving teacher training programmes.

Figure 1 shows the teacher demand and supply elements that may be used to determine if the teacher labor market is in shortage or in surplus. Determining the demand for teachers is relatively more straightforward, as demand is dependent on the number of pupils in the country and on the Government's desired Pupil Teacher Ratio (PTR). The higher the number of pupils enrolled in schools along with a lower PTR target set by the Government will boost demand for teachers.

The supply of teachers as outlined in Figure 1 can be divided into two: the current supply of teachers and the potential supply. The current supply of teachers, consists of those who are currently in service in the teaching workforce. These teachers in service are denoted by "s" in Figure 1 and would contain those who are continuing teachers, the new entrants (e) and the re-entrants (rf). The new entrants are those who are first timers teaching in public schools while re-entrants are those with previous teaching experience in public schools, who left and are now returning to teaching. The number of students enrolled in the Initial Teacher Training (ITT) courses sustains the flow of new entrants as they can enter into teaching upon completion of their training. A shortage (ex) occurs when the demand for teachers is not matched by supply and a surplus occurs when the current supply of teachers exceeds the demand of teachers.

To complete the teacher supply and demand model, the outflow of teachers needs to be considered as well. Wastage makes up the outflow of teachers from the current supply. This group of leavers can be divided into those who leave at retirement age and those who leave for reasons other than retirement (i.e., those below the age of 60–65). When teachers (and those who are qualified to teach) leave the profession, they become inactive and enter the stock of potential teachers in the Pool of Inactive Teachers (PIT). In addition to the leavers below retirement age, the PIT also contains the ITT graduates who do not enter into teaching. A second component in the potential supply of teachers is the Pool of Recoverable Teachers (PRT). The teachers in the PRT are those who leave the profession but can be enticed to return to teaching and are therefore the main source of potential supply.

Using the distinctions in Figure 1 it is possible to argue that several of the variables which may exist in national data may serve as an adequate proxy for the state of teacher supply. It should be appreciated that there are limitations with all these proxy measures of the supply of teachers.

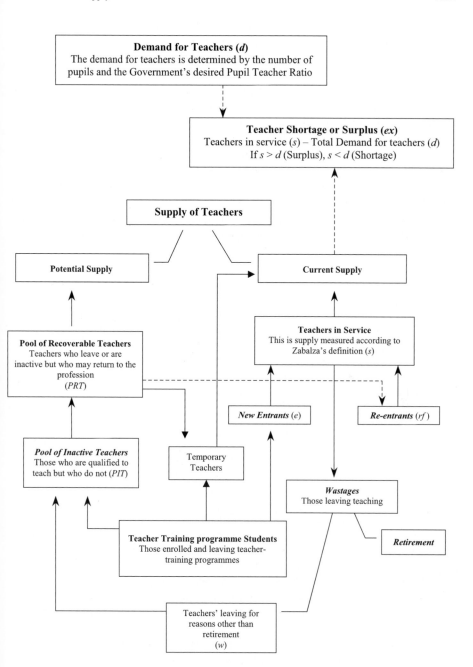

Figure 1. Teacher demand and supply.

The problem with using the PIT figures is that the calculation of these figures is subject to various assumptions about the retirement rate. The same is true of the PRT. Using the Zabalza, Turnbull and Williams (1979) definition of supply – as the number of people actually in teaching – does not give an adequate idea of the number of people who could teach. The number of people in post determines the actual number of people in teaching. It takes no account of the number of vacancies or the number of unemployed teachers who are seeking jobs but cannot find them. Importantly there may be a geographical mismatch of those seeking teaching jobs and where the vacancies are. In the UK there are many more vacancies in London and the South East but many more trained teachers who are not in work but seeking jobs in the North of England.

Using the wastage from teaching as a measure of supply is clearly indicative of the outflow rate from teaching but takes no account of the inflow rate. The problems with using the numbers entering and leaving ITT are that this gives one an impression of only part of the inflow rate. Other streams in the inflow are those who are possible re-entrants to teaching.

2.2. Evidence from the US

The empirical position on teacher supply and demand in the USA has been documented by Maaske (1951), Kershaw and McKean (1962), Kelsall and Kelsall (1969), Graybeal (1974), Corrigan (1974), Weaver (1983), Dimmock (1980), Haggstrom, Darling-Hammond and Grissmer (1988), Darling-Hammond (1989), Boe and Gilford (1992), Billingsley (1993), Boe, Bobbitt and Cook (1997), Grissmer and Kirby (1997), Flyer and Rosen (1997) and Darling-Hammond and Berry (1999). The account of the teacher supply position in the USA is brought up to date in Dolton, Tremayne and Chung (2003) and Dolton, McIntosh and Chevalier (2003).

In the USA, each Federal state is autonomous in acting as the teacher employer, deciding on the teacher training requirement, recruitment and pay issues. Therefore Dimmock (1980) suggests that the teacher labor market in the USA conforms to a *laissez faire* model. The USA does not have a set of consistently collected aggregate national education statistics. This means that although it is possible to obtain data on pupil enrollment changes and teacher numbers over time, other statistics such as the number of new entrants, new graduate teachers, re-entrants and wastage rates are unavailable for the USA. The actual data on some of these groups of teachers (mainly leavers, mover and new entrants) are limited to the years when the National Center of Educational Statistics' School and Staffing Survey (SASS) is conducted, that is, 1987–1988, 1990–1991 with follow-up surveys in 1988–1989, 1991–1992 and 1994–1995. In Figure 2 we graph the change in the pupil enrollment over the 1960–2000 period. From this graph it can be seen that the school pupil population was growing up until the 1970s then it declined until the 1980s before growing again from 1986. These trends will be reflected directly in the demand for teachers.

Figure 3 shows the number of teachers in the USA from 1960 to 2000. Teacher numbers in the USA were increasing throughout the 40-year period. Breaking it down into

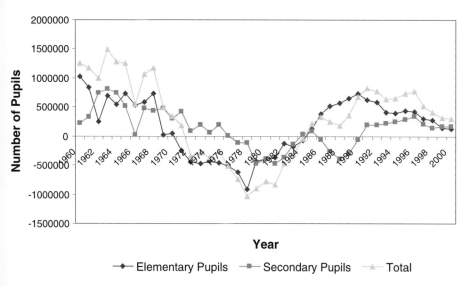

Figure 2. Pupil enrollment change in the USA, 1960–2000. *Source*: NCES.

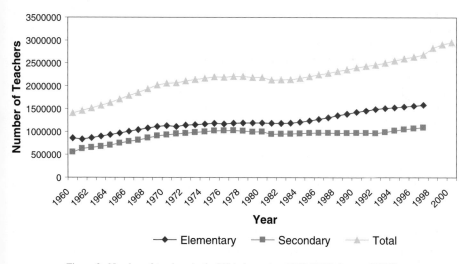

Figure 3. Number of teachers in the USA, by sector, 1960–2000. *Source*: NCES.

the different decades, the 1960s saw the highest growth in the number of teachers (at all levels) in the USA. This high growth in teacher supply was encouraged by the post-war baby boom. The total number of teachers was growing at an average of 4% in the 1960s, decreasing to 0.8% in the 1970s and the 1980s and increased substantially by 2.07% in the 1990s. The growth in the teacher numbers by each schooling level is similar to that found at the total level. Secondary school teachers were increasing faster than the Elementary school teachers with the exception of the 1980s where the Secondary school teacher's growth was negative (-0.23%).

Putting the data on teacher and pupil numbers together it is possible to graph the teacher pupil ratio for the USA over the period 1965–2000. Figure 4 shows the trend of the teacher–pupil ratio in the USA from 1965 to 2000. In essence this is the pattern of teacher supply relative to pupil numbers. It suggests that on average pupils in the USA were taught in classes of 23 in 1965 – but this has fallen to classes of 16 by 2000. This represents a dramatic growth in teacher supply over the last 35 years in the USA.

In examining the teacher supply and demand situation in the USA, we can apply the model used by Weaver (1983) who looked at the number of additional teachers required in the event a change in 3 factors, i.e., the change in the teacher turnover rate, the change in the pupil–teacher ratio and the change in pupil enrollment. Additional demand was then derived from taking the total number of teachers required as a result of these 3 factors.

On the supply side, Weaver's model looked at how this additional demand could be filled by new graduates and re-entrants in the profession. The supply of new graduates in Weaver's model is limited due to the lack of data on the number of new graduates in teaching. While he was able to obtain actual numbers of new graduates in teaching for 1970–1980, he had to estimate the number of new graduates in teaching for his remaining years of 1980–1990.

Weaver used linear extrapolation to estimate the number of new graduates for the years 1980–1990. This extrapolation of the supply of new graduate teachers is based

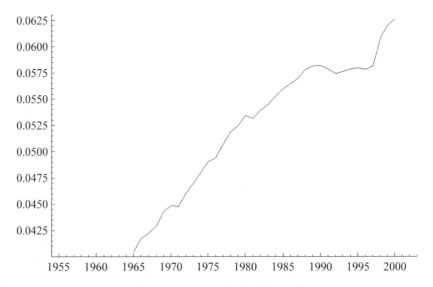

Figure 4. Teacher–pupil ratio in the USA, 1965–2000.

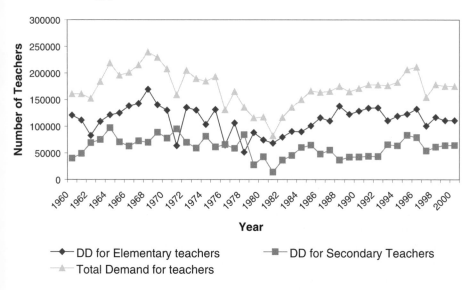

Figure 5. Additional demand for teachers in the USA, 1960–2000. *Source*: Weaver (1983) and own calculations.

on the average rate of change for the previous five years of information. Therefore, if supply shows a net decline for the period 1975–1980, the 1981 supply and supplies to the subsequent years to 1990 will show a continuous decline. Applying this same method it is possible to extend Weaver's data set to the year 2000. The total number of additional teachers required in the USA for the period 1960–2000 is shown in Figure 5.

One important factor which this research on teacher supply ignores is the quality dimension in the teacher stock. This is an important aspect of supply which has been variously treated by Ballou (1996), Ballou and Podgursky (1997, 1998a, 1998b), Lakdawalla (2001) and Corcoran, Evans and Schwab (2002). The suggestion has been that teacher quality has been falling in the US mainly due to the opening up of alternative career options for women. If this was correct then the "effective supply" as measured by the TPR in efficiency units may not be rising as graphed in Figure 4. This assertion has been questioned by Corcoran, Evans and Schwab (2002).

While we do not have a trend of the number of teachers leaving in the USA, in a NCES report on the "characteristics of stayers, movers and leavers: results from the Teacher Follow-up Survey of 1994–1995", it is reported that the teacher attrition rate in public schools in the USA was 6.6 percent between the 1993–1994 and 1994–1995 school years. In the USA, teachers who were likely to leave are teachers in their first years, younger woman teachers, white teachers compared to black teachers, secondary school teachers, teachers with high scores on standardized tests and teachers who were paid the least [Murnane et al. (1991)].

In the 1994–1995 Teacher Follow-up Survey, the main reasons cited for leaving were retirement and pregnancy/child rearing. Many teachers in the USA were leaving the profession due to dissatisfaction in the teaching conditions at school. In the NCES (1997) report, student discipline and related problems were some of the reasons given for teachers wanting to leave the profession. There is also evidence that indicates that relative wages play a role in the decisions that teachers take in deciding whether to continue in their teaching career or not. The NCES (1997) reported that 53.1% of public school teachers were of the opinion that higher salaries would be the most effective way of retaining teachers at schools. This indicates that the teacher labor market would need to be competitive enough to attract and retain teachers in the profession.

When the two elements of teacher supply and demand are interacted, the picture is that between 1945 and 1969, the USA faced a shortage of teachers but that there was a surplus of teachers in the decade after 1969 [Dimmock (1980)]. The main reason for this surplus of teachers in the 1970s was the falling number of pupils enrolled during this period. From Figure 2, the pupil number declined dramatically in the 1970s, especially among the elementary pupils. The decrease in the number of pupils enrolled caused the number of teachers required to decrease and hence, caused a teacher surplus.

In the past two decades there has been a shortage of teachers in the USA because of the increasing number of pupils. The shortage has been exacerbated by the fact that the teachers who were hired during the baby boom years are now approaching retirement. There has also been considerable political pressure at the federal level to reduce class size. Hence, there is now a need to fulfill additional demand for teacher as a results of the changing pupil teacher ratio and pupil enrollment, as well as a need to fill the vacancies left by retiring teachers. In Hussar (2002), it is predicted that by 2008–2009, 1.7 million to 2.7 million teachers would need to be hired by public schools in the USA.

Figure 6 graphs the trend in the relative teacher wages in the USA from 1959 to 2000. We can see that teachers earned 19% and 24% above the average wage in 1970 and 1990 respectively, but that in between these years teacher's relative pay has declined to between 6–8% of average earnings in 1959, 1979 and 1999. A major factor in the decline of teacher salaries in the 1970s was the surplus of teachers over these years. However, since teacher salaries are set at the state level it is more difficult to explain the process by which these salaries adjust to market forces.

In the next section of this chapter, we will examine why not only average relative wages in teaching are important for teacher supply but also the pattern of teacher and nonteacher pay over the life cycle is important. Figure 7 shows what the profile of female average teacher pay and nonteacher pay by college graduates is over the life cycle. We see from this figure that nonteacher pay is higher for most of the life cycle but that the two curves cross after about 30 years of work experience. The corresponding graph for men (not shown) does not have these two functions crossing. This finding is consistent with that described by Flyer and Rosen (1997). This suggests that the occupational choice of becoming a teacher or a nonteacher must be made not only on financial grounds. We return to this important question in the next section.

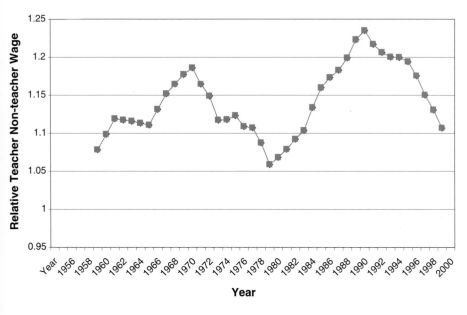

Figure 6. Teacher relative wages in the USA.

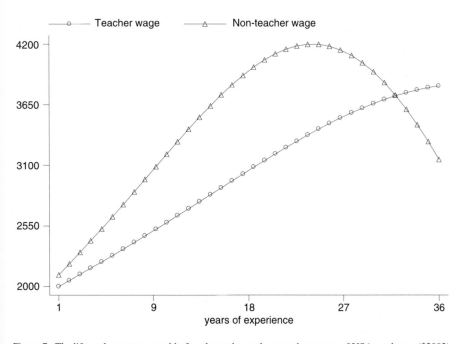

Figure 7. The life cycle average monthly female teacher and nonteacher wages of USA graduates ($2002).

2.3. Evidence from the UK

There has been a large literature summarizing the labor market situation for teachers in the UK over the last 30 years [Tropp (1957), Ahamad (1970, 1973), Zabalza, Turnbull and Williams (1979), Dimmock (1980), Blackstone and Crispin (1982), Booth (1989), Straker (1991a, 1991b), Grace (1991), Grace and Lawn (1991), Fidler, Fugl and Esp (1993), Wilson and Pearson (1993a, 1993b), Dolton (1996), Hutchings et al. (2000), Smithers and Robinson (2000a, 2000b, 2001)]. Edmonds, Sharp and Benefield (2002), Godwin (2002) and Ross and Hutchings (2003) all survey the alternative policies for attracting and retaining teachers in the UK. These papers provide a thorough overview of the institutional and administrative detail of the UK system of teacher pay and school organization. They include a description of the UK funding. They detail the various initiatives which have been used in the UK to attempt to overcome the problems with teacher shortage. This section reviews the empirical position regarding teacher supply and demand and the factors like relative teacher salaries which influence it.

Figure 8 graphs the trend in pupil numbers in the UK over the 1947–2000 period. The "switchback" nature of these trends show clearly the nature of the baby boom periods of the immediate post war period and that of the late 1960s. The graph shows how the balance of the demographic structure of the school population will shift the demand for teachers. In 1947 there were 3.7 million primary school pupils and only 1.2 secondary pupils. By 1984 there were 4 million of both primary and secondary pupils. This pattern will have a dramatic impact on the relative demand for primary and secondary school teachers.

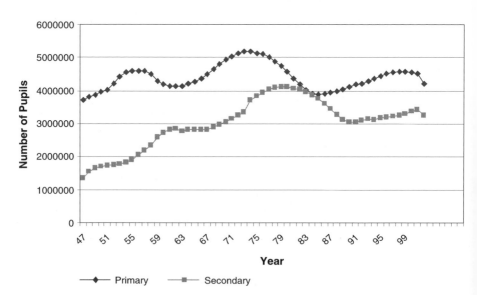

Figure 8. Primary and secondary school pupil numbers in the UK, 1947–2001.

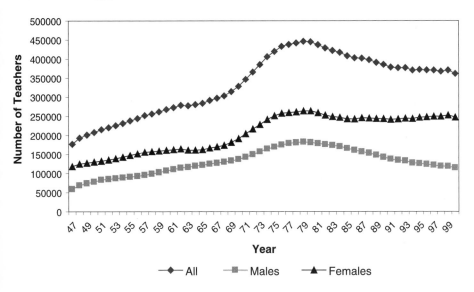

Figure 9. Teachers in service, UK 1947–2000. *Source*: Statistics of education.

Figure 9 depicts the situation of teachers in service in the UK for the period 1947–2000. The number of teachers in service rose markedly up until 1980 and has been declining since then. The number of teachers in service will be determined directly by the number of pupils to be taught and the pupil teacher ratios which are used. A similar pattern is observed among the male and female teachers. The ratio of female–male teachers in the UK for the period 1947–2000 is 60:40. Teaching is also a predominantly female occupation in most other OECD countries.

Looking at the information in Figures 8 and 9 we can derive the overall supply position by graphing the teacher pupil ratio experienced by pupils in the UK over the 1947–2000 period. This is graphed in Figure 10. It shows that the average child in a UK primary school was taught in a class of 29 in 1947; that this declined to 20 by 1990 and has subsequently risen to 23 in 2000. The average secondary school pupil was taught in a class of 27 in 1947, 16 in 1990 and 22 in 2000.

The interaction between supply and demand will tell us if there is a shortage or surplus of teachers in the UK. The number of pupils and the Government's published target pupil teacher ratio determines the demand for teachers. For example, in 2000, there were 4,278,123 primary school children (full-time equivalents). According to the Government's target pupil teacher ratio[1] there would be 21.2 primary school children for every primary school teacher, implying that over 210,000 primary school teachers are

---

[1] Successive government publications have included a figure for a desired target pupil teacher ratio for primary and secondary schools. See Bee and Dolton (1995) for the details of the UK government's published desired PTR.

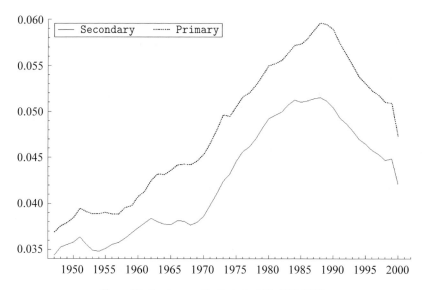

Figure 10. Teacher–pupil ratio in the UK, 1947–2000.

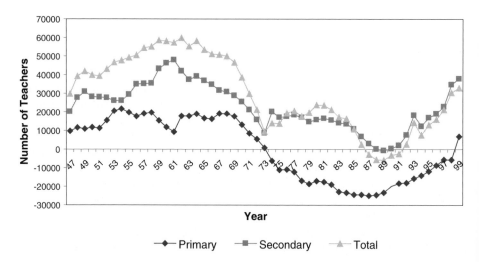

Figure 11. Excess demand of teachers, by sector, UK, 1947–2000. *Source*: Own calculations.

needed. In actual fact, there were over 183,000 primary school teachers in 2000, implying an excess demand of around 27,000 primary school teachers. A similar analysis for secondary school teachers reveals that there was an excess demand of nearly 16,000 teachers, giving the overall excess demand figure of approximately 34,000. Figure 11 uses this logic to chart the situation for all years since 1947.

The graph shows that there has been an overall excess demand for teachers almost continuously throughout this period. However, closer inspection shows that there has, in fact, been a surplus (negative excess demand) of primary school teachers over the 1973–1998 period. This is a feature of the market in the UK – namely that in some segments of the market there is a shortage and in others a surplus. Overall there is a shortage but this disguises the surplus of primary school teachers which is offset by the shortage of secondary school teachers and in particular science and maths teachers and teachers in London and the South East of England.

A major part of the structural determinants of teacher supply relates to the rate at which males and female teachers leave the profession during their careers, the extent of wastage from the profession and how it has changed over time and what has happened to the stock of inactive teachers and those who could return to the profession. We examine these factors for the UK in Figures 12–14. Figure 12 shows how women leave the occupation in much larger numbers during their child rearing and household production years than men but subsequently return to the job in their later life.

The average wastage rate by gender is graphed in Figure 13. It shows how on average around 10% of female teachers in the UK leave the job each year. Traditionally male wastage from teaching was much lower at around 5% up until the mid-1980s. Since then the rate of male wastage from the profession has risen markedly to around 8% per year in the 1990s. These trends give cause for concern for the UK government since male teachers are predominantly secondary school teachers and are more likely to be in science and maths subjects.

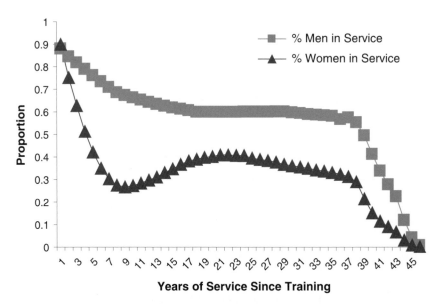

Figure 12. Exit rates of trained teachers by gender over experience.

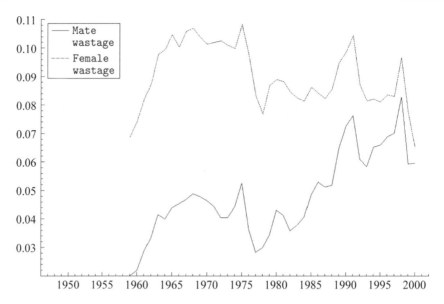

Figure 13. Male and female wastage rates in the UK, 1959–2000.

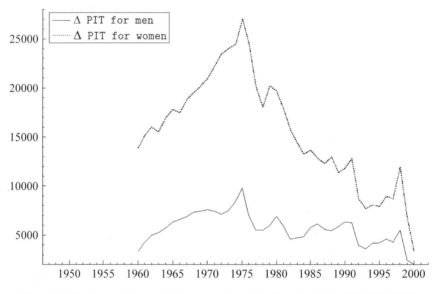

Figure 14. The change in the pool of inactive male and female teachers in the UK, 1960–2000.

The trend of the change in the male PIT and female PIT as presented in Figure 14 show an upward trend with a decreasing change over the years. This means that in every

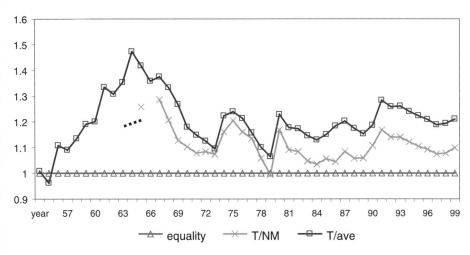

Figure 15. UK relative teachers' wages. *Source*: Own calculations.

year the PIT and the PRT is growing but that this growth has slowed down over the last 25 years.

Having observed the trends of teacher supply in the UK and from the literature that is available on teachers, we recognize that teachers' pay relative to other graduate occupations is of prime importance, since it is relevant to consider how graduates make choices between becoming a teacher and taking up another occupation. Figure 15 graphs the relative earnings of teachers compared to average nonmanual earnings and national average earnings.[2] The highest relative wages were paid to teachers in the mid-1960s, followed by a considerable deterioration in the period up to 1973. There followed a series of dramatic adjustments after the Houghton Report (1974) and the Clegg Commission (1980) recommended that teachers' pay had been allowed to decline too far. More recently, the 1990s have seen a continuous decline in the relative wage of teachers, although of less dramatic extent than the decline of the late 1960s and early 1970s.

---

[2] Data on earnings are available from two sources, the October survey of earnings and, since 1968, the New Earnings Survey (NES). With respect to average earnings of all employees, the two surveys give similar estimates over the period that they are both in existence, and so the reported average earnings is a simple average of the two estimates. For specifically nonmanual earnings, the DfES's *Labour Market Trends* (formerly the *Employment Gazette*) reports an index based upon the October Survey until 1970, and from then onwards, the NES. However, the resulting estimate is considerably above the estimate of nonmanual earnings supplied by the NES, and so in Figure 3, we only display teachers' earnings relative to the nonmanual average from 1968 onwards using the NES. We estimate the position relative to nonmanual earnings for 1966 (to gauge the situation for our first cohort), by adding the average difference between the October Survey and NES estimates of teachers' earnings relative to nonmanual earnings (approximately 20 percentage points), to the October Survey estimate of the relative position for that year.

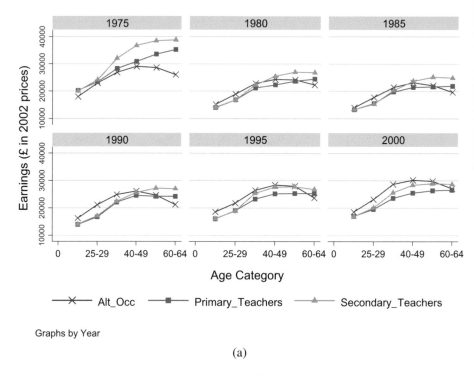

Figure 16. Age-earning profile of primary school teachers, secondary school teachers and an alternative occupation, (a) males and (b) females, 1975–2000. *Source*: DfES publications, NES and LFS.

Of course in the decision to become a teacher it is possible that the individual would
consider the lifetime profile of earnings in the alternative career destinations. In Figure 16(a) we graph the average salary profile over the life cycle[3] of a male teacher and a
graduate who works in an alternative occupation.[4] The figure displays the age-earning
profile for males for selected years. The alternative occupation (Alt_Occ) legend represents the earnings in the alternative occupation for those with a teaching qualification
who do not teach. In recent years we can see that the male nonteacher in the UK has

___

[3] This figure is complied from Labour Force Survey data and represents only the life-time earnings as measured in 2001 prices for teachers and other graduates based on salary data for people aged less than 25, 25–29,
30–39, 40–49, 50–59, 60–64 in each year from 1975, 1980, 1985, 1995 and 2000. They of course do not necessarily reflect what will be the lifetime earnings of those beginning their career in each year based on what
they could observe people of different ages in teaching and alternative occupations earning in each of these
years.

[4] Early studies of teacher salaries in the UK are Greenhalgh (1968), Conway (1962a, 1962b), Thomas
(1973), Turnbull and Williams (1974).

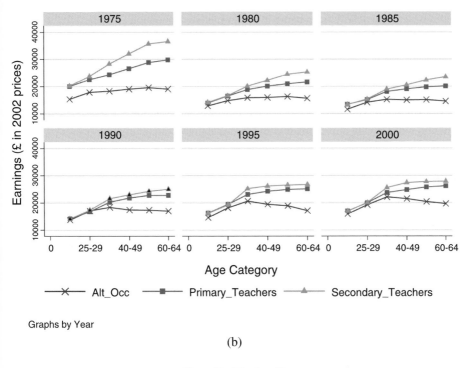

Figure 16. (*Continued.*)

an average salary which always exceeds that of the teacher. The position is completely reversed for women as we see in Figure 16(b).[5]

Overall, in Figure 16(a), it is quite clear that the earnings of male teachers were uniformly higher than earnings in the alternative occupation in 1975. But over time, the earnings profile in the alternative occupation has been shifting up whilst that of teachers has been moving down. By 2000, it is clear that the wage in the alternative occupation is almost uniformly above that of teaching.

Additionally, the lower age categories appear to be earning a much higher level of earnings in the alternative occupation in all years after 1975, while in the later age categories, earnings from teaching exceed earnings from the alternative occupation. This gap between the older age grouped teachers and nonteachers is clear in the 1980s. However, the age-earnings profile in the 1990s and into the new century appear to indicate a slow erosion of the higher level of earnings for the older age group in teaching compared to the alternative occupation. Calculations based on these graphs indicate strongly that

---

[5] These life-cycle earning profiles do not cross even if we plot the teacher wage at the 90th percentile and the nonteacher wage at the 10th percentile.

males benefit financially from being in an alternative occupation compared to the teaching profession. The same analysis for women in Figure 16(b) shows that although the age-earnings profile in teaching drifts down over time, it is still above that in the alternative composite occupation. In Dolton and Chung (2004) full details of the analysis is reported. The authors show that internal rate of return to teaching has been declining for the last 25 years and is now negative for men and this means that on average men lose up to £40,000–67,000 in terms of the Pet Present Value of Earnings over their lifetime whereas women gain approximately the same relative to an alternative occupation.

The above analysis begs the question about why an individual male graduate will decide to enter the teaching profession. There are several explanations which must be borne in mind: firstly that nonpecuniary factors (like hours of work, job satisfaction and the type of vocational element to work) loom large in the individual's choice, second that the average graduate who enters teaching has a lower ability or exam performance making it less likely that they will get a nonteacher graduate job; or finally that compositional differences between the teacher and nonteacher populations regarding subject specialty, gender and other factors are the cause. We will return to these explanations in considering the theory of teacher/nonteacher occupational choice and examine the empirical validity of these explanations in the empirical econometric literature we examine.

2.4. Evidence from the rest of the world

The literature on aspects of teacher supply in the other countries in the rest of the world is large. See Macdonald (1999) for an international review of teacher attrition. There have been studies on Argentina by Vegas, Pritchett and Experton (1999), Australia by Lewis and Norris (1992), Belgium by Van den Berghe (2000), Bolivia by Piras and Savedoff (1998), Brazil by Vegas (1999), Delannoy and Sedlacek (2000) and the OECD (2001), Canada by Tremblay (1997), Press and Lawton (1999) and McIntyre (1998), Cote d-Ivoire by Komenan and Grootaert (1990), Ghana by Glewwe and Jacoby (1994), Israel by Angrist and Lavy (2001), Mexico by Nelson, Lutenbacher and López (2001) and Lopez-Acevedo and Salinas (2001), Nigeria by Abubakar (1983), Norway by Falch and Storm (2002), Bonnesronning, Falch and Strom (2003), the Netherlands by Borghans (1991), New Zealand by Gilbert, King and Cregan (2002), Oman by Al-Salmi (1994), Philippines by Acedo (1999), South Africa by Black and Hosking (1997) and Kgobe (1995), Switzerland by Wolter and Denzler (2003), Trinidad and Tobago by Premdas (1971) and Zimbabwe by Chivore (1985). Chapman (1983) provide a review for the developing countries of the world.

The single most comprehensive source of comparative information about teachers in different countries around the world is in OECD (2001). Together with the "Education at a Glance" publications from the OECD (2002a, 2002b) and earlier years it is possible to build up a picture of what has happened with teachers in different countries. These publications provide information on teacher salaries, both starting, as well as 15 years into the profession, educational expenditure, the percentage of teachers who are women, teacher work hours, educational personnel as a percentage for the labor force, instruction time by subject. In addition much of this information is available across primary, lower secondary and upper secondary school sectors.

Data of the kind we have examined for the USA and the UK relating to pupil numbers, teacher numbers, teacher wages and other factors relating to teacher supply are difficult to obtain on a consistent basis for most other countries for any reasonable time series.[6] Hence, in order to understand what is happening across countries we turn to an examination of evidence from a cross section of OECD countries data. Until now we have explored the evidence relating to the different aspects of the teacher labor market in the UK and USA over time over the whole post war period. In this section, we will attempt to shed light on the relationship between teachers' salaries and some economic and educational variables for most of the OECD countries.[7]

It should be noted that a major difficulty in any study of this sort is the existence of heterogeneity in the educational systems of the different countries that cannot be easily observed. This is an inevitable shortcoming in the data set that we have used in this section. Nevertheless an examination of this nature, i.e., using a cross-country set of data would be interesting. In such an analysis, each country would be at different points in the economic cycle and hence, any significant relationship between the variables representing teacher supply and the economic cycle in this data set would be evidence of a link between these two components.

Our task is to explain the variation in teacher's salaries across different countries by relative supply and demand factors having controlled for the basic cross country heterogeneity which can be observed. In the OECD data there is information on teacher: starting salaries, salaries after 15 years, and salaries at the top of the professional pay scale for the Primary, Lower Secondary and Upper Secondary levels in the education system. All this data is presented in terms of indexed purchasing power parity in US dollars and are therefore directly comparable. From this information it is possible to derive relative teachers pay compared to GDP per head and teachers pay per hour. Dolton and Marcenaro-Guiterrez (2004) discuss all these different possible dependent variables of interest. Here we report only their results for the last two, most interesting, variables.

The data which is available from the OECD "Education at a Glance" publications allows us to construct a panel data set relating to 1995, 1996, 1998, 1999, 2000 and 2001.[8] For most of these years up to 35 countries are observed. At the maximum this gives us in our unbalanced panel data set of 425 observations (i.e., 35 countries, times 3 education sectors times 6 years minus missing values). However, for some variables not all years are observed. This means that our resulting panel data is unbalanced. In this data basic characteristics of the educational system are observed (or derived).

---

[6] Waterreus (2003) plots age/wage profiles in teaching and nonteaching for 7 countries France, Germany, US, UK, Sweden, Australia and the Netherlands for men and women separately.

[7] The data is available for countries which participated in the WEI Project. This project was carried out by the OECD and UNESCO, with the support of The World Bank.

[8] There are unfortunately no data for 1997 published by the OECD.

In the endogenous growth literature the relationship between education and growth has been extensively examined. The relationship between teacher supply and economic growth is therefore one of interest [see Tamura (2001)]. We measure the nature of the country's investment in education by the level of educational expenditure as a fraction of GDP and we control for the rate at which a country is growing, since clearly this will constraint its choice set of educational investment possibilities. The relative supply of teachers is measured by the number of teachers (and other educational staff) as a fraction of the labor force and the student–teacher ratio in the education system. An additional supply factor relates to the composition of the teacher stock in terms of the proportion of teachers in the country who are women. We also control for the number of teacher hours supplied in the country, as obviously fewer teachers can compensated for by a lower number of teachers working more hours. The changing nature of the demand for teacher services is proxied for in this data by the demographic growth in the size of the population of school age. In addition we are able to control for the salary differences in the three education sectors: primary, lower secondary and secondary schools.

We also collected data to try to control for the quality of educational output – by using results on the PISA tests – and the relative importance of science and mathematics in the curriculum of each country – by using the fraction of time spent on these subjects in the curriculum. The suggestion here is that since there is a relative shortage of teachers in these subjects in most schools then this might show up in the relative earnings of teachers if the fraction of time devoted to science and mathematics was higher. In the event neither of these two variables were significant in our regressions and since they reduced our sample size somewhat further we have omitted these results.

Table 1 presents the regression estimates of the aggregate factors that have an impact on the teachers salaries (expressed in PPP) relative to GDP per head and average teachers' salaries per hour in primary education, lower secondary education and upper secondary education. It shows the results of two different specifications for each of the two different dependent variables, those obtained by using OLS on the whole data and random effects when treating the data as a panel.

Looking at the table as a whole there are some clear indications that the relative supply of teachers, as measured by the stock of teachers in the labor force, has a clear effect on teacher salaries in the intuitively sensible way – that it to say – the greater the potential supply, the lower will be teacher's earnings. Likewise the pupil–teacher ratio has a supply effect which is picked up in the OLS results but not significant when the data is recognized as a panel. On the demand side it appears that as the stock of school age children grows then this demand push will factor into higher teacher wages per hour – although not into higher teacher's wages relative to GDP per head.

Further evidence of the influence of supply factors is present in the significance of the percentage of teachers who are women for both of the dependent variables under consideration. This variable has a negative impact on teachers' salaries. This may result from the possibility of gender wage discrimination or from the occupational segregation which takes place in most countries where teaching is still regarded as predominantly a female occupation. Alternatively, it may be a consequence of the different career pro-

Table 1

Estimation explaining the variation in teachers' salaries across 35 countries from 1995–2001

Variables	Teachers wage/GDP per head				Teachers wage per hour			
	OLS		Random effects		OLS		Random effects	
	Coefficient	S.E.	Coefficient	S.E.	Coefficient	S.E.	Coefficient	S.E.
Constant	1.1302***	0.272	1.5344***	0.5833	32.8512***	6.4504	25.9023**	12.3274
Teachers and educational staff as a fraction of the labor force (%)	−0.1917***	0.0451	−0.2908***	0.1075	−3.2530***	1.0246	−2.1446	2.4813
Teaching hours per year	0.00003	0.0002	0.0003	0.0003				
Women fraction of teaching staff (%)	−0.0073***	0.0024	−0.0018	0.0027	−0.5717***	0.0545	−0.2796***	0.0523
Lower secondary dummy	0.1083	0.0662	0.1579***	0.0605	−0.4816	1.5716	2.5731**	1.1642
Upper secondary dummy	0.1413	0.0811	0.2533***	0.0866	−1.7056	1.9602	5.2414***	1.6747
GDP growth (%)	−0.0098***	0.0019	−0.0089***	0.0016				
GDP per head					0.0014***	0.0001	0.0009***	0.0001
Expenditure on educational institutions as a percentage of GDP	0.2452***	0.0355	0.1617*	0.0893	6.1510***	0.9495	4.1793**	1.9743
Student–teacher ratio	0.0287***	0.0045	0.0085	0.0059	0.0921	0.1326	−0.0443	0.1330
Growth in the size of the population at the age of primary/lower secondary and upper secondary education (%)	0.0001	0.0030	0.0035	0.0039	0.2415***	0.0626	0.1071	0.0755
Number of observations	425		425 in 30 countries		388		388 in 30 countries	
F-statistic	26.35				89.29			
R-squared within			0.118				0.4011	
R-squared between			0.471				0.7659	
R-squared overall	0.349		0.327		0.646		0.6289	

*Coefficient significantly different from zero at 10% confidence level.

**Coefficient significantly different from zero at 5% level.

***Coefficient significantly different from zero at 1%.

motion prospects faced by the male and female teachers in the various countries that we examine.

With our two different dependent variables we must be careful how we control for the relative wealth of a country and the effect of economic growth. When using the teacher's wage relative to GDP per head we can clearly only control for economic growth and not the absolute size of the wealth in the country. However in the teachers wage per hour equation we must control for this absolute wealth effect although this will limit the specification to exclude growth in GDP. This specification strategy will hopefully allow us to assess the importance of wealth in explaining teachers' salaries in the different countries.

The results relating GDP growth to teachers' relative salaries compared to GDP per head indicate that there exists a negative relationship between the changing wealth of a country and their teachers' salaries. This may be due to the rate at which an economy grows is largely determined by the productivity of the private sector. Those countries which have private sectors which are growing more rapidly are more likely to be leaving their public sector workers behind – in relative pay terms. Looking at the teacher pay per hour results we find that the wealthier a country is (as measured by GDP per head) the more likely they are to pay their teachers more per hour. As expected, any increase in the expenditure on educational institutions (as a percentage of GDP) has a significant and positive effect on teachers' salaries.

Two dummy variables are used to measure the differences among teachers' salaries in the lower secondary, upper secondary and primary education levels (the latter is the reference group). These variables are have positively significant coefficients when the panel models are estimated suggesting that when cross country heterogeneity is accounted for then there is some evidence that teachers in lower or upper secondary schools are paid up to 15% or 25% more, respectively, than their primary school counterparts.

The overall goodness of fit of these estimated equations is reasonable with around 32–35% of the variation in teacher's wages relative to GDP per head explained and 62–65% of the variation in teachers wages per hour explained. This indicates that the included variables have a reasonable capacity to explain the variance observed in teachers' salaries in the countries sampled. Moreover, the results of the F-test indicate that the model estimated is significant at the 1% confidence level (for both specifications).

3. Modeling teacher supply

A variety of theoretical econometric models have been used to estimate aspects of teacher supply. The OECD (2002a, 2002b) report on teacher supply is careful to distinguish the different components of a satisfactory explanation of teacher supply. These would include: an explanation of the choice of training to be a teacher by those eligible, the initial occupational choice and entry into the profession, what conditions whether an individual leaves or stays in the job and the length of duration in the job, and who returns to teaching after an interruption to working in the job. Additional supply considerations are the hours of teaching and nonteaching time an individual teacher chooses to supply and whether the individual will be absent from work on any specific day. Finally, how can individual's teachers supply decisions be aggregated to provide a national picture about aggregate supply?

This section starts with a simple characterization of the aggregate market in diagrammatic terms before examining, in some detail, the models which have been used to model individual training and occupational choice, entry to the job, exit from the job and duration in the job.

3.1. A simple model of the aggregate teacher labor market

In the Zabalza, Turnbull and Williams (1979) model of the labor market, the demand for teachers is formulated in terms of the number of children of school age, and the government's own desired pupil–teacher ratio. Clearly, if the government was willing to accept larger class sizes then it could cut the demand for teachers immediately by increasing its desired pupil–teacher ratio. Since in many countries the current political climate puts pressure on governments to cut class sizes and improve SAT examination performance, this option is unlikely to be adopted. The other factor determining the level of demand for teachers, the number of children who require teaching, is outside government control. It would therefore appear that the most feasible route for reducing the excess demand for teachers is via an increase in their supply. The supply of teachers is the focus of this chapter.

The supply of teachers can be regarded as all those currently in teaching, plus those currently not teaching, but who are qualified to teach, and would consider teaching if the conditions were right. The supply issues at stake are therefore ones of recruitment and retention, as well as inducing the return of qualified individuals who have left the profession. There are many factors that are likely to influence the supply of teachers, such as the relative earnings on offer in teaching and other careers, other labor market opportunities, and varying relative nonpecuniary conditions of work. To a certain extent, some of these factors can be controlled by the government (or federal authorities), for example, the earnings that teachers receive, and so public policy can have an influence on supply.

Much of the analysis that follows focuses on the earnings that individuals can earn as teachers, relative to what they could earn in alternative occupations, as one of the key determinants of the decision to become a teacher. It is likely that nonpecuniary factors such as workload, job stress, physical surroundings and related factors also play an important role in the decision to enter teaching. Indeed, anecdotal evidence would suggest that such conditions are adversely perceived by current and potential teachers, which can have a real effect on reducing the supply of labor to teaching [Kyriacou and Coulthard (2000)].

We now outline a simple model of the labor market for teachers, illustrating how a situation of excess demand (or insufficient supply) can arise. Following Zabalza, Turnbull

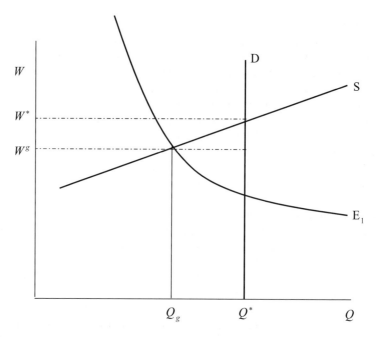

Figure 17. The labor market for teachers.

and Williams (1979), the labor market for teachers can be thought of within a traditional supply and demand framework, with the additional complication that the government is virtually the sole hirer of labor.[9]

The demand for teachers can determined by the number of children in the country of school age, and the government's desired pupil–teacher ratio. For a given such ratio, the demand for teachers is therefore a constant, denoted by Q^* in Figure 17. Under the reasonable assumption that the supply of teachers is a positive function of average teacher earnings, an upward-sloping labor supply schedule can be drawn as S. In a perfectly competitive market, a teacher wage of W^* would therefore clear this labor market. However, the teachers' labor market is of course not competitive, and the government, in its role as (almost) exclusive purchaser of teaching labor, has other considerations, prime among which is the level of expenditure on teachers' salaries in total. For a given level of such expenditure, an inverse relationship can be plotted between teachers' earnings and the number of teachers hired, labeled E_1 in Figure 17; if the government wants to raise the salaries of teachers, it can afford to hire fewer of them, given a fixed budget. The number of teachers hired is therefore Q_g at average earnings of W^g, and the excess demand for teachers is $Q^* - Q_g$. This can only be eradicated by a relaxing of the budget

---

[9] The private sector in most countries accounts for no more than 5–7% of all teachers hired.

constraint leading to higher earnings, or other factors changing to make teaching more attractive, so that more potential teachers supply their labor at any given wage.

Of course, the above analysis is simplistic in that it treats all teachers as being the same. In reality, within the same country, there may be teacher shortages in particular geographical locations or regions or in particular subjects, with an over-supply elsewhere. In addition, the real market position is very different for primary and secondary school teachers. We can amend Figure 17 to allow for such possibilities by creating a simple distinction of different kinds of teachers. A simple analysis would suggest that the possibility of differential wages by subject, in different regions or between primary and secondary sectors could be adopted to solve the problems of short supply in particular areas. Whether this solution is actually viable, given the demands of teachers' unions and the political process in general, is another question. In any detailed empirical analysis, we would wish to allow for the possibility that supply responses differ by subject of study among potential teachers. In addition, there are of course other conceptual problems with the simple concepts of supply and demand which have be used in the literature [see Zabalza, Turnbull and Williams (1979) for a discussion].

3.2. Initial occupational choice models

In this section we review the basic static model of occupational choice as applied to the initial decision to become a teacher. This model is taken from Zabalza (1979a, 1979b), Willis and Rosen (1979) and Dolton (1990). The basic form of this model is that the individual is assumed to be making the choice of becoming a teacher or not when teaching is compared to the best of the other alternative occupations. Let regime A refer to those who make the choice of becoming "a teacher" and regime N models the behavior of those who choose "not to become a teacher". In the basic Willis and Rosen model it is assumed that earnings streams in two occupational regimes may be parameterized by a simple geometric growth process. The model can then be written out formally.

To consider the model in detail it is necessary to examine the individual's choices. If individual i chooses to enter teaching after graduation then his expected earnings stream is

$$\begin{cases} W_i^a(t) = 0, & 0 \leqslant t \leqslant T_i^a, \\ W_i^a(t) = W_{si}^a \exp[g_i^a(t - T_i^a)], & T_i^a \leqslant t \leqslant \infty, \end{cases} \tag{1}$$

where T_i^a is the fixed period of postgraduate teacher training for individual i, W_{si}^a is the starting salary on commencing work after T_i^a months, and g_i^a is the per period growth of earnings of the individual i in group A. Notice that salary at any time $W_i^a(t)$ is assumed to be a function of the length of service $t - T_i^a$, and the growth of earnings.

If individual i chooses not to enter teaching then the individual may, or may not, enter vocational or academic postgraduate study after graduation, prior to taking a job. The expected earnings stream for a nonteacher is

$$\begin{cases} W_i^n(t) = 0, & 0 \leqslant t \leqslant T_i^n, \\ W_i^n(t, T_i^n) = W_{si}^a \exp[g_i^n(T_i^n)(t - T_i^n)], & T_i^n \leqslant t \leqslant \infty, \end{cases} \tag{2}$$

where T_i^n is the period of full time study to be chosen by individual i, W_{si}^n is the starting salary on commencing work after T_i^n months, and g_i^n is the per period growth of earnings of the individual i in group N. Notice that salary at any time is assumed to be a function of T_i^n, as is initial renumeration and the growth in earnings. If the individual has made a rational decision the human capital model would predict that $W_t^a(t)$, W_{si}^n and g_i^n would be increasing functions of T_i^n.

The present value of earnings for individual i in group A is

$$V_i^a = \int_{T_i^a}^{\infty} \left[W_i^a(t) \exp(-r_i t) \right] dt. \tag{3}$$

The maximum present value of earnings, chosen over alternative investment periods for any individual i in group N is

$$V_i^n = \underset{T_i^n}{\text{Max}} \int_{T_i^n}^{\infty} \left[W_i^n(t, T_i^n) \exp(-r_i t) \right] dt, \tag{4}$$

where it is assumed that the choice of the full time study months investment by individuals is rational. Denote this optimal choice by T_i^{*n}. One important problem with the choice of T_i^n is that most courses are of a fixed duration e.g. one year. This creates problems in any model which assumes continuous investment possibilities in T_i^n. Rather it is convenient to acknowledge that T_i^n may only be available in discrete lumps and assume for modeling purposes that each graduate has rational expectations of future earnings (and earnings growth) with different levels of T_i^n and makes the choice which maximizes his present value of future earnings.

Assume that a person i chooses not to go into teaching if $V_i^n > V_i^a$. Defining $I_{1i} = \ln(V_i^n / V_i^a)$ and substituting from Equations (1) and (2) into (3) and (4) would give[10]

$$I_{1i} = \ln W_s^n - \ln W_s^a - r_i (T^{*n} - T^a) - \ln(r_i - g^n) - \ln(r_i - g^a). \tag{5}$$

One consideration which has been overlooked in this simple model is the possibility that graduates entering different occupations may face different employment prospects. Zabalza (1979a, 1979b) and Zabalza, Turnbull and Williams (1979) raise this possibility and explicitly introduce the probability that having trained for a job a graduate may be unemployed for a period of time – which may be different in different jobs. Let the per period probability that a trained teacher finds a job be π^a, then the expected time until a trained teacher finds a job will be $\tau^a = 1/\pi^a$. Likewise the typical nonteacher will have a per period probability of finding a job of π^n then the expected time until they find a job will be $\tau^n = 1/\pi^n$. Without rehearsing all the notation presented above, it is straightforward to see that the time taken to find a teaching job after training, will now be the training time and the average waiting time, i.e., $[T^a + \tau^a]$. Likewise the time taken to find a nonteaching job will now be $[T^{*n} + \tau^n]$. This means we can rewrite the

---

[10] After a Taylor series expansion and some mathematical manipulation Willis and Rosen (1979) show.

occupational choice function (5) as

$$I_{1i} = \ln W_s^n - \ln W_s^a - r_i\left(\left[T^{*n} + \tau^n\right] - \left[T^a + \tau^a\right]\right)$$
$$- \ln(r_i - g^n) - \ln(r_i - g^a),$$

$$I_{1i} = \ln W_s^n - \ln W_s^a - r_i\left(T^{*n} - T^a\right) - r_i\left(\frac{1}{\pi^n} - \frac{1}{\pi^a}\right)$$
$$- \ln(r_i - g^n) - \ln(r_i - g^a). \tag{6}$$

Hence, we can see that the choice of entering one occupation or another will also depend on the relative probability of being offered a job in the different destinations. We will return to this expression when we consider the derivation of the aggregate supply function.

3.3. Nonpecuniary considerations and subsequent occupational choice

An important aspect of modeling an individual's decision to be a teacher is the potential nonpecuniary aspects of teaching compared to other jobs. The theory of compensating wage differentials and equalizing differences [Rosen (1986)], would suggest that individuals weight such nonpecuniary considerations as well as the pecuniary rewards in decision making. Hence the "actual wage" has components of both pecuniary and nonpecuniary rewards in jobs. Following the model suggested in Dolton (1990) we can assume that this can be captured in one parameter, μ, so that "real" earnings in teaching ω^a, and outside teaching, ω^n, are money wages, W^a and W^n respectively, weighted by the individual's perception of the nonpecuniary rewards in teaching relative to non-teaching, μ_{it} ($0 < \mu_{it} < 1$) at time t:

$$\omega_{it}^a(t) = \frac{\mu_{it}}{1 - \mu_{it}} W_{it}^a(t), \tag{7}$$

$$\omega_{it}^n(t) = \frac{1 - \mu_{it}}{\mu_{it}} W_{it}^n(t). \tag{8}$$

We assume that this μ parameter is simultaneously an index measuring the characteristic "propensity to teach" which each individual has but is unknown before working and is learned and revised as the individual spends time in the labor market. For convenience we assume that prior to entry into any job any individual i has $\mu_i = 0.5$ so that nonpecuniary rewards to jobs are considered equal. After some time in the labor market the individual may modify their subjective evaluation of μ. At time t, μ_{it} could also be used to capture the difference in short term "actual earnings" of changing jobs caused by transition costs, extra training and other factors.

Assume that the individual is considering a change in occupation at time t'. Assume also that wages continue to grow at their constant rates in the two regimes so that the expected earnings stream for teachers and nonteachers are given by

$$W_t^a(t) = W_{si}^a \exp\left[g_t^a(t - t')\right], \qquad t' \leqslant t \leqslant \infty, \tag{9}$$
$$W_t^n(t, T_i^n) = W_{si}^n(t') \exp\left[g_t^n(T_i^n)(t - t')\right], \quad t' \leqslant t \leqslant \infty. \tag{10}$$

The difference in the present value, V_{it}^{an} of future "actual" earnings of an individual who is a teacher but decides to become a nonteacher at time t' is

$$V_{it}^{\mathrm{an}} - V_{it}^{\mathrm{a}} = \int_{t'}^{\infty} \left\{ \left[\omega_i^{\mathrm{a}}(t) - \omega_i^{\mathrm{n}}(t) \right] \exp(-r_i t) \right\} dt. \tag{11}$$

If $V_{it}^{\mathrm{an}} - V_{it}^{\mathrm{a}} > 0$ the individual who started in the labor market as a teacher will change his occupation at time t'. The corresponding expression for the present value of earnings of individuals who were nonteachers but considering a change into teaching at time t' is

$$V_{it}^{\mathrm{na}} - V_{it}^{\mathrm{a}} = \int_{t'}^{\infty} \left\{ \left[\omega_i^{\mathrm{n}}(t) - \omega_i^{\mathrm{a}}(t) \right] \exp(-r_i t) \right\} dt. \tag{12}$$

3.4. Modeling using cross-section data

Using equation (6) a Taylor series approximation to the nonlinear terms around their population mean yields a "reduced form" determination of the I_{1i} as a function of the independent variables in (6). Therefore the statistical representation of I_{1i} may be written as

$$I_{1i} = \delta_0 + \delta_1 \left(\ln W_s^{\mathrm{n}} - \ln W_s^{\mathrm{a}} \right) + \delta_2 \tau^{\mathrm{n}} + \delta_2 \tau^{\mathrm{a}} + \delta_2 g^{\mathrm{n}} + \delta_2 g^{\mathrm{n}} + X_{1i} \beta_1, \tag{13}$$

where X_{1i} measures the postgraduate training variables and includes a vector of other relevant exogenous variables and cannot be observed directly but the decision by each individual concerning his or her preferred regime is recorded. The implication of this decision criteria is that the individual will make the choice of whether or not to become a teacher on the basis of comparative salaries, their expected earnings growth and the employment prospects in the different regimes.

There are inevitably clear problems in reconciling the theoretical model described above with the data which is usually available for the econometric modeling of the teacher decision. There are many econometric problems with such estimation procedures.

One of the most difficult problems in the modeling of a system of equations is obviously that of determining which variables can be regarded as exogenous in order to ensure identification via exclusion restrictions. Typically relative wages and previous occupation choices are endogenous variables in the current occupational choice decision. Most importantly to identify the decision equation we have to find exclusion restrictions which are factors which influence occupational choice but do not influence the earnings and earnings growth equations. In practice this means finding regressors for the determination of occupational choice which are exogenous to the determination of wages. In many datasets this will be a difficult task. This means that (at least) two stage estimation procedures are required to derive consistent estimates of these variables in order to use their predicted value in a second (or subsequent) stage of estimation. Commonplace in econometric models of this kind is to employ the Willis and Rosen (1979) type structural model combining both earnings determination, earnings growth and occupational choice into a simultaneous structure. This is the procedure adopted by Dolton (1990).

A second and related problem that has received a lot of attention in the economics literature in the issue of sample selection bias. The problem directly affects our ability to estimate a model relating to one group in the population when entry into that group is determined in a way which is not unrelated to the original dependent variable we wish to explain. For example, estimating an equation for teachers only when teachers as a group may be a nonrandom subset of the population will lead to biased estimates of the coefficients in the relevant equations. Hence in modeling teacher earnings equations we would first need to make the appropriate corrections for the fact that the sample observed earning wages as teachers are only those who have chosen to be teachers and that such a decision may be related to the wage prospects on offer in teaching relative to other jobs. Care must therefore be exercised in attempting to model the correlations between the relevant structural equations.

A related problem plagues the estimation of an equation relating to the occupational choice of women when the choice is only being observed for those women who are participating in the labor market. Hence this means that a teacher choice equation needs to be jointly estimated in a bivariate probit model to allow for the simultaneity of the occupational choice and participation decisions. Such a model is estimated by Dolton and Makepeace (1993). A more complete econometric representation of this problem would require the dynamic modeling of the women's occupational choice and participation decision jointly with fertility and even marital decisions.

An associated important problem is that the theory relies on a comparison of the lifetime earnings in different regimes. Naturally it is only possible to approximate the earnings of any individual in the regime chosen. This presents us with the problem of how to estimate the foregone earnings in other regimes which will influence an individual's investment decision. The approach adopted in Dolton (1990) was adapted from Willis and Rosen (1979). It suggested using a structural model of the joint decision to enter teaching with the determination of earnings and earnings growth in the teaching and nonteaching regimes. From these equations the predicted level of earnings and earnings growth that a teacher would have got in nonteaching and a nonteacher would have got in teaching are predicted. This then enables us to estimate the equation relating to the teacher/nonteacher decision via the use of the predicted wage differential terms included as regressors.

3.5. Duration modeling and exit from teaching

A natural corollary of the modeling of the occupational decision at any specific point in time is to model the length of time someone stays in a given labor market state. This is possible if the econometrician has available to them panel data which tells them what state the person occupied at various points in time. Alternatively if we have good retrospective data from a survey which asks when the respondent changed labor market state we may also model the duration of time in the state. This is of particular importance in studying the market for teachers as we wish to know how long people stay in teaching, what state they exit to (i.e., is it another job outside teaching or is it to household production) and what influences the timing of these decisions.

A commonly used econometric model for this problem is to analyze the duration of the stay in teaching as a continuous time reduced form proportional hazard specification with unrestricted baseline hazard:

$$h_i(t) = \underline{h}(t) \exp\{X_i(t)'\beta\}, \tag{14}$$

where $\underline{h}(t)$ is the baseline hazard at time t, $X_i(t)'$ is a vector of possibly time dependent explanatory variables for individual i at time t and β is a vector of unknown parameters. In many cases the explanatory variables will include the relative earnings in the two destinations of teaching and nonteaching. This basic model, or variants of it have been used by Dolton and Van der Klaauw (1995a, 1995b), Brewer (1996), Stinebrickner (1998a, 1998b) and Van den Berghe (2000) to model the duration of stay in the teaching occupation. An important generalization of this model involves the using of a competing risks specification to allow the possibility of exit to several different labor market states. Dolton and Van der Klaauw (1999) and Stinebrickner (2002) use this model to consider the exit of women teachers to either other jobs outside teaching or directly into household production.

The econometric problem which has received the most attention in the duration data literature is the modeling of the presence of unobserved heterogeneity. That is to say that there are influences on the dependent duration variable which are not captured in the measured regressors available to the econometrician. If unobserved heterogeneity is present but erroneously the model specification assumes it absent then the estimated parameters may exhibit erroneous negative duration dependence. The models of duration in teaching estimated by Dolton and Van der Klaauw (1995a, 1995b, 1999) explicitly model this unobserved heterogeneity both in a Gamma form and in the nonparametric way using mass points.

A second important problem in the estimation of duration models for teacher job duration is that of the most appropriate specification for the baseline hazard. The models of duration in teaching estimated by Dolton and Van der Klaauw (1995a, 1995b, 1999) explicitly model this baseline in a variety of ways. The most appropriate specification turns out to be that of the flexible baseline hazard estimated nonparametrically for each month or each quarter. When estimated using this method the baseline hazard reveals the distinctive pattern of job tenure, which exhibits clearly defined spikes for the periods which coincide with school term ends and academic year ends. Indeed, the use of any other modeling assumption on the baseline hazard can understandably be shown to be a model misspecification as clearly the institutional nature of the restrictions imposed on possible lengths of job tenure by the duration of school years and academic terms requires the use of the flexible baseline hazard. This is clearly another example of a situation in which the correct econometric model yields new insights into the economic structure of the data to be explained and where use of the wrong technique would give rise to biased results.

Modeling the exit from teaching should undoubtedly distinguish between the different types of reasons for leaving teaching. Most importantly, a women leaving teaching for family reasons is quite distinct from one leaving teaching to enter a job in a different sector. Modeling job durations by different types of exit is most often estimated using the independent competing risks framework which assumes that the underlying error structure for each type of exit is independent of each other type. A new departure in this literature is to recognize that the reason for exit from teaching for one reason may not be independent of the latent variable of the time to exit for another reason. Such a model of dependent competing risks estimation is estimated by Dolton and Van der Klaauw (1999).

3.6. Dynamic models and uncertainty

So far in our discussion we have assumed that the individual makes a decision to enter a job in the initial period, or leave a job in a subsequent period, based on a single calculation relating to the wage and nonwage benefits as calculated at the time the decision is being made. In reality, the decision maker will not know the wage on offer in the alternative careers with certainty or their growth into the future.

One simple model of occupational choice with uncertainty is presented by Flyer and Rosen (1997). In this model, which essentially attempts to capture this crucial feature of the teacher labor market, it is suggested that the individual faces the choice between a low variance earnings occupation (teaching) and high variance earnings occupation. They show that there is an increasing propensity to choose the high variance occupation as θ increases (where θ is the time devoted to work). This result is consistent with results found by Polachek (1981) which suggests that female dominated occupations have lower human capital depreciation rates.

The static occupational choice model in the previous section is myopic in its assumptions about individual decision making because it assumes: that current period decisions do not affect the utility of future decisions and that current period decisions do not influence the state variables that will affect the utility that the person receives from the different available alternatives into the future. For example the acquisition of an extra year's experience in teaching now could affect the future wages in teaching since it may affect promotion and advancement prospects.

More complex models which attempt to capture the dynamic nature of the career decision process for teacher entry and exit have been suggested by Van der Klaauw (1997), Stinebrickner (2001a, 2001b) and Csellack (2002) based on dynamic programming models adapted from other the occupational choice literature [Miller (1984), Siow (1984)], or other applications in economics [Eckstein and Wolpin (1989)]. A further important complication which we have so far ignored is the possibility that the individual may not wish to work in any career at various points in their life cycle to be primarily engaged in home production. We can now introduce this possibility into the theoretical framework. We follow closely the exposition of Stinebrickner (2001a, 2001b) as it is most directly relevant to our concern to model the supply of teachers.

Let W_{it}^j and Z_{it}^j represent respectively the wage and nonwage utility of person i at time t for some employment option j. Let $j = A, N, H$, where A denotes the teaching alternative, N the nonteaching alternative career and H the household production alternative,

$$U_{it}^j = W_{it}^j + Z_{it}^j. \tag{15}$$

Assume that the individual is assumed to know their current utility associated with each option but that they do not know the utility of each option in the future. Hence we assume that both W_{it}^j and Z_{it}^j are partly determined by stochastic factors which represent the randomness in wage and nonwage utility (respectively) of each person in each option into the future.

The value function of an option, which depends on the person's state variables, can be written as

$$V_{it}^j = U_{it}^j + \beta E \max\left[\{V_{it+1}^j \mid d_{it} = j\}\right], \tag{16}$$

where β is the discount rate, E is the expectation operator, and the set $\{V_{it+1}^j \mid d_{it} = j\}$ includes the value functions associated with the set of available options for the person in the next period, $t + 1$, conditional on the choice at time t, d_{it}, being equal to j.

In principle this model is sufficiently general to allow the econometrician to consider modeling a panel data set of individuals entering and leaving teaching and nonteaching jobs or engaging in home production throughout their working lifetime. The use of the dynamic model of teacher choice requires detailed panel data in which the participation and occupational choice are observed at each point in time.

3.7. The aggregate teacher supply function and time series models

It is relatively straightforward to derive [see Zabalza (1979a, 1979b) for formal details] an aggregate time series model of teacher supply directly from the simple microeconometric model set out in Section 3.2. In this framework (in which only monetary factors condition decisions) then it is possible to show that a direct consequence of the decision rule (16) is that there exists an individual specific reservation relative wage ζ such that for each person in the eligible labor force (L) such that if the wage is below this level the person becomes a teacher and below it they become a nonteacher. Out of a possible total potential labor force L, the proportion selecting $A(L_a/L)$ will be given by those whose reservation wage is less than, or equal to, the market relative wage; that is $P(\xi \leqslant W_a/W_n)$. Given a distribution of the reservation wage in the population, the proportion choosing to enter teaching will change if the relative wage on offer changes. This aggregate supply function will also change as the relative employment prospects in the alternative occupations change, the reservation wage changes and the discount rate changes. We can write this basic aggregate supply function in the following simple form

$$\frac{L_a}{L} = S\left(\underset{+}{\frac{W_a}{W_n}}, \underset{+}{\pi_a}, \underset{-}{\pi_n}, \underset{+}{r}, \underset{-}{\xi}\right). \tag{17}$$

Variants of this aggregate teacher supply function have been estimated by Thomas (1975), Zabalza (1979a, 1979b), Zarkin (1985), Court, Reilly and Williams (1995), Dolton, Tremayne and Chung (2003) and others.

Such aggregation ignores: regional disparities in pupil–teacher ratios, the deployment of teachers as opposed to the total numbers and the overall total level of unfilled vacancies, ad hoc temporary or part time supply teacher arrangements and the substitution of untrained teachers into specialist subjects. Obviously the huge variation indifferent the demand for different subjects also complicates the position.

A structural form model of the aggregate working of the teacher labor market over time would have the determinants of market supply and market demand in its structural equations and be estimated using time series data. A commonly used reduced form of such a model is written in terms of a market adjustment equation describing how movements in relative earnings change with the changing level of excess demand. This equation was first suggested by Arrow and Capron (1959) to model the market for scientists. It has been used to model the market for teachers by Dahlby (1981), Zabalza (1979a, 1979b), Dolton and Robson (1996) and Bee and Dolton (1995). Such a "Market Adjustment Equation" has the form

$$rw_t - rw_{t-1} = g(ED_{t-1}, X_t) + u_t, \tag{18}$$

where excess demand, $ED_{t-1} = (d_{t-1} - s_{t-1})$, where d_{t-1}, s_{t-1} are respectively demand and supply in period $t - 1$, rw_t is the average relative wage of teachers at time t and X_t are the set of exogenous variables affecting demand or supply at time t.

In its simplest form the market adjustment model is a naïve specification with regard to the implicit assumed perfect market structure. In practice the public sector demand for teachers predominates and several authors have been concerned to model the role of monopsony power in the market. Research by Dahlby (1981) in the UK found some support for the monopsony model with supply elasticities ranging from 0.20 to 0.75. A later paper by Luizer and Thorton (1986) has been concerned to measure the concentration of the monopsony power over local education authority boundaries, claiming that previous, more naive, measures of monopsony which ignore concentration, are flawed.

3.8. Government and manpower planning models

Manpower planning models were developed in the 1960s and 1970s in response to the need of governments to model the flows of workers into and out of occupations and forecast the need for qualified manpower into the future. Such models were extensively used by governments in various countries to model the demand for and supply of teachers. For early expositions of the operation and application of these models see IBE/UNESCO (1967), Hansen (1966), Ahamad (1970, 1973), Edmonston and

Knapp (1979), Williams (1975, 1979), Denton, Feaver and Spencer (1994). The statistical theory of the most sophisticated versions of these models are well described in Bartholemew, Forbes and McClean (1991). The manpower planning model is still the basis of the government's model for the teacher labor force in the UK, see DES (1965, 1990), DfEE (1997, 1998).

The demand for teachers in these models is calculated by using the available figures on pupil numbers and desired pupil–teacher ratios. This will give a crude estimate of the required number of teachers to staff the existing school system under various assumptions. This demand calculation may be made more complex by allowing for subdividing the aggregate demand into demand for teachers into primary school teacher and secondary school teacher demand and examining the demand for teachers of different subjects and factoring into the calculation the regional variations in the population of school children or the enrollment rate trends. Other factors which may be brought into the calculation are: the size of the existing stock of qualified teachers who are trained but not yet employed, the numbers who may return to the job after a household or family break, any changes in the structure of the school day, class size or teaching load or conditions of work. In any year, to compute the required additional demand for new teachers it is also necessary to model the rate of retirement and resignations from the existing stock of teachers.

In the manpower planning context the supply of teachers is modeled using a formal model of the process described in Figure 1. This involves estimating the number of teachers who are in service in any year and into the future by modeling the process of entrance, re-entrance retirement and wastage from the profession. This includes modeling the process by which those who are being trained as teachers either enter the workforce or drop into the pool of inactive teachers, PIT on graduation. It also involves establishing which teachers from the PIT are in fact likely to return to teaching – i.e., are really in the pool of recoverable teachers, PRT. Again such modeling can become fairly complex, if it takes into account the demographic age structure of the existing teacher workforce and the pattern of wastage by gender and age which may operate. Further complications arise if the differential demand by geographical region is considered or the primary or secondary balance is taken into account and the existing subject specialist stock of teachers is considered.

In general, the manpower planning approach is to collect as much data on the exogenous factual variables, like pupil numbers by age, existing numbers of teachers by age, gender, sector and subject, as possible, then making the most appropriate use of this data make assumptions about the existing set of relationships between variables – by extrapolating from, for example, recent wastage trends and retirement rates into the future. This technique allows the planner to forecast the demand for and supply of teachers into the future. It must be stressed that such forecasts will only be relevant estimates of the future state of supply and demand if the assumptions used to generate the prediction are reliable. By and large these models are fairly deterministic and do not usually ascribe any role to economic variables like relative teacher salaries. The excess demand/excess supply figure (Figure 11) relating to the UK was constructed using the most basic form of a manpower planning model as it relied on the existing stock of serving teachers as an estimate of supply and the fulfillment of the government's target pupil–teacher ratio as the driver of demand when pupil numbers are given exogenously. Although the calculation is naïve – it does – nevertheless provide a basic benchmark for the determination of pattern of shortage or surplus over the last 40 years.

3.9. Other models

Surprisingly in a consideration of teacher supply there are relatively few studies which actually model the conventional labor supply hours of work decision for teachers. This is because – for the most part – teachers have little scope to choose their hours of work as the school day is fixed in terms of length and the school terms are already set prior to the individual choosing to become a teacher. Two exceptions to this are when we consider the decision to be a part time or full time teacher or if we consider the pattern of teacher absence as part of the labor supply decision. Waterreus and Dobbelsteen (2001) have considered the former and Lindeboom and Kerkhofs (2000) have considered the latter. We need not rehearse the standard labor supply model in order to discuss their contributions as this is available elsewhere [see Blundell and McCurdy (1999)].

4. The determinants of teacher recruitment, turnover, retention, mobility and re-entry

A large literature exists on the factors affecting the supply decisions of teachers, most of it originating in the US. This literature can be divided into studies that examine the factors that influence the decision to enter teaching, and those that influence the decision to exit from teaching. The key explanatory variable in most of these studies is the wages that teachers receive, and thus this review will concentrate on these results. Since the empirical literature is so large we will focus attention on those studies which report the most important econometric results. Our approach will be to summarize the details of these key studies in Table 2 and focus on the qualitative conclusions in the exposition. Other factors will however be mentioned where appropriate. In particular we will attempt to draw out a synthesis of conclusions relating to studies which assess the effect on teacher supply of: school and subject differences; conditions of work and career structure; and female work patterns. Inevitably many studies cross over these different factors in teacher supply so we will only discuss them in the section which relates to their major findings.

It is inevitable that many studies in the literature on teacher supply consider the quality of teachers and the relationship between teacher inputs and pupil outcomes. A part of this literature also considers the possibility that other methods of payment for teachers, like merit pay, or performance related pay may affect teacher performance or pupil outcomes. We do not consider any aspects of this literature. These studies are the subject of a separate chapter in this volume.

Table 2

Summary of selected applied econometric articles on teacher supply

Author (Year)	Dependent variable	Country/Sample	Estimation method	Wage effect	Other comments
I. Entry and staying decision					
Manski (1987)	Entry	2952 respondents from the National Longitudinal Study of the High School Class of 1972, who gain a degree, and are in work in October 1979	Estimate probit of occupation choice, as a function of sex and academic ability. Estimate weekly earnings equation as a function of sex, academic ability and occupation, corrected for selection into occupation	Use the results to predict the proportion of the cohort who enter teaching, and their average ability. $25 increase in weekly earnings (about a 10% increase), raises the supply of teachers from 19% to 24% of the cohort. $100 increase in weekly earnings (about a 40% increase), raises the supply of teachers from 19% to 44% of the cohort. Thus wage elasticity of supply ranges from 2.4 for small salary increases to 3.2 for large changes	Average ability of supply of teachers barely changed by these wage increases (since both high and low ability individuals are attracted). A $25 per week increase, together with a minimum. requirement of 800 on SAT tests, would maintain the supply of teachers at 19% of the cohort, while raising average academic ability to the national average for college graduates
Dolton (1990)	Entry and staying decisions	UK, 1980 Graduate Cohort, information for 1980–1987 on 4,982 graduates, of whom 633 chose teaching as a first job	Probit on decision to become a teacher 4 stage modeling. Reduced form probit on becoming a teacher, and then staying a teacher. Use selectivity terms in teacher, nonteacher wage equations, finally use predicted earnings in structural form for entry decision probit and continuation probit	Relative nonteacher/teacher starting wages, expected wage growth for teachers and nonteachers. Nonteacher starting wages relative to teacher starting wages and expected nonteacher wage growth have significant negative effect on probability of becoming a teacher, while expected teacher wage growth has significant positive effect. Higher current predicted non teacher earnings relative to predicted teacher earnings has a significant negative effect on whether currently a teacher (7 years in)	Include predicted decision whether to become teacher upon graduation as a regressor in current job equation. Significant positive effect – suggests importance of first occupational decision or nonpecuniary factors

Table 2
(*Continued*)

Author (Year)	Dependent variable	Country/Sample	Estimation method	Wage effect	Other comments
Dolton and Makepeace (1993)	Choice of participation in the labor force and choosing teaching as a career	UK, 1980 2,056 female graduates	Bivariate probit of participation and teacher occupational choice with selectivity corrections	Finds significant relative earnings effects on the choice of occupation. A rise in the relative earnings of teachers from 1970 to 1990 increases the proportion who would choose teaching by 8.2%	Finds that the participation decision and the decision to enter teaching are endogenously related. Typically women choosing careers in teaching are partly doing so because it is a compatible career with household production
Hanushek and Pace (1995)	Probability of being in a teacher training program	USA, 1,299 graduates	Probit estimation of the probability of teaching	Participation in teacher training is not significantly affected by relative teacher earnings	Potential teachers perform lower on tests that other graduates and teacher training completion is lowered by state requirements for courses and teacher tests

Table 2
(Continued)

Author (Year)	Dependent variable	Country/Sample	Estimation method	Wage effect	Other comments
Dolton and Mavromaras (1994)	Staying in teaching	UK, 1970 and 1980 Graduate Cohorts, providing information for 1970–1977 and 1980–1987. Usable samples sizes equal to 3,990 and 4,980	Probit on decision to continue as a teacher. Reduced form probit on becoming a teacher, and then staying a teacher. Use selectivity terms in teacher, nonteacher wage equations, finally use predicted earnings in structural form for entry decision probit and continuation probit	Predicted nonteacher minus teacher-log earnings. Significant negative effect on probability of continuing as a teacher for both males and females. A 10% rise in relative teacher earnings would increase probability of currently being a teacher by 9.67% for 1970 men, 1.37% for 1980 men, 3.03% for 1970 women and 2.38% for 1980 women. 12% (32%) of 1970 men (women) choose teaching – would fall to 6% (16%) if facing 1980 conditions. 7% (25%) of 1980 men (women) choose teaching – would rise to 18% (32%) if facing 1970 conditions. The average man is 5% more likely to become a teacher in 1970 than in 1980. Due entirely to deteriorating market conditions – characteristics of 1980 men actually more favorable to teaching than those of 1970 men. Similarly, women are 8% more likely to teach in 1970 than in 1980, almost all of which is due to market conditions (favorability of characteristics barely changed)	Men's current decision to be a teacher more strongly influenced by original occupation choice than for women

Table 2
(*Continued*)

Author (Year)	Dependent variable	Country/Sample	Estimation method	Wage effect	Other comments
Dolton and Kidd (1995)	Entry into different career destinations including teaching	UK, 1980 male and female graduates	Multinomial logit estimation with endogenous wage determination	Finds relative wage effects are important in career choice	Simulations suggest that if men had chosen "like" women more of them would enter teaching. Likewise if women had chosen like men more of them would have entered the private sector
Flyer and Rosen (1997)	Linked to entry into teaching	Female college graduates in 1979–1991 NLSY, with less than 18 years of education, who worked 500 hours in any year after graduation, and earned hourly rates between $3 and $50 (1990 $'s)	Estimate log wage growth equations, including time spent out of the labor force and its interaction with teacher status	Fall in wage growth equals to 10% per year out of the labor force. However, offset completely by out of labor force – teacher interaction. Female teachers do not suffer wage penalty for time out of the labor force that other women suffer. May make teaching more attractive to family-orientated women	Results are not typical of other female-dominated occupations. Interaction term insignificant for both nurses and administrative, support – suggesting these occupations suffer the usual wage penalty for time out of labor force
Chevalier, Dolton and McIntosh (2006)	Entry and staying in teaching	UK, 1960, 1970, 1980, 1985, 1990 and 1995 cohorts of graduates surveyed 6–11 years after graduation	Sample selection correction on earnings from the reduced form probit decision to be a teacher	Relative wages in teaching have a significant impact on the likelihood of graduates choosing to teach. Impact depends on the cohort and changes over time	School exam performance, subject of degree, class of degree, postgraduate qualifications, type of school, parents occupation, region, and gender all have a significant effect on the entry decision. Cross-cohort simulations suggest that wage effect on the supply of teachers is strongest at times of low relative teacher's earnings

Table 2
(Continued)

Author (Year)	Dependent variable	Country/Sample	Estimation method	Wage effect	Other comments
II. Exit decision					
Zabalza, Turnbull and Williams (1979), Chapter 6	Exit	UK, Time series, 1963–1972. 8 observations per year, defined by age groups	OLS	Relative wages defined as above (replacing subject specific with age specific earnings in the first case). Elasticity of trained graduate separation rate, with respect to relative wages is −2.4 to −3.0 for men, and −0.6 to −0.7 for women. Elasticity of trained graduate separation rate with respect to relative starting wage is −2.6 for women and −0.7 for women, and with respect to the relative growth in earnings is −1.2 for men and −0.1 for women	
Rumberger (1987)	Percentage of teacher shortages and turnover of Maths and Science teachers by district	USA, 346 school districts from 1983–1984	OLS	Salary differentials between teachers and alternative occupations influence teacher shortages	The basic relationship is influenced by gender and geographic area
Eberts (1987)	Exit from teaching	USA (New York), 7,714 individuals working as full-time teachers in 1972–1975, taken from Personnel Files	Logit estimation	Difference between actual and predicted salary not significant in separation probability	Finds union negotiated contract provision sand class size limitation provisions reduce the probability of separation in unionized districts

Table 2
(Continued)

Author (Year)	Dependent variable	Country/Sample	Estimation method	Wage effect	Other comments
Theobald (1990)	Exit from district (may still be teachers elsewhere. Can't distinguish vol/invol, perm/temporary)	USA, all certified teachers in Washington state 1984–1987	Probit	Salary per day that they should receive next year. Significant negative for men in all years. Significant negative for women in some years. Prospective earnings 10% above the mean leads to a 6.9% fall in the probability of leaving	Outside options captured by qualifications. Teachers with Masters degree 35% more likely to leave (doctorate; 40%). Only significant for men
Rees (1991)	Exit (if leave to teach in another district of New York, treated as first spell)	USA (New York), 49,396 individuals working as full-time teachers in 1975–1976, taken from Personnel Files	Logit model on separations.	Current salary. Significant negative effect on quits. Predicted probability of separations, at different salary levels: 0.097 at $13,000, 0.075 at $16,400, 0.057 at $20,000	Teachers with higher educational attainments (measuring outside opps) are significantly more likely to quit
Beaudin (1993)	Returning to teaching after an interruption	USA (Michigan), 3,060 teachers in 1972–1975	Logit model	Those teachers least likely to return are those with better paying employment outside schools	Teachers most likely to return are those with subject specialties. Females return in higher proportions than males. Those who interrupt at a younger age and with higher qualifications are less likely to return

Table 2
(Continued)

Author (Year)	Dependent variable	Country/Sample	Estimation method	Wage effect	Other comments
Gritz and Theobald (1996)	Stay in teaching	USA (Washington), 9,756 white teachers who began teaching in 1981–1990. Followed until 1992	Generalized transition probability model	Finds significant salary effects in the probability of staying in teaching but these diminish with experience	Examines the teacher decision to teach in the same school district and the considers the role of inter-district mobility. Finds that expenditure and resources at the district level can impact on teacher stay
Theobald and Gritz (1996)	Exit from first teaching post, to a teaching post in another Washington school district, or out of teaching altogether	USA (Washington), 9,756 white teachers who began teaching in 1981–1990. Followed until 1992	Multinomial logit	Annual salary paid to teacher. Raising salaries reduces probability of exiting school system, and increases probability of remaining within teaching if they do exit. Raising all teacher salaries by $3000 decreases the proportion of females leaving education system in 10 years from 59% to 54% (males 31% to 23%). Of those leaving, the proportion transferring to another school within state increases from 28% to 33% for women and from 49% to 53% for men	Average earnings in county has positive, mainly insignificant effect on leaving. A $3,000 fall in outside wages leads to a fall in proportion of teachers leaving profession over 10 years, from 59% to 57% for women, and from 31% to 30% for men

Table 2
(*Continued*)

Author (Year)	Dependent variable	Country/Sample	Estimation method	Wage effect	Other comments
Hanushek, Kain and Rivkin (1999)	Exit (includes changing school district) and quality	USA. Texas Schools Project database – a matched panel of entire cohorts of students and all teachers. Use 1993–1996 data	Linear probability models for exit. OLS and IV for quality	Base year salary. Negative, and significant for teachers with up to 5 years experience. A 10% increase in starting salary is associated with a 2% decrease in the probability of leaving for probationary teachers (0–2 years of experience) and a 1% decrease for those with 3–5 years of experience. Note, when include district fixed effects, salary effect becomes insignificant (in contrast to Murnane and Olsen studies above). Maybe insufficient salary variation across small time span	Quality effects: 1. Effects of starting salary on a teachers' test scores (at district level): Salary coefficient insignificant. Split by district size – salary has positive and significant effect on teacher test scores in districts that hire at least 7 new teachers – a 10% rise in starting salary in such districts increases district average test score by 5 percentiles. Maybe larger districts make better use of enlarged applicant pool. 2. Effects of starting salary on change in student test scores. When use IV for measurement error on starting salary, and include student fixed effects, salary effect is positive and significant. A 10% increase in starting salaries raises maths achievement by 0.17 standard deviations, and reading achievement by 0.11 standard deviations. Note, not affected when control for turnover, and effect is larger where there are no probationary teachers – suggests salary effect works through motivating existing teachers

Table 2
(Continued)

Author (Year)	Dependent variable	Country/Sample	Estimation method	Wage effect	Other comments
III. Duration of stay in teaching					
Murnane, Singer, Willet (1989)	Time spent in teaching	USA (North Carolina) teachers hired between 1976–1978	Hazard function estimation	Find that higher than average salaries induce lower than average leaving hazard	Underlying hazard of leaving declines with the length of service. Found evidence of higher hazard for those with higher examination scores and subject specialty differences
Murnane and Olsen (1989a, 1989b)	Time spent in teaching (includes movement within the state but not outside the state)	USA (Michigan Statist. Dept.) of Education on all teachers who began teaching in 1972–1975, followed through to 1985	Estimate probability density function for duration of continuous teaching spell	Annual salaries teachers earned (or would have earned if they had stayed in teaching in the same district), expressed in 1967 dollars. Significant negative effect – stay longer in teaching if paid more. An increase of $1,000 in 1967$'s in each step of salary scale is associated with an increase in median length of teaching spell of greater than 4 years	Salary effect 1/3 smaller if exclude district fixed effects (assume fixed effects pick up bad working conditions, that are positively associated with salary through compensating differentials). Include opportunity cost, as salary paid to graduates who participate in subject training. A $1,000 increase in opportunity cost salary (in 1967$'s) reduces median length of teaching spell by 4 years

Table 2
(Continued)

Author (Year)	Dependent variable	Country/Sample	Estimation method	Wage effect	Other comments
Murnane and Olsen (1990)	Time spent in teaching (includes movement within the state but not outside the state)	USA, 13,890 white teachers who began teaching in North Carolina public schools between 1975 and 1984	Estimate probability density function for duration of continuous teaching spell	Annual salaries teachers earned (or would have earned if they had stayed in teaching in the same district), expressed in 1987 dollars. Significant negative effect – stay longer in teaching if paid more. An increase of $1,000 in 1967$'s in each step of salary scale is associated with an increase in median length of teaching spell of 2–3 years, for teachers who started teaching in 1975. Influence then falls in later years (effect half as big for those starting teaching in 1979) – perhaps due to declining student enrollments making teachers wary about getting back in to teaching if they leave	No significant interaction effect between salary and subject specialty. Influence of salary 30% less for teachers with National Teachers Exam (NTE) score in the top quartile (viewed as indicator of ability and ease of getting job elsewhere, rather than measure of teacher effectiveness). Salary effect 35% smaller if exclude district fixed effects (assume fixed effects pick up bad working conditions, that are positively associated with salary through compensating differentials)
Dolton and Van der Klaauw (1995a)	Duration to exit from first continuous teaching spell (i.e., maybe across different jobs).	UK, 1980 Graduate Cohort. Uses information for 1980–1987 on 923 graduates who chose teaching as a first job	Hazard model of length of first teaching spell	Relative wage – predicted difference in log of teacher and nonteacher graduate earnings at each month of experience. Elasticity of the hazard with respect to the relative wage equals to −1.5 (higher relative teacher wages reduce the probability of leaving). A 10% rise in teacher relative earnings reduces exit probability at 5 years' tenure by 9% (retention rate after 5 years increases from 66% to 69%, and to 73% if a 25% rise in relative wage)	Teachers with a B.Ed. have a lower probability of leaving teaching

Table 2
(Continued)

Author (Year)	Dependent variable	Country/Sample	Estimation method	Wage effect	Other comments
Mont and Rees (1996)	Time to exit (if leave to teach in another district treated as end of first spell)	USA (New York), 525 individuals newly hired as teachers in the fall of 1979, followed through until 1987, taken from Personnel Files	Discrete hazard model on length of teaching spell	Starting salary in 1979$'s. Significant negative on hazard of exiting teaching job. A 10% increase in starting salary lowers attrition rates by about 6%	Finds that probability of exit is higher for teachers with higher class load characteristics and below average quality of students. Also finds evidence of median household income effects in the district
Brewer (1996)	Exit (if leave to teach in another district of New York, as end of first spell)	Panel of teachers newly hired in New York, treated through to 1989, from New York State Dept. of Education data	Discrete time hazard model on length of spell in teaching	Current salary, in 1980$'s. Negative effect on probability of quitting, but significant only for women. Include mean salary of newly appointed educational administrators, and number of such positions in district created per year (represents pinnacle of career). Administrators wage has negative effect on probability of quitting, significant only for males (more likely to get the post). Number of posts has insignificant effect. A 10% increase in district administrator salaries reduces quit probability by 0.3%	Include county mean teaching salary relative to teacher's own salary as measure of outside opportunities. Increases quit probability for men and women. Dividing male new hires into new entrants and re-hires, effects of own salary and administrators' salary are significant only for new entrants. Interacting wage effects with length of spell, effect of district administrators' salaries and number of administrator posts opened becomes greater (more negative) with length of spell, while effect of own salary becomes smaller (less negative) with length of spell

Table 2
(Continued)

Author (Year)	Dependent variable	Country/Sample	Estimation method	Wage effect	Other comments
Stinebrickner (1998a, 1998b)	Exit from first continuous teaching spell (i.e., maybe across different jobs)	USA, National Longitudinal Study (NLS) of the High School Class of 1972. Followed for 14 years. Use data on 341 certified to teach between 1975–1985	Hazard model of length of first teaching spell	Log weekly wage. Significant negative effect – higher wages increase the length of first teaching spell. Probability that a person with a wage 1 standard deviation above the mean will stay in teaching more than 5 years is 9% higher than the probability that a person with the mean wage will stay in teaching	Opportunity cost captured by degree subject. Teachers with a science degree are significantly more likely to leave
Dolton and Van der Klaauw (1999)	Duration to exit from first continuous teaching spell, and re-entry to teaching after leaving teaching as a first job	1980 Graduate Cohort. Info for 1980–1987 on 6,098 graduates, of whom 923 chose teaching as a first job	Hazard model of length of first teaching spell. Competing risks of exit into nonteaching job or nonemployment allowed for. Also, hazard model for length of time spent out of teaching	Predicted earnings in teaching, at each level of experience. Significant negative effect on hazard of leaving to nonemployment (large but not significant effect on nonteaching employment hazard). Uniform 10% increase in teacher salaries will raise percentage of teachers still teaching after 5 years from 66% to 69% (equal reductions in numbers going into nonteaching employment and nonemployment). Positive effect (almost significant) on hazard of returning to teaching. A uniform 10% increase in expected teacher salary reduces percentage of former teachers who do not return within 4 years from 41% to 37%	Also include predicted earnings in nonteaching employment, at each level of experience. Significant positive effect on exit to nonteaching employment (but not nonemployment) and significant negative effect on hazard of returning. 10% increase in expected nonteacher earnings reduces percentage still in teaching after 5 years from 69% to 62%, and increases percentage who do not return within 4 years from 41% to 44%

Table 2
(Continued)

Author (Year)	Dependent variable	Country/Sample	Estimation method	Wage effect	Other comments
Van den Berghe (2000)	Staying in teaching	Belgium, 50,041 administrative records of teachers between 1973–1996	Proportional hazard Model. Weibull and non-parametric baseline	Finds a significant but very small effect of increased wages in teaching increasing the hazard of men leaving teaching. Wages have no effect for women	Finds that increasing workload, part time work and centralized decision making increase the leaving hazard but that if the individual works in several schools this reduces the hazard
Stinebrickner (2002)	Duration, exit	USA, NLS 1972, 422 female teachers	Duration Competing Risks with exit to non-teaching job and out of the labor force. Flexible baseline hazard	Wage coefficients have negative sign suggesting that individuals are less likely to exit to nonteaching or OLF if their teaching wage is higher	Finds that there is a very large positive effect of leaving teaching on nonteaching option with the birth of a new baby
IV. Dynamic programming model of stay in teaching					
Van der Klaauw (1997)	Entry and mobility	USA, NLS of the High School Class of 1972. 2,940 high school graduates. Followed for 14 years	Dynamic utility maximization model of occupational choice and occupational mobility estimated by Maximum likelihood. Model accounts for first and subsequent choice and nonpecuniary aspects of the decisions	Estimated model could be used to evaluate the effectiveness of several policy experiments designed to improve the composition and quality of the teacher labor force	Finds that teacher salaries and opportunity wages are important determinants of the supply and retention of teachers

Table 2
(*Continued*)

Author (Year)	Dependent variable	Country/Sample	Estimation method	Wage effect	Other comments
Stinebrickner (2002)	Entry and exit	USA, NLS of the High School Class of 1972. 22,652 high school graduates. Followed for 14 years. Use data on 450 certified to teach between 1975–1985	Estimate wage and nonpecuniary utility equations for teaching and nonteaching. Maximum likelihood estimation, estimating coefficients on characteristics to make the labor force choices that we actually observe most likely (as individuals evaluate wages and nonpecuniary utility from different options)	Simulation. Calculate individuals' value functions, given their characteristics and the estimated coefficients, then change wages, via 1 of 2 policies. Policy 1: 25% pay increase for all teachers. Policy 2: on average, a 25% pay increase, but depending linearly on teachers' SAT scores. Proportion of time spent in teaching increase from 0.48 to 0.72 under both policies more choose to teach initially and those that do stay longer, particularly the former – therefore greatest effect on males. Both policies reduce time in nonteaching rather than time out of workforce – therefore again, greatest effect for males	Interaction with SAT scores. Ratio of time spent in teaching among high ability relative to low ability is 0.88 (0.44:0.50). Under policy 1, this ratio increases to 0.94, and under policy 2 to 1.11 (i.e., policy 2 more successful in attracting high ability teachers)
Csellack (2002)	Teacher occupational choice by year	USA, NLSY 1979. 1,839 individuals from 1979 to 1998 of whom 276 chose teaching as an occupation	Dynamic structural model of occupational choice	Simulates the effect of wage policies on teacher supply. Finds that a 2% increase in teacher's wages increases teacher supply by 2.6% but has no effect on the ability of those choosing to be teachers	Considers the effect of marriage, fertility college major and post graduate study on the teacher decision

Table 2
(*Continued*)

Author (Year)	Dependent variable	Country/Sample	Estimation method	Wage effect	Other comments
V. Time series studies of aggregate supply relative wages and excess demand					
Thomas (1975)	Relative supply as measured by the Proportion of Graduates entering teaching	UK time series 1962–1970	OLS	Find significant salary effects suggesting a 1% fall in relative starting salaries will induce a 2–5% fall in the relative supply of male graduates entering teaching and similar effects for average salaries of teachers. Effects for female graduates are up to twice as big	Find for male graduates that the unemployment to vacancy ratio for administrative, technical and professional workers is positively significant for male graduates but not female graduates
Zabalza, Turnbull and Williams (1979) Chapter 5	Entry	UK time series, 1963–1971. 5 obs per year, defined by numbers of teachers in 5 subject groups	OLS	Relative teacher wages (compared to subject specific salaries from NES, or average annual earnings of nonmanual workers). Elasticity of graduate new entrants with respect to wage equals to 2.4–3.9, depending on definition of alternative wages, for men, and 0.3–1.8 for women (prefers higher estimates based on average earnings of all nonmanuals). Also, look at relative starting wage, and relative growth in wages. Elasticity of graduate entrants with respect to relative starting wages is 3.4 for men and 2.8 for women, while elasticity with respect to relative growth in earnings is, 1.6 for men and 0.4 for women. Therefore wage effects greater for men primarily because of their consideration of career prospects	Split results by degree subject (sciences and arts). For men, wage elasticity is greater for arts than for science students (insignificant for latter), while for women the reverse is true

Table 2
(*Continued*)

Author (Year)	Dependent variable	Country/Sample	Estimation method	Wage effect	Other comments
Dahlby (1981)	Shortage of school teachers	UK time series 1948–1973	OLS using a dynamic adjustment model on changes in relative wages	Number of students entering teaching is related to wage adjustment	Uses the data to argue that the monopsony model explains the shortage of teachers
Zarkin (1985)	Numbers completing teacher training	USA time series from 1950–1979 on teacher enrollment data	OLS	NA	Finds an important role for future demand conditions in the supply of graduates entering teacher training
Lewis and Norris (1992)	Supply and demand for teachers	Australia, time series data from 1972–1989 for Western Australia	No formal estimation	NA	Discusses the role of market forces in shaping supply and demand for teachers in Australia
Bee and Dolton (1995)	Teachers relative pay	UK 1956–1998 time series	OLS	Finds evidence of higher salaries link with excess demand for teachers	Links the time series evidence with the cross-section evidence to suggest the importance of excess demand in the determination of relative wages in cross-section data
Dolton and Robson (1996)	Teachers relative pay	UK 1956–1990 time series	OLS	Finds evidence of higher salaries link with excess demand for teachers	Finds that higher teacher union concentration of membership is positively related to teacher relative pay

Table 2
(Continued)

Author (Year)	Dependent variable	Country/Sample	Estimation method	Wage effect	Other comments
Court, Reilly and Williams (1995)	Relative supply as measured by the Proportion of Graduates entering teaching	UK 1986–1992 using time series data	OLS	Find significant salary effects suggesting a 1% fall in relative starting salaries will induce a 4% fall in the relative supply of graduates entering teaching	Find additional effects for the subject mix and proportions of women reading social science and language degrees. Do not find any evidence of unemployment or salary progression effects
Dolton, Tremayne and Chung (2003)	Teacher supply as proxied by various variables	UK time series data from 1947–2000	OLS using time series stationarity tests	Find that teacher supply is countercyclical. Evidence that supply is higher if graduate unemployment and relative wages are more favorable. Also find differences in the strength of effects by gender. Men are much more likely to be affected by aggregate conditions than women	Use different measures to proxy for teacher supply – wastage rates, changes in the size of the PIT and fractions entering the profession from all graduates in a given year
VI. Other studies					
Antos and Rosen (1975)	Earnings	USA, 5,454 teachers from a 5% sample from 1965 Equality of Educational Opportunity Survey	OLS	NA	Examined the spatial distribution of teachers based on the theory of equal advantage. School characteristics, racial composition, intelligence of students and neighborhood hazards are found to be important in wage variation. Estimates an increment of at least $300 would be required to get the average white teacher into the average black teachers school

Table 2
(Continued)

Author (Year)	Dependent variable	Country/Sample	Estimation method	Wage effect	Other comments
Edmonston and Knapp (1979)	Teacher aggregate supply and demand	USA, time series from 1934–1978	Demographic manpower model	NA	Uses a manpower planning model projecting pupil, teacher and new teacher numbers and fertility rates to project demand and supply for teachers. Predicts an over supply of teachers in the USA in the late 1970s
Denton, Feaver and Spencer (1994)	Demand and supply of teachers	Simulation	Dynamic simulation	NA	Simulation experiments investigate the changes in fertility rates on supply and demand for teachers. Results suggest that teacher imbalance is found to be highly volatile in response to fertility variations
Ballou and Podgursky (1998a, 1998b)	Quality	None	Simulation, using estimates of entry and exit behavior from other studies	Increase salary by 20%. Share of teaching workforce in top 5% of SAT scores increase from 5% to 7.6%. Most still have SAT scores below the college graduate average. If a high weight is put on attracting high ability (greater chance of them getting job) then 9.0% of workforce are high ability (top 5% of SAT distribution)	Problem is higher wages reduce exit rates, reducing number of vacancies, thus putting off people from training, esp. those with good alternative options (i.e., high ability). If the 20% salary increase is restricted to top 2 levels of ability, get 9.2% of workforce as high ability (similar effect to giving all teachers the raise, and targeting high ability, but of course cheaper)

Table 2
(Continued)

Author (Year)	Dependent variable	Country/Sample	Estimation method	Wage effect	Other comments
Lindeboom and Kerkhofs (2000)	Duration of absence from teaching job	Holland, 4,969 teachers in 426 schools with 21,137 spells of absence in 1987–1991	Mixed proportional hazard, partial likelihood, nonparametric baseline hazard with fixed school effects		Teachers are more likely to be absent: if they are very young or old, if they teach lower or small groups, if anticipated replacements are difficult or unanticipated replacements less difficult and if they are on permanent contract rather that a part time contract
Waterreus and Dobbelsteen (2001)	Hours of work in the labor supply equation	Holland, 1324 Dutch Secondary school teachers in 1998	OLS and IV. Endogeneity of net wage is corrected by using gross hourly wage and household income as IVs	Wage elasticity of supply at average weekly hours worked (33.48) is 0.24, i.e. to induce a teacher to supply 34 instead of 33 hours a week a 13% increase in salary is required. Male wage elasticity is 0.19 and female is 0.39	Simulation suggests that 3.5 million guilders would need to be spent on teachers wages to increase the number of hours by 8%. Whereas they suggest a full time premium would produce some effects for only 0.5 million guilders
Gilbert, King and Cregan (2002)	Earnings of teachers	New Zealand, 125 teachers observed 20 years after graduation	OLS		40% of the wage differential cannot be explained by experience, qualifications and mobility an hence attributed to discrimination and unobservables

4.1. Overview of the market and sources of supply

At the beginning of this chapter Figure 1 detailed the potential sources of teacher supply. At the outset in the determination of teacher supply we must be interested in the numbers who enroll in teacher training as this is the source of potential teachers. There are relatively few studies of what determines entrance into teacher training. In several studies in the USA, Hanushek and Pace (1994, 1995) examine the decision of college students to enter teacher training or not. They use the NLSY High School and Beyond survey from 1980–1986. They find that potential teachers perform lower on tests than other graduates and teacher training completion is lowered by state requirements for courses and teacher tests. They suggest that would be teachers are less likely to complete their qualification if the state imposes a pre-specified cut-off on a standardized test (national Teacher's Examination). They also suggest that students are less likely to complete their training in states which require their trainee teachers to complete a large number of education related courses. Their results suggest that teacher salaries do not have an important influence on student choices. Although the relative earnings of teachers compared to all college graduates varies considerably across different states in the US, they do not have a significant impact on the decision to enter teacher training.

There is a limited amount of evidence of a time series nature relating to the pattern of what influences initial teacher training recruitment. Zabalza (1979a, 1979b), using time series data for the UK over the 1963–1971 period, examines entry into teacher training by faculty of degree. He finds that relative wages and graduate unemployment have an effect on entry. Higher relative wages and higher unemployment induce higher rates of entry into teaching. This work has been brought up to date by Dolton, Tremayne and Chung (2003) who also find evidence of the importance of unemployment and relative wage effects in the initial teacher entry decision as modeled by entry to teacher training. They model entry into teacher training by faculty of study over the time period 1960–2000.

A further source of supply are the teachers that are created under crisis "emergency certification" measures which are, from time to time, instituted to ease the crisis in teacher supply. Examples of these measures have been used in the UK over the period 1960–1970, and at various times since, when graduates and those with suitable levels of experience were considered for short term training courses. Other such schemes have been introduced in various US states at different points in time. Little or no evaluation of how well these teachers work out or how long they stay in the profession has been conducted.

Another source of potential supply is to encourage part time working of those ex-teachers who are considering a return to work but may be constrained by family and other obligations. HMSO (1994) explicitly examines part time and returning teachers into the profession in the UK. It suggests that more could be done to make provision for part time and returning teachers to be able to adapt to the changes in the school curriculum and ensure that part time staff had improved lines of communication with full time staff. It also suggests that supply problems could be alleviated by more effective job share arrangements.

4.2. Aggregate labor market conditions, government intervention and the market mechanism

An early study, based only on time series data at the average aggregate level in the UK for the years 1963–1971 by Zabalza, Turnbull and Williams (1979), estimates the elasticity of the supply of labor into teaching, with respect to relative teacher earnings. The estimated elasticities range from 2.4–3.9 for men, and from 0.3–1.8 for women, depending on the definition of alternative wages used. When teaching wages are split into starting wages and wage growth, the authors find that the effect of the relative level of starting wages in teaching is similar for both sexes, while the effect of teacher wage growth over time is much greater for men. This suggests that the wage effects are greater for men primarily because of their consideration of career prospects.

As with the entry into teaching decision, Zabalza, Turnbull and Williams (1979) also undertake a time series analysis of the exit decision, considering the years 1963–1972. Dolton and Mavromaras (1994) find that males are much more likely to be influenced by the wage rates on offer than females, the elasticity of the trained graduate separation rate with respect to relative wages being -2.4 to -3.0 for men, and -0.6 to -0.7 for women. Unlike their analysis of the entry decision, Zabalza, Turnbull and Williams (1979) find that this gender differential in wage effects exists for both starting wages and the growth in wages.

Chevalier, Dolton and McIntosh (2001, 2006) overview the market position for teachers in the UK from 1960 to the 2002 using graduate cohort data from six separate cohorts of university graduates. The use of this data allows them to simulate the effect of possible teacher pay rises over time. They find that relative wages in teaching compared to alternative professions have a significant impact on the likelihood of graduates choosing to teach, although the impact depends on the market situation at the time. The wage effect on the supply of teachers is strongest at times of low relative teachers' wages, or following a period of decline in those wages. It is also strongest for those individuals who have more recently graduated. For example, increasing wages of teachers by 10% would have led to an increase of nearly 10% in the supply of teachers in the mid-1980s but only 2% in the mid-1960s or early 1990s.

Labor market conditions at the time the occupational choice is made are also important. The most recent evidence from Dolton, Tremayne and Chung (2003) looks at time series data over the whole post war period in the UK and finds that aggregate labor market conditions, particularly unemployment levels, are important determinants of teacher supply. They use various different proxies of teacher supply including the wastage rate from the profession and changes in the size of the pool of inactive teachers. They find that the supply of graduates to teaching is counter-cyclical with most graduates' perception of teaching (and willingness to enter the profession) improving when teacher pay is high compared to alternative occupations and when graduate unemployment is high.

4.3. Earnings, relative pay and the opportunity wage

Most of the empirical work on teacher supply that has been published has focused on the role of salary, and most specifically, relative salaries in teaching in an econometric explanation of those who decide to initially become teachers, and those who subsequently decide to stay in teaching. Naturally higher relative salaries are a possible way of offsetting poor working conditions in a compensating wage type explanation of the relative attractiveness of the teaching profession. In this section and in Table 2 we review the most important contributions to this literature.

There are a small number of US studies to have considered the entry decision into the teaching profession. One of the first significant contributions to have used an econometric approach to teacher supply is the contribution of Manski (1987). He uses data from the National Longitudinal Survey of the High School Class of 1972. The results of his probit equation on occupational choice (teacher/nonteacher) suggest a 10% increase in weekly teaching earnings will raise the supply of teachers from 19% to 24% of the graduate cohort. Moreover, a 40% increase in weekly teaching earnings raises the supply of teachers to 44% of the cohort. Thus the elasticity of teacher supply ranges from 2.4 from small salary increases, to 3.2 for larger increases. Manski also considers the quality aspect, and in particular is concerned by the fact that the average ability of those who choose teaching is below the average among all college graduates, quality or ability being measured by SAT scores. He suggests that a general pay increase does not improve teacher quality, since both low- and high-quality teachers are increasingly attracted to the profession. However, Manski calculates that a 10% increase in weekly teaching earnings, coupled with a minimum requirement for entrance to the profession of an 800 SAT score, would maintain the supply of teachers at 19% of the cohort, while raising the average academic ability among that group to the national average for college graduates.

Other early cross-section evidence of the importance of teacher salaries as a determinant of the decision to stay in teaching was provided by the papers of Murnane and Olsen (1989a, 1989b, 1990). Their results suggested that those teachers who have the highest salaries stay in teaching longer and those with the higher opportunity cost – as measured by test scores and degree subject – stay in teaching for less time.

Considering the entry decision, British work on this topic is limited. Dolton (1990) uses data from the 1980 Graduate Cohort, which follows 4,982 graduates for up to seven years after they have graduated. The paper suggests that it is the relative level of teachers' wages, rather than the absolute level, that affects the decision whether to become a teacher. In order to test this hypothesis empirically of course requires estimates of alternative earnings in jobs that individuals did not choose, as well as data on actual earnings received in whatever job graduates choose to do. In order to obtain estimates of alternative earnings, Dolton estimates wage equations for each of the possible cases (teacher

and nonteacher), to derive an estimate of earnings for each individual in their nonchosen state.[11] Similarly, wage growth equations are also estimated in both states, so that
estimated wage growth in the nonchosen state can be compared to actual wage growth
in the chosen state. The results are very much as expected, in that relative starting wages
in teaching (compared to estimated potential earnings elsewhere) are positively related
to the probability of becoming a teacher. In addition, individuals are more likely to become teachers the greater is the growth over time in teachers' earnings, and the lower is
the growth in earnings of nonteachers. The other variables in the equation suggest that,
among the individual characteristics, belonging to an ethnic minority, and having parents of a higher social class, are both associated with a lower probability of becoming a
teacher. As expected, individuals with degrees in education are more likely to become
teachers than those individuals with degrees in other subjects. The results also reveal
something about the quality of graduates who decide to become teachers, since individuals with a higher class of first degree, who went to university instead of a polytechnic,
and who hold a PhD are all, on average, less likely to become teachers. This quality
effect is over-and-above the simple fact that the high-achievers at degree level can earn
more in nonteaching occupations, since alternative wages are controlled for.

One important problem in the econometric estimation models which were reviewed in
the previous section was the difficulty of identifying the precise nature of wage effects.
In a simple static choice framework, under restrictive assumptions, we saw that we
could reduce the problem of choice to a consideration of starting salaries and the growth
in earnings. Typically we do not have good data on earnings growth in teaching and
nonteaching or indeed on a more general rate of return to becoming a teacher compared
to the rate of return of having an alternative career. Hence what little evidence there
is on this is important. Wilson (1983) shows that there has been a declining rate of
return to becoming a teacher over the 1962–1979 period in the UK. The paper follows
the method of Birch and Calvert (1973) by simply calculating a rate of return based
on national salary data for teachers. Such a task requires good cross-section data on
a country wide basis over many years. In addition it also really requires the equivalent
data for nonteachers in order to make a valid comparison about what has happened to the
relative rate of return in teaching and alternative occupations. A recent paper by Dolton
and Chung (2004) addresses these issues by comparing teachers life time earnings with
those of people who are qualified to teach but do not do so. They find in computing
rates of return for men and women over the 1960–2000 period that the rate of return in
teaching has been falling for both genders over this time period but that teaching is still
a relatively good job for women compared to the alternative available to those who are
qualified to teach but do not do so. In contrast, teaching has a negative rate of return for
men over the nonteaching alternative.

There are many more studies examining the decision to exit from teaching. This
is presumably due to the existence, particularly in the US, of administrative data sets

---

[11] Note that the wage equations were corrected for selectivity into the chosen state.

containing information on large numbers of teachers, allowing the "quitters" to be compared to the "stayers". Most of the British work in this area has been undertaken using information on various cohorts of university graduates, for example Dolton (1990), Dolton and Van der Klaauw (1995a, 1995b, 1999) and Dolton and Mavromaras (1994). With the exception of the last of these studies, all use data from the 1980 Graduate Cohort. The Dolton (1990) study estimates a probit equation on whether an individual is in a teaching job seven years after graduating (conditional on choosing a teaching job as the first job upon graduation). The results suggest that the factors affecting the decision to continue teaching are very similar to those that affect the decision to become a teacher in the first place. The selectivity term controlling for those who became teachers in the first job after graduation attracts a positive and significant coefficient, suggesting that the original choice has a strong influence on later choices, which may be caused by inertia and the transition costs of moving jobs or a persistent effect of attractive nonpecuniary benefits associated with teaching.

The three papers by Dolton and van der Klaauw all adopt a hazard approach to model the length of time spent in the first job after graduation among teachers. Each uses data on 923 1980 graduates who chose teaching as their first job, following the individuals for seven years after their graduation. The econometric model used analyses the factors associated with the "hazard" of leaving this job. As in the Dolton (1990) paper, a lot of attention is given to the role of relative wages, with wage equations again being estimated to provide the relative wage variable, measured as the predicted difference in the log of teacher and nonteacher graduate earnings at each month of experience. The results show that the elasticity of leaving a teaching job with respect to this relative wage measure is about −1.5, suggesting a large reduction in quit behavior among teachers, following a rise in earnings. For example, a 10% rise in teachers' relative earnings is estimated to increase the retention rate after five years from 66% to 69%, while a 25% rise in relative earnings would further increase this retention rate to 73%. The importance of the outside labor market and alternative opportunities is also clearly demonstrated by the significance of other variables in the estimated equation. In particular, teachers are more likely to leave their jobs, if their local unemployment rate is low, if they have a professional qualification, if they hold a noneducation first degree, if they are from a higher social class and if they attended an independent school. In addition, those teachers who claim that they only entered teaching because they could not find more suitable work are, not surprisingly, more likely to leave teaching in the following years, presumably as more appropriate work becomes available.

Dolton and Van der Klaauw (1995b, 1999) extend their earlier (1995a) work by adopting a "competing risks" approach to their hazard rate modeling. In particular, they allow the explanatory variables to have a differential impact on the likelihood of leaving for nonteaching work, and the likelihood of leaving the labor force altogether. The fact that a large proportion of teachers are women, who are more likely to leave the labor force in order to raise a family, could make such a distinction appropriate. The results show that this is indeed the case. Specifically, a higher teaching wage reduces the probability of teachers leaving the labor force altogether, while a higher predicted wage in the nonteaching sector is related to an increased likelihood of moving into a nonteaching job. The individual characteristics identified as having a significant impact on teacher turnover in the Dolton and Van der Klaauw (1995a) paper, are shown to work specifically through their impact on the probability of leaving the labor force altogether, and have a much smaller effect on the likelihood of moving into alternative employment, with the exception of the effect of having a professional postgraduate qualification, for which the reverse is true.

Turning back to the US literature on the exit decision, the evidence closest in spirit to the UK studies using the graduate cohort data sets is provided in two papers by Stinebrickner (1998a, 1998b, 2001a, 2001b), using data from the National Longitudinal Study of the High School Class of 1972. The two papers follow a small number of individuals who chose teaching as their first job (341 and 450 respectively) over the period 1975–1985. The earlier paper estimates a hazard model of the duration of this first teaching job. As was found with the UK studies, teachers are more likely to stay in their job, the higher are the wages that they receive. Stinebrickner estimates that a teacher earning one standard deviation above the mean teaching wage will have a 9% higher probability of staying in that teaching post more than five years. The Stinebrickner (2001a, 2001b) paper is interesting, in that it follows a different strategy to all other papers in this area. Essentially, he estimates wage and nonpecuniary utility equations for both teaching and nonteaching. The coefficients are maximum likelihood estimates, chosen so that it is more likely that we observe individuals in the occupation (in this case teaching or nonteaching) that they actually choose, on the basis that individuals are more likely to choose the occupation in which their predicted wages and nonpecuniary benefits are highest. Given an individual's characteristics and the estimated coefficients, the author can then predict whether that individual will become and remain a teacher, and can simulate the effects of changing teacher wages. Two policies are considered, the first being a 25% pay increase for all teachers, and the second being a 25% pay increase on average, the actual amount depending linearly on teachers' SAT scores. The results of the simulation show that the proportion of time, that the initial teachers spend in teaching, rises from 0.48 to 0.72 under both of these policies. As in the Dolton and Van der Klaauw (1995b, 1999) papers discussed above, both nonteaching jobs and time out of the labor force are considered as alternatives to teaching. Stinebrickner reports that the wage rises are more likely to reduce the amount of time spent in nonteaching employment, than they are to reduce time spent out of the labor force altogether. Consistent with other research reviewed here, the wage effect on the decision to continue working as a teacher is therefore greater for men than for women.

Although both wage policies in the Stinebrickner (2001a, 2001b) study raise the amount of time spent in teaching by approximately the same amount, they do differ in the extent to which they attract high quality teachers (quality being measured in terms of SAT scores). Not surprisingly, the second policy, whereby wages are increased in proportion with teacher quality, leads to a change in the mix of teachers towards a greater proportion of those of high quality. Other papers have also considered this relationship between relative wages, teacher supply and teacher quality. For example,

Ballou and Podgursky (1997) undertake a simulation exercise, using estimates of entry and exit behavior from other studies, to estimate the impact of changing teacher wages. They conclude that a general 20% increase in wages would do little to increase teacher quality, the problem being that higher wages reduce exit from the profession, hence lowering the number of teaching vacancies and so reducing the incentive to invest in teacher training, particularly for those high ability individuals with good opportunities elsewhere. The authors therefore suggest that the wage increase should be implemented together with an attempt to target those of higher ability, or, more cost effectively, making the 20% pay rise conditional on having a certain minimum SAT score, thus removing the need to pay higher wages to all teachers, including those of lower ability. In a similar vein, Hanushek, Kain and Rivkin (1999) use data for the years 1993–1996 from the UTD Texas Schools Project database, which is a matched panel of entire cohorts of pupils and teachers. The authors show that a 10% increase in starting wages is associated with a 2% fall in the probability of leaving for probationary teachers, and a 1% fall for those with 3–5 years of experience. The same wage increase is also associated with higher maths and reading achievement among pupils of 0.17 and 0.11 standard deviations respectively. These results are not affected when the authors control for turnover, and the effects are larger when probationary teachers are removed from the sample, suggesting that the greatest quality effects arising from wage increases occur through motivating existing teachers, rather than attracting new higher-quality ones.

Summarizing the remaining US papers to have studied the exit decisions of teachers, many have used city or state level data on all teachers registered within particular states, including Brewer (1996), Rees (1991), Mont and Rees (1996) (all studying New York), Murnane and Olsen (1989a, 1989b) (Michigan), Murnane and Olsen (1990) (North Carolina), Theobald (1990), Richards and Sheu (1992), Theobald and Gritz (1996) (both Washington) and Greenbaum (2002) (Pennsylvania). These papers all adopt either a dichotomous dependent variable approach based on whether teachers have left their job after a certain amount of time, or undertake a duration analysis of the time spent in teaching. In each case, only individuals who started teaching in a particular year, rather than all teachers in the state, are considered, so as not to confuse wage effects with seniority effects. A problem with using administrative data of this type is that if individuals move states they automatically fall out of the data set, whether or not they have continued as a teacher. The results should therefore be seen as the factors affecting the length of the first job in teaching, rather than the length of time spent in the teaching profession as a whole. The results across all of the studies named above agree that the salary paid to teachers is negatively related to their propensity to leave, or positively related to the duration spent in first teaching jobs. Where studies allow for gender differences, a common finding is that these wage effects are larger for men than for women. There is also some evidence [for example, in the Murnane and Olsen (1990) study] that the influence of teacher earnings declined over time during the 1970s, which is consistent with the UK evidence of Dolton and Mavromaras (1994). Finally the US studies do not consider relative earnings or alternative earnings in the same detail as the UK studies outlined above, with none estimating wage equations to obtain estimates of wages that could be earned in nonteaching jobs, although most include proxies for outside alternatives, such as qualifications held by teachers, or average district-level wages. The results generally show that teachers with higher level qualifications, or who live in areas with higher average nonteaching wages, and more likely to leave their teaching jobs.

Another aspect of teacher supply relates to the mobility of teachers between different locations. Hanushek, Kain and Rivkin (1999), in the study cited above, assess the role that salary schedules played in the composition of teachers within a district and how pay affected mobility and specifically transitions both between and within Texas public schools. Their evidence suggests that student characteristics play an important role in these decisions and that there is only weaker evidence of the importance of salaries affecting transitions. The typical Texas teacher places a high weight on high achieving nonminority students and such factors act as clear compensating differentials in the decisions to move to another location or exit teaching all together.

An important element to teacher supply are those who return to teacher after a break. Murnane (1996) suggests that in the USA only one in four teachers return to teaching after a career interruption. The decision to re-enter teaching would also appear to be influenced by pecuniary factors. Beaudin (1993) finds those teachers least likely to return are those with better paying employment outside schools.

Econometric evidence from other countries aside from the USA and the UK is limited. Wolter and Denzler (2003) use data on university graduates in Switzerland over the period from 1981–1999 to assess the wage elasticity of teacher supply. They find that teacher supply is responsive to wage levels. However their results indicate that this relationship is not so strong in their data as that reported in other countries. It is possible that part of the explanation for their finding is that teachers are paid relatively well in Switzerland compared to other workers.

4.4. School differences and conditions of work

A most important set of factors which may condition individual labor supply decisions relate to working conditions in schools. In addition the labor market faced by teachers working in some subjects or in certain schools may be radically different from those faced by others. Teaching is quite a different job if you face a large class of 16 year old inner city pupils from deprived homes who simply do not want to be there – than if you face a small class of middle class 5 year olds for whom school is fun. More specifically, variations in working conditions may involve: class size, teaching load, the extent of teaching outside one's area of expertise, the composition and background of the pupils to be taught, the fabric of the buildings and equipment one has to work with, the nature of one's colleagues, the extent of administrative support from local or federal agencies, the degree of classroom assistance by pupils or trained support staff, the opportunities for training and advancement of skills, the flexibility of working practices and many other factors. The issue of the relationship between teacher shortage and class size and teaching loads is of crucial importance to policy makers trying to solve the problems of teacher supply. If there is evidence that teachers are more likely to quit when class size is higher and other conditions are more adverse then this poses logical questions for policy associated with spending budgets on more teachers – possibly instead of raising the salaries of existing teachers.

There has been relatively little research devoted to the relationship between working conditions and the supply of teachers. Mont and Rees (1996) examine the effect of class load and other factors on teacher turnover. Specifically they examine the role of factors like the number of classes taught, class size and whether a teacher is teaching in the subject area of certification. They suggest that increasing class size, and the greater the number of classes taught, and the higher the percentage of time a teacher has to teach outside their specialist area do have an impact by increasing teacher turnover. They also find that the school district characteristics also play a role in this turnover. Again this research was conducted using data from the New York State Department over the years 1979–1989.

Other studies have also found a role for working conditions effects. Stinebrickner (1999a) finds that the pupil teacher ratio is an important determinant of teacher turnover. However he also finds that the ability level of students is less significant in determining a teacher's view of the school. Likewise Hanushek, Kain and Rivkin (1999) find that the characteristics of the study body are important in why teachers may switch locations. Van den Berghe (2000), using data from Belgium, finds that increasing workload, part time work and centralized decision making increase the leaving hazard but that if the individual works in several schools this reduces the hazard. One of the main conclusions of his study is that nonmonetary working conditions, namely access to teaching jobs with permanent contracts is a more important determinant of supply than salary levels.

There are few studies of the effects of organizational conditions in schools and teacher turnover. Ingersoll (2001a, 2001b) investigates this relationship using data from the Schools and Staffing Survey from the US Department of Education. His results indicate that low salaries, inadequate support from administrative authorities, the presence of student discipline problems and the remoteness of teaching staff from decision making all contribute to higher teacher turnover – even if teacher and other school characteristics are controlled for. The wider issue of the extent to which making teachers accountable but also giving them more control over their working environment has not really been examined in the literature. Indeed will know little about whether there is any relationship between teachers becoming more professional and their decisions relating to their labor supply and turnover.

There is a further literature, which is small but growing, on the relationship between teacher mobility and the social class and ethnic makeup of the school. Greenberg and McCall (1974) in an empirical investigation of San Diego schools finds that new teachers tend to be placed in low SES schools and those teachers who move tend to move to higher SES schools having teachers with greater experience and higher educational attainment. The authors suggest that teacher upward mobility and the fact that higher SES schools have better qualified teachers are both outcomes of the process whereby better qualified teachers gravitate to the more privileged schools. Antos and Rosen (1975) using the 1965 Equality of Educational Opportunity Survey found that an additional

$300 per year (in 1965 prices) would be necessary to induce the average white teacher to teach in a predominantly black school. Undoubtedly there is evidence of teacher supply and mobility decisions being affected by the kind of children in the school. Such factors are important in an explanation of the schools that find it hard to recruit teachers but the consequences for the persistence of inequality of opportunity are potentially massive.

4.5. Subject specialism differences

Another important difference in the teacher supply position relates to the different conditions which exist in the market for school teachers of different subject specialisms. Rumberger (1987) examines the impact of salary differences on teacher shortage for Mathematics and science teachers in the USA. He uses data on a sample of medium and large schools districts in metropolitan areas. Using the salaries of engineers to proxy for wage prospects in alternative occupations outside teaching for science and maths graduates he finds that larger salary differentials between alternative occupations and teaching do induce bigger teacher shortages. Murnane, Singer, Willet (1989) also finds (using his sample of North Carolina teachers from the 1970s) that teachers of chemistry and physics tend to leave teaching sooner than teachers so of other subject specialties. Moreover, they are much less likely to return to teaching once they had left.

Stinebrickner (1998a, 1998b) finds that teachers with a science degree are significantly more likely to leave the profession. Beaudin (1993) finds that teachers most likely to return are those with subject specialties that provide only limited opportunities for alternative employment outside of schools. Such findings are repeated in a number of other studies and suggest that decisions to enter or return to teaching are related to opportunity costs. Clearly those individuals with good outside options because of their skills and qualifications are more likely to be attracted into another profession.

Guthrie and Zusman (1982) discuss the serious shortage of maths and science teachers in the US in the early 1980s. They describe the cause of the problem and suggest a variety of policies to deal with it. Not surprisingly they suggest that relative salaries in teaching compared with other science career alternatives are at the root of the problem. They suggest that more differential pay, more in service staff development and more industry and school cooperation may alleviate the problem.

One solution to the shortage of teachers in the mathematics and science field is to ask teachers of other subjects to teach these subjects. This is an increasingly important phenomena in many countries, including the UK. The issue of the extent of "out of field teaching", i.e. teaching outside one's are area of expertise, is a topic which has been given detailed consideration by Ingersoll (1997, 2000, 2001a, 2001b, 2001c, 2002) for selected areas of the US but has been virtually ignored in other countries. Ingersoll has good reason to suggest that this out of field teaching is commonplace and hides the true extent of teacher shortage.

4.6. Career structure considerations

There is scattered evidence that the career structure in teaching actually affects teacher supply. Issues relating to, if and when, a teacher chooses to move to another school, or into a different kind of job, may relate to the structure of teaching as a career. Specifically, the possibility of moving up the occupational hierarchy and getting promoted to a headteacher or not could be relevant to whether someone chooses to leave the profession early. The actual profile of the age at which an individual teacher chooses to leave the job, and return or not, may well be related to career concerns. Likewise the possibility that a teacher may choose an "optimal time to quit teaching to enter a related field" – like educational administration – may also be related to their age, promotion ladders, and their inability to get advancement in their own school or school district. Alternatively, they could choose to leave teaching as a result of the cumulative occupational stress of successive years at the "chalkface". This evidence is contained in the detailed findings of many different studies – we highlight only some of the more important contributions.

In considering the possible career path for teachers one logical possibility is that teachers may enter educational administration. Brewer (1996) examines this possibility by considering the responsiveness of teachers to opportunities in school administration. Using a sample of newly hired teachers in New York from 1978 to 1988 he finds that male teachers are sensitive to expected administrative salaries. The argument is that teachers often move to fill up the jobs as administrators. Higher district administrator's wages decrease the probability that a teacher will leave the district. Specifically a 10% increase in district administrator salaries reduces quit probability by 0.3%. Dividing male new hires into new entrants and re-hires, effects of own salary and administrators' salary are significant only for new entrants. In addition he finds that if administrative salaries in surrounding districts rise then teachers are more likely to leave their own district. These effects are significant only for males which indicates that female careers in teaching are less likely to consider the administrative route – possibly because such jobs are less compatible with family responsibilities.

Boyd et al. (2002a, 2002b) describe the "career paths" of teachers using administrative individual teacher data from New York State over the last 20 years. The data show that: there is a substantial turnover in teaching in the first years; that students from more selective colleges tend to quit earlier, as do those whose initial job is in an urban area. They find that the age of entry into teaching has been rising. They also find that the proportion of teachers who have failed a Teacher Certification exam have been rising, as has the proportion with Master's degrees. This suggests a wider dispersion in the quality of teacher provision.

Using the same data set Boyd et al. (2002b) examine teacher preferences over their job location. They find that teachers exercise a strong preference to teach close to where they grew up. They suggest that if the location of a job is not considered in modeling individual supply decisions then this may results in an econometric misspecification.

The responsiveness of teacher supply is related to the age of the teacher or their years of experience. There is good evidence that teacher attrition is higher at the beginning of the career and at the end than in the middle. Grissmer and Kirby (1997) found that younger teacher tend to have higher attrition rates. The hazard for leaving teaching rises during the mid-career and then declines with professional experience. Stinebrickner (1999b) also finds this pattern. He suggests that the early years of experience are an important determinant of whether a person stays in the job. He suggests that the hazard rises in the first four years in the job but declines thereafter. These results would suggest that policies to increase retention rates of teachers would be best focused on young teachers and making their conditions of work more acceptable. However this conclusion should be tempered with the fact that much of this age/experience pattern of attrition will be induced by women leaving teaching to have family career breaks. It seems clear that the real problem for policy makers is the men who quit teaching early in their career as they are much less likely to return to the profession.

One aspect of the teacher career choice which is relatively under-researched is the role that expectations of school pupils and students of teaching as a possible future career for themselves play in the formation of subsequent occupational choices. Why is it that the sons and daughters of doctors often want to be doctors but that the sons and daughters of teachers seldom want to follow in the footsteps of their parents? Kyriacou and Coulthard (2000) examine this subject using data from undergraduates views on teaching as a career in the UK. Their work suggests that students have a poor impression of teaching as a potential career due to salary prospects and also to the stressful image of the job.

In a related paper Chevalier, Dolton and McIntosh (2001), consider reported job satisfaction with a number of aspects of working life, using data from the UK 1985 and 1990 Graduate Cohort Data Sets. The results suggest that teachers are less satisfied than other graduates concerning key aspects of their jobs, such as pay and hours worked. However this work does show that teachers are more content with other aspects of their job than those graduates who enter alternative careers. Specifically they are more content with the match of their qualifications with the nature of their work and also their sense of job security.

In their investigation of teacher mobility Theobald and Gritz (1996) examine the teacher decision to teach in the same school district and considers the role of inter-district mobility. They find that expenditure and resources at the district level can impact on the length of time a teacher stays in the profession. Shen (1997) using data from the 1990–1991 US Schools and Staffing Survey examines the teachers who stay in the same school, move to another school voluntarily and those who left teaching of their own accord. The author finds that stayers are statistically distinct from the movers and the leavers. Osei Bempah et al. (1994) using data from a beginning teacher survey in Missouri estimate a model of migrant and nonmigrant teachers. They find that the migration decision is most strongly influenced by home ownership and leadership style of the school administration.

4.7. Female career patterns

The role that gender considerations play in the supply of teachers cannot be under-estimated. From the OECD data on different countries we know that around 62% of teachers are women and that in some countries the fraction is as high as 94%. Not only do women choose teaching as a career in their initial occupational choice they also return to the career if they leave it. Beaudin (1993) finds that females return to teaching in higher proportions than males. Those who interrupt at a younger age and with higher qualifications are less likely to return. This means that the teacher labor market is unlike other in terms of its reliance on female labor. As a result – more than in nearly any other professional labor market – we need to be aware of the issues of female labor force participation and the wishes of women to have career interruptions or work part time.

Many of the econometric studies report findings separately for men and women and as a result explicitly show how the labor supply decision of women is particularly important in the context of the teacher labor market. Dolton and Van der Klaauw (1999) make a distinction between exiting teaching for family reasons and exiting to another job. This distinction is a particularly important aspect of female labor supply. They also find that women from higher social classes and privileged schools are more likely to leave the workforce; those with education degrees are less likely to quit teaching for a nonteaching job and those with postgraduate qualifications are more likely to quit teaching and those who entered the profession reluctantly are more likely to exit involuntarily or for family reasons.

An important aspect of female teacher labor supply has been the changing opportunity set in terms of alternative careers for women over time. Corcoran, Evans and Schwab (2002) examine how the propensity for educated women to enter teaching has changed over time in the US over the period 1957–1992. They find that although the quality of the average new female teacher has fallen slightly over this period, the likelihood that a women from the top of her high school class will enter teaching has fallen from 20% in 1964 to under 4% in 1992. A major part of the explanation of this change has been that other employment opportunities for women have changed remarkably over this time period.

One particularly important dimension of teaching as a career for women is the flexibility of working time. Flyer and Rosen (1997) using the NLSY from 1979–1991 examine the transitions of women college graduates between the home and the market sector. They suggest that teaching provides for more flexible allocation of time between market and home production. They investigate whether teaching as a career for women provides a more flexible alternative which is compatible with home production. They suggest that teaching does provide a more flexible market to facilitate this intermittent pattern of participation in work combined with periods of household production. Such interruptions are shown to be less costly for women teachers than women graduates who have alternative careers in that that women teachers do not suffer such big pay penalties for taking time out of the labor market. Women college graduates who take jobs outside teaching face an average 9% pay penalty for each year spent out of the labor market. Flyer and Rosen suggest that the flexibly afforded by a teaching career offers an important attraction to the profession for women.

Personal circumstances relating to family obligations play a very important role in the decision to become and remain in teaching. Dolton and Makepeace (1993) show that for women the decision to become a teacher and participate in the labor market need to be considered simultaneously as these decisions are endogenously related. This is true in the sense that unobserved factors, which make a woman more likely to select a career outside teaching, make them less likely to participate in the labor market and vice versa. This generates a positive correlation in the teaching occupational choice decision and the decision to work.

For many women – up to 60% in the US [see Stinebrickner (1999b)] – leaving teaching can mean leaving the workforce all together. Stinebrickner (1999a, 2001a, 2001b) finds that changes in marital status and the birth of a child play a key role in teacher supply. Clearly for a women the decision to continue in teaching after the birth of a child have to be assessed very carefully in relation to the extra cost associated with child care. Since remaining in full time teaching after the birth of a child will require day care provision then the birth of a child lowers the effective wage on offer and this may effect whether a women decides to continue in her job. Stinebrickner suggest that child-care subsidies may represent an efficient way to increase teacher supply relative to increasing teacher salaries. Further work by Csellack (2002) using a dynamic occupational choice model suggests that the marital and fertility decisions need to be treated endogenously to the modeling of teacher career choice and specifically whether a person actually works in teaching in any specific year.

Dolton and Mavromaras (1994), use data from both the UK graduate cohort surveys of 1970 and the 1980 to provide comparisons over time for men and women. The results show that the influence of relative earnings on the decision to remain in teaching declines between these two dates. Specifically, the authors estimate that a 10% rise in relative teacher earnings would increase the probability of currently being a teacher by 9.67% for 1970 men, but only by 1.37% for 1980 men, and by 3.03% for 1970 women, but only 2.38% for 1980 women. The authors also decompose the cause of the fall in the likelihood of becoming a teacher into changes in the characteristics of the individuals themselves, and changes in the characteristics of the job market that they face, with the latter dominating. The average man is 5% more likely to become a teacher in 1970 than in 1980, with this fall being due entirely to deteriorating market conditions for teachers. The characteristics of 1980 men are actually more favorable to becoming a teacher than those of 1970 men. Similarly, women are 8% more likely to teach in 1970 than in 1980, almost all of which is due to market conditions, the favorability of individual characteristics having barely changed.

4.8. Other aspects of teacher supply

There are many other factors which impact on teacher supply, some of which have been rarely examined in the literature. A particularly important feature of the teacher labor market is the presence, in many countries, of quite strong trade unions. Much of the literature on teacher unions has sought to examine the relationship between unions and pupil outcomes or school choice [e.g. Hoxby (2000), Eberts (1987)]. Such studies have little to say about the teacher supply consequences of the presence of trade unions or their activities. There are a few studies however that do address the issue (albeit briefly) of the relationship between teacher trade unions and aspects of teacher wages and teacher supply [Currie (1991), Baugh and Stone (1982) and Easton (1988)].

Historically, in the UK and the USA, teaching has been a heavily unionized profession. This is partly due to the nature of the union in this occupation is that it acts as a professional club and also provides members with a degree of insurance against allegations of negligence or abuse, or accident when in charge of children. Nevertheless, there are clear supply and wage consequences of the heavy presence of unions in teaching. Eberts (1987) finds union negotiated contract provisions and class size limitation provisions reduce the probability of teacher separation in unionized districts in New York State in the 1970s. Rees (1991) examines the relationship between teacher quits and the strength of grievance procedure. Using data from New York State public teachers in the mid 1970s he finds that teachers with the strongest types of grievance procedures in their contracts had a lower probability of quitting that those working under weaker grievance procedures. The author suggests that this provides evidence that unionization can reduce quits through a voice effect.

5. Future research

The overwhelming conclusion of much of the empirical econometric research on the supply of teachers is that problems of teacher shortage could be alleviated with higher relative teacher salaries. If relative teacher salaries were higher then the problems of teacher recruitment, retention and duration would be alleviated. This is a relatively straightforward prediction given any simple economic model of occupational choice which is based on the choice of career based on the criteria of the maximization of expected future lifetime earnings. There are many important assumptions in such a model which were discussed in Section 3. Here we recap the most limiting of these assumptions as they provide directions for future research. Explicitly the model assumes that: the only element to the decision criteria is expected future lifetime earnings and that nonpecuniary factors do not matter, secondly that the agents have perfect foresight about the path of these expected future lifetime earnings which are naively assumed to grow at a constant rate and thirdly that there are no radical changes to these initial conditions.

There are further technical econometric problems in the modeling of teacher supply in that there are many other decisions which the individual takes simultaneously with deciding to become (or remain) a teacher. Firstly the decision to participate in the labor market and secondly how much labor to supply are not exogenous of the decision of becoming a teacher. Also, for a woman, the decision to get married and have children may not be independent of her decision to study education and become a teacher. We have seen that there is already some empirical evidence that occupational choice, participation decisions, and marital and fertility decisions are all inter-related for women teachers. The problem with all these interrelated decisions are that they are complex to model simultaneously and so far there has only been modest progress on models which incorporate these complexities. The early dynamic programming papers on teacher supply have attempted to unravel the main elements of these decisions. These models of teacher supply represent one promising avenue of future investigation with the advent of larger, more comprehensive, data – but much work remains to be done. In this context it is possible that more use could be made of merged exogenous data. Likewise attempts to model these decisions using static cross-section data have fallen foul of the problem of the lack of appropriate instrumental variables or exclusion restrictions which could be used to identify the different elements to these distinct but related decisions.

Further econometric difficulties are apparent whenever one wishes to evaluate the nature of any policy change in the field of teacher supply. For example, it is unclear exactly how to model the effect of any change in teacher's wages on the overall supply of teachers. The complexity of this process has been outlined in this chapter but there are many opportunities for good empirical work which could use actual policy regime shifts to identify the effect of policy changes. Techniques of quasi or natural experiments and regression discontinuity design could be profitably used in this area. Features like changing administrative regimes for the hiring or remuneration of teachers over time could be used to identify the effects of relative wage effects on teacher supply.

One of the important assumptions in almost all of the models of teacher supply which have been investigated is that both the wage in teaching and the wage in nonteaching will grow at a constant rate. Not only is this assumption very naive but potentially wrong. By using various data sets it could prove possible to not only retrieve teacher wages, but also that of nonteachers, over the whole lifecycle. [See Dolton and Chung (2004) for a first step in this direction.] This would mean that rather than assuming that earnings grew at a constant rate in the alternative careers – real data could be used to more accurately reflect the true empirical position. However it is clear that there needs to be more work on the issues of modeling educational investment decisions under uncertainty.

Another area for fruitful research would be in the role that nonpecuniary factors play in the decision to become (or remain) a teacher. There is only a very limited literature which recognizes that such factors could be important in the decision to enter or stay in the teaching profession. Examination of the pattern of life cycle earnings for men in the USA and the UK in teaching and nonteaching alternatives shows that if earnings were the only criteria used to decide a career then no men would become teachers in these countries. Hence other factors must play an important role in this decision. This is a topic worthy of careful research, not least because one of the perennial problems of teacher supply is how to recruit the highest ability individuals into the career. If it was clearer as to exactly what the nonpecuniary benefits of teaching were, we could target individuals who most highly rated these attributes of a job. In addition, good research in this area might also reveal what were the most important negative aspects of a teaching career in terms of working conditions and appropriate measures may be devised to ameliorate these negative aspects of the job. More specifically there is scope for detailed empirical work on the relationship between job-satisfaction, nonpecuniary work conditions and the rate of turnover of teachers. New data sets are being collected which emphasize the role of these factors in occupational choice and satisfaction. They could be profitably used to shed light on why graduates enter the job of teaching and why they stay in the occupation when their remuneration could be much higher in an alternative occupation.

There are many possible directions for future empirical econometric research into the labor market for teachers. Perhaps the most promising lines for future research have been opened up by important new data sources. Particularly exciting are the prospects of being able to use detailed administrative data on teachers over their working careers. Specifically, many countries now have census like databases of teachers. In the UK the Database of Teacher Records (DTR) has detailed information on all 1.9 million people who had become teachers since 1961. Likewise some US states now have good administrative data on teachers [e.g. Boyd et al. (2002a, 2002b)]. The data allows us to track who is in and who is out of the teacher labor force at any given time – knowing precisely when they entered the teacher profession, when they left and when they returned. One advantage of administrative data over survey data is that there is no problem with nonresponse and the bias that this may cause. Another advantage of administrative data is that it is possible to conduct realistic analysis of important subgroups which are difficult to study with survey data due to lack of sample size. Specifically with administrative data it is now possible to further study the supply of teachers in key subjects and particular geographical locations as the literature is relatively thin in this area.

There are many other areas in which our knowledge about teacher supply is scant. Although teacher shortage is widespread we know from empirical evidence that many young people still choose to be teachers despite the low pay. Clearly nonpecuniary factors matter in occupational choice but we know relatively little about this part of the process and how it operates. We also know relatively little about the role of expected future lifetime earnings in the decision process and how people trade this off against a job which is rewarding. We also know little about young people's perceptions of teaching as a career or their real relative perceptions of earnings in teaching. In some countries there are a sizable number of teachers who enter the profession in mid-career after working in the private sector for some time. One interesting earlier exception is Pavalko (1970). We need to know more about what motivates these individuals to make these choices and if they are more effective teachers due to their outside perspective on the real world.

Further opportunities to study the problems of teacher supply may be possible by the collection of reliable data on teacher vacancies. Hitherto, this data has been patchy as not all vacancies are recorded centrally. But the signs are that good data on teacher vacancies is now being recorded nationally via comprehensive data collection and website accessibility to these records. It is not impossible that fruitful analysis of this data by subject and geographical location over time might provide further insights into the problem of teacher supply.

A further natural area for research work is to compare the position on the state of teachers across different countries. There is now a large amount of data in different countries – some administrative and some survey data which can be used to study how different the problems of teacher supply are in different countries. Such data also raise the possibility of genuine comparative work across countries. The natural direction for this work is to consider studying the aggregate labor market for teachers in a panel dataset of all countries over time. Section 2.4 of this chapter has made a first step in the analysis of inter country teacher salary variation but it is possible, with improved data from the OECD and other sources, that other aspects of the international market for teachers and its variation across countries and over time might be examined in the future.

Another further empirical challenge is the opportunity of modeling teacher supply decisions in a time series context. Longer runs of data collected nationally are becoming available in order to model the role of changing relative wages and unemployment prospects on teacher supply at the aggregate level. Although sometimes the problems with such data are an insufficient number of years worth of data there is also the possibility of using panel data by considering the supply of teachers in different subject areas in different geographical locations over different time periods. A further challenge in this area is the possible integration of the times series data with individual cross section data from different cohorts. Such data could be used to estimate a dynamic programming model of individual choices allowing for the changing relative wages and unemployment conditions faced by different cohorts at different points in time.

A perennial problem of teacher supply is that it is not simply about recruiting a specific number of teachers. The real challenge of teacher supply is to get high-quality individuals into teaching who have the most appropriate personalities to be good teachers. To some extent this does not necessarily mean the most able individuals – but often those with the capacities to be good teachers. What makes a good teacher is not something which can be easily measured.

Teacher quality is extremely difficult to observe and there is a principal-agent type relationship between individual teachers and their administrative authorities. [See Dixit (2000).] That is to say – it is very difficult to observe, or accurately measure, the amount of effort exerted or output produced by any individual teacher. Naturally governments and state agencies should try to maximize the effective use of the tax-payers money spent on education – this means that there should be appropriate attempts to monitor spending on teachers. The problem with this is that we do not fully understand: how to measure teacher quality, how teacher quality affects pupil performance, how to measure effective teacher input or effort. [See Figlio (1997), Odden and Kelley (1997), Ehrenberg and Brewer (1994, 1995), Loeb and Page (2000) and Nickell and Quintini (2002).] Under these circumstances it is tempting for government to try to introduce various incentive mechanisms and even performance related pay for teachers. Such pay schemes have created a vibrant debate over the value of teachers but there is insufficient understanding of the effects that such schemes could have on incentives and outputs or recruitment and retention. The current state of knowledge is overviewed in Adnett

(1999) and Dolton, McIntosh and Chevalier (2003) but this is a very fruitful are for future research.

The consequences of the teacher supply problem are inequitably felt across different socioeconomic groups in any society. There is some evidence that the pupils from the poorest homes are the ones who have problems in getting teachers to teach them in the sense that it is the schools in the least well-off areas that have the biggest problems with recruitment, retention, turnover and even absence of teachers.[12] These factors must act as a force which continues to generate educational and hence later income inequality [Darling-Hammond and Berry (1999) and Darling-Hammond (2000)]. There has been little systematic research into the inequality consequences of teacher supply and this topic should be on the agenda for future research.

6. Conclusion

It is clear in most countries that there are teacher supply problems. There would appear to be a lot of evidence from many different states in the USA and from other countries around the world that there are persistent episodic shortages of teachers. This manifests itself in terms of not enough recruits entering the profession and too many leaving it prematurely. However, it is also clear that there is not a universal shortage of all categories of teacher. Specifically, teachers are in short supply in difficult schools in areas with inner city urban problems and in subjects which have a high opportunity wages for those with specific technical skills. The problems seem to be worst in the scientific and mathematical subjects. Hence the real challenge of teacher supply is to get teachers into teaching the subjects and areas that are not appealing. The straightforward economic answer is to consider higher pay for those shortage categories. It is unclear whether teacher trade unions would be prepared to countenance these proposals but good economic and econometric research in these areas could calibrate the problem and provide some simulations as to the effective salary scale differences which may be required in these key areas to solve the problem. There is a considerable body of time series and cohort evidence that the shortage problems could be alleviated with higher relative salaries for teachers. What is less clear are the long term consequences of having children taught by temporary, or low quality teachers. High teacher turnover probably has a price in terms of the quality of educational instruction that children receive – but there is little evidence on this issue.

The perennial challenge for governments and education administrators is to establish a high-quality teacher labor force which is hard working and effective. Such problems could easily be solved by paying teachers higher wages. The problem of course is that governments are reluctant to throw more money at such problems and that even if they

---

[12] In the USA 15% of teachers are unlicensed in some inner cities – indeed in California 1 in 5 kids are taught by underqualified teachers.

did it, is not clear what the outcome of increased expenditure is – precisely. Hence more research on the relationship between educational resource inputs, teacher quality and outcomes must inevitably have important lessons for the importance of teacher supply. For example, if we knew categorically that the size of teacher pupil ratios had no effect on pupil outcomes then we could simply solve teacher shortage problems by having larger classes. In addition, we do not know in much detail, the effect of teacher working conditions on their relative effectiveness. To what extent do we alienate teachers from their jobs if we ask them to keep more detailed pupil records and does this induce significant numbers to leave the profession? There are many unanswered questions relating to teacher supply which deserve the attention of research in the future.

Acknowledgements

I gratefully acknowledge research assistance from Tsung-Ping Chung, Oscar Marcenaro, Steve McIntosh and David Newson. They are not responsible for my errors.

References

Abubakar, I.A. (1983). "The education, training and supply of technical teachers for schools and colleges in Nigeria". University of Wales, Cardiff.

Acedo, C. (1999). "Teachers supply and demand in the Philippines". World Bank Organisation, 1–29.

Adnett, N. (1999). "Rewarding performing teachers? Theory, evidence and UK policy". Working papers. Business School, Staffordshire University.

Ahamad, B. (1970). "A post-mortem on teacher supply forecasts". Higher Education Review 2 (3).

Ahamad, B. (1973). "Teachers in England and Wales". In: Ahamad, B., Blaug, M. (Eds.), The Practice of Manpower Forecasting. Elsevier, Amsterdam.

Al-Salmi, T.I. (1994). "Teacher education in Oman, selection and training of primary school teachers". Ph.D. thesis, University of Birmingham.

Angrist, J., Lavy, V. (2001). "Does teacher training affect pupil learning? Evidence from matched comparisons in Jerusalem public schools". Journal of Labor Economics 19 (2), 343–369.

Antos, J.R., Rosen, S. (1975). "Discrimination in the market for public school teachers". Journal of Econometrics 3 (2), 123–150.

Arrow, K., Capron, W. (1959). "Dynamic shortages and price rises: The engineer–scientist case". Quarterly Journal of Economics 73 (2), 292–308.

Ballou, D. (1996). "Do public schools hire the best applicants?". Quarterly Journal of Economics 111 (1), 97–134.

Ballou, D., Podgursky, M. (1997). "Teacher pay and teacher quality". W.E. UpJohn Institute for Employment Research. Kalamazoo, MI.

Ballou, D., Podgursky, M. (1998a). "Recruiting smarter teachers". Journal of Human Resources 30 (2), 326–338.

Ballou, D., Podgursky, M. (1998b). "Teacher recruitment and retention in public and private schools". Journal of Policy Analysis and Management 17 (3), 393–417.

Bartholemew, D., Forbes, A.F., McClean, S.I. (1991). Statistical Techniques for Manpower Planning. Wiley, New York.

Baugh, W.H., Stone, J.A. (1982). "Teachers, unions and wages in the 1970s: Unionism now pays". Industrial and Labor Relations Review 35 (3), 368–376.

Beaudin, B.Q. (1993). "Teachers who interrupt their careers – characteristics of those who return to the classroom". Educational Evaluation and Policy Analysis 15 (1), 51–64.

Bee, M., Dolton, P. (1995). "The remuneration of school teachers: Time series and cross-section evidence". Manchester School of Economic and Social Studies 63 (1), 1–22.

Billingsley, B. (1993). "Teacher retention and attrition in special and general education – a critical review of the literature". Journal of Special Education 27 (2), 137–174.

Birch, D., Calvert, T. (1973). "How profitable is teaching". Higher Education Review 6 (1), 35–44.

Black, P.A., Hosking, S.G. (1997). "The teacher crisis in South Africa: Quitting, shirking and 'inferior substitution'". South African Journal of Economics 65 (4), 500–509.

Blackstone, T., Crispin, A. (1982). "How many teachers? Issues of policy, planning and demography". Bedford Way Papers No. 10. London.

Blundell, R., McCurdy, T. (1999). "Labour supply: A review of alternative approaches". In: Ashenfelter, O., Card, D. (Eds.), Handbook of Labor Economics, vol. 3A. Elsevier, Amsterdam.

Boe, E.E., Bobbitt, S.A., Cook, L.H. (1997). "Why didst thou go? Predictors of retention, transfer, and attrition of special and general education teachers from a national perspective". Journal of Special Education 30 (4), 390–411.

Boe, E.E., Gilford, D.M. (1992). Teacher Supply, Demand and Quality: Policy Issues, Models and Databases. National Academy Press, Washington, DC.

Bonnesronning, H., Falch, T., Strom, B. (2003). "Teacher quality, student composition and school characteristics". Norwegian University of Science and Technology, Trondheim.

Booth, M.B. (1989). "Teacher supply & teacher quality: Solving the coming crisis". Department of Education, University of Cambridge, Cambridge.

Borghans, L. (1991). "Occupational choice: The market for primary school teachers". University of Maastricht.

Boyd, D., Langford, H., Loeb, S., Wyckoff, J. (2002a). "Initial matches, transfers and quits: Career decisions and the disparities in average teacher qualifications across schools". University of Albany, Albany.

Boyd, D., Langford, H., Loeb, S., Wyckoff, J. (2002b). "Analyzing the determinants of the matching of public school teachers to jobs: Estimating compensating differentials in imperfect labor markets". University of Albany, Albany.

Brewer, D.J. (1996). "Career paths and quit decisions: Evidence from teaching". Journal of Labor Economics 14 (April), 313–339.

Chapman, D.W. (1983). "A model of the influences on teacher retention". Journal of Teacher Education 34 (5), 43–49.

Chevalier, A., Dolton, P., McIntosh, S. (2001). "The Job Satisfaction of UK Teachers". Mimeo.

Chevalier, A., Dolton, P., McIntosh, S. (2006). "Recruiting and retaining teachers in the UK: An analysis of graduate occupation choice from the 1960s to the 1990s". Centre for the Economics of Education Discussion Paper Series 21, London. Economica, in press.

Chivore, B.S.R. (1985). "Recruitment and training of non-graduate secondary teachers in Zimbabwe". Institute of Education, University of London, London.

Conway, F. (1962a). "School teachers' salaries 1945–1959". Manchester School 30, 153–179.

Conway, F. (1962b). "Salary indices for school teachers". Manchester School 30, 69–81.

Corcoran, S.P., Evans, W.N., Schwab, R.S. (2002). "Changing labor market opportunities for women and the quality of teachers, 1957–1992". NBER Working Paper Series #9180.

Corrigan, D. (1974). "Do we have a teacher surplus". Journal of Teacher Education 25 (Fall), 196–198.

Court, M.S., Reilly, B., Williams, M. (1995). "Teachers: Recruitment and the labour market". Institute for Employment Studies.

Csellack, J. (2002). "The effects of wages on teacher labor supply". University of North Carolina, Chapel Hill.

Currie, J. (1991). "Employment determination in a unionized public-sector labor market – the case of Ontario's school teachers". Journal of Labor Economics 9 (1), 45–66.

Dahlby, B. (1981). "Monopsony and the shortage of school teachers in England and Wales, 1948–73". Applied Economics 13 (3), 303–319.

Darling-Hammond, L. (1989). "Teacher supply, demand, and standards". Educational Policy 3 (1), 1–17.

Darling-Hammond, L. (2000). "Solving the dilemmas of teacher supply, demand and standards: How we can ensure a competent, caring and qualified teacher for every child". National Commission on Teaching and America's Future.

Darling-Hammond, L., Berry, B. (1999). "Recruiting teachers for the 21st century: The foundation for educational equity". Journal of Negro Education 68 (3), 254–279.

Delannoy, F., Sedlacek, G. (2000). "BRAZIL: Teachers development and incentives: A strategic framework". Human Development Department, World Bank Organisation, 1–84.

Denton, F.T., Feaver, C.H., Spencer, B.G. (1994). "Teachers and the birth rate: The demographic dynamics of a service population". Journal of Population Economics 7, 307–329.

DES (1965). "The demand for and supply of teachers 1963–1986: Ninth report of the National Advisory Council of the Training and Supply of Teachers". Department for Education and Science, HMSO, London.

DES (1990). "Projecting the supply and demand of teachers: A technical description".

DfEE (1997). Teacher Supply and Demand Modelling: A Technical Description. Stationary Office, London.

DfEE (1998). Teachers Meeting the Challenge of Change. DfEE, London.

Dimmock, C. (1980). "Teacher supply as a problem in the USA and England". LACE Occasional Paper 3, London Association of Comparative Educationists.

Dixit, A. (2000). "Incentives and organizations in the public sector: An interpretative review". University of Princeton.

Dolton, P.J. (1990). "The economics of UK teacher supply – the graduates decision". Economic Journal 100 (400), 91–104.

Dolton, P.J. (1996). "Modelling the labour market for teachers: Some lessons from the UK". Education Economics 4 (2).

Dolton, P.J., Chung, T.P. (2004). "The rate of return to teaching". National Institute Economic Review 190, 89–104.

Dolton, P.J., Kidd, M. (1995). "Wage discrimination and occupational access". Oxford Bulletin of Economics and Statistics 56, 457–474.

Dolton, P.J., Makepeace, G.H. (1993). "Female labor-force participation and the choice of occupation – the supply of teachers". European Economic Review 37 (7), 1393–1411.

Dolton, P.J., Marcenaro-Guiterrez, O. (2004). "Teachers salaries and economic growth: A cross country comparison". London School of Economics. Mimeo.

Dolton, P.J., Mavromaras, K. (1994). "Intergenerational occupational choice comparisons: The case of teachers in the UK". Economic Journal 104, 841–863.

Dolton, P.J., McIntosh, S., Chevalier, A. (2003). Teacher Pay and Performance. Institute of Education, London.

Dolton, P.J., Robson, M. (1996). "Trade union concentration and the determinants of wages: The case of teachers in England and Wales". British Journal of Industrial Relations 34 (4), 539–556.

Dolton, P.J., Tremayne, A., Chung, T.P. (2003). "The economic cycle and teacher supply". OECD: 96, Paris.

Dolton, P.J., Van der Klaauw, W. (1995a). "Leaving teaching in the UK – a duration analysis". Economic Journal 105 (429), 431–444.

Dolton, P.J., Van der Klaauw, W. (1995b). "Teaching salaries and teacher retention". In: Nelson, R.R. (Ed.), Assessing Educational Practices: The Contribution of Economics. MIT Press, Cambridge MA.

Dolton, P.J., Van der Klaauw, W. (1999). "The turnover of teachers: A competing risks explanation". Review of Economics and Statistics 81 (3), 543–550.

Easton, T. (1988). "Bargaining and the determinants of teacher salaries". Industrial and Labor Relations Review 41 (2), 263–278.

Eberts, R.W. (1987). "Union-negotiated employment rules and teacher quits". Economics of Education Review 6 (1), 15–25.

Eckstein, Z., Wolpin, K. (1989). "The specification and estimation of dynamic discrete choice models". Journal of Human Resources XXIV (4), 562–598.

Edmonds, S., Sharp, C., Benefield, P. (2002). "Recruitment to and retention on initial teacher training: A systematic review". Teacher Training Agency: 83, London.

Edmonston, B., Knapp, T.R. (1979). "A demographic approach to teacher supply and demand". American Research Journal 16, 351–366.

Ehrenberg, R.G., Brewer, D.J. (1994). "Do school and teacher characteristics matter? Evidence from high school and beyond". Economics of Education Review 13, 1–17.

Ehrenberg, R.G., Brewer, D.J. (1995). "Did teachers' verbal ability and race matter in the 1960s? Coleman revisited". Economics of Education Review 14 (1), 1–21.

Falch, T., Strom, B. (2002). "Teacher turnover and non-pecuniary factors". Norwegian University of Science and Technology, Dragvoll.

Fidler, B., Fugl, B., Esp, D. (1993). The Supply and Recruitment of School Teachers. Longman, Harlow.

Figlio, D.N. (1997). "Teacher salaries and teacher quality". Economics Letters 55 (2), 267–271.

Flyer, F., Rosen, S. (1997). "The new economics of teachers and education". Journal of Labor Economics 15 (1(2)), 104–139.

Gilbert, A., King, A., Cregan, C. (2002). "Gender and wages: A cohort study of primary school teachers". Applied Economics 34 (3), 363–376.

Glewwe, P., Jacoby, H. (1994). "Student-achievement and schooling choice in low-income countries – evidence from Ghana". Journal of Human Resources 29 (3), 843–864.

Godwin, C. (2002). "Government policy and the provision of teachers". British Journal of Educational Studies 50 (1), 76–99.

Grace, G. (1991). "The state and teachers: Problems in teacher supply, retention and morale". In: Teacher Supply and Teacher Quality: Issues for the 1990's. Grace, G., Lawn, M. (Eds.). Multilingual Matters Ltd, Clevedon, Avon.

Grace, G., Lawn, M. (1991). Teacher Supply and Teacher Quality: Issues for the 1990's. Multilingual Matters Ltd, Clevedon, Avon.

Graybeal, W. (1974). "States and trends in public school teacher supply and demand". Journal of Teacher Education 25 (Fall), 200–208.

Greenbaum, R. (2002). "A spatial study of teachers' salaries in Pennsylvania school districts". Journal of Labor Research XXIVI (1), 69–86.

Greenberg, D.H., McCall, J.J. (1974). "Teacher mobility and allocation". Journal of Human Resource 9 (4), 480–502.

Greenhalgh, V. (1968). "The movement of teachers salaries 1920–1968". Journal of Educational Administration and History 1, 23–36.

Grissmer, D.W., Kirby, S.N. (1997). "Teacher turnover and teacher quality". Teachers College Record 99 (1), 45–56.

Gritz, M.R., Theobald, N.D. (1996). "The effects of school district spending priorities on length of stay in teaching". Journal of Human Resources 31 (Summer), 477–512.

Guthrie, J.W., Zusman, A. (1982). "Teacher supply and demand in mathematics and science". Phi Delta Kappa 64 (1), 28–33.

Haggstrom, G.W., Darling-Hammond, L., Grissmer, D.W. (1988). Assessing Teacher Supply and Demand. The RAND Corporation, Santa Monica.

Hansen, L.W. (1966). "Human capital requirements for educational expansion: Teacher shortages and teacher supply". In: Anderson, C., Bowman, M.-J. (Eds.), Education and Economic Development. Frank Cass and Co Ltd, London.

Hanushek, E., Kain, J., Rivkin, S. (1999). "Do higher salaries buy better teachers?". Working Paper 7899. National Bureau of Economic Research.

Hanushek, E., Pace, R.R. (1994). "Understanding entry into the teaching profession". In: Ehrenberg, R.G. (Ed.), Choices and Consequences: Contemporary Policy Issues in Education. ILR Press, New York, Ithaca.

Hanushek, E., Pace, R.R. (1995). "Who chooses to teach (and why)?". Economics of Education Review 14 (2), 101–117.

HMSO (1994). "Teacher supply: The work of part-time and returning teachers". Office of Her Majesty's Chief Inspector of Schools: 21, London.

Hoxby, C.M. (2000). "Would school choice change the teaching profession?". Working Paper 7866. National Bureau of Economic Research: 55.

Hussar, W.J. (2002). "Predicting the need for newly hired teachers in the United States to 2008–2009". National Center for Education Statistics (NCES).

Hutchings, M., Menter, I., Ross, A., Thomson, D., Bedford, D. (2000). "Teacher supply and retention in London 1998–99: A study of six London boroughs: A Report for the Teacher Training Agency". Teacher Training Agency, London.

IBE/UNESCO (1967). "The shortage of secondary school teachers". IBE/UNESCO, Geneva/Paris.

Ingersoll, R.M. (1997). "Teacher turnover and teacher quality: The recurring myth of teacher shortages". Teachers College Record 99 (1), 41–44.

Ingersoll, R.M. (2000). "Turnover among mathematics and science teachers in the U.S". Paper prepared for the National Commission on Mathematics and Science Teaching for the 21st Century.

Ingersoll, R.M. (2001a). "A different approach to solving the teacher shortage problem". Policy Brief, Center for the Study of Teaching and Policy, University of Washington.

Ingersoll, R.M. (2001b). "Teacher turnover and teacher shortages: An organisational analysis". American Educational Research Journal 38 (3), 499–534.

Ingersoll, R.M. (2001c). "Teacher turnover, teacher shortages and the organization of schools". Research Report, Center for the study of Teaching and Policy, University of Washington.

Ingersoll, R.M. (2002). "Out-of field teaching, educational inequality and the organization of schools". Research Report, Center for the Study of Teaching and Policy, University of Washington.

Kelsall, R.K., Kelsall, H.M. (1969). The School Teacher in England and the United States: The Findings of Empirical Research. Pergamon Press, London.

Kershaw, J.A., McKean, R.N. (1962). Teacher Shortages and Salary Schedules. McGraw-Hill, New York.

Kgobe, M.P. (1995). "Restructuring teacher supply in South Africa: Overcoming inefficiency and inequity". Department of Education, Institute of Education, University of London: 95, London.

Komenan, A., Grootaert, C. (1990). "Pay differences between teachers and other occupations: Some empirical evidence from Cote d'Ivoire". Economics of Education Review 9 (3), 209–217.

Kyriacou, C., Coulthard, M. (2000). "Undergraduates' views of teaching as a career choice". Journal of Education for Teaching 26 (2), 117–126.

Lakdawalla, D. (2001). "The declining quality of teachers". Working paper. National Bureau of Economic Research: 68.

Lewis, P., Norris, K. (1992). "Demand, supply and adjustment in the teachers labor-market". Australian Journal of Education 36 (3), 260–277.

Lindeboom, M., Kerkhofs, M. (2000). "Multistate models for clustered duration data-an application to workplace effects on individual sickness absenteeism". Review of Economics and Statistics LXXXII (4), 668–684.

Loeb, S., Page, M.E. (2000). "Examining the link between teacher wages and student outcomes: The importance of alternative labor market opportunities and non-pecuniary variation". Review of Economics and Statistics LXXXII (3), 393–408.

Lopez-Acevedo, G., Salinas, A. (2001). "Teacher salaries and professional profile in Mexico". Mimeo. The World Bank.

Luizer, J., Thorton, R. (1986). "Concentration in the labor market for public school teachers". Industrial and Labor Relations Review 39 (4), 573–584.

Maaske, R.J. (1951). "Analysis of trends in teacher supply and demand". Journal of Teacher Education 2 (December), 263–268.

Macdonald, D. (1999). "Teacher attrition: A review of literature". Teaching and Teacher Education 15 (8), 835–848.

Manski, C.F. (1987). "Academic ability, earnings and decision to become a teacher: Evidence from the national longitudinal study of the high school class of 1972". In: Wise, D. (Ed.), Public Sector Payrolls. University of Chicago Press, Chicago.

McIntyre, F. (1998). "Shortage looms: Almost half of Ontario teachers to retire in the next 10 years". Professionally Speaking XXXIV, 10–16.

Miller, R. (1984). "Job matching and occupational choice". Journal of Political Economy 92 (6), 1086–1120.

Mont, D., Rees, D.I. (1996). "The influence of classroom characteristics on high school teacher turnover". Economic Inquiry XXXIV (1), 152–167.

Murnane, R.J. (1996). "Staffing the nation's schools with skilled teachers". In: Hanushek, E., Jorgenson, D. (Eds.), Improving America's Schools, The Role of Incentives. National Academy Press, National Research Council, Washington, DC.

Murnane, R.J., Olsen, R.J. (1989a). "Will there be enough teachers?". American Economic Review 79 (2), 242–246.

Murnane, R.J., Olsen, R.J. (1989b). "The effects of salaries and opportunity costs on the length of stay in teaching: Evidence from Michigan". Review of Economics and Statistics 71 (2), 347–352.

Murnane, R.J., Olsen, R.J. (1990). "The effects of salaries and opportunity costs on the length of stay in teaching". Journal of Human Resources Winter, 106–124.

Murnane, R.J., Singer, J.D., Willet, J.B. (1989). "The influences of salaries and opportunity costs of teachers' career choices: Evidence from North Carolina". Harvard Education Review 59 (3), 325–346.

Murnane, R.J., Singer, J.D., Willet, J.B., Kemple, J.J., Olsen, R.J. (1991). Who Will Teach: Policies that Matter. Harvard University Press, Cambridge, MA.

NCES (1997). National Center for Education Statistics 'School and staffing survey: Characteristics of Stayers, Movers and Leavers: Results from the Teacher Follow-up Survey: 1994–95'. Office of Educational Research and Improvement, US. Department of Education.

Nelson, G., Lutenbacher, C., López, M.E. (2001). "A cross-cultural study of Mexico and the United States: Perceived roles of teachers". Journal of Multilingual and Multicultural Development 22 (6), 463–474.

Nickell, S., Quintini, G. (2002). "The consequences of the decline in public sector pay in Britain: A little bit of evidence". Economic Journal 112 (477), 107–118.

Odden, A., Kelley, C. (1997). Paying Teachers for what They Know and Do: New and Smarter Compensation Strategies to Improve Schools. Corwin Press, Thousand Oaks, CA.

OECD (2001). Teachers for Tomorrow's Schools. Organisation for Economic Cooperation and Development, Paris.

OECD (2002a). Education at a Glance. Organisation for Economic Cooperation and Development, Paris.

OECD (2002b). Attracting, Developing and Retaining Effective Teachers. Organisation for Economic Cooperation and Development, Paris.

Osei Bempah, E., Kaylen, M., Osburn, D., Birkenholz, R. (1994). "An econometric analysis of teacher mobility". Economics of Education Review 13 (1), 69–77.

Pavalko, R.M. (1970). "Recruitment to teaching: Patterns of selection and retention". Sociology of Education 43, 340–355.

Piras, C., Savedoff, B. (1998). "How much do teachers earn?". Working Paper 33, Inter-American Development Bank.

Polachek, S. (1981). "Occupational self-selection: A human capital approach to sex differences in occupational structure". Review of Economics and Statistics 63, 60–69.

Premdas, S. (1971). "Recruitment of teachers in Trinidad and Tobago". Department of Education, University of Newcastle Upon Tyne.

Press, H., Lawton, S. (1999). "The changing teacher labor market in Canada patterns and conditions". The Alberta Journal of Educational Research XLV (2), 154–169.

Rees, D.I. (1991). "Grievance procedure strength and teacher quits". Industrial and Labor Relations Review 45, 31–43.

Richards, C., Sheu, T.M. (1992). "The South Carolina school incentive reward program: A policy analysis". Economics of Education Review 11, 71–86.

Rosen, S. (1986). "The theory of equalizing differences". In: Ashenfelter, O., Layard, R. (Eds.), Handbook of Labor Economics. North-Holland, New York. Chapter 12.

Ross, A., Hutchings, M. (2003). "Attracting, developing and retaining effective teachers in the United Kingdom of Great Britain and Northern Ireland". Institute for Policy Studies in Education, London: 109.

Rumberger, R. (1987). "The impact of salary differentials on teacher shortages and turnover: The case of mathematics and science teachers". Economics of Education Review 6, 389–399.

Shen, J.P. (1997). "Teacher retention and attrition in public schools: Evidence from SASS91". Journal of Educational Research 91 (2), 81–88.

Siow, A. (1984). "Occupational choice under uncertainty". Econometrica 52 (3), 631–645.

Smithers, A., Robinson, P. (2000a). "Attracting teachers". University of Liverpool 67.

Smithers, A., Robinson, P. (2000b). "Coping with teacher shortages". NUT 71, London.

Smithers, A., Robinson, P. (2001). "Teachers leaving". NUT: 46, London.

Stinebrickner, T. (1998a). "Serially correlated wages in a dynamic, discrete choice model of teacher attrition". Working Paper 9821. UWO Department of Economics, Western Ontario, Ontario, Canada.

Stinebrickner, T. (1998b). "An empirical investigation of teacher attrition". Economics of Education Review 17 (2), 127–136.

Stinebrickner, T. (1999a). "Using latent variables in dynamic discrete choice models: The effect of school characteristics on teacher decisions". Research in Labor Economics 18, 141–176.

Stinebrickner, T. (1999b). "The reasons that elementary and high school teachers leave teaching: An analysis of occupational change and departure from the labor force". University of Western Ontario.

Stinebrickner, T. (2001a). "Compensation policies and teacher decisions". International Economic Review 42 (3), 751–780.

Stinebrickner, T. (2001b). "A dynamic model of teacher labor supply". Journal of Labor Economics 19 (1), 196–230.

Stinebrickner, T. (2002). "An analysis of occupational change and departures from the labor force: Evidence of the reasons teachers quit". Journal of Human Resource 37 (1), 192–216.

Straker, N. (1991a). "Teacher supply in the 1990s: An analysis of current developments". Evaluation and Research in Education 5 (1–2), 17–33.

Straker, N. (1991b). "Teacher supply in the 1990s: An analysis of current developments". In: Grace, G., Lawn, M. (Eds.), Teacher Supply and Teacher Quality: Issues for the 1990s. Multilingual Matters Ltd, Clevedon.

Tamura, R. (2001). "Teachers, growth, and convergence". Journal of Political Economy 109 (5), 1021–1059.

Theobald, N.D. (1990). "An examination of the influence of personal, professional and school district characteristics on public school teacher retention". Economics of Education Review 9, 241–250.

Theobald, N.D., Gritz, M.R. (1996). "The effects of school district spending priorities on the exit path of beginning teachers leaving the district". Economics of Education Review 15, 11–22.

Thomas, R.B. (1973). "Post-war movements in teachers' salaries". Industrial Relations Journal 4, 12–46.

Thomas, R.B. (1975). "The supply of graduates to school teaching". British Journal of Industrial Relations 13 (March).

Tremblay, A. (1997). "Are we headed toward a teacher surplus or a teacher shortage?". Education Quarterly Review 4 (1), 53–85.

Tropp, A. (1957). The School Teachers: The Growth of the Teaching Profession in England and Wales from 1800 to the Present Day. Heinemann Ltd, London.

Turnbull, P., Williams, G. (1974). "Sex differentials in teacher's pay". Journal of the Royal Statistical Society 137 (2).

Van den Berghe, V. (2000). "Leaving teaching in the French-speaking community of Belgium: A duration analysis". Education Economics 8 (3), 221–239.

Van der Klaauw, W. (1997). "The supply and early careers of teachers". Department of Economics, New York University.

Vegas, E., Pritchett, L., Experton, W. (1999). "Attracting and retaining qualified teachers in Argentina: Impact of the structure and level of compensation". LCSHD Paper Series No. 38. The World Bank, Washington, DC, pp. 1–67.

Vegas, E. (1999). "Teachers in Brazil: Who are they and how well do they fare in the labour market?". Mimeo.

Waterreus, I., Dobbelsteen, S. (2001). "Wages and teachers' hours of work". De Economist 149 (3), 277–298.

Waterreus, I. (2003). "Lessons in teacher pay". Universiteit van Amsterdam.

Weaver, W.T. (1983). America's Teacher Quality Problem: Alternatives for Reform. Praeger Publishers, New York.

Williams, P. (1975). "Planning teacher supply". University of London Institute of Education, Department of Education in Developing Countries.

Williams, P. (1979). Planning teacher demand and supply. International Institute for Educational Planning, UNESCO, Paris.

Willis, R., Rosen, S. (1979). "Education and self-selection". Journal of Political Economy 87 (5), S7–S36.

Wilson, R. (1983). "The declining return to becoming a teacher". Higher Education Review, 22–37.

Wilson, A., Pearson, R. (1993a). "The problem of teacher shortages". Education Economics 1 (1), 69–75.

Wilson, A., Pearson, R. (1993b). The Problem of Teacher Shortages. Heinemann, London.

Wolter, S., Denzler, S. (2003). "Wage elasticity of the teacher in Switzerland". Working Papers IZA DP no. 733, Bonn.

Zabalza, A. (1979a). "The determinants of teacher supply". Review of Economic Studies 46 (1), 131–147.

Zabalza, A. (1979b). "From shortage to surplus: The case of school teachers". Applied Economics 11, 55–69.

Zabalza, A., Turnbull, P., Williams, G. (1979). The Economics of Teacher Supply. Cambridge University Press, Cambridge, MA.

Zarkin, G. (1985). "Occupational choice: An application to the market for public school teachers". Quarterly Journal of Economics 100, 409–446.

Chapter 20

PRE-SCHOOL, DAY CARE, AND AFTER-SCHOOL CARE: WHO'S MINDING THE KIDS?

DAVID BLAU

University of North Carolina, Chapel Hill

JANET CURRIE

UCLA
and
NBER

Contents

Handbook of the Economics of Education, Volume 2
Edited by Eric A. Hanushek and Finis Welch
© 2006 Elsevier B.V.   *All rights reserved*
DOI: 10.1016/S1574-0692(06)02020-4

Abstract

The majority of children in the US and many other high-income nations are now cared for many hours per week by people who are neither their parents nor their school teachers. The role of such pre-school and out-of-school care is potentially two-fold: First, child care makes it feasible for both parents or the only parent in a single-parent family to be employed. Second, early intervention programs and after school programs aim to enhance child development, particularly among disadvantaged children. Corresponding to this distinction, there are two branches of literature to be summarized in this chapter. The first focuses on the market for child care and analyzes factors affecting the supply, demand and quality of care. The second focuses on child outcomes, and asks whether certain types of programs can ameliorate the effects of early disadvantage. The primary goal of this review is to bring the two literatures together in order to suggest ways that both may be enhanced. Accordingly, we provide an overview of the number of children being cared for in different sorts of arrangements; describe theory and evidence about the nature of the private child care market; and discuss theory and evidence about government intervention in the market for child care. Our summary suggests that additional research is needed in order to better characterize interactions between government programs and market-provided child care.

Keywords

pre-school, child care, day care, early intervention, Head Start, after school programs, subsidies, regulations

JEL classification: I21, I28, I38

1. Introduction

For good or ill, the majority of children in the US and many other high-income nations are now cared for many hours per week by adults other than their parents and school teachers. The role of such pre-school and out-of-school care is potentially two-fold: First, child care can make it feasible for both parents or the only parent in a single-parent family to be employed. This role has become increasingly important in an era of welfare reform, in which able bodied mothers are expected to work regardless of the age of their children. Second, early intervention programs and after school programs can enhance child development, particularly among disadvantaged children. Consistent with this distinction, child care is typically provided by the private market, while early intervention programs are generally publicly provided.

Corresponding to this distinction, there are two branches of literature to be summarized in this chapter. The first focuses on the market for child care and analyzes factors affecting the supply, demand and quality of care. The second focuses on child outcomes, and asks whether certain types of programs can ameliorate the effects of early disadvantage. However, child care and early intervention are intrinsically linked: The quality of child care is likely to affect child development, and programs such as Head Start which seek to enhance child development also provide child care. Moreover, National Research Council and Institute of Medicine (2003) estimates that in the US one third of the costs of child care for children under age six is paid for by government subsidies or provided directly by the public sector. The primary goal of this review is to bring the two literatures together in order to suggest ways that both may be enhanced. Our summary suggests that additional research is needed to analyze how government programs and market provided child care interact with each other.

Section 2 provides an overview of the number of children being cared for in different sorts of arrangements. Section 3 describes theory and evidence about the nature of the child care market. Section 4 discusses theory and evidence on government intervention in the market for child care, while Section 5 discusses direct government provision of services. Section 6 offers conclusions and suggestions for further research. This review follows the literature in focusing on the United States. As Waldfogel (2001) emphasizes, there are dramatic differences among high-income countries in the involvement of the public sector in child care. Cross-country analysis of child care policy would be an interesting topic for future research.

2. Who is minding the kids?

The dramatic increase in female labor force participation is one of the most important developments in the postwar US economy. This increase has been greatest among married women with children. For example, in 1950 11.9% of married women with children under six were in the labor force, compared to 62.8% in 2000. Never married, separated and divorced mothers also increased their labor force participation dramatically, with the most rapid growth in the last three decades. In 2000, 65.3% of single women with children under 6 were in the work force [U.S. Bureau of Labor Statistics (2001)], and the National Institute for Child Health and Development (NICHD) Early Child Care Study found that most infants were placed in some sort of nonmaternal care by four months of age [NICHD ECCRN (1997)]. In a recent press release calling attention to the "record" participation rates of women with young children, the Census Bureau noted that "The large increase in labor force participation rates by mothers since 1976 is an important reason why child-care issues have been so visible in recent years" [U.S. Census Bureau (2000), October 24].

However, child care is also increasingly utilized by families with stay-at-home parents. Tables 1 and 2 present tabulations of the type of child care used by children aged 0–4 and 5–14 in 1999, disaggregated by the mother's employment status. Table 1 shows that almost a third of 0–4 year old children with mothers who are not employed are in nonparental child care, compared to three quarters of children of employed mothers (lower panel, first row). The former group spends an average of 16–20 hours per week in the primary mode of nonparental care, and 20–27 percent also spend a further 7–11 hours in a secondary mode of nonparental care. This is a substantial amount

Table 1

Characteristics of households with children age 0–4 by type of child care arrangement, and distribution of households across child care arrangements, 1999

| | Primary child care arrangement | | | | | | |
| | Mother employed | | | | Mother not employed | | |
	Parent	Relative	Nonrelative	Center	Parent	Relative	Nonrelative	Center
Hours/week in primary arrangements	22	32.4	34.4	34.7	16.7	17.3	20.2
Percent who paid cash	0	23.5	90.1	78.9	10.6	54.5	52.2
Amount paid/week if > 0	0	47.6	70.7	79.7	27.6	59.0	42.6
Percent of income paid	0	6.3	6.9	6.9	5.9	9.4	5.7
Percent who receive government subsidy	0.8	1.3	4.6	7.1	2.7	12.7	8.3
Mother's hours of work/week	29.2	35.1	37.7	36.2			
Percent who with a secondary arrangement	33.1	28.5	30.0	37.1	20.5	19.9	27.2
Type of secondary arrangement							
Parent	69.2	84.0	87.9	76.4	82.1	83.2	76.5
Relative	16.3	6.6	7.1	12.5	11.3	16.2	11.8
Nonrelative	8.8	3.5	0.9	3.8	4.2	0.0	8.5
Center	5.6	5.8	4.0	7.3	2.5	0.6	3.2
Hours in secondary arrangements	11.4	14.6	16.0	16.7	6.7	10.5	8.8
Total number of arrangements	1.26	1.38	1.44	1.52	1.25	1.24	1.33
Total hours of care	25.2	37.3	40.4	42.2	18.2	19.6	22.9

Table 1
(*Continued*)

	Primary child care arrangement							
	Mother employed				Mother not employed			
	Parent	Relative	Nonrelative	Center	Parent	Relative	Nonrelative	Center
Distribution of children across types of primary arrangements								
All	24.9	28.9	20.8	25.4	68.4	14.5	5.5	11.6
Age 0	33.4	31.2	19.3	16.1	78.7	14.7	4.8	1.8
Age 1	25.0	30.5	26.1	18.4	74.3	15.1	7.0	3.6
Age 2	26.4	28.7	21.8	23.0	71.4	16.9	6.4	5.3
Age 3	24.0	31.7	18.9	25.5	63.6	16.2	5.0	15.1
Age 4	18.7	23.6	18.0	39.8	56.0	9.4	3.8	30.8
Married	29.1	24.1	21.7	25.1	73.1	11.0	4.7	11.2
Widowed, divorced, or separated	15.8	35.4	20.3	28.5	49.7	25.1	7.1	18.0
Never married	13.4	44.6	17.6	24.4	55.6	25.5	8.3	10.6
White (non-Hispanic)	26.5	23.7	23.4	26.3	70.0	12.5	5.7	11.7
Black (non-Hispanic)	16.7	36.2	13.4	33.6	46.7	25.4	10.7	17.2
Hispanic	26.2	38.4	20.0	15.3	76.2	14.0	1.9	7.9
Annual income								
<18(000)	21.1	36.1	19.2	23.6	64.4	18.8	5.7	11.1
18–35.999	27.6	36.6	16.4	19.4	75.2	12.8	2.5	9.5
36–53.999	28.1	24.6	21.4	25.9	69.6	15.6	6.1	8.7
54+	22.8	24.2	23.8	29.2	65.7	10.2	7.6	16.5
Income < poverty line	22.7	36.0	17.7	23.6	64.8	17.9	5.8	11.6
Income 1–2 times poverty line	28.4	38.0	15.9	17.6	72.0	15.4	3.1	9.6
Income 2+ times poverty line	24.1	24.5	23.1	28.3	68.7	11.7	6.8	12.8
Income ⩾ poverty line	25.2	27.9	21.3	25.6	70.0	13.1	5.4	11.6
Northeast	30.2	27.3	18.2	24.3	67.4	10.7	9.4	12.5
Midwest	27.9	24.2	24.9	23.0	70.2	15.8	3.9	10.1
West	26.2	33.0	21.4	19.4	70.1	15.4	5.2	9.3
South	19.2	30.1	19.0	31.6	66.7	15.2	4.3	13.8
Non-South	27.9	28.3	21.7	22.1	69.2	14.2	6.1	10.5
Metro	25.8	28.9	19.8	25.5	68.5	13.5	6.0	12.0
Nonmetro	19.8	28.9	26.7	24.6	68	20.4	2.7	8.9
Receives public assistance	14.0	42.0	16.5	27.5	58.4	19.3	7.4	14.9
No public assistance	25.8	27.8	21.2	25.2	70.4	13.6	5.1	10.9
Mother works full time	17.5	30.1	24.1	28.3				
Part time	38.2	26.9	15.7	19.2				

Source: Tabulations from wave 10 of the 1996 panel of the Survey of Income and Program Participation (Spring 1999).

Notes. Parent includes the mother while working, the father, and cases in which no regular child care arrangement is used. Most of the parent care cases for children of nonemployed mothers report no regular arrangement, and in these cases information on hours of care etc. is not available. Relative includes grandparents, siblings, and other relatives. Nonrelative includes family day care, nannies, and babysitters. Center includes day care centers, pre-schools, and Head Start. Public assistance includes TANF, other cash assistance, and Food Stamps. Figures are weighted by the child's sample weight. The distributions in the lower panel sum to 100% conditional on the mother's employment status.

of time, although much less than the 32–35 hours per week that children of employed mothers spend in their primary nonparental care arrangement. It is striking that a large fraction of care is not paid for, particularly in families in which the mother is not employed. For the latter group, about half of nonrelative and center care is unpaid, compared to 10–20 percent for employed mothers. Families with a nonemployed mother are also more likely to receive government assistance in paying for child care.

Table 1 also shows that there are distinct demographic patterns in the use of child care modes. Relative to white non-Hispanic mothers, black mothers are more likely to use care from relatives, or child care centers, and less likely to use nonrelative care. Hispanic mothers are most likely to use relative care, and least likely to use centers, a pattern that has been noted previously [cf. Fuller, Holloway and Liang (1996), Hofferth et al. (1991)]. The use of center-based care is distinctly U-shaped with respect to income, with both poor and rich families more likely to use such care than middle-income households, and families on public assistance being more likely to use such care than other families.

Table 2

Characteristics of households with children age 5–14 by type of child care arrangement (excluding school), and distribution of households across child care arrangements, 1999

	Primary child care arrangement						
	Mother employed				Mother not employed		
	Parent	Relative	Nonrelative	Organized activity	Parent	Relative	Nonrelative	Organized activity
Hours/week in primary arrangements	12.1	16.4	20.4	15.9	10.7	11.2	7.3
Percent who paid cash	0.0	8.1	72.1	73.4	1.7	47.8	67.9
Amount paid/week	0.0	40.1	48.6	44.1	27.8	37.1	19.8
Percent of income paid	0.0	4.8	13.6	5.4	9.1	7.0	2.9
Percent who receive government subsidy	0.5	1.2	3.1	5.0	1.2	8.6	3.0
Mother's hours of work/week	33.5	37.0	38.1	36.5			
Percent with a secondary arrangement	47.5	87.7	77.5	79.9	82.0	66.2	82.3
Type of secondary arrangement							
Parent	67.9	66.6	60.2	52.9	72.6	66.3	51.7
Relative	12.0	12.2	9.1	18.2	14.6	22.4	13.6
Nonrelative	1.8	1.3	0.7	2.0	0.6	0.0	5.4
Center	18.3	19.9	30.0	26.9	12.1	11.4	29.2
Hours in secondary arrangements	14.2	12.2	14.5	9.7	8.8	8.3	5.1
Total number of arrangements	1.18	1.63	1.82	2.0	1.41	1.62	1.81
Total hours of care	17.9	22.5	29.5	23.2	13.6	15.0	10.5

Table 2
(*Continued*)

	Primary child care arrangement							
	Mother employed				Mother not employed			
	Parent	Relative	Nonrelative	Organized activity	Parent	Relative	Nonrelative	Organized activity
Distribution of children across types of primary arrangements								
All	37.0	36.3	9.6	17.1	68.7	18.6	2.0	10.6
Age 5	29.9	24.5	18.5	27.1	67.4	16.0	4.4	12.2
Age 6	35.9	27.4	16.2	20.5	71.0	14.9	1.5	12.6
Age 7	36.5	31.9	11.8	19.8	76.8	11.9	1.7	9.6
Age 8	38.6	31.8	12.0	17.6	69.9	13.6	2.0	14.6
Age 9	37.8	33.4	13.5	15.3	74.7	14.0	1.3	9.9
Age 10	40.7	32.3	9.1	17.9	68.7	17.6	1.9	11.8
Age 11	37.6	37.8	7.9	16.8	67.7	19.6	2.1	10.6
Age 12	38.1	44.5	4.6	12.8	64.6	23.8	2.5	9.1
Age 13	38.7	47.7	2.3	11.4	61.4	30.7	1.1	6.7
Age 14	35.6	49.6	1.8	13.0	59.7	32.6	1.0	6.7
Married	42.5	31.5	9.1	16.9	70.9	15.4	1.6	12.1
Widowed, divorced, or separated	24.3	47.6	10.2	17.9	61.6	29.5	3.5	5.4
Never married	22.6	49.4	11.9	16.1	62.3	27.8	3.3	6.6
White (non-Hispanic)	39	33.4	9.3	18.3	66.5	18.2	1.6	13.7
Black (non-Hispanic)	31.6	43.1	8.3	17.0	63.8	26.5	2.4	7.3
Hispanic	33.6	41.4	12.6	12.4	77.5	14.3	2.9	5.3
Annual income								
<18(000)	34.3	42.1	10.1	13.4	69.7	22.0	2.6	5.8
18–35.999	36.6	39.9	9.7	13.8	73.1	16.4	2.4	8.2
36–53.999	40.9	34.9	8.8	15.5	69.9	17.7	0.7	11.8
54+	36.1	33.3	9.8	20.8	62.7	17.1	2.0	18.2
Income < poverty line	37.3	41.6	8.8	12.3	69.8	21.6	2.5	6.1
Income 1–2 times poverty line	38.0	39.0	9.7	13.3	72.5	18.0	2.4	7.1
Income 2+ times poverty line	36.6	34.5	9.7	19.2	65.4	16.5	1.5	16.7
Income ⩾ poverty	37.0	35.7	9.7	17.6	68.2	17.1	1.9	12.9
Northeast	42.2	32.4	9.8	15.7	65.9	16.1	3.5	14.5
Midwest	38.5	35.2	11.5	14.8	63.3	21.6	1.2	13.9
West	36.3	37.5	9.9	16.3	69.8	19.5	1.9	8.8
South	33.8	38.4	8.0	19.8	72.7	17.3	1.9	8.2
Non-South	38.7	35.2	10.5	15.7	66.7	19.3	1.9	11.8
Metro	37.1	35.8	9.7	17.4	69.7	16.9	2.0	11.3
Nonmetro	36.5	38.6	9.3	15.6	63.2	27.8	2.0	7.1
Receives public assistance	25.4	50.8	10.9	12.8	65.5	25.5	3.0	6.1
No public assistance	37.9	35.3	9.5	17.4	69.5	17.0	1.8	11.7
Mother works full time	32.3	39.0	10.7	17.9				
Part time	48.3	30.0	7.6	14.2				

Notes. See Table 1. Organized activity includes centers and institutional before-school and after-school programs.

There are also pronounced regional differences, though urban and rural families tend to have fairly similar patterns of mode choice. For example, mothers in the South are more likely to use center-based care than those in the rest of the country.[1] Not surprisingly, younger children are more likely to be cared for by parents than older children, as are children of married mothers.

Table 2 indicates that 63% of school age children of employed mothers regularly spend time in some form of nonschool, nonparental care, compared to 31 percent of children of nonemployed mothers. Children of employed mothers spend an average of 22–30 hours a week in such arrangements. Considering that most children spend about 30 hours a week in school, it is evident that what they do during this nonschool care time is likely to be important to their development. In contrast to younger children, school-age children spend relatively little time in nonrelative care, and greater amounts of time in organized activities. Two thirds to three quarters of these activities involve a monetary payment, so it is not surprising that white children are more likely to be involved than black and especially Hispanic children, or that poorer children are less likely to have organized activities than richer ones.

The vast increase in maternal employment has generated a large literature on the effects of maternal employment on child outcomes [cf. Baum (2002), Belsky and Eggebeen (1991), Blau and Grossberg (1992), Desai, Chase-Lansdale and Michael (1989), Greenstein (1993), Hill et al. (2003), Han, Waldfogel and Brooks-Gunn (2001), Neidell (2000), Parcel and Menaghan (1990, 1994), Ruhm (2004), Waldfogel, Han and Brooks-Gunn (2002), James-Burdumy (2005)]. This literature finds at most small effects of maternal employment on children. Although OLS estimates often show negative effects of employment in the first year, these effects are not generally robust to attempts to deal with the endogeneity of employment. The small or negligible effects may be because the increased income earned by employed mothers offsets the effect of reduced time spent with their children. However, time use studies indicate that except for very young children, maternal employment has only modest effects on the amount of time mothers spend with their children, and tends to increase the amount of time that fathers spend with their children in two-parent households. Mothers apparently reduce both leisure time and housework in order to maintain their time inputs into child raising [National Research Council and Institute of Medicine (2003)].

The most consistent evidence of negative effects of maternal employment comes from families in which some or all of the following are true: the mother returns to work when the child is less than one year old; young children spend very long hours in care; the mother's employment does not raise family income (as in some households where families have been forced off welfare); there is a single parent with few family members to draw on so that time spent in employment cannot be compensated by drawing on the time of other family members either for child care or for housework; and/or the work

---

[1] Blau (2001) notes that mothers in the South are substantially more likely to be employed full time than are mothers in other regions.

Table 3a

Trends in child care arrangements: Primary child care arrangement used by employed mothers
of children age 0–4

	Parent	Relative	Nonrelative	Organized facility
Winter 1985	23.9	24.1	28.2	23.9
Fall 1988	22.8	21.1	28.9	27.3
Fall 1990	22.9	23.1	25.1	28.7
Fall 1991	28.7	23.5	23.3	24.7
Fall 1993	22.1	26.0	21.6	31.0
Fall 1995	24.3	21.4	28.4	25.7
Spring 1997	28.4	25.8	22.1	23.7
Spring 1999	24.9	28.9	20.8	25.4

Source: Smith (2000, 2002) and tabulations from wave 10 of the 1996 Survey of Income and Program Participation (Spring 1999).

Notes. Parent includes the mother while working, and the father. Relative include grandparents, siblings, and other relatives. Nonrelative includes family day care, nannies, and babysitters. Organized facility includes day care centers, pre-schools, and Head Start. Beginning in 1995, the SIPP child care module was changed to allow "no regular arrangement" as a response. These cases are classified here as parent care. In 1997 they were 6% of all cases. Figures are weighted by the child's sample weight.

itself is very stressful and reduces the resources the mother brings to parenting. Some studies of shift-work, for example, suggest that it may have this effect. Adolescents may also suffer more negative effects of maternal employment than younger children, particularly if they are left unsupervised [National Research Council and Institute of Medicine (2003)].

Table 3a focuses on trends in the use of child care by employed mothers. Perhaps surprisingly, the percentage of pre-school children in organized facilities shows no clear trend between 1985 and 1999, although the number of children reporting relative care as their primary arrangement increases.[2] Table 3b shows that the fraction of families who report paying for child care increased over time, from 33.7% in 1985 to 43% in 1999, although the average amount paid fell in real terms. Since the percentage of income paid for child care increased over the same period, Table 3 suggests that more low-income families are paying for child care.

Table 4 addresses the issue of so-called "latch-key" children, who spend some part of the day without any adult supervision. In 1999, 16.4% of children age 5–14 of employed mothers [10.5/(10.5 + 53.4)] were in unsupervised self-care for part of the day, compared to 8.9% of children of nonemployed mothers [3.2/(3.2 + 32.9)]. Most of these

---

[2] A CPS supplement in June 1977 collected data on child care used by children of employed mothers. There were 4.37 million children under age 5 at that time, and their distribution of modes of care was father: 14.4%; relative (including grandparent): 30.9%; babysitter in the child's home: 7.0%; family day care home: 22.4%; day care center/pre-school: 13.0%; mother while working: 11.4% [Casper (1997)]. Thus, the major increase in use of centers occurred between 1977 and 1985.

children were in relative care as their primary child care arrangement. This suggests that employed mothers who rely on care from relatives are often unable to schedule activities so that all of the child's time can be supervised. As one might expect, the fraction of children who are unsupervised rises sharply with age: among 9-year-old children of employed mothers, 8.1% are sometimes unsupervised [5.2/(5.2 + 59.1)] compared to 18.1% among 11-year-olds [11.5/(11.5 + 51.9)] and 44.9% of 14-year-olds [32.3/(32.3 + 39.7)]. The probability of being unsupervised is higher for single parents, and rises with income. It is lower for Hispanics and blacks than for whites.

There is evidence that unsupervised children are at increased risk of truancy, poor grades, and risk-taking behaviors such as substance abuse [Dwyer, Ron and Daley

Table 3b
Trends in child care expenditures: Total family expenditure on child care, employed mothers with children age 0–14

	Percent who pay anything	Weekly expense (1999$), if pay	Percent of income
Winter 1985	33.7	90.6	NA
Fall 1987	33.3	94.7	6.6
Fall 1988	39.9	97.2	6.8
Fall 1990	38	87.6	6.9
Fall 1991	34.5	86.4	7.1
Fall 1993	35.5	85.1	7.3
Fall 1995	40.5	92.9	7.4
Spring 1997	44.1	74.7	7.4
Spring 1999	43	75.6	7.5

Source: Smith (2000, 2002) and tabulations from wave 10 of the 1996 Survey of Income and Program Participation (Spring 1999).
Notes. See Table 3a. NA indicates not available.

Table 4
Distribution of children ages 5–14 by use of self-care and mother's employment status, 1999

	Uses any self-care		Does not use any self-care	
	Mother employed	Mother not employed	Mother employed	Mother not employed
Percent in each primary care arrangement				
Parent	11.1	0.9	42.1	75.3
Relative	76.9	89.2	28.4	11.8
Nonrelative	3.0	1.0	10.9	2.1
Organized activity	9.0	8.8	18.6	10.8
Total	100	100	100	100

Table 4

(*Continued*)

	Uses any self-care		Does not use any self-care	
	Mother employed	Mother not employed	Mother employed	Mother not employed
Distribution of children across any self-care and mother's employment status				
All	10.5	3.2	53.4	32.9
Age 5	0.7	0.3	56.5	42.6
Age 6	1.3	0.6	58.2	40.0
Age 7	1.4	1.1	60.2	37.3
Age 8	2.8	1.2	58.8	37.2
Age 9	5.2	1.5	59.1	34.1
Age 10	8.3	2.4	57.7	31.5
Age 11	11.5	4.4	51.9	32.2
Age 12	19.6	5.5	47.3	27.6
Age 13	25.0	7.5	42.4	25.1
Age 14	32.3	8.0	39.7	20.0
Married	10.0	3.2	52.4	34.4
Widowed, divorced, or separated	14.3	3.0	56.5	26.1
Never married	7.6	3.1	55.7	33.6
White	12.3	3.6	53.6	30.5
Black	9.0	2.8	59.2	29.0
Hispanic	5.3	2.0	47.3	45.4
Annual income				
<18(000)	5.4	4.3	35.9	54.4
18–35.999	9.2	2.6	55.2	33.0
36–53.999	11.5	3.0	56.0	29.5
54+	13.6	3.0	60.5	22.8
Income < poverty line	4.3	4.5	33.1	58.1
Income ⩾ poverty	12.0	2.9	58.3	26.9
Northeast	8.9	2.3	56.9	31.9
Midwest	14.6	4.6	52.1	28.7
West	9.7	3.5	49.1	37.6
South	9.1	2.5	55.6	32.9
Metro	10.0	2.9	53.1	34.0
Nonmetro	12.8	4.5	55.0	27.7
Receives public assistance	4.7	5.7	33.5	56.1
No public assistance	11.2	2.9	55.9	30.0

Source: Tabulations from wave 10 of the 1996 panel of the Survey of Income and Program Participation (Spring 1999).

Notes. Parent includes the mother while working, the father, and cases in which no regular child care arrangement is used. Relative include grandparents, siblings, and other relatives. Nonrelative includes family day care, nannies, and babysitters. Organized activity includes before and after school programs, lessons, clubs, sports, and day care centers. Public assistance includes TANF, other cash assistance, and Food Stamps. Figures are weighted by the child's sample weight.

(1990)]. Juvenile crime rates triple in the after school hours between 3 and 6 in the afternoon when children are most likely to be left unattended, and children are most likely to be victims of violent crimes committed by nonfamily members in these hours [Fox and Newman (1997), U.S. Office of Juvenile Justice and Delinquency Prevention (1996)]. These facts suggest that lack of supervision is a serious problem, at least for some children – an issue we revisit in Section 6.

In summary, large numbers of children spend many hours each week in some form of nonparental, nonschool child care. While children of employed mothers are most likely to be in child care, a significant share of children with nonemployed mothers are also in child care. Many children spend time in more than one mode of nonparental care, and routinely spend time unsupervised, suggesting that it is difficult for some parents to patch together enough child care to completely cover the necessary hours.

3. The market for child care

3.1. Demand for child care

3.1.1. Theory

A simple one-person static labor supply model augmented with assumptions about child care provides a useful starting point for analyzing demand for child care. The mother is the agent in the model, making decisions about care for her children. Suppose that child care is homogeneous in quality and commands a market price of p dollars per hour of care per child, taken as given by the mother.[3] There is no informal unpaid care available and the mother cannot care for her children while she works, so paid child care is required for every hour the mother works. By assumption, the mother cares for her children during all hours in which she is not working. There are no fixed costs of work, and the wage rate w is the same for each hour of work. For simplicity, suppose there is only one child who needs care. The mother's budget constraint is $c = y + (w - p)h$, where c is consumption expenditure other than child care, y is nonwage income, and h is hours of work. The time constraint is $h + l = 1$, where l is hours of leisure, and the utility function is $u(c, l)$. The monetary cost of child care reduces the net wage rate $(w - p)$. A higher price of child care increases the likelihood that the net market wage is below the reservation wage, thereby reducing the likelihood of employment.

Some families have access to care by a relative, including the father or another family member, at no monetary cost. But not all families with access to such care use it, because it has an opportunity cost: the relative sacrifices leisure or earnings in order to provide care. The quality of such care compared to the quality of market care is also

---

[3] Homogeneous quality means that we can ignore the effect of child care on child outcomes for now. This assumption will be relaxed below.

likely to influence the use of informal care, but consideration of quality is taken up below and ignored here. If the mother pools income with the relative or has preferences over the relative's leisure hours, then the mother will behave as if unpaid child care has an opportunity cost. To illustrate in the simplest possible setting, take as given that the relative who is the potential unpaid child care provider is not employed.[4] Let H represent hours of *paid* child care purchased in the market and U hours of *unpaid* child care. Maintaining the assumption that the mother is the care giver during all hours in which she is not employed, we have $h = H + U$ and $h \geqslant H, U \geqslant 0$. The budget constraint is $c = y + wh - pH$. The utility function is $u(c, l, l_r)$, where l_r is leisure hours of the relative. The time constraints are $l + h = 1$ for the mother and $l_r + U = 1$ for the relative. If U and H are both positive, then the shadow price of an hour of relative care is the marginal utility of the relative's leisure. In this case relative care is used for the number of hours U^* for which the marginal rate of substitution between consumption and leisure of the relative equals the market price of care: $u_{l_r}/u_c = p$; and paid care is used for the remaining $H^* = h - U^*$ hours for which child care is required.

In order to examine work incentives in this model, classify outcomes as follows A

Outcome	Mother employed	Unpaid care used	Paid care used
1	no	no	no
2	yes	yes	no
3	yes	yes	yes
4	yes	no	yes

higher price of child care increases the cost of using paid care, but does not affect the cost of unpaid relative care, because no money changes hands for such care. A higher price therefore decreases the probability of choosing outcomes 3 and 4, and increases the probability of choosing outcomes 1 and 2. In addition to providing a work disincentive for the mother (outcome 1 is more likely) a higher price also provides an incentive to use unpaid care conditional on working (outcome 2 is more likely).

If the quality of paid child care is variable and if the quality of care affects child outcomes, then the mother will be concerned about the quality of care she purchases. The simplest case to consider is uni-dimensional quality: quality is a single "thing". The price of an hour of child care is $p = \alpha + \beta q$, where q is the quality of care and α and β are parameters determined in the market. This hedonic price function is determined by the market supply of and demand for quality (a linear price function is not essential to the argument). The mother cares about the quality of child care because it affects her child's development outcome d. Let the child development production function be

---

$d = d(lq_m, hq)$, where q_m is the quality of the care provided by the mother. The effect of purchased child care on development depends on its quantity (h) and quality (q). For simplicity, no distinction is made between the mother's leisure and her time input to child development, and assume also for simplicity that no unpaid care is available. Relaxing these assumptions does not change the main implications of this model. The utility function is $u(c, l, d)$ and the budget constraint is $c = y + (w - [\alpha + \beta q])h$.

Blau (2003a) demonstrates the following results in this model. A higher price of child care resulting from an increase in either α or β decreases the incentive to be employed. An increase in α has a bigger negative effect on employment than an equivalent increase in β. So, if the goal of a subsidy program is to facilitate employment, this is best accomplished by an "α-subsidy" unconditional on quality. In a quality–quantity model such as this one, the substitution effect of a change in price on the level of quality demanded is ambiguous, and this holds for changes in both α and β. But it can be shown that (1) if the substitution effects $\partial q/\partial \alpha|_{\bar{u}}$ and $\partial q/\partial \beta|_{\bar{u}}$ are both negative, then $\partial q/\partial \beta|_{\bar{u}}$ is larger in absolute value than $\partial q/\partial \alpha|_{\bar{u}}$; and (2) if $\partial q/\partial \alpha|_{\bar{u}} > 0$ then either $\partial q/\partial \beta|_{\bar{u}}$ is positive but smaller than $\partial q/\partial \alpha|_{\bar{u}}$, or $\partial q/\partial \beta|_{\bar{u}} < 0$. Thus an increase in β has a bigger negative effect or a smaller positive effect on the level of quality demanded than an increase in α. So if the goal of a subsidy is to improve the quality of child care, a "β-subsidy" that provides a more generous subsidy for higher-quality care is more effective than an α-subsidy. There is a clear tradeoff in subsidy policy between the goals of increasing employment and improving the quality of child care.

3.1.2. Evidence

Table 5 summarizes results from 20 studies that estimated the effect of the price of purchased child care on the employment of mothers.[5] Estimated price elasticities reported in the studies range from 0.06 to −3.60. The studies differ in the data sources used and in sample composition by marital status, age of children and income. Sample composition does not explain much of the variation in the elasticity estimates; the range of estimates is large within studies using the same sample composition. Differences in the data sources also do not appear to account for much variation in the estimates, since there is substantial variation in estimates from studies using the same source of data. Hence specification and estimation issues most likely play an important role in producing variation in the estimates.

The dozen studies listed in the upper panel of the table use very similar methods. These studies estimate a binomial discrete choice model of employment by probit or

---

[5] Reviews of this literature can be found in Anderson and Levine (2000), Blau (2003a), Connelly (1991) and Ross (1998). Chaplin et al. (1999) review the literature on the effect of the price of child care on child care mode choice. Some studies are not included in the table because the elasticity of employment with respect to the price of child care was not estimated or reported. Some of the latter studies estimated an hours of work (or a marginal rate of substitution) equation instead of an employment equation [Averett, Peters and Waldman (1997), Heckman (1974), Michalopoulos, Robins and Garfinkel (1992)]. Others did not report enough information to determine the method of estimation or the elasticity [Connelly (1990), Kimmel (1995)].

Table 5

Studies of the effect of the price of child care on employment of mothers

Study	Data	Population	Employment	Price	Method	Elasticity
Anderson and Levine (2000)	SIPP 1990–1993	Child < 13	Binary: LFP	Total c.c. expenses per mother's hours worked	Probit; standard	Married, < 13: −0.30 Single, < 13: −0.47 Married, < 6: −0.46 Single, < 6: −0.58
Baum (2002)	NLSY 1988–1994	Women who gave birth 1988–1994	Month of return to work following birth	Total c.c. expenditure per hour worked	Discrete time logit hazard	Low income: −0.59 Others: −0.02* (one year after birth)
Blau and Robins (1991)	NLSY 1982–1986	Child < 6	Binary: employed in last 4 weeks	Total c.c. expenses per hour of care	Probit; standard	0.04*
Connelly (1992)	SIPP 1984	Married, child < 13	Binary: LFP	Total c.c. expenses per mother's hours worked	Probit; standard	−0.2
Connelly and Kimmel (2003a)	SIPP 1992–1993 (data for 1994)	Child < 6	FT, PT, OLF	Expenditure per hour on primary arrangement of youngest child	Ordered probit on FT, PT, OLF	Married: FT: −0.71, PT: −0.08 Single: FT: −1.22, PT: −0.37
Connelly and Kimmel (2003b)	SIPP 1992–1993 (data for 1994)	Single, child < 6	Binary: LFP	Expenditure per hour on primary arr. of youngest child	Probit; standard	−1.03
U.S. GAO (1994)	NCCS 1990	Child < 13	Binary: LFP	Total weekly c.c. expenses	Probit; standard	Poor: −0.50 Near poor: −0.34 Not poor: −0.19
Han and Waldfogel (2001)	CPS 1991–1994	Child < 6	Binary: employed	Total c.c. expenses per mother's hours worked (from SIPP)	Probit; standard	Married: −0.30 Single: −0.50

Table 5
(Continued)

Study	Data	Population	Employment	Price	Method	Elasticity
Hotz and Kilburn (1997)	NLS72, 1986	Child < 6	Binary: employed	Total c.c. expenses per hour of care	Probit	−1.26
Kimmel (1998)	SIPP 1987	Child < 13	Binary: worked last month	Total c.c. expenses per mother's hours worked	Probit; standard	Married: −0.92 Single: −0.22
Powell (1997)	Canadian NCCS	Married, child < 6	Binary: employed	Total family work-related expenditure per mother's hours worked	Probit; standard	−0.38
Ribar (1992)	SIPP 1984	Child < 15	Employed	Total c.c. expenses per hour of care	Probit	−0.74
Blau and Hagy (1998)	NCCS 1990	Child < 6	Employed	Quality-adjusted location-specific price from provider survey	Multinomial logit	−0.2
Blau and Robins (1988)	EOPP 1980	Married, child < 14	Employed	Average location-specific weekly c.c. expenditure	Multinomial logit	−0.34
Fronstin and Wissoker (1995)	NCCS 1990	Child < 6	Employed	Average location-specific price from c.c. provider survey	Binary logit	Low-income area: −0.45 High-income area: 0.06*
Michalopoulos and Robins (2000)	Canadian and U.S. NCCS	Married, child < 5	FT, PT, OLF	Expenditure per hour of child care	Multinomial logit	−0.156

Table 5
(*Continued*)

Study	Data	Population	Employment	Price	Method	Elasticity
Michalopoulos and Robins (2002)	Canadian and U.S. NCCS	Single, child < 5	FT, PT, OLF	Expenditure per hour of child care	Multinomial logit	−0.259
Powell (2002)	Canadian NCCS	Married, child < 6	Employed	Expenditure on primary arr. of youngest child per hour of care	Multinomial logit	Center user: −1.40 Nonrelative user: −3.60 Relative user: −0.80
Ribar (1995)	SIPP 1984	Married, child < 15	Employed FT, employed PT	Total c.c. expenses per hour of care	Structural multinomial	−0.09
Tekin (2004)	NSAF 1997	Single, child < 13	Employed FT, employed PT	Total c.c. expenses per hour of care	Multinomial logit	Full time: −0.15 Part time: −0.07

Notes. Standard – A binomial employment model estimated by probit or logit. The price of child care is usually measured using the fitted value from a model of child care expenditures per hour estimated on the sample of families with an employed mother who pays for care. These child care price equations are usually corrected for selection. SIPP – Survey of Income and Program Participation. NLSY – National Longitudinal Survey of Youth. NCCS – National Child Care Survey. CPS – Current Population Survey. NLS72 – National Longitudinal Survey of the Class of 1972. EOPP – Employment Opportunity Pilot Projects. NSAF – National Survey of America's Families. FT – Full-time. PT – Part-time. OLF – Out of the labor force. LFP – Labor Force Participation. c.c. – child care.
*Underlying coefficient estimate on the price of care was *insignificantly* different from zero at the 10% level.

logit. The price of child care is measured by the fitted value from an hourly child care expenditure equation estimated by linear regression on the subsample of families in which the mother was employed and paid for child care. The expenditure equation is corrected for selectivity on employment and paying for care using either a standard two stage approach [Heckman (1979)] or a reduced form bivariate probit model of employment and paying for care, following Maddala (1983) and Tunali (1986). For identification, some variables that are included in the child care expenditure equation are excluded from the employment probit in which the fitted value from the expenditure equation appears as a regressor. Also, some variables that are included in the probit selection equations are excluded from the child care price equation in order to help identify the selection effects. A selectivity-corrected wage equation is used to generate a fitted value for the wage rate, which is included in the employment model.[6]

Blau (2003a) discusses two problems with this approach. First, it does not account for the existence of an unpaid child care option. In the theoretical model described above, the price of child care affects the employment decision through its effect on the utility of the employment–child care options in which paid child care is used, compared to the utility of not being employed and the utility of being employed and using unpaid care only. A multinomial choice model accounts for these various choices, but the standard binomial model used in these studies does not. As a result, the price effect estimated in a binomial employment model is a biased estimate of the true effect of the price of child care on employment.

The second problem is how to measure the price of child care. The studies listed in the upper panel of Table 5 use the fitted value from a selection-corrected child care expenditure equation estimated on the subsample of employed mothers who use paid care. This approach provides a price measure for all sample cases, not just those who used paid care, and one that is more likely to be exogenous than observed expenditure for mothers who pay for care. The effect of price on employment is identified by exclusion restrictions. Researchers have typically used child care regulations, average wages of child care workers, and other factors that vary across geographic locations as identifying variables, under the assumption that such variables affect household behavior only insofar as they affect the price of child care. Some studies have also used less defensible identifying variables such as the number of children by age.

If the unobserved factors that influence employment and child care behavior are correlated with the unobserved determinants of the price of care, then estimating a reduced

---

[6] Exceptions to this general approach among the eleven studies include the following. Baum (2002) specifies the employment equation as a discrete-time monthly hazard model of return to work following birth of a child. Blau and Robins (1991) estimate the employment probit jointly with equations for the presence of a preschool age child and use of nonrelative care. Connelly and Kimmel (2003a) estimate an ordered probit model for full-time employment part-time employment, and nonemployment. U.S. GAO (1994) used weekly child care expenditure. Ribar (1992) estimates the employment equation jointly with equations for hours of paid and unpaid care. Hotz and Kilburn (1997) estimate the binary employment equation jointly with equations for use and hours of paid child care, child care price and the wage rate.

form price equation on a sample of mothers who are employed and pay for care yields biased estimates. Most researchers have specified reduced form employment and pay-for-care equations that are used to correct the child care price equation for selection effects in a two-stage estimation. However, if quality of care is a choice variable for the family, then there are no justifiable exclusion restrictions to identify the selection effects: after substituting for quality the price function is a reduced form, so it contains all of the exogenous variables in the model. Hence the only basis for identification of a child care price equation using consumer expenditure data in a manner consistent with economic theory would be functional form or covariance restrictions (i.e., assume that the unobserved factors that influence employment and child care behavior are uncorrelated with the unobserved determinants of the price of care).

The estimated elasticity of employment with respect to the price of child care ranges from 0.04 to −1.26 in the studies listed in the upper panel of Table 5. Without a detailed examination of specification and estimation differences, it is difficult to explain why these estimates are so varied. Some of this variation may be due to the two problems discussed here: ignoring unpaid child care, and inappropriate exclusion restrictions to identify the child care price equation. Different identification restrictions are used in each study, possibly leading to different degrees of bias. Different data sources containing different proportions of mothers who use paid care are used in each study, and the bias caused by ignoring unpaid child care is likely to depend on this proportion.

The eight studies listed in the lower panel of Table 5 use variants of the multinomial choice framework discussed above. Of these, three studies – Ribar (1995), Tekin (2004) and Blau and Hagy (1998) – are most consistent with an underlying framework in which informal care is dealt with appropriately. Ribar specifies a structural multinomial choice model. Paid child care is *not* treated as if it was the best option for all mothers: the price of child care influences behavior by affecting the utility of the options in which paid care is used, consistent with the theory described above. Tekin specifies a discrete choice model with outcomes defined by cross-classifying employment status (full-time, part-time, not employed) with indicators for use of paid child care conditional on employment and receipt of a child care subsidy conditional on employment and use of paid care. Like the studies in the upper panel, Ribar and Tekin use consumer expenditure data to measure the price of child care. Blau and Hagy specify a multinomial choice model with categories defined by cross-classifying binary indicators of employment and paying for care with an indicator of type of care, accounting appropriately for unpaid child care. They derive the price of child care from a survey of day care providers.

These three studies produce estimates of the elasticity of employment with respect to the price of child care at the lower end of the range (in absolute value) in Table 5: −0.09 in Ribar, −0.15 in Tekin and −0.20 in Blau and Hagy. It is risky to generalize from only three studies, but the fact that the studies that accounted for unpaid child care in ways consistent with the existence of an informal care option produced small elasticities suggests that the true elasticity may be small.

The effect of the price of child care on the intensive labor supply margin is of interest as well. Several of the studies in Table 5 provide estimates of the effect of the price of child care on hours of work by the mother, conditional on employment. Blau and Hagy (1998) estimate the price effect on weekly hours of work separately by the mode of child care used, and find uncompensated elasticities 0.06, 0.08 and −0.05, respectively for users of centers, family day care and other nonparental care. Michalopoulos, Robins and Garfinkel (1992) and Baum (2002) also find small elasticities, not significantly different from zero. On the other hand, Averett, Peters and Waldman (1997) report an uncompensated labor supply elasticity with respect to the price of child care of −0.78. This large estimate could be a result of Averett et al.'s use of a kinked budget constraint method, which imposes a substitution effect with a sign consistent with economic theory whether or not this is consistent with the data [MaCurdy, Green and Paarsch (1990)].

One additional response to a child care price change deserves mention although it is not included in Table 5. The price of child care may have an impact on welfare participation. Using the standard approach to measuring price, Connelly and Kimmel (2003b) find an elasticity of AFDC participation of 0.55 with respect to the price of child care from an ordinary probit model, and an elasticity of 0.28 from a probit model of AFDC participation estimated jointly with an employment probit. Tekin (2001) uses a multinomial model of employment, welfare participation, and payment for child care similar to the approach in Tekin (2004) described above. He estimates the elasticity of TANF enrollment with respect to the price of child care to be just 0.098.

In summary, the best available estimates suggest that the effects of the price of paid child care on labor force participation, hours of work, and welfare use are small.

3.2. Supply of child care

3.2.1. The quantity of child care supplied

Since nationally representative data on the supply of child care are unavailable, the quantity of child care *labor* typically serves as a proxy for the quantity of child care. Examining trends in child care labor makes sense in this context because child care is a very labor-intensive activity and the technology of providing care is unlikely to have changed much over time. This proxy does not allow us to determine with certainty how much child care is supplied in a given year, but we can be reasonably confident that trends in child care labor supply will track trends in child care supply.[7]

Consider the following simple conceptual framework developed in Blau (1993, 2001). Assume that during a given period of time, a person can engage in one of the following three activities: (1) work for pay in the child care sector, (2) work for pay in another sector of the labor force, or (3) not work for pay (the "home sector"). She chooses the option that gives her the highest utility, and in sectors (1) and (2) she also chooses

---

[7] Changes over time in the mix of child care by type (center, family day care, etc.) could cause divergence between trends in child care labor supply and child care supply. Day care centers have the highest child–staff ratio and if more care is provided in centers over time, then a given change in the number of child care workers would be associated with a different change in the number of children in care over time.

the number of hours of work. Utility in sectors (1) and (2) depends on the wage rate in the sector, and on the direct satisfaction she gets from working in the sector, measured by observed covariates and an unobserved disturbance. A multinomial model of the discrete choice among the three sectors and a regression model of hours of work per week for those employed in child care can be derived from this framework. The key explanatory variables of interest in both models are wage rates. The coefficient estimates on the child care wage rate can be used to measure the supply responsiveness of child care labor: the amount by which the quantity of child care labor supplied increases as a result of an increase in the child care wage relative to the wage rate available in other employment. Note also that one must account for selectivity bias in this scenario since the unobserved characteristics that influence a person's choice of sectors also likely affect the wage rate that a person could earn as a child care worker and hours of work in child care.

Blau (2001) uses pooled data from the Current Population Survey (CPS) for the years 1977–1998 to estimate the model described above. He estimates the total elasticity of supply of child care labor to be 1.15, accounting for both new entrants to the sector and increased hours supplied by workers already in the child care sector.

The large increase in demand for child care in recent years should drive up the wages of child care workers. Blau estimates that there was a 24 percent increase in demand for child care during the period 1983–1998 and uses a demand elasticity of −0.24. The supply elasticity of 1.15 implies that a 24 percent increase in the demand for child care should have caused the child care wage rate to rise by 17 percent. The actual increase in the average child care wage rate was only 8 percent, so some other factors that affects child care labor supply must account for why the child care wage rate increased by as little as it did. One possibility is that the supply of child care workers increased as a result of increased immigration of low-skilled women for whom child care is a relatively attractive employment option. Another possibility is that day care centers use less labor per child than home-based arrangements, so the increase over time in the share of child care provided in centers could help explain why child care wages have not grown as much as expected in response to the enormous increase in labor force participation of mothers. This argument suggests that an analysis that does not distinguish between the center and home-based sectors may be overly simple.

3.2.2. The supply of quality in child care centers

The quality dimension of child care is arguably as important as the quantity supplied because in many cases the alternative to high quality child care is not home care, but lower-quality child care. In this section, we define quality and give some descriptive statistics for measures of quality in US day care centers. We describe findings from the child care quality literature and analyze the relationship between child care price and quality.

Reviews of the literature on child care quality by Hayes, Palmer and Zaslow (1990), Lamb (1998) and Love, Schochet and Meckstroth (1996) note that there are two distinct concepts of quality in the literature. The first type is variously referred to as "process" quality, "global" quality and "dynamic features of care", while the second is called "structural" quality or "static features of care". Process quality characterizes the interactions between children and their caregivers, their environment and other children. A child care arrangement is considered high quality according to this concept when

> ". . . caregivers encourage children to be actively engaged in a variety of activities; have frequent, positive interactions with children that include smiling, touching, holding, and speaking at children's eye level; promptly respond to children's questions or requests; and encourage children to talk about their experience, feelings, and ideas. Caregivers in high-quality settings also listen attentively, ask open-ended questions and extend children's actions and verbalizations with more complex ideas or materials, interact with children individually and in small groups instead of exclusively with the group as a whole, use positive guidance techniques, and encourage appropriate independence". [Love, Schochet and Meckstroth (1996), p. 5.]

Structural quality refers to characteristics of the child care environment such as the child–staff ratio, group size, teacher education and training, safety, staff turnover and program administration. A child care arrangement is considered to be of high quality according to the structural definition when it meets standards specified by professional organizations such as the National Association for the Education of Young Children (NAEYC). The NAEYC and other standards specify maximum child–staff ratios and group sizes by age of the children in care; curriculum content; minimum staff qualifications for alternative levels of responsibility; health and safety standards; and standards for other program characteristics [see Hayes, Palmer and Zaslow (1990) for details of the NAEYC and other standards].

The surveys cited above argue that process quality is more closely related to child development than structural quality. The authors contend that structural features of child care "appear to support and facilitate more optimal interactions" [Hayes, Palmer and Zaslow (1990), p. 84] and "potentiate high-quality interaction and care but do not guarantee it" [Lamb (1998), p. 13]. For example, caring for children in a smaller group will only lead to better child development if a smaller group makes it easier for caregivers to provide developmentally appropriate care. But despite the widespread agreement on the importance of process quality, there are no nationally-representative data available on process measures. Researchers must rely on structural measures under the assumption that the two types of quality are related. Complicating matters further, is the failure of the US child care data collection system to collect quality data on a regular basis. The most recent nationally representative data on the structural measures of child care quality are from 1990. Here, we summarize the available information on the quality of child care in the US.

Table 6 summarizes characteristics of centers and regulated family day care homes [see Kisker et al. (1991) for more details]. Average group size is 16 in centers and 7 in family homes. Group size increases with the age of children in centers, but remains within the range of maximum group size recommended by the National Association for the Education of Young Children [see Hayes, Palmer and Zaslow (1990), p. 333] for each age group. Average child–staff ratios, on the other hand, generally fall on the high

Table 6
Characteristics of day care centers and regulated family day care homes, 1990

	Day care centers	Regulated family day care homes
Average group size[a]	16	7
Infants only	7	7
1-year-olds only	10	7
2-year-olds only	12	7
3–5-year-olds only	17	8
Average child–staff ratio[a]	9	6
Infants only	4	5.9
1-year-olds only	6.2	6.2
2-year-olds only	7.3	6.2
3–5-year-olds only	9.9	6.5
Annual rate of teacher turnover	25	
Percent of centers with any turnover	50	
Turnover rate in centers with turnover	50	
Average percentage of teachers with		
At least a BA/BS	47	11
Some college	39	44
High school degree or GED	13	34
No degree or GED	1	11
Percentage of teachers who have had[b]		
Child Development Associate (CDA) training	25	6
Teacher training	35	
Other education training	40	
Child care workshops or courses	54	43
Child development or psychology courses	36	28
Nurse or health training	26	
Training by a Resource & Referral or government agency	5	5
Social service training	4	2
Other training	6	

Source: Kisker et al. (1991).

[a]Excluding programs that serve primarily handicapped children.

[b]The training information for centers refers only to private, nonreligious-sponsored centers.

end or outside the NAEYC's recommended range. The average child–staff ratio of 6.2 for one-year-olds and 7.3 for two-year-olds exceed the recommended ranges for these age groups, while the average of 9.9 for 3–5-year-old children is at the high end of the NAEYC recommended level. The great majority of children in centers are 3–5 years old, so the majority of classrooms are (barely) within the range recommended by the NAEYC.

Half of the centers in the sample report no staff turnover, and the other half report turnover averaging 50% annually. Thus some centers appear to be quite stable, while others have a significant amount of turnover. From the perspective of a child, however, turnover is not exceptionally high. If a child enrolls in a center on her third birthday and remains in the center for two years, she will be in the center for the same duration as the average teacher (expected duration equals the inverse of the turnover rate).

Teachers in day care centers are well educated on average, with almost half (47%) having a four-year degree, 39% with some college, 13% with a high school diploma or GED, and virtually no high school dropouts (1%). Operators of regulated family day care homes are much less educated, with only 11% having graduated from college, 44% with some college, 34% with a high school diploma or GED, and 16% high school dropouts. Specialized training in early education, child development, or child care is also more common among center staff than in family day care homes.

As indicated above, there are no nationally representative samples of day care centers with measures of process quality. But two studies with reasonable sample sizes, the Cost, Quality, and Outcomes Study (CQOS) and the National Child Care Staffing Study (NCCSS) (see the Data Appendix for further information), measured process quality in site-specific samples of day care centers using the Early Childhood Environment Rating Scale (ECERS) and its infant–toddler counterpart (ITERS) to assess quality. These instruments rate each observed classroom on 30–35 items using a scale of 1–7 for each item. As a guide to the intended interpretation of the scores, ratings of 1, 3, 5 and 7 are designated by the instrument designers as representing inadequate, minimal, good and excellent care, respectively [Harms and Clifford (1980), Harms, Cryer and Clifford (1990)]. Summary scores are obtained by averaging over the items.

Table 7 presents descriptive statistics on quality ratings in day care centers from these two studies, by site, age of children in the classroom, and the type of center (for-profit or nonprofit). The overall average rating in both studies is just under 4, or about halfway between minimal and good. The authors of the CQOS report refer to this level of quality as "mediocre" [Helburn (1995), p. 1]. Quality varies substantially across locations, with the highest-quality sites (California, Connecticut and Boston) rated about one standard deviation above the lowest-quality sites (North Carolina, Atlanta and Seattle). Classrooms with pre-school age children are almost always rated to be of higher quality than infant–toddler rooms, by a fairly wide margin in the CQOS data.[8] With only a few exceptions, nonprofit centers receive higher average quality ratings than for-profits.[9]

Day care centers (the only type of provider with the necessary data on quality) can be thought of as cost-minimizing firms facing a quality production function. Since labor is the most important input to this production function in terms of cost, and little information is available for other inputs such as materials and rent, the price of teacher labor is the primary focus. If providers choose group size and the amounts of the different types of labor to minimize the cost of providing child care of the desired level

---

[8] The ECERS and ITERS instruments are similar but not identical. It is not clear whether quality differences by age of children in the classroom are real or reflect different scales of the instruments.

[9] There is little systematic information on process quality in family day care homes. Kontos et al. (1995) studied about 200 family day care homes and relatives providing child care. They concluded that the majority of providers were providing care of adequate quality, about one third were providing inadequate-quality care, and only 9% were providing good-quality care.

Table 7

The distribution of child care quality in day care centers as measured by the early childhood and infant–toddler environment rating scales. Mean (and standard deviation)

	All centers	For-profit		Nonprofit	
		Pre-school	Infant–toddler	Pre-school	Infant–toddler
Cost, quality, and outcomes study (1993)					
All sites	3.99 (1.07)	4.07 (0.99)	3.33 (1.02)	4.41 (0.96)	3.57 (1.07)
California	4.36 (0.96)	4.27 (0.88)	3.86 (0.70)	4.66 (0.97)	3.60 (1.07)
Colorado	3.94 (0.95)	4.09 (0.85)	3.40 (0.89)	4.25 (0.89)	3.66 (1.04)
Connecticut	4.24 (1.05)	4.46 (1.02)	4.00 (1.07)	4.33 (0.99)	3.85 (1.13)
North Carolina	3.44 (1.08)	3.28 (0.83)	2.54 (0.60)	4.31 (0.95)	3.29 (1.02)
National child care staffing study (1989)					
All sites	3.92 (0.99)	3.59 (0.90)	3.43 (0.98)	4.39 (0.97)	4.09 (1.07)
Atlanta	3.57 (0.96)	3.32 (0.84)	3.04 (0.86)	4.30 (0.87)	3.89 (1.05)
Boston	4.44 (0.72)	3.66 (0.86)	3.16 (0.57)	4.72 (0.61)	4.51 (0.72)
Detroit	3.96 (1.24)	4.23 (1.04)	3.86 (1.37)	4.14 (1.40)	3.69 (1.45)
Phoenix	4.09 (0.90)	3.74 (0.75)	3.84 (0.83)	4.79 (0.89)	4.48 (0.97)
Seattle	3.62 (0.84)	3.30 (0.86)	3.37 (1.06)	3.99 (0.73)	3.63 (0.96)

Source: Tabulations from the Cost, Quality, and Outcomes Study (CQOS) and the National Child Care Staffing Study (NCCSS).

Notes. See Cryer et al. (1995) for description of the CQOS, and Whitebook, Howes and Phillips (1990) for description of the NCCSS. Sample size is 731 classrooms in 401 centers for the CQOS and 665 classrooms in 227 centers for the NCCSS. The public release data set from the NCCSS does not include the scores on the individual ECERS and ITERS items or the average score. Rather, it includes two summary measures derived from factor analysis of the underlying items. The figures presented here are the unweighted average of the two summary measures. This has the same scale as the ECERS and ITERS scores from the CQO but was derived differently, so comparisons between the CQO and NCCSS should be made with caution.

of quality, given the labor prices and technology the provider faces, the relationship between cost and quality can be characterized by a standard cost function. The quantity of care is assumed to be determined by consumer decisions conditional on the quality and price distributions available in the market. The price per hour of care that a provider can charge depends on the quality of care offered, as determined by the equilibrium price function in its local market.

Given the cost function and the price function in its local market, a provider chooses the quality of care to maximize its utility, where utility of the provider is a function of profit and quality. The relative weight placed on quality versus profit in the utility function may differ across providers (e.g., between for-profit and nonprofit providers). With estimates of the parameters of the cost function, the price function, and the relative weight on quality, it is then possible to derive the *quality supply function*: the relationship between price and the level of quality offered by providers.

We begin with estimates of the cost function part of the puzzle. Several studies have estimated cost equations for day care centers: Powell and Cosgrove (1992), Preston

(1993), Mukerjee and Witte (1993), Mocan (1997) and Blau and Mocan (2002). We focus on results from the latter study because it is most recent, and because it uses data from the large scale Cost, Quality and Outcomes Study. Blau and Mocan (2002) find that the logarithm of total cost is positively related to quality, with a coefficient estimate of 0.056 (significantly different from zero at the 5% level). The interpretation of this estimate is that a one unit increase in quality (for example, a change in the ECERS score from 3 to 4, equal to about a one standard deviation increase) would raise cost by 5.6 percent. By this metric, raising the quality of a center from "minimal" (3) to "good" (5) would only raise costs by 11.2 percent. This is a small effect, and it suggests that with the current structure of teacher wages it is not very costly to raise the quality of child care in centers. Cost is positively related to wages of teachers of various education levels, with the wage rate of the least educated workers showing the biggest impact.

The results for the price function in Blau and Mocan (2002) indicate that the market rewards higher-quality care with a significantly higher price in three of the four states examined, with elasticities of 0.40 in California, 0.32 in Colorado, 0.22 in Connecticut and 0.13 in North Carolina. Further estimates indicate that the relative weight on quality in the providers' utility function is approximately zero for both for-profit and nonprofit centers. This is not a surprising finding for the for-profit centers: they are in business to make a profit, and presumably care about quality only in so far as it affects their profit. The finding that nonprofits also put no weight on quality is surprising given evidence that nonprofits have higher average quality, but it is very robust.

Having estimated the cost function, the price function, and the relative weight on quality, Blau and Mocan use these to calculate the quality supply function. The simulated quality supply function yields an average price elasticity of 0.66 among for-profits and 0.48 among nonprofits. These moderately large elasticities result from the fact that cost is estimated to increase only modestly with increases in quality, while the market price can be increased fairly substantially as quality increases. Since the major cost of child care is labor, another policy of interest is a wage subsidy for child care labor. Quality supply appears to be fairly sensitive to the wage rate, with average elasticities of −0.77 to −0.80, suggesting that even small wage subsidies have the potential to substantially improve the quality of care. These results suggest a puzzle: If raising the quality of child care is relatively inexpensive and well rewarded, then why is so much privately provided child care of low quality? One possible resolution of this puzzle is discussed below: parents may not be willing to pay even the small additional amount required to cover the cost of improved quality. The increase in market price that is observed with increased quality may be due to public subsidies.

3.3. The effects of child care quality on children

Many studies of the effects of structural inputs on "process quality" and of the effects of child care inputs and child care quality on child outcomes are reviewed in National Research Council and Institutes of Medicine (2000, 2003), Love, Schochet and Meckstroth (1996) and Lamb (1998). The great majority of such studies are relatively uninformative by the standards of economic research. For example, many use small nonrandomly selected convenience samples, include few or no measures of family and child characteristics, and lack measures of child development prior to exposure to the child care arrangement being studied. A few of the better studies on child care quality are summarized in Table 8. It is important to note, however, that only a few of these studies consider the possibility that families select child care arrangements on the basis of unobserved aspects of the home environment, or unobserved characteristics of the child, which limits the inferences that can be drawn.

The National Day Care Study [Ruopp et al. (1979)] is remarkable for using random assignment of children within centers to classrooms with different staff–child ratios and teachers with different training levels. Other studies listed in Table 8, use the CQOS and the NICHD Study of Early Child Care data, which are large-scale observational studies. These data are described in more detail in the Appendix. An important limitation of these observational studies is that it is difficult to control for nonrandom selection of children into centers.

Some studies using these data simply compare the developmental outcomes of children according to whether their child care arrangement is classified as low-quality or high-quality based on inputs. These studies typically find that high-quality care has a positive and statistically significant association with child cognitive development [Peisner-Feinberg et al. (2001), NICHD Early Child Care Research Network (NICHD ECCRN) and Duncan (2003), NICHD ECCRN (2000)], behavior [NICHD ECCRN (1998)] and peer interactions [NICHD ECCRN (2001)]. However, this approach does not provide estimates of the impact of varying each input separately, which would be useful for policy analysis.

Other studies examine the effects of inputs separately. Ruopp et al. (1979) report that both low staff–child ratios and higher teacher training were associated with better child outcomes. Similarly, Mocan et al. (1995) use data from the CQOS to examine the effect of structural inputs such as staff–child ratios, wage rates, teacher training, teacher turnover, and group size, and find that all but group size have an effect on "process" measures of the quality of care. Their study is notable for including a large number of control variables, relative to other studies. However, Blau (2000) shows using the same data that when center fixed effects are included in the model, only teacher training has an effect on child care quality. This finding replicates his earlier analysis of data from the National Child Care Staffing Survey [Blau (1997)]. The center fixed effects may be viewed as an attempt to control for fixed characteristics of centers (such as location) that might attract families of a particular type.

The Florida Child Care Quality Study was designed to exploit changes in Florida's child care regulations that mandated higher staff–child ratios, and more training for staff in day care centers. A sample of 150 child care centers was selected, and Center directors and children were interviewed before and after the changes. The study found that the regulations did appear to affect the regulated inputs (for example, staff–teacher ratios increased), but had no significant impact on measures of process quality. There were some significant improvements in children's psychological well-being as measured by their attachment security. However, there was no comparison group in this study.

Table 8

Studies of the effects of child care inputs on quality and on child outcomes

Data	Author	Design	Age of participation	Sample size	Outcomes
National day care study (NDCS)	Ruopp et al. (1979)	Children given baseline developmental assessments and evaluated again after nine months. Random assignment of children to classrooms with different staff–child ratios and teachers with different levels of training, but day care centers not randomly chosen	Age 1–5	64 centers, 1,600 children, T_1 = low staff–child ratio, T_2 = high teacher training, low-income urban	Language receptivity: all $T > C$ (age 3–5) General knowledge: all $T > C$ (age 3–5) Cooperative behavior: all $T > C$ (age 3–5) Child development: $T_1 > C$ (age 1–2), $T_1 = C$ (age 3–5) Larger group sizes associated with poorer outcomes, but group size not randomly assigned
Cost, quality, and outcomes study (CQOS)	Helburn (1995)	Observational data on measures of quality, inputs, and costs of centers in four states. Children who spent at least one full year at the sampled centers were given developmental assessments in Kindergarten and second grade		400 centers, Initial: 828 children, Final: 757 children, T = high-quality centers	
	Peisner-Feinberg et al. (2001)	Controls for maternal education, child gender, ethnicity, and relationship with teacher, but does not control for home environment or a baseline assessment		Same as above	Mental development: $T > C$ Math achievement: $T > C$ Behavior: $T > C$

Table 8
(*Continued*)

Data	Author	Design	Age of participation	Sample size	Outcomes
	Mocan et al. (1995)	Estimates a model of classroom quality as a function of child care inputs. Includes many controls		Same as above	Inputs with significant effects on process quality Staff–child ratio Wage rates for teachers with low education Proportion of staff with college degree Lead teacher turnover Inputs which do not affect quality Group size
	Blau (2000)	Uses center fixed effects approach to compare different classrooms in the same centers as Mocan et al. (1995)	Age 0–5	Same as above	Inputs with significant effects on process quality Workshop training Inputs which do not affect quality Staff–child ratio Wage rates for teachers with low education Proportion of staff with college degree Lead teacher turnover Group size
National child care staffing survey (NCCS)	Blau (1997)	Uses center fixed effects approach to compare different classrooms in the same centers	Infants to children of age 5+	204 centers, 567 classrooms, 1,094 teachers	Similar to Blau (2000) results

Table 8
(Continued)

Data	Author	Design	Age of participation	Sample size	Outcomes
Florida child care quality improvement study	Howes et al. (1998)	Evaluates changes in regulation of staff–child ratio and training in Florida. Center directors and teachers in three classrooms were interviewed. Two children from each class were randomly selected for developmental assessments. Process conducted before regulations changed in 1992 and again in 1994 and 1996. No comparison group and no way to isolate changes resulting from regulations. Different children assessed in each wave		150 centers in 4 Florida counties	Significant changes in inputs 1992–1994 Staff–child ratios up Teacher detachment down Complexity of peer and object play up Attachment security up Inputs which did not change 1992–1994 Teacher sensitivity Teacher harshness Overall classroom quality Behavior problems Cognitive development Significant changes in inputs 1994–1996 Teacher responsiveness up Teacher detachment up Attachment security up Inputs which did not change 1994–1996 Overall classroom quality Behavior problems Cognitive development

Table 8
(Continued)

Data	Author	Design	Age of participation	Sample size	Outcomes
NICHD study of early child care (SECC)	U.S. Department of Health and Human Services (1998)	Monitors children from birth in 1991 until present. Selected healthy births to English-speaking mothers over age 18 who planned to remain in the state for one year. Families and child care facilities of every type were visited periodically. The effects of child care quality on child development analyzed in many studies by the NICHD early child care research network (ECCRN). See below		1,300 children English-speaking	
	NICHD ECCRN (2001)	Regression model of cognitive development. Controls for five family and child characteristics and site dummies in addition to the type, quantity, and quality of child care	Age 15, 24, 36 months	Same as above. T = high-quality care. Children in nonmaternal child care at time of assessment	Cognitive development: $T > C$
	NICHD ECCRN (1998)	Models behavior problems. Controls for family income, psychological adjustment of the mother, gender, child temperament, quality of home environment, character of mother–child interactions, and child's security of attachment to mother	Age 24, 36 months	Same as above. T_1 = high-quality care, T_2 = stable care arrangement. Children in nonmaternal child care at 24 or 36 months	Caregiver-reported behavior problems: $T_1 < C$ (age 24 months) Mother-reported behavior problems: $T_1 = C$ (age 24 months) Noncompliance of children in care: $T_2 < C$ (age 24 months) Problem behavior: $T_1 < C$ (age 36 months)
	NICHD ECCRN (2001)	Controls for several family characteristics as well as child's cognitive development, temperament, and mother's sensitivity when analyzing peer interactions		Same as above. T = high-quality care	Peer interactions: $T > C$

Table 8
(*Continued*)

Data	Author	Design	Age of participation	Sample size	Outcomes
	NICHD ECCRN (2000)	Models the effects of child care inputs on child care quality. Regression controls for site, but not child, family, or center characteristics. Only characteristics of room, teacher, and type of child care	Age 15, 24, 36 months	Same as above	Inputs with significant effects on quality Group size (age 15, 24 months) Staff–child ratio (age 15, 24 months) Caregiver education (age 24, 36 months) Caregiver specialized training (age 15 months) Caregiver experience (age 24, 36 months)
	NICHD ECCRN and Duncan (2003)	Controls for many home and child characteristics and estimates change score models	Age 54 months	Same as above. T = high-quality care	Cognitive functioning: $T > C$
National Longitudinal Survey of Youth 1979 (NLSY79)		Began with sample of 12,652 individuals age 14–21 in 1979. Data collected annually until the present. Beginning in 1986, children of sample women were given developmental assessments every other year			
	Blau (1999)	Analyzes the effect of child care inputs on child development. Controls for type of care, payment, time spent in care, and family and child characteristics. Models with and w/o family fixed effects	Variable, depends on outcome	$N = 2{,}503$–$4{,}031$ depending on outcome	Inputs with significant effects on development Group size (wrong sign) Generally, inputs small and not significant Home environment large and significant

Notes. T – Treatment, C – Control.

The results from the NICHD Study of Early Child Care (SECC) are potentially more credible than those of many other studies because of the longitudinal design of the SECC, the inclusion of children in all types of child care, and the availability of extensive information on nonchild care factors. The recent analysis of these data by NICHD ECCRN and Duncan (2003) takes advantage of the richness of the data by controlling for more home and child characteristics than the other SECC studies, and by also examining changes in outcomes. The results indicate that a two standard deviation (SD) improvement in child care quality in early childhood is associated with a one-sixth to one-seventh of an SD increase in cognitive functioning in a model that controls for cognitive functioning at age 24 months as well as extensive controls.

Blau (1999) uses data from the National Longitudinal Survey of Youth (NLSY), which is a large general purpose study which includes women who were 14–21 in 1978, and follow-ups of their children (see the Appendix for further information). He examines the effects of maternally reported group size, staff–child ratios, and teacher training, as well as of type of care, cost of care, hours per week, and month per year spent in the arrangement on a series of cognitive and test scores as well as a behavioral problems index. The models control for a large number of background variables, including measures of the quality of the home environment. Some models also include family fixed effects, and/or lagged measures of child development. Blau finds that the effects of child care quality are generally insignificant, and sometimes wrong-signed. In contrast, measures of the home environment are all statistically significant and have relatively large effects. It is possible that maternal reports are measured with error, which biases the estimated effects toward zero.

The overall message of this section is that there is little convincing evidence that structural child care inputs affect child outcomes, while there is more evidence that "process quality" has a positive effect on child development. These findings are rather similar to those in the school quality literature, in which many studies find that structural inputs such as class size, teacher education and experience, and teacher pay have little impact on student outcomes, while more intangible teacher characteristics (captured by teacher fixed effects) are strongly associated with student outcomes [Hanushek (1992, 2007)]. It is interesting to note that French pre-school programs, which are generally thought to be of high quality, employ a different input mix than American programs, with small staff–child ratios, more highly trained staff, and centrally-planned curricula [Boocock (1995)]. It may be that part of the difficulty in making a strong connection between inputs and outputs is that there are different ways to produce care of a given quality level, so that focusing on levels of a few inputs in isolation yields a misleading picture.

4. Government intervention in the child care market

4.1. Rationale

To this point, we have mostly ignored the role of the government in the child care market. The government does in fact play an important role, and an economic case for government intervention in the child care market can be made on several grounds. First, the government may be concerned with equity; second, the government may want to encourage parents to work; and third, there may be market failures, such as liquidity constraints, information failures and externalities.

The first argument in favor of government intervention in the child care market is on the grounds of equity, just as the case is sometimes made for government involvement in the public school system. For example, Bergmann (1996, p. 131) argues that high-quality child care can be thought of as a "merit good, something that in our ethical judgment everybody should have, whether or not they are willing or able to buy it". Bergmann argues that the usual economic considerations in favor of cash transfers over in-kind subsidies do not apply to merit goods. The main arguments she advances are that children have little or no say in how parents spend a cash grant; that society has a responsibility to ensure that children are well cared for while the parents work; and that high-quality child care has benefits to children that parents may not fully account for in their spending decisions. Economic actors who start out with very unequal endowments (in terms of ability, environment, or opportunities) are likely to end up with very unequal allocations, even if the outcome is efficient [Inman (1986)]. Meyers et al. (2002) discuss inequalities in access to quality early childhood educational experiences.

A government that is concerned with equity can compensate for differences in final outcomes, attempt to equalize initial endowments, or both. In principal, spending on programs of each type can be increased until the marginal benefit associated with an additional dollar of spending is equalized. However, to the extent that it is possible, equalizing endowments through intervention in the child care market may be a superior approach to the problem of unequal allocations compared to providing compensation for unequal outcomes later in life, both because it avoids many of the moral hazard problems that arise when society attempts to compensate those with poor outcomes, and because it may be more cost-effective [Heckman (2000)].

For example, Furstenberg, Brooks-Gunn and Morgan (1987) present evidence that it is important for children to get "off on the right foot" in school, and that children who started school with disadvantaged families had worse average performance than other children even if their parents' situation improved subsequently. To the extent that initiatives such as after-school programs can prevent high school dropout and juvenile crime, they may be very cost effective approaches to such societal problems. Earlier intervention is also attractive because of the sheer difficulty of overcoming poor endowments later in life. Public sector efforts to train low-skilled adult workers have generally found very small returns. Lalonde's (1995) survey of the training literature points out that most training programs for adult males and youths have been ineffective (the exception for youths being the costly Job Corps program). And among poor adult women, the evidence shows rapidly diminishing returns to training investments, suggesting that it may not be possible to raise earnings much with this kind of intervention.

A quite different rationale for government intervention in the child care market is to encourage parents – particularly low-income women – to work. There are two main reasons for this type of policy. First, it may be less costly to taxpayers to require low-income women to work and to provide child care subsidies than it is to support the same women via the welfare system. That is, child care subsidies may be able to help low-income families be economically self-sufficient. Self-sufficient in this context means employed and not enrolled in cash-assistance welfare programs. Self-sufficiency may be a desirable goal for noneconomic reasons, but also may be considered desirable if it increases future self-sufficiency by inculcating a work ethic and generating human capital, thereby saving the government money in the long run [Robins (1991)]. Child care and other subsidies paid to employed low-income parents may cost the government more today than would cash assistance through TANF. But if the dynamic links suggested above are important, then these employment-related subsidies could result in increased future wages and hours worked and lower lifetime subsidies than the alternative of cash assistance both today and in the future. But there is little evidence either for or against the existence of strong enough dynamic links to make means-tested, employment-conditioned, child care subsidies cost-effective for government.[10]

Second, there may be positive externalities associated with employment of low-income mothers. For example, younger women may be more likely to stay in school and less likely to get pregnant if they see that work is always required of recipients of public assistance. The children of women who move into the workforce may gain a positive role model. Third, liquidity constraints could prevent some women from paying for the child care that they need in order to enhance their own human capital through on-the-job training.[11] These potentially positive effects of encouraging maternal employment will be undermined if sending women to work results in children being cared for in a way that harms their development. For example, taxpayers could end up spending more rather than less, if neglected children are more likely to engage in future crime. Thus, there is a potential conflict between these two goals of government intervention in the child care market. Policies that enhance child development will not always encourage maternal employment, and vice versa.

A third broad justification for government intervention in the child care market is that there is a market failure that the government can address. Indeed, several market

---

[10] There is substantial evidence of positive serial correlation in employment. Whether this is due to "state dependence" (working today changes preferences or constraints in such a way as to make working in the future more attractive) or unobserved heterogeneity (working today does not affect the attractiveness of future work; some people find work more attractive than others in every period) is unclear. See Heckman (1981) for an early discussion and Hyslop (1999) for recent evidence. Gladden and Taber (2000) analyze the effect of work experience on wage growth for less-skilled workers. Card and Hyslop (2004) discuss evidence from a Canadian welfare to work program which suggests that the program increased employment, but that there was little growth in earnings over time.

[11] Walker (1996) has argued, however, that difficulties in attaining economic self-sufficiency are caused by imperfections in the credit market, not the child care market. If the dynamic links suggested above are important, then a family could borrow against its future earnings in a perfect credit market to finance the child care needed in order to be employed today and gain the resulting higher future earnings. Imperfection in the credit market caused by moral hazard and adverse selection prevent this, but the remedy according to Walker lies in government intervention in the credit market, not the child care market.

failures are potentially relevant in this case, including liquidity constraints, information failures, and externalities. Liquidity constraints may prevent parents from making optimal investments in the human capital of their children. But the existence of liquidity constraints alone would only justify financial assistance to certain parents, not direct government intervention in the provision of child care services. However, information failures are also likely to be important. There is increasing evidence that parents find it difficult to evaluate the quality of child care centers and that some parents pay for care of such low quality that it may be harmful to their children [Cryer and Burchinal (1995), Helburn and Howes (1996), U.S. Department of Health and Human Services (1998)].

Information failures provide a possible explanation for the poor average quality of child care available in the United States.[12] There is imperfect information in the child care market because consumers are not perfectly informed about the identity of all potential suppliers, and because the quality of care offered by any particular supplier identified by a consumer is not fully known. A potential remedy for this problem is government subsidies to Resource and Referral (R&R) agencies to maintain comprehensive and accurate lists of suppliers. This may not solve the problem in practice because of very high turnover and unwillingness to reveal their identity among informal child care providers. The second information problem is that consumers know less about product quality than does the provider, and monitoring is costly. This can lead to moral hazard and/or adverse selection. Moral hazard is a plausible outcome in day care centers (e.g., changing diapers just before pick-up time). Adverse selection of providers is plausible in the more informal family day care sector: family day care is a very low-wage occupation, so women with high wage offers in other occupations are less likely to choose to be care providers. If the outside wage offer is positively correlated with the quality of care provided, then adverse selection would result. Regulations are often suggested as a solution to the information problem, but Walker (1991) notes that the conditions under which regulations are beneficial to consumers may not be satisfied in the child care market.[13] We address this issue in more detail below.

Some evidence suggests that parents do not obtain much information about the child care market before making a choice. Walker (1991) reports that 60–80 percent of child care arrangements made by low-income parents are located through referrals from friends and relatives or from direct acquaintance with the provider. A referral may not be a good signal of the developmental appropriateness of child care if parents are not good judges of the quality of care. Cryer and Burchinal (1995) report a direct comparison of parent ratings of various aspects of the developmental appropriateness of their child's day care center classroom with trained observer ratings of the same aspects, using data from the Cost, Quality, and Outcomes study. The results show that parents give

[12] See Walker (1991), Council of Economic Advisors (1997), Magenheim (1995), Robins (1991), and U.S. Department of Health and Human Services (2001). This paragraph draws heavily on Walker (1991).
[13] See Walker (1991, pp. 68–69), which is based on applying Leland's (1979) model of regulations to the child care market. The conditions are low price elasticity of demand, quality matters to consumers, the marginal cost of quality is low, and consumers place a low value on low-quality care.

higher average ratings on every item than do trained observers, by about one standard deviation on average for pre-school age classrooms and by about two standard deviations on average for infant–toddler rooms. The instrument containing these items is of demonstrated reliability when administered by trained observers, so this suggests that parents are not well informed about the quality of care in the arrangements used by their children.[14]

Similarly, Mocan (in press) finds that parents use less information than trained observers when making quality assessments. He finds that parents tend to incorrectly associate some characteristics of centers (such as clean reception areas) with quality and fail to use other more relevant signals. Parents who are more educated, and married parents, assess quality in a way more similar to the trained observers. Mocan finds that the vast majority of parents claimed that they valued the quality attributes measured by the process-oriented scales, suggesting that parents are not choosing centers on the basis of some entirely different criteria (such as location). These findings suggest that government may be able to improve outcomes by developing and publicizing standards, but there is little evidence available about the efficacy of this type of market intervention.

The evidence about whether parents are willing to pay for better quality (and how much) is conflicting. On the one hand, Blau and Mocan (2002) find that the price centers can charge rises appreciably with quality. On the other hand, Blau (2001) reports a small correlation between family income and quality, and a generally flat price-quality gradient. In their study of consumer-demand functions for child care quality inputs, Blau and Hagy (1998) also find that parents do not seem to be willing to pay more for regulated aspects of care such as lower staff–child ratios.

Externalities provide perhaps the strongest theoretical justification for direct government involvement in the provision of quality child care. However, even the best justifications in terms of equity or market failures are moot if it is not actually possible to improve child outcomes through intervention. Hence, we will return to this question in the next section. In the remainder of this section we examine two types of government interventions in the private child care market: subsidies and regulation.

4.2. Subsidies

Table 9, which is based on Blau (2003a) shows the history, goals, and main provisions of the major child care subsidy programs in the US.[15] The oldest program is the Dependent Care Tax Credit, which, since it is not refundable, does not benefit low-income

---

[14] The instrument is the Early Childhood Environment Rating Scale (ECERS) and its counterpart for infants and toddlers, the Infant–Toddler Environment Rating Scale (ITERS). See Harms and Clifford (1980) and Harms, Cryer and Clifford (1990) for discussion of the instruments. Helburn (1995) discusses their reliability in the Cost, Quality and Outcomes study. The correlation between parent and observer scores was 0.21 for infant–toddler rooms and 0.29 for pre-school rooms [Cryer and Burchinal (1995, p. 206)]. Thus parents do appear to have some ability to distinguish among programs of different quality. However, from a child development perspective it is the absolute level of quality that matters, not relative quality.

[15] One significant program not included in Table 9 is military child care. Government expenditure on military child care was estimated to be $352 million in 2000 [Campbell et al. (2000)]. This program is not discussed

Table 9

Summary of the history, goals, and provisions of major federal child care programs

Program	Dependent Care Tax Credit	Exclusion of Employer-Provided Dependent Care Expenses	Aid to Families with Dependent Children Child Care	Transitional Child Care	At-Risk Child Care	Child Care and Development Block Grant	Title XX Social Services Block Grant
(Acronym)	(DCTC)	(EEPDCE)	(AFDC-CC)	(TCC)	(ARCC)	(CCDBG)	(TXX-CC)
Year Began	1954	1981	1988[c]	1988	1990	1990	1975[a,b]
Goal	Subsidize employment-related dependent care expenses	Subsidize employment-related dependent care expenses	Facilitate participation in the JOBS program	Help families who recently left AFDC for work maintain self-sufficiency	Help families who need child care in order to work and are at-risk of going on AFDC if child care is not provided	Provide child care services for low-income families, and improve the overall supply and quality of child care	Help low-income families achieve self-sufficiency; prevent child neglect
Original form	Tax deduction	Amounts paid or incurred by an employer for dependent care assistance provided to an employee are excluded from the employee's gross taxable earnings	Open-ended entitlement. Vouchers, contracts, or reimbursement of expenses. No fee for recipients	Same as AFDC-CC; limited to 1 year. Sliding fee for recipients	Capped entitlement. State match required. Sliding fee for recipients. Income limits set by states	Block grant to states. No state match. 75% of funds for direct subsidies (income < 75% of SMI); 25% for quality improvement and consumer education	Capped entitlement; population-based distribution to states
Major changes	1976: Credit replaced deduction. 1982: Subsidy rate and maximum allowable expenses raised. 1983: Added to short form 1040A. 1988: Required Social Security Number of provider	None	1996: Personal Responsibility and Work Opportunity Reconciliation Act (PRWORA) consolidated AFDC-CC, TCC, ARCC, and CCDBG into a single program: the Child Care and Development Fund (CCDF)				1981: Converted to block grant. 1996: States allowed to transfer up to 10% of TANF funds to TXX

Table 9
(Continued)

Program	Dependent Care Tax Credit	Exclusion of Employer-Provided Dependent Care Expenses	Aid to Families with Dependent Children Child Care	Transitional Child Care	At-Risk Child Care	Child Care and Development Block Grant	Title XX Social Services Block Grant
(Acronym)	(DCTC)	(EEPDCE)	(AFDC-CC)	(TCC)	(ARCC)	(CCDBG)	(TXX-CC)
Current form	Nonrefundable tax credit	Same as original	Combination discretionary and entitlement block grant. States must meet maintenance of effort and matching requirements for some of the entitlement funds. States may transfer up to 30% of their Temporary Assistance for Needy Families (TANF) block grant funds into the CCDF. States may also use TANF funds directly for child care, without transferring them to CCDF.				Block grant to states that can be used for many social services; 15% of funds on average used for child care
Current provisions	30% tax credit on expenses up to $4,800 for 2 children for AGI ⩽ 10 K; subsidy rate falls to 20% for AGI > 28 K. Effective 2003, 35% credit on expenses up to $6,000 for 2 children for AGI ⩽ 15 K	Up to $5,000 per year excludable. Expenses excluded from gross income are not eligible for the DCTC	Sliding fee scale, but states may waive fees for families below the poverty line. At least 4% of funds must be spent on quality-improvement and consumer education. Child care must meet state licensing and regulatory standards. Contracts or vouchers. Relative care eligible if provider lives in a separate residence				Child care must meet state regulatory and licensing standards
Current eligibility criteria	Both parents (or only parent) employed	None, other than being employed by a firm that offers this benefit	Family income no more than 85% of SMI, but states can (and most do) impose a lower-income eligibility limit. Children < 13. Parents must be in work-related activities				States choose income eligibility. Employment required

Source: Committee on Ways and Means (1998, 2000); Blau (2001, 2003a).

Notes. AGI – adjusted gross income. SMI – state median income.

[a]Earlier provisions of the Social Security Act provided federal matching funds to the states for social services.

[b]Less than two percent of the funds in the food program go to adult care centers.

[c]Before explicit child care subsidies were added to the AFDC program in 1988, states could choose to disregard from earnings up to $200/month in child care expenses incurred by employed AFDC recipients in determining AFDC eligibility and benefit amounts.

families without tax liabilities. The Exclusion of Employer-Provided Dependent Care Expenses (EEPDCE) allows expenses paid or incurred by an employer for dependent care assistance provided to an employee to be excluded from the employee's gross taxable earnings. This subsidy is also of little benefit to low-income families.

The 1988 Family Support Act (FSA) and the Omnibus Budget Reconciliation Act (OBRA) of 1990 instituted four different means-tested child care subsidy programs, with different target populations, eligibility requirements, and subsidy rates. This resulted in a fragmented system in which families had to switch from one program to another as a result of changes in employment or welfare status, which may have depressed takeup below already low levels [cf. U.S. Advisory Commission on Intergovernmental Relations (1994), U.S. General Accounting Office (1995), Ross (1996), Long et al. (1998)]. The 1996 Personal Responsibility and Work Opportunity Reconciliation Act (PRWORA) consolidated the programs created by FSA and OBRA into a single block grant called the Child Care and Development Fund (CCDF). Under the new system, states can allow families that move from welfare to work to remain in the same subsidy program. Rules governing the types of child care that can be subsidized are determined by the states, and hence vary widely across states. States have substantial flexibility in designing their CCDF programs, as shown in Table 10.

The data in Table 10 show that only four states plus Puerto Rico set income eligibility at the maximum allowed by law, 85 percent of State Median Income (SMI). Fourteen states set the income eligibility limit at less than 50 percent of SMI. States are permitted to waive fees (co-payments) for families with income below the poverty line, and the fourth column of Table 10 shows that there is substantial variation across states in use of this provision. Fees are determined in many different ways, including flat rates, percent of cost, percent of income, and combinations of these. States are required to have sliding scale fee structures, with fees that rise with family income. The minimum fee shown in the fifth column of the table is the co-payment required of the lowest-income families, and the maximum fee shown in the sixth column is the co-payment for the highest-income eligible families. The reimbursement rates listed in the last two columns represent the amount of the subsidy exclusive of the family co-payment. States that provide relatively generous reimbursement also tend to have higher income eligibility limits. Federal guidelines for implementation of the CCDF law require that the subsidy rate be set at the 75th percentile of the price distribution from a recent local market rate survey. In practice many states use out-of-date market rate surveys or set the subsidy rate lower than the 75th percentile of the price distribution [Adams, Schulman and Ebb (1998)]. States frequently change the characteristics of their CCDF plans.

---

here because it is not available to civilians. The military child care system was drastically reformed in the 1990s, and the current military child care system is often taken as a model of how a publicly-run child care program should be organized. See Campbell et al. (2000), U.S. General Accounting Office (1999b) and Lucas (2001) for information on military child care.

Table 10
Characteristics of state child care and development fund plans, 2003

State	Monthly income eligibility level ($)	Income eligibility as a percent of state median income (%)	Are families at or below poverty required to pay a fee?	Minimum fee (full-time rate)	Maximum family fee (full-time rate)	Reimbursement rate for pre-school age child[a,c]	Implied weekly reimbursement rate[b] ($)
Alabama	1,653	43	Some	$5.00/week	$72.5/week	$99/week	99.00
Alaska	3,853	77	Some	$13/month	$766/month	$880/month	203.00
Arizona	2,099	53	Some	$1.00/day + $0.50 additional c.	$10/day + $5 additional c.	$23.20/day	116.00
Arkansas	2,009	60	None	0	100% of fee	$17/day	85.00
California	2,925	75	None	$2/day	$10.50/day	$27.59/day	137.95
Colorado	2,862	61	Some	$6/month	$560/month + $20 each additional c.	$28/day	140.00
Connecticut	2,889	50	Some	2% of gross income	10% of gross income	$135/week	135.00
District of Columbia	3,470	78	Some	$0	$13.08/day (1 c.) $22.89/day (2 c.)	$23.55/day	117.75
Delaware	2,544	52	Some	1% of cost	80% of cost	$86.25/week	86.25
Florida	2,543	66	Some	$0.80/day	$11.20/day	$90/week	90.00
Georgia	2,034	46	Some	$0	$45/week	$80/week	80.00
Hawaii	3,678	85	None	0	20% of reimbursement rate ceiling	$425/month	98.15
Idaho	1,706	45	Some	7% of cost	100% of cost	$396/month	91.45
Illinois	2,328	50	All	$4.33 (1 c.) $8.67/month (2 c.)	$186.32 (1 c.) $320.64/month (2 c.)	$24.34/day	121.70
Indiana	1,615	37	None	$0	9% of gross income	$33/day	165.00
Iowa	1,780	41	None	$0	$12/day	$10.50/half-day	105.00
Kansas	2,353	59	Some	$0	$243/month	$3.12/hour	124.80

Table 10
(Continued)

State	Monthly income eligibility level ($)	Income eligibility as a percent of state median income (%)	Are families at or below poverty required to pay a fee?	Minimum fee (full-time rate)	Maximum family fee (full-time rate)	Reimbursement rate for pre-school age child[a,c]	Implied weekly reimbursement rate[b] ($)
Kentucky	1,908	50	Some	$0	$10.50 (1 c.) $11.50/day (2 + c.)	$20/day	100.00
Louisiana	2,596	75	Some	30% of cost of care	70% of cost	$15/day	75.00
Maine	3,343	85	Some	2% of gross income	10% of income	$150/week	150.00
Maryland	2,499	50	Some	$4/month + $4 per additional c.	$146/month + $116 each additional c.	$433/month	100.00
Massachusetts	2,414	50	None	$0	$120/week	$31.5/day	157.50
Michigan	1,990	41	Some	5% of reimbursement rate ceiling	30% of reimbursement rate ceiling	$2.25/hour	90.00
Minnesota	2,225	44	Some	$5/month	$741/month	$55/day	275.00
Mississippi	2,513	85	Some	$10.00 (1 c.) $20/month (2 c.)	$180 (1 c.) $190/month (2 c.)	$77/week	77.00
Missouri	1,482	35	Some	$1 per year	$4.00/day	$15.30/day	76.50
Montana	1,878	56	Some	$5	$263	$17.25/day	86.25
Nebraska	1,463	37	None	$10/month	$214/month (1 c.) $428/month (2 c.)	$21/day	105.00
Nevada	3,112	75	Some	0%	85% of child care benefit	$30/day	150.00
New Hampshire	2,407	48	Some	$0	$0.50/week	$24.40/day	122.00
New Jersey	3,179	58	Some	$0	$294.90/month + $221.20, 2nd c.	$121.40/week	121.40

Table 10
(Continued)

State	Monthly income eligibility level ($)	Income eligibility as a percent of state median income (%)	Are families at or below poverty required to pay a fee?	Minimum fee (full-time rate)	Maximum family fee (full-time rate)	Reimbursement rate for pre-school age child[a,c]	Implied weekly reimbursement rate[b] ($)
New Mexico	2,543	72	Some	$0	$205/month (1 c.) $307.50/month (2 c.)	$386.48/month	89.26
New York	2,543	56	Some	Varies by locality	Varies by locality	$45/day	225.00
North Carolina	2,946	75	Some	10% of gross income	10% of gross income	$477/month	110.20
North Dakota	2,463	64	Some	20% of reimbursement. rate ceiling, to a max of $42/month	80% of cost of care	$100/week	100.00
Ohio	1,272	28	Some	$1/month	$203/month	$113/week	113.00
Oklahoma	2,825	83	Some	0	$263/month	$13/day	65.00
Oregon	1,908	46	Some	$43/month	$399/month	$372/month	85.91
Pennsylvania	2,543	55	Some	$5.00	$70/week	$28/day	140.00
Puerto Rico	1,279	85	None	$5.00/month	$43/week	$243/month	56.12
Rhode Island	2,861	58	None	0	14% of gross income	$140/week	140.00
South Carolina	1,908	48	Some	$3/child/week	$11/child/week	$83/week	83.00
South Dakota	2,544	61	None	$10/month	15% of family income	$2.15/hour	86.00
Tennessee	2,355	60	Some	$1/week (1 c.) $2/week (2 c.)	$47/week (1 c.) $83/week (2 c.)	$90/week	90.00
Texas	3,368	85	Some	11% (1 c.) 13% (2 + c.) of gross monthly income	11% (1 c.) 13% (2 + c.) of gross monthly income	$20.09/day c.	100.45

Table 10
(Continued)

State	Monthly income eligibility level ($)	Income eligibility as a percent of state median income (%)	Are families at or below poverty required to pay a fee?	Minimum fee (full-time rate)	Maximum family fee (full-time rate)	Reimbursement rate for pre-school age child[a,c]	Implied weekly reimbursement rate[b] ($)
Utah	2.244	56	Some	$10/week (1 c.) $15/week (2 c.) $18/week (2 + c.)	$255/week (1 c.) $281/week (2 c.) $306/week (2 + c.)	$3/hour	120.00
Vermont	2.586	83	None	$0	90% of reimbursement rate ceiling	$20.81/day	104.05
Virginia	1.908	39	Some	10% of gross monthly income	10% of gross monthly income	$161/week	161.00
Washington	2.544	57	Some	$15/month	$50/month + 0.44* (family income – 137.5% of FPL)	$26.50/day	132.50
West Virginia	1.769	51	Some	$0	$5.75/child	$18/day	90.00
Wisconsin	2.353	51	Some	$4/week (1 c.)	$55/week (1 c.) $9/week (2 c.)	$5.50/hour	220.00
Wyoming	2.544	65	All	$0.40/day/child	$4.00/day/child	$2.43/hour	97.20

Source: National Child Care Information Center: nccic.org/pubs/stateplan/stateplan-intro.html.

Notes. FPL – federal poverty line; c. – "child" or "children".

[a] In most states reimbursement rates vary by location.

[b] Figures in the last column are calculated from figures in the next-to-last column, assuming 8 hours of care per day, 5 days per week, and 4 and 1/3 weeks per month.

[c] The rate for Texas is from an earlier year.

Table 11 summarizes federal and state expenditures on child care subsidies in recent years, and the numbers of children served by the subsidy programs. A rough figure for total expenditure on child care subsidies in Fiscal Year 1999 is $13 billion. A meaningful total for the number of children cannot be computed, because the DCTC lists only the number of families served, and data are not available for TXX. The CCDF is the biggest

Table 11
Federal and state expenditures and children served by major child care subsidy programs

	DCTC	EEPDCE	TXX-CC	CCDF
Federal + state expenditures (billions of current dollars)				
FY1999	2.675	0.995	0.285	9.132
FY1998	2.649	0.910		6.399
FY1997	2.464	0.862	0.370	4.369
FY1996	2.663	0.823	0.352	
FY1995	2.518	0.792	0.414	3.1
Children served (millions)				
FY1999	6.182			1.760
FY1998	6.120			1.515
FY1997	5.796			1.248
FY1996	6.003			
FY1995	5.964			1.445

Notes. See Table 9 for definition of the program acronyms. Expenditures are given in current dollars to facilitate checking with the original sources. To convert expenditures to 2001 dollars using the Consumer Price Index, multiply dollar figures for 1995–2000 by 1.162, 1.129, 1.103, 1.0865, 1.063 and 1.028, respectively.
Sources:
DCTC. Committee on Ways and Means (2000, p. 816), except 1999: Internal Revenue Service (2001). Figures in the lower panel are number of returns filed claiming the credit, not the number of children.
EEPDCE. Office of Management and Budget, Budget of the United States Government Fiscal Year 1997. These figures are for the calendar year. The method used to compute them is unclear, and in budget statements for subsequent years they are different. They are also different in the Joint Committee on Taxation, JCS-13-99. These are probably the least reliable figures in the table.
TXX-CC. Committee on Ways and Means (2000, pp. 600 and 634): 15% of $1.9 billion for 1999; 13% of $1.775 billion for 2000; Committee on Ways and Means (1998, pp. 714 and 720): 14.8% of $2.800, $2.381, $2.500 for FY1995, 1996, 1997.
CCDF. Expenditure: 1997–1999: We computed expenditure figures by summing all federal and state expenditures on the CCDF, either directly or through transfers to TANF, using data from the Annual TANF Reports to Congress (U.S. Department of Health and Human Services, various years) and reports from the U.S. Administration for Children and Families (various years). The latter source provides allocations to the CCDF for FY2000 and 2001, but there are no data available on transfers from TANF for these years. Transfers to TANF constituted about half of CCDF spending in FY1999. 1995: U.S. General Accounting Office (1998, p. 4): total funding for the four programs later consolidated in to the CCDF: AFDC-CC, TCC, ARCC, CCDBG. Children served: 1999: U.S. Administration for Children and Families (2000); 1998: U.S. Administration for Children and Families (2001); 1997: Adams, Schulman and Ebb (1998); 1995: U.S. Administration for Children and Families (1995).

program in terms of expenditure, at about \$9 billion. Much of the CCDF funding was transferred from TANF; the CCDF appropriation for 1999 was \$5.285 billion.[16]

Table 12 shows data on the incidence of child care subsidy receipt and characteristics of recipients in 1999, tabulated from the SIPP. The respondents who used nonparental

Table 12
Incidence of child care subsidy receipt and characteristics of recipients, 1999

A. Incidence		B. Characteristics of households with annual income < 25,000				
Annual household income (\$000)	Proportion with subsidy		Receives public assistance		Does not receive public assistance	
			Subsidy	No subsidy	Subsidy	No subsidy
All	0.021	Center	0.45	0.05	0.41	0.05
0–4.999	0.040	Nonrelative	0.44	0.10	0.33	0.11
5–9.999	0.053	Other nonparent	0.10	0.31	0.20	0.30
10–14.999	0.042	Pay for care	0.42	0.10	0.46	0.14
15–19.999	0.029	Cost/hour	2.55	1.76	2.81	3.07
20–24.999	0.033	Mother employed	0.61	0.28	0.79	0.49
25–29.999	0.025	Hours worked if > 0	39	33	37	37
30–34.999	0.029	Wage rate	6.62	6.58	6.71	7.1
35–39.999	0.013	Annual earnings if > 0	10,760	7,575	11,053	11,953
40+	0.009	Education > 12	0.45	0.18	0.52	0.32
Public assistance (PA) status		Married, spouse present	0.12	0.12	0.35	0.51
Receives PA	0.112	Other adults in household	0.09	0.28	0.17	0.21
Does not receive PA	0.022	Number kids < 5	1.09	0.72	0.84	0.68
		Black	0.34	0.40	0.28	0.21
		Hispanic	0.23	0.29	0.17	0.24
		White	0.43	0.25	0.52	0.50
Sample size	15,747		89	762	88	3,875

Source: Tabulations from the Survey of Income and Program Participation, Spring 1999.
Notes. Unit of analysis is a child. Figures are weighted by the child's sample weight. A child is coded as receiving a subsidy if the mother reports that a government agency helps pay for child care, or one of the child's arrangements is Head Start. Public assistance includes cash (Temporary Assistance for Needy Families, General Assistance, and Supplemental Security Income) and food stamps. Center care includes nursery, pre-school, and Head Start. Nonrelative care includes family day care homes, nannies, babysitters, and other nonrelatives except centers.

---

[16] Expenditure on other programs such as Head Start, Title I, and the Child Care Food Program are discussed below.

child care were asked if they received any assistance from a government agency in paying their child care expenses. Overall, only 2.1% of respondents reported receiving a subsidy. This seems quite low. It is likely that tax-based subsidies were not reported, and subsidies paid directly to child care providers may have been under-reported. The highest incidence of subsidy receipt by income, 5.3%, was reported by respondents with annual income of $5–10,000, and the incidence generally declines with income. Recipients of public assistance (TANF, Food Stamps, General Assistance) reported a subsidy receipt rate of 11.2%. Among households with income less than $25,000, subsidy recipients were much more likely to use center care than nonrecipients, and were more likely to pay some out-of-pocket expenses than nonrecipients. The maternal employment rate was much higher among recipients than nonrecipients, no doubt reflecting the fact that most child care subsidies require employment or employment-related activities such as education and training. On the other hand, average hours worked and wage rates conditional on employment are similar for recipients and nonrecipients. Subsidy recipients have higher education, a lower marriage rate (among nonrecipients of public assistance), fewer adults in the household other than the mother and father, and more young children than nonrecipients.

If we assume for the moment that all child care is of the same quality, and that the mother must purchase one hour of child care for every hour that she works, then we can use the simple model outlined in Section 3 to examine the effects of subsidized child care on maternal employment. A linear child care subsidy of s dollars per hour changes the budget constraint by raising the wage net of child care costs, and hence increases the probability that the mother works a positive number of hours. The effect on hours of work is ambiguous, given that there is both an income and a substitution effect. However, most subsidy programs are highly nonlinear. As Table 10 shows, most states structure CCDF subsidies so that they decline as income rises, up to some maximum level at which the family is no longer eligible. This is also true of TXX child care subsidies and the DCTC. This type of structure results in a "notch" in the budget constraint at the point when the subsidy drops to zero [Blau (2003a, p. 469)]. Like a linear subsidy, a nonlinear subsidy creates an incentive to work. But it is even more difficult to determine effects on hours of work given that women now have incentives to locate on particular portions of the budget constraint.

By making paid care relatively cheaper, a subsidy will increase the probability that the mother is employed and that paid care is used. But subsidies for paid child care will also have effects on the use of unpaid care. Some women who would have worked and used unpaid care will switch to paid care. Thus, a subsidy to paid care "crowds out" unpaid care. Moreover, a child care subsidy will have income effects on the purchases of all goods, so that the additional expenditures on child care will be less than the amount of the subsidy. However, even given these crowd out effects, Blau (2003a) shows that a child care subsidy is usually a less expensive way to increase labor supply than a wage subsidy. The intuition is that the wage subsidy provides benefits to all working mothers, including the many mothers who use unpaid care, while the child care subsidy provides benefits only to mothers who use paid care.

We can go one step further, by relaxing the assumption that all care is of the same quality, and assuming that higher-quality care costs more; that is, $p = \alpha + \beta q$, where q is child care quality, as in the model in Section 3. Most existing child care subsidies affect α but not β, because they are independent of quality. Others, such as the CCDF, can only be used in child care arrangements that satisfy state licensing standards or are legally exempt from such standards. These subsidies can be thought of as being subject to a quality threshold, but they are independent of quality once that threshold is crossed. Thus, they do not alter the marginal price of quality (ignoring general equilibrium effects). As discussed in Section 3, a subsidy that is independent of quality (which we can call an α-subsidy) has a bigger positive effect on employment than a quality specific or β-subsidy. On the other hand, a β-subsidy has a bigger effect on the quality of care that is chosen. Hence, there is a direct policy tradeoff between those subsidy policies that are most effective in supporting maternal employment and those that are most effective in improving child care quality.

In the remainder of this section we describe evidence on how child care subsidies affect maternal employment and child care quality. The evidence discussed is from two types of studies: evaluations of experimental demonstration projects and evaluations of actual child care subsidy programs. Note also that the literature reviewed above on the effect of the price of child care on employment is relevant as well. One of the motivations for that literature is to infer how child care price subsidies would affect employment decisions. Whether inferences about the effects of subsidies drawn from this literature are useful depends on several factors. If there are substantial costs to taking up a subsidy, either in the form of time costs required to negotiate the subsidy bureaucracy or psychic costs ("stigma") of participating in a means-tested program, then price effects on employment may not be a reliable guide to subsidy effects. Also, the price effects estimated in this literature are generally assumed to be linear, while most subsidies are nonlinear. Nonlinearity of a subsidy does not affect the qualitative result that a child care price subsidy increases the incentive to be employed, but it could affect the magnitude of the employment effect. Thus estimates of linear price effects could be an unreliable guide to the effects of typical nonlinear subsidies.

Several demonstration programs designed to help low-income families achieve economic independence included child care subsidies along with other benefits and services. These programs were evaluated using randomized assignment methods, so the average effects of the programs on outcomes of interest are estimated without bias by simple comparisons of treatment and control group averages. However, in each case the child care subsidy was only one of several services provided as part of the program, so it is not possible to determine how much of the program impacts were due to the child care subsidy.[17] We discuss one example of a demonstration program in order to illustrate the nature of the evidence from such programs.

---

[17] A 1989 randomized experiment in Mecklenberg County, North Carolina offered a treatment group of 300 AFDC mothers guaranteed access to subsidized child care for up to one year within two weeks of taking a full-time job, while a control group of 302 AFDC mothers had access to subsidized child care only through a long

New Hope was a program intended to reduce poverty among the low-income population in Milwaukee [Bos et al. (1999)]. It operated from 1994 through 1998 with broad eligibility rules that made virtually anyone with low income eligible to enroll, regardless of employment and family status. The program was voluntary and provided an earnings supplement, affordable health insurance, a child care subsidy, and a full-time community service job if no other employment was available. The program required full-time employment (30 hours per week) and provided benefits for up to three years. Participants made their own child care arrangements and were reimbursed for most of the expenses, with a co-payment that increased with family income. 39% of participants with children used child care at an average subsidy of $2,376 over two years. An early evaluation based on two years of data from the program found that among individuals who were not employed at entry to the program, participation in the program increased employment by seven percentage points, boosted earnings by about $700 per year (13%), raised income by 12%, and had no impact on welfare participation. The program had no statistically significant effects on employment and earnings for those who were employed for at least 30 hours per week at entry, although the sample size was small (the point estimate of the earnings impact was −$571 per year), but reduced AFDC and Food Stamp participation by 7–10% in year two. The program increased use of formal child care by 7.4% for boys and 12.5% for girls, and resulted in improved academic performance, study skills, social competence, and behavior among boys but not girls.[18]

Turning now to studies that examine the effect of child care subsidies more directly, we discuss four studies that have estimated the impact of actual child care subsidies on employment. The studies are summarized in Table 13. In each of these studies the subsidy recipients are self-selected, and the studies recognize and attempt to deal with the possibility of selectivity bias.

Two of these studies evaluate means-tested state subsidies for low-income families funded by Federal programs prior to the 1996 welfare reform [Berger and Black (1992),

---

waiting list with an average wait of 6–10 months. However, the offer was made by mail with no telephone or personal contacts, and the take up rate was very low: only 1/6 of the treatment group applied for and received a subsidy. The treatment had no significant impact on welfare participation or expenditure. See Bowen and Neenan (1993) for details.

[18] Other demonstrations and experiments that included child care subsidies were the Teenage Parent Demonstration [Kisker, Rangarajan and Boller (1998)], New Chance [Quint, Bos and Polit (1997)], GAIN in California [Riccio, Friedlander and Freedman (1994)], the National Evaluation of Welfare-to-Work Strategies, formerly known as the JOBS program [Hamilton et al. (1997)], the Minnesota Family Investment Program [Miller et al. (1997)], the Florida Family Transition Program [Bloom et al. (1999)], and the Gary, Seattle, and Denver Income Maintenance Experiments. The GAIN demonstration excluded children under age 6. Granger and Cytron (1999) report that the effects of the Teenage Parent Demonstration and New Chance (which was also targeted at teenage mothers) on use of center-based child care were smaller than in New Hope and often statistically insignificant. Robins and Spiegelman (1978) estimate that eligibility for a SIME-DIME child care subsidy increased use of market child care by 18 percentage points in Seattle and 14 percentage points in Denver. Results for child care use in the other demonstrations are not available. See Hamilton, Freedman and McGroder (2000) for a summary of the effects of all of the recent demonstration programs.

Table 13
Studies of the effect of child care subsidies on employment

Study	Data	Population	Subsidy	Method	Identification	Effect of subsidy receipt on employment
Berger and Black (1992)	Survey of single mothers in Kentucky; Current Population Survey (CPS), May 1988	Single, child mean age 3.6	Title XX centers only	Probit for employment before and after subsidy receipt/waitlist	Before–after subsidy/waitlist comparison	8.4–25.3 percentage point increase, depending on whether "waitlist effect" is included
Blau and Tekin (2006)	National Survey of American Families (NSAF), 1999	Single, child age < 13	Assistance with child care expenses from government agency	Two stage least squares linear probability model (LPM)	County dummies	33 percentage point increase
Gelbach (2002)	1980 U.S. Census	Single, youngest child age 5	Kindergarten	2SLS LPM	Eligibility for Kindergarten (quarter of birth dummies)	4–5 percentage point increase for both single and married mothers
Meyers, Heintze and Wolf (2002)	Survey of California Aid to Families with Dependent Children (AFDC) recipients in 4 counties, 1995	Single, child age < 14	Assistance with child care expenses from govt. agency under several subsidy programs	Probits for nonparental child care use and subsidy receipt. Predicted value included in probit for employment	Knowledge of child care subsidy system excluded from employment probit	Increase in probability of subsidy receipt from 0.0 to 0.5: 52 percentage point increase

Meyers, Heintze and Wolf (2002)]. Berger and Black compare the employment of mothers with subsidies to those on a wait list and find that subsidies increase employment by 8.4–25.3 percentage points depending on the assumptions made about unobservables in the model. Meyers, Heintze and Wolf use the mother's knowledge of subsidy programs to identify the effects of child care subsidies on employment. They find much larger effects of subsidies – on the order of 52 percentage points increase – but the lack of a convincing comparison group weakens their results.

A third study by Gelbach (2002) evaluates the labor supply effects of the implicit child care subsidy provided by free Kindergarten for five year old children in public school. To identify the effect of the subsidy, Gelbach exploits variation in quarter of birth of children and the fact that all states impose a date-of-birth requirement for entry to Kindergarten. His instrumental variable estimates indicate that access to free public school increased the employment probability of single mothers whose youngest child was age five by five percentage points at the interview date and by four percentage points during calendar year 1979. Gelbach's approach is creative and provides credible evidence of the impact of a child care subsidy on employment of mothers whose youngest child is five years old. However, it is unclear whether his results can be generalized to children younger than five.

The fourth study evaluates the impact of subsidies in the post-PRWORA era, using data from the 1999 National Survey of America's Families. Blau and Tekin (2006) identify the employment effect of subsidy receipt using county-level dummies as instruments for subsidy receipt. Two stage least squares (2SLS) estimates show an effect of 33 percentage points on employment, a result that is significantly different from zero. The identification strategy may be problematic if, after controlling for 21 county characteristics, county-level differences in subsidy receipt are not exogenous. Moreover, as in the Meyers, Heintze and Wolf study, there is no natural comparison or control group.

These results indicate that there are at least some positive effects of subsidies on employment. But it is also interesting to note that there is a low rate of take-up of child care subsidies. Meyers and Heintze (1999) asked mothers why they did not receive subsidies from the programs for which they appeared to be eligible, and the majority response for every type of subsidy program was that they were not aware of the program. The acceptance rate for mothers who applied averaged 72% across all programs. Similarly, Fuller et al. (1999) estimate a model of child care subsidy take-up for TANF mothers using data from San Francisco, San Jose, and Tampa in 1998. Of the women using any nonmaternal child care, only 37–44 percent received a subsidy.

4.3. Regulations

In addition to providing price subsidies, the government intervenes in the child care market by imposing regulations on providers. As with many other consumer products and services, the goal of these regulations is to reduce the risk of harm to children. Potential risks include harm from injury as well as from disease and developmental impairment [Morgan and Azer (1997)]. Regulations stipulate such things as the educational requirements for child care providers, the maximum number of children per child care staff member, and the frequency with which facilities are inspected.

Three aspects of regulations are important. First, they are determined by state governments, not the federal government. The federal government can impose standards that child care providers must meet in order to be eligible for federal subsidies, but the federal government is not authorized to regulate child care.[19] Child care regulations therefore differ across states, sometimes substantially. Second, child care regulations impose minimum standards but do not define or attempt to enforce "optimal" standards, such as those specified by the National Association for the Education of Young Children [Morgan and Azer (1997)]. Thus it is possible for a child care provider to comply with all state regulations but nevertheless receive a low score on quality rating scales. Third, regulations differ for day care centers and family day care homes, and in most states some providers are legally exempt from regulation. For example, many states exempt day care centers affiliated with a church or family day care homes that provide care for only a few children. This means that such providers are not required to register or obtain a license, though they must comply with some health and safety standards.

Table 14 summarizes a few of the many child care regulations by state. The regulations are typically very detailed. For example, in most states the maximum group size (GS) and child–staff ratio (CSR) standards differ by single year of child age, and staff training requirements differ by type of position. The regulations shown in the table are a small excerpt from the regulatory structure of each state, but comparisons across states on the basis of the examples shown in the table are a reasonable guide to the overall relative standards of different states. The maximum allowable CSR for infants younger than one year old in day care centers ranges from 3:1 in Kansas and Maryland to 6:1 in five states. Maximum group size for infants ranges from 8 to 20, and is not regulated at all in 11 states. The maximum allowable CSR for four-year old children in centers ranges from 10:1 in 17 states to 20:1 in 2 states, and the maximum group size for four year olds ranges from 20 to 36. Thirty six states have no pre-service child care experience or early education/training requirement for teachers in day care centers. In these states it is legal to employ a teacher with no education, training, or experience in child care or early education. Many of these states do impose a nonchild-care-specific education requirement such as a high school diploma, and some require in-service training. In the other states, pre-service requirements range from eight clock hours of training in early childhood education in Texas, to Rhode Island's requirements of a Bachelor's degree in any field, 24 credits in early childhood education, and six credits in student teaching. The most common requirement is a Child Development Associate credential, which can be

---

[19] Federal Interagency Day Care Requirements (FIDCR) were developed in the 1960s to standardize the requirements for receiving federal funding for child care services. These requirements were eliminated in 1981. Head Start imposes uniform federal standards that providers must meet in order to qualify for funding, and Title IA also uses the Head Start standards. Hayes, Palmer and Zaslow (1990, Appendix B) describe the FIDCR. Head Start program standards are listed at http://www2.acf.dhhs.gov/programs/hsb/regs/regs/rg_index.htm.

Table 14
Selected state child care regulations, 2004

State	Day care centers					Family day care homes	
	Infants		Four-year-olds		Pre-service education, experience, and training requirement for teachers	Number of annual inspections	Minimum size for licensing
	CSR	GS	CSR	GS			
AL	4	10	16	20		1	1
AK	5	10	10	20		1	5
AZ	5		15			1	1
AR	6	12	15	30		2	6
CA	4		12		16 semester hours ECE or child development	a	2
CO	5	10	12	24		0.5	2
CT	4	8	10	20		0.5	1
DE	4		15		Vocational c.c. program and 6 months experience	1	1
DC	4	8	10	20	CDA and experience	1	1
FL	4		20			2	2
GA	6	12	18	36		0.5	3
HI	4	8	16		CDA or certificate in ECE; 1 year experience	2	3
ID	6		12			0.5	7
IL	4	12	10	20	CDA or CCP	1	4
IN	4	8	12	24		1	6
IA	4		12			1	6
KS	3	9	12	24	CDA	1	1
KY	5	10	14	28		1	4
LA	5		15			1	
ME	4	8	10	30		NA	3
MD	3	6	10	20	90 clock hours in ECE and 1 year experience	0.5	1
MA	3.5	7	10	20	2 year vocational c.c. course	1	1
MI	4		12			1	1
MN	4	8	10	20	CDA and 1,560 hours experience	0.5	2
MS	5	10	16	16		1	6
MO	4	8	10			2	5
MT	4		10			1	3
NE	4	12	12			1	4
NV	4		13			2	5
NH	4	12	12	24	2 year vocational c.c. course	1	4
NJ	4	20	12	20	CDA or CCP and 1 year experience	1	
NM	6		12			1	5
NY	4	8	8	21		0.5	3
NC	5	10	20	25		1	3
ND	4	8	10	20		1	4
OH	5	12	14	28		2	7
OK	4	8	15	30		2	1

Table 14
(*Continued*)

State	Day care centers					Family day care homes	
	Infants		Four-year-olds		Pre-service education, experience, and training requirement for teachers	Number of annual inspections	Minimum size for licensing
	CSR	GS	CSR	GS			
OR	4	8	10	20		2	4
PA	4	8	10	20		1	4
RI	4	8	10	20	Bachelor's degree plus 24 credits in ECE plus 6 credits student teaching	2	4
SC	6		18			2	2
SD	5	20	10	20		1	13
TN	4	8	13	20		2	5
TX	4	10	18	35	8 hours ECE training	1	4
UT	4	8	15	30		1	5
VT	4	8	10	20	CDA	2	3
VA	4		12			2	6
WA	4	8	10	20		1	1
WV	4	8	12	24		1	4
WI	4	8	13	24	2 courses in ECE and 80 days experience	2	4
WY	4	10	12	30		2	3

Sources: National Child Care Information Center (http://nccic.org); U.S. General Accounting Office (2004).
Notes. Blank cell indicates no regulation. c.c. – child care. ECE – Early Childhood Education. CDA – Child Development Associate Credential awarded by the Council for Professional Recognition. CCP – Certified Child Care Professional Credential awarded by the National Child Care Association. GS – Group Size. CSR – Child Staff Ratio. NA indicates the information is not available.
[a]California reports that it does not inspect child care facilities on a regular basis.

obtained through a one year training program or through certified on-the-job experience (http://www.cdacouncil.org).

States inspect child care providers and give them information on how to comply with regulations. Table 14 includes a summary measure of state enforcement: the average annual number of inspections per day care center. This varies from a low of 0.5 (every other year) to 2.0 (two pear year).

The last column of Table 14 shows the minimum number of children in a family day care home for which a license is required. Eleven states require all family day care homes to be licensed or registered, while 13 states exempt those caring for fewer than five children.

An important question is whether child care regulations have any effect on the well-being of children. In principle, imposing more stringent minimum standards on child care arrangements should improve child well-being. But this conclusion presumes that: (1) the standards are binding on the existing practices in child care settings; (2) regulations are enforced; and (3) parents do not "avoid" the regulations by the child care arrangements they choose. Whether or not the regulations are circumvented will depend in part on how costly they are to implement and enforce. To the extent that higher-quality and safer child care arrangements are costly to produce, binding child care regulations are likely to increase the price of child care, causing some parents to be "priced out" of regulated care. As a result of this "crowd-out" effect, it is unclear whether imposing more stringent standards on regulated child care will actually increase the quality of care to which children are exposed on average.

Table 15 summarizes the literature about crowd-out in child care markets. Using data from a national sample of child care centers, Chipty and Witte (1997) find that a lower required child–staff ratio for pre-school children reduces the probability that child care centers care for pre-school rather than school age children, and vice versa.[20] Blau (2003b) uses data from the SIPP and considers a more comprehensive set of child care regulations. He finds that child care regulation affects the type of child care that is chosen (though he finds no impact on child care expenditures or hours in care). Currie and Hotz (2004) use data from the NLSY and find that tougher child care regulations are associated with lower probabilities of using regulated child care services. However, Currie and Hotz also show that regulating the education of care givers improves the safety of children at these centers. Evidence from some household surveys indicates that stricter child–staff ratio and training regulations are associated with lower rates of use of nonparental child care and lower hours of care per week among users [Hotz and Kilburn (1997), Hofferth and Chaplin (1998)]. However, Ribar (1992) finds no impact of a stricter child–staff ratio on hours of child care used, and Chipty (1995) finds mixed results on the effects of regulations on use of child care.

Evidence on the effects of child care regulations on labor force participation of mothers shows small negative effects, often insignificantly different from zero [Hotz and Kilburn (1997), Blau (1993), Ribar (1992)]. Hotz and Kilburn (1997) and Hofferth and Chaplin (1998) find that tougher regulations are associated with higher family expenditure per hour of child care among families paying for care. Chipty (1995) finds that a stricter group size regulation in both family day care and centers raises family expenditure per hour in both settings, but a stricter child–staff ratio regulation reduces expenditure in both settings. Imposing a training requirement in a given sector is associated with lower family expenditure in that sector.

As discussed above, parents may be uncertain about the quality of care their children will receive from a particular child care provider. For example, parents may not know exactly how attentive a provider is to their child or how safe a particular setting is. Informational deficiencies among consumers with respect to quality are a common concern in markets for many goods and services and the potential for adverse selection in such markets is well known. Imposing minimum quality standards, via regulation, represents

---

[20] See also Fuller et al. (1993), Gormley (1991), Lowenberg and Tinnin (1992), Queralt and Witte (1997) and Rose-Ackerman (1983).

Table 15

Studies on the effect of regulations on child care use

Author	Data	Design	Sample size	Outcomes
Chipty and Witte (1997)	1990 Profile of Child Care Setting (PCS)	PCS data merged to 1990 Census and state and local regulations. Random effect probit estimation to account for unobserved market specific heterogeneity	945 market-oriented centers	Lower required child–staff ratios for pre-school children reduce the probability that child care centers care for pre-school children rather than school age children, and vice versa
Blau (2003b)	Survey of Income and Program Participation (SIPP) and Current Population Survey (CPS)	Data from SIPP merged to state-level data on child care regulation. Estimates include state fixed effects	17,370 families with at least one pre-school age child	Child care regulations are associated with lower probabilities of using regulated child care services, although no impact on price or quality of care was found
Currie and Hotz (2004)	National Longitudinal Survey of Youth (NLSY)	NLSY data merged to state-level data on child care regulations. Multinomial logit estimation of choice of child care on state child care regulations	44,369 quarters of child life, from 3,394 mothers and 6,290 children	Regulations are associated with lower probabilities of using regulated child care services. Regulating education of caregivers improves child safety
Hotz and Kilburn (1997)	National Longitudinal Survey of the High School Class of 1972 (NLS72)	NLS72 data merged to state-level data on child care regulations		Stricter child:staff ratio and training regulations are associated with lower rates of use of nonparental child care and lower hours of care per week among users. Effects of child care regulations on labor force participation of mothers shows small negative effects, often insignificantly different from zero Tougher regulations are associated with higher family expenditure per hour of child care among families paying for care

Table 15
(*Continued*)

Author	Data	Design	Sample size	Outcomes
Hofferth and Chaplin (1998)	1990 National Child Care Survey (NCCS)	NCSS data merged to data on county and state level demographics and regulatory requirements	1,206 children under 6 whose mothers are working, in training or in school	Stricter child:staff ratio and training regulations are associated with lower rates of use of nonparental child care and lower hours of care per week among users. Tougher regulations are associated with higher family expenditure per hour of child care among families paying for care
Ribar (1992)	Survey of Income and Program Participation (SIPP)	SIPP data merged to data on state-level regulations	3,738 married families with at least one child under the age of 15	No impact of a stricter child–staff ratio on hours of child care used
Chipty (1995)	1990 National Child Care Survey (NCCS)	NCSS data merged to data on county-level demographics and state-level regulatory requirements. OLS estimation of reduced forms on equilibrium price, hours and staff–child ratio for family day care and day care centers	Family day care: 67 day care centers: n.a.	Mixed results on the effects of regulations on use of child care. Stricter group size regulation in both family day care and centers raises family expenditure per hour in both settings, but a stricter child–staff ratio regulation reduces expenditure in both settings. Imposing a training requirement in a given sector is associated with lower family expenditure in that sector
Blau (1993)	Current Population Survey (CPS), March Public Use Tape for 1977–1987	CPS data merged to data on state and federal child care subsidy parameters and regulations	15,195 women between the ages of 18 and 64, consisting of 4,305 child care workers, 7,180 other workers and 3,710 nonworkers	Effects of child care regulations on labor force participation of mothers shows small negative effects, often insignificantly different from zero

one mechanism for solving the informational problems faced by consumers.[21] For example, Klein and Leffler (1981) argue that the maintenance of licensure systems that impose minimum quality standards on service providers may have beneficial welfare effects in markets for goods and services in which product quality is difficult to monitor. Imposing standards in such markets can "assure" consumers of the quality of the goods and services they receive to the extent that a provider's investment in meeting such standards either generates a higher stream of earnings or results in higher costs (fines) to the provider if these minimum standards are violated.

Regulations may change the production function for child quality, making it easier to avoid unintentional injury with a given level of parental effort. As a result, such regulations may increase both the actual quality of care in the regulated sector and the amount that parents are willing to pay for it. Chipty and Witte (1997) find, using individual-level data from the National Child Care Survey, that increasing the number of mandatory inspections increases both the price of child care and the number of hours that children spend in care. This finding is consistent with the idea that minimum quality standards may encourage consumers to purchase more child care.

On the other hand, Blau (in press) finds that a substantial portion of day care centers fail to comply with regulations, which limits the usefulness of regulation as a means of providing quality assurance. The weak association between those structural aspects of quality that can be regulated, such as staff–pupil ratios and more global measures of quality suggest that it would be very difficult to substantially increase the quality of child care centers through regulation alone. For example, the estimates presented in Mocan et al. (1995) suggest that to increase the quality of a child care center from average to good through reductions in staff–pupil ratios would require a reduction in staff–pupil ratios from 5.4 children per staff member to 1.6.

Thus, it may be unrealistic to expect regulation to do much more than to weed out centers with unacceptably low levels of quality. There is evidence from the Head Start program that detailed government oversight of observable aspects of quality can eliminate poor quality programs. Head Start centers have consistently been found to be of higher quality on average than other pre-school programs [Resnick and Zill (undated)], because in contrast to the private child care market, there are few very low-quality Head Start programs.[22]

An interesting alternative approach to the regulation of child care quality would be to encourage the use of credentialing services, as suggested by Shapiro's (1986) model.

---

[21] Also see Leland (1979) for more on the role of licensing and imposing minimum quality standards in markets for goods and services with hard-to-monitor quality attributes. See Lowenberg and Tinnin (1992), Chipty and Witte (1997) and Hotz and Kilburn (1997, 2000) for more on the application of such arguments to the market for child care services.

[22] However, the quality of Head Start should not be regarded as uniform, either. Zigler and Styfco (1994) argue that funds are insufficient to allow for proper enforcement of Head Start program standards, which may be one reason for the variation in quality. Still, it is interesting that the sheer existence of these standards, even with little enforcement, seems to be associated with a minimum level of quality higher than the minimum observed in the private sector.

Xiao (2004) studies a voluntary quality certification mechanism for child care centers. She presents evidence that relatively few child care centers bother to get certification although it is inexpensive to do so. She argues that certification conveys information to parents, but most parents have already gleaned the same information from other sources. Hence, certification has little effect on demand for child care centers, which explains why few centers obtain the certification.

In summary, regulating the child care market by imposing minimum standards on some segments of the market can be a two-edged sword. While children in child care settings subject to binding regulation may receive higher-quality care, regulation is also likely to drive some children out of the regulated sector. Thus, the overall effect of regulation is ambiguous, with the potential crowd out effect balanced against the quality assurance effect. Estimating the magnitudes of these separate effects is difficult, requiring the imposition of considerable structure on the parental child care choice process and child quality production functions in order to separately identify these effects. The utility of regulation is also limited by failure to comply and by the fact that only the most obvious (and not necessarily most important) aspects of quality can be regulated.

5. Publicly provided child care

As discussed above, most child care subsidy programs do not attempt to influence the quality of care, and regulatory policy must balance potential crowd out with quality assurance. In contrast, publicly provided care is usually explicitly intended to improve the quality of care that children receive in order to enhance their development. This section provides an overview of the literature on early intervention, and of the emerging literature on after school programs.

5.1. Model early intervention programs

A recent National Research Council and Institutes of Medicine (2000) report on early childhood education and intervention divides skill development into three areas: cognitive skills, school readiness, and social and emotional development. Until very recently, the economics literature on this topic has focused primarily on the development of cognitive skills as measured by test scores, and especially on IQ. The gains in test scores associated with early intervention are often short lived, which has cast doubt on the effectiveness of these programs. However, there is increasing evidence that the absence of obvious behavior problems and the development of skills such as self-control may be at least as important to future success in life as formal cognitive skills [Lee et al. (1990), Heckman (2000), Heckman, Hsse and Rubinstein (2000)]. Noncognitive attributes – even in a form as basic as the ability to sit still and pay attention – may even be necessary for the full development of formal cognitive skills. Thus, the focus in the early intervention literature has recently shifted toward trying to measure outcomes such as success in school (i.e., reductions in remedial education placements and grade repetition) and the earnings of children who participated in early intervention programs.

The excellent literature reviews of early childhood education programs in Barnett (1995) and Karoly et al. (1998) list 16 studies of model programs. Table 16 shows the results of the seven such studies that followed a randomized methodology. These programs were typically funded at higher levels and run by more highly trained staff than large-scale, publicly-funded programs. The sample sizes for treatment and control groups in these model studies are small, often less than 100 children. However, evidence from these studies can be used to shed light on the issue of whether it is possible to use early intervention to improve child outcomes. In a randomized trial, children are randomly assigned to treatment and control groups. The importance of random assignment is that researchers can be reasonably certain that there are no pre-existing, unobserved, and uncontrolled differences between the treatments and controls on average. In contrast, when comparison groups are created by some method other than random assignment, one can never be certain that the differences between the treatments and controls reflect the effects of the experimental intervention rather than the effects of some other unobserved difference between the groups. However, even in a randomized trial, problems can arise: Some of the more serious problems mentioned in Heckman and Smith (1995) include differential attrition from treatment and control groups, the fact that people randomized to the control group may seek "treatment" outside the experiment, and the fact that it is often difficult to generalize the results of experiments to differing settings.

For example, the Institute for Developmental Studies program summarized in Table 16 [Deutsch et al. (1983)] started with 503 participants but was able to conduct long-term follow-up at grade 7 on only 97 of them. The 97 who were followed may not be very representative of the initial sample since they are likely to be from more stable families. Unless attrition is random, it is difficult to draw any inferences about the long-term outcomes of the whole group from this small subset. Four studies from Table 16 stand out because they used random assignment, are relatively free of attrition, and follow children at least into middle school. They are the Early Training Project, the Carolina Abecedarian Project, the Perry Pre-School Project, and the Milwaukee Project. (The Infant Health and Development Project also used a randomized design and had low attrition, but followed children only to age 8. A long-term followup is currently in the field.[23])

The first conclusion that can be drawn from these studies was alluded to above: Only the Milwaukee Project found any long-term effect on IQ. However, the Early Training, Carolina Abecedarian, and Perry Pre-School Projects all found positive effects on measures of scholastic success, which strongly suggests that boosting IQ is not the only way to affect this important outcome.

---

[23] The IHDP data has been extensively analyzed. In addition to the positive effects on IQ and other outcomes at age 8, analysts have shown using propensity score analysis that the largest effects were for the children who would otherwise have been least likely to have been in center based care [Hill, Waldfogel and Brooks-Gunn (2002)], and that the largest effects were for children of the least educated mothers.

Table 16
Model early childhood programs with randomized designs[a]

Program name[b]	Program description	Age of participation	Sample size[c]	Outcomes[d]
Carolina Abecedarian [Campbell and Ramey (1994), Campbell et al. (2002)]	Pre-schoolers: full-day child care; School age: parent program	Entry 6 weeks to 3 months; Exit: 5–8 years	Initial: $T = 57$, $C = 54$; Age 8: $T = 48$, $C = 42$; Age 15: $T = 48$, $C = 44$; Age 21: $T = 53$, $C = 51$	IQ: $T > C$ at age 12, $T = C$ at age 15; Achievement tests: $T > C$ at ages 8, 15, 21; Special education: $T < C$ at age 15; Grade retention: $T < C$ at age 15; School dropout: $T < C$ at age 21; College attendance: $T > C$ at age 21; Employment status: $T = C$ at age 21; Average age first child born: $T > C$ at age 21
Houston Parent Child Development Center [Johnson and Walker (1991)][e]	Home visits; Full-day child care; Center-based program for parents	Entry: 1–3 years; Exit: 3–5 years	Initial: $T = 97$, $C = 119$; Grades 2–5: $T = 50$, $C = 87$	Achievement tests: $T = C$; Grades: $T = C$; Bilingual education: $T < C$; Special education: $T = C$; Grade retention: $T = C$
Infant Health and Development Project [McCarton et al. (1997)[f], Hill, Waldfogel and Brooks-Gunn (2002)]	Home visits; Full-day child care	Entry: birth (home visits); 1 year (care); Exit: 3 years	Initial: $T = 377$, $C = 608$; Age 8: $T = 336$, $C = 538$	IQ: $T > C$ ages 3, 5, 8; Behavioral problems: $T < C$, at ages 3, 5; $T = C$ at age 8; Math achievement: $T > C$ at age 8; Grade retention: $T = C$ at age 8; Special education: $T = C$ at age 8; General health: $T = C$ at age 8
Milwaukee Project [Garber (1988)]	Full-day child care; Job and academic training for mothers	Entry: 3–6 months; Exit: 5 years	Initial: $T = 20$, $C = 20$; Grade 4, 8: $T = 17$, $C = 18$	IQ: $T > C$, grade 8; Achievement tests: $T = C$; Grades: $T = C$; Special education: $T = C$; Grade retention: $T = C$
Early Training Project [Gray, Ramsey and Klaus (1983)]	Home visits; Summer part-day pre-school program	Entry: 4–5 years; Exit: 6 years	Initial: $T = 44$, $C = 21$; Post-high school: $T = 36$, $C = 16$	IQ: $T = C$ at age 17; Achievement tests: $T = C$; Special education: $T < C$, grade 12; Grade retention: $T = C$; High school graduation: $T = C$

Table 16
(*Continued*)

Program name[b]	Program description	Age of participation	Sample size[c]	Outcomes[d]
High/Scope Perry Pre-School Project [Schweinhart, Barnes and Weikart (1993)][f]	Home visits Pre-school program	Entry: 3–4 years Exit: 5 years	Initial: $T = 58$, $C = 65$ Age 27: $T = 58$, $C = 63$	IQ: $T > C$ at ages 5, 7; $T = C$ at ages 8, 14 Achievement tests: $T > C$ at ages 9, 14 High school GPA: $T > C$ Special education: $T = C$, grade 12 Grade retention: $T = C$, grade 12 High school graduation: $T > C$ Post-secondary education: $T = C$ at age 27 Arrests: $T < C$ at age 27 Employment: $T > C$ at age 19, $T = C$ at age 27 Monthly earnings: $T > C$ at age 27 Receive public assistance: $T < C$ at age 27 Teen pregnancies: $T = C$ at age 19
Institute for Developmental Studies [Deutsch et al. (1983)]	Home visits Part-day pre-school program Parent center school (K-3)	Entry: 4 years Exit: 9 years	Initial: $T = 312$, $C = 191$ Grade 7: $T = 63$, $C = 34$	Special education: $T = C$ Grade retention: $T = C$

[a] See Barnett (1995) and Karoly et al. (1998) for more detailed information about studies described in this table.

[b] Programs are grouped such that those enrolling children younger than three years old appear first, followed by those enrolling children after age three.

[c] Throughout the table, 'T' refers to treatment group and 'C' refers to control or comparison group.

[d] Outcomes listed as $T > C$ or $C > T$ were statistically significant at the 5% level.

[e] Most recent published document. See Barnett (1995) for description of other studies.

[f] See Karoly et al. (1998) for description of earlier studies.

The Early Training Project was the least intensive intervention of this group. It served four- and five-year-olds, and involved weekly home visits during the year in addition to a ten-week part-day pre-school for either two or three summers. It showed dramatic reductions in use of special education by age 12: 5 percent of the treatment group compared to 29 percent of the controls. Although there were no statistically significant differences between treatments and controls in achievement test scores, grade retention, or high school graduation, differences in the latter two outcomes were in the right direction. For example, 68 percent of the treatment group graduated compared to only 52 percent of the controls. The lack of statistical significance is likely to be due to the small sample size: 44 treatments and 21 controls.

The Carolina Abecedarian Project involved a somewhat larger group of 57 treatments and 54 controls. At birth, children were randomized into a treatment group that received enriched center-based child care services emphasizing language development for eight hours per day, five days a week, 50 weeks per year, from birth to age five, and a control group that did not receive these services. The teacher–student ratio ranged from 1:3 to 1:6 depending on the child's age. At school entry, the children were again randomized into two groups. One received no further intervention, and the other had a "Home–School Resource Teacher" who provided additional instruction, a liaison between parents and school, and served as a community resource person for the family [Campbell and Ramey (1994, 1995)].

At age 15, the Carolina Abecedarian Project found that the children who had received the pre-school intervention had higher scores on achievement tests (especially reading) and reductions in the incidence of grade retention and special education, regardless of whether or not they had been assigned a Home–School Resource Teacher once they entered school. Retention in grade and being placed in the special education "track" are viewed by educators as predictors of dropping out of school. They also create additional costs to society that must be weighed against the costs of providing the early intervention. In contrast, the effects of the Home–School Resource Teacher were generally either small or statistically insignificant. The investigators have now completed a follow-up assessment of the Abecedarian children at age 21.[24] Of the original 111 infants, 104 were assessed. At age 21, the children who received the pre-school intervention had higher average tests scores and were twice as likely to still be in school or to have ever attended a four-year college.

A recent cost benefit analysis based on follow-ups through age 21 suggested that each dollar spent on Abecedarian saved tax payers four dollars [Barnett and Masse (in press)]. Both the study children and their mothers had higher earnings, and costs for special education and health care were reduced in the treatment group relative to the controls.

The most famous of these interventions is the Perry Pre-School Project, which involved 58 children in the treatment group and 65 controls. The intervention involved

---

[24] The following discussion is taken from the Executive Summary of the Carolina Abecedarian Project which is available at http://www.fpg.unc.edu/verity.

a half-day pre-school every weekday plus a weekly 90 minute home visit for eight months of the year, for two years. Teacher–student ratios were 1:6, and all teachers had a Masters degree and training in child development [Schweinhart, Barnes and Weikart (1993)]. The intervention had positive effects on achievement test scores, grades, high school graduation rates, and earnings, as well as negative effects on crime rates and welfare use (as of age 27). It is estimated that each dollar spent on this program saved up to seven dollars in social costs [see Karoly et al. (1998) for a more detailed discussion].

Studies of model early intervention programs do not show universally positive results. In particular, studies with nonrandomized designs frequently find insignificant or even wrong-signed effects. However, well-designed studies of intensive educational interventions show that it is possible for intervention to make a positive difference in children's lives.

5.2. Head Start

There is a large gap between the model programs for early childhood education and the large-scale publicly funded interventions that are currently in place. The largest and best known public program is Head Start, a pre-school program for disadvantaged children which aims to improve their skills so that they can begin schooling on an equal footing with their more advantaged peers. Begun in 1965 as part of President Johnson's "War on Poverty", Head Start now serves almost 800,000 children in predominantly part-day programs, about 60% of eligible 3 and 4 year old poor children [U.S. Administration for Children, Youth and Families (1999)]. Over time, federal funding has increased from $96 million in 1965 to $6.2 billion in FY2001.

These numbers can be compared to those in Table 1, which shows that 21% of 3-years-olds and 36% of 4-year-olds had some sort of center based care as their primary arrangement in 1999. This figure should include Head Start cases, since Head Start is classified as center care in Table 1. However, it is likely that this number excludes many children who are in Head Start. The Census Bureau currently asks the SIPP child care questions between April and July, when many part-year Head Start centers are closed. The 1999 SIPP yields less than 200,000 children in Head Start, far lower than the number indicated by administrative records. Still, we conclude that the fraction of children served by Head Start is quite large relative to the total number of children of this age range in any sort of center-based care.

Head Start is run at the local level, but local operators are subject to federal quality guidelines. These guidelines specify that Head Start is to provide a wide range of services in addition to providing a nurturing learning environment. For example, Head Start is required to facilitate and monitor utilization of preventive medical care by participants, as well as to provide nutritious meals and snacks. This multidimensional aspect of the program has generated controversy, since some observers feel that Head Start should focus more narrowly on "education". The program is not an entitlement, but is funded by appropriation, which means that when funds run out, eligible children cannot be served.

Head Start provides child care services that are of much better quality than those commonly available to low income parents, though they are not usually full-day programs.[25] However, the most recent available estimates suggest that as of 1995, 28 percent of Head Start parents were employed full time, and 17 percent were employed part-time [Smith (2000)]. These percentages may have become much higher in recent years due to welfare reform. Head Start parents typically combine Head Start with relative care, in order to obtain the required number of child care hours.

The successful model programs discussed in the previous section were funded at higher levels than a typical publicly funded program. For example, in 1998 it cost $5,021 to keep a child in a part-day Head Start program for 34 weeks a year, implying that it would cost approximately $10,000 to send a child for two years. The part-day Perry Pre-School intervention cost $12,884 per child (in 1999 dollars) for a program that lasted eight months a year over two years. Since 20 percent of the children participated only for one year, the figures imply that the cost per child was approximately $7,000 per year, so that Head Start costs approximately 71 percent of what Perry Pre-School cost [Karoly et al. (1998)].

The U.S. Administration for Children, Youth and Families estimates that it would cost $2,394 to extend the Head Start program to full-year care, and an additional $1,615 to extend it to full-day/full-year care. Taking these figures together, it would cost approximately $9,000 per child per year to have a child in a full-year, full-day Head Start program [Bourdette (1999)]. The pre-school component of the Carolina Abecedarian intervention (which was full-day) cost about $15,000 per child, per year and this part of the intervention lasted five years. Children entered the pre-school component of the program between 1972 and 1983.[26] Fewell and Scott (1997) report that the IHDP program also cost about $15,000 per year per child, though 20 percent of the costs were in the form of transportation expenses. These figures suggest that a full-year, full-day Head Start program would cost roughly 60 percent of what these model programs cost.

Since the model programs offered more intensive services with smaller group sizes and more highly trained personnel, it is reasonable to expect that they would have larger effects than Head Start or similar public programs. The reviews of early childhood education studies in Barnett (1995) and Karoly et al. (1998) list 22 studies of the effects

---

[25] Tabulations from the CQOS show that among families using for-profit day care centers, 40% of the lowest income quartile used care with ECERS quality less than or equal to 3, compared to only 9% of the top income quartile. The distribution of quality by income was much more even among users of nonprofit child care.

[26] Ramey, Campbell and Blair (1998) state that on average the pre-school component of the program cost about $6,000 per year in 1978 dollars, which is approximately $15,000 in 1999 dollars. It is not completely clear that the CPI is the right deflator to use in making this adjustment, however, since the bulk of child care costs are for labor and wages of less skilled workers fell over this period. A cost-benefit analysis of the Abecedarian program by Barnett and Masse (in press) estimates that using a discount rate of 5%, the PDV of the program costs was $34,600, and the PDV of the benefits was $76,000. The benefits included in the calculation were the treatment-control differences in participant earnings, earnings of future generations, earnings of the participant's mother, savings in K-12 education costs, savings in smoking-related health expenditure, differences in higher education costs (a "negative" benefit, since the treatments attended college at a higher rate than the controls), and savings in welfare expenditure.

of Head Start programs, as well as similar programs funded under Title 1 of the Federal Elementary and Secondary Education Act of 1965. (Title 1 provides about $8 billion per year to school districts with disadvantaged students, but makes few stipulations regarding how the funds can be spent. It is estimated that in FY1999 about $2 billion was spent on services for pre-school age children [U.S. General Accounting Office (1999a, p. 6)].)

It is surprising that there has never been a large-scale, randomized trial of a typical Head Start program.[27] Moreover, few existing studies have attempted to follow children past the elementary grades. The most recent federally-sponsored study of Head Start is FACES which stands for Family and Child Experiences Survey [Zill, Resnick and McKey (1999)]. Unfortunately this study took a short-term perspective and had no control group. The study focused on documenting improvements in the skills of Head Start children over the course of a year in the program. The children showed gains in social skills over the course of a year in Head Start. However, these gains could not be compared to any national norms, so it is unclear what to make of the finding; after all, surely one would expect all pre-school children to improve their social skills over the course of a year. The cognitive gains of the Head Start children were assessed by comparing the Head Start children to national norms. These findings were consistent with those of many other studies that have documented short-term gains to some cognitive skills, particularly to verbal skills.

Table 17 provides an overview of selected studies of large-scale publicly funded early childhood intervention programs, focusing on those which are most recent and prominent and on those which have made especially careful attempts to control for other factors that might affect outcomes.[28] The Educational Testing Service's Longitudinal Study of Head Start began by conducting a spring canvas of all the children in a neighborhood who would be eligible to enter Head Start in the fall [Lee et al. (1990)]. The children who actually attended Head Start had lower scores on average than those who did not, although much of the difference could be accounted for by family characteristics. The children were followed into second grade, and it was found that Head Start

---

[27] The Advisory Committee on Head Start Research and Evaluation recently recommended that the Department of Health and Human Services conduct an evaluation that relies on random assignment of children in sites in which funds are insufficient to serve all eligible children; that is, if some children are to be denied access to services in any case, the committee recommends that this be done randomly so that the effects of Head Start can be assessed. This proposed random-assignment evaluation of Head Start was recently initiated, but results will not be available for some time. See http://www.acf.hhs.gov/programs/core/ongoing_research/hs/impact_intro.html. The evaluations are to focus on the intermediate outcome of school readiness. Longer-term followup of treated children would be very useful, but raises many practical problems to do with tracking substantial numbers of individuals over long periods of time.

[28] McKey et al. (1985) offers a meta-analysis of many of these Head Start studies. They argue that while the effects generally do not reach statistical significance in individual studies, the studies taken together suggest positive effects on schooling attainment, school attendance, health care utilization, and social development. Here, we take a different approach by focusing on those studies that we judge to be most methodologically sound.

Table 17
Selected studies of large-scale public early childhood programs

Program name[a]	Study design	Age of participation	Sample size	Outcomes
Chicago Child–Parent Center (CPC) and Expansion Program [Fuerst and Fuerst (1993)]	Compared former CPC children with non-CPC children from same feeder schools	Entry: 3–4 years Exit: 9 years	Initial: $T = 684$, $C = 304$ Post-high school: $T = 513$, $C = 244$	Achievement tests: $T > C$, grade 2, $T = C$, grade 8 High school graduation: $T > C$
Chicago Child–Parent Center and Expansion Program [Reynolds et al. (2000), Temple, Reynolds and Miedel (2000)]	Compared former CPC children with similarly poor children eligible for CPC but it was not offered in neighborhood	Entry: 3–4 years Exit: 9 years	$T = 837$, $C = 444$	School dropout: $T < C$ at age 20 High school completion: $T > C$ at age 20 Delinquency and crime: $T < C$ at age 17 Grade retention: $T < C$ at age 15 Special education: $T < C$ at age 18 Proficiency skills test: $T > C$ at ages 14, 15
ETS Longitudinal Study of Head Start [Lee et al. (1990)]	Compared attenders with children who attended other or no pre-schools at grade 3	Entry: 4 years Exit: 5 years	$T = 333$, $C = 313$	Achievement tests: $T > C$, grade 1; $T = C$ in grades 2, 3
Head Start Family and Child Experiences Survey [Zill, Resnick and McKey (1999)]	Studied gains made by Head Start children at age 4 or older	Entry: 3–4 years Exit: 4–5 years	$T = 1,580$, no control	Achievement tests: $T > C$ Other gains cannot be compared to any control

Table 17
(Continued)

Program name[a]	Study design	Age of participation	Sample size	Outcomes
Florida and Colorado Head Start [Oden, Schweinhart and Weikart (2000)]	Compared attenders (at age 22 in 1988) with those who did not attend any early childhood education program and lived in the same census tract	Entry: 3–4 years Exit: 4–5 years	$T = 290$, $C = 332$	Achievement tests: $T = C$ ($T < C$ in Colorado) Elementary GPA: $T = C$ ($T > C$ in Florida) Middle and high school GPA: $T = C$ Special education: $T = C$ High school graduation: $T = C$ ($T > C$ for females) Postsecondary education: $T = C$ Employed/enrolled at interview: $T = C$ Teen parent status: $T = C$ Use of public assistance: $T = C$ Arrests: $T = C$ ($T < C$ for females) Convictions: $T = C$
National Longitudinal Survey of Youth (NLSCM) Head Start [Currie and Thomas (1995, 1999)]	Compared difference between attended and nonattended siblings with difference between pre-school and non-pre-school siblings at various grades	Entry: 3–5 years Exit: 5–6 years	$T = 896$, $C = 911$ Hispanic study: $T = 182$, $C = 568$	Achievement tests: $T > C$ (whites only) Grade retention: $T > C$ (whites only) Immunization rates: $T > C$ Child height-for-age: $T = C$ Achievement tests: $T > C$ (Hispanics only) Grade retention: $T > C$ (Hispanics only)
Panel Study of Income Dynamics (PSID) Head Start [Garces, Thomas and Currie (2002)]	Compared Head Start participants to nonparticipants between ages 18 and 31	Entry: 3–4 years	$T = 583$, $C = 3,502$	Grade retention: $T = C$ High school graduation: $T = C$ Teen pregnancy: $T = C$ Welfare: $T = C$ Arrests: $T < C$ College: $T > C$

Table 17
(Continued)

Program name[a]	Study design	Age of participation	Sample size	Outcomes
National Evaluation of Early Head Start [U.S. Administration for Children, Youth, and Families (2002)]	17 EHS sites selected to reflect program approaches and demographic characteristics of all EHS programs funded in 1995–1996. Random assignment conducted within each site to compare participants with eligible nonparticipants	Entry: 0–1 year Exit: 3 years	Initial: $T = 1{,}513$, $C = 1{,}488$	Mental Development Index: $T > C$ at age 2, 3 Low Mental Development Index: $T < C$ at age 2, $T = C$ at age 3 Vocabulary production score: $T > C$ at age 2 Sentence complexity score: $T > C$ at age 2 Percentage combining words: $T = C$ at age 2 Vocabulary: $T > C$ at age 3 Low vocabulary score: $T < C$ at age 3 Aggressive behavior: $T < C$ at ages 2, 3 Emotional regulation: $T = C$ at ages 2, 3 Orientation/engagement: $T = C$ at ages 2, 3 Engagement of parent during play: $T = C$ at age 2, $T > C$ at age 3 Negativity w/parent during play: $T = C$ at age 2, $T < C$ at age 3 Attention to objects during play: $T = C$ at age 2, $T > C$ at age 3 Child frustration during parent–child task: $T = C$ at age 3 Engagement of parent during task: $T = C$ at age 3 Persistence during parent–child task: $T = C$ at age 3

Notes. See Barnett (1995) and Karoly et al. (1998) for more information about the studies described in this table. None of these evaluations were randomized except for Early Head Start. "*T*" refers to the treatment, "*C*" refers to the control or comparison group. $T > C$ means that the difference was significant at the 5% level.

[a]Most recent published document. See Barnett (1995) for description of other studies.

attendance had positive effects on both verbal test scores and measures of social adjustment such as impulse control. Unfortunately, it was not possible to follow the children further to see whether these effects were sustained.

The Chicago Child–Parent Centers is an early intervention that began with an enriched pre-school program, and followed up with an enriched curriculum for school-aged children up to age nine. This intervention is similar to providing a Head Start-like pre-school program and then improving the school subsequently attended by the Head Start children. Reynolds (1998) followed a sample of children who had all participated in the pre-school and Kindergarten components of the program through 7th grade. Some participated after Kindergarten (the treatments) and some did not (the controls). In addition, some attended schools in which the extended program was offered for two years, while some attended schools in which it was offered for three years. Reynolds finds significant reductions in the rates of grade retention, special education, and delinquency in the treatment group, as well as higher reading scores. He uses several different statistical methods to control for the possibly unobserved characteristics of the (nonrandomly assigned) treatment and control children.[29] His results are robust to the use of different methodologies.

In other studies of the Chicago Child–Parent Center population, Temple, Reynolds and Miedel (2000) follow the children to the end of high school and find that the program reduced the high school dropout rate by 24 percent, and that the size of the effect grows with the time that children spent in the program. Reynolds et al. (2000) look at several additional outcomes including delinquency, crime, and a skills test and find beneficial effects of the program on all of the outcomes they examine. They include a simple cost-benefit analysis which suggests that a dollar spent on the program saved $3.69 in future costs to government.

The National Longitudinal Survey of Youth, which has followed a nationally representative group of people who were between the ages of 14 and 21 in 1979, began following the children born to the female sample members in 1986. Currie and Thomas (1995) use these data to evaluate Head Start. They attempt to control for unobserved characteristics of children by comparing siblings who participated in Head Start to those who did not. The idea is that by using siblings as the controls, any shared characteristics of family background will be controlled. As discussed above, unobserved characteristics such as the parents' views on the importance of education are likely to contaminate estimates of program effects if they are not accounted for.

---

[29] Reynolds (1998) uses three different methods. First, he conducts an analysis of the initial differences in test scores between the two groups, and finds that most of it can be explained by observable characteristics; that is, there do not appear to be large pre-existing unobservable differences between the treatments and the controls. Second, he estimates a model in which selection into the treatment group is controlled for by including the inverse Mill's ratio from a first-stage selection equation. In this model, it is assumed that the characteristics of each school site affected selection into the treatment group without having additional direct effects on child outcomes. A third approach is to compare children in schools which offered the treatment for two years to those in schools that offered it for three.

The Currie and Thomas (1995) evaluation is one of very few to have included significant samples of the 60 percent of Head Start children who are not African-American. The estimates of gains for African-American children parallel those of studies in which subjects were randomly assigned, which lends them additional credibility: initial gains in vocabulary and reading test scores "faded out" while the children were still in elementary grades. For white children, in contrast, there were persistent gains in test scores, as well as reductions in grade repetition. It is worth emphasizing that the initial gains in test scores were the same for whites and blacks – thus, the real difference was not in the initial impact of the Head Start program but in what happened to the children after they left.

In conjunction with results from Reynolds' work on the Chicago Parent–Child program and with evidence that Head Start children often go on to attend poor schools [Lee and Loeb (1995)] these results suggest that the fade out of Head Start gains among African-American children may be due not to deficiencies in the Head Start program but to problems of subsequent school quality. Currie and Thomas (2000) find that black children who attended Head Start go on to attend schools of lower quality than other black children. However, the same is not true among whites. Moreover, when they stratify by an indicator of school quality, gaps in test scores between Head Start and other children are very similar for blacks and whites. Hence, the effects of Head Start may fade out more rapidly among black students at least in part because black Head Start children are more likely to subsequently attend inferior schools.

Most recently, Currie and Neidell (2006) combine administrative data about Head Start programs with data from the NLSY to examine the effect of spending on the outcomes of Head Start children. They find that the gap between Head Start and non-Head Start children is smaller in counties that had higher per capita Head Start spending, suggesting that funding Head Start at the level of model programs would indeed increase the beneficial effect of the program.

Only two published studies have attempted to follow Head Start children into adulthood. Oden, Schweinhart and Weikart (2000) report on an attempt to follow up a group of young adults who participated in Head Start between 1970 and 1971 in both urban and rural areas in Colorado and Florida. These children were compared to a group of children who had never participated in any form of early childhood education program. In order to construct the comparison group, researchers found young adults who had lived on the same streets, or in the same census tracts as the Head Start children, and who had initially enrolled in the same elementary school. They recognize that this method of constructing a comparison group is imperfect, and note that in the final sample, the Head Start children were more disadvantaged than the control children along a number of dimensions. A statistical analysis of differences in many different outcomes between the Head Start and no intervention children is presented, but none of the differences are statistically significant at conventional levels of significance.

In contrast, Garces, Thomas and Currie (2002) find that Head Start generates long-term improvements in important outcomes such as schooling attainment, earnings and crime reduction. The data for this study come from the Panel Study of Income Dynamics

(PSID), which began in 1968 with a survey of 4,802 households containing 18,000 individuals. In 1995, adults in the PSID who were age 30 or younger were asked whether they had ever been enrolled in Head Start or any other pre-school or day care program. These adults have been followed since childhood, and also answered questions about labor force participation, earnings, schooling, and criminal activity. There are roughly 4,000 respondents in the survey for whom both information about pre-school and information about these adult outcomes is available.[30] They find that disadvantaged whites who had been enrolled in Head Start were more likely to graduate from high school and to have attended college than siblings who did not, while African-Americans who attended Head Start were significantly less likely to have been booked or charged with a crime compared to siblings who did not participate in Head Start.

The existing evidence from both model programs and Head Start studies suggests that the benefits of early intervention may be greater for more disadvantaged children than for other children, though again, this needs to be more rigorously demonstrated. For example, in the Carolina Abecedarian project, researchers found positive effects that were twice as large for children from the poorest and least educated families as they were for the other children. The Infant Health and Development Project listed in Table 16 found positive effects on math scores only for a group of relatively high birthweight children within their low birthweight sample. But within this group, the children of the poorest and least educated mothers gained the most. Currie and Thomas (1999) find that in a sample of Hispanic children in Head Start, the largest gains in test scores were among children of mothers who had been interviewed in Spanish, suggesting that at least some of the positive effect of the program is due to increased pre-school exposure to "mainstream" language.

In summary, the evidence in support of favorable long-term effects of public programs is less conclusive than the evidence showing positive effects of model programs, mostly because there have been very few well-designed studies of longer-term effects. Thus, the jury is still out on whether Head Start is cost effective, although Currie (2001) calculates that the short and medium-term benefits of Head Start (in terms of reducing ills such as grade repetition) pay back 40–60% of the cost of the program. Thus, if Head Start has long-term benefits even a quarter as large as those of some of the model programs, then the intervention pays for itself.

5.3. Early Head Start

The Early Head Start (EHS) program was created in 1994 as part of a Congressional mandate to address the needs of infants and toddlers within the existing Head Start

---

[30] A possible problem is that the Head Start questions refer to events that took place many years ago. Aware that survey participants might have problems remembering pre-school attendance, the authors compare self-reported PSID Head Start enrollment rates and the racial composition of enrollments in the PSID with those reported by the Head Start Bureau. They find no evidence that poor memories contaminate their results.

framework. The 1994 legislation set aside three percent of the 1995 Head Start budget for the creation of EHS. The proportion of funding designated for EHS has grown steadily since then, reaching ten percent in 2002 [Raikes and Love (2002)]. In response, EHS has grown from 68 programs in 1995 to 664 programs serving over 55,000 families in 2002. EHS is organized and evaluated according to the same performance standards as the Head Start Program. However, programs are allowed considerable flexibility and can offer several options, including: a home-based program with weekly home visits and at least two group socializations per month for each family; a center-based program which also provides a minimum of two home visits per year; or a mixed approach. EHS can also contract out child care services to existing providers in the community. Paulsell et al. (2002) and Buell, Pfister and Gamel-McCormick (2002) find evidence that the involvement of EHS enhances the quality of child care at these locations.

Perhaps because of controversy regarding the wisdom of encouraging mothers to place infants in child care, an evaluation component was built into EHS. Seventeen sites have been chosen to be part of the national evaluation. At each site, randomly assigned treatments and controls are being tracked. It is interesting to note that in the relatively short time since the program's inception, the 17 sites in the national evaluation have all but abandoned the home-based approach in favor of center-based care.

The results to date of the national evaluation are reported in Table 17. As of age three, the effects appear to be very positive. The EHS children have significantly higher scores on several tests of cognitive development, exhibit less aggressive behavior, and less negative behavior toward parents during play, and are also better able to devote sustained attention to an object during play. Given the results suggesting some "fade out" in effects of Head Start, at least for some children, it will be very important to see how well these gains are maintained over time.

5.4. State programs

Head Start has served as a model for state pre-schools targeted to low-income children in states such as California [U.S. General Accounting Office (1995)], and also for new (voluntary) universal pre-school programs in Georgia, Oklahoma and New York.[31] In many states, the state program has a contractual arrangement with local Head Start agencies, but may also operate through the public schools. It is common for state programs to use the Head Start Performance Standards as guidelines for their program. It is also common for these programs to emphasize the "comprehensive services" mandated by Head Start – that is parent involvement, health referrals, case workers, and home visits in addition to educational services.

---

[31] Georgia established a universal voluntary program for 4-year olds in 1995. New York followed in 1997, and Oklahoma expanded an existing program serving disadvantaged kids into a universal 4-year old program in 1998. In New York, only 200 out of 700 school districts were participating in 2002, and the continued existence of the program is in jeopardy due to budget crises.

Table 18 shows state spending on pre-school education at three points in time, by program. Most states have shown significant growth in their expenditures on these programs between 1987 and 1999. The Children's Defense Fund (1999) reports that as of the 1998–1999 school year, 724,610 children were participating in state-funded enriched pre-school programs. A recent NCES report [NCES (2003)] finds that in 2000–2001, 822,000 children were served by pre-Kindergarten classes operated by public schools. One impetus for this growth is the federal Individuals with Disabilities Education Act (IDEA), which provides funding to states to support educational services for children with disabilities. In 1999–2000 five percent of US pre-schoolers (588,300) received some IDEA services at a cost of $374 million. In order to be eligible for these funds, states must make free appropriate public education available to all three to five year old children with disabilities. The NCES report indicates that 51% of public elementary schools that provided pre-Kindergarten classes used funds from federal or local programs for children with disabilities. Twenty five percent reported using Title 1 funds, and 13 percent used Head Start funds (nationally, about 13 percent of Head Start centers are operated by public schools). These figures indicate that while there is considerable overlap between different types of public programs serving pre-school children, the number of children in state-funded early education initiatives is roughly equal to the 800,000 participants in Head Start. However, we know very little about the effectiveness of these programs, a problem that has become more urgent given their rapid growth.

The best available summary of research on these programs is a meta-analysis by Gilliam and Zigler (2001). They note that by 1998, only 13 of 33 state funded pre-school programs providing classroom-based educational services had completed any formal evaluation of the program's impact on children. Of these 13, three did not include any comparison group. The remaining 10 generally chose comparison groups from either eligible nonattendees or randomly chosen classmates who may or may not have been eligible. The evaluation of the New York program selected a control group from the waiting list for the program, which is perhaps the best nonexperimental design of the group. However, this evaluation is extremely dated (1977).

The evaluations of these programs yielded results quite similar to those of the nonexperimental evaluations of Head Start discussed above. There generally seem to be positive short-term effects on measures of social-emotional, cognitive, motor, language, academic and literacy skills, which are sustained through Kindergarten. Most evaluations followed children only into first grade, but noted some positive effects in academic and literacy domains. The few studies that followed children beyond first grade found no positive effects, and an evaluation in Kentucky found negative effects when children from the state program were compared to random classmates.

In contrast, evaluations that looked beyond test scores, sometimes reported sustained positive effects. For example, a Florida evaluation that examined actual reported incidents of corporal punishment, suspensions and expulsions found significant effects as late as fourth grade: eligible nonattendees without pre-school experience were significantly more likely to have been disciplined than participants. Similarly, most states that examined attendance found significant impacts that persisted beyond school entry. For

Table 18
State spending on pre-Kindergarten initiatives

State	Program		State spending 1987–1988	State spending 1991–1992	State spending 1998–1999
Alabama	Pre-School Collaboration Project		–	–	$690,000
Alaska	Comprehensive Pre-School		$197,000	–	–
	Alaska Head Start Program (State-Funded Head Start Model)		$2,700,000	$5,728,174	$5,489,951
		total	$2,897,000	$5,728,174	$5,489,951
Arizona	Early Childhood State Block Grant (PreK component)		–	$1,500,000	$10,013,423
Arkansas	Arkansas Better Chance			$5,000,000	$10,000,000
California[a]	State Pre-School Program		$35,500,000	$83,335,000	$127,000,000
Colorado	Colorado Pre-School Program			$3,204,000	$21,640,000
Connecticut	School Readiness and Child Care Initiative			–	$39,000,000
	State-Funded Head Start Model		$400,000	$400,000	$5,100,000
		total	$400,000	$400,000	$44,100,000
Delaware	Early Childhood Assistance Program (State-Funded Head Start Model)		$189,000	–	$3,600,000
District of Columbia	Public School Pre-School Program		$12,200,000	$11,483,850	$14,591,000
	District-Funded Head Start Model		$1,100,000	$1,556,241	$2,570,000
		total	$13,300,000	$13,040,091	$17,161,000
Florida	PreK Early Intervention Program		$1,600,000	$69,000,000	$97,000,000
	State Migrant PreK Program		$2,900,000	$3,064,540	$3,295,172
	State-Funded Head Start Model		–	$6,000,000	–
		total	$4,500,000	$78,064,540	$100,295,172

Table 18
(*Continued*)

State	Program		State spending 1987–1988	State spending 1991–1992	State spending 1998–1999
Georgia	PreK Program for Four-Year-Olds		–	–	$217,000,000
Hawaii	Pre-School Open Doors		–	n/a	$2,700,000
	State-Funded Head Start Model		$291,790	$529,700	$3,087,387
		total	$291,790	$529,700	$5,787,387
Illinois	Early Childhood Block Grant (PreK component)		$12,700,000	$71,500,000	$136,000,000
	State-Funded Head Start Model		–	$500,000	–
		total	$12,700,000	$72,000,000	$136,000,000
Iowa	Comprehensive Child Development Program ("Shared Visions")		–	$4,958,315	$7,633,087
Kansas	Four-Year-Old At-Risk Children Pre-School Program		–	–	$3,000,000
	State-Funded Head Start Model		–	–	$2,500,000
		total			$5,500,000
Kentucky	Kentucky Pre-School Program		$232,123	$30,595,270	$39,700,000
Louisiana	Pre-School Block Grant		$1,800,000	$3,501,500	$6,650,000
Maine	Two-Year Kindergarten		$27,730	n/a	$1,300,000
	State-Funded Head Start Model		$1,900,000	$2,407,393	$2,329,000
	Early Childhood Demonstration Grants		–	$150,000	–
		total	$1,927,730	$2,557,393	$3,629,000
Maryland	Extended Elementary Education Programs (EEEP)		$3,300,000	$8,948,914	$19,263,000
Massachusetts	Community Partnerships for Children		$10,300,000	$7,500,000	$78,500,000
	State-Funded Head Start Model		$4,500,000	$6,000,000	$6,900,000
		total	$14,800,000	$13,500,000	$85,400,000

Table 18
(Continued)

State	Program		State spending 1987–1988	State spending 1991–1992	State spending 1998–1999
Michigan	Michigan School Readiness Program		$2,300,000	$32,917,700	$67,083,000
Minnesota	Learning Readiness		—	—	$10,300,000
	State-Funded Head Start Model		$2,000,000	$6,500,000	$18,400,000
		total	$2,000,000	$6,500,000	$28,700,000
Missouri[b]	Missouri Pre-School Project		—	—	—
Nebraska	Early Childhood Projects		—	—	$500,000
New Hampshire	NH Head Start-State Collaboration (State-Funded Head Start Model)		—	$201,000	$230,000
New Jersey	Early Childhood Program Aid (PreK component)		$7,900,000	—	$70,000,000
	State Equalization Aid for Four-Year-Old Kindergarten		—	$9,500,000	—
	Urban PreK Pilot Program/Good Starts		—	$2,500,000	—
	State-Funded Head Start Model		—	$1,300,000	$1,400,000
		total	$7,900,000	$13,300,000	$1,400,000
New Mexico	Child Development Program		—	$145,106	$1,300,000
	State-Funded Head Start Model		—	—	$5,000,000
		total	—	$145,106	$6,300,000
New York	Universal PreK		—	—	$67,000,000
	Experimental PreK		$27,000,000	$47,000,000	$50,200,000
		total	$27,000,000	$47,000,000	$117,200,000
North Carolina[c]	Smart Start		—	—	—

Table 18
(*Continued*)

State	Program		State spending 1987–1988	State spending 1991–1992	State spending 1998–1999
Ohio	Public School Pre-school		$18,000	$13,386,236	$17,900,000
	State-Funded Head Start Model		–	$19,878,559	$92,562,977
		total	$18,000	$33,264,795	$110,462,977
Oklahoma	Early Childhood Four-Year-Old Program		$832,275	$2,132,120	$36,500,708
	Head Start State-Appropriated Funds (State-Funded Head Start Model)		–	–	$3,316,918
		total		$2,132,120	$39,817,626
Oregon	Oregon Head Start PreK (State-Funded Head Start Model)		$1,100,000	$8,200,000	$16,272,167
Pennsylvania[d]	Education Aid for Kindergarten for Four-Year-Olds		$1,700,000	n/a	$5,700,000
Rhode Island[e]	State-Funded Head Start Model		$365,000	$1,958,558	$1,965,000
	Early Childhood Investment Fund		–	–	–
	Legislative Allocations for Special Projects		–	$200,000	–
		total	$365,000	$2,158,558	$1,965,000
South Carolina	Early Childhood Program (Half-Day Child Development Program)		$10,900,000	$15,163,447	$22,356,688
Tennessee	Tennessee Early Childhood Education Pilot Program		–	–	$3,100,000
Texas	Public School PreK		$46,200,000	$181,000,000	$235,000,000
Vermont	Early Education Initiative		$500,000	$1,414,000	$1,315,000
Virginia	Virginia Pre-school Initiative		–	–	$23,500,000

Table 18
(Continued)

State	Program		State spending 1987–1988	State spending 1991–1992	State spending 1998–1999
Washington	Early Childhood Education & Assistance Program		$4,700,000	$17,190,000	$28,897,592
	Head Start State Match Program (State-Funded Head Start Model)		$660,000	$530,763	$470,000
		total	$5,360,000	$17,720,763	$29,367,592
West Virginia	Public School Early Childhood Education		$258,574	$1,035,006	$6,232,702
Wisconsin	Four-Year-Old Kindergarten		$4,300,000	$5,800,000	$19,800,000
	State-Funded Head Start Model		–	$2,250,000	$4,950,000
		total	$4,300,000	$8,050,000	$24,750,000
All states		total	$202,600,000	$697,065,392	$1,675,455,100

Sources: 1987–1988 data from Marx and Seligson (1988). 1991–1992 and 1998–1999 from Children's Defense Fund (1999).
[a]California: The data presented here is for 1997–1998.
[b]Missouri: The Missouri Pre-School Project was introduced in 1998–1999, but the first year of funding (estimated to be $9.2 million) was 1999–2000.
[c]North Carolina: Total state funding for Smart Start was $140 million but the program supports a range of services and it cannot be determined how much of the total was spend on preK.
[d]Pennsylvania: The data presented for the Education Aid for Kindergarten for Four-Year-Olds is for 1997–1998.
[e]Rhode Island: The Early Childhood Investment Fund provided $5.3 million of funding for a range early childhood-related programs including preK, but no funds were used for this purpose.

example, New York found statistically significant impacts at the fifth and sixth grade when comparing state pre-school attendees to nonattendees drawn from the waiting list for the program, and Maryland found positive effects at tenth grade when participating children were compared to random classmates. Several studies also reported that participants had higher scores on school-administered academic achievement tests, although the effect sizes were small. The Maryland and New York evaluations found statistically significant positive effects at grades 5, 8, 9 and 10, and in grade 6, respectively. Finally, every state that evaluated retention in grade found that program participants were significantly less likely to have been retained than controls.

In sum, like Head Start, state pre-school programs have not been adequately evaluated. However, the limited available information suggests that while effects on cognitive test scores may fade out, there may well be longer-term effects on actual achievement.

5.5. Programs for school-aged children

Data from the National Survey of America's Families suggests that in 1997, about seven percent of children 6–12 were enrolled in some sort of after-school program. Concern about the plight of "latch key" children has led to increasing interest in after school (and before-school) programs for children of school age. Between 1997 and 2002, the U.S. Department of Education increased funding for 21st Century Community Learning Centers, which are school-based after school programs, from $40 million to $1 billion. In 2001, 1.2 million elementary and middle school students participated in this program in 3,600 schools. State governments have also increased their spending on these initiatives. California recently passed Proposition 49, which increased state funding for before- and after-school programs up to $455 million dollars, beginning in 2004. Proponents of the measure argued that up to a million California children under the age of 15 were left unsupervised after-school, and that after-school programs could reduce crime rates by 40 percent or more [California Secretary of State (2002)].

There are many studies examining correlates of self-care among children [cf. Belle (1997), Vandell and Posner (1999)]. Some of the more recent studies are summarized in Table 19. With the exception of Aizer (2004), none of the studies attempt to deal with heterogeneity between students who take care of themselves after school and other students. There are many reasons to expect selection bias in simple comparisons of children who are and are not in self-care: If parents are less likely to leave children with problems alone, then the estimated effects of self-care could be biased toward zero. On the other hand, self-care could be correlated with other characteristics of families that cause negative outcomes.

Many of these observational studies report behavior problems in children left in self-care [Galambos and Maggs (1991), Marshall et al. (1997), McHale, Crouter and Tucker (2001), Pettit et al. (1997, 1999), Rodman, Pratto and Nelson (1985)]. Pettit et al. (1997) also report negative correlations between self-care and the test scores of children in self-care in grade 1, though they find no significant effect on grade 2 test scores. On the other hand, Vandell and Ramanan find that among 3rd to 5th grade children, children in

Table 19
Studies of the effects of self-care on child outcomes

Report	Study design	Definition of self-care	Age of participation	Sample size[a]	Outcomes[b]
Aizer (2004)	Uses ordinary least squares (OLS), family fixed effects, and instrumental variables (IV) estimation to look at self-care in the National Longitudinal Survey of Youth 79 Child–Mother file through 1998	Child responds that there is not usually an adult present when he returns from school	Age 10–14	Final: 5,838 $T = 1{,}518$ (self-care) $C = 4{,}320$ (supervised)	Skipping school: $T > C$; Using alcohol or drugs: $T > C$; Stealing: $T > C$; Hurting someone: $T > C$
Galambos and Maggs (1991)[c]	No random assignment. Students answered a questionnaire to determine what category of care they were in. No discussion of methodology	Same definition as Steinberg (1986)	6th grade	Final: 112 $T_1 = $ *Unsup* at friends $T_2 = $ *Unsup* at home $T_3 = $ *Unsup* hanging out $C = $ *Supervised* (by parent or after-school program)	Peer involvement: all $T > C$; Problem behavior: $T_2, T_3 > T_1, C$ (girls only); Impulse control: $T_2, T_3 < T_1, C$ (girls only); Ability to cope: $T_2, T_3 < T_1, C$ (girls only)
Marshall et al. (1997)	Grade 1–4 children recruited from 30 Boston public schools and 8 parochial schools. Data collected through face-to-face interviews and questionnaires with the parent and through observations at the child's after-school setting. OLS regression of the child's behavioral problems on the types of care	Any time spent alone or only with siblings and no adult	1st–4th grade	Final: 181	Self-care had negative effects for poor children

Table 19
(Continued)

Report	Study design	Definition of self-care	Age of participation	Sample size[a]	Outcomes[b]
McHale, Crouter and Tucker (2001)	A short-term longitudinal study with 2 year interval for families who responded to a recruiting letter. Children's behavior evaluated and reported by the parent through home interviews. Children's time use reported by the children and collected through telephone interviews	Time alone, or with unsupervised peers	10 and 12	Final: 198 $T_1 =$ time alone $T_2 = w$ peers	Depression: $T_1 > C$ Behavior problems: $T_2 > C$
Pettit et al. (1997)	A longitudinal study of children (and families) recruited at the time of Kindergarten preregistration and observed through grade 7. Data collected through telephone interviews with children (on after-school time use), mother interview (on parental monitoring) and teacher rating (on children's behavior)	Time spent alone or with siblings	6th grade	Initial: 585 $T_1 =$ self-care in grade 1 or 3 $T_2 =$ self-care in grade 5	Grades $T_1 < C, T_2 = C$ Achievement test scores $T_1 < C, T_2 = C$ Significant interactions T_1 and poverty, behavior problems in Kindergarten
Pettit et al. (1999)	Same as Pettit et al. (1997)	Time spent unsupervised in 6th grade	7th grade	Final: 342 $T_1 = w$ peers $T_2 = $ alone $T_3 = w$ siblings	Externalizing problems $T_1 > C$, greatest effects for students with low parental monitoring and unsafe neighborhoods, $T_2 = C, T_3 = C$

Table 19
(Continued)

Report	Study design	Definition of self-care	Age of participation	Sample size[a]	Outcomes[b]
Richardson et al. (1989)	Eighth grade students in 169 classrooms in LA and 67 classes in San Diego filled out a survey on their supervision and substance abuse. Calculated relative risks of substance abuse for those with more than 11 hrs of self-care vs. those with 0 hrs of self-care (calculated the ratio of the proportion of kids in each group who abused also stratified by covariates)	More than 11 hours of self-care per week	8th grade	Final: 4,932 $T = 1,411$ (self-care) $C = 3,521$	Cigarette use: $T > C$ Alcohol use: $T > C$ Marijuana use: $T > C$
Rodman, Pratto and Nelson (1985)	Matched kids in self-care with those in adult care by age, sex, race, family composition, and father's occupation. Well-matched on these characteristics. Only difference between groups is mother's employment and no difference in parental permission to participate. No random assign. Used child interviews, tests, and teacher surveys. T-tests for differences in means	Children who report that they usually go home after school and either no one or only a younger sibling at is at home. Adult care children were those who reported an adult was at home	4th and 7th grade	Final: 96 4th grade: $T = 26$, $C = 26$ 7th grade: $T = 22$, $C = 22$	Self-esteem inventory: $T = C$, 4th and 7th Personal reaction (self-control): $T = C$, 4th and 7th Behavior problems: $T = C$, 4th and 7th

Table 19
(Continued)

Report	Study design	Definition of self-care	Age of participation	Sample size[a]	Outcomes[b]
Steinberg (1986)	Uses existing data set on Madison, WI school district. Analysis of variance (ANOVA) and analysis of covariance (ANCOVA) [controlling for age, socioeconomic status (SES), family structure, and mother's employment]. Survey includes hypothetical peer pressure situations	Categorization based on child's response to "where you usually go after school" and "are there adults present"	5th–9th grade	Final: 768 T_1 = 177 Unsupervised at home T_2 = 85 Unsupervised at friend's T_3 = 57 Unsupervised "hanging out" C_1 = 243 Supervised at home C_2 = 48 Supervised at neighbor or relative's C_3 = 93 Supervised at friend's C_4 = 82 Supervised at school	Susceptibly to peer pressure: $T_1 = C_1$[d] all T > all C (girls) all T = all C (boys) $T_1 < T_2, T_3$
Vandell and Corasaniti (1988)	Parents of 349 third-graders in a suburban Dallas school district filled out surveys describing type of care. Of these, 150 white students were deliberately chosen for study. Most day care centers were proprietary. Teacher, parent, peer, and self-ratings as well as standardized test scores and grades analyzed with ANOVA, MANOVA and Duncan post-hoc. Controls for parents' education and marital status	Parents filled out survey with the 4 choices of after school care listed along with "other". Those who reported a combination of types of care under "other" were categorized in the type of care used for the majority of days/week	3rd grade	Final: 150 T_1 = 54 (self-care) C_1 = 26 (center) C_2 = 42 (mother care) C_3 = 25 (other adult) White suburban	Peer ratings: $T_1 = C_2$ Grades: $T_1 = C_2$ Standardized test scores: $T_1 = C_2$. C_1 < all T and C Conduct grades: $T_1 = C_2$ Self-perception: $T_1 = C_2$ Parent ratings: $T_1 = C_2$ Teacher ratings: $T_1 = C_2$ Negative peer ratings: $C_1 > T_1, C_2$ Academic grades: C_1 < all T and C

Table 19
(Continued)

Report	Study design	Definition of self-care	Age of participation	Sample size[a]	Outcomes[b]

Vandell and Ramanan (1991)	Used the NLSY79 with data from home visits of NLSY staff. ANOVA then Duncan's post hoc analyses	Parents report "primary" after school care arrangement	3rd–5th grade	Final: 390
				$T = 28$ (self-care)
				$C_1 = 114$ (other adult)
				$C_2 = 248$ (mother care)
				
				Overrepresentative of single-parent and low-income
					Headstrong: $T >$ all C
					  (but $T = C$ w/family controls)
					Hyperactive: $T >$ all C
					  (but $T = C$ w/family controls)
					Anxious: $T =$ all C
					Peer conflicts: $T =$ all C
					Antisocial: $T =$ all C
					Dependent: $T =$ all C
					Harter self-rating, Cognitive:
					  $T =$ all C
					Harter self-rating, General:
					  $T =$ all C
					Digit span: $T =$ all C
					Peabody Picture Vocab. Test:
					  $T =$ all C
					Peabody Indiv. Achievement Test:
					  $T =$ all C

[a]Throughout the table, "T" refers to treatment group and "C" refers to control or comparison group.

[b]Outcomes listed as $T > C$ or $C > T$ were statistically significant at the 5% level unless otherwise noted.

[c]In Galambos and Maggs (1991).

[d]Steinberg (1986) also break the unsupervised group into children whose parents know their whereabouts and those who do not. There is some evidence that those children whose parents know their whereabouts (no matter where they go after school) are less susceptible to peer pressure.

self-care are significantly more likely to be "headstrong" and hyperactive, but have test scores similar to other children, and are equally likely to report peer conflicts.

Looking at 8th grade children, Richardson et al. (1989) reports that self-care children are significantly more likely to use cigarettes, alcohol and marijuana than other children. Using data from the National Longitudinal Survey of Youth, Aizer examines children 10–14, and attempts to control for unobserved family background characteristics using family fixed effects. Her estimates indicate that children in self-care are significantly more likely to report that they skip school, use alcohol or drugs, have stolen, or have hurt someone. Thus, these studies offer some support for the view that self-care can be harmful.

However, it is considerably more difficult to demonstrate, on the basis of the available evidence, that formal after school programs are the solution to this problem. The first problem facing the researcher, is that there is little consensus in the literature about the definition of an after-school program. Seppanen et al. (1993) offer a coherent definition as well as the first national overview of such programs. Following them, we define an after-school program as one offering "formally organized services for five to thirteen year olds that occur before and/or after school during the academic year and all day when school is closed and parents are at work". We further narrow our attention to school or center-based programs that operate at least one hour per day and at least three days per week. As Seppanen et al. (1993, p. 6) explain, "Such programs augment the school day, and typically also the school calendar, creating a second tier of services that provide supervision, enrichment, recreation, tutoring, and other opportunities for school-age youth".

Seppanen et al. report several surprising findings. First, they find that before and after school programs are underutilized nationally – enrollments were at an average of only 59 percent of the capacity of licensed programs, and only one-third of programs were operating at 75 percent or more of capacity. Thus, the widespread perception that after school programs are unavailable seems to be incorrect, though it is of course possible that existing programs are "too expensive". In the 2000 competition for the 21st Century Community Learning Centers (a federal program intended to support after school care), 2,252 communities applied for funds that were sufficient to fund only 310 grantees [National Research Council and Institute of Medicine (2003)].

Seppanen et al. also report that 90 percent of the before school enrollments, and 83 percent of the after-school enrollments are of children in pre-Kindergarten through grade three. Thus, it would appear that these programs are used primarily as child care for children deemed by their parents to be too young to be on their own, but that the programs are not used very much for the older children who are apparently most at risk of negative effects of self care. Moreover, the largest drop off in enrollments occurs between Kindergarten and grade one. It may be that the generally somewhat longer school day for children in grade school allows parents to find alternative child care arrangements more easily than they can for Kindergartners.

According to Seppanen et al. most after school programs offer the following low-cost, easy to organize activities: socializing, free time, games and puzzles, reading independently or in small groups, time for homework, unstructured play time, and construction or building (with sand, Legos, etc.). Less than 75 percent of programs offered activities such as dramatic play or dressing up, music, storytelling, or theater. Fewer than half of all programs offered creative writing, sports, field trips, or science activities at least once a week or more. There was also a great deal of heterogeneity in structural measures of program quality. The education of care-givers ranges from less than high school through graduate degrees. Staff turnover averaged 60 percent, although some programs reported no turnover. Child–staff ratios ranged from four to one to 25 to one.

The existing evaluations of after-school programs, summarized in Table 20, tend to focus on special after-school programs rather than on the more typical programs surveyed in Seppanen et al.[32] Two other limitations of the existing studies are almost immediately apparent from Table 20. First, very few studies have used a randomized treatment and control design. Second, while proponents of after-school programs generally focus on keeping older kids out of trouble, many of the "model" after-school programs that have been evaluated focus on improving the scholastic outcomes of younger children.

Two of the better studies of this type are the Howard Street Tutoring Program and the Memphis City Schools Extended Day Tutoring program. Both used a design in which students with poor reading test scores were randomly assigned to a treatment group which received tutoring or a control group. In their evaluation of the Howard Street program, Morris, Shaw and Penney (1990) report significant gains in basal passage reading, timed word recognition, basal word recognition, and spelling in their sample of second and third grade children. Ross et al. (1996) also report significant gains in reading scores in the Memphis City Schools program. However, rather than simply comparing treatments and controls, Ross et al. conduct comparisons which add treatment children who did not attend the program more than a threshold amount of the time to the control group. Even with this modification to a standard experimental design, they find significant effects only for third graders, and not for either second graders or fourth graders.

One of the after-school programs which has received most attention (and is the subject of three of the evaluations in Table 20) is LA's BEST. This program offers comprehensive after-school tutoring, cultural enrichment, recreation, computer, and nutrition services to Kindergarten and elementary school children in 19 of Los Angeles' poorest schools, and is probably what proponents of California's proposition 49 had in mind. Brooks, Mojica and Land (1995) conducted a study of 146 LA's BEST children over academic years 1992/93 and 1993/94. Children in the program were compared to a nonrandomly selected group of control students whose parents had agreed to let them participate in the study. The control group started with significantly higher grades, and also showed differences in family background characteristics and ethnic composition when compared to the treatments.

---

[32] Note that some of the studies summarized in Table 19 essentially compare self-care to care in some sort of after-school program. These include Vandell and Corasaniti (1988), Posner and Vandell (1994), Marshall et al. (1997) and Pettit et al. (1997). We have not repeated these studies in Table 20.

Table 20
Studies of the effects of after-school programs on child outcomes

Program name	Program description	Study design	Age of participation	Sample size[a]	Outcomes[b]
Random					
Gevirtz Homework Project [Cosden et al. (2001)]	Homework assistance with a credentialed teacher after school 3–4 days per week (no drop-in)	Stratified random assignment of 4th graders to treatment and control groups, students followed from 4th–6th grades	4th–6th grade	Final: 90 $T = 36$, $C = 54$	No difference between treatment and control. Dosage correlated with achievement
Howard Street Tutoring Program [Morris, Shaw and Penney (1990)]	One-on-one adult reading tutors work with 20 low reading ability second and third graders at a public school. Operates after school 4 days/wk from October–May, but students attend only 2 days/wk for 50 hrs. of total tutoring over the year	Teachers identify the lowest 50 readers in second and third grade. Then kids are ranked according to 3 reading and spelling tests. The 2 lowest scoring are paired, then the next two, etc. and one of each pair is randomly assigned to participate in the program. Study compares students in program to the control group in each of two years using the same 3 tests that were administered prior to the program. No significant differences between control and treatment group on tests at pretest. Compared mean gains for T and C using t-tests	2nd–3rd grade	Final: 60 $T = 30$, $C = 30$ Low socio-economic status urban school	Word recognition: $T = C$ Basal word recognition: $T > C$ Basal passages: $T > C$ Spelling (correct score): $T > C$ Spelling (qualitative score): $T > C$

Table 20
(*Continued*)

Program name	Program description	Study design	Age of participation	Sample size[a]	Outcomes[b]
Memphis City Schools Extended-Day Tutoring Program [Ross et al. (1996)]	Goal was to improve students' reading in grades 1–4 with group tutoring in the after-school hours. Focus on reading, with occasional writing, computer, and test-taking skills. One hour a day, 3 days/wk	Matched students on the basis of standardized test scores, then attitude and behavior. One student from each pair assigned to participate (supposedly randomly, although 2 outlier schools may have assigned students first, then found a match. These 2 (out of 13) had different mean test scores for T and C and were left out of the analysis. Study uses standardized test scores to evaluate students. ANCOVA and matched-pairs	Program: 1st–4th grade Study: 2nd–4th grade	Final: 656 $T = 328, C = 328$ Title I students	Reading test score: $T > C$, grade 3, $T = C$, grades 2, 4

Table 20
(Continued)

Program name	Program description	Age of participation	Sample size[a]	Study design	Outcomes[b]
Quantum Opportunities [Hahn, Leavitt and Aaron (1994)]	After-school educational activities (250 hrs), development activities such as mentoring and peer tutoring (250 hrs), community service activities (250 hrs) each year for 4 years. Students receive hourly bonuses and stipends for completing each part of program	9th–12th grade	Initial: 250 $T = 125, C = 125$ Final: 170 $T = 88, C = 82$ All students from families receiving public assistance	Entering 9th grade students whose families were on public assistance randomly selected from schools near program sites. Then randomly assigned to control or intervention. Those assigned to the program were then called and encouraged to join. Surveys conducted before and throughout the 4-year program. Final evaluation in autumn after completion	High school graduation or GED: $T > C$ Post-secondary attendance: $T > C$ Honors/awards: $T > C$ Attending high school: $T = C$ Dropout of high school: $T < C$ Have children: $T = C$ ($T < C$ at 10% level) Number of children: $T < C$ In trouble with police in past year: $T = C$ ($T < C$ at 10% level) On welfare, AFDC, food stamps: $T = C$ Do community service in past 6 months: $T > C$ Volunteer mentor/tutor in past 6 months: $T > C$ Start business or self-employed: $T = C$ Family life is happy: $T = C$ Hopeful about future: $T > C$ Depressed about life: $T = C$ Bothered about things: $T = C$ Lonely: $T = C$ Life has been a success: $T > C$ Have future plans: $T = C$ Need reading/math skill improvements: $T = C$ Need training for a good job: $T = C$ Need help finding a job: $T = C$ Need help with alcohol/drug problem: $T < C$

Table 20
(Continued)

Program name	Program description	Study design	Age of participation	Sample size[a]	Outcomes[b]
Nonrandom					
The ADEPT Project [Ross et al. (1992)]	Comprehensive after-school program focusing on building positive self-esteem and providing homework assistance and activities for social and emotional growth. Kids participated in 2 hours sessions with free play, creative dramatics, and homework assistance throughout the school year	Teachers and social workers chose 60 kids at each school site who they considered to be latchkey. Families were invited to an orientation and teachers then selected 20 to participate based on "need". Those youths whose parents were not interested became the control group. Quasi-experimental. Use data from parents, teachers, and school records. ANOVA with gain scores used	K–6th grade	Initial: 836; $T = 540, C = 296$; $T_2 =$ self-esteem building curriculum; Final: 667; $T = 443, C = 224$; Mostly low-income African-American	Self-esteem: all $T < C$; Depression: all $T = C$; Risk-taking: all $T = C$; Impulsivity: all $T = C$; Sulking: all $T = C$; Egotism: all $T < C$; Learning: all $T = C$; Shyness: all $T = C$; Acting: all $T = C$; Pressure: $T = C, T_2 < C$; Motivation: $T = C, T_2 > C$; Frustration: $T = C, T_2 < C$; Peer interaction: $T = C$; Standardized test scores: $T = C, T_2 > C$
Boston After School Study [Marshall et al. (1997)]	Regular after-school programs at public and parochial schools in Boston	Grade 1–4 children recruited from 30 Boston public schools and 8 parochial schools. Data collected through face-to-face interviews and questionnaires with the parent and through observations at the child's after-school setting. OLS regression of the child's behavioral problems on the types of care	1st–4th grade	Final: 181	Behavior problems, $T < C$ for "regular attenders"

Table 20
(Continued)

Program name	Program description	Study design	Age of participation	Sample size[a]	Outcomes[b]
Extended Services School Initiative [Grossman et al. (2002)]	Comprehensive after-school program seeking to promote the well-being and positive development of young people in their out of school hours	Teachers identify the lowest 50 readers	2nd–3rd grade	Final: 60 T = regular attenders	Word recognition: $T = C$ Skip school: $T < C$
Kindergarten After-School Program [Howes, Olenick and Der-Kiureghian (1987)]	After-school program designed to provide a service to working parents by providing extended day care beyond the morning – only Kindergarten class. Also aims to enhance socio-emotional development. Located on school grounds. Operates 5 days/wk. Children may stay until 3 or 5:30 pm	Sociometric interviews and classroom observations used to assess differences in social adjustment between participants in the after-school program and nonparticipants at the end of one school year. Nonrandom, but T and C groups had similar demographic composition. Chi-square and F tests of means	Kinder-garten	Final: 100 $T = 30$, $C = 70$ School admissions reflect ethnic diversity of US	Identified as "friend" by peers: $T > C$ Teacher talk to child, spontaneous: $T = C$ Teacher talk to child, responsive: $T > C$ Teacher talk to child, social: $T = C$ Teacher talk to child, information: $T = C$ Teacher talk to child, directions: $T = C$ Teacher talk to child, praise: $T = C$ Teacher talk to child, reprimands: $T = C$ Child talk to teacher, spontaneous: $T > C$ Child talk to teacher, responsive: $T = C$ Child talk to teacher, social: $T = C$ Child talk to teacher, information: $T > C$ Child talk to teacher, demands: $T = C$ Teacher responsiveness to child, positive: $T > C$ Teacher responsiveness to child, negative: $T = C$ Teacher responsiveness to child, unaware: $T = C$

Table 20
(*Continued*)

Program name	Program description	Study design	Age of participation	Sample size[a]	Outcomes[b]
LA's BEST [Brooks, Mojica and Land (1995)]	Comprehensive after-school program intended to combat obstacles to educational achievement. Academic tutoring and instruction, cultural enrichment, recreation, computer activities, and nutrition for K–6th graders after-school until 6 pm M–F in 19 of LA's poorest schools	2-year longitudinal study of some participants in the 10 longest-running LA's BEST sites. These participants had attended program for at least 2 yrs, had complete school records, and parental permission. No random assignment. Comparison group formed from kids in same school whose parents agreed to participate. Comparison group significant. different in grades (higher), family characteristics, and ethnicity. Data collected for 1992–1993 and 1993–1994 school years. Compared the improvement in scores of treatment and controls	Program: K–6th grade Study: 5th–8th grade	Initial: 146 $T = 80, C = 66$ Final: 127 $T = 69, C = 58$	The following outcomes did not have significance tests GPA math: $T = C$ Reported effort in math: $T = C$ GPA reading: $T = C$ Reported effort in reading: $T = C$ GPA composition: $T = C$ Reported effort in composition: $T = C$ GPA social studies: $T > C$ Reported effort in social studies: $T > C$ GPA science: $T > C$ Reported effort in science: $T > C$ The following outcomes were reported as significant (or not) at the 5% level Feel that grown-ups in after-school life care: $T = C$ Feel that grown-ups in after-school life expect you to do well: $T = C$ Feel that grown-ups in after-school life are easy to talk to: $T = C$ Feel that grown-ups in after-school life are helpful: $T > C$ Include teachers to help with a problem: $T > C$ Include student aides for help with a problem: $T > C$ Positive attitude toward school: $T > C$ Felt safe during after-school hours: $T > C$ Educational expectations (how far you will go in school): $T > C$[c]

Table 20
(*Continued*)

Program name	Program description	Study design	Age of participation	Sample size[a]	Outcomes[b]
LA's BEST [Huang et al. (2000)]	Same as above	Compares participants to schoolmates who did not participate. Followed students for five years. Broke down participants into those who attended 75% of days (high), 25–74% (med), and less than 25% (low). Control for gender, ethnicity, income, and language status (English profic). Not random assignment	2nd–5th grade	Initial: $T = 4,312$, $C = 15,010$	Language redesignation (English profic): $T > C$ (grades 4, 6, 8), $T = C$ (grades 5, 7) School absence: $T < C$ (grade 6, 7), $T = C$ (grades 8, 9) Math achievement test scores: $T = C$ (but started with $T < C$) Felt safe after school: $T > C$ Like school: $T > C$ Engagement in school: $T > C$ Educational expectations: $T > C$ Standardized math tests: *High > Low* Standardized reading tests: *High > Low* Standardized language arts tests: *High > Low* School attendance: *High > Low*
LA's BEST [Huang, Lin and Henderson (2001)]	Same as above	Surveys 74 of the 76 LA's BEST sites in June 2001. Participants whose parents gave permission (27% of all participants). No control group. Students tested in 1998–1999 and again in 1999–2000	2nd–5th grade	Initial: 3,717	Reading SAT-9: Proportion of LA's BEST students scoring above 50th National Percentile Rank (NPR) rose by 1 percentage pt. Math SAT-9: Proportion of LA's BEST students scoring above 50th NPR rose by 3 percentage pts Language arts SAT-9: Proportion of LA's BEST students scoring above 50th NPR rose by 5 percentage pts

Table 20
(Continued)

Program name	Program description	Age of participation	Study design	Sample size[a]	Outcomes[b]
Milwaukee Public School District [Posner and Vandell (1994)]	Formal After-school Program (ASP) participants were in 8 different programs at 5 elementary schools. 21 kids attended the same on-site ASP sponsored by the district that offered academic, recreational, and remedial activities at the end of the school day. The other programs attended typically had a recreational focus with some optional assisted homework time. Participants in all categories had to spend at least 3 days per week in these arrangements	3rd grade	Parents volunteered for the study and 216 children were selected if they participated in one of the arrangements for 3 days a week or more. Children evaluated with teacher and parent reports of behavior, the child's grades, and a standardized reading test. Not random. Chi-square tests for selection on categorical variables lead them to control for race, mother's education, and family income. Use ANCOVA and MANCOVA. Then Fisher tests for differences between T and all C	Initial: 216 $T = 34$ formal ASP $C_1 = 121$ maternal care $C_2 = 45$ informal adult supervision $C_3 = 15$ self-care Low income	GPA math: $T > C_1, C_2$ GPA reading: $T > C_1, C_2$ GPA other subjects: $T >$ all C GPA conduct: $T > C_1, C_2$ Wisconsin 3rd grade reading test: $T =$ all C Antisocial: $T < C_2, C_3$ Work habits: $T >$ all C Peer relations: $T >$ all C Emotional adjustment: $T > C_1, C_2$ Adult relations: $T =$ all C Anxious: $T =$ all C Dependent: $T =$ all C Hyperactive: $T =$ all C Time engaged in academic activities: $T >$ all C Time engaged in enrichment: $T >$ all C Time watching TV: $T <$ all C Time in outdoor unorganized activities: Time in transit: $T =$ all C Time eating: $T =$ all C Time in indoor unorganized activities: $T =$ all C Time with adults present: $T >$ all C Time with peers present: $T >$ all C Actively engaged with peers: $T >$ all C Actively engaged with adults: $T >$ all C Actively engaged with siblings: $T <$ all C Academic activities with adults: $T >$ all C

Table 20
(Continued)

Program name	Program description	Study design	Age of participation	Sample size[a]	Outcomes[b]
Milwaukee Public School District [Posner and Vandell (1999)]	Same as above	Followed the same children as above for 2.5 yrs. Used t-tests to contrast the outcomes of kids in formal programs with others	3rd–5th grade	Initial: Same as above Final: 194 no differential attrition $T = 26$ formal After-School Program $C_1 = 121$ maternal care $C_2 = 30$ informal adult supervision $C_3 = 17$ self-care Low income	Time on academics: $T >$ all C (grades 3, 4), $T =$ all C (grade 5) Time on nonsport extracurriculars: $T >$ all C (grades 3, 4, 5) Time in outdoor unorganized activities: $T <$ all C (grades 3, 4, 5) Time in coached sports: $T =$ all C (grades 3, 4), $T >$ all C (grade 5) Time in indoor structured activities: $T =$ all C (grades 3, 4), $T >$ all C (grade 5) Time watching TV: $T <$ all C (grades 3, 4, 5) Time socializing: $T =$ all C (grades 3, 4), $T <$ all C (grade 5) Time doing chores: $T <$ all C (grades 3, 4, 5) Time in transit: $T =$ all C (grades 3, 4, 5)[d]

Table 20
(Continued)

Program name	Program description	Study design	Age of participation	Sample size[a]	Outcomes[b]
The After-school Corporation (TSAC) [Welsh et al. (2002)]	Community-based organizations (CBOs) and other nonprofit organizations are funded by TASC to operate in-school after-school programs from 3:00 pm to 6:00 pm Monday through Friday throughout the public school year. TASC programs include educational enrichment through activities in language arts, science, mathematics, fine and performing arts and sports	Compares the actual changes in academic indicators (performance on standardized tests and school attendance) of TASC participants over a three year period to projected changes for nonparticipants, derived from OLS regressions controlling for factors including prior year's test scores, and demographic and educational background. Data were collected from TASC sites	K–8th grade	$T = 25{,}909$, $C = 39{,}780$	Gains in math: $T > C$, especially for students from disadvantaged circumstances Increase in attendance: $T > C$

[a] Throughout the table, "T" refers to treatment group and "C" refers to control or comparison group.

[b] Outcomes listed as $T > C$ or $C > T$ were statistically significant at the 5% level unless otherwise noted.

[c] All outcomes reported are based on Brooks, Mojica and Land (1995) "method 1" which compares improvements in test scores of the treatment and control groups (as described above). "Method 2" finds stronger evidence of positive effects of LA's BEST as cited in other meta-analyses. However, method 2 simply excludes low-scoring students from the treatment group, thereby biasing the results.

[d] Posner and Vandell (1994, 1999) also report the effects that these activities had on GPA, emotional adjustment, work habits and behavior problems in 5th grade. They find that time spent on unorganized outdoor activities is associated with worse outcomes for whites. Considering this finding in conjunction with the list of results above, suggests that formal after-school programs may have some positive effects. On the other hand, time in nonsport extracurriculars lowers emotional adjustment among blacks, so to the extent that after-school programs increase time spent in these types of activities, they may have detrimental effects on student outcomes.

Brooks et al. report that at the end of two years in the program, the LA's Best children had higher GPAs in reading and science than the control children, as well as reporting generally more positive attitudes toward school, higher aspirations, etc. Perhaps notably, treatment children were also more likely than controls to report that they felt safe after school. However, the estimates discussed by Brooks et al. and cited in other analyses of after school programs are based on an analysis that deletes "outliers" from the comparison. From the pattern of results, it appears that the effect of deleting these outliers was to raise the mean scores of the LA's Best kids relative to the controls. Alternative estimates reported in the appendix to Brooks et al. show treatment children with lower GPAs than control children, although "gains" in GPAs in social studies and in science were still significantly larger for the LA's Best children than for the other children. These are the estimates that we have reported in Table 20.

Huang et al. (2000) offer a much larger study of almost 20,000 children in LA's Best schools. The study compares children who participated in the program with schoolmates who did not, and controls for gender, ethnicity, income, and English proficiency. Relative to nonparticipants, the LA's Best students were more likely to have been redesignated into the English proficient group, had fewer absences, had better attitudes and were more likely to be in the "high" group on standardized tests rather than the "low" group. However, no effort was made in this study to control for nonrandom selection into the program. Huang, Lin and Henderson (2001) report increases in the Stanford 9 test scores of children in the LA's Best children, but does not compare them to Stanford 9 test scores of other children. This is a potentially important omission as test scores in the Los Angeles Unified School District have shown overall increases in recent years. For example, the mean percentile on the Stanford 9 reading, language, and mathematics tests increased from 27 to 38, 29 to 40, and 36 to 44 for Grade 2 LA Unified School District students between 1998–1999 and 2000–2001 [Los Angeles Unified School District (2001)].

The only study which addresses public concern about keeping older children in school and out of trouble, is Hahn, Leavitt and Aaron (1994), which evaluates the Quantum Opportunities program. This program randomly selected ninth grade students with families on public assistance, who were then randomly assigned to control or treatment status. The program involved after-school educational activities and community service activities each year for four years. Students received monetary rewards for completing each portion of the program. Participants in this program were more likely to graduate from high school or to obtain a GED than controls, and they were more likely to go on to post-secondary education. They also had significantly fewer children and reported being more hopeful about the future than other teens. There was no significant difference in the probability that participants had been "in trouble with police" in the past year, which is interesting in view of the focus of after-school proponents on crime.

There are many programs that do not fit our definition of after-school programs, but are sometimes mentioned in this context. Table 21 summarizes some of the more notable of these "positive youth development" programs, which in contrast to the programs in Table 20, are largely privately funded. The Tiernay, Grossman and Resch (1995)

Table 21

Studies of the effects of positive youth development programs on child outcomes

Program name	Program description	Study design	Age of participation	Sample size[a]	Outcomes[b]
Across Ages[c,d] [LoSciuto et al. (1996)]	Mentoring by adults over age 55 at least 2 hr/wk, community service 1 hr/wk, 26 sessions of social problem solving, workshops for parents	Random assignment of sixth grade classes in three schools to either program or control group. Used ANCOVA	6th grade	Initial: 729 Final: 562 no diff.	Increased positive attitudes: $T > C$ Inc. knowledge of older people: $T > C$ Likely to have negative reaction to drug use: $T > C$ More community service: $T > C$ School attendance: $T > C$
Big Brothers/Big Sisters [Tiernay, Grossman and Resch (1995)]	Mentors from the community are matched with eligible youth (typically those with only one adult involved in life). Mentors are usually required to interact with youth 9–12 hours per month for the first year	Randomly assigned eligible youth to treatment or wait list at eight sites with large case loads across the country. Surveys were administered to parents and youth at the time of assignment and 18 months later (note: those assigned to wait list remained on it for all 18 months). Case managers also completed data collection forms throughout the study. Interestingly, 22% of youth in the treatment group were never matched, usually because the youth became ineligible or no longer wished to be matched. This is typical for the program. The treatment group represents the opportunity to be matched. Outcomes were usually based on several survey questions and established scales of peer relationships, scholastic competence, etc. Used ordinary least squares controlling for age, race, gender, abuse, home environment, and site. Used logit for dichotomous outcomes	Program: Age 5–18 Study: Age 10–16	Initial: 1,138 $T = 572$, $C = 567$ Final: 959 $T = 487$, $C = 472$ From single-parent households	Likelihood of initiating drug use: $T < C$ Likelihood of initiating alcohol use: $T = C$ ($T < C$ at 10%) Number of times hit someone: $T < C$ Number of times stole something: $T = C$ Number of times damaged property: $T = C$ Perceived ability to complete schoolwork: $T > C$ Grade point average: $T = C$ ($T > C$ at 10%) Number times skipped class: $T < C$ Number of times skipped day of school: $T < C$ Weekly hours of homework: $T = C$ Weekly hours spent reading: $T = C$ School value scale: $T = C$ Overall positive parental relationship: $T > C$ Improved parental relationships (trust): $T > C$ Improved communication with parent: $T = C$ Anger/alienation in parental relationship: $T = C$ Number of times lied to parents: $T < C$[e]

Table 21
(*Continued*)

Program name	Program description	Study design	Age of participation	Sample size[a]	Outcomes[b]
I Have a Dream (IHAD) [Kahne and Bailey (1999)]	A sponsor adopts a sixth grade class and offers long-term financial, academic, and social support including after-school programs, tutoring, summer programs, and college scholarships	Natural experiment where participants are compared to the sixth graders of the previous year (in the same school). Study focuses on two IHAD programs in Chicago	6th–12th grade	Final: $T = 92$, $C = 89$	High school graduation: $T = 70.6\%$, $C = 35.5\%$ College enrollment: $T = 64.7\%$, $C = 18.9\%$ (approx.) No significance tests reported
Teen Outreach[c,d] [Allen et al. (1997)]	45 hrs of volunteer service and weekly small class discussions of values, decision making, parenting, life options. Can be in-school or after	25 schools nationwide randomly assigned to treatment or control from 1991 to 1995, but students in those schools elected to participate. Sites with more interested students than could participate held lotteries. Immediate post-tests after 1-year of participation	9th–12th grade	Initial: $T = 342$, $C = 353$ Final: $T = 324$, $C = 323$	School failure: $T < C$ School suspension: $T < C$ Teen pregnancy: $T < C$

Table 21
(Continued)

Program name	Program description	Age of participation	Sample size[a]	Study design	Outcomes[b]
Woodrock Youth Development Project [LoSciuto et al. (1997)][c]	Weekly classes (skills for human relations), daily mentoring, peer tutoring, homework assistance, extracurricular activities, and some home visits. Also, out-of-school special events. In-school classes once a wk and an after-school program	Age: 6–14	Initial: 453 T = 161, C = 292 Final: 367 T = 130, C = 237 Age 6–9: n = 170 Age 10–14: n = 197 Attrition differences in age (older attrited more) and more from T group among older and more from C for younger	Classes in 4 Philadelphia schools were randomly assigned to treatment or control. Different pre- and post-tests given to younger children (age 6–9) and older children (age 10–14). ANCOVA to compare outcomes	Self-esteem: $T = C$ (age 6–9, age 10–14) Relationship w/ and perception of students of other races: $T > C$ (age 6–9), $T = C$ (age 10–14) Alcohol, tobacco, or drug use in last year: $T < C$ (age 6–9), $T = C$ (age 10–14) Alcohol, tobacco, or drug use in last month: $T < C$ (age 6–9, age 10–14) Negative attitude toward alcohol, tobacco, and drug use: $T = C$ (age 6–9), $T < C$ (age 10–14) (Note that paradoxically, among the older group, T had a less negative attitude toward drugs.)

[a] Throughout the table, "*T*" refers to treatment group and "*C*" refers to control or comparison group.

[b] Outcomes listed as $T > C$ or $C > T$ were statistically significant at the 5% level unless otherwise noted.

[c] In Catalano et al. (1999).

[d] In Roth et al. (1998).

[e] Other social and behavioral outcomes were also reported, such as self-confidence, social acceptance, conflict with peers, and time spent in cultural activities, but none were significantly different for the treatment and comparison groups.

survey of Big Brothers/Big Sisters is notable both for its rigorous design and for the positive effects, which range from reductions in the probability of hitting people or initiating drug use, to improved schooling attendance. Kahne and Bailey's (1999) study of the "I Have a Dream" program reports very large increases in the probability of high school graduation in participating schools after the implementation of the program. Other programs demonstrate positive effects in terms of reduced probability of teen pregnancy, and reductions in alcohol and tobacco use.

Taken together, the evidence reviewed in these tables suggests that concern for latch-key children is well founded, and that model after school programs and other programs that focus on improving outcomes for youth can be effective in improving child outcomes. However, it is a leap to argue that the average available after-school program has any effect on child outcomes, since the model programs appear to be significantly better than the typical program. Moreover, despite the focus on reducing crime among advocates of after-school programs, few evaluations include any measure of violence or criminal activity among older children. Finally, more attention should be paid to uncovering the reasons that parents of older children are not using the available after-school programs.

6. Unanswered questions

Rather than summarize the preceding survey, we end this chapter with some unanswered research questions. First, the preceding discussion highlights the need for additional, rigorous research on the effects of all types of child care and early intervention programs on children. Existing analyses are often limited by a weak design (e.g., no control group, or a poorly chosen control group), small sample sizes, limited followup, and/or attrition. Another major problem is the lack of comprehensive data on child care quality. Analysts are often in the position of the proverbial three men trying to understand what an elephant is like when one observes only an ear, the second a tail and the third a tusk. As states become increasingly active in the child care market, this problem is likely to become more acute, as it is difficult to collect comparable data from disparate state systems.

Second, there has been little research documenting the interactions between the private and the public sectors of the child care market. For example, there has been no analysis of the extent to which programs like Head Start "crowd out" private sector provision of child care to low income children, or of the effects of such crowdout on the care provided to children. Moreover, little is known about the extent to which child care subsidies are passed through to child care prices. There has also been little systematic analysis of the takeup of public programs such as child care subsidies, and of the reasons why eligible families choose alternative child care modes. As a result of these gaps in our knowledge, there is currently little basis for evaluating the tradeoffs between different types of interventions in the child care market, such as different types of subsidy programs, regulation, and direct provision of care.

Finally, there is a pressing need for more information about the child care arrangements of older children, given increasing public expenditures in this area and the large numbers of children in care.

Acknowledgements

We would like to thank Ilya Berger, Stephanie Riegg and Jwahong Min for excellent research assistance, and Jeanne Brooks-Gunn and participants in the Handbook on the Economics of Education Conference of March 2003 for helpful comments.

Appendix: Child care data sources

The Cost, Quality, and Outcomes Study [CQOS; Helburn (1995)]. Collected data from a sample of 400 day care centers in four states in 1993. Observational measures of quality were recorded, along with rich data on inputs and costs. Children who were expected to spend another full year at one of the sampled centers and then enroll in Kindergarten in Fall 1994 were selected to be given developmental assessments. They were reassessed in Kindergarten and second grade. The sample included 828 children, of whom 757 provided usable data.

National Child Care Staffing Survey (NCCSS) was conducted in 227 centers in 5 cities in 1988. Approximately 45 centers were randomly selected from the licensed programs in each city. In each center, an infant, toddler, and pre-school classroom was randomly selected and two teachers from each of these classrooms were interviewed about their training, education, wages, experience, and background. In total, 1,309 teachers were interviewed. Classrooms were also rated on the ECERS scale, as well as the ITERS and the Arnett scale of teacher sensitivity.

The National Day Care Study [NDCS; Ruopp et al. (1979)] closely monitored a sample of 64 day care centers and approximately 1,600 of the children they served for about nine months. The children were given baseline developmental assessments and were assessed again at the end of the nine-month period during which classroom activities and inputs were monitored. The study design included two experiments in which some children were randomly assigned to classrooms with different staff–child ratios and teachers with different levels of training.

NICHD Study of Early Childhood Care [SECC; U.S. Department of Health and Human Services (1998)] has followed a sample of over 1,300 children from their birth in 1991 through the present, closely monitoring their home and child care environments and their development. The study used hospital birth records in ten sites in the US during 1991 to select a sample of healthy births to English-speaking mothers over age 18 who planned to remain in the site during the next year. Families were visited periodically for assessments of the home environment, and children who were in nonmaternal child care arrangements were visited in their child care arrangement. The quality of the arrangement was measured using a variety of assessment instruments, and data on child care inputs were recorded by direct observation. A novel feature of the study was the inclusion and assessment of all types of nonmaternal child care arrangements, not just centers and family day care homes. Child development was assessed at regular intervals and extensive psycho-social data on the mother and data on the home environment were collected as well. As children changed child care arrangements, the new arrangements were visited and observed.

National Longitudinal Survey of Youth (NLSY) began with a sample of 12,652 individuals aged 14–21 in 1979. Data was collected annually through 1994 and biannually thereafter. Beginning in 1986, the children of the women in the sample were given developmental assessments every other year. In addition, mothers are asked a series of questions about the home environment and home inputs to child development. And extensive data on child care is collected from the mothers as well. The main disadvantages of the NLSY are that the child care questions are not consistent across survey waves or children (e.g. some questions are asked only for the youngest child, or for infants), there are no data on child care quality (because this would require visits to thousands of child care arrangements), and the child care input data are reported by the mother instead of being recorded by trained observers in visits to the arrangement. The advantages are the very large random sample of children, the availability of extensive measures of the home environment and inputs, and the availability of repeated measures of the inputs and developmental outcomes. Unlike most other studies (with the exception of the NICHD SECC), the sample is not limited to children in a single mode of child care.

The Profile of Child Care Settings [PCS; Kisker et al. (1991)]. Collected information on structural classroom characteristics from a nationally representative sample of 2,089 day care centers and 583 regulated family day care homes by telephone survey in 1990. Regulated family day care homes are unlikely to be representative of unregulated day care homes, and the latter are thought to be far more numerous than the former.

The National Child Care Survey [NCCS; Hofferth et al. (1991)]. Collected information on child care from a nationally representative sample of 4,392 families with children aged 0–12 in 1990. The 100 primary sampling units in the NCCS were the same as in the PCS, so the two surveys together provide consumer and provider information about the same child care markets. Extensive data on child care arrangements were collected for all children.

Survey of Income and Program Participation (SIPP) . The SIPP consists of a series of national panels that are interviewed at frequent intervals for a period of 2½–4 years (depending on the panel) with sample sizes ranging from 14,000 to 36,700 households. Each panel of the SIPP is interviewed every 4 months to collect data on the "core content" – labor force status, program participation and income information. In addition, there are topical modules administered at least once to each panel on a variety of topics like assets and liabilities, health and disability, education and work history, child care, etc. Information from these topical modules can be merged to the core data.

The topical module on child care contains information on all child care arrangements for all children under age 15 in the household for the last reference month prior to the interview. Information is collected on mode of care, weekly number of hours of care, location of care and cost of child care. There are specific questions on whether a relative or nonrelative provided care, whether the child took care of herself or whether the child was in school. If the child care arrangement is a facility outside the child's home, parents are asked if the facility is licensed and who is in charge of transporting the child to the facility. Parents are also asked to provide information on whether child care problems adversely affected them at school or at work. Information is available for the following Panels (waves): 1984 (5), 1985 (6), 1986 (3, 6), 1987 (3, 6), 1988 (3, 6), 1989 (3), 1990 (3), 1991 (3), 1992 (6, 9), 1993 (3, 6, 9), 1996 (4, 10), 2001 (4).

National Survey of America's Families (NSAF; Urban Institute) was conducted by the Urban Institute in two rounds in 1997 and 1999, with two different samples. It was designed to analyze the consequences of devolution of responsibility for social programs from the federal government to the states. The survey was conducted by telephone on a sample derived primarily from random-digit dialing. Residents of 13 states were over-sampled in order to allow detailed within-state analysis, and low-income households (income less than twice the federal poverty level) were over-sampled as well. The full 1999 NSAF sample includes 42,360 households, and the 1997 sample includes 44,361 households. There are extensive questions on child care and other topics.

References

Adams, G., Schulman, S., Ebb, N. (1998). Locked Doors: States Struggling to Meet the Child Care Needs of Low-Income Working Families. Children's Defense Fund, Washington, DC.

Aizer, A. (2004). "Home alone: Child care and the behavior of school-age children". Journal of Public Economics 88 (9–10), 1835–1848.

Allen, J.P., Philliber, S.P., Herrling, S., Kuperminc, G.P. (1997). "Preventing teen pregnancy and academic failure: Experimental evaluation of a developmentally-based approach". Child Development 64, 729–742.

Anderson, P., Levine, P.B. (2000). "Child care and mothers' employment decisions". In: Blank, R.M., Card, D. (Eds.), Finding Jobs: Work and Welfare Reform. Russell Sage Foundation, New York, pp. 420–462.

Averett, S.L., Peters, H.E., Waldman, D. (1997). "Tax credits, labor supply, and child care". Review of Economics and Statistics 79 (1), 125–135.

Barnett, S. (1995). "Long-term effects of early childhood programs on cognitive and school outcomes". The Future of Children 5 (3), 25–50.

Barnett, W.S., Masse, L.N. (in press). "Early Childhood program design and economic returns: Comparative benefit-cost analysis of the Abecedarian program". Economics of Education Review.

Baum, C.L. (2002). "Child care costs and work decisions of low-income mothers". Demography 39 (1), 139–164.

Belle, D. (1997). "Varieties of self-care: A qualitative look at children's experiences in the after-school hours". Merrill–Palmer Quarterly 43 (3), 478–496.

Belsky, J., Eggebeen, D. (1991). "Early and extensive maternal employment and young children's socioemotional development: Children of the National Longitudinal Survey of Youth". Journal of Marriage and the Family 53 (4), 1083–1098.

Berger, M.C., Black, D.A. (1992). "Child care subsidies, quality of care, and the labor supply of low-income single mothers". Review of Economics and Statistics 74 (4), 635–642.

Bergmann, B. (1996). Saving Our Children from Poverty: What the United States Can Learn From France. Russell Sage Foundation, New York.

Blau, D.M. (1993). "The supply of child care labor". Journal of Labor Economics 11 (2), 324–347.

Blau, D.M. (1997). "The production of quality in child care centers". Journal of Human Resources 32 (2), 354–387.

Blau, D.M. (1999). "The effect of child care characteristics on child development". Journal of Human Resources 34 (4), 786–822.

Blau, D.M. (2000). "The production of quality in child care centers: Another look". Applied Developmental Science 4 (3), 136–148.

Blau, D.M. (2001). The Child Care Problem: An Economic Analysis. The Russell Sage Foundation, New York.

Blau, D.M. (2003a). "Child care subsidy programs". In: Moffitt, R. (Ed.), Means Tested Social Programs. University of Chicago Press, Chicago, pp. 443–516, for NBER.

Blau, D.M. (2003b). "Do child care regulations affect the child care and labor markets?". Journal of Policy Analysis and Management 22 (3), 443–465.

Blau, D.M. (in press). "Unintended consequences of child care regulations". Labour Economics.

Blau, D.M., Hagy, A.P. (1998). "The demand for quality in child care". Journal of Political Economy 106 (1), 104–146.

Blau, D.M., Mocan, H.N. (2002). "The supply of quality in child care centers". Review of Economics and Statistics 84 (3), 483–496.

Blau, D.M., Robins, P.K. (1988). "Child care costs and family labor supply". Review of Economics and Statistics 70 (3), 374–381.

Blau, D.M., Robins, P.K. (1991). "Child care demand and labor supply of young mothers over time". Demography 28 (3, August), 333–352.

Blau, D.M., Tekin, E. (2006). "The determinants and consequences of child care subsidies for single mothers". Journal of Population Economics, in press.

Blau, F.D., Grossberg, A.J. (1992). "Maternal labor supply and children's cognitive development". Review of Economics and Statistics 74, 474–481.

Bloom, D., Farrell, M., Kemple, J.J., Verma, N. (1999). "The family transition program: Implementation and three-year impacts of Florida's initial time-limited welfare program". Manpower Demonstration Research Corporation, New York, April.

Boocock, S. (1995). "Early childhood programs in other nations: Goals and outcomes". The Future of Children 5 (3, Winter), 94–114.

Bos, J.M., Huston, A.C., Granger, R.C., Duncan, G.J., Brock, T.W., McCloyd V.C. (1999). "New hope for people with low incomes: Two-year results of a program to reduce poverty and reform welfare". Manpower Demonstration Research Corporation, New York, August.

Bourdette, M. (1999). Personal communication to I. Sawhill of the Brookings Institution, June 17, 1999. From M. Bourdette, the Deputy Assistant Secretary for Legislation, Department of Health and Human Services.

Bowen, G.L., Neenan, P.A. (1993). "Does subsidized child care availability promote welfare independence of mothers on AFDC: An experimental analysis". Research on Social Work Practice 3 (4, October), 363–384.

Brooks, P.E., Mojica, C.M., Land, R.E. (1995). "Final evaluation report. Longitudinal study of LA's BEST after school education and enrichment program". Mimeo. University of California, Los Angeles, Center for the Study of Evaluation, Los Angeles.

Buell, M.J., Pfister, I., Gamel-McCormick, M. (2002). "Caring for the caregiver: Early head start/family child care partnerships". Infant Mental Health Journal 23 (2), 213–230.

California Secretary of State (2002). "California general election official voter information guide". Sacramento, CA, State of California, Fall.

Campbell, F.A., Duff, N., Applebaum, J.C., Martinson, S., Martin, E. (2000). "Be all that we can be: Lessons from the military for improving our nation's child care system". National Women's Law Center, Washington, DC, April.

Campbell, F.A., Ramey, C.T. (1994). "Effects of early intervention on intellectual and academic achievement: A follow-up study of children from low-income families". Child Development 65, 684–698.

Campbell, F.A., Ramey, C.T. (1995). "Cognitive and school outcomes for high-risk African-American students at middle adolescence: Positive effects of early intervention". American Educational Research Journal 32 (4), 743–772.

Campbell, F.A., Ramey, C.T., Pungello, E.P., Miller-Johnson, S., Sparling, J.J. (2002). "Early childhood education: Young adult outcomes from the Abecedarian Project". Applied Developmental Science 6 (1), 42–57.

Card, D., Hyslop, D. (2004). "Estimating the dynamic effects of an earnings subsidy for welfare leavers". Working Paper 10647. NBER.

Casper, L.M. (1997). "Who's minding our preschoolers? Fall 1994 update". Current Population Reports, P70-62, November. U.S. Bureau of the Census, Washington, DC. http://www.census.gov/population/www/socdemo/childcare.html.

Catalano, R.F., Berglund, M.L., Ryan, J.A., Lonczak, H.S., Hawkins, J.D. (1999). "Positive youth development in the United States: Research findings on evaluations of positive youth development programs". Social Development Research Group, University of Washington School of Social Work, Seattle, WA.

Chaplin, D.D., Robins, P.K., Hofferth, S.L., Wissoker, D.A., Fronstin, P. (1999). "The price elasticity of child care demand: A sensitivity analysis". Working paper. The Urban Institute, Washington, DC.

Children's Defense Fund (1999). Seeds of Success: State Prekindergarten Initiatives 1998–1999. Children's Defense Fund, Washington, DC.

Chipty, T. (1995). "Economic effects of quality regulations in the day care industry". American Economic Review 85 (2), 419–424.

Chipty, T., Witte, A.D. (1997). "An empirical investigation of firms' responses to minimum standards regulation". Working Paper 6104, July. NBER, Cambridge, MA.

Committee on Ways and Means, U.S. House of Representatives (1998). 1998 Green Book. Washington, DC. http://www.access.gpo.gov/congress/wm001.html, May.

Committee on Ways and Means, U.S. House of Representatives (2000). 2000 Green Book. Washington, DC. http://www.access.gpo.gov/congress/wm001.html, May.

Connelly, R. (1990). "The cost of child care and single mothers: Its effect on labor force participation and AFDC participation". Working paper. Bowdoin College, Brunswick, ME.

Connelly, R. (1991). "The importance of child care costs to women's decision making". In: Blau, D. (Ed.), The Economics of Child Care. Russell Sage Foundation, New York, pp. 87–118.

Connelly, R. (1992). "The effects of child care costs on married women's labor force participation". Review of Economics and Statistics 74 (1, February), 83–90.

Connelly, R., Kimmel, J. (2003a). "Marital status and full-time/part-time work status in child care choices". Applied Economics 35 (7, May), 761–777.

Connelly, R., Kimmel, J. (2003b). "The effect of child care costs on the labor force participation and welfare recipiency of single mothers: Implications for welfare reform". Southern Economic Journal 69 (3, January), 498–519.

Cosden, M., Morrison, M.G., Albanese, A.L., Macias, S. (2001). "When homework is not homework: After-school programs for homework assistance". Educational Psychologist 36 (3), 211–221.

Council of Economic Advisors (1997). The Economics of Child Care. U.S. Government Printing Office, Washington, DC, December.

Cryer, D., Burchinal, M. (1995). "Parents as child care consumers". In: Helburn, S.W. (Ed.), Cost, Quality, and Child Outcomes in Child Care Centers. Department of Economics, Center for Research in Economic and Social Policy, University of Colorado at Denver, Denver, CO, pp. 203–220. Technical report.

Cryer, D., Peisner-Feinberg, E.S., Culkin, M.L., Phillipsen, L., Rustici, J. (1995). "Design of study". In: Helburn, S.W. (Ed.), Cost, Quality, and Child Outcomes in Child Care Centers. Department of Economics,

Center for Research in Economic and Social Policy, University of Colorado at Denver, Denver, CO. Technical report.

Currie, J.J. (2001). "Early childhood education programs". Journal of Economic Perspectives 15 (2), 213–238.

Currie, J.J., Hotz, V.J. (2004). "Accidents will happen? Unintentional injury, maternal employment, and child care policy". Journal of Health Economics 23 (1, January), 25–59.

Currie, J., Neidell, M. (2006). "Getting inside the black box of head start program quality: What matters and what doesn't". The Economics of Education Review, in press.

Currie, J.J., Thomas, D. (1995). "Does head start make a difference?". American Economic Review 85 (3), 341–364.

Currie, J.J., Thomas, D. (1999). "Does head start help Hispanic children?". Journal of Public Economics 74 (2), 235–262.

Currie, J.J., Thomas, D. (2000). "School quality and the longer-term effects of head start". Journal of Human Resources 35 (4), 755–774.

Desai, S., Chase-Lansdale, P.L., Michael, R.T. (1989). "Mother or market? Effects of maternal employment on the intellectual ability of 4-year-old children". Demography 26 (4), 545–561.

Deutsch, M., Deutsch, C.P., Jordan, T.J., Grallo, R. (1983). "The IDS Program: An experiment in early and sustained enrichment". In: Consortium for Longitudinal Studies Staff (Ed.), As the Twig is Bent . . . Lasting Effects of Preschool Programs. Erlbaum, Hillsdale, NJ, pp. 377–410.

Dwyer, K.M., Ron, J.L., Daley, K.L. et al. (1990). "Characteristics of eight grade students who initiate self care in elementary and junior high school". Pediatrics 86 (3), 448–454.

Fewell, R.R., Scott, K.G. (1997). "The cost of implementing the intervention". In: Goss, R.T., Spiker, D., Haynes, C.W. (Eds.), Helping Low Birth Weight, Premature Babies: The Infant Health and Development Program. Stanford University Press, Stanford, CA, pp. 479–502.

Fox, J.A., Newman, S.A. (1997). "After school crime or after school programs?". Report to the U.S. Attorney General. Fight Crime Invest in Kids, Washington, DC.

Fronstin, P., Wissoker, D. (1995). "The effects of the availability of low-cost child care on the labor-supply of low-income women". Working paper. The Urban Institute, Washington, DC. January.

Fuerst, J.S., Fuerst, D. (1993). "Chicago experience with an early childhood program: The special case of the child parent center program". Urban Education 28, 69–96.

Fuller, B., Holloway, S.D., Liang, X.Y. (1996). "Family selection of child care centers: The influence of household support, ethnicity, and parental practices". Child Development 67 (6), 3320–3337.

Fuller, B., Kagan, S.L., McCarthy, J., Caspary, G., Lubotsky, D., Gascue, L. (1999). "Who selects formal child care? The role of subsidies as low-income mothers negotiate welfare reform". Paper presented at the Society for Research in Child Development Meeting, Albuquerque, NM, April.

Fuller, B., Raudenbush, S.W., Wei, L.-M., Holloway, S.D. (1993). "Can government raise child care quality? The influence of family demand, poverty, and policy". Educational Evaluation and Policy Analysis 15 (3, Fall), 255–278.

Furstenberg, F., Brooks-Gunn, J., Morgan, S.P. (1987). Adolescent Mothers in Later Life. Cambridge University Press, New York.

Galambos, N.L., Maggs, J.L. (1991). "Children in self-care: Figures, facts, and fiction". In: Lerner, J., Galambos, N. (Eds.), Employed Mothers and Their Children. Garland Press, New York, pp. 131–157.

Garber, H.L. (1988). The Milwaukee Project: Prevention of Mental Retardation in Children at Risk. American Association on Mental Retardation, Washington, DC.

Garces, E., Thomas, D., Currie, J.J. (2002). "Longer-term effects of head start". American Economic Review 92 (4), 999–1012.

Gelbach, J. (2002). "Public schooling for young children and maternal labor supply". American Economic Review 92 (1, March), 307–322.

Gilliam, W., Zigler, E. (2001). "A critical meta-analysis of all evaluations of state-funded preschool from 1977 to 1998: Implications for policy, service delivery, and program evaluation". Early Childhood Research Quarterly 4, 441–473.

Gladden, T., Taber, C. (2000). "Wage progression among less skilled workers". In: Blank, R.M., Card, D. (Eds.), Finding Jobs: Work and Welfare Reform. Russell Sage Foundation, New York, pp. 160–192.

Gormley, W.T. (1991). "State regulations and the availability of child care services". Journal of Policy Analysis and Management 10 (1), 78–95.

Granger, R.C., Cytron, R. (1999). "Teenage parent programs: A synthesis of the long-term effects of the new chance demonstration, Ohio's learning, earning, and parenting program, and the teenage parent demonstration". Evaluation Review 23 (2), 107–145.

Gray, S.W., Ramsey, B., Klaus, R. (1983). "From 3 to 20: The early training project". In: Consortium for Longitudinal Studies Staff (Ed.), As the Twig is Bent . . . Lasting Effects of Preschool Programs. Erlbaum, Hillsdale, NJ, pp. 171–200.

Greenstein, T.N. (1993). "Maternal employment and child behavioral outcomes – A household economics analysis". Journal of Family Issues 14 (3, September), 323–354.

Grossman, J.B., Price, M.L., Fellerath, V., Jucovy, L., Kotloff, L., Raley, R., Walker, K. (2002). "Multiple choices after school: Findings from the extended-service schools initiative". Public/Private Ventures, Philadelphia.

Hahn, A., Leavitt, T., Aaron, P. (1994). "Evaluation of the quantum opportunities program. Did the program work? A report on the postsecondary outcomes and cost-effectiveness of the QOP 1989–1993". Brandeis University Heller Graduate School Center for Human Resources, Waltham, MA.

Hamilton, G., Brock, T., Farrell, M., Friedlander, D., Harknett, K. (1997). "The national evaluation of welfare-to-work strategies. Evaluating two welfare-to-work approaches: Two-year findings on the labor force attachment and human capital development programs in three sites". Manpower Demonstration Research Corporation. New York, December.

Hamilton, G., Freedman, S., McGroder, S.M. (2000). "Do mandatory welfare-to-work programs affect the well-being of children? A synthesis of child research conducted as part of the national evaluation of welfare-to-work". Manpower Demonstration Research Corporation. New York, June.

Han, W.-J., Waldfogel, J. (2001). "The effect of child care costs on the employment of single and married mothers". Social Science Quarterly 82 (3), 552–568.

Han, W.-J., Waldfogel, J., Brooks-Gunn, J. (2001). "Long-run effects of early and extensive maternal employment on children's achievement and behavior". Journal of Marriage and the Family 63 (2), 336–354.

Hanushek, E. (1992). "The tradeoff between child quantity and quality". Journal of Political Economy 100 (1), 84–117.

Hanushek, E. (2007). "School resources". In: Hanushek, E., Welch, F. (Eds.), Handbook on the Economics of Education. North-Holland, Amsterdam, pp. 865–908. This volume.

Harms, T., Clifford, R. (1980). Early Childhood Environment Rating Scale. Teachers College Press, New York.

Harms, T., Cryer, D., Clifford, R. (1990). Infant/Toddler Environment Rating Scale. Teachers College Press, New York.

Hayes, C., Palmer, J., Zaslow, M. (1990). Who Cares for America's Children? Child Care Policy for the 1990s. The National Academy of Sciences Press, Washington, DC.

Heckman, J.J. (1974). "Effects of child-care programs on women's work effort". Journal of Political Economy 82 (2, March/April, Part 2), S136–S163.

Heckman, J.J. (1979). "Sample selection bias as a specification error". Econometrica 47 (1, January), 153–162.

Heckman, J.J. (1981). "Heterogeneity and state dependence". In: Rosen, S. (Ed.), Studies in Labor Markets. University of Chicago Press, Chicago, pp. 91–139.

Heckman, J.J. (2000). "Policies to Foster human capital". Research in Economics 54 (1, March), 3–56.

Heckman, J.J., Hsse, J., Rubinstein, Y. (2000). "The GED is a mixed signal: The effect of cognitive and non-cognitive skills on human capital and labor market outcomes". Xerox. University of Chicago.

Heckman, J.J., Smith, J. (1995). "Assessing the case for social experiments". Journal of Economic Perspectives 9 (2), 85–110.

Helburn, S.W. (Ed.) (1995). Cost, Quality, and Child Outcomes in Child Care Centers. Department of Economics, Center for Research in Economic and Social Policy, University of Colorado at Denver, Denver, CO. Technical report, June.

Helburn, S., Howes, C. (1996). "Child care cost and quality". The Future of Children 6 (2), 62–82.

Hill, J., Brooks-Gunn, J., Waldfogel, J., Han, W. (2003). "Towards a better estimate of causal links in child policy: The case of maternal employment and child outcomes". Unpublished paper. Columbia University School of International and Public Affairs.

Hill, J., Waldfogel, J., Brooks-Gunn, J. (2002). "Differential effects of high quality child care". Journal of Policy Analysis and Management 21 (4), 601–627.

Hofferth, S.L., Brayfield, A., Deich, S., Holcomb, P. (1991). "National child care survey, 1990". Report 91-5, Urban Institute, Washington, DC.

Hofferth, S.L., Chaplin, D.D. (1998). "State regulations and child care choice". Population Research and Policy Review 17, 111–140.

Hotz, V.J., Kilburn, R. (1997). "Regulating child care: The effects of state regulations on child care demand and its cost". Xerox. Department of Economics, UCLA, October.

Hotz, V.J., Kilburn, R. (2000). "The effects of state regulations on child care prices and choices". Xerox. Department of Economics, UCLA, March.

Howes, C., Galinsky, E., Shinn, M., Gulcur, L., Clements, M., Sibley, A., Abbott-Shim, M., McCarthy, J. (1998). "The Florida child care quality improvement study". Families and Work Institute, New York.

Howes, C., Olenick, M., Der-Kiureghian, T. (1987). "After-school child care in an elementary school: Social development and continuity and complementarity of programs". Elementary School Journal 88, 93–103.

Huang, D., Gribbons, B., Kim, K.S., Lee, C., Baker, E.L. (2000). "A decade of results: The impact of LA's BEST after school enrichment program on subsequent student achievement and performance". Mimeo. Graduate School of Education and Information Studies, UCLA Center for the Study of Evaluation.

Huang, D., Lin, S.-J., Henderson, T. (2001). "Evaluating the impact of LA's BEST on students' social and academic development: Study of 74 LA's BEST sites 2001–2002". Phase I, Preliminary Report. Mimeo. Graduate School of Education and Information Studies, UCLA Center for the Study of Evaluation, Los Angeles, CA.

Hyslop, D. (1999). "State dependence, serial correlation, and heterogeneity in intertemporal labor force participation of married women". Econometrica 67 (6, November), 1255–1294.

Inman, R. (1986). "Markets, government, and the 'new' political economy". In: Auerbach, A., Feldstein, M. (Eds.), Handbook of Public Economics, vol. 2. North-Holland, Amsterdam, pp. 647–674.

Internal Revenue Service (2001). "Individual tax statistics, complete report publications, tax year 1999". Available at http://www.irs.gov/taxstats.

James-Burdumy, S. (2005). "The effect of maternal labor force participation on child development". Journal of Labor Economics 23 (1, January), 177–211.

Johnson, D., Walker, T. (1991). "A follow-up evaluation of the Houston parent child development center: School performance". Journal of Early Intervention 15 (3), 226–236.

Kahne, J., Bailey, K. (1999). "The role of social capital in youth development: The case of "I have a dream" Programs". Educational Evaluation and Policy Analysis 21 (3), 321–343.

Karoly, L. et al. (1998). "Investing in our children: What we know and don't know about the costs and benefits of early childhood interventions". RAND, Santa Monica.

Kimmel, J. (1995). "The effectiveness of child care subsidies in encouraging the welfare-to-work transition of low-income single mothers". American Economic Review Papers and Proceedings 85 (2, May), 271–275.

Kimmel, J. (1998). "Child care costs as a barrier to employment for single and married mothers". Review of Economics and Statistics 80 (2, May), 287–299.

Kisker, E., Hofferth, S.L., Phillips, D.A., Farquhar, E. (1991). "A profile of child care settings: Early education and care in 1990". Mathematica Policy Research, Washington, DC. Report prepared for U.S. Department of Education.

Kisker, E.E., Rangarajan, A., Boller, K. (1998). Moving Into Adulthood: Were the Impacts of Mandatory Programs for Welfare-Dependent Teenage Parents Sustained After the Programs Ended? Mathematica Policy Research, Inc., Princeton, NJ, February.

Klein, B., Leffler, K. (1981). "The role of market forces in assuring contractual performance". Journal of Political Economy 89, 615–641.

Kontos, S., Howes, C., Shinn, M., Galinsky, E. (1995). Quality in Family Child Care and Relative Care. Teachers College Press, New York.

Lalonde, R. (1995). "The promise of public sector sponsored training programs". Journal of Economic Perspectives 9 (2, Spring), 149–168.

Lamb, M.E. (1998). "Nonparental child care: Context, quality, correlates, and consequences". In: Sigel, I., Renninger, K. (Eds.), Child Psychology in Practice, fifth ed. In: Damon, W. (Ed.), Handbook of Child Psychology. Wiley, New York.

Lee, V.E., Brooks-Gunn, J., Schnur, E., Liaw, F.R. (1990). "Are head start effects sustained? A longitudinal follow-up comparison of disadvantaged children attending head start, no preschool, and other preschool programs". Child Development 61, 495–507.

Lee, V., Loeb, S. (1995). "Where do head start attendees end up? One reason why preschool effects fade out". Educational Evaluation and Policy Analysis 17 (1), 62–82.

Leland, H. (1979). "Quacks, lemons, and licensing: A theory of minimum quality standards". Journal of Political Economy 87, 1328–1346.

Long, S.K., Kirby, G.G., Kurka, R., Waters, S. (1998). "Child care assistance under welfare reform: Early responses by the states". Assessing the New Federalism Occasional Paper 15. The Urban Institute, Washington, DC.

Los Angeles Unified School District (2001). "Rapid gains reflected in 2000–2001 Stanford 9 results". Office of Communications News Release, LAUSD, Los Angeles, CA, August 14.

LoSciuto, L., Freeman, M.A., Harrington, E., Altman, B., Lanphear, A. (1997). "An outcome evaluation of the Woodrock Youth Development Project". Journal of Early Adolescence 17 (1), 51–66.

LoSciuto, L., Rajala, A.A., Townsend, T.N., Taylor, A.S. (1996). "An outcome evaluation of across ages: An intergeneration mentoring approach to drug prevention". Journal of Adolescent Research 11 (1), 116–129.

Love, J.M., Schochet, P.Z., Meckstroth, A.L. (1996). "Are they in any real danger? What research does – and doesn't – tell us about child care quality and children's well-being". Mathematica Policy Research, Inc., Princeton, NJ, May.

Lowenberg, A., Tinnin, T. (1992). "Professional versus consumer interests in regulation: The Case of the U.S. child care industry". Applied Economics 24, 571–580.

Lucas, M.A. (2001). "The military child care connection". The Future of Children 11 (1), 129–133.

MaCurdy, T., Green, D., Paarsch, H. (1990). "Assessing empirical approaches for analyzing taxes and labor supply". Journal of Human Resources 25 (3, Summer), 415–490.

Maddala, G.S. (1983). Limited and Qualitative Dependent Variables in Econometrics. Cambridge University Press, New York.

Magenheim, E.B. (1995). "Information, prices, and competition in the child care market: What role should government play?". In: Pogodzinksi, J.M. (Ed.), Readings in Public Policy. Blackwell, Cambridge, MA, pp. 289–307.

Marshall, N.L., Garcia Coll, C., Marx, F., McCartney, K., Keefe, N., Ruh, J. (1997). "After school time and children's behavioral adjustment". Merrill-Palmer Quarterly 43 (3), 497–514.

Marx, F., Seligson, M. (1988). "The public school early childhood study: The state survey". Bank Street College, New York, NY.

McCarton, C.M. et al. (1997). "Results at age 8 years of early intervention for low-birth-weight premature infants. The infant health and development program". Journal of the American Medical Association 277 (2), 126–132.

McHale, S.M., Crouter, A.C., Tucker, C.J. (2001). "Free-time activities in middle childhood: Links with adjustment in early adolescence". Child Development 72 (6), 1764–1778.

McKey, R. et al. (1985). "The impact of Head Start on children, families and communities: Final Report of the Head Start evaluation". Synthesis and Utilization Project. CSR Inc., Washington, DC.

Meyers, M.K., Heintze, T. (1999). "The performance of the child care subsidy system: Target efficiency, coverage adequacy and equity". Social Service Review 73 (1), 37–64.

Meyers, M.K., Heintze, T., Wolf, D.A. (2002). "Child care subsidies and employment of welfare recipients". Demography 39 (1, February), 165–180.

Meyers, M., Rosenbaum, D., Ruhm, C., Waldfogel, J. (2002). Inequality in Early Childhood Education and Care: What Do We Know? Social Inequality Series. Russell Sage Foundation, New York, November 15.

Michalopoulos, C., Robins, P.K. (2000). "Employment and child care choices in the United States and Canada". Canadian Journal of Economics 33 (2), 435–470.

Michalopoulos, C., Robins, P.K. (2002). "Employment and child care choices of single parent families in the United States and Canada". Journal of Population Economics 15 (3), 465–493.

Michalopoulos, C., Robins, P.K., Garfinkel, I. (1992). "A structural model of labor supply and child care demand". Journal of Human Resources 27 (1), 166–203.

Miller, C., Knox, V., Auspos, P., Hunter-Means, J., Orenstein, A. (1997). "Making welfare work and work pay: Implementation and 18-month impacts of the Minnesota family investment program". Manpower Demonstration Research Corporation, New York, September.

Mocan, H.N. (1997). "Cost functions, efficiency, and quality in child care centers". Journal of Human Resources 32, 861–891.

Mocan, H.N. (in press). "Can consumers detect lemons? Information asymmetry in the market for child care". Journal of Population Economics.

Mocan, H.N., Burchinal, M., Morris, J.R., Helburn, S. (1995). "Models of quality in center child care". In: Helburn, S. (Ed.), Cost Quality and Child Outcomes. Center for Research on Economic and Social Policy University of Colorado at Denver, Denver, CO, pp. 279–304.

Morgan, G., Azer, S. (1997). "A primer of child care licensing 1997: Its role in public policy". Institute for Leadership and Career Initiatives, Wheelock College, Boston, MA.

Morris, D., Shaw, B., Penney, J. (1990). "Helping low readers in grades 2 and 3: An after-school volunteer tutoring program". The Elementary School Journal 91 (2), 133–150.

Mukerjee, S., Witte, A.D. (1993). "Provision of child care: Cost functions for profit-making and non-profit day care centers". Journal of Productivity Analysis 4 (1/2), 145–163.

National Center for Education Statistics (2003). "Prekindergarten in U.S. public schools: 2000–2001". NCES 2003-019. U.S. Department of Education, Washington, DC.

National Research Council and Institutes of Medicine (2000). Shonkoff, J., Phillips, D., Keilty, B. (Eds.), Early Childhood Intervention: Views from the Field. National Academy Press, Washington, DC.

National Research Council and Institutes of Medicine (2000). Shonkoff, J., Phillips, D. (Eds.), From Neurons to Neighborhoods: The Science of Early Childhood Development. National Academy Press, Washington, DC.

National Research Council and Institute of Medicine (2003). Smolensky, E., Gootman, J.A. (Eds.), Working Families and Growing Kids: Caring for Children and Adolescents. National Academy Press, Washington, DC.

Neidell, M. (2000). "Early time investments in children's human capital development: Effects of time in the first year on cognitive and non-cognitive outcomes". Xerox. Department of Economics, UCLA, October.

NICHD Early Child Care Research Network (1997). "Child care during the first year of life". Merrill–Palmer Quarterly 43, 340–360.

NICHD Early Child Care Research Network (1998). "Early child care and self-control, compliance, and problem behavior at twenty-four and thirty-six months". Child Development 69 (4), 1145–1170.

NICHD Early Child Care Research Network (2000). "The relation of child care to cognitive and language development". Child Development 71 (4), 960–980.

NICHD Early Child Care Research Network (2001). "Child care and children's peer interactions at 24 and 36 months: The NICHD study of early child care". Child Development 72 (5), 1478–1500.

NICHD Early Child Care Research Network, Duncan, G.J. (2003). "Modeling the impacts of child care quality on children's preschool cognitive development". Child Development 74 (5), 1454–1475.

Oden, S., Schweinhart, L., Weikart, D. (2000). Into Adulthood: A Study of the Effects of Head Start. High/Scope Press, Ypsilanti, MI.

Parcel, T.L., Menaghan, E.G. (1990). "Maternal working conditions and children's verbal facility: Studying the intergenerational transmission of inequality from mothers to young children". Social Psychology Quarterly 53 (2), 132–147.

Parcel, T., Menaghan, E. (1994). Parent's Jobs and Children's Lives. Aldine de Gruyter, New York.

Paulsell, D., Kisker, E.E., Love, J.M., Raikes, H. (2002). "Understanding implementation in early Head Start programs: Implications for policy and practice". Infant Mental Health Journal 23 (1/2), 14–35.

Peisner-Feinberg, E.S., Burchinal, M.R., Clifford, R.M., Culkin, M.L., Howes, C., Kagan, S.L., Yazejian, N. (2001). "The relation of preschool child-care quality to children's cognitive and social development trajectories through second grade". Child Development 72 (5), 1534–1553.

Pettit, G.S., Bates, J.E., Dodge, K.A., Meese, D.W. (1999). "The impact of after-school peer contact is moderated by parental monitoring, perceived neighborhood safety, and prior adjustment". Child Development 70, 768–778.

Pettit, G.S., Laird, R.D., Bates, J.E., Dodge, K.A. (1997). "Patterns of after-school care in middle childhood: Risk factors and developmental outcomes". Merrill–Palmer Quarterly 43, 515–538.

Posner, J.K., Vandell, D.L. (1994). "Low-income children's after-school care: Are there beneficial effects of after-school programs?". Child Development 65, 440–456.

Posner, J., Vandell, D.L. (1999). "After-school activities and the development of low-income urban children: A longitudinal study". Developmental Psychology 35 (3), 868–879.

Powell, I., Cosgrove, J. (1992). "Quality and cost in early childhood education". Journal of Human Resources 27 (3), 472–484.

Powell, L.M. (1997). "The impact of child care costs on the labour supply of married mothers: Evidence from Canada". Canadian Journal of Economics 30 (3), 577–594.

Powell, L.M. (2002). "Joint labor supply and child care decisions of married mothers". Journal of Human Resources 37 (1), 106–128.

Preston, A. (1993). "Efficiency, quality, and social externalities in the provision of day care: Comparisons of nonprofit and for-profit firms". Journal of Productivity Analysis 4 (1/2), 165–182.

Queralt, M., Witte, A.D. (1997). "Effects of regulations, consumer information, and subsidies on child/staff ratios at child care centers". Working Paper 97-2. Florida International University, Miami, FL.

Quint, J.J.C., Bos, J.M., Polit, D.F. (1997). "New chance: Final report on a comprehensive program for young mothers in poverty and their children". Manpower Demonstration Research Corporation, New York, October.

Raikes, H.H., Love, J.M. (2002). "Early Head Start: A dynamic new program for infants and toddlers and their families". Infant Mental Health Journal 23 (1/2), 1–13.

Ramey, C., Campbell, F., Blair, C. (1998). "Enhancing the life course for high-risk children". In: Crane, J. (Ed.), Social Programs That Work. Russell Sage Foundation, New York, pp. 184–199.

Resnick, G., Zill, N. (undated). "Is Head Start providing high-quality educational services? Unpacking Classroom Processes". Xerox. Westat, Inc.

Reynolds, A. (1998). "Extended early childhood intervention and school achievement: Age thirteen findings from the Chicago longitudinal study". Child Development 69 (1), 231–246.

Reynolds, A. et al. (2000). "Long term benefits of participation in the Title 1 Chicago child–parent centers". Working paper. University of Wisconsin, Madison, Madison, WI.

Ribar, D. (1992). "Child care and the labor supply of married women: Reduced form evidence". Journal of Human Resources 27 (1), 134–165.

Ribar, D. (1995). "A structural model of child care and the labor supply of married women". Journal of Labor Economics 13 (3), 558–597.

Riccio, J., Friedlander, D., Freedman, S. (1994). "GAIN: Benefits, costs, and three-year-impacts of a welfare-to-work program". Manpower Demonstration Research Corporation, New York, September.

Richardson, J., Dwyer, K., McGugan, K., Hansen, W.B., Dent, C., Johnson, C.A., Sussman, S., Brannon, B., Flay, B. (1989). "Substance abuse among eighth-grade students who take care of themselves after school". Pediatrics 84 (3), 556–566.

Robins, P.K. (1991). "Child care policy and research: An economist's perspective". In: Blau, D. (Ed.), The Economics of Child Care. Russell Sage Foundation, New York, pp. 11–42.

Robins, P.K., Spiegelman, R. (1978). "An econometric model of the demand for child care". Economic Inquiry 16, 83–94.

Rodman, H., Pratto, D.J., Nelson, R.S. (1985). "Child care arrangements and children's functioning: A comparison of self-care and adult care children". Developmental Psychology 48, 413–418.

Rose-Ackerman, S. (1983). "Unintended consequences: Regulating the quality of subsidized day care". Journal of Policy Analysis and Management 3 (1), 14–30.

Ross, C. (1996). "State child care assistance programs for low-income families". Mathematica Policy Research, Washington, DC, April.

Ross, C. (1998). "Sustaining employment among low-income parents: The role of child care costs and subsidies". Mathematica Policy Research, Washington, DC, December.

Ross, J.G., Saavedra, P.J., Shur, G.H., Winters, F.N., Felner, R.D. (1992). "The effectiveness of an after-school program for primary grade latchkey students on precursors of substance abuse". Journal of Community Psychology 20, 22–38.

Ross, S.M., Lewis, T., Smith, L., Sterbin, A. (1996). "Evaluation of the extended-day program in Memphis county schools: Final report to CRESPAR". Center for Research in Educational Policy, University of Memphis, TN, Memphis.

Roth, J., Brooks-Gunn, J., Murray, L., Foster, W. (1998). "Promoting healthy adolescents: Synthesis of youth development program evaluations". Journal of Research on Adolescents 8 (4), 423–459.

Ruhm, C.L. (2004). "Parental employment and child cognitive development". Journal of Human Resources 39 (1), 155–192.

Ruopp, R., Travers, J., Glantz, F., Coelen, C. (1979). Children at the Center. Abt Books, Cambridge.

Schweinhart, L.J., Barnes, H., Weikart, D. (1993). Significant Benefits the High/Scope Perry Preschool Study Through Age 27. High-Scope Educational Research Foundation, Ypsilanti, MI, Monograph #10.

Seppanen, P.S., Love, J.M., deVries, D.K., Bernstein, L., Seligson, M., Marx, F., Kisker, E.E. (1993). "National study of before- and after-school programs". U.S. Department of Education, Washington, DC.

Shapiro, C. (1986). "Investment, moral hazard, and occupational licensing". Review of Economic Studies LIII, 843–862.

Smith, K. (2000). "Who's minding the kids? Child care arrangements, Fall 1995". Current Population Reports P70-70. October. U.S. Census Bureau, Washington, DC. http://www.census.gov/population/www/socdemo/childcare.html.

Smith, K. (2002). "Who's minding the kids? Child care arrangements, Spring 1997". Current Population Reports P70. U.S. Census Bureau, Washington, DC. http://www.census.gov/population/www/socdemo/childcare.html.

Steinberg, L. (1986). "Latchkey children and susceptibility to peer pressure: An ecological analysis". Developmental Psychology 22, 433–439.

Tekin, E. (2001). "The responses of single mothers to welfare and child care subsidy programs under the new Welfare Reform Act". Doctoral dissertation. University of North Carolina, Chapel Hill.

Tekin, E. (2004). "Child care subsidy receipt, employment, and child care choices of single others". Working Paper 10459. National Bureau of Economic Research.

Temple, J., Reynolds, A., Miedel, W. (2000). "Can early intervention prevent high school dropout?". Urban Affairs 35 (1), 31–56.

Tiernay, J.P., Grossman, J.B., Resch, N. (1995). Making a Difference: An Impact Study of Big Brothers/Big Sisters. Public/Private Ventures, Philadelphia, PA.

Tunali, I. (1986). "A general structure for models of double-selection and an application to a joint earnings/migration process with remigration". Research in Labor Economics 8, Part B, 235–282.

U.S. Administration for Children and Families (1995). "Federal child care programs in FY1995". Washington, DC. http://www.acf.dhhs.gov/programs/ccb/research/1995.htm.

U.S. Administration for Children and Families (2000). "New statistics show only small percentage of eligible families receive child care help". Washington, DC, December 6. http://www.acf.dhhs.gov/news/press/2000/ccstudy.htm.

U.S. Administration for Children and Families (2001). "Final 1998 state data tables and charts". Washington, DC, February 15. http://www.acf.dhhs.gov/programs/ccb/research/archive/98acf800/index.htm.

U.S. Administration for Children, Youth and Families (1999). "Head Start fact sheet, 1998". Head Start Bureau, Washington, DC.

U.S. Administration for Children, Youth, and Families (2002). "Making a difference in the lives of infants and toddlers and their families: The impacts of early Head Start". U.S. Department of Health and Human Services, Washington, DC. http://www.acf.dhhs.gov/programs/core/ongoing_research/ehs/ehs_intro.html.

U.S. Advisory Commission on Intergovernmental Relations (1994). "Child care: The need for federal-state-local coordination". Report A-128, March. U.S. Advisory Commission on Intergovernmental Relations, Washington, DC.

U.S. Bureau of Labor Statistics (2001). "Report on the American workforce". Bureau of Labor Statistics, Washington, DC.

U.S. Census Bureau (2000). "Record share of new mothers in labor force". Census Bureau Reports. October 24. U.S. Census Bureau, Washington, DC.

U.S. Department of Health and Human Services (1998). "The NICHD study of early child care". National Institute of Child Health and Human Development, Washington, DC. April.

U.S. Department of Health and Human Services (2001). "The economic rationate for investing in children: a focus on child care." Office of the Assistant Secretary for Planning and Evaluation, Washington, DC. December.

U.S. General Accounting Office (1994). "Child care subsidies increase the likelihood that low-income mothers will work". Report GAO/HEHS-95-20, December. Washington, DC. http://www.gpo.gov.

U.S. General Accounting Office (1995). "Early childhood centers: Services to prepare children for school often limited". Report GAP/HEHS-95-21, March. Government Printing Office, Washington, DC.

U.S. General Accounting Office (1998). "Welfare reform: States' efforts to expand child care programs". Report GAO/HEHS-98-27, January. Washington, DC. http://www.gpo.gov.

U.S. General Accounting Office (1999a). "Early education and care: Early childhood programs and services for low-income families". Report GAO/HEHS-00-11, November. Washington, DC. http://www.gpo.gov.

U.S. General Accounting Office (1999b). "Child care: How do military and civilian center costs compare?". Report GAO/HEHS-00-7, October. Washington, DC. http://www.gpo.gov.

U.S. General Accounting Office (2004). "Child care: State efforts to enforce safety and health requirements". Report GAO-04-786, September. http://www.gao.gov/new.items/d04786.pdf.

U.S. Office of Juvenile Justice and Delinquency Prevention (1996). "Juvenile offenders and victims: A national report". Washington, DC.

Vandell, D.L., Corasaniti, M.A. (1988). "The relations between third graders' after-school care and social, academic, and emotional functioning". Child Development 59, 868–875.

Vandell, D.L., Posner, J.K. (1999). "Conceptualization and measurement of children's after-school environments". In: Friedmen, S.L., Wachs, T.D. (Eds.), Measuring Environment Across the Lifespan Emerging Methods and Concepts. American Psychological Association Press, Washington, DC. Ch. 6.

Vandell, D.L., Ramanan, J. (1991). "Children of the national longitudinal survey of youth: Choices in after-school care and child development". Developmental Psychology 27 (4), 637–643.

Waldfogel, J. (2001). "International policies towards parental leave and child care". The Future of Children 11 (1), 99–111.

Waldfogel, J., Han, W.-J., Brooks-Gunn, J. (2002). "Early maternal employment and child cognitive development". Demography 39 (2), 369–392.

Walker, J. (1991). "Public policy and the supply of child care services". In: Blau, D. (Ed.), The Economics of Child Care. Russell Sage Foundation, New York, pp. 51–77.

Walker, J. (1996). "Funding child rearing: Child allowance and parental leave". The Future of Children 6 (2, Summer/Fall), 122–136. Available at http://www.futureofchildren.org/information2826/information_show.htm?doc_id=73300.

Welsh, M.E., Russell, C.A., Williams, I., Reisner, E., White, R.N. (2002). "Promoting learning and school attendance through after-school programs: Student level changes in educational performance across TASC's first three years". Policy Studies Associates, Washington, DC.

Whitebook, M., Howes, C., Phillips, D. (1990). "Who cares? Child care teachers and the quality of care in America". Final Report of the National Care Staffing Study. Child Care Employee Project, Oakland, CA.

Xiao, M. (2004). "Is quality certification effective: Evidence from the child care market". Working paper. Department of Economics, Iowa State University, January.

Zigler, E., Styfco, S.J. (1994). "Head Start: Criticisms in a constructive context". American Psychologist 49 (2), 127–132.

Zill, N., Resnick, G., McKey, R.H. (1999). "What children know and can do at the end of Head Start and what it tells us about the Program's Performance". Westat Inc., Rockville, MD.

Chapter 21

THE COURTS AND PUBLIC SCHOOL FINANCE: JUDGE-MADE CENTRALIZATION AND ECONOMIC RESEARCH

WILLIAM A. FISCHEL

Dartmouth College

Contents

Handbook of the Economics of Education, Volume 2
Edited by Eric A. Hanushek and Finis Welch
© 2006 Elsevier B.V.   *All rights reserved*
DOI: 10.1016/S1574-0692(06)02021-6

Abstract

This paper explores for economists how the school-finance litigation movement, which began with Serrano v. Priest in 1971, ought to be characterized in economic models. Its primary message is that this has become a national movement, not one confined to individual states. Economists should be wary of characterizing these cases as discrete events in which a state that loses to reform-minded plaintiffs is distinctly different from a state that succeeds in defending its system. I describe numerous instances in which states have attempted to head off defeat in the courts by conceding to reform-demands by the plaintiffs. School finance litigation does make a difference, however. Win or lose, states have been induced to reformulate their state-aid formulas. I show that the most common of these reforms, which focus on differences in tax-base per pupil, have altered the local tax price for education. This alteration causes the "property rich" districts to pay more for education. However, the correlation between "property rich" and "income rich" is essentially zero, largely because low-income communities are more willing to tolerate the nonresidential uses that lower their tax price. The result is that school-finance reform in most states is likely to reduce the efficiency of local public education because of tax-price distortion but not improve the lot of low-income students and taxpayers in any systematic way.

Keywords

state constitutions, education finance, tax price, school district, median voter

JEL classification: I22, H70

1. Centralized in law, decentralized in practice

The financing of American public schools is unusual in public finance because of the long-standing tension between the forces of decentralization to local districts and centralization to the state government. Decentralization models incorporate the market-like location choice of households (Tiebout-style demanders) and the supply decisions of competitive school districts, which are conceived of as median-voter models of political organization. Centralization models dwell on the national spillover benefits of education and the effects of unequal educational expenditures on the distribution of income.

Up until the 1970s, the level of centralization in most states was a political decision that balanced the decentralizing inclinations of parents and other local residents against the centralizing forces of education professionals. In the last thirty years, numerous state courts have tipped the balance in favor of centralization (at the state level) of funding and regulation of public education. This essay explores the law and economics of these judge-made reforms. Their primary implications have been an exogenous change in the local tax price for public education and the detachment of local fiscal decisions from school spending. Empirical evidence suggests that both of these changes have contributed to the declining efficiency of public education.

The federal constitution does not mention education as an obligation of the national or the state governments. Most state constitutions, which are always more detailed and usually more practical-minded than the federal Constitution, do list education as one of the government functions for which the legislature is to make provision. Except for prohibitions on aiding sectarian schools, the directions are seldom specific. For example, the Michigan constitution requires the legislature to "maintain and support a system of free public elementary and secondary schools".

Until about 1970, it had been assumed by nearly all state courts that state legislatures were entitled to delegate to geographic subdivisions of the state as much responsibility for school funding as they wished. (Some state constitutions do specify minimum funding levels for the state, but such amounts were almost always a small fraction of actual spending.) The "education clauses" of state constitutions do not speak to this issue directly. Some contain hortatory language about education along the lines of "knowledge is good". Phrases urging comprehensiveness, such "thorough and efficient" and "general and uniform" are found in several dozen states. These requirements should be taken in the nineteenth-century context in which they were written. Public schools in rural areas were often irregular in operation and a good deal less than comprehensive, and their local constituency was often resistant to state-mandated regulations, especially when the state did not put up much money [Tyack (1972)].

Local governmental entities such as municipalities, counties, and school districts are, with the exception of the District of Columbia, entirely the creatures of state governments. The states, as the U.S. Supreme Court ruled in Hunter v. Pittsburgh (1907), have almost complete discretion about local government structure and powers [Briffault (1990)]. They could adopt a unitary, state-run school system with no local variation. The state of Hawaii is the only current example of such a system, though California and New

Mexico verge on it in practice. Or the state can offer almost complete decentralization, allowing local governments to make tax and spending decisions entirely on their own.

There are no current examples of such a decentralized system in the United States. The closest is New Hampshire, which uses local property taxes to fund about 90 percent of school spending, as shown in Table 1. (This and subsequent calculations exclude federal programs, which fund about 7 percent of school spending nationally, not counting

Table 1
Percent of revenues for public K-12 schools, 1997–1998, from most local to least local

	Local percent of total	State percent of total	Federal percent of total	Private percent of total
United States	42.3	48.4	6.8	2.5
(ten largest states in **bold**)				
New Hampshire	84.5	9.3	3.8	2.4
Vermont	63.6	29.4	5.2	1.8
Illinois	62.5	28.5	6.8	2.2
Virginia	60.2	31.4	5.2	3.2
Nevada	60.1	31.8	4.6	3.5
Connecticut	56.1	37.3	3.9	2.7
Nebraska	54.7	33.1	6.7	5.5
New Jersey	54.3	39.8	3.6	2.3
New York	53.9	39.7	5.4	0.9
Pennsylvania	53.6	38.7	5.9	1.8
Rhode Island	53.1	40.1	5.4	1.3
Massachusetts	52.9	40.7	5.0	1.4
Maryland	52.7	39.0	5.2	3.1
South Dakota	51.4	35.6	10.0	3.0
Missouri	50.1	39.7	6.2	3.9
Ohio	48.9	41.2	5.8	4.1
Colorado	47.6	43.4	5.1	3.9
Maine	46.4	45.5	7.0	1.1
Texas	45.8	44.2	7.6	2.4
Wyoming	44.5	47.0	6.7	1.7
Arizona	43.2	44.3	10.2	2.2
North Dakota	41.1	41.1	12.4	5.4
Indiana	40.9	51.4	4.8	2.9
Georgia	40.1	51.2	6.8	1.9
Minnesota	39.8	52.3	4.9	3.0
Wisconsin	39.7	53.7	4.5	2.1
Florida	39.7	48.8	7.6	3.9
Montana	38.7	46.9	10.2	4.2
Iowa	38.2	51.3	5.3	5.2
Tennessee	36.4	47.7	8.8	7.0
Louisiana	35.9	50.4	11.3	2.4
South Carolina	35.7	51.5	8.5	4.3

Table 1
(*Continued*)

	Local percent of total	State percent of total	Federal percent of total	Private percent of total
Oregon	33.6	56.8	6.4	3.2
Kansas	33.5	57.9	5.9	2.7
California	30.6	60.2	8.2	1.1
Utah	29.5	61.0	6.9	2.5
Idaho	28.6	62.7	7.0	1.7
Mississippi	27.1	55.4	14.1	3.4
West Virginia	26.8	62.7	9.2	1.3
Delaware	26.7	64.4	7.6	1.4
Kentucky	26.5	61.7	9.6	2.2
Arkansas	26.0	57.7	10.8	5.6
Michigan	25.4	66.0	6.6	1.9
Oklahoma	24.5	61.6	8.6	5.3
Washington	24.4	66.0	6.4	3.2
Alabama	23.2	62.5	9.4	5.0
Alaska	22.9	62.2	12.3	2.7
North Carolina	22.7	67.3	7.2	2.7
New Mexico	12.3	72.2	13.2	2.2
Hawaii	0.5	89.0	8.6	1.9

Source: U.S. Department of Education, National Center for Education Statistics, Common Core of Data survey. (Table 159, prepared November 2001.) Available at http://nces.ed.gov/pubs2002/digest2001/tables/dt159.asp.

the substantial tax–expenditure arising from deductions of state income and property taxes from taxable federal income [Loeb and Socias (2004)].) The next closest states, Illinois and Vermont, rely on local property taxes for about 70 percent of state and local spending, and the corresponding figure for the median state is 43 percent. As Table 2 indicates, the mean local share of state and local spending declined steadily from 1920, when it was about 83 percent, to a little less than half of the state and local total in 1980, and it has hovered around that fraction since then.

The modest growth of state sources since 1980 is somewhat deceptive. This is because many of the court decisions since 1970 have called for states to "offset" the inequalities in property tax base. If this were followed exactly, most local property taxes would actually not be subject to local control. To take the example of the largest state, California, Table 1 indicates that local funds finance 30.6 percent of school spending. However, because of the *Serrano* decision (discussed further) and Proposition 13, the state legislature controls all of school spending, regardless of whether it comes from property taxes or other taxes. Simply because property taxes are classified as local does not mean that economists should assume that local units from which they are collected actually control the disposition of the revenue.

Table 2
Historical trends in local, state and federal financing of K-12 public schools, 1919–1998

School year	Local percent	State percent	Federal percent
1919–1920	83.2	16.5	0.3
1929–1930	82.7	16.9	0.4
1939–1940	68.0	30.3	1.8
1949–1950	57.3	39.8	2.9
1959–1960	56.5	39.1	4.4
1969–1970	52.1	39.9	8.0
1979–1980	43.4	46.8	9.8
1989–1990	46.8	47.1	6.1
1998–1999	44.2	48.7	7.1

Source: U.S. Department of Education, National Center for Education Statistics, Statistics of State School Systems; Revenues and Expenditures for Public Elementary and Secondary Education; and Common Core of Data surveys. (Table 157, prepared November 2001.) Available at http://nces.ed.gov/pubs2002/digest2001/tables/dt157.asp.

Despite substantial interstate variety in the state-local split and the long-term decline in the importance of local funds in most states, many researchers persist in characterizing American public school finance as being an entirely local function. In reality, state funding (and accompanying regulation) has for more than a century been an important supplement for local funding. There is nothing constitutional about local funding. Any state government can alter its school finance system without raising issues of within-state federalism. Local school districts can be expanded, contracted, consolidated, or abolished at the discretion of the state's legislative machinery. Unlike municipalities, many of which have acquired a constitutionally-protected home-rule status, school districts are legally creatures of the state [Garber and Edwards (1962)].

With this constitutional framework, one would expect that school districts would seldom be more than administrative arms of the state government. They would be like counties, which were originally intended as dispensers for state-established courts, public records systems, and public works. (Many urban counties have since been granted home-rule charters and assumed the role of local self-governance that municipalities have.) Yet for most of their history, American public schools have been the quintessential local public service, the focus of the most intense expressions of local preferences. Efforts to detach schools from local control are almost always resisted, and the expanding role of state and national funding has had to accommodate local demands for autonomy [Kaestle (1983)].

The Federal constitution's failure to mention schools does not disable Congress from legislating on the subject. The spending power of Congress has been construed sufficiently liberally that nearly any configuration of subsidies can be offered to local education. It might be politically wise for Congress to channel such funds through the states, and it usually does, but there is no requirement that funds be allocated in any particular way. Federal funds can be made subject to conditions without, in the eyes of the U.S. Supreme Court, infringing on powers reserved to the states.

What is slightly more hedged is Congress' power to make the states and their schools subject to direct regulation. One of the anomalies of studying constitutional law is that the student is told at the outset that the federal government has only specific "enumerated" powers. The "police power" is the ability to make regulations and enforce them with legal penalties, and neither Congress nor the President is granted such general authority. Much of the rest of the course, however, demonstrates that circumventions of this disability have since the 1930s been tolerated by the federal courts. All Congress has to do is say that the regulation is necessary to promote interstate commerce, whose regulation is explicitly granted to Congress.

The Supreme Court originally regarded interstate commerce as applying only to goods shipped across state boundaries, but in the 1930s, under pressure from New Deal reforms, the Court relented and has until very recently not questioned federal authority to regulate even the most local of activities, including schools. However, in United States v. Lopez (1995), the Court made a small but definite step in the direction of limiting congressional powers. The case coincidentally involved schools in that it overturned a conviction in federal court of a man who had possessed a firearm in violation of a recent federal statute limiting their possession near any public school.

Despite the *carte blanche* for federal spending authority, federal support for public education has always been small. One area in which they have played a role is in facilitating desegregation. Federal funds were dangled as a reward for compliance with intradistrict desegregation by funding such experiments as magnet schools. Aside from this, federal funding for schools has usually been part of an anti-poverty program rather than an educational endeavor. The 2001 "No Child Left Behind" school funding legislation advanced by the Bush administration must be evaluated in this light. Although the program is quantitatively modest, it occurs in a background of a historically small role for the federal government and in the uncertain future of Supreme Court jurisprudence concerning regulatory authority. A close watch on litigation involving these initiatives might reveal to economists opportunities for examining important changes in school finance and governance.

One final legal point involves the tension between compulsory education and parental control. All states have laws that compel parents to send their children to school. Alternatives to the public school, including private, religious and home-schooling, are permitted but are subject to state regulation. Compulsory education itself is controversial mainly among religious sects like the Amish, and wary compromises involving sectarian schools seem to be the rule in these cases [Wisconsin v. Yoder (1972)]. But no state can compel attendance at public schools exclusively. The movement to eliminate nonpublic schools arose in the 1920s in several states. Instruction of recent immigrants in religious schools, sometimes in a language other than English, was thought to undermine American values. In Oregon, the Ku Klux Klan and, to a lesser extent, public school teachers, pressed for an initiative that compelled public school attendance [Tyack (1968)]. The U.S. Supreme Court struck it down in Pierce v. Society of Sisters (1925), which has become the lodestar of private schools for its dictum about parental rights and responsibilities in education.

2. Origins of localism in American public schools

The theory of public finance is difficult to reconcile with the public's attachment to localism in funding and governing public education. Education is not a local public good in the sense that economists understand that term. It fails in most respects to meet the conditions of nonexclusion or nonrivalry. Would-be free riders can easily be excluded, as the viability of private schools has long demonstrated. The concern about class size is evidence that education is rivalrous in that dimension, and most evidence suggests that schools and school administrative systems achieve optimal size at levels that could easily be attained by private providers [Brasington (1997)].

On the other side of the size issue is the distribution of the spillover benefits of education. The spillover benefits of having educated neighbors or co-workers are realized at a geographic area that is unlikely to correspond to any school district's boundaries for the simple reason that Americans are so mobile. The benefits of even New York City's huge school system accrue to people in Los Angeles and College Station as well as in Manhattan and the Bronx. (New York City high school reunions are common in southern California.) One puzzle of American education finance is why there is so much localism, especially since most other high-income countries have largely centralized their education–finance systems.

One approach to explaining the role of localism in American education is historical. Cubberley (1919), a pioneer historian of education, summed up the origins of American schooling as "completely local... Everywhere development has been from the community outward and upward, and not from the State downward" (p. 155). To illustrate this localism, Cubberley pointed out that New England towns, which were the national leaders in public education, financed schools by property taxation of separate districts within the town itself, not by taxation of the town as a whole (pp. 43, 162, 235–240). The submunicipal district system spread to most other states in the North and to much of the West, and it persisted well into the twentieth century, with critics constantly decrying its tax-base inequalities and inadequacies [Reisner (1930)].

One line of investigation for this historical localism would be to investigate education as a local economic development device. European settlement of the American continent was a gradual and largely decentralized affair. Many entrepreneurs established towns as a way of attracting settlers and thereby increasing the value of their real estate [Reps (1965)]. One of the attractions for would-be settlers was the availability of a primary school. One such entrepreneur was William Cooper, who established Cooperstown, New York, in the 1790s and incidentally sired the novelist James Fenimore Cooper. The senior Cooper laid out lots, provided financing for new farms, and established a public school all with an eye toward attracting settlers [Taylor (1995)]. Similar anecdotes can be found in other sources, but I am unaware of any that systematically explores the connection between competitive town-founding and the system of education that was developed subsequently. Studies of the development of the American high school in the early twentieth century do emphasize competitive impetus of the movement, which propelled American education far ahead of European nations [Goldin (1998)]. Competition among districts has been convincingly established as an important contributor to the quality of public schools [Hoxby (2000)].

The system of education that developed in northern states in the nineteenth century was based on districts whose dimensions were determined by walking distances. Most municipalities thus had numerous districts. The first consolidation movement occurred in larger cities in the late nineteenth century, according to Tyack (1974). Many had inherited the rural system of local districts, and even urban schools that were consolidated into a city-wide district often had a decentralized ward governance system. But the impetus to enlarging their geographic scope had little to do with internalizing spillover benefits. The movement was largely promoted by professional educators.

One of the drawbacks of the district system for teachers and administrators was employment insecurity. Teachers complained of having too many masters and of arbitrary treatment by parents, community members, and meddling politicians. Administrators complained of political resistance to curricular changes. Even where job conditions were satisfactory, continuation of schools for more than a year was often uncertain. (As an aside, I found that most nineteenth-century rural school systems had regular sessions in the winter and the summer. The twentieth-century tradition of summer vacation was not an agrarian holdover, as is popularly thought [Fischel (2003)].)

The response to these conditions was primarily organizational, and it was inspired by the managerial revolution in business that was going on in early twentieth century. Consolidation of authority into a corporate-like board of education, with its powerful CEO – the superintendent of education – was a major political goal of educators. It paralleled the rise of the council–manager system in municipal governance, in which a professional manager, consciously imitative of the new business manager, was selected by an elected council [East (1965)]. The city manager, like the superintendent of schools, was intended to displace day-to-day administration by council members, who were generally expected afterward only to be lawmakers and passive overseers of the professional manager.

This same movement produced the nominal divorce between municipality and school district. Most local school districts are now governed and financed separately from the municipality. (Municipal boundaries and school-district boundaries are seldom exactly congruent any more, which raises both empirical and theoretical problems for economists which will be discussed in Section 4.) The first "centralization" movement wrested direct control over education from parents and municipal politicians and gave rise to the CEO-style superintendent of schools and the subservient elected school board [Tyack (1974)].

3. Capitalization, asset risk, and the persistence of localism

The historical account of the centralization of school districts moves a bit too quickly, though, in its implication that voter and parental control was usurped by a powerful education establishment. There are economic reasons to suspect that local control would remain strong in municipalities and school districts. Unlike boards of directors of the business corporation, who got in bed with the CEO and let him run the show at the expense of stockholders, elected city councils and school boards closely monitored the city managers and the school superintendents they hired. They were more faithful agents of their principals, the local voters, than business boards of directors [Fischel (2001)].

One explanation for retention of representative governance in school districts is risk spreading. The conventional reason for why CEOs control their boards is stockholder diversification. Since no single stock greatly affects the wealth of a holder of a diversified portfolio, few stockholders have much interest in making costly efforts to monitor boards and managers. In local governments, by contrast, the "stockholders" are property owners, and the most numerous property owners are homeowners. They are the residual claimants of the success and failures of their cities and school districts. Starting with Oates (1969), innumerable studies have found that better local services and lower taxes raise owner-occupied home values.

Both the current flow of services and taxes and the capitalized value of future flows, which affect their home values, make homeowners highly interested in managerial slacking. Unlike corporate stockholders, most homeowners cannot diversify the risk of managerial failures. They can indeed "vote with their feet" if schools get bad, taxes rise without offsetting benefits, or environments deteriorate. But because these conditions are usually observable by potential homebuyers, sellers would suffer a large and concentrated capital loss. So they become much more watchful of what happens in local government.

This offers one possible explanation for the persistence of localism in providing public schools. The local property market gives voters incentives to monitor the performance of their elected boards and superintendents. Studies too numerous to name have found that better schools are capitalized in home values [Haurin and Brasington (1996), Jud and Watts (1981)]. One form of monitoring is fairly obvious, since the local consumers of education are parented by a subset of local voters. They do not need to wait for distant analysts to provide them with news about a poorly run school.

The fraction of local adults who have children in school, however, is low. Even at the height of the baby-boom generation's attendance in school it seldom exceeded fifty percent of households. Nationally, about 15 percent of the population is in public school in the year 2000, and only about a third of the adult population are parents of children under 18 [Fields and Casper (2001)]. If school expenditures served only the interests of currently-existing families with children, majoritarian preferences would tend to underfund schools.

Voters without children in public schools are nonetheless interested in their operation. Most of them are homeowners who know that an important set of potential homebuyers will be interested in school quality as well as tax rates [Mayer and Hilber (2002), Sonstelie and Portney (1980)]. Capitalization of local schools and school taxes makes for more attentive stockholder–voters [DiPasquale and Glaeser (1999)]. Such capitalization is much less likely to occur at the state level because the larger area of a state precludes the land-scarcity necessarily for capitalization and because supplier interests are apt to be more successful in manipulating politicians at the state level.

So much research has established the importance of schools for home values that a interesting variant is how the conditions in which capitalization might not work well as a guide to local education policy. One possibility arises when a significant fraction of voting adults hold no interest in property that would be adversely affected by poor school performance. Cities with large fractions of renters might be less interested in local schools [Carroll and Yinger (1994)]. Indeed, long stayers might want to discourage competition for existing housing. But renters tend to participate less in local government anyway, so their greater numbers might not be accompanied by greater influence [Verba and Nie (1972)]. And rent-control, formal or informal, allows them to capitalize, to some extent, the benefits of local improvements.

Better candidates for alienation of voters from school capitalization might be communities with a large fraction of the population living in adults-only retirement communities. Another might be homeowners whose communities are undergoing transition to rental housing or commercial development, for which schools might be less important to potential buyers. Still another might be racial or ethnic hostility to newcomers [Poterba (1997)], though the capitalization principle says that trashing the schools for this reason is a costly form of racial animosity, since it would reduce the value of the old-timers' homes.

Capitalization can also provide incentives for efficiency even if local voters are not very successful at monitoring school superintendents' performance. As long as the superintendent is dependent on the level of local taxes, she will have some incentive to adopt efficient policies [Hoxby (1999)]. This is because local tax collections, particularly property-tax collections, will be sensitive to the quality of schools. Thus as long as homebuyers can tell a good school district from a bad one, the school superintendent will have more revenue at her disposal if she makes efficient decisions about schools. Again, this will generally not be true when the state provides the marginal dollars to the district. In that case, a revenue-maximizing superintendent will be dedicated to obtaining more revenue from the state legislators or administrators, and education that is valued by homebuying parents will only coincidentally be provided.

A potentially interesting area of research is how homebuyers know which schools are good. Recent studies suggest that housing prices respond to test scores more than to spending itself. Even when neighborhood characteristics are controlled for in sophisticated ways, it appears that a good school can raise housing prices by amounts that are comparable to the cost of private-education alternatives [Black (1999), Bogart and Cromwell (1997)]. Yet surveys of homebuyers with children in school reveal that most cannot accurately rank test scores, taxes, or spending in their own district compared to nearby districts. Some theories suggest that people use heuristics to judge schools [Bickers and Stein (1998)]. Absence of graffiti turns out to be a reasonable proxy for a well-run school [Schneider et al. (1998)]. But the microeconomics of the operation of this market are not well specified.

4. School district boundaries and municipal zoning

The Tiebout–Hamilton model of property taxation describes the conditions under which public school spending can be privatized. [Tiebout (1956) and Hamilton (1975) are discussed in Nechyba's essay in this volume.] A necessary condition for its operation is that localities have control over their land use. They must be able at least to prevent land developers from building homes whose property-tax revenues do not exceed the anticipated expenditures on schools that the new occupants will generate. I have argued that most municipalities have the power to do something very much like that through existing zoning requirements and monetary and in-kind exactions on development that is permitted [Fischel (1992)].

What has not been addressed at any length is that school districts themselves lack zoning authority. Only general municipal governments – cities, towns and, in states where they serve municipal functions, counties – can do zoning or impose exactions. This would not seem to be much of a problem where the school district is coterminous with the municipality. There still are some "dependent" school districts in the United States, in which the city council controls school funds as well as other municipal revenues. The zoning side of city hall could surely coordinate its efforts with the school finance side. But the dominance of the "independent" school district would still not be problematic where boundaries of districts and municipalities are coterminous. City commissions making zoning and planning rules have every incentive to do what the school-board itself would do if it had the authority.

Only in New England and New Jersey do municipal and school district boundaries match for almost the entire population. (Users of the U.S. Census of Governments will miss this fact because the Census perversely refuses to regard New England towns and the townships of several Northeastern states as true municipalities.) In much of the rest of the country, school districts cross municipal and even county lines with apparent impunity. The reason for this is the school consolidation movement. The number of districts fell from 83,642 to 15,987 between 1950 and 1980, and it has now leveled off [Kenny and Schmidt (1994)].

Most of the loss in districts is statistically inconsequential, since it involved lightly populated and often declining rural areas. More important have been the unification of urban districts that were formerly divided between several elementary districts and a single high school district. The resulting "unified" district governs all schools from kindergarten through high school. The creation of large unified districts often combines several municipalities and unorganized county areas. In these, the congruence of zoning authority and schooling would appear to be weak. A possible question for economic research is whether either land use or school policies and outcomes are different in areas in which school and city are more or less congruent.

Several cautions are in order. It could be that the constituent municipal governments of the school district are cooperative with regard to zoning decisions, so that fragmentation of authority does not lead to disregard for the well being of the fiscal condition of the district. Some studies indicate that zoning decisions by one locality are imitated by nearby municipalities [Rolleston (1987), McMillen and McDonald (1991)], though whether this indicates cooperation is not clear. I have seen instances of school impact fees being assessed by a municipality and handing the money over to a school district of which it was only one part. There may be more cooperation among municipal governments because of the many opportunities for repeated interactions and from the fact that their constituents know each other through participation in school affairs. The "beggar thy neighbor" strategy of putting noxious land uses on downwind borders is more common on the blackboard than in reality.

I should not give the impression that the overlap between city and school district is nil. In most states that have smaller than county districts, it is rare for a city to be divided among several districts. The most common type of district encompasses an entire municipality and its surrounding hinterland or another municipality. The internalization of land use decisions may be less problematic than it looks on the maps. My preliminary (unpublished) survey of school district structure in the states suggest that district boundaries are chosen with some consideration for municipal boundaries. It is uncommon, for instance, for a city to be divided into more than one district.

One consideration in district formation is including enough tax base to finance schools. One objective of California's district unification was to create districts whose tax bases were not too unequal [California State Board of Education (1998)]. Thus low-income cities would often be included in an area that had substantial commercial tax base, while high-income residential districts would not get such a tax-base enhancement. This possibility may be important for understanding tax-base issues. Far from being the "accidents of geography" that school-finance litigators decry, school districts represent at some point conscious attempts to have sufficient tax base. Sonstelie, Brunner and Ardon (2000) found that even before *Serrano*, school districts with lower-income housing often had a substantial nonresidential tax base, and Hoxby (2001) found that California spending and wealth disparities were relatively low even prior to the *Serrano* litigation.

A further subdivision of school districts is also worth scholarly attention. Most districts have several schools, and allocation of students among those of the same type (elementary, middle and high school) are usually by contiguous neighborhoods. (There are intriguing exceptions: West Bend, Wisconsin, has two high schools next to one another, and students are assigned on the basis of odd and even birthdates.) One way of preserving some sense of municipal identity within a large school district would be to have attendance boundaries coincide with municipal borders.

In areas with relatively little housing construction, these boundaries can be stable for a long time. This offers an opportunity to examine samples of students who attend different schools, which may differ in quality, in settings in which the financial conditions are presumably the same. (One would be wise to check the validity of this, as there has been litigation about it, too.) Sandra Black has exploited a Massachusetts sample of this type to obtain more precise estimates of the extent of capitalization of school quality into housing values. Bogart and Cromwell (2000) have examined the consequences of changing attendance boundaries in a Cleveland suburb, though it is not apparent from this article why the district would have undertaken a program that appears to have lowered their home values.

5. The decline of localism in the twentieth century

The principle of capitalization of school quality in home values offers one explanation for why localism persists in American education, but local control may also be the product of particular institutional settings. One of these is the geographic districting of state legislative boundaries. The proportional voting systems of Europe never got a foothold in the United States. Although electoral districts do not necessarily correspond to school-district boundaries, state legislative districts are usually drawn with some respect for local boundaries. Thus local governments and school districts are apt to have a strong collective voice in their state legislature. Of course, it could be that Americans' interest in local control is why all states select representatives in winner-take-all elections in distinct and fairly stable geographic districts. Legislatures elected in such a manner are apt to be sensitive to the preferences of local voters.

What the foregoing does not explain, however, is why localism in education has been in decline for the latter two-thirds of the twentieth century. An event that might explain some of this is the imposition of the one-person, one-vote rule on state legislatures in the 1960s. Up until Baker v. Carr (1962), the apportionment of state legislatures was regarded by the U.S. Supreme Court as a political question beyond the reach of the courts. Baker v. Carr changed that, and subsequent rulings by both federal and state courts quickly required that both houses of the bicameral state legislatures (only Nebraska is unicameral) had to be apportioned on the basis of population. Many states had explicitly used counties or towns as the basis for representation in the upper house, with the result that large cities were often underrepresented and rural counties overrepresented in the state senate. Reluctance to reapportion in response to population change (rural decline and suburban growth) also contributed to malapportionment.

By 1970, all state legislatures conformed fairly well to the one-person, one-vote standard. This resulted in less correspondence between local boundaries and state legislative boundaries, which could have weakened the voices of local governments and provided an opening for teacher unions and other supplier interest-groups to increase the state's role in funding education. I know of no research into this particular implication of reapportionment, but before undertaking it, one should ask how much malapportionment there was previously.

One of the reasons for the general success of judge-made reform of legislative apportionment may be that it did not make too much of a difference. Lower houses of most state legislatures usually were represented by approximately equal-sized districts, and even most upper houses had only a few egregious outliers. (The national champion was Los Angeles County, which with a quarter of the state's population had but one representative in the 40-seat senate, since no county could have more than one.) Political scientists have shown that the most numerous gainers from reapportionment were suburban districts [Reichley (1970)], and the suburbs have long been a mainstay for local control of schools.

A Pollyannaish but possibly valid reason for the decline in localism is that the wider-than-local benefits of education are perceived to have risen. If either the area over which educational benefits has expanded or the percent of education's benefits internalized in wages and personal utility has declined, a larger area and larger population government might better handle either externality than local school districts.

This explanation does not fit the facts, though. Geographic mobility among Americans has always been high. If anything, it has declined in the last two or three decades [Fischer (2002)]. The education of children has for more than a century returned only a fraction of whatever spillover benefits education may have to the community that financed it. It is also not clear that spillover benefits to education have increased. There is evidence that returns to education have risen in the last two or three decades, but most of the economic benefit is internalized by the educated person in the form of higher wages. The part that cannot be internalized does not seem to have grown by any measurable statistic, though one must admit that such a metric would be hard to come by. For these reasons, the centralization of education finance does not seem to have resulted from a desire to get a better match between the area benefited and the area paying the cost.

A public-choice account of the centralization of education would have to begin with the rise of teacher unionization. Teacher unions are the biggest – indeed, almost the only – success story of American labor unions in the last forty years. Most unions, if not most teachers, appear to benefit from having a state legislature to deal with rather than a group of fragmented local districts whose attentive taxpayers are well represented on local school boards [Hoxby (1996)]. In this respect, state funding is just another step in the centralization movement that brought the strong-manager approach to city governance earlier in the twentieth century. But just asking *qui bono* is not satisfactory by itself when the mechanism for gain is not well specified. Municipal governments have become unionized without enduring as much pressure for centralization of their finance. Unlike school districts, the number of municipalities has risen over the century, and the ideology of decentralization still seems to hold sway.

I will presently identify the court system as a prime mover of centralization in the last thirty years. Teacher unions have often offered friend of the court support for plaintiffs who seek more centralized finance, but none to my knowledge has ever taken the lead role in recruiting plaintiffs and prosecuting the cases. Perhaps the reformist lawyers who bring these cases are stand-ins for teacher unions, but the connection is not at all obvious. As I think it is worth recounting in some detail, judge-made centralization in education came from a particular concern and in a form that continues to influence education funding to the present day.

6. Are judges doing what voters want but politicians will not deliver?

I will presently trace the sequence of events in which judges got into school finance. A preliminary question is whether the judiciary was undertaking something that the majority of voters wanted but which the political market failed to deliver. After all, polls that ask people about equality of educational resources find that large majorities favor the principle [Reed (2001)]. Most such polls, however, do not frame the question in terms of giving something up (like local control) in order to get more equality of expenditure.

Whether voters favor local control has a fairly unambiguous answer. Prior to the onset of successful litigation, school-finance activists of the 1960s and early 1970s took their case to the people. Half of the states allow for some form of statewide voter initiatives. The clearest and cleanest evidence comes from statewide referenda and initiatives prior to the *Serrano* decision. (Those that came later give less clear signals because of the spreading influence of the court cases.) The issue of whether school financing should be shifted from the local property tax to a statewide tax was put on the ballot in several states. As Carrington (1973) pointed out, voters rejected these proposals in 1972 in California, Colorado, Michigan and Oregon. A proposed constitutional amendment to centralize school financing was also rejected by voters in Michigan in 1971 [Hain (1974)]. Voters in Maine overwhelming rejected a *Serrano*-inspired statewide property tax system for school finance after four years experience with it in 1977. Even the towns that supposedly benefited from the plan voted against it [Perrin and Jones (1984)]. A few years before a court-ordered reform in 1979, voters in the state of Washington rejected two referenda that proposed an income tax and a corporation tax to relieve local districts of the obligation to fund schools [Gale (1981), Theobald and Hanna (1991)].

Even after *Serrano*, referenda that asked voters to approve the taxes required by plaintiff victories were rejected. West Virginia voters declined in 1984 to approve a revenue-equalization bill that responded to its court's *Serrano*-style decision of Pauley v. Kelly (1979). On May 5, 1998, Ohio voters rejected by a four-to-one margin a proposal to replace local property taxes, whose variations were found unconstitutional by the Ohio Supreme Court in DeRolph v. State (1997), with a two percentage point increase in the state sales tax. New Jersey's incumbent governor, Jim Florio, is widely believed to have been defeated for reelection in 1992 as a result of his attempt to comply with court-ordered school finance in Abbott v. Burke (1990) [Harrison and Tarr (1996)]. I cannot locate a single statewide initiative or referendum in the post-World-War-II era that proposed to equalize school spending or taxable resources by centralizing funding and came anywhere close to passing without a court-ordered reform preceding it.

California's Proposition 13, adopted by a 2-1 margin in 1978, cut rates to one percent, which reduced property taxes by half. Its limit on reassessments to no more than two percent per year has kept property taxes extremely low. It is often given as an instance in which voters did choose to send school taxing responsibility to the state. It would be a counterexample to my rule if Proposition 13 did not come directly after legislative compliance with the *Serrano* decision. In the decade before 1978, voters in California had rejected by wide margins at least four initiatives that proposed to increase the state's role in funding education and reduce reliance on local property taxes [Allswang (2000)]. Once *Serrano* had made state control a *faite accompli*, voters had no reason to want to retain the local property tax and grabbed the first initiative available [Fischel (1989, 2004)]. When property taxes buy better schools, voters are unwilling to give up local control by switching from local property taxes to state taxes. It was not a failure of the political system that maintained the local finance system.

There is actually some evidence that the political failure was not a matter of politicians failing to deliver school-finance reform that voters desired. It was instead a matter of politicians persuading judges to give them cover to undertake reforms that voters did not want. While most litigation was sponsored by civil rights lawyers who were more-or-less independent of state politics, they often got a boost from elected officials whose reforms would result in their defeat if proposed by the elected officials themselves. In California, the named defendants for the state actually switched sides after the trial court ruled against them. In the critical *Serrano II* case in 1976, which was decided by a one-vote margin, Wilson Riles, the State Superintendent named as a defendant, provided material assistance to the plaintiffs and left the appeal to the understaffed lawyers of Los Angeles County [Elmore and McLaughlin (1982)].

Another example was Kentucky. According to Dove (1991), the litigation in Rose v. Council (1989) that resulted in Kentucky's landmark decision was the product of a "friendly suit", one in which the nominal parties have no real disagreement. The trial judge had co-authored a book on education law with the plaintiffs' principal expert, but the defense declined his offer to recuse himself. The state governor switched sides after the trial judge ruled for the plaintiffs. The plaintiff's victory on appeal was the occasion for the governor to reverse his campaign pledge not to raise taxes. Of course, these and other examples of friendly suits in Washington, Massachusetts and Connecticut might actually be the stuff of ordinary politics in these states [Enrich (1995)]. Even if they are, they do illustrate the importance of the school finance litigation movement in changing the shape of political outcomes.

7. Judges entered school finance via Brown v. Board of Education

Brown v. Board of Education (1954), held that legally segregated facilities violate the Equal Protection Clause of the U.S. Constitution. The case has become an icon to the public. Critics can denounce the Supreme Court for all sorts of decisions, but hardly anyone criticizes the result in *Brown*. Even Bork (1990), whose jurisprudential philosophy is as far removed as possible from the Warren Court that decided *Brown*, found it necessary to fit *Brown* into his view of what courts ought to do.

In the process of becoming the symbol of Civil Rights, *Brown's* interpretation has expanded. Its original importance was its reversal of Plessy v. Ferguson (1896). Louisiana had required its railroads to provide "separate by equal" accommodations for whites and blacks. Neither blacks nor railroads cared for the law, but the U.S. Supreme Court upheld it in *Plessy* against the charge that it violated the equal protection clause. In 1954, the Supreme Court changed its mind about separate but equal in a case involving racial segregation in public schools. *Brown* was no more about schools than Plessy was about passenger railroads. Both addressed legally-enforced separation of the races in any situation.

Brown became a public education case only in retrospect. School desegregation was among the more contentious issues arising from the Court's attempt to enforce *Brown*. The tradition of local control made public schools more resistant to changes imposed from above. President Truman could desegregate the armed forces with a single command (which he issued in 1948, well before *Brown*), but 20,000 school districts had for centuries regarded themselves as equal partners with the states and not a partner at all with the federal government. A nontrivial minority of them actively resisted desegregation, and many that did not resist were nonetheless hostile to broader remedies to desegregate schools across district lines.

Civil rights lawyers were disturbed that school desegregation did not seem to benefit blacks very much [Wise (1967)]. The flight of whites and better-off blacks to suburban jurisdictions and private schools made many urban desegregation victories Pyrrhic. In the South, it was not so difficult to implement busing because most Southern school districts encompassed entire counties. County school districts were probably the Southern norm because they facilitated state-imposed segregation [Margo (1990)]. If so, it was a strategy that boomeranged. After passage of Civil Rights legislation in the mid-1960s, the U.S. Justice Department usually blocked attempts by white groups to secede from the county school district in order to avoid being subject to busing [Motomura (1983)].

School districts in the north were another matter. Integration would have required busing across the boundaries of its many small districts. However, the U.S. Supreme Court in Milliken v. Bradley (1974) held that interdistrict busing could not be ordered unless the (usually) suburban district could be shown to have a direct party to intentional segregation. That was usually not the case, or at least not provable, so central-city schools in northern and western states became disproportionately black. (One state court, Connecticut, has ordered interdistrict remedies in Sheff v. O'Neill (1996) after finding that school finance reform ordered in a previous case, Horton v. Meskill (1977) was ineffective [Ryan (1999)].)

8. School finance enters the court on tax-base differences

Observing that the busing remedies the followed *Brown* had not brought much desegregation, several civil rights attorneys tried a different approach [Henke (1986)]. They took the position that if the poor and minorities were going to be stuck in central cities as whites left, at least their children should be eligible to be educated in decent schools. Several cases were brought in federal court to remedy this under the claim that poor students and poor districts were discriminated against because they had inadequate economic resources for education. Their chief constitutional platform was the Fourteenth Amendment's guarantee of equal protection of the laws.

It was not fanciful to do so in the 1960s. A few Supreme Court decisions in that era had seemed to move Equal Protection jurisprudence from political discrimination and toward economic inequalities. One milestone was the requirement in Gideon v. Wainwright (1963), that indigent defendants in criminal cases had to be provided with a state-funded attorney. It did not seem too great a step for the Court to require the state to provide a competent lawyer for impecunious criminal defendants to having the Court require a competent education system for people who had done nothing to deserve the wretched systems they were stuck with.

This approach did not work. The federal courts in the late 1960s did not agree that education should be regarded as a right subject to strict-scrutiny analysis under the Equal Protection Clause. ("Strict scrutiny" places a high burden of proof on the government to defend its laws, in contrast to the easily-met "rational relationship" to some government purpose that ordinary legislation is subject to. The former burden is hardly ever met when either a "fundamental right", such as speech, or a "suspect classification", such as race, is burdened by the law in question.) As a practical matter, the federal trial court in McInnis v. Shapiro (N.D. Ill. 1968) regarded the desired remedy in the early school-finance cases as beyond their ability to establish or monitor. How would a judge know when enough resources had been provided to remedy the deficiency? Judges also wondered how to distinguish the right to a good education from the right to other economic benefits. If poverty were a "suspect classification" that raised equal protection scrutiny in public schooling, what other inequalities of a capitalist system would survive litigation? The Supreme Court implicitly agreed by declining to review this and related cases.

After this initial defeat, the civil rights lawyers needed a backup plan to attack the inequalities left by the respect for school district boundaries in *Milliken*. Plan B was the brainchild of Professor John Coons and two of his Northwestern law students, Clune and Sugarman [Coons, Clune and Sugarman (1969, 1970)]. They argued that inequalities in school-district *property-tax bases* should be the object of equal protection remedies. Tax-base inequalities had a quality that personal inequalities lacked. As a matter of formal law, school districts were the product of state government, and state governments had, by creating districts with unequal tax bases, flouted the canons of equal protection, according to this argument. The focus on an inequality of state-authorized tax bases got around the problem of extending the equal protection clause to an indefinite class of economic outcomes. Judges could thus distinguish cases about financing schools – something provided in the public sector – from the financing of ordinary private goods.

The remedy that Coons, Clune and Sugarman argued for had another advantage. It did not seem to require that the courts get involved in allocating educational resources, a problem that had made judges in the previous cases so wary. Coons, Clune and

Sugarman argued simply that local tax bases be pooled in a fashion that they called district power equalization (DPE). It required districts with a large tax base (per pupil) to, in effect, share their taxable wealth with districts that had smaller tax bases. Their defining rule was that for any given tax rate, each district should be able to generate the same amount of revenue per pupil, regardless of its own wealth. (I will examine the economic implications of this in Section 12.)

DPE seemed like an ideal way around judicial reluctance to enter the school finance field because its remedy was easily monitored – local tax rates and tax bases are readily calculated – and did not require complex political and educational judgments. Tax base sharing seemed to have a stopping point on the economic spectrum. Judges could see that private goods did not have to be allocated by pooling wealth, since the Fourteenth Amendment applied only to public actions, not private decisions. Although some additional footwork was required to differentiate fiscal equality for schools from fiscal equality for municipal golf courses, beaches, and recreation areas, DPE seemed profoundly reasonable, even conservative. It left schools and taxes in the hands of local voters. Even its critics in academic law found little to object to. Feldstein's (1975) argument that DPE did not make for true wealth neutrality seemed excessively technical and too difficult to administer. "Let not the best be the enemy of the good" is another common saying among lawyers.

9. Central-city residents might not benefit from tax-base sharing

One objection to DPE was noticed by Coons, Clune and Sugarman but largely ignored by others. DPE was contrived as an indirect way to add educational resources to inner-city schools. Since the federal courts would not order direct aid to such districts, equalizing the tax base seemed like a reasonable second best. But some of these school districts in fact stood to lose taxable resources by a straightforward application of tax-base equalization. Inner cities had high concentrations of poor and minorities, so their residential valuations were often low, but they often had disproportionate amounts of nonresidential property to tax. And many had relatively low public-school populations, as whites and middle-class families with school-age children had left for the suburbs or sent their children to private schools. Even the back-to-the-city movements by middle class are dominated by the childless and those able to afford private schools.

Coons et al. apparently assumed that the evidence that the poor and blacks would be hurt by DPE was not general. One reason for believing this was that prior to special studies of 1970 census data, one could not match school district data, from which tax-base per pupil could be calculated, with U.S. census data for income and other personal data. Thus most of what was known about tax base and family income was anecdotal. In any event, Coons et al. regarded the role of DPE as establishing a "rational" system from which the state could make appropriate transfers to help the needy students [Coons (1978)].

Most other members of the school finance litigation group, however, assumed that DPE would help almost all of the poor, and where it did not, more ad hoc equal protection arguments would prevail. This faith was apparently not shared by the NAACP Legal Defense Fund, the mainstay of the original civil rights movement, which politely declined to get involved with school-finance litigation [Greenberg (1994)]. The NAACP may also have been concerned that centralization of school funding would undermine the authority of locally-elected officials who, in an increasing number of larger cities, were African-American.

I have personified the school-finance litigation movement as civil-rights lawyers and legal scholars. Lawyers are normally supposed to be agents for their clients, who are the aggrieved parties. Searching for clients was once frowned upon. The common-law crime of recruiting clients with no real grievances is called "barratry", and it and the related tort of "champerty" (contingent-fee agreements) have been almost entirely expunged from American law. It is nonetheless of some interest in examining the school-finance litigation movement to observe that it was not popular movement. Residents of low-wealth districts did not initiate most of the suits, though those that were recruited were usually pleased when their side won.

Funding for the school-finance litigators came initially from foundations, especially Ford and Carnegie, and from federally-financed poverty-law programs [Lee and Weisbrod (1978)]. Although most of this financing dried up in the 1980s, litigation has been partly financed by the courts themselves. Beginning with Serrano v. Unruh (Cal. 1982), some state courts began granting victorious plaintiffs legal fees under the doctrine of "private attorney general" [Friesen (1985)]. This holds that a private citizen who vindicates a constitutionally-guaranteed right ought to be compensated. Thus some of the school finance litigation has involved parties who face asymmetric costs. If the government (representing the defendants) prevails, it does not collect any fees from the losing plaintiffs. But if the plaintiffs prevail, they are paid out of the government's funds. An interesting question might be the extent to which the implicit state subsidy, where there is one, accounts for the litigation itself.

10. The state courts took up school finance litigation after *Rodriguez*

The school-finance litigators tried the new argument about tax-base inequality (rather than student disadvantage) in both state and federal court. The first decision was obtained in California, to which Coons and Sugarman, the bearers of the DPE standard, had both moved as law professors. In Serrano v. Priest (1971), the California Supreme Court bought into the DPE argument – and seemingly every other argument that the plaintiffs made. Although the 1971 case only reversed the trial judge's ruling that California law did not grant them relief even if all their facts were proved, its opinion made it clear that it would not tolerate spending inequalities that resulted from inequalities in local tax bases, and it affirmed this remedy in its second decision, Serrano v. Priest (1976).

DPE also succeeded in lower federal courts, which distinguished it from the previous more general claims on equal protection grounds. San Antonio v. Rodriguez (1973), was the first to reach the U.S. Supreme Court, which accepted it after the *Serrano* decision was made by the state supreme court of California. (*Serrano* itself was not heard by the U.S. Supreme Court.) *Rodriguez* presented the same issues as *Serrano*, though, and the Coons DPE remedy was presented in an *amicus curiae* brief by Coons. (Friend of the court briefs are common and sometimes influential supplements for the Court to consider in major cases.)

The *Rodriguez* plaintiffs lost. Justice Powell's opinion held specifically that education was not a fundamental right subject to strict scrutiny under the Court's equal protection jurisprudence. He said that states' preference for local control provided an acceptable rationale for inequalities in tax base. Beyond that, Powell ridiculed the statistical comparisons of selected extremes that enabled plaintiffs to argue that property-rich and income-rich were the same. It's worth reading Powell's opinion to offset the otherwise ample evidence that statistical illiteracy is a prerequisite for a judgeship.

The vote in *Rodriguez* was 5–4. It precluded federal relief, but it did not preclude litigation under state constitutions. Litigation has been brought in almost every state. [For a recent scorecard, see Lukemeyer (2003).] This has allowed a variety of decisions among the states, which presents the opportunity for a quasi-experimental examination of changes in school finance, with the control group possibly being the states in which plaintiffs lost their case.

I say "possibly" because one would want to know why some cases succeed and others do not before using court decisions as random variables in a national study. Some states may have seemed more ripe for equalization litigation than others, which could imply that more general political and economic factors were at work. One would also want to know the extent to which governors and legislators were surprised by the litigation and, if they were not, whether they had done things to forestall its effect.

One thing does seem clear. The language of the state's constitution does not seem to make any difference for plaintiffs' success. Hermeneutic examination by constitutional scholars has failed to come up with either necessary or sufficient constitutional conditions to predict state courts outcomes [McUsic (1991), Underwood (1994)]. Kitchensink-style regression analysis has not yielded much, either [Figlio, Husted and Kenny (2000)]. State courts reading seemingly identical constitutional language can arrive at opposite conclusions.

This is less surprising than it might seem to people who have not studied constitutional law. As was described in Section 1 above, state constitutional provisions concerning education are largely hortatory and nebulous. The only clear violations of having a "thorough and efficient" system would be for the legislature to neglect to set up a school district in some part of the state in which school-age children could reside. School districts are actually almost as pervasive as counties. Except for large government reservations, school districts blanket the entire United States. Beyond that, there is nothing that compels the judiciary to get involved in school finance. The great majority of the education clauses are not placed in the state's bill of rights.

At the same time, there is almost nothing that compels judges to stay away from the issue. The mention of schools and the deployment of various state equal protection clauses opens the schoolhouse door to the judiciary in almost every state. Moreover, the common-law tradition of judging, which is most active at the state level, encourages borrowing ideas from other states [Langer (2002)]. In this respect, the *Serrano* decision in 1971 was very important, since it came from a large state whose judiciary has had considerable influence on the American development of common law, and whose constitutional authority for its decision was less than explicit, as the dissent in *Serrano II* pointed out. Other state judges who might be nervous about inventing new law could point to an influential sister court that had ruled for plaintiffs on even thinner textual basis.

The more obvious puzzle is why judicial review of school funding started to succeed in the 1970s. Most of the education clauses date to the nineteenth century. Here again the influence of *Brown* and the growing acceptance of judicial leadership in politics that followed from it seems like the most plausible explanation [Carrington (1998)]. Consider the 1854 Indiana case, Greencastle Township v. Black (1854). It bore a remarkable similarity to *Serrano* in holding, on state constitutional grounds, that local property financing of schools discriminated against low-wealth districts and was therefore unconstitutional.

There the similarity ends. The Indiana legislature ignored the court's decision, and 18 years later, the state supreme court acknowledged that there was nothing it could do, and it simply reversed its previous decision, remarking that the schools had done rather well without their reform [Stark (1992)]. Contrast this with the experience of New Jersey, whose legislature in 1976 refused to pass an income tax supported by the governor in order to fund a court-ordered school finance reform in Robinson v. Cahill (1973). The court responded by ordering the schools closed (in July). The legislature caved in within a few weeks and passed the state's first income tax [Lichtenstein (1991)].

The other means by which courts can put legislators in line would be to declare a particular tax unconstitutional. Taxpayers could then refuse to pay it without penalty. Bond rating systems would threaten to downgrade the state's credit rating well in advance of any suit, which would make litigation unnecessary. Talk among New Hampshire legislators of refusing to go along with a court's school-finance reform ruling brought just such a threat, and the legislators promptly ceased talking about stonewalling the court [Campbell and Fischel (1996)].

11. The ongoing influence of tax-base equalization (and spending equality)

After *Rodriguez*, the California Supreme Court promptly declared that its application of the state's equal protection doctrine was more expansive than the U.S. Supreme Court's holding, and *Serrano* was upheld and the DPE criterion became part of the decision. Some other state courts felt obliged to follow the U.S. Supreme Court. Even this did not necessarily deter litigation in these states, though. School-finance plaintiffs shifted their arguments to the state education clauses. In doing so, they also shifted the grounds for relief from equality of distribution to adequacy of resources. It is possible that the latter shift was made in light of California's Proposition 13, which so limited the total amount of property-tax revenues available that compliance with the *Serrano* decision resulted in an equality of paupers.

Despite the shift of the courts away from equal protection, DPE and tax-base inequalities have remained as central issues in school-finance litigation. In the three recent plaintiff victories, Vermont [Brigham v. State (1997)] and New Hampshire [Claremont v. Governor (1997)] and Ohio [DeRolph v. State (1998)], property-tax inequalities were central to the court's decision. The more recent plaintiff victory in Campaign for Fiscal Equity v. State of New York (2003), however, deliberately slighted tax-base arguments, since plaintiffs were suing on behalf of New York City's school children, who lived in a district that would normally be regarded as property-rich, as had been pointed out by the New York Court in Board v. Nyquist in 1982 [Board of Education v. Nyquist (1982)], when plaintiffs lost. In most cases, the source of a system's inadequacies was traced to its inequalities in local tax base. Reforms that complied with an adequacy standard that left substantial tax-base inequalities were an invitation to the state government's lawyers for another unhappy day in court.

DPE's centrality in school-finance litigation might be regarded as a fluke of history, a substitute that plaintiffs grabbed once the real problem, poor education for the inner-city poor, was not amenable to direct assault. DPE was the wedge to get into court, a wedge, it turns out, was not really necessary after the state courts began to use education clauses instead of equal protection. Even one of its original progenitors, Stephen Sugarman, concedes that claims based on tax-base inequality are no longer necessary to get into state court [Minorini and Sugarman (1999)].

Yet the persistence of tax base as a major concern in school-finance litigation may not be just inertia. The federal judges were right in the pre-*Serrano*, pre-*Rodriguez* era. Education is complicated, and courts do not have the wherewithal to monitor remedies that focus on outcomes, processes, and goals. Tax-base per pupil really is an easy standard to say and monitor, one in which inequalities look largely unjustified. Even relatively sophisticated economists often characterize it as an exogenous constraint that only the state (as opposed to the district) can do anything about. I shall explore why this view of the local property-tax base is at odds with more sophisticated models of economic behavior. The intention is not simply to criticize the view. It is to make economists think about what they should consider endogenous to their models and how they might investigate the outcomes of school finance litigation.

12. Tax prices, tax rates and tax-base per pupil

Homebuyers with children put a substantial premium on residences with good schools. Good schools thus raise housing values, creating the sort of virtuous cycle to promote efficiency alluded to earlier. To the extent that higher-income communities demand better education, homes in these district will be more valuable. But this observation would make one assume, as many economists do, that high income and large tax-base per student are positively and strongly correlated. After all, goes the usual story, the major element of the tax base is residential property, so high-income communities should have more valuable tax bases. This is best expressed in the median voter analysis of local public school spending decisions [Inman (1978), Romer, Rosenthal and Munley (1992)]. In this model, potential voters within a community are ranked from lowest to highest income (or wealth or home value). Political transparency is assumed; public officials do what the majority wants, which, in the model's formulation, means the preferences of the median voter always prevail. This permits the analysis of collective goods through the preferences of a single individual. (Operationally, the median voter is not a particular person but a vector of characteristics, which makes the model stable even if there is population turnover. As long as the emigrant is replaced by an immigrant with the same characteristics, the model's predictions are unchanged.)

Figure 1 represents such a tradeoff for two separate communities, Richdale and Poorville, juxtaposed on a single graph. The vertical axis is private disposable income (other goods), and the horizontal axis is school services. The tax price is the amount the median voter must pay in taxes for an additional unit of school services. Richdale and Poorville are assumed to be able to tax only residential property, and the value of their residential property is exactly proportional to personal income. The measurement of school services has been normalized so that the tax price in this baseline example is

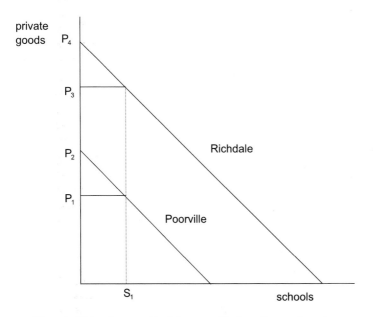

Figure 1. Rich and poor residential communities have the same tax price.

minus one. (The chief adjustment would be for the "pureness" of public goods, since in that case the tax price declines as more people join the community. Schools are assumed here to be private goods offered in the public sector, so that per household tax prices would be the same under the previously stated assumptions.)

Proportionality of personal income to residence value is assumed throughout this discussion to allow tax rates on housing to be expressed graphically as tax rates on income. This does not reach the important capitalization point that Hoxby (2001) makes, which is that positive capitalization rewards successful districts. But my formulation does address a point she neglects, which is that the tax price can be greatly affected by the presence of nonresidential property and differences in school enrollment among communities, both of which are important in school-finance cases.

Figure 1 illustrates a persistent source of confusion between school finance lawyers and economists. Lawyers, particularly DPE advocates, often argue that the school property-tax *rate* is the price of education [e.g., Coons (1978)]. Richdale obviously has a lower tax rate to obtain school services S_1. Richdale's rate (as a percent of income) is $(P_4 - P_3)/P_4$, which is much less than Poorville's rate, $(P_2 - P_1)/P_2$. Economists, however, would say that the *tax price* of schools in the two districts is exactly the same. In order to obtain S_1, Richdale must spend $P_4 - P_3$ in taxes, and Poorville must spend $P_2 - P_1$ in taxes, and $P_4 - P_3 = P_2 - P_1$, since the budget lines are parallel.

If DPE were to be adopted, the net budget lines of both communities would change as shown in Figure 2. The broken lines are the new net budget lines for a DPE system. DPE

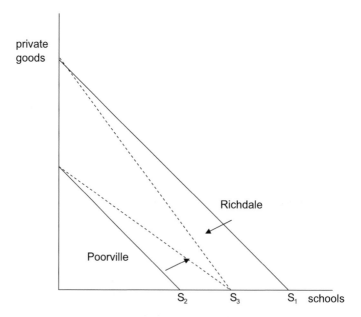

Figure 2. DPE transfers (tax-base equalization) creates different tax prices.

requires that each district (and hence each median voter) must pay the same fraction of her income (same tax rate) if they both choose the same level of schooling. The shape of the DPE budget lines is easiest to see from the intercepts. On the vertical axis intercept, no schools are provided, so there is no transfer and DPE and local finance are the same. At the horizontal intercepts, both districts spend 100 percent of their income. DPE would require that for the same tax rate (100 percent, in this case), both must get the same level of schooling. To do this, Richdale must disgorge $S_1 - S_3$ of its school services to Poorville, which gets an additional $S_3 - S_2$ in schooling. Thus S_3 is midway between S_2 and S_1 on the horizontal axes, and the two new lines are linear in order to maintain the same ratio of taxes to income for any given level of school services, as can be seen by the geometry.

I will be examining the DPE system through this graph, which may seem to readers excessive for a system that for all its rhetorical influence is actually seldom applied in its pure form. However, the graphical comparisons illustrate a more general quality of school finance reform systems that Hoxby (2001) pointed out. They are tax systems by the higher government (the state) imposed on local school districts. DPE shows this quite clearly in that tax prices of both jurisdictions are changed by DPE. The effect of the DPE reform is to tax local school spending in Richdale and to subsidize it in Poorville. But other popular reforms are also tax systems and alter tax prices. A system of state grants funded by income or sales taxes but distributed on the basis of district tax base is also a tax system, even if no locally generated revenues are transferred from one district to another. Withholding funds from Richdale because it has sufficient tax base in the state's opinion is a tax, while giving funds to Poorville for lack of local tax base is a negative tax and thus reduces its tax price.

Figure 2 shows that a multiple jurisdiction DPE system could allow districts to choose to spend different amounts. The broken lines are budget lines, and districts can choose any point on them. But there would be, as advocates of DPE expected, a tendency toward convergence in spending. Poorville faces a lower tax price and so would choose more schooling, while Richdale faces a higher tax price and presumably would choose less in the long run. (School finance advocates often assumed that the Richdales of the world had zero price elasticity of demand while Poorville had elastic demand, which is why they generally expected DPE systems to increase total expenditures on education.) DPE is not the only transfer system that raises the tax price to the higher spending district, but it does so in an obvious fashion.

It is tempting to see the subsidy that Poorville gets as a higher government subsidy of the type suggested to internalize the spillover benefits of education. The analogy is not apt, though. Higher government subsidies for education in general are intended to increase average spending because, the external benefits story goes, local decisions will not reflect statewide or national benefits of education. DPE does not do this, since there is not guarantee that net spending will be higher after the higher tax price to Richdale is taken into account. Only if Richdale's educational spending is regarded as having a negative externality proportional to the positive externality in Poorville would DPE make sense as a means of correcting some market failure in local education decisions.

13. Tax-base per pupil and commercial development

Figure 3 presents a comparison of two districts paired along a criterion other than personal income and home value. The median voters in "Homeburg" and "Office Park" have the same private incomes (the vertical intercept of their budget lines is the same), but Office Park has twice the tax base and hence a tax price that is one-half that of Homeburg. The names of the two places suggest the reasons: Office Park has half of its land use in nonresidential property. Because commerce and industry pay half of the taxes, Office Park's tax price is lower than Homeburg's. The broken line that bisects the distance between the two district's horizontal axis represents the effect of DPE. It lowers Homeburg's tax price and raises Office Park's tax price.

The nonresidential fraction of the property-tax base tends to be underemphasized by economists. In most states, nonresidential property constitutes almost half of the property tax base. This is partly because residential properties, and owner occupied homes in particular, are subject to exemptions based on age and disability and sometimes veteran status. Some states also amended their constitutions to allow for lower rates (or assessments) for homes, though in most states, assessment and taxation of property cannot discriminate by type of use. The distribution of nonresidential property varies a great deal among taxing units, however, so there can be substantial differences in tax base that require scholarly attention. The frequent assumption that residential property values are a good proxy for property-tax base is seldom warranted by the facts.

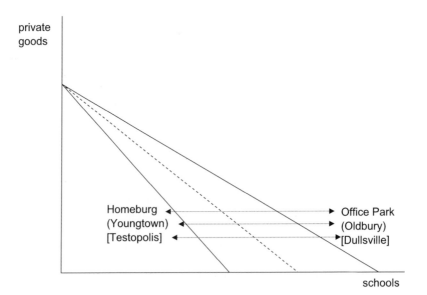

Figure 3. Tax prices in equal-income communities can differ for several reasons.

There is a sense in which without DPE Office Park is better off than Homeburg. While its private incomes may be the same, Office Park's families can get better schools, and the evidence is that lower tax prices do account for higher spending. However, there is a dimension of income or well-being that is not accounted for by the budget lines shown here. Office Park's residents must put up with the disamenities of commercial activity, while Homeburg's residents do not. How much this changes the picture of well-being cannot be determined, but much of the evidence about location preferences is that higher-income cities tend *not* to have as much commercial and industrial property per capita. This is both because higher-income families move to communities that lack major disamenities and because higher-income communities use zoning to keep disamenable industry out [Fischel (2001)].

Office Park's residents may have previously zoned for industry in order to lower their tax price and get better schools [Ladd (1975), Fischel (1975)]. Unforeseen adoption of DPE, of course, eliminates the advantage without also eliminating the disamenity. This may account for part of the resentment that "property rich" districts often express about DPE or similar attempts to raise their tax price to the level of their neighbors. Indeed, it is not difficult to find comparisons that are shown in Figure 4, in which the high-income community, Whitewine, zones out all nonresidential uses and thus has the higher tax price than low-income Sixpack, which is "property rich" by virtue of its teeming, disamenable factories. Adoption of DPE in this latter situation has unambiguously regressive effects, lowering the tax price of the high-income community and raising the

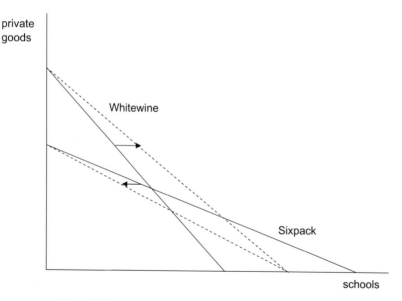

Figure 4. Tax-base sharing can penalize low-income communities.

tax price in the poorer community but leaving the latter with all of the disamenities of its commercial and industrial neighborhoods.

Returning to Figure 3, one can think of other reasons for the differences in tax prices. Instead of their original labels, Homeburg and Office Park, consider the names in parentheses: "Youngtown" and "Oldbury". Youngtown has many families with children, and Oldbury is dominated by retirees. The median voter in Oldbury has a lower tax price only because of life-cycle reasons. Its taxes are only temporarily lower, and Oldbury's residents are no less supportive of school spending (per student), since they want to be able to sell their homes to families with children. DPE again penalizes a district solely for having a presumably temporary reduction in the number of children. As I have shown for California in the late 1970s, most of the variation in tax-base per pupil was accounted for by the fraction of the population attending public schools [Fischel (2004)]. One of the figures from this article that illustrates this is reproduced as Figure 5. For the thirty-six districts in Los Angeles County whose boundaries corresponded to a city, the simple correlation between percent of population over age 65 and tax-base per pupil was 0.85.

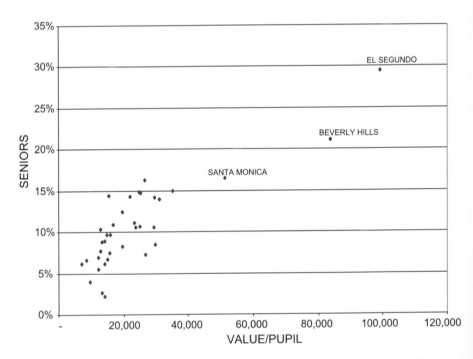

Figure 5. SENIORS & VALUE/PUPIL, Los Angeles County. Scatter diagram of SENIORS (city percent of 1980 population over age 65 in city) and VALUE/PUPIL (school district tax-base per pupil in 1977–1978) for the 36-district Los Angeles County sample, in which city and school-district boundaries were closely related.

The other characterization of the two districts, with their names in brackets in Figure 3, is along Tiebout lines. Testopolis offers an efficient, high quality school system, while Dullsville plods along with the state-required minimum curriculum. Families with children move to Testopolis, thereby raising the tax price. With more children per family, the tax-base per pupil will go down. There is an important secondary effect that is not shown here, which is that the immigration of more families bids up the price of housing and thus raises the total income (flow and capital gains) of Testopolis. This capital gain rewards the citizens of Testopolis for their foresight, and in raising property values it reduces the tax price of the median voter, as Hoxby (2001) emphasizes. This last situation cannot be represented by the simple diagrammatic comparison proposed here, since it would not normally be an equilibrium. Aside from capital gains in Testopolis, it overlooks that voters in Dullsville might smarten up as their home values decline, and they might try to improve their schools. Communities that go into decline seldom passively accept their fates.

Research into the effect of changes in tax prices due to school finance litigation has found that their net effect has been to raise local tax prices. This would seem counterintuitive in the DPE case, since at least as many districts would have tax prices reduced by DPE. But, as Hoxby (2001) has shown, communities with good schools tend to value schooling more. Raising their tax price both causes them to choose less schooling and lowers their home values. By the same token, communities of similar income that spend less on schools tend to value them less. The lower tax price will induce only a modest increase in spending and not raise housing values much. Thus the net effect will be lower aggregate home values and lower levels of local school spending.

The other reason for lower spending is that the impetus for DPE has generally been accompanied by a desire to equalize spending. Since DPE does this only imperfectly, states subject to this pressure attempt to restrain high-spending districts with caps and force low spending districts to spend more than they would choose even with low tax prices. In this situation, no voter is happy with the level of school spending. High spending districts pay more in taxes and get less in schools, and low spending districts are forced to use tax money to buy more schools than they would otherwise choose. In such a situation, most voters would generally choose a lower level of common spending and taxation rather than a higher level, especially if there are private supplements to public education that high-demanders can purchase.

14. *Serrano* spread to other courts – and to state legislatures

Many econometric studies of the effects of school finance litigation has assumed, at least implicitly, that each case can be treated as an independent event [e.g., Murray, Evans and Schwab (1998)]. Thus the litigation that began in Vermont in the 1990s was unrelated to litigation that began in California in the 1960s. This is essential to any project that wants to examine the decisions as random variables. There are numerous examples that attempt to explain the effects of school finance litigation by using the time of a state supreme court victory as one set of observation, and the absence of a plaintiff victory as the control group. This section explains why this procedure is flawed. [This and the following sections draw extensively from Fischel (2001).]

The success of the original school-finance cases in California in 1971 and New Jersey in 1972 sent a message to state legislature in all states, not just those in which litigation was pending. This has important implications for research on school finance. Attorneys general in other states had good reason to advise their governors and legislatures that the seemingly novel interpretation of the hortatory education clause in their constitutions could be a license for judges to redirect the financing of education. Their best defense might be an orderly surrender in advance to the forces of equalization and centralization.

Even if elected officials succeeded in defending their system once in court, turnover of supreme court justices and creative reformulation of complaints – first "equity" then "adequacy" – made anything less than full state control and absolute equality of expenditure a constitutionally risky path. No state actually went that far, but that is the outcome consistent with most plaintiffs' positions. As a well-traveled team of school-finance consultants observed, "Even where litigation has not occurred or has not succeeded, the prospect of litigation has prompted revisions of state funding policies" [Augenblick, Myers and Anderson (1997), p. 63]. While the formal legal complaints have varied over time, they share a common concern about unequal spending and unequal local tax bases.

I present below several instances in which legislatures responded to a *Serrano*-style suit before it even got to its state supreme court. This is not an exhaustive list. The evidence for *Serrano's* extrajudicial influence is necessarily episodic. One can generate from Lexis and Westlaw lists of court victories and defeats, but not of legislative committee compromises and out-of-court settlements on school finance. Nonetheless, the accounts in this section demonstrate the immediate and persistent influence of *Serrano* in other state legislatures.

According to a history of school finance in New Mexico by Coulton (1996), legislators there were told in 1974 that their state supreme court was about to issue a *Serrano*-style decision, and they responded with legislation to pre-empt it. New Mexico's school finance, already highly centralized, became almost completely so after this action.

The Michigan Supreme Court decision in Governor v. State Treasurer (Mich. 1972), was clearly *Serrano* inspired and directed at getting the legislature to pass an equalitarian school-finance bill [Hain (1974), Hirth (1994)]. The bill was passed, and its features were highly redistributive in that it took from the property-rich and gave to the property-poor districts [Rothstein (1992)]. After the legislation was passed, the Michigan Supreme Court withdrew its decision, and so Michigan is counted as a state whose school finance arrangements have been untouched by the courts. Justice T.E. Brennen's tart dissent (203 N.W. 2d at 475) remarked: "The majority opinion... is a political position paper, written and timed to encourage action by the state Legislature through the threat of future court intervention." (It should be noted that the Michigan court, like many other state supreme courts, is authorized to issue advisory opinions, and the opinion in Governor v. State Treasurer was sought by the state governor, not by the usual appellants.)

Ohio's *DeRolph* decision [DeRolph v. State (1997)] actually mentions (at p. 218) in the majority opinion that the legislature had tried to anticipate and head off an adverse decision in the past: "In *Walter* [a 1979 case that had provisionally upheld Ohio's system], this court reviewed the constitutionality of the Equal Yield Formula for school funding and, in 1979, upheld that formula as constitutionally acceptable. There is a body of thought," the Court goes on in *DeRolph*, "that the General Assembly created the Equal Yield Formula in anticipation of the filing of the *Walter* case.".

The experience of Kansas, as related by Berger (1998), shows that from 1972, when a trial court invoked *Serrano*-style principles, to the present the state courts have constantly set the agenda for school finance legislation. The judge in the most recent case held meetings with the governor and legislative leaders to plan the state's most recent reform. The state did not appeal the judge's decision because it anticipated losing, so Kansas, too, can be classified as a state that has not been subject to court-ordered reform.

The Massachusetts Supreme Judicial Court, which found for the plaintiffs in McDuffy v. Secretary (1993), likewise sets out a history of legislation induced by the threat of litigation. The litigation previous to McDuffy was initially filed as Webby v. Dukakis. *Webby* was brought in 1978 when the legislature was considering what Morgan (1985) describes as a equalitarian and centralizing school-finance bill. The bill, which was sponsored by Governor Michael Dukakis, was having a rough time in the legislature. The lower house was balking, and the plan looked dead in the water. Then the *Webby* litigation was filed. As a Brandeis University doctoral dissertation by Perlstein (1980, p. 569) points out, "The suit was officially filed before the state's Supreme Judicial Court on May 9 (1978), on the eve of the House vote, in an attempt to influence the outcome.". The House promptly caved in and adopted the Dukakis reform, and the litigation was immediately dropped (*Boston Globe*, May 16, 1978, p. 16).

15. Does school-finance reform increase spending?

The previous section demonstrated that school-finance litigation has been influential even where state courts ostensibly did not interfere with existing arrangements. Thus in one sense we now have a national experiment in school funding theory. The state judiciary has provided a experiment in what happens when school funding responsibilities are shifted from local districts to the state to a degree not demanded by the electorate. The first question of some interest is whether spending per pupil rises or falls as a result of the centralization of funding induced by the courts.

The answer in California is clear. Silva and Sonstelie (1995) compared the trend in California spending per pupil to the rest of the US from before *Serrano* to years after Proposition 13. California fell well below the trend-line of growth with the onset of *Serrano*. Silva and Sonstelie concluded that half of California's drop was caused by the state's increasing enrollments, which generally cause spending per pupil to fall (just as falling enrollments cause them to rise). The other half of the decline they attributed to the centralizing effects of the *Serrano* decision. [In contrast, Sonstelie, Brunner and Ardon (2000, chap. 5) conclude that the spending decline was more likely caused by the loss of nonresidential tax revenues that had previously been earmarked for education under the local property-tax.] A noneconometric but numerically transparent study by Joondeph (1995) also documents California's fall from fiscal grace after *Serrano*.

Whether *Serrano's* descendents in other state courts increased funding for schools in the rest of the nation is not so clear, which in itself is surprising. The expectation of the plaintiffs in these cases has been that putting the responsibility for funding on the state rather than the local fisc (or, to be more accurate about pre-*Serrano* practice, dividing responsibility between the state and the local districts) should increase resources available to schools. Perhaps not to the very highest spending or richest districts, but generally pulling up the lower tail while not reducing the spending of the average.

The national, econometric studies of the fiscal effects of the *Serrano*-style decisions in other states have yielded mixed results. The pioneer econometric study by Downes and Shah (1995) found that sometimes states with *Serrano*-style decisions raised spending per pupil above the national trend, but in other instances it fell, as in California. Similarly mixed results were found by Manwaring and Sheffrin (1997). Less ambivalent were Evans, Murray and Schwab (1997), who concluded that the average of the 11 *Serrano*-style decisions prior to 1992 caused spending per pupil to rise in those states compared to those without a court decision. Murray, Evans and Schwab (1998) concluded that these states tended to both equalize and "level up". Neither of the latter two studies separated out individual states, so their conclusions, though not their rhetoric, may be consistent with the mixed results of Downes and Shah and of Manwaring and Sheffrin.

The mixed results of the aforementioned econometric studies are partly due to lumping all of the plaintiff-victory cases into a single category of "reform". All but Wisconsin's did require more equalization and a larger fiscal role for the state, but the exact nature of that role was not specified in the studies. Hoxby (2001) found that legislative responses to *Serrano*-style decisions varied. Some legislatures adopted school-aid formulas that encouraged spending, while others (the majority of those with a plaintiff victory) adopted formulas that penalize higher spending by local districts. The effect of the newly adopted school-funding formula on local districts' tax prices, she found, was a good predictor of whether statewide spending fell or rose after it was enacted.

The other problem that afflicts attempts to assess school funding litigation as a group is that we don't know how much individual states anticipated the court decision. As the previous section indicated, we do know that state legislatures had ample warning that a school-finance decision could be forthcoming. Some may have lowered spending before the decision in order to collect a reserve for compliance. States in the "control group" of those without court decisions might have increased state funding to forestall an adverse decision. This is not to say that court decisions do not matter. It does suggest that broad-brush econometric studies are a less appropriate way to assess this movement than a detailed history of individual states. (As mentioned in Section 10, the search for instrumental variables that might independently predict court decisions has not gone well so far.)

Most of the individual state accounts indicate that the court decisions reduced or left unchanged previous spending levels. Theobald and Picus (1991) titled their introduction to studies of California's and Washington's experience with judge-made reform, "Living with Equal Amounts of Less". An econometric comparison of Washington to neighboring Oregon, which did not have a similar court decision, found that Washington's ruling reduced instructional spending growth by one percent per year in comparison with neighboring Oregon [Garvey (2000)]. It was especially hard on the "property rich" but low-income Seattle school district, which, ironically, had been the plaintiff in the case, Seattle School District v. State (1978).

Michael Heise (1995) examined the experiences of New Jersey and Wyoming, whose courts had overturned local financing in 1973 and 1980, respectively (though both states had subsequent decisions that again overturned the legislature's response). Heise found that, when other factors that influence per pupil spending are controlled for, the court decisions had little or no effect on spending trends. Harrison and Tarr (1996) concluded that New Jersey's considerable rise in spending per pupil after litigation began merely continued previous trends and could not be attributed to court decisions.

Murray, Evans and Schwab's (1998) econometric study of all states found that *Serrano*-style victories did not result in high spending districts being held back by the resulting reforms. Studies of individual states suggest that this was not true for the three largest states whose courts ordered reforms in their 1972–1992 sample. (Murray, Evans and Schwab did not weight the states by size, nor did they break out results for individual states.) The three big states, California, Texas and Washington, have more than two-thirds of the students in the ten plaintiff-victory states in that period.

California, as mentioned above, clearly pulled the high-spending districts down after Proposition 13. Washington State imposed binding caps on local efforts to supplement the state's constitutionally required (as declared by its supreme court in 1979) "basic grant". Most of Seattle's suburban districts as well as Seattle itself bump up against those caps [Plecki (1997)]. While local voters and many legislators would like to lift the caps, insiders to Washington politics believe that doing so would invite a lawsuit that the state would lose [Narver (1990)]. Texas reforms that responded to Edgewood v. Kirby (1991) likewise show that high-spending districts were considerably constrained in their spending following the court-ordered Texas reforms [Picus (1994)]. Grosskopf et al. (1997) were similarly impressed with how the Texas reforms tended to constrain the high-spending districts.

None of these individual state accounts by themselves prove that school finance reform adversely affects spending. Collectively, however, they cast considerable doubt on the validity of national econometric studies, especially since the observations these studies use are not random variables.

16. Does court-ordered reform improve education?

Public education in California has without a doubt suffered from the effects of what I regard as the *Serrano*-induced fiscal regime that has prevailed since 1978 [Sonstelie, Brunner and Ardon (2000, chap. 7)]. Almost no one without an office in the capitol has a good word for the state's school system, which in the late 1960s was almost as well regarded as California's university system [Schrag (1998, pp. 69, 87)]. California's average class size in the 1980s and 1990s has become the second-largest (after Utah's) in the United States. The late Charles Benson, a founder of modern school-finance research and a *Serrano* advocate, glumly conceded before a Congressional Committee in the early 1990s, "You must be very careful when you wish for things because you may just get what you wish for. We worked hard for equity in California. We got it. Now we don't like it" [quoted in Hickrod et al. (1995)]. A study of Tennessee districts that successfully sued the state for more funds found that after five years there was no trend toward convergence of test scores between the seventy-one plaintiff districts and the rest of the state [Peevely and Ray (2001)].

The evidence from other states is less clear but still generally pessimistic. Average scores on the Scholastic Aptitude Test (SAT) are a reasonable metric for comparing student academic accomplishment among states once differing participation rates are taken into account [Graham and Husted (1993)]. There is a fair amount of evidence that SAT scores are worse, not better, in states that have gone down the centralization and equalization road farther than others [Peltzman (1993)]. Peltzman (1996) also found that noncollege students in states with more centralized funding did worse on the Armed Forces Qualifying Test. Two studies that focused on other interstate differences among schools found incidentally that states with more centralized financing had lower SAT scores [Southwick and Gill (1997)] and lower NAEP scores [Fuchs and Reklis (1994)]. A study of Kentucky's court-induced reforms by Clark (2003, p. 1) concluded, that "Black students in Kentucky have experienced modest test score gains since KERA's implementation, but the scores of white students have remained unchanged relative to their peers in surrounding states. I also find no evidence that KERA has narrowed the gap in test scores between rich and poor districts.".

Like the studies mentioned in the previous section, the test-score studies do not account for anticipation of and possible endogeneity of centralization itself. One study has taken this into account. Husted and Kenny (2000) obtained records of individual test-takers of the SAT and their personal characteristics for the 34 states in which the SAT is taken by a nontrivial fraction of high school seniors. Husted and Kenny constructed a measure not only of average state SAT scores, but the variance in SAT scores within the state. Instead of looking at court orders, they looked at how much centralization and equalization of school funding actually changed over the period 1972–1992 and compared it to how much it would have been expected to change (as a result of demographic and political factors) after 1972.

Husted and Kenny's results show that centralization of school funding – more state money, less reliance on local property taxes – appears to have statistically significant, large, negative effects on average SAT scores. They also find that equalization (which is not the same as centralization) of spending likewise reduced SAT scores. On the less gloomy side, Husted and Kenny found that within-state variance in SAT scores was somewhat reduced by both equalization and centralization, though this result was not as robust as the pessimistic result about average scores. They conclude that equalization and centralization may make the previously lower-scoring students better off relative to the higher scoring students, but it seems largely to be a "dumbing down" effect, since the average scores are clearly reduced by both centralization and equalization.

The lack of evidence that school finance reform has improved education generally should be juxtaposed onto the issue of whether reform has increased spending. If spending has risen as a result of school-finance reform, then the additional taxes required to finance that spending would seem to be entirely deadweight loss. A useful project for economist might be to estimate the welfare losses under alternative assumptions about spending and efficiency.

17. Has court-ordered reform helped low achievers?

My description in Section 8 of the development of school-finance litigation indicated that reformers were primarily interested in educational opportunities of the poor within central cities. Their strategy of litigating on the basis of local property tax-base inequalities was thought of as a detour around federal court reluctance, not a change in destinations. Even most of those who realized that low tax base and personal poverty were poorly correlated expected that a more centralized and equalized system of finance would work for the benefit of the poor.

There is little evidence that the goal of equal opportunity is improved in California, where the combination of *Serrano* and Proposition 13 promoted substantial equalization. Students in previously low-scoring districts did not close the test score gap after spending becomes more equalized, as Downes (1992) has shown. His much-cited evidence comes from California, where court-induced centralization resulted in an equality of paupers. [See also Sonstelie, Brunner and Ardon (2000, Chapter 10).] Perhaps it worked better in "level-up" states. Connecticut's response to the *Horton* decision did cause expenditures in its largest city, Hartford, to rise above the suburban average, but with no measurable improvement in student performance. As a sympathetic commentator, Ryan (1999, p. 538) pointed out, "successful school finance reform did not make a significant difference in the academic achievement of Hartford students.".

Two studies suggest a note of optimism. Card and Payne (2002) found that poor students did slightly better on SATs in states whose courts ordered more equalized spending. But their most elaborate regression was not statistically significant, and it is also questionable because of the low participation by the poorest students in the SAT test. (The previously mentioned studies using SAT scores looked at state averages, not the poor by themselves.) Unless one controls for participation rates, the SAT is useless as a means comparing states and districts.

Dee (2000) examined states whose courts had undertaken *Serrano*-style reforms. He hypothesized that formerly low-spending districts should have their property values increased as a result of the additional state aid. If their schools were getting better as a result, more people would want to live there and drive up housing prices. His results suggest that at least for the formerly low-spending districts, the reforms improved education. My only objection to his clever study is his labeling of these low-spending districts as the "poor districts", which implies that the reforms helped most poor people. As I mentioned earlier, there is no evidence that the majority of poor people live in the "property-poor" districts that are the focus of school-finance litigation.

Although the Card and Payne and Dee studies suggest some note of optimism about the educational results of the school-finance cases, the bulk of the evidence seems pessimistic. An important long-range goal of school-finance equalization is to narrow the gap between high- and low-wage workers Benabou (1996). A study by Hanushek and Somers (1999) concluded that "the three-decade-old movement toward reducing the variation in school spending within states appears to have done nothing to reduce subsequent income variations of workers.". Three decades may be too short a period to fully judge the effects, but their finding is certainly not cause for optimism.

18. Consequences of equalization on location

Although there is controversy about school-finance litigation's influence on spending and school quality, there is little debate about its impact on the within-state distribution of spending among districts. Both national studies and before-and-after studies of individual states concur that by almost all measures, spending per pupil in states subject to judicial reform has become more equal [Evans, Murray and Schwab (1997)]. This is all the more impressive because income inequality and income segregation by location have generally increased over the same period [Abramson, Tobin and VanderGoot (1995)]. The extent of inequality may actually be understated by most measures. States that did not have court orders may have headed it off by adopting policies that tended to equalize. This was certainly true in the Massachusetts and Ohio examples described above. If promoting a trend toward equality of spending was the sole object of school-finance litigation, there is little evidence to suggest that it has failed.

This raises the question of the importance of tax-base remedies. Since tax base is not closely related to income, why would tax-base remedies promote equality of spending among districts? One possibility is that in fashioning remedies, judges have assumed that most variation in spending is due to tax-base differences. Tax-base remedies are typically unpalatable to legislatures because in most states the central city, which is both needy and an important political entity, would stand to face higher taxes rather than lower taxes for the same level of spending. The less politically-disruptive approach to ridding the influence of tax base on spending may be simply to make spending equal by displacing local funds with state funds.

19. School-finance litigation and private schools

Downes and Schoeman (1998) found that private school enrollment rose in California just after *Serrano II* and Proposition 13. Downes and Greenstein (1996) found that individual private schools in California opened in response to concerns by high-demand residents that public schools had declined. But the increase in private schooling in California, from ten to twelve percentage points, is hardly massive, and its growth does not seem to have persisted into the 1990s [Brunner and Sonstelie (1997)]. This is perhaps because the high-income suburbs have adjusted to the public constraints with private financing, as Brunner, Murdoch and Thayer (2002) suggest. Nechyba (2003) finds in a computable general equilibrium model that fiscal centralization does not necessarily lead to increased private school enrollments even though it may diminish the quality of public schools.

But the stability of private school enrollments in California and elsewhere after *Serrano* and similar suits in other states may hide an important nationwide shift. Catholic schools, which are the largest category of private schools, have changed radically over the last twenty-five years [Byrk, Lee and Holland (1993)]. Their clientele up to the 1960s consisted largely of immigrant families who sent their children to parochial schools for religious and cultural reasons. That component of Catholic school clientele is now much reduced. Nowadays Catholic schools are sought by both Catholic and non-Catholic refugees from urban public schools who seek an education that is, by most measures, more successful than in the big-city public sector [Evans and Schwab (1995)].

Moreover, Catholic schools' share of education enrollments has slipped from 12 percent in 1965 to 5.4 percent in 1990 [Byrk, Lee and Holland (1993), p. 33]. For the national private-school attendance fraction to have remained steady (at around 12 percent of school-age children) over this period, other types of private schools, in which matriculation is more likely to be for academic reasons, must have expanded during the period. Some of this represents the effects of public-school desegregation, but even in this case, many if not most of the refugees from big-city busing are families concerned about educational quality, not the race of their children's classmates. Big-city parochial schools are fully integrated with respect to local racial conditions [Byrk, Lee and Holland (1993)]. Hence the national stability of overall private school enrollment masks the extent to which public school decline has driven educationally ambitious families to private schools.

There is some evidence of a reverse migration to the central cities so that the metropolitan area is less segregated by income groups. Downes and Figlio (1999) suggest, however, that relocation of higher-income people to central cities does not necessarily result in integration of the public schools. They conclude (p. 107), "The evidence is wholly consistent with the notion of highly educated families moving to central cites in response to school finance reforms and sending their children to private schools.".

20. Conclusion: What has changed?

If one simply looks at the ratio of local to state funding nationally, it would appear that little has changed as a result of school-finance litigation. The local share of state and local spending declined to 48 percent by 1980, but it has not moved more than a point or two from there since then. There has been lots of school finance litigation since then, so it seems unlikely that all of the impact was felt before 1980.

Some of this could be that the available data miscount what is local. Almost all summaries of school-finance data assume that if the property tax is collected locally, it must be a local tax. That may be formally true, but if the local entity that pays the tax has no control on how it is spent, it should not really be called a local tax. California is again an example. With about 12 percent of the nation's population, it is responsible for much of the drop in local taxes as a result of Proposition 13 in 1978, which cut local property tax revenues by over fifty percent. But that actually understates the reduction in local school taxation that occurred in that era.

California is typically listed as funding thirty percent of education through local taxes, since property taxes, collected locally, pay for thirty percent of expenditures. But because of *Serrano* and Proposition 13, all property taxes are allocated by the state legislature. School officials in Santa Monica have no more claim on property taxes generated there than they do on property tax revenues generated in San Francisco. The amount of spending on local schools is determined by the state for almost all districts. The only exceptions are a few small "out of formula" districts and the modest local tax revenues that can, with a two-thirds majority, be generated from property taxes that are not based on property values. (These parcel taxes typically are assessed as a dollar amount per ownership parcel, which makes them extremely regressive.)

No other state has gone as far as California in divorcing local taxes from local spending, but it is worth considering how local a tax is in a system in which the state sets a maximum rate or maximum revenue that is actually binding. One of the underexplored legacies of school-finance litigation is that it has made it more difficult to say just what a local tax is.

Even if one concedes that local to state funding has not changed much as a result of school-finance litigation, there may still have been an important change in the underlying structure of state and local relationships. Prior to *Serrano*, most state governments relied on a foundation system coupled with block grants. A minimum level of spending was assured by requiring a minimum local tax effort and supplying state funds based on both local income conditions such as the incidence of poverty. Although many of these formulas had some perverse effects on local incentives, legislators had considerable latitude to adjust the formulas for individual cases. A formula that penalized a central city district because its low-income residents happened to have a large tax base could be tweaked in an *ad hoc* fashion to transfer more resources to it.

After *Serrano* and related cases began to succeed, legislators perceived that they had less discretion to fix perverse formulas. A system that allowed the state to give more resources to the "property rich" was more likely to be challenged in court. Thus all legislatures had an incentive to make their systems more regular in this dimension. As a result, the total amount of state funding might not have changed much, but the way it was allocated did change. Thus studies of the impact of school finance litigation need to examine in more detail how state funds were allocated rather than just how much funds the state was providing.

A final lesson that attention to school finance litigation offers pertains to education production functions [Hanushek (1986)]. Prior to the 1970s, capitalization studies suggested that spending itself was a reasonable proxy for education quality [e.g., Oates (1969)]. More recently, though, spending seems to have little to do with output at the local level. This may be because of a change in the way funds are allocated by state governments. The shift in resources caused by the courts may have reduced the discretion that local decision makers have in spending them. It also reduces the feedback rewards that successful managers got from local property taxation. A better school made local property more valuable and thus painlessly generated more tax revenue. Increased reliance on state funds reduces the importance of this to managers. A state system of transfers based on property wealth also taxes some of the manager's reward: The increased local home values will cause the state to reduce its aid to the district, so what the manager gains in local taxes she loses, in part, in state aid [Timar (1994)].

The study of school finance through the lens of school-finance litigation offers economists numerous opportunities for additional research. This research will be most productive if it is informed by an understanding of what courts have done and what they seem capable of actually accomplishing. The problematic record of judicial intervention in school finance may yet be improved by serious economic analysis that is made accessible to those who undertake policy changes.

References

Abramson, A.J., Tobin, M.S., VanderGoot, M.R. (1995). "The changing geography of metropolitan opportunity: The segregation of the poor in us metropolitan areas, 1970 to 1990". Housing Policy Debate 6 (1), 45–72.

Allswang, J.M. (2000). The Initiative and Referendum in California, 1898–1998. Stanford University Press, Stanford, CA.

Augenblick, J.G., Myers, J.L., Anderson, A.B. (1997). "Equity and adequacy in school funding". Future of Children 7 (Winter), 63–78.

Benabou, R. (1996). "Heterogeneity, stratification, and growth: Macroeconomic implications of community structure and school finance". American Economic Review 86 (June), 584–609.

Berger, C. (1998). "Equity without adjudication: Kansas school finance reform and the 1992 School District Finance and Quality Performance Act". Journal of Law and Education 27 (January), 1–46.

Bickers, K.N., Stein, R.M. (1998). "The microfoundations of the Tiebout model". Urban Affairs Quarterly 34 (September), 76–93.

Black, S.E. (1999). "Do better schools matter? Parental valuation of elementary education". Quarterly Journal of Economics 114 (May), 577–599.

Bogart, W.T., Cromwell, B.A. (1997). "How much more is a good school district worth?". National Tax Journal 50 (June), 215–232.

Bogart, W.T., Cromwell, B.A. (2000). "How much is a neighborhood school worth?". Journal of Urban Economics 47 (March), 280–305.

Bork, R.H. (1990). The Tempting of America: The Political Seduction of the Law. Free Press, New York.

Brasington, D.M. (1997). "School district consolidation, student performance, and housing values". Journal of Regional Analysis and Policy 27 (2), 43–54.

Briffault, R. (1990). "Our localism: Part I – The structure of local government law". Columbia Law Review 90 (January), 1–115.

Brunner, E.J., Murdoch, J., Thayer, M. (2002). "School finance reform and housing values: Evidence from the Los Angeles metropolitan area". Public Finance and Management 2, 535–565.

Brunner, E.J., Sonstelie, J. (1997). "Coping with Serrano: Voluntary contributions to California's local public schools". 1996 Proceedings of the Eighty-Ninth Annual Conference on Taxation. National Tax Association, Washington, DC.

Byrk, A.S., Lee, V.E., Holland, P.B. (1993). Catholic Schools and the Common Good. Harvard University Press, Cambridge, MA.

California State Board of Education (1998). School District Organization Handbook. State Board of Education, Sacramento.

Campbell, C.D., Fischel, W.A. (1996). "Preferences for school finance systems: Voters versus judges". National Tax Journal 49 (March), 1–15.

Card, D., Payne, A.A. (2002). "School finance reform, the distribution of school spending, and the distribution of student test scores". Journal of Public Economics 83 (1, January), 49–82.

Carrington, P.D. (1973). "Financing the American dream: Equality and school taxes". Columbia Law Review 73 (October), 1227–1260.

Carrington, P.D. (1998). "Judicial independence and democratic accountability in highest state courts". Law and Contemporary Problems 61 (Summer), 79–126.

Carroll, R.J., Yinger, J. (1994). "Is the property tax a benefit tax? The case of rental housing". National Tax Journal 47 (June), 295–316.

Clark, M.A. (2003). "Education reform, redistribution, and student achievement: Evidence from the Kentucky education reform act". PhD dissertation. Economics Department, Princeton University.

Coons, J.E. (1978). "Can education be equal and excellent?". Journal of Education Finance 4 (Fall), 147–157.

Coons, J.E., Clune III, W.H., Sugarman, S.D. (1969). "Educational opportunity: A workable constitutional test for state financial structures". California Law Review 57 (April), 305–421.

Coons, J.E., Clune III, W.H., Sugarman, S.D. (1970). Private Wealth and Public Education. Belknap Press of Harvard University Press, Cambridge, MA.

Coulton, D.L. (1996). "The weighting game: Two decades of fiscal neutrality in New Mexico". Journal of Education Finance 22 (Summer), 28–59.

Cubberley, E.P. (1919). Public Education in the United States: A Study and Interpretation of American Educational History. Houghton Mifflin, Boston.

Dee, T.S. (2000). "The capitalization of education finance reforms". Journal of Law and Economics 43 (April), 185–214.

DiPasquale, D., Glaeser, E.L. (1999). "Incentives and social capital: Are homeowners better citizens?". Journal of Urban Economics 45 (March), 354–384.

Dove, R.G. Jr. (1991). "Acorns in a mountain pool: The role of litigation, law and lawyers in Kentucky education reform". Journal of Education Finance 17 (Summer), 83–119.

Downes, T.A. (1992). "Evaluating the impact of school finance reform on the provision of public education: The California case". National Tax Journal 45 (December), 405–420.

Downes, T.A., Figlio, D.N. (1999). "Economic inequality and the provision of schooling". Federal Reserve Bank of New York Economic Policy Review 5 (September), 99–110.

Downes, T.A., Greenstein, S.M. (1996). "Understanding the supply decisions of nonprofits: Modeling the location of private schools". RAND Journal of Economics 27 (Summer), 365–390.

Downes, T.A., Schoeman, D. (1998). "School finance reform and private school enrollment: Evidence from California". Journal of Urban Economics 43 (May), 418–443.

Downes, T.A., Shah, M.P. (1995). "The effect of school finance reforms on the level and growth of per pupil expenditures". Discussion Paper 95-05. Department of Economics, Tufts University.

East, J.P. (1965). Council-Manager Government: The Political Thought of Its Founder, Richard S. Childs. University of North Carolina Press, Chapel Hill.

Elmore, R.F., McLaughlin, M.W. (1982). Reform and Retrenchment: The Politics of California School Finance Reform. Ballinger, Cambridge, MA.

Enrich, P.D. (1995). "Leaving equality behind: New directions in school finance reform". Vanderbilt Law Review 48 (January), 101–194.

Evans, W.N., Murray, S., Schwab, R.M. (1997). "School houses, court houses, and state houses after Serrano". Journal of Policy Analysis and Management 16 (January), 10–31.

Evans, W.N., Schwab, R.M. (1995). "Finishing high school and starting college: Do Catholic schools make a difference?". Quarterly Journal of Economics 110 (November), 941–974.

Feldstein, M.S. (1975). "Wealth neutrality and local choice in public education". American Economic Review 65 (March), 75–89.

Fields, J., Casper, L.M. (2001). "America's families and living arrangements". Current Population Report P20-537. U.S. Census Bureau, Washington, DC.

Figlio, D.N., Husted, T.A., Kenny, L.W. (2000). "Constitutions, court decisions, and inequality in school spending". Working paper. Department of Economics, University of Florida, Gainesville.

Fischel, W.A. (1975). "Fiscal and environmental considerations in the location of firms in suburban communities". In: Mills, E.S., Oates, W.E. (Eds.), Fiscal Zoning and Land Use Controls. Heath-Lexington Books, Lexington, MA.

Fischel, W.A. (1989). "Did *Serrano* cause Proposition 13?". National Tax Journal 42 (December), 465–474.

Fischel, W.A. (1992). "Property taxation and the Tiebout Model: Evidence for the benefit view from zoning and voting". Journal of Economic Literature 30 (March), 171–177.

Fischel, W.A. (2001). The Homevoter Hypothesis: How Home Values Influence Local Government Taxation, School Finance, and Land-Use Policies. Harvard University Press, Cambridge, MA.

Fischel, W.A. (2003). "Will I see you in September? An economic explanation for the summer school vacation". Working paper. Dartmouth College Economics Department.

Fischel, W.A. (2004). "Did John Serrano vote for Proposition 13? A reply to Stark and Zasloff". UCLA Law Review 51, 887–932.

Fischer, C.S. (2002). "Ever-more rooted Americans". City and Community 1, 177–199.

Friesen, J. (1985). "Recovering damages for state bills of rights claims". Texas Law Review 63 (March/April), 1269–1311.

Fuchs, V.R., Reklis, D.M. (1994). "Mathematical achievement in eighth grade: Interstate and racial differences". Working Paper W4784. NBER.

Gale, D.H. (1981). "The politics of school finance reform in Washington State, 1975–1979". Ph.d. dissertation. Department of Urban Planning, University of Washington.

Garber, L.O., Edwards, N. (1962). The Law Relating to the Creation, Alteration, and Dissolution of School Districts. Interstate Publishers, Danville, IL.

Garvey, D.L. (2000). "Does school finance centralization reduce the growth of instructional spending? The case of reform in Washington". Working paper. Office of Population Research, Princeton University.

Goldin, C. (1998). "America's graduation from high school: The evolution and spread of secondary schooling in the twentieth century". Journal of Economic History 58 (June), 345–374.

Graham, A.E., Husted, T.A. (1993). "Understanding state variations in SAT scores". Economics of Education Review 12 (September), 197–202.

Greenberg, J. (1994). Crusaders in the Courts: How a Dedicated Band of Lawyers Fought for the Civil Rights Revolution. Basic Books, New York.

Grosskopf, S., Hayes, K.J., Taylor, L.L., Weber, W. (1997). "Budget-constrained frontier measures of fiscal equality and efficiency in schooling". Review of Economics and Statistics 79 (February), 116–124.

Hain, E. (1974). "Milliken v. Green: Breaking the legislative deadlock". Law and Contemporary Problems 38 (Winter/Spring), 350–365.

Hamilton, B.W. (1975). "Zoning and property taxation in a system of local governments". Urban Studies 12 (June), 205–211.

Hanushek, E.A. (1986). "The economics of schooling: Production and efficiency in public schools". Journal of Economic Literature 24 (September), 1141–1177.

Hanushek, E.A., Somers, J.A. (1999). "Schooling, inequality, and the impact of government". Working Paper W7450. NBER.

Harrison, R.S., Tarr, G.A. (1996). "School finance and inequality in New Jersey". In: Tarr, G.A. (Ed.), Constitutional Politics and the States. Greenwood Press, Westport, CT.

Haurin, D.R., Brasington, D. (1996). "School quality and real house prices: Inter- and intrametropolitan effects". Journal of Housing Economics 5 (December), 351–368.

Heise, M.R. (1995). "The effect of constitutional litigation on education finance: More preliminary analyses and modeling". Journal of Education Finance 21 (Fall), 195–216.

Henke, J.T. (1986). "Financing public schools in California: The aftermath of Serrano v. Priest and Proposition 13". University of San Francisco Law Review 21 (Fall), 1–39.

Hickrod, G.A., Chaudhari, R., Pruyne, G., Meng, J. (1995). "The effect of constitutional litigation on educational finance: A further analysis". In: Selected Papers in School Finance 1995. National Center for Education Statistics, Washington, DC.

Hirth, M.A. (1994). "A multistate analysis of school finance issues and equity trends in Indiana, Illinois, and Michigan: The implications for 21st century school finance policies". Journal of Education Finance 20 (Fall), 163–190.

Hoxby, C.M. (1996). "How teachers' unions affect education production". Quarterly Journal of Economics 111 (August), 671–718.

Hoxby, C.M. (1999). "The productivity of schools and other local public goods producers". Journal of Public Economics 74 (October), 1–30.

Hoxby, C.M. (2000). "Does competition among public schools benefit students and taxpayers?". American Economic Review 90 (December), 1209–1238.

Hoxby, C.M. (2001). "All school finance equalizations are not created equal". Quarterly Journal of Economics 116 (November), 1189–1231.

Husted, T.A., Kenny, L.W. (2000). "Evidence on the impact of state government on primary and secondary education and the equity-efficiency tradeoff". Journal of Law and Economics 43 (April), 285–308.

Inman, R.P. (1978). "Testing political economy's 'as if' proposition: Is the median income voter really decisive?". Public Choice 33 (4), 45–65.

Joondeph, B.W. (1995). "The good, the bad, and the ugly: An empirical analysis of litigation-prompted school finance reform". Santa Clara Law Review 35, 763–824.

Jud, G.D., Watts, J.M. (1981). "Schools and housing values". Land Economics 57 (August), 459–470.

Kaestle, C.F. (1983). Pillars of the Republic: Common Schools and American Society, 1780–1860. Hill and Wang, New York.

Kenny, L.W., Schmidt, A.B. (1994). "The decline in the number of school districts in the United States – 1950–1980". Public Choice 79 (April), 1–18.

Ladd, H.F. (1975). "Local education expenditures, fiscal capacity, and the composition of the property tax base". National Tax Journal 28 (June), 145–158.

Langer, L. (2002). Judicial Review in State Supreme Courts: A Comparative Study. State University of New York Press, Albany.

Lee, A.J., Weisbrod, B.A. (1978). "Public interest law activities in education". In: Weisbrod, B.A. (Ed.), Public Interest Law. University of California Press, Berkeley, CA.

Lichtenstein, J. (1991). "Note: Abbott v. Burke: Reaffirming New Jersey's constitutional commitment to equal educational opportunity". Hofstra Law Review 20 (Winter), 429–493.

Loeb, S., Socias, M. (2004). "Federal contributions to high-income school districts: The use of tax deductions for funding K-12 education". Economics of Education Review 23 (February), 85–94.

Lukemeyer, A. (2003). Courts as Policymakers: School Finance Reform Litigation. LFB Scholarly Publishing, New York.

Manwaring, R.L., Sheffrin, S.M. (1997). "Litigation, school finance reform and aggregate educational spending". International Tax and Public Finance 4 (May), 107–127.

Margo, R.A. (1990). Race and Schooling in the South, 1880–1950: An Economic History. The University of Chicago Press, Chicago.

Mayer, C., Hilber, C. (2002). "Why do households without children support local public schools? House price capitalization, school spending, and the elderly". Working paper. University of Pennsylvania, April.

McMillen, D.P., McDonald, J.F. (1991). "A Markov chain model of zoning change". Journal of Urban Economics 30 (September), 257–270.

McUsic, M. (1991). "The use of education clauses in school finance litigation". Harvard Journal on Legislation 28 (Summer), 307–340.

Minorini, P.A., Sugarman, S.D. (1999). "School finance litigation in the name of educational equity: Its evolution, impact, and future". In: Ladd, H.F., Chalk, R., Hansen, J.S. (Eds.), Equity and Adequacy in Education Finance: Issues and Perspectives. The National Academies Press, Washington, DC.

Morgan, E. (1985). "Obstacles to educational equity: State reform and local response in Massachusetts, 1978–1983". Journal of Education Finance 10 (Spring), 441–459.

Motomura, H. (1983). "Preclearance under section five of the Voting Rights Act". North Carolina Law Review 61 (January), 189–246.

Murray, S.E., Evans, W.M., Schwab, R.M. (1998). "Education-finance reform and the distribution of education resources". American Economic Review 88 (September), 789–812.

Narver, B.J. (1990). "Schools for the '90s: Washington's education choices". In: Williams, W., Zumeta, W., Narver, B.J. (Eds.), Washington Policy Choices 1990s. Institute for Public Policy and Management, Seattle.

Nechyba, T.J. (2003). "Centralization, fiscal federalism, and private school attendance". International Economic Review 44 (February), 179–204.

Oates, W.E. (1969). "The effects of property taxes and local public spending on property values: An empirical study of tax capitalization and the Tiebout hypothesis". Journal of Political Economy 77 (November), 957–971.

Peevely, G.L., Ray, J.R. (2001). "Does equalization litigation effect a narrowing of the gap of value added achievement outcomes among school districts?". Journal of Education Finance 26 (Winter), 319–332.

Peltzman, S. (1993). "The political economy of the decline of American public education". Journal of Law and Economics 36 (April), 331–370.

Peltzman, S. (1996). "Political economy of public education: Non-college-bound students". Journal of Law and Economics 39 (April), 73–120.

Perlstein, B.W. (1980). "Taxes, schools, and inequality: The political economy of the property tax and school finance reform in Massachusetts". Ph.d. dissertation. Department of Politics, Brandeis University.

Perrin, A.F., Jones, T.H. (1984). "Voter rejection of a school finance recapture provision". Journal of Education Finance 9 (Spring), 485–497.

Picus, L.O. (1994). "The local impact of school finance reform in four Texas school districts". Educational Evaluation and Policy Analysis 16 (Winter), 371–404.

Plecki, M. (1997). "Conditions of education in Washington State". Institute for the Study of Education Policy, Seattle.

Poterba, J.M. (1997). "Demographic structure and the political economy of public education". Journal of Policy Analysis and Management 16 (Winter), 48–66.

Reed, D.S. (2001). On Equal Terms: The Constitutional Politics of Educational Opportunity. Princeton University Press, Princeton, NJ.

Reichley, A.J. (1970). The Political Constitution of the Cities. Prentice-Hall, Englewood Cliffs, NJ.

Reisner, E.H. (1930). The Evolution of the Common School. Macmillan, New York.

Reps, J.W. (1965). The Making of Urban America: A History of City Planning in the United States. Princeton University Press, Princeton, NJ.

Rolleston, B.S. (1987). "Determinants of restrictive suburban zoning: An empirical analysis". Journal of Urban Economics 21 (January), 1–21.

Romer, T., Rosenthal, H., Munley, V.G. (1992). "Economic incentives and political institutions: Spending and voting in school budget referenda". Journal of Public Economics 49 (October), 1–33.

Rothstein, P. (1992). "The demand for education with 'power equalizing' aid". Journal of Public Economics 49 (November), 135–162.

Ryan, J.E. (1999). "Sheff, segregation, and school finance litigation". NYU Law Review 74 (May), 529–573.

Schneider, M., Teske, P., Marschall, M., Roch, C. (1998). "Shopping for schools: In the land of the blind, the one-eyed parent may be enough". American Journal of Political Science 42 (July), 769–793.

Schrag, P. (1998). Paradise Lost: California's Experience, America's Future. The New Press, New York.

Silva, F., Sonstelie, J.C. (1995). "Did Serrano cause a decline in school spending?". National Tax Journal 48 (June), 199–215.

Sonstelie, J., Brunner, E., Ardon, K. (2000). For Better or for Worse? School Finance Reform in California. Public Policy Institute of California, San Francisco.

Sonstelie, J.C., Portney, P.R. (1980). "Take the money and run: A theory of voting in local referenda". Journal of Urban Economics 8 (September), 187–195.

Southwick, L., Gill, I.S. (1997). "Unified salary schedule and student SAT scores: Adverse effects of adverse selection in the market for secondary school teachers". Economics of Education Review 16 (April), 143–153.

Stark, K.J. (1992). "Rethinking statewide taxation of nonresidential property for public schools". Yale Law Journal 102 (December), 805–834.

Taylor, A. (1995). William Cooper's Town: Power and Persuasion on the Frontier of the Early American Republic. Vintage Books, New York.

Theobald, N.D., Hanna, F. (1991). "Ample provision for whom? The evolution of state control over school finance in Washington". Journal of Education Finance 17 (Summer), 17–33.

Theobald, N.D., Picus, L.O. (1991). "Living with equal amounts of less: Experience of states with primarily state-funded school systems". Journal of Education Finance 17 (Summer), 1–6.

Tiebout, C.M. (1956). "A pure theory of local expenditures". Journal of Political Economy 64 (October), 416–424.

Timar, T.B. (1994). "Politics, policy, and categorical aid: New inequities in California school-finance". Educational Evaluation and Policy Analysis 16 (Summer), 143–160.

Tyack, D.B. (1968). "The perils of pluralism: The background of the Pierce case". American Historical Review 74 (October), 74–98.

Tyack, D.B. (1972). "The tribe and the common school: Community control in rural education". American Quarterly 24 (1, March), 3–19.

Tyack, D.B. (1974). The One Best System: A History of American Urban Education. Harvard University Press, Cambridge.

Underwood, J.K. (1994). "School finance litigation: Legal theories, judicial activism, and social neglect". Journal of Education Finance 20 (Fall), 143–162.

Verba, S., Nie, N.H. (1972). Participation in America: Political Democracy and Social Equality. Harper and Row, New York.

Wise, A.E. (1967). Rich Schools, Poor Schools: The Promise of Equal Educational Opportunity. University of Chicago Press, Chicago.

Cases cited

Abbott v. Burke, 119 N.J. 287 (1990).

Baker v. Carr, 369 U.S. 186 (1962).

Board of Education v. Nyquist, 57 N.Y. 2d 27 (1982).

Brigham v. State, 166 Vt. 246 (1997).

Brown v. Board of Education, 347 U.S. 483 (1954).

Campaign for Fiscal Equity v. State of New York, 744 N.Y.S. 2d 130 (2003).

Claremont v. Governor, 142 N.H. 462 (1997).
DeRolph v. State, 78 Ohio St. 3d 193 (1997).
DeRolph v. State, 78 Ohio St. 3d 193 (1998).
Edgewood Independent School District v. Kirby, 804 S.W. 2d 491 (Tex. 1991).
Gideon v. Wainwright, 372 U.S. 335 (1963).
Governor v. State Treasurer, 389 Mich. 1 (1972).
Greencastle Township v. Black, 5 Ind. 56 (1854).
Horton v. Meskill, 172 Conn. 615 (1977).
Hunter v. Pittsburgh, 207 U.S. 161 (1907).
McInnis v. Shapiro, 293 F. Supp. 327 (N.D. Ill. 1968).
McDuffy v. Secretary, 415 Mass. 545 (1993).
Milliken v. Bradley, 418 U.S. 717 (1974).
Pauley v. Kelly, 162 W. Va. 672 (1979).
Pierce v. Society of Sisters, 268 U.S. 510 (1925).
Plessy v. Ferguson, 163 U.S. 537 (1896).
Robinson v. Cahill, 62 N.J. 473 (1973).
Rose v. Council, 790 S.W. 2d 186 (Ky. 1989).
San Antonio v. Rodriguez, 411 U.S. 1 (1973).
Seattle School District v. State, 90 Wn. 2d 476 (1978).
Serrano v. Priest, 5 Cal. 3d 584 (1971) (*"Serrano I"*).
Serrano v. Priest, 18 Cal. 3d 728 (1976) (*"Serrano II"*).
Serrano v. Unruh, 32 Cal. 3d 621 (1982).
Sheff v. O'Neill, 238 Conn. 1; 678 A. 2d 1267 (1996).
United States v. Lopez, 514 U.S. 549 (1995).
Wisconsin v. Yoder, 406 U.S. 205 (1972).

Chapter 22

INCOME AND PEER QUALITY SORTING IN PUBLIC AND PRIVATE SCHOOLS

THOMAS J. NECHYBA

Duke University
and
NBER

Contents

Handbook of the Economics of Education, Volume 2
Edited by Eric A. Hanushek and Finis Welch
© 2006 Elsevier B.V. All rights reserved
DOI: 10.1016/S1574-0692(06)02022-8

Abstract

Any system of primary and secondary schools involves explicit or implicit mechanisms that ration not only financial but also nonfinancial inputs into education production. This chapter focuses primarily on such mechanisms as they relate to the sorting of parents and children into schools and classrooms. Three primary mechanisms are reviewed: (1) sorting that emerges through residential location choices within housing markets that are linked to schools; (2) sorting that arises from parental choices to send children to private rather than public schools; and (3) sorting within schools that results from explicit tracking policies. The equilibrium level of sorting (along parental income and child peer quality dimensions) then depends on both the specifics of how education production works and the overall characteristics of the general equilibrium environment within which schools operate. We review the theoretical as well as the related simulation-based literature in this area and suggest that much potential exists for increasing empirical relevance of the emerging models for policy analysis, particularly as a related empirical literature comes to better terms with the nature of peer effects in education production.

Keywords

sorting, peers, segregation, peer effects, school competition, vouchers

JEL classification: I21, H70, H73, R21

1. Introduction

Over half of parents choosing public schools in the US explicitly state that their residential location choice was influenced by public school considerations [Benson and McMillan (1991)]. Residential choices thus result in nonrandom sorting of students across public schools that differ widely in both inputs and outcomes [Hoxby (2000, 2001), Murray, Evans and Schwab (1998)]. Furthermore, the percentage of children sorting into private schools ranges from just over 5% in Wyoming to over 20% in Delaware (with a national average close to 13 percent for the US) [Nechyba (2003b)]. Such schools include elite secular as well as more common religious (and particularly Catholic) schools, with studies suggesting that – even when selection of students on unobservables is treated seriously, at least Catholic schools offer higher quality at lower cost, particularly for minority students [Evans and Schwab (1995), Neal (1997), Grogger and Neal (2000)]. Beyond such decentralized sorting within the public sector and into the private school market, individual public schools often deliberately sort students by ability, with nearly 75% of public primary and secondary schools offering programs for gifted children [Benson and McMillan (1991)] and close to 90% tracking in math by tenth grade [Rees, Argys and Brewer (1996)].[1] Finally, increasing numbers of deliberately differentiated schools within the public sector – including charter and magnet schools – are emerging as states experiment with different forms of decentralized public school choice beyond what emerges through inter-district residential sorting.[2]

Sorting in education markets thus takes many forms within the public school sector as well as between public and private schools – with some sorting arising from purely decentralized household choices and other sorting arising from deliberate tracking policies. Given the large variance in inputs and outcomes across different schools and the clearly nonrandom allocation of students across these institutions, there is little question that sorting is empirically important in the US and represents a prime candidate for explaining the variance in student achievement (and other outcomes). Furthermore, while sorting mechanisms may differ across countries, there is little reason to doubt that sorting itself is a critical component of most primary and secondary school systems [Ladd and Fiske (2001), McEwan (2001)]. This chapter therefore provides an overview of different types of centralized and decentralized sorting forces – focusing particularly on sorting along income and household peer quality dimensions. At the same time, the chapter deliberately steers away from a separate analysis of the important issue of sort-

---

[1] Private schools tend to track less frequently and less selectively [Epple, Newlon and Romano (2002)].

[2] Since the early 1990s, 39 states (as well as the District of Columbia and Puerto Rico) have passed charter school laws, with approximately one percent of US students attending roughly 1,800 charter schools nationwide [Loeb and Strunk (2003)].

ing across racial dimensions that may arise independently of income and peer quality sorting.[3] Such questions are treated in other chapters of this volume.

Section 2 then begins with a discussion of different forms of income and peer quality sorting that might impact educational opportunities for primary and secondary school-aged children. Section 3 continues by exploring the extent to which the literature has succeeded in moving theoretical models toward empirically plausible computational frameworks or structural models that can be employed for policy analysis in a general equilibrium setting. Finally, Section 4 discusses some of the more recent reduced-form empirical evidence on the nature of sorting in education markets as well as the likely impact (through peer effects) that such sorting has on achievement. Finally, Section 5 concludes with some general reflections and likely avenues for future research.

2. Causes of different forms of sorting in primary and secondary education: Theory

There are essentially three distinct ways in which sorting of families and peers could arise. First, families may *self-select into different traditional public schools* because housing markets, local public finance institutions and/or spatial constraints induce residential household segregation which in turn results in school-level segregation.[4] Second, in the presence of private school markets or nontraditional public schools (like charter schools or magnet schools), some families may select *out of traditional public schools*. Finally, traditional public schools themselves may choose to *sort students within the public system through tracking* – leading in some cases to partial segregation of peers (as, for example, when tracking is undertaken in certain but not all subjects) and in other cases to full segregation (as in European systems that set up different schools for different tracks). While the first two types of sorting arise from decentralized household decisions conditional on particular economic environments, the third form of sorting is explicitly imposed by public school authorities. We discuss these in Sections 2.1–2.3 respectively.[5] The issue of centrally imposed sorting in public schools then raises the larger issue of how public school objective functions should be modeled and what this

---

[3] This issue is treated in an intriguing new framework in Bayer and McMillan (2005b). Cooley (2005) suggests that while peer effects in schools can explain some of the persistent racial achievement gap, further desegregation of schools holds only limited promise for reducing this gap.

[4] Kremer (1997) questions the degree to which residential sorting plays a large role in educational attainment and the persistence of income inequality. While his analysis provides a persuasive case that such sorting may have only small effects on attainment, it does not focus on *quality* as opposed to *quantity* of education. The models discussed below explicitly ask whether residential (and other) forms of sorting into different types of schools leads to access to substantially different levels of educational quality.

[5] A separate literature investigating intergenerational sorting issues linked to the transmission of preferences or particular skills from parents to children in models that may include such factors as marital sorting is beyond the scope of this chapter. Recent examples include Fernandez (2001) and Fernandez, Fogli and Olivetti (2002).

implies for sorting of students and teachers. While much of the literature has implicitly assumed a passive public school sector, Section 2.4 discusses some implications of modeling a more active public sector.

2.1. Sorting across schools within the traditional public school system – school production, housing markets and residential segregation

Much of the focus of US education finance policy in the last three decades has centered around the explicit recognition (often by state courts) that public school systems are characterized by vastly different levels of school quality. Equal protection clauses in state constitutions are often interpreted as guaranteeing either equal access to public school quality or minimal access to "adequate" public schools regardless of the economic circumstances of particular households. Yet it is not immediately clear how – in a system where all public schools are in principle accessible to all households – public school quality can differ so dramatically in equilibrium and why optimizing behavior by households choosing "free" public schools does not lead to equalization of school quality. An understanding of the economic forces leading to equilibrium sorting of households into different quality public schools is therefore crucial for attempts to address perceived or real inequities within the public school system. And it has become increasingly clear from theoretical work on this issue that such an understanding ultimately requires a model that comes to terms with the spatial role of housing markets, the functioning of local public finance institutions and the link of residential location to public school access for households whose choices are constrained by general equilibrium forces.

The earliest attempts to arrive at local public finance models that lead to household income segregation and unequal provision of local public goods relied on approaches that seem in retrospect too simplistic to adequately incorporate the complexities of education markets. Westhoff (1977) provides an early example of such a model where income taxes are set through local majority rule and used by jurisdictions to provide local public goods whose quality is characterized solely by per capita spending on these goods. With no spatial or housing dimension to the model, Westhoff demonstrates conditions under which households endogenously segregate into jurisdictions that are composed of continuous intervals of the income distribution, with higher income jurisdictions using higher income tax rates that deter low income households from residing there despite the fact that those jurisdictions provide better public goods. Rose-Ackerman (1979) extends this model to include housing markets, and Epple, Filimon and Romer (1993) provide additional restrictions on preferences that guarantee a similar "perfect segregation" result – with local property taxes combined with housing prices taking the place of Westhoff's local income taxes.

While this literature has important implications for the role local financing institutions play in supporting differences in public good provision, it is ultimately unsatisfying as a basis for studying sorting in education markets on both theoretical and empirical grounds. As theoretical exercises, the models lack generality because of the severity of assumptions on preferences and technologies.[6] At the same time, when interpreted as models of public education markets, the models employ empirically questionable assumptions regarding school production and lead to empirically false predictions regarding segregation, local tax rates and housing prices. More precisely, they assume that per capita (or per pupil) spending is the only relevant input into school production, an assumption that is questionable given the empirical evidence reviewed elsewhere in this volume and leads to the conclusion that the sole source of public school differences lies in the institution of local financing.[7] Furthermore, they predict property tax rates that monotonically increase in community income[8] as well as local income and house price distributions that do not overlap between jurisdictions.[9]

This brief review of the applied local public finance models suggests that an explanation of the economic forces that support sorting of households into unequal public schools requires a more subtle approach that goes beyond a focus only on local spending in schools. The combined introduction of richer school production functions as well as more complex economic environments in which households choose schooling and housing has been shown to generate theoretically more satisfying models that give rise to more plausible empirical predictions. Two possibilities have emerged in the most recent literature, with each approach giving a substantial role to nonfinancial inputs into public school production.[10] The first of these models housing markets as an exogenously given set of discrete houses partitioned into school districts with the potential of housing quality distributions overlapping in ways that are consistent with the data [Dunz (1985), Nechyba (1997, 1999)]. This approach therefore takes the implicit view that housing is durable, has arisen to take its present form through some previous unspecified historical process, and now serves as a major constraint to households that must choose residential locations and access to local public schools as a lumped bundle of goods. Alternatively, a recent second approach is emerging and focuses on the

---

[6] Epple, Filimon and Romer (1993), for instance, resolve existence problems pointed out by Rose-Ackerman (1979) by assuming single crossing of indirect indifference curves in the house price/tax space. While examples of combinations of utility and production functions that satisfy this certainly exist and have been employed with great success in applied analysis, some common examples of functional forms do not satisfy this condition [Konishi (1996)].

[7] The empirical evidence suggests that states which have largely equalized public school spending by abandoning local school financing (as in California) have not experienced equalization of public school quality.

[8] Property tax rates often show the opposite pattern, with lower income jurisdictions imposing higher tax rates to finance lower levels of public expenditures due to lower tax bases.

[9] Empirical analysis suggests greater *intra*-jurisdictional variation in income and property values than inter-jurisdictional variation [Epple and Sieg (1999)]. Epple and Platt (1998) extend the Epple, Filimon and Romer model to include heterogeneity in preferences that can yield intra-jurisdictional income variation, but local house price distributions remain nonoverlapping and local tax rates remain monotonically increasing in local income.

[10] An alternative approach simply assumes exogenously that households will perfectly sort into jurisdictions such that each jurisdiction is occupied by a single type of household [Fernandez and Rogerson (1999, 2003)]. While this literature has provided interesting insights into education finance debates as well as political economy issues, its use of exogenously imposed sorting makes it less relevant to the issues treated in this chapter.

role of local transportation costs within a more homogeneous housing market [Epple and Romano (2003)]. The key similarities in these approaches are the introduction of school production functions that incorporate nonfinancial inputs combined with an economic force that can support sorting within the public system in equilibrium even when school financing is equalized. These similarities are discussed in more detail in Sections 2.1.1 and 2.1.2, respectively.

2.1.1. School production functions

School quality S is typically modeled as a function of the form

$$S = f(x, q), \tag{1}$$

where x represents financial inputs – usually per pupil spending,[11] and q represents nonfinancial inputs – often labeled "peer effects". The output S may then directly enter household utility functions [as, for example, in Nechyba (1999)]. Alternatively, an individual *achievement function* may combine individual ability with S, with the resulting individual achievement levels entering household utility functions [as, for example, in Epple and Romano (1998)].

The input q into school production can be interpreted in a number of different ways. One possibility is to simply assume that it represents one or more moments of the distribution of child abilities within the school. All else equal, a model would typically assume that higher average ability within the school leads to higher quality. The precise shape of the relationship between school quality and average ability, however, has important efficiency implications regarding sorting Arnott and Rowse (1987).[12] In addition, assumptions regarding the independent impact of the variance in abilities within a school may be added. It is not immediately apparent what the appropriate assumptions regarding ability variance would be. One view might be that there are benefits to diversity – thus leading to higher variances as being desirable. A different view (often implicitly assumed in many European school systems) suggests that narrow variances allow for more precise targeting of curricula to the particular needs of subgroups.

Interpreting nonfinancial inputs as measures of child ability distributions could be characterized as the purest form of a "peer effects" approach. Some [e.g., Nechyba (2003a)], however, have argued that q could be interpreted much more broadly as representing a number of different kinds of nonfinancial inputs that are correlated with

---

[11] Some models take a more minimalist approach by assuming that a fixed per pupil set up cost is required, with no marginal benefit from additional spending [e.g., Epple and Romano (1998)].

[12] Care should be taken here to be careful by what one means by efficiency. In terms of maximizing S in society, complete mixing of students is efficient whenever the relationship between S and average ability is concave. A full analysis of efficiency, however, depends on other elements of particular models. In models where S enters achievement functions that also take individual ability as arguments, we may for instance be more interested in maximizing total achievement rather than overall S, or we may be interested in analyzing efficiency using a full Pareto criterion based on household utility.

household income, with moments of child ability distributions representing only one possibility. For instance, the inclusion of nonfinancial parental inputs into school production – either through direct volunteering in schools or simple monitoring of public school performance, extends the nonfinancial input q to a household rather than child specific peer effect.[13] Similarly, in the presence of union wage scales that do not permit additional financial compensation for high-quality teachers, teacher labor markets are likely to compensate high quality teachers with better assignments – typically thought of as assignments in higher-income public schools. Thus, teacher quality can emerge as a nonfinancial school input correlated with district income.[14] And, recent evidence suggests that direct financial contributions by parents can play an important role under certain institutional settings – again suggesting an effect correlated with parental income.[15]

The inclusion of nonfinancial inputs into public school production introduces the empirically relevant possibility that public school sorting and public school quality differences may arise not only because of local financing institutions but also because of nonfinancial input differences due to sorting. However, while the presence of nonfinancial inputs is necessary for equilibrium sorting within the public system to emerge under equalized public school financing, it is not sufficient. In the absence of some constraints on household choices of public schools, differences between public schools would still disappear in equilibrium [as, for example, in Epple and Romano (1998)] when financing is equalized across public schools because households would have an incentive to switch schools whenever differences exist. In private school markets, such constraints emerge endogenously (as discussed in Section 2.2) as private schools use tuition prices to ration access. Since public schools do not charge explicit tuition, public school markets must give rise to implicit rationing mechanisms – typically through housing markets and capitalization – in order to sustain inequalities within the public system as an equilibrium outcome. We turn to these rationing mechanisms next.

2.1.2. Housing market and spatial constraints that support sorting within public schools

As suggested already, two types of constraints have been employed in local public finance models of public schooling. In school systems where admission to particular public schools is determined by residential location, housing markets (and capitalization of school quality) represent the natural mechanism through which sorting could arise. In

---

[13] McMillan (2000) finds empirical evidence of a correlation of parental income and parental monitoring of schools. Higher income parents may also be more effective at introducing innovation into school bureaucracies that have shown to be handicapped by the presence of strong teacher unions [Hoxby (1996)].

[14] Loeb and Page (2001) provide empirical evidence in favor of this assumption.

[15] Brunner and Sonstelie (2003) suggest that parental contributions play an important role in California school districts where spending limitations are in place.

open enrollment systems where multiple public schools can be accessed from any residential location, on the other hand, the spatial distance of houses to different schools (combined with a different type of capitalization effect) may emerge as a rationing mechanism under the assumption that transportation is costly. Each of these mechanisms explicitly recognizes the link between residential location and public school access – and thus the constraints households face as they are forced to make a "bundled" choice of housing and schooling simultaneously.

Public school choice in the context of neighborhood or district-based school admission has been linked most directly to housing markets in the local public finance model introduced by Dunz (1985), developed further by Nechyba (1997) and modified to focus on schools in Nechyba (1999).[16] The model begins with a fixed set of houses of varying quality partitioned into a set of school districts. While the model does not permit endogenous changes in housing stocks, it places no restrictions on the intra- and inter-district distribution of housing quality, and it permits housing quality to reflect both house- and community-specific characteristics. Thus, existing housing stocks can be varied so as to give rise to different inter- and intra-district distributions of house prices and household incomes, with later models focusing on empirically relevant equilibrium distributions. Households are endowed with incomes and child abilities, and school production is described by the production function in Equation (1). Per pupil spending x in each district is determined through a political process (that can include a mixture of state income and local property tax financing), while q is endogenously determined by the characteristics of households attending local public schools.

Sorting arises in this context through several channels. First, the housing market itself – absent any distortions introduced by public school institutions – gives rise to residential income segregation so long as some jurisdictions have disproportionately more high-quality houses than others. Second, given the presence of per pupil spending (x) in school production, local financing of public schools generally gives rise to spending that is monotone in local income. Similarly, the correlation of nonfinancial inputs (q) with household income leads to higher nonfinancial school inputs in wealthier districts. Combined, this implies that housing prices for the same quality house will differ across jurisdictions as higher public school quality must be capitalized into local house prices in equilibrium (especially in light of the fact that empirically plausible versions of the model predict no strong correlation of property tax *rates* and local wealth). Under local financing of public schools, housing prices are therefore distorted upward

---

[16] Rangazas (1995) offers a somewhat earlier treatment of education in a two-district context based on the Epple, Filimon and Romer (1993) model, with school quality defined solely by spending. Like the Nechyba approach, a link between housing markets and education is supported in part by exogenously imposed zoning and community amenity differences. Fernandez and Rogerson (1996) also discuss public school choice in a two-district context but also do so within the context of a school production model that equates quality solely with per pupil spending. DeBartolome (1990) offers a nice earlier treatment of peer effects in a two community/two family type setting – demonstrating the efficiency implications of decentralized finance in the presence of peer effects.

in wealthier communities and downward in poorer communities – leading to sorting by income above what is predicted by inter-jurisdictional differences in housing quality. Under state financing (that equalizes spending across schools), on the other hand, x is independent of the school district but q remains higher in wealthier districts. Thus, a portion of the segregating force introduced by locally-financed public schools remains under state financing. While these results are primarily presented as simulation results (treated more explicitly in Section 3) in the literature [Nechyba (1999, 2000, 2003a, 2003b, 2003c, 2003e)], they could in principle be derived analytically in more simplified settings.[17]

Similar results emerge in models that rely on the introduction of a more explicitly spatial element linked to transportation costs to ration entry into equally financed public schools of different quality. A recent model by Epple and Romano (2003) investigates sorting across public schools when multiple schools are nominally available for all households regardless of residential location but where houses are located at different distances from the various public schools.

The potential costs of residential segregation in education markets has been investigated in various frameworks. Benabou (1993, 1996), for instance, focuses on human capital accumulation in a general equilibrium framework with locally financed public schools and peer effects. Low human capital "ghettos" may form in these models – giving rise to inefficiencies (aside from inequities) when the negative impact of peer segregation on education in such ghettos is greater than the gains from such segregation in other communities. As in the models discussed above, such stratification may persist despite equalization of expenditures. Durlauf (1996) focuses on the dynamics of income inequality when education depends on both expenditures and neighborhood effects. Persistent income inequality arises in the model under certain conditions that lead to particular forms of household segregation across communities. In each of these models, the efficiency and distributional implications of segregated peer groups depend on the way peer effects are assumed to impact different groups, much as had already been discussed in a different setting in the theoretical treatment of peer sorting by Arnott and Rowse (1987).

2.2. Sorting out of the traditional public school system – private, charter and magnet schools

In our discussion of decentralized sorting across public schools in the previous section, our sole focus was on household choices within a traditional public school system that offers hierarchically ranked school quality options linked to housing markets. Choice, of course, increasingly extends beyond traditional public schools, with nontraditional

---

[17] While alternative models of housing markets [e.g., continuous housing good models such Epple, Filimon and Romer (1993)] have not been introduced as vehicles for investigating public school sorting within a framework that specifically incorporates features important in education, one can conjecture that similar analytic results could arise under the necessary theoretical restrictions.

public schools such as charter schools and magnet schools emerging within the public sector and private schools competing with it. Sorting therefore extends beyond different neighborhood or district schools as decentralized household choices lead some to exit the traditional public school system. Because of a greater focus of the current literature on private (as opposed to nontraditional public) schools, we focus much of this section on a discussion of private schools (Sections 2.2.1 and 2.2.2) and then discuss nontraditional public schools in Section 2.2.3.

2.2.1. Modeling private schools

Because private schools charge tuition, any model of private schools must choose between a number of different competitive advantages that a private school might have over what "free" public schools can offer. Such advantages generally fall into one or both of the following categories:

(a) the ability of private schools to select inputs (both x and q) into school production, and/or

(b) access by private schools to different school production technologies.

An additional advantage emerges in multijurisdictional settings where private schools permit the unbundling of residential location and housing choices, but discussion of this is deferred to Section 2.2.2.

(a) *Cream skimming private schools.* The simplest form of the first type of private school advantage is one that assumes private schools set minimum household peer quality standards in order to produce a vertically differentiated product that can attract households away from public schools. Nechyba (1999) introduces such an assumption by characterizing private schools as announcing x (per pupil spending) and q_{min} (the minimum household peer quality level accepted into the private school). Under perfect competition and constant returns to scale in production, this gives rise to private schools that each serve a single household type with peer quality level q_{min} and tuition equal to the spending level that is most preferred by that household type. Households thus sort based on both income and peer quality, with high income and high peer quality households gaining the most from choosing private schools. Within private school markets, sorting is "perfect" in the sense that no two household types attend the same private school. And while private schools are able to target spending levels specifically to households, simulations of this framework (discussed in Section 3) suggest that the primary force supporting private school markets under empirically relevant parameterizations rests with the private school market's "cream skimming" through minimum peer quality levels.

Although this model of private school markets is simple and easily incorporated into multicommunity public school models (see Section 2.2.2), it imposes the artificial assumption that private schools cannot price discriminate between different observable household peer types. This assumption is relaxed by Epple and Romano (1998) and Caucutt (2001). Instead of assuming that private schools "cream skim" by setting q_{min}, these models allow profit maximizing private schools to manipulate q through tuition policies linked to household peer quality. More precisely, the models assume that, aside from a fixed per pupil cost of education, the determining factor of school quality is the average child ability level within a school.[18] Private schools can then directly price the peer externality associated with a child's ability level, leading them to offer scholarships to high ability, low-income children while charging high tuition to lower ability, high income families. Epple and Romano (1998) illustrate how such price discrimination leads to a hierarchy of private schools of different qualities, with each private school offering higher quality than the one public school in the model.[19] As in the Nechyba framework, households sort out of public schools based on both income and peer quality, but sorting *within* the private sector takes on a richer and more subtle form. Specifically, with price discrimination (rather than minimum peer quality levels) serving as the primary tool supporting sorting in equilibrium, each private school targets a continuous combination of income/ability types composed of higher-income/lower-ability attendees who pay high tuition and lower-income/higher-ability attendees who pay less tuition (or receive a scholarship).

(b) *Private school access to different technologies.* While "cream skimming" of this kind has provided the most common theoretical explanation for the existence of private school markets in formal models, various modifications of school production functions are increasingly being explored – typically within the context of private schools also being able to choose inputs. To fix ideas, one might for instance extend the production function in Equation (1) to take the form

$$S = \phi_i\big(f(x, q)\big) \tag{2}$$

where the transformation ϕ_i depends on whether a school is public or private. For instance, one simple approach in the spirit of Epple and Romano (2002) treats ϕ_i as a parameter and sets

$$\phi_{\text{pub}} < \phi_{\text{priv}}, \tag{3}$$

---

[18] An additional difference between the Epple and Romano and the Nechyba approach arises from the assumed technology available to households to convert school quality into academic achievement. Epple and Romano assume an achievement function $a(S, b_n)$, where b_n represents an individual child n's ability and S represents school quality as measured by average ability within the school [q in Equation (1)]. It is the child achievement a which enters household utility, not S. Nechyba, on the other hand, takes a more reduced form approach of S entering household utility functions.

[19] Unlike Epple and Romano (1998), Caucutt (2001) abstracts away from public schools and models only private schools. The two approaches have much in common in terms of theoretical insights, although Caucutt solves the existence problem common to "club models" by having families randomize over private schools while Epple and Romano appeal to an ε-equilibrium concept. Caucutt (2002) introduces a public school into her earlier model.

where the subscripts "pub" and "priv" refer to public and private schools respectively. Public schools are thus exogenously assumed to be productively less efficient than private schools in the sense that they produce lower quality S for any given set of inputs (x, q).[20] This public school inefficiency could be endogenized [as in Nechyba (2003c)] by letting

$$\phi_i = \left(1 - \lambda_i(PUB)\right), \tag{4}$$

where $\lambda_{priv} = 0$ and λ_{pub} is some positive monotone transformation of the fraction of students attending public schools (PUB). This yields a model in which public school inefficiency declines as the degree of private school competition faced by public schools increases.[21] While this does not introduce an explicit optimization model for public school administrators (as discussed further in Section 2.4), it represents a reduced form model of a public sector responsive to external incentives. One interpretation of this approach suggests an underlying rent seeking model of public schools [Manski (1993)], where the λ_{pub} function specifies the degree to which rent seeking is part of what public schools do.[22]

The introduction of public school inefficiency then has the potential of impacting the type of sorting that is predicted by the various models. In the extreme, one could assume a framework where private schools either do not have the ability to choose peer inputs or where school production functions place no weight on peer quality. Private schools would thus rely solely on their cost advantage as they compete with public schools, with only higher-income households sorting out of public schools. In models with empirically plausible parameters, however, cost advantages by themselves are unlikely to produce a sufficiently strong force to support private school markets, implying that models which introduce public school inefficiency typically continue to rely on the previously discussed private school advantage of peer input selection. When combined,

---

[20] Evans and Schwab (1995), Neal (1997) and Grogger and Neal (2000) for instance, suggest that Catholic schools are more effective at producing school quality, in particular for minority children, and Figlio and Ludwig (2000) find a positive impact of private schooling on other adolescent behavior (such as sexual activity and hard drug use). Rouse (1998) documents faster math achievement gains among private school attendees in the Milwaukee Parental Choice Program, and Angrist et al. (2001) document substantial performance increase in various dimensions for students randomly assigned to a private school voucher program in Columbia. Ballou and Podgursky (1998) provide evidence that private schools are more successful at retaining high-quality teachers and developing their teaching skills, and Toma (1996) – in a study of five different countries – finds that the extension of government restrictions to private schools diminishes private school effectiveness.

[21] In principle this could of course be extended to include competition between public schools which Hoxby (2000), Bayer and McMillan (2005a) and Hanushek and Rivkin (2003) suggest raises the quality of public schools while McHugh (2003) finds less evidence. Positive impacts of private school competition on public school quality have been demonstrated in Hoxby (1994) and Dee (1998) but were not found by Sander (1999) and McMillan (2000).

[22] Manski (1993) uses this approach to present the classic trade-off under private school vouchers – with public school quality suffering from private competition unless rent seeking within public schools is sufficiently large and thus productively constrained by increased competition.

this would tend to lead to sorting based on both household income and peer quality, with household income playing a larger role than in models without public school inefficiencies (assuming both lead to the same overall level of private school attendance).

In all of these formulations of private school advantages, it is implicitly assumed that households agree on a definition of school quality, which implies that the ranking of public and private schools is independent of households and their circumstances. A further extension of private school models could therefore arise from an explicit incorporation of *horizontal* differentiation rather then *vertical* differentiation, with private school markets less constrained than public schools in offering a menu of alternatives targeted to particular household tastes. For instance, preferences for schools of a particular vertical quality dimension may differ along a horizontal dimension denoted by μ, with the school production function (2) extended such that

$$S^n = \phi_i(f(x, q), \mu). \tag{5}$$

The superscript "n" on school quality S then denotes a particular household who evaluates both the vertical quality considerations modeled above as well as the proximity of the horizontal school type μ to the household's own preferences over μ. Public schools in such a model might be constrained to offering a particular value of μ, with private schools free to choose different values.

Examples of such a formulation are offered by Ferrayra (2002) and Cohen-Zada and Justman (2002) who introduce a preference parameter for religious education and permit private schools to differentiate themselves by offering a religious dimension to the curriculum. Other interpretations of μ might include diversity in pedagogical approaches or subject concentration. In terms of sorting of households across public and private schools, this formulation introduces a form of sorting that is beyond the "cream skimming" associated with the other approaches mentioned above. Put differently, sorting now occurs not only along household peer and income dimensions but also along the preference dimension over which households differ, and it therefore becomes a more unambiguously positive phenomenon. Ferris and West (2002) also formalize this in a framework where cream skimming private schools serve as an avenue for low-income students to escape the uniformity of public schools. This analysis leads them to suggest that concerns over cream skimming and peer group effects are insufficient to dismiss other potentially positive impacts of private school differentiation.[23]

2.2.2. *Private schools in heterogeneous public school markets*

While sorting into private schools is often analyzed in models that assume a homogeneous public school sector (with all public schools of the same quality),[24] additional

---

[23] More specifically, Ferris and West (2002) consider the combined effect of cream skimming on the one hand and lower drop out rates induced by additional school choices.

[24] One interpretation of this homogeneity assumption is that households are free to choose any public school and are thus unconstrained by housing market or spatial consideration. As discussed in Section 2.1, public school differences cannot be supported in equilibrium under these assumptions.

sorting effects emerge when private school markets are introduced into heterogeneous public school settings of the type discussed in Section 2.1. An early analytic treatment of the intuition behind the new forces introduced into a heterogeneous local public goods environment when merged with private markets is offered by Goldstein and Gronberg (1986) and extended in a more school-specific context in Mora (2003), Nechyba (1999) and subsequent simulation papers. In an environment where a link between housing markets and access to public schools supports equilibrium public school differences, private school markets have a competitive advantage in that they are able to allow households to unbundle their housing and schooling choices. More precisely, with housing prices depressed (due to capitalization of public school quality) in poorer districts, private school attending households can obtain "bargains" in lower-income public school districts while avoiding the public schools that are the cause of depressed housing prices.

Under empirically plausible parameterizations (see Section 3), this private school advantage is by itself typically not sufficient to support an empirically relevant private school market.[25] But when combined with the other types of private school advantages raised in Section 2.2.1, it suggests a pattern of residential location that results in higher-income and higher peer quality households mixing with lower-income and lower-ability households in residential housing markets while sorting into different public and private schools. It further gives rise to the possibility that sorting out of public schools is less continuous than what is suggested by models discussed in the previous section, with some higher-ability and higher-income households choosing good public school districts and others choosing private schools in lower-income districts. Models that incorporate both heterogeneous public school and private school markets have, however, been analytically too intractable to yield many closed form solutions, relying instead on computable general equilibrium simulations discussed in more detail in Section 3. An exception is offered by Mora (2003) who provides a simplified version of Nechyba (1999) model with identical housing stocks across two jurisdictions and with education production depending only on per pupil spending. While a one community version of the model predicts perfect sorting of higher-income households into private schools, the housing market in a two jurisdiction model gives rise to the possibility that sorting takes on a more subtle form. Examples are offered in which middle-income households reside in the lower-income jurisdiction and send their children to private schools that are of lower quality than public schools frequented by higher-income households in the other jurisdiction. Other examples illustrate different possible patterns of sorting, all of which can also emerge in the more complex simulation models based on Nechyba (1999) but none of which is established analytically in the more complex settings.

---

[25] In a more theoretical context, however, Mora (2003) demonstrates that private school markets in multi-jurisdiction settings can indeed emerge solely based on production technologies that take per pupil spending as their only input.

2.2.3. Nontraditional public schools

While public school reforms in a number of states have gone beyond the traditional residence-based public school system explored in Section 2.2.1, theoretical explorations of the introduction of nontraditional public schools like charter schools and magnet schools have remained largely absent from the literature. At the same time, some of the likely sorting effects of such reforms can be discussed to some degree based on the theoretical treatment of sorting within (traditional) public and private school markets. Charter schools, for instance, often represent attempts at horizontal differentiation within the public system, with school charters specifying particular nontraditional goals for each such school. Because admission is not based on residential location, such schools are likely to give rise to some of the effects of private schools in that they divorce (at least to some extent) residential location from school choices. In the absence of explicit tuition prices, however, models of charter schools would likely have to include an alternative rationing mechanism – either a spatial transportation cost [as in Epple and Romano (2003)] or a cost measured in terms of effort required to assure admission. Sorting may therefore arise along preference and peer quality dimensions (as in the case of private schools) but may also include an additional "opportunity cost" dimension. Magnet schools, on the other hand, represent attempts to provide greater vertical differentiation within the public system and, as in the case of charter schools, such attempts are typically not linked to residential location requirements. Sorting in such cases is therefore likely to lead to greater ability sorting within the public system, a topic we now turn to more explicitly within a traditional public school setting.

2.3. Sorting within the traditional public school system – tracking and public school objectives

In all the frameworks discussed above, it has implicitly been assumed that *within* any particular public school, quality is the same for all students and that no explicit attempt is made by the public school sector to sort students on the basis of ability or peer quality. To one degree or another, however, public schools frequently attempt to provide a differentiated product within individual schools (or across very different public schools within the same geographic area), whether through partial or complete tracking. Conceptually, public school designers determine not only the degree of centrally directed sorting that is appropriate within public schools but also the grade level at which such sorting should begin. In fact, virtually all societies have chosen to introduce fairly complete tracking within publicly supported schools at some stage, although the timing and precise form of public school tracking takes many different forms. In the US, partial sorting may take place in public primary and secondary schools with the more complete sorting introduced at the post-secondary stage of schooling, while other societies accelerate the transition from no tracking to complete tracking within the primary and secondary years of schooling.

From the outset, it should be noted that – while the sorting *among* public schools in Section 2.1 and *into* private schools in Section 2.2 emerges from *decentralized* choices of households operating in particular economic environments, public school tracking represents a more *centralized* form of sorting. Its presence in public school systems does not obviate the decentralized sorting forces described in the previous section, but it does alter the economic environment under which these decentralized forces operate. While no theoretical work to date has explored fully the degree to which the decentralized sorting forces are impacted by public sector attempts to sort students explicitly, some initial work in the area has paved the way to a fuller investigation of the problem.

The issue has been tackled most directly by Epple, Newlon and Romano (2002) within a model where the degree of tracking within public schools is set exogenously and the nature of the competition between public and private schools is investigated in the context of the Epple and Romano (1998) model of tuition-based cream skimming in private school markets. Public schools are therefore still modeled as passive agents except that now, unlike in models discussed in Sections 2.1 and 2.2, the fraction of time that students mix with other students is set exogenously below 1. More specifically, the model imposes an exogenous ability cut off B, with students whose ability falls above B attending a separate track for an exogenously specified fraction m of the day. The impact of varying B and m is then investigated computationally. The analytic result in Epple and Romano (1998) indicating that all private schools must dominate the public school in terms of quality is then modified – all private schools must be of higher quality than the lower track in the public school, but the model may give rise to some private schools (composed of students whose ability falls below B) whose quality falls below that of the upper track in the public school. The upper track in public schools attracts some households that would attend private schools in the absence of public school tracking, thus changing the sorting into private schools as sorting within the public school is implemented. This suggests a possible avenue through which public schools may choose to respond to private school competition, but a full exploration of this issue would require an explicit model of the objective function for public school administrators – an issue to which we turn next.

2.4. Modeling public school objectives and their impact on sorting of students (and teachers)

In almost all theoretical models of public and private school markets discussed above, it has implicitly been assumed that public schools are largely passive institutions that take inputs provided by the political process (spending) and the selection of students (peers) as given and do little to themselves manipulate these. As noted above, even in the Epple, Newlon and Romano (2002) model of public school tracking, the tracking policy itself does not emerge from a public school optimization problem. The school production function in Equation (4) deviates from this somewhat by incorporating a reduced form specification of public responsiveness to competition, but it also does so without specifying an underlying optimization problem for public schools. Two micro-based models of public school objective functions have, however, recently been developed. The first assumes that public schools are rent-seeking institutions that produce school quality only to the extent to which this raises rents for school administrators or teachers, while the second assumes that public schools are maximizing some measure of achievement within the public school. In light of increasing empirical evidence that public schools indeed alter behavior as a response to changes in incentives,[26] the theoretical exploration of public school objectives represents a potentially important avenue for future research.

Until recently, the common presumption has been that the presence of rent seeking motives on the part of public schools leads to an unambiguous positive and efficiency enhancing effect of increased private school competition that constrains rents by public schools and forces them to raise productive effort even as private schools cream skim from the public sector Manski (1993). McMillan (2004), however, questions this in a model where parents are given both "voice" within the public schools as well as the opportunity to "exit" into the private sector, with some parents assumed to be more active in pressuring public school officials than others. While the possibility that public schools may respond to increased private school competition by raising productive effort exists within this framework, McMillan also demonstrates that public schools may choose to behave *more inefficiently* under greater competition if it is less costly for them (in terms of sacrificing rents) to simply allow motivated parents to exit the public system and thus be left free to obtain greater per pupil rents in a smaller public school. Sorting into private schools along the dimension of parental involvement – which can in principle be modeled as a household specific rather than student specific peer effect – thus plays a critical role in this framework. The issues raised imply that the implicit assumption of λ_{pub} as a positive monotone transformation in Equation (4) may be an over simplification as more explicit micro foundations of public school behavior are introduced.

Lazear (2001), on the other hand, assumes that public schools optimize overall student achievement as they assign students to classrooms in the presence of peer effects. He develops a "disruption model" of peer effects where the emphasis is on the disruptive role of particular students rather than the average ability of students within a classroom. His optimizing framework then implies that it may be optimal for schools to concentrate disruptive students in smaller classrooms, a prediction that would help explain the common empirical finding that class size has little impact on measured student achievement.

---

[26] Cullen (1999) and Figlio and Getzler (2002), for instance, provide evidence that public schools alter their classification of students with disabilities in response to changes in fiscal incentives; Cullen and Reback (2003) suggest ways in which schools game rules under accountability systems and Jacob and Levitt (2003) find evidence of rather dramatic cheating on standardized tests in Chicago under fairly mild incentives for schools. Figlio and Winicki (2002) even suggest that schools may alter school lunch content to boost performance on standardized tests.

While Lazear focuses on the assignment and sorting of students, the potential for developing explicit models in which public school systems assign different teacher qualities (in the presence of external opportunities for teachers) may offer a fruitful avenue for further theoretical analysis, especially in light of evidence that higher-quality teachers tend to be assigned to higher peer quality and higher-income households [Loeb and Page (2001)]. Just as parental involvement can be viewed as a household level peer effect in the equations of Section 2.2, it may be that a similar household level peer effect emerges in micro modeling of teacher assignments if indeed it is the case that higher-income and higher-ability households are assigned higher-quality teacher inputs. At this stage, the literature simply treats this possibility in the reduced form fashion implicit in the specifications of productions functions with household level peer effects, and it does not treat the possibility of differential teacher assignments within a single public school.[27] A final idea that may be incorporated into multijurisdictional models of education in the future is offered by Hoyt and Lee (2003) who suggest that local policy (such as school policy) may be shaped in part with an eye toward making communities more attractive for high peer quality households.

3. From theoretical to computational models of school markets

Much of the theoretical discussion of Section 2 arises within research programs that ultimately aim to provide an empirically richer description of the relevant economic forces through computational versions of the underlying theoretical models. The increasing emphasis of computational approaches to modeling school markets has arisen for two basic reasons: First, more complex theoretical models – while incorporating a richer and empirically more relevant economic framework, are simply too involved to yield clear, closed form analytic solutions; and second, increasingly powerful computer platforms provide previously unavailable avenues to advance a research agenda aimed at characterizing the interaction of complicated general equilibrium forces. This section therefore begins with a discussion of the appropriate interpretation of computational models of education (Section 3.1), followed by an overview of some of the results (Section 3.2) and a review of current research aimed at linking computational models increasingly to data (Section 3.3).[28]

---

[27] Ballou (1996) suggests that the empirical evidence supports the notion that public schools generally do not hire the most-qualified teachers from their applicant pool and speculates that this may change if public schools face increased competition. Hoxby (2002) provides evidence from traditional forms of Tiebout and private school choice suggesting that increased competition causes schools to pay closer attention to teacher quality, and Hanushek (2002) reports that, while teacher quality is typically not correlated with observable characteristics of teachers, principals seem to be able to discern quality differences (and presumably use these when making teacher assignments). In addition, Hanushek (2001) provides evidence that teacher attrition is affected strongly by student characteristics, suggesting that schools have a strong interest in using teacher assignments as a compensation and retention tool.

[28] Portions of this section draw heavily on discussions in Nechyba (2003d).

3.1. Interpreting computational structural models

Computational equilibrium models attempt to provide internally consistent frameworks for analyzing not only the impact of policies on individual incentives but also the degree to which policies change the general economic environment in which individual decisions are made. Empirically relevant work needs to come to terms with a number of challenges, including the fact that parental choices about education involve judgments about school production functions that remain controversial among researchers, that these decisions are often made in environments in which school choices are bundled with choices over residential housing and local amenities, that parents take into account the possibility of private alternatives to public schooling and that their decisions are made in environments where families are credit constrained because it is generally difficult to borrow against human capital investments. It is in large part because of the complexity of these challenges that purely analytic approaches are often insufficient to yield empirically relevant insights.

Computational models therefore represent attempts to bridge theoretical and empirical work – avoiding the simplicity that is necessary for purely theoretical treatments to yield closed form solutions while at the same time recognizing that traditional (reduced-form) empirical work is often unable to characterize important general equilibrium interdependencies between individual behavior and the evolution of the general economic environment. Such models span a continuous spectrum from theoretical to empirical work, with some computational models primarily used for exploring the theoretical properties of complex economic models and others aimed at empirically estimating models that can be used to simulate out-of-sample policy changes. Few models are on either extreme of this spectrum and most contain elements of both theoretically and empirically motivated simulations. All such approaches, however, begin with the specification of the underlying mathematical *structure* of the economic environment that is modeled, thus leading to the frequent label for such approaches as *structural models*. This structure includes the detailed specification of preference and production functions, a determination of appropriate distributions of characteristics for the economic agents in the model (such as income distributions), and a mathematical description of the political (voting) and economic environment (tax instruments, housing and private school markets) that determines school inputs. A purely theoretical application of simulation techniques then proceeds to a computational analysis of how equilibrium outcomes change as values for the underlying structural parameters change.

Beyond such explorations of the theoretical properties of equilibrium models, researchers then typically proceed to developing ways of identifying the empirically "correct" values for key structural parameters in order to investigate policy simulations within the most relevant portion of the parameter space. Key aspects of the models (such as elasticities, income distributions, etc.) may simply be set so as to be consistent with estimates from traditional empirical work, or they may be calibrated to yield equilibrium outcomes that are consistent with certain aspects of observed outcomes under a particular economic setting. More ambitious attempts to move computational models along the spectrum from theoretical to empirical work may furthermore employ structural estimation techniques to estimate (rather than calibrate) underlying parameters. With critical aspects of theoretical models linked to data, the models then permit simulations of out-of-sample policies under the assumption that the estimated structural parameters remain unchanged even as the general equilibrium environment may change dramatically. The empirical relevance of simulation results then depends on both an empirically plausible underlying structure as well as a high level of confidence that the structural parameters are sufficiently linked to empirical realities. Confidence in the model is bolstered by successful replication of observed equilibrium outcomes under existing institutions. An even stronger criterion would involve estimating the structural model for a data set using the institutions relevant for the setting from which the data were drawn, and then simulating equilibrium outcomes under a different observed institutional setting to check whether the estimated model can replicate outcomes under that new setting.[29]

In interpreting computational policy analysis, it is therefore important to come to terms with the approximate position occupied by the particular model on the continuum between theoretical and empirical work. Extraordinarily valuable insights regarding the relevance of different competing economic forces can be obtained even with models that fall on the more theoretical end of that spectrum without the need to interpret specific simulation results as empirical estimates to be used directly for policy analysis. At the same time, as computational models find their way toward the more empirical end of the spectrum, more confidence can be placed in the precise estimates of policy impacts. With this in mind, we now turn to an overview of some of the results from current simulation approaches.

3.2. Selected simulation results and general lessons on sorting: school finance policies, tracking and vouchers

Computational models have tackled the issue of sorting in two separate settings: those that involve a single homogeneous public school sector (which is equivalent to assuming a single public school competing against endogenously emerging private schools) and those that explicitly model heterogeneous public schools supported in equilibrium by spatial or housing market constraints. A common theme across these literatures involves the importance of sorting along peer characteristics and household income, with both types of sorting emerging between public and private schools as well as within each school market. While the primary type of sorting that is investigated has been hierarchical (with higher-income and higher peer quality households sorting into separate schools), an emerging literature is beginning to investigate horizontal forms of sorting (with different types of peer quality sorting into separate schools or tracks). Below, we focus separately on sorting within computational models that model public schools as homogeneous (Section 3.2.1) and those that incorporate economic forces leading to heterogeneity in quality within the public sector (Section 3.2.2).

---

[29] Few, if any, computation models have been subjected to this stronger test.

3.2.1. *Sorting in private schools in the presence of homogeneous public schools*

Epple and Romano (1998) build the foundation for the most common approach to investigating sorting in the presence of a single public school.[30] As detailed in Section 2.2, the theoretical model that underlies the computational analysis models private schools as profit maximizing institutions that gain a competitive advantage over the public school by selecting peer inputs into school production through price-discriminating tuition policies. While per pupil spending is relegated to play a minor role in this model, more recent generalizations that include a more prominent role for marginal impacts of private school spending on school quality [Epple and Romano (2002)] do little to alter the general lessons regarding sorting. The primary policy applications of this model have been to private school voucher policy and to a computational analysis of tracking within the public schools, with some other approaches providing additional nuances.

School production in the Epple and Romano work is modeled as in equation (1) (Section 2.1.1), with no marginal impact of school spending once a minimum per pupil spending level is in place. School quality (or in this case, average ability within a school) combines with individual ability to determine individual achievement. In equilibrium, private schools are composed of continuous slices of the household income/child ability type space, with each school combining relatively higher-income/lower-ability students (who pay high tuition) with lower-income/higher-ability students (who pay less tuition or receive scholarships). Because of the higher average ability in private schools, all private schools dominate the public school in terms of quality, and private schools themselves can be ranked by average ability (and thus quality).

3.2.1.1. *Private school vouchers.*   This sorting along both household income and child ability is intensified as private school vouchers are introduced, with additional private schools serving students that previously attended the public school and reallocating students among previously existing private schools. The central intuition behind the impact of vouchers arises from the increased competition for high-ability students, which in equilibrium lowers tuition for such students by substantially more than the amount of the voucher.

Vouchers then have two separate effects: First, they alter the nature of ability sorting across schools, leaving public schools with lower quality because of the "cream skimming" by private schools. Second, vouchers implicitly redistribute income. For this reason, an analysis of which children benefit and which are hurt in terms of their access to school quality differs from a household welfare analysis that also includes the impact of income redistribution. Achievement gains are greatest (between 12.9% and 20.2% for a $2,000 voucher) for children whose households are induced to switch from public

---

[30] The single public school assumption can be interpreted as a model of open enrollment public schools in the absence of housing market or spatial constraints that can sustain public school differences in equilibrium. Caucutt (2001) presents an alternative model with many of the same implications but abstracts away from the existence of a public school sector.

to private schools, while students who remain in the public school experience a decline in achievement of 4.9%. Not all households that switch to private schools are, however, better off in terms of household welfare because they are induced to switch to private schools (and pay partial tuition) due to the declining quality of public schools. While their children have access to better schools, the decline in income from having to pay tuition may outweigh the benefit of higher school quality. Overall, the largest gains occur for low-income, high-ability households. Because private schools have only the advantage of being able to select peers through tuition pricing (and none of the other possible advantages discussed in Section 2.2), all of these (and other) results of the impact of vouchers on the access to different levels of school quality are due to the changes in sorting induced by vouchers. Furthermore, because peer externalities are priced explicitly in private schools, an increase in private schooling is efficiency enhancing in the model.

In a continuation of this work, Epple and Romano (2002) extend their model in the direction suggested by Equations (2) and (3) in Section 2.2.1 – combining a larger role for school spending effects with an assumed higher cost effectiveness of private schools. These extensions are motivated by an attempt to see whether more finely tuned voucher policies can take advantage of private school efficiencies without giving rise to equity concerns raised by the type of sorting from cream skimming private schools that is central to the results in Epple and Romano (1998). More precisely, the model investigates the impact of different forms of targeting. It demonstrates that targeting of vouchers to child ability does little to alter the results of their previous work because of the unintended policy consequence of the emergence of private schools with lower quality than the public school. These private schools would find clients among low-income, low-ability households who are attracted to the schools by scholarships given in exchange for their vouchers. While this increases household welfare of such low-income families through redistribution of income, it leads to a decline in achievement for their children. The paper then demonstrates that ability targeting of vouchers will undermine cream skimming only to the extent to which the targeting is appropriately structured and accompanied by constraints on schools that accept vouchers. More precisely, when vouchers are set to be equal to the effective marginal cost of an ability type for a school with average ability equal to the population average, and when schools are prohibited from accepting tuition above the voucher amount, cream skimming is neutralized as a homogeneous (and more cost effective) private school sector replaces the public school system.

Voucher design issues are also raised in recent work by Cohen-Zada and Justman (2002) who present a computational model with homogeneous public schools and private schools that may horizontally differentiate themselves by offering religious education. Peer effects play no role in this model, but private subsidies for religious schools are permitted – offering an additional advantage for such schools. The paper then simulates different types of voucher targeting to schools and households, with a focus on means testing at the household level and limitations of vouchers to nonreligious schools. The results, echoed in Ferrayra (2002) multijurisdictional analysis of the same question (see Section 3.2.2), suggest that vouchers limited to nonreligious private schools and targeted to low-income families would have significantly less of an impact than similar vouchers that permit participation of religious schools. The work simultaneously highlights the possibility that the private subsidies received by religious schools may also play an important role. As the model is calibrated to different states with different religious enrollments, the model also suggests that states with high religious enrollments are likely to experience more of a response to vouchers than states with lower religious enrollments.

3.2.1.2. Tracking and public schools.   In an important related project, Epple, Newlon and Romano (2002) investigate sorting issues *within* the public school rather than across public and private schools. Specifically, they model exogenously set levels of tracking within public schools and demonstrate that increased sorting within the public sector may have profound impacts on the nature of public/private school competition. They predict large within-school differences in school quality for different ability levels, with the potential of some private schools offering higher quality than the lower public school track but lower quality than the higher public school track. The existence of two tracks within the public system fundamentally alters the sorting into private schools as the upper track in public schools essentially cream-skims within public schools by setting a minimum ability level. A potentially large segment of relatively higher-ability students that might be attracted to private schools in the absence of public school tracking therefore remains within the segregated track in the public school.

On the spectrum of computational analysis between theoretical and empirical extremes, these models could reasonably be said to fall toward the middle. Most of the models give no role to heterogeneity in public school systems or to large advantages for private schools other than the ability to select peers, but the computable versions of the models are calibrated to replicate some important features of US public schools. While Cohen-Zada and Justman (2002) introduce horizontal differentiation and cost advantages of religious schools, they abstract away from residential sorting, peer group effects and potential competitive responses by public schools. However, the important lessons emerging from these research programs place the issue of sorting that results from competition at center stage and suggest important avenues for future research as the models are enriched and as voucher *design* becomes a greater focus of policy-motivated research.

3.2.2. Sorting within heterogeneous public and private school markets

In models with heterogeneous public school systems, sorting generally occurs in quite similar ways and for quite similar reasons, but additional subtleties are introduced by the presence of public school heterogeneity. It is, for instance, no longer the case in models such as Nechyba (1999) that all private schools are of higher quality than all public schools [as in Epple and Romano (1998)]. Rather, within each jurisdiction or attendance zone, all private schools must be of higher quality in equilibrium than that jurisdiction's public school (for the same reasons as in Epple and Romano's model), but private schools in low-quality public school districts may be of lower quality than public schools in higher-income public school districts. Sorting along the lines suggested in the homogeneous public school literature therefore extends throughout the combined public and private system in ways that are similar to the sorting that occurs over private schools in the absence of public school heterogeneity. In addition, issues regarding equilibrium sorting now extend beyond policy simulations related to vouchers and tracking to more general public school finance policies involving various degrees of centralization. The additional economic forces that play a key role within the heterogeneous public school models primarily involve general equilibrium mobility and price adjustments that alter the economic environment within which household choices regarding schooling are made.

The theoretical model developed in Nechyba (1999) and expanded into more involved computational frameworks in Nechyba (2000, 2003b) and Ferrayra (2002) offers the approach most directly related to research questions involving sorting within heterogeneous public school models with private school markets. The models are calibrated to various data sets from New York and New Jersey [Nechyba (2000, 2003b)] and structurally estimated with a more national data set in Ferrayra (2002). Nechyba (2003b) derives income distributions as well as housing quality distributions from these data[31] and sets preference parameters to yield accurate levels of public school spending (through a voting process) and production parameters to accurately replicate observed levels of private school attendance.

It is in this calibration exercise that the model provides interesting insights into the degree to which the underlying structure of a multidistrict economic model requires different aspects of school production to play a role. More specifically, when a constant returns to scale Cobb–Douglas version of the school production function in Equation (1) places little weight on household peer quality, private school markets do not arise in equilibrium because private schools do not have a sufficient competitive advantage to attract tuition-paying households (even if relatively high private school vouchers are introduced). If, on the other hand, too much weight is placed on household peer quality, public school systems cannot survive in equilibrium because the private school advantage from being able to select peer inputs is too large. As a result, the underlying structure of the model implies that parents in the model must place weight on both spending and peer quality (in roughly equal proportions) in the absence of other private school advantages. When private schools have additional cost advantages [as in versions of Equation (4)], on the other hand, the role assigned to peer quality in the production function declines as the model is re-calibrated to once again replicate observed private

---

[31] Housing quality for different house types across three stylized school districts are calibrated to give rise to housing prices that are observed in the data. Given that prices incorporate both house quality as well as neighborhood amenities and externalities, the calibrated "house quality" values thus represent a combination of housing and neighborhood characteristics as reflected in house prices.

school attendance rates [Nechyba (2003c)]. And when private schools have the additional opportunity to engage in horizontal differentiation in the presence of differences in household tastes [as in Equation (5)], peer quality again plays a less important role [Ferrayra (2002)].

In each of these versions of the computational model, sorting among households takes on a somewhat different form. When the production function is simply as specified in Equation (1) with private schools being able to select inputs but having no additional advantages, those that gain most from segregating into private schools are families with relatively high peer quality, and those that can most easily afford to separate are families with high income. With the option of different school districts offering different qualities in the presence of housing markets that capitalize quality differences, it is similarly higher-income and higher-ability households that have a greater incentive to segregate within the public sector into better public school districts. Thus, sorting across schools is such that relatively higher-income and relatively higher peer quality households sort into better schools, whether these are in the public or the private sector. The lowest quality public school in the poorest district is attended by primarily low-income and lower peer quality households. This result changes somewhat when the production function is altered to that of equation (4) where private schools enjoy an additional cost advantage, with household income playing somewhat less of a role and household peer quality somewhat more of a role in the sorting of families into privates schools. However, when the possibility of horizontal differentiation is introduced [as in Ferrayra (2002)], sorting arises not only along the dimensions of income and peer quality but also in the taste parameter that differentiates households in terms of the value they place on a horizontally differentiated product. The particular application explored by Ferreyra is tastes for religious education as represented by Catholic schools.

3.2.2.1. Private school vouchers. When private school vouchers are then introduced into the model, sorting across schools increases and follows a similar pattern. The most consistent result across all specifications of school production assumptions, however, involves predictions regarding residential sorting. Because of the distortions in housing prices that are introduced through capitalization of public school quality (and local tax rates) in different districts, vouchers (without eligibility restrictions) tend to result in substantial declines in residential sorting as marginal households who attend public schools in better school districts uncouple their housing and schooling choices and thus migrate to lower-income districts to take advantage of depressed housing prices [Nechyba (2000, 2003a, 2003c, 2003e), Ferrayra (2002)]. Simulation results suggest that this effect is initially increasing in the size of the voucher until the voucher approaches public school spending levels in the poor district when the model predicts that some public schools collapse entirely.

Even in the absence of vouchers, the private school market has such a desegregating effect, providing direct incentives for relatively higher-income and peer quality households to choose private schools in poorer districts. In fact, Nechyba (2003c, 2003e) reports that, while public schools in the absence of private school markets lead to substantially more income segregation than is attributable to mere inter-district housing quality differences, a mixed public/private system of the type we observe in the data actually gives rise to *less* residential income sorting than would arise without distortions from the existence of public schools. Residential segregation patterns within heterogeneous public school systems are then predicted to be quite different from school segregation patterns, with private school markets fostering *reduced* residential segregation by income and peer quality but *increased* school segregation along these same dimensions.

Although the predictions from simulation models of the impact of policies such as private school vouchers on residential segregation seems to be robust to alternative specifications of private school advantages (and public school responses) [Nechyba (2003c), Ferrayra (2002)], the effect such policies have on access to educational opportunities for different groups depends critically on these specifications. The model as described by equation (1) with cream skimming as the only advantage for private schools and no response by the public sector predicts a decline in public school quality with the introduction of vouchers. This decline, however, is not primarily centered on public schools in districts where private schools emerge but rather spread throughout the public system as high peer quality households exit better public schools to reside in worse public school districts as they switch to private schools. In fact, many simulations suggest that public schools in richer districts are more adversely affected by private school cream skimming under private school vouchers than are public schools in poorer districts.[32]

Under alternative specifications [such as those of equation (4)], on the other hand, the model predicts increasing public school quality as public schools become more cost effective under increased competition due to private school vouchers [Nechyba (2003c)]. And under horizontal differentiation of private schools targeted to household tastes [Ferrayra (2002)], the model predicts additional preference sorting that has fewer of the negative cream skimming effects emphasized in the Nechyba models. As in the case of homogeneous public school models, the role for horizontal differentiation on the basis of religious education plays a particularly important role as voucher design issues come into play, with Ferreyra predicting substantially different effects for vouchers

---

[32] This result holds more frequently when voucher levels are modest and disappears when voucher levels approach public school spending in poorer districts. In some instances, simulations suggest that public schools (under modest voucher levels) in poor district actually improve as increased per pupil spending (resulting from fewer public school students) outweighs the negative impact of declining peer quality [Nechyba (1999, 2003c)]. The latter result is more likely to hold in a locally financed than a state-equalized public school system (where increases in per pupil spending are spread across all school districts). In an earlier model in which school quality was defined only as a function of spending, Rangazas (1995) offers calibrated simulations in which all public schools improve when vouchers are introduced because a declining public school population, while causing some to withdraw political support from public schools, leads to a lower effective tax price for raising per pupil expenditures. This intuition is also at work in simulations based on the Nechyba model, although the impact on school quality is muted by the smaller role of spending in school production. Rangazas' model also predicts migration effects that are qualitatively similar to those found in the Nechyba framework.

that can be used in religious schools than vouchers targeted only at nonreligious private schools.

The models have also been used to clarify the extent to which targeting of private school vouchers might change both residential and school level sorting. Recall the result that, under modest levels of vouchers available to all, vouchers would be taken up primarily in low-income districts by households that migrate into these districts from higher quality public schools elsewhere. This implies that targeting of vouchers to poor districts differs quite fundamentally from targeting to poor households – with only the former proposal giving rise to the bulk of migration effects of untargeted vouchers. At least for modest voucher levels, vouchers targeted to poor districts are thus more similar to untargeted vouchers than they are to household income targeted vouchers [Nechyba (2000)]. Similar results are likely for investigations of other forms of nontraditional schools such as magnet and charter schools.

3.2.2.2. Public school finance policies. The interaction of private school markets, public schools and residential housing markets can also give rise to predicted general equilibrium price and mobility effects as more general public school finance policies change. Under the production function specification of equation (1), the model predicts greater private school attendance under local property tax financing of public schools than under equalized state income tax financing [Nechyba (2003b)]. This occurs in part because the higher predicted public school quality in poor districts under state equalization provides less of a reason to lower-income/high peer quality households to use private schools in the poor district, and a greater extent because the effective opportunity cost of housing in wealthy districts relative to those in poor districts declines substantially as local financing is changed to state financing.[33] Sorting within the public system and into the private system therefore decreases as financing moves to the state level under the assumption that state and locally financed schools are equally productive.[34] Hybrid state/local financing policies can have similar effects, with general equilibrium effects often outweighing the impact arising under partial equilibrium assumptions [Nechyba (2003a, 2003b, 2002)].

---

[33] This, in turn, arises both because of the capitalization of higher-quality public schools in poor districts (and lower-quality public schools in richer districts) under state equalization, and because local property taxes are part of the opportunity cost of residential location choices while state income taxes are not [Nechyba (2003b)].

[34] Given the empirical evidence that private school attendance tends to increase under equalization [Downes and Greenstein (1996), Downes and Schoeman (1998), Husted and Kenny (2002)], the computational model of Nechyba (2003b) therefore does not accurately predict responses of private school markets to equalization within the public sector. To replicate this increase in private school attendance, the structure of the model requires that public school productivity be linked to the degree of local input into school production (with declining productivity under centralization). Hoxby (1999) suggests that local property tax finance may be a key factor in yielding information to school producers that allows local financing to reach efficiency levels that state income tax financing cannot.

Models such as those reviewed in this section attempt to narrow the gap between strictly empirical and theoretical approaches, but more work on both ends of the spectrum is required for that gap to close further. Currently, the models are strictly static – giving policy outcomes without any sense of transition paths and associated costs. This lack of dynamics also leads to simplifying assumptions. For instance, it is commonly assumed that each household has a child when a more dynamic model could contain life cycle elements that permitted not all residents in each district to have children at any given time. Similarly, housing stocks are assumed, at least in the Nechyba/Ferreyra models, to be exogenously set, with no possible improvements or depreciation. These issues present major challenges for future research, some of which are discussed in more detail in Epple and Nechyba (2004). Finally, while peer effects have become quite central to computational investigations of sorting across schools and neighborhoods, the conceptually separate impact of residential neighborhood and school peer effects has yet to be modeled explicitly in these frameworks. To this end, Bayer, Ferreira and McMillan (2003, 2005) have developed a new method for estimating preferences for school and neighborhood amenities, and their results suggest a "social multiplier" from increased public school quality – because public school quality attracts higher income and more highly educated households to neighborhoods (beyond what one would predict from simply considering the partial equilibrium impact of schools).

3.3. From calibration to structural estimation

The promise of computational approaches to become increasingly empirically relevant is strengthened by recent efforts to use structural estimation techniques to estimate theoretical models rather than rely on relatively crude methods of calibration. Epple and Sieg (1999) and Epple, Romer and Sieg (2001), for instance, develop techniques to estimate general local public finance models that allow for household mobility, housing market adjustments and voting. While this work has not at this point been focused on studying the public and private markets for education, it provides a basis from which future structural work may estimate models more directly focused on issues of sorting across communities and schools. Epple, Romano and Sieg (2003) have investigated peer effects and educational sorting at the college level and without some of the local public finance complexities of primary and secondary education markets. Ferrayra (2002) extends the theoretical model of Nechyba (1999) to include preference variation with regard to religious (Catholic) education and structurally estimates a model with housing, voting, public schools and both secular and religious private schools. Her model is then used to simulate different types of vouchers as discussed in the previous section. And a series of recent empirical papers combine structural and instrumental variable techniques in an attempt to estimate household preference parameters for school and neighborhood amenities while explicitly taking into account the general equilibrium nature of the economic environment in which residential segregation takes place [Bayer, Ferreira and McMillan (2003, 2005), Bayer, McMillan and Reuben (2005), Bayer and Timmins (2003)]. This work promises to bridge much of the gap between theoretical, simulation and empirical work and is providing strong evidence to support conclusions from the computational work cited above that partial equilibrium estimation approaches often yield results that are quite unreliable. Each of these approaches is still in its early stages, with structural estimation of school markets emerging as a likely avenue for much future work.

4. The impact of sorting on outcomes

The fact that nonrandom sorting of students across schools is pervasive is not in dispute and has been documented extensively in the empirical literature. The earliest indication of the importance of residential sorting arises from school capitalization studies dating back to Oates (1969), with more recent estimation techniques focused on discontinuities in housing prices at public school attendance zone boundaries [Black (1999), Weimer and Wolkoff (2001)].[35] Discrete choice models [Nechyba and Strauss (1998), Bayer, McMillan and Reuben (2005), Bayer, Ferreira and McMillan (2003, 2005), Epple and Sieg (1999), Ferrayra (2002)] similarly identify the importance of local school and neighborhood qualities in household utility functions. And in her investigation of the impact of Tiebout style competition on public school quality, Hoxby (2000) documents that much of the segregation along race and income happens across schools within districts – again linked to residential location.[36] These literatures, using very different methodologies and reviewed more extensively elsewhere [Epple and Nechyba (2004)], all suggest an important public school sorting force arising from household mobility, with Bayer, Ferreira and McMillan (2005) illustrating the importance of both partial and general equilibrium effects as the impact of good schools on neighborhoods causes substantial (general equilibrium) sorting on top of the (partial equilibrium) sorting induced by schools themselves.

Equally important is empirical work investigating the extent to which private school sorting is affected by the general equilibrium forces emphasized in the theoretical and computational literature. Lankford and Wyckoff (1992) suggest that parental choices with respect to private schooling are sensitive to the quality of school offerings, to peer characteristics and tuition, all consistent with the theoretical predictions in models reviewed earlier, and Epple, Figlio and Romano (2004) find evidence that private schools engage in the type of price discrimination predicted by Epple and Romano (1998) leading to sorting on observed ability within the private sector. And studies of Catholic school effectiveness have explicitly tackled selection of higher-ability children into private schools in various ways, with Altonji, Elder and Taber (2002) (among others) providing an overview of the econometric problems of estimating private school quality in light of such selection.

---

[35] Complementing this literature are recent studies documenting an impact of new information about local schools on housing prices [Figlio and Lucas (2000)] and the effect of open enrollment within public school districts on property values [Reback (2002)].

[36] This suggests that district level analysis of sorting within public schools is likely to be misleading.

While sorting in school markets is thus well documented, it has been considerably more difficult to identify the degree to which such sorting is responsible for observed differences in student outcomes. Clear correlations between observable household and peer characteristics within schools and school outcomes are easily documented, but the empirical challenge lies in determining the extent to which such correlations are indicative of underlying causation. We begin therefore in Section 4.1 with a brief discussion of the general identification problem faced by researchers who seek to document a causal link between observable sorting patterns and actual outcomes and then proceed in Section 4.2 with an outline of alternative means of addressing these challenges. Section 4.3 then provides a brief review of the initial (and limited) evidence that is emerging from this literature.

4.1. The problem of identifying peer effects

Researchers face several challenges in estimating the importance of peer or neighborhood characteristics on student achievement. The first, treated most extensively in the theoretical econometrics literature, arises from the difficulty in econometrically separating a group's influence on an individual's outcome from the individual's influence on the group [Manski (1993), Moffitt (1998), Brock and Durlauf (2001)], a challenge that has become labeled the "reflection problem" [Manski (1993)]. Thus, if the performance by student X is influenced by the presence of student Y, then student Y's performance is presumably also affected by the presence of student X leading to a classic simultaneous equation bias.

Second, rarely (if ever) are peer groups or neighbors assigned randomly. An important selection issue then arises as peer group choice is endogenous – with the econometrician not observing the full set of individual characteristics determining this choice. Put differently, individuals who choose to associate with a "good" peer group may be "good" in ways that are difficult to quantify or observe, causing peer characteristics to serve merely as good proxies for omitted (or mismeasured) factors. A positive correlation between peer and individual might therefore reflect these omitted factors rather than any causal relationship, suggesting that peer effects will tend to be overestimated.

Finally, data limitations (rather than well-grounded theoretical considerations) generally place tight constraints on how researchers can define peer groups and measure their quality. Thus, researchers are typically limited to using such variables as "average school characteristics" when classroom characteristics might be more relevant, or "average classroom characteristics" when sub-groups within classes may represent the best peer definition. Similarly, measuring peer quality (once peer group has been defined) is not trivial, with most data sources typically limiting researchers to only certain measures such as particular test scores or test score gains. Those concerned about peer effects will point out that theoretically important aspects of peers such as motivation, drive, maturity, etc. are not easily captured. Data limitations may thus lead to a focus on certain types of peer effects (the impact of high achievers on low achievers, for instance) without addressing the much larger issue of how peers influence each other in many other important dimensions [Harris (1998)].

4.2. Empirical approaches to conceptual challenges of identifying peer effects

Awareness of each of the three challenges identified above – the simultaneity bias of the reflection problem, the omitted/mismeasured variables bias arising from the endogenous selection into peer groups, and the limits of defining peer groups and peer quality arising from data constraints – have led to recent empirical research aimed at addressing these problems. The most recent developments in each of these areas are identified below.

4.2.1. The reflection problem

Two very different approaches to the reflection problem have emerged in the empirical literature. One strategy has involved a focus on the relationship between "exogenous" characteristics of a peer group, such as race or gender, and the outcomes of an individual – rather than a focus on the relation of endogenous outcomes between individual and peer. Manski (1993) conceptually distinguishes this "exogenous" peer effect that arises from exogenous peer characteristics from "endogenous" peer effects that arise from current (endogenous) behavior of peers. While some insights have emerged from this approach to the reflection problem, it limits the types of questions that can be addressed.

A second strategy to confronting the reflection problem involves the use of lagged peer outcome measures. Thus, the past performance by student Y is used to quantify the peer quality experienced by student X whose current peer group is composed of student Y. This period's performance gain by individual X is then related to lagged achievement of student Y. Of course this approach requires observations on current and past performance, data that are available in some but not all relevant education data sets (as, for example, in the well-known data set of Texas schools [Hanushek et al. (2003)]), and a more recent data set of North Carolina schools [Vigdor and Nechyba (2006)].[37] Hanushek et al. (2003) provide a thorough discussion of how this does and does not fully address the reflection problem, arguing that this strategy would likely lead to lower bound estimates of peer effects.

4.2.2. Endogenous selection into peer groups

The second challenge – the selection of peers into peer groups, has also been tackled through several different avenues. Some have exploited situations or policy experiments where individuals are randomly assigned to peer groups [Sacerdote (2001)] or neighborhoods [Hanratty, McLanahan and Pettit (1998), Katz, Kling and Liebman

---

[37] Similar data are also available in other more regional data sets such as one explored by Betts and Zau (2002) in San Diego.

(2001), Ludwig, Duncan and Hirschfield (2001), Ludwig, Duncan and Pinkston (2000), Ludwig, Ladd and Duncan (2001), Leventhal and Brooks-Gunn (2001), Rosenbaum (1991)].[38] A variation of this strategy is to use idiosyncratic variation in the composition of peer groups from "natural" experiments. Different cohorts within a school or across classrooms in an elementary school, for instance, might arise from random differences in cohort compositions [Hoxby (2000), Hanushek et al. (2003)]. Or, changes in school attendance zone boundaries caused by the opening of new schools or broader changes in school integration strategies may result in different peer group formations. Such policy "experiments" offer potentially fruitful avenues for partially addressing the selection problem when such changes provide sufficient variation in a district's boundaries to identify quasi-random variation in peer group composition and when family responses to such changes can be adequately controlled for.

Finally, the recent literature [Hanushek et al. (2003), Vigdor and Nechyba (2006)] has made increasing use of fixed effects techniques to control for unobserved characteristics, with student-level fixed effects aimed at controlling for unobserved student characteristics in data sets with multiple observations per student and school or grade fixed effects similarly controlling for other unobserved school and grade characteristics.

4.2.3. Defining peer groups and quality

The last challenge identified in the previous section relates most directly to data limitations – limitations that constrain the researcher's definition of peer groups as well as the measure of peer quality. The explosion of empirical investigations of issues in the general area of economics of education during the past decade has led to considerable efforts by researchers to construct better data sets, with statewide data sets such as those for Texas and North Carolina representing some of the most ambitious attempts to construct better data in part to address the impact of sorting. Other data sources are also emerging or being used more productively. This increasing availability of more detailed student-level data not only allows for the use of econometric techniques to address the simultaneity and selection problems raised above but also is beginning to permit a more flexible approach to specifying different peer groups that might have causal effects on achievement. As a result, it is conceivable that more clarity with regard to the appropriate definition of peer groups will emerge from research that is currently in progress. A nice overview of the impact of different data sets, combined with new approaches to educational data, is given by Loeb and Strunk (2003).

4.3. Empirical findings

As suggested above, the empirical literature investigating the impact of peer sorting on student achievement is still in its early stages and only now coming to terms with

---

[38] Note that random assignment does not resolve the reflection problem.

the challenges outlined above. As a result, there is little definitive that can be stated at this time.[39] Within this literature, there exists great variation in terms of the outcomes considered,[40] the definition of an individual's peer group[41] and the degree to which data sets and methodologies combine to truly identify causation rather than mere correlation. One common theme in studies that find ways of addressing the econometric challenges discussed above is that estimates of peer effects tend to decline in magnitude, particularly as endogeneity issues are addressed.

Hanushek et al. (2003) and Hoxby (2000) confront the selection issue by identifying peer effects from small differences in peer groups for successive *cohorts* within schools – both using data from Texas. Betts and Zau (2002) and Vigdor and Nechyba (2006) focus on *classroom* level variations. The latter approach has the clear disadvantage that certain endogenous aspects of within school sorting could drive the results, although attempts are made to at least partially control for this.[42] Even in these most recent papers, all of which aim to address the selection and simultaneity issues discussed above, results do not yet provide a coherent picture of how peer effects operate. Hoxby, for instance, identifies relatively large peer effects while Hanushek et al. finds smaller but still quite significant effects. Betts and Zau suggest that cohort level fixed effects dissipate as the analysis aims to identify the same effects at the classroom level, while Vigdor and Nechyba suggest they increase. At the same time, preliminary work toward a more causal interpretation of results in Vigdor and Nechyba (to control for sorting in schools) suggests that initial estimates of peer effects are once again biased upward. Variance in achievement is found to have an impact in some papers but not in others.

A different strand of the literature has considered the implications of neighborhood rather than school characteristics for individual outcomes, particularly the developmen-

---

[39] A common view is that low-ability students are helped by high-ability students but high-ability students are not hurt significantly by the presence of low-ability students. Implications for optimal sorting would then be clear, but the empirical literature that has given rise to this view is deeply flawed in that it has not typically come to terms with the inherent econometric difficulties of estimating peer effects. The most often cited early attempts to uncover peer group effects are those of Summers and Wolfe (1977) and Henderson, Mieszkowski and Sauvagean (1978) which provided strong suggestive evidence for the existence of such effects. For more complete reviews of some of the intervening literature, see Slavin (1987, 1990) and Nechyba, McEwan and Older-Aguilar (1999).

[40] Recent examples of non-education related outcomes considered in the literature include teenage pregnancy [Evans, Oates and Schwab (1992)] and welfare participation [Bertrand, Luttmer and Mullainathan (2000)].

[41] Peer groups are most commonly defined at the school level in primary and secondary school investigations as well as higher education studies [Arcidiacono and Nicholson (2005), Caldas and Bankston (1997), Gaviria and Raphael (2001), Jencks and Mayer (1990), Link and Mulligan (1991), Mayer (1991), Robertson and Symons (1996), Zimmer and Toma (1999)], although other investigations [summarized in Slavin (1987, 1990) and Nechyba, McEwan and Older-Aguilar (1999)] have focused on within school and within classroom groupings – often, however, without paying sufficient attention to simultaneity and endogeneity issues.

[42] Clotfelter, Ladd and Vigdor (2004) suggest that, at least for North Carolina public schools, across school sorting is significantly more important than within school sorting. They use the same data set as Vigdor and Nechyba.

tal consequences of growing up in a poor neighborhood.[43] A few of these studies have considered the impact of neighborhood characteristics on educational outcomes, but none have had access to the type of comprehensive panel data on individual's residential locations and academic achievement that is ultimately necessary for a definitive empirical investigation of the causal link between neighborhood peers and educational outcomes. Several recent attempts to analyze random assignments to neighborhoods through "Moving to Opportunity" experiments have suggested the presence of at least some impact of neighborhood characteristic on outcomes.

Overall, it is clear that the empirical literature on peer and neighborhood effects is very much in its early stages, with much future research in this area likely in the coming years. This process should be aided by the increasing availability of better data sets and a more thorough understanding of the underlying econometric challenges.

5. Future research and conclusion

This chapter has reviewed an increasingly extensive literature on income and ability sorting as it relates to schools. Such sorting arises through a variety of channels – through residential sorting linked to public school access; through sorting out of traditional public schools and into private, charter or magnet schools; and through deliberate tracking policies within schools. Much of this sorting arises from decentralized choices by individual households who operate within an economic environment defined by past evolutions of housing stocks and school district boundaries and shaped by current public policies and market forces.

The theoretical and simulation literature on sorting has explicitly recognized the general equilibrium nature of sorting and its dependence on institutions that help shape the economic environment in which decentralized choices are made. Much progress has been made in this literature, and much fertile ground for future research remains. In particular, the theoretical general equilibrium analysis has not yet reached full maturity in that it is only now beginning to move from calibration to estimation. Given the inherent general equilibrium nature of peer group formation and sorting, a particularly strong argument for structural estimation and analysis exists in this area. As a result, it is likely that much research energy should be and will be devoted to advancing well-grounded theoretical model toward a full empirical treatment.

Well before the theoretical and simulation models on sorting gained attention over the last decade, a separate reduced form empirical literature has aimed to identify peer

---

[43] Brooks-Gunn et al. (1993), Case and Katz (1991), Chase-Lansdale et al. (1997), Duncan (1994), Duncan, Connell and Klebanov (1997), Ensminger, Lamkin and Jacobson (1996), Halpern-Felsher et al. (1997), Hanushek et al. (2001), Katz, Kling and Liebman (2001), Leventhal and Brooks-Gunn (2001), Ludwig, Duncan and Hirschfield (2001), Ludwig, Duncan and Pinkston (2000), Ludwig, Ladd and Duncan (2001), Rosenbaum (1991), Rosenbaum and Harris (2000), Solon, Page and Duncan (2000); see Jencks and Mayer (1990), Ellen and Turner (1997) and Gephardt (1997) for literature reviews.

effects without the direct use of theoretical general equilibrium models. Over the past decade, it has become increasingly clear that this literature had glanced over a number of econometric difficulties, and these difficulties in turn have become thoroughly explored from a theoretical (econometric) perspective. The increased understanding of the difficult identification problem has now given rise to new and significantly more sophisticated reduced form approaches to estimating peer effects. While these approaches continue to be largely disconnected from the theory literature on sorting, they are increasingly informed by progress made on the theoretical econometric issues involved in estimating peer effects.

Within the field of the economics of education, sorting thus remains an area of need for much additional research. Theoretical and simulation approaches can use refinement, but, even more importantly, such approaches still have some way to go before representing the kind of empirically rooted structural analysis that can truly inform public policy. At the same time, reduced form estimates of peer effects – to the extent that consensus may at some point emerge – can directly inform simulation approaches as to the appropriate calibration of key parameters. Thus, a better link between theoretically rooted simulation models and reduced form peer effect estimates can emerge as the reduced form empirical literature generates more reliable estimates of the true nature of peer effects in today's schools.

References

Altonji, J., Elder, T., Taber, C. (2002). "Selection on observed and unobserved variables: Assessing the effectiveness of Catholic schools". Working paper. Northwestern University.

Angrist, J., Bettinger, E., Bloom, E., King, E., Kremer, M. (2001). "Vouchers for private schooling in Columbia: Evidence from a randomized natural experiment". Working Paper 8343. NBER.

Arcidiacono, P., Nicholson, S. (2005). "Peer effects in medical school". Journal of Public Economics 89 (2/3), 327–350.

Arnott, R., Rowse, J. (1987). "Peer group effects and educational attainment". Journal of Public Economics 32, 287–306.

Ballou, D. (1996). "Do public schools hire the best applicants?". Quarterly Journal of Economics 111 (1), 97–133.

Ballou, D., Podgursky, M. (1998). "Teacher recruitment and retention in public and private schools". Journal of Public Policy and Management 17 (3), 393–417.

Bayer, P., Ferreira, F., McMillan, R. (2003). "A unified framework for measuring preferences for schools and neighborhoods". Working Paper 872. Yale Economic Growth Center.

Bayer, P., Ferreira, F., McMillan, R. (2005). "Tiebout sorting, social multipliers and the demand for school quality". Working Paper 10871. NBER.

Bayer, P., McMillan, R. (2005a). "Choice and competition in local education markets". Working Paper 11802. NBER.

Bayer, P., McMillan, R. (2005b). "Racial sorting and neighborhood quality". Working Paper 11813. NBER.

Bayer, P., McMillan, R., Reuben, K. (2005). "An equilibrium model of sorting in an urban housing market". Working Paper 10865. NBER.

Bayer, P., Timmins, C. (2003). "Estimating equilibrium models of sorting across locations". Working paper. Department of Economics, Yale University.

Benabou, R. (1993). "Workings of a city: Location, education and production". Quarterly Journal of Economics 108 (3), 619–652.

Benabou, R. (1996). "Equity and efficiency in human capital investment: The local connection". Review of Economic Studies 63 (2), 237–264.

Benson, P., McMillan, M.M. (1991). Private Schools in the United States: A Statistical Profile, with Comparisons to Public Schools. NCES 91-054. U.S. Department of Education, Washington, DC.

Bertrand, M., Luttmer, E., Mullainathan, S. (2000). "Network effects and welfare cultures". Quarterly Journal of Economics 115 (3), 1019–1055.

Betts, J., Zau, A. (2002). "Peer groups and academic achievement: Panel evidence from administrative data". Working paper. University of San Diego.

Black, S. (1999). "Do better schools matter? Parental valuation of elementary education". Quarterly Journal of Economics 114 (2), 577–599.

Brock, W., Durlauf, S. (2001). "Interactions-based models". In: Heckman, J., Leamer, E. (Eds.), Handbook of Econometrics, vol. 5. North-Holland, Amsterdam, pp. 3299–3381.

Brooks-Gunn, J., Duncan, G., Klebanov, P., Sealand, N. (1993). "Do neighborhoods influence child and adolescent development?". American Journal of Sociology 99 (2), 353–395.

Brunner, E., Sonstelie, J. (2003). "School finance reform and voluntary fiscal federalism". Journal of Public Economics 87 (9/10), 2157–2185.

Caldas, S., Bankston, C. (1997). "The effect of school population socioeconomic status on individual student academic achievement". Journal of Educational Research 90, 269–277.

Case, A., Katz, L. (1991). "The company you keep: The effects of family and neighborhood on disadvantaged youth". Working Paper 3705. NBER.

Caucutt, E. (2001). "Peer group effects in applied general equilibrium". Economic Theory 17, 25–51.

Caucutt, E. (2002). "Educational vouchers when there are peer group effects – size matters". International Economic Review 43 (1), 195–222.

Chase-Lansdale, L., Gordon, R., Brooks-Gunn, J., Klebanov, P. (1997). "Neighborhood and family influences on the intellectual and behavioral competence of preschool and early school-age children". In: Brooks-Gunn, J., Duncan, G., Aber, L. (Eds.), Neighborhood Poverty: Context and Consequences for Children. Russel Sage Foundation, New York, pp. 79–118.

Clotfelter, C., Ladd, H., Vigdor, J. (2004). "Teacher sorting, teacher shopping and the assessment of teacher effectiveness". Working paper. Duke University.

Cohen-Zada, D., Justman, M. (2002). "The religious factor in private education". Occasional Working Paper 53. National Center for the Study of Privatization in Education, Teacher's College, Columbia University.

Cooley, J. (2005). "Desegregation and the achievement gap: Do diverse peers help?". Working paper. Department of Economics, Duke University.

Cullen, J. (1999). "The impact of fiscal incentives on student disability rates". Working Paper 7173. NBER.

Cullen, J., Reback, R. (2003). "Tinkering toward accolades: School gaming under a performance accountability system". Working paper. University of Michigan.

DeBartolome, C. (1990). "Equilibrium and inefficiency in a community model with peer group effects". Journal of Political Economy 98 (1), 110–133.

Dee, T. (1998). "Competition and the quality of public schools". Economics of Education Review 17 (4), 419–427.

Downes, T., Greenstein, S. (1996). "Understanding the supply decisions of nonprofits: Modeling the location of private schools". RAND Journal of Economics 27 (2), 365–390.

Downes, T., Schoeman, D. (1998). "School finance reform and private school enrollment: Evidence from California". Journal of Urban Economics 43 (3), 418–443.

Duncan, G. (1994). "Families and neighbors as sources of disadvantage in the schooling decisions of white and black adolescents". American Journal of Education 103, 20–53.

Duncan, G., Connell, J., Klebanov, P. (1997). "Conceptual and methodological issues in estimating causal effects of neighborhoods and family conditions on individual development". In: Brooks-Gunn, J., Duncan, G., Aber, J. (Eds.), Neighborhood Poverty, vol. 2. Russell Sage Foundation, New York, pp. 219–250.

Dunz, K. (1985). "Existence of equilibrium with local public goods and houses". Discussion Paper 201. SUNY, Albany Department of Economics.

Durlauf, S. (1996). "A theory of persistent income inequality". Journal of Economic Growth 1, 75–93.

Ellen, I., Turner, M. (1997). "Does neighborhood matter? Assessing recent evidence". Housing Policy Debate 8, 833–866.

Ensminger, M.E., Lamkin, R.P., Jacobson, N. (1996). "School leaving: A longitudinal perspective including neighborhood effects". Child Development 67, 2400–2416.

Epple, D., Figlio, D., Romano, R. (2004). "Competition between private and public schools: Testing stratification and pricing predictions". Journal of Public Economics 88 (7/8), 1215–1245.

Epple, D., Filimon, R., Romer, T. (1993). "Existence of voting and housing equilibrium in a system of communities with property taxation". Regional Science and Urban Economics 23, 585–610.

Epple, D., Nechyba, T. (2004). "Fiscal decentralization". In: Thisse, J., Henderson, V. (Eds.), Handbook of Regional and Urban Economics, vol. 4: Cities and Geography. North-Holland, Amsterdam, pp. 2424–2480.

Epple, D., Newlon, E., Romano, R. (2002). "Ability tracking, school competition, and the distribution of educational benefits". Journal of Public Economics 83, 1–48.

Epple, D., Platt, G. (1998). "Equilibrium and local redistribution in an urban economy when households differ in both preferences and income". Journal of Urban Economics 43 (1), 23–51.

Epple, D., Romano, R. (1998). "Competition between public and private schools, vouchers and peer group effects". American Economic Review 88 (1), 33–62.

Epple, D., Romano, R. (2002). "Educational vouchers and cream skimming". Working paper. Carnegie Mellon University.

Epple, D., Romano, R. (2003). "Neighborhood schools, choice, and the distribution of educational benefits". In: Hoxby, C. (Ed.), The Economics of School Choice. Chicago University Press, Chicago, pp. 227–286.

Epple, D., Romano, R., Sieg, H. (2003). "Peer effects, financial aid and selection of students into colleges and universities: An empirical analysis". Journal of Applied Econometrics 18 (5), 501–525.

Epple, D., Romer, T., Sieg, H. (2001). "Interjurisdictional sorting and majority rule: An empirical analysis". Econometrica 69 (6), 1437–1466.

Epple, D., Sieg, H. (1999). "Estimating equilibrium models of local jurisdictions". Journal of Political Economy 107 (4), 645–681.

Evans, W., Oates, W., Schwab, R. (1992). "Measuring peer group effects: A study of teenage behavior". Journal of Political Economy 100, 966–991.

Evans, W., Schwab, R. (1995). "Finishing high school and starting college: Do Catholic schools make a difference?". Quarterly Journal of Economics 110, 941–974.

Fernandez, R. (2001). "Education, segregation and marital sorting: Theory and an application to UK data". Working Paper 8377. NBER.

Fernandez, R., Fogli, A., Olivetti, C. (2002). "Marrying your mom: Preference transmission and women's labor and education choices". Working Paper 9234. NBER.

Fernandez, R., Rogerson, R. (1996). "Income distribution, communities, and the quality of public education". Quarterly Journal of Economics CXI, 135–164.

Fernandez, R., Rogerson, R. (1999). "Education finance reform and investment in human capital: Lessons from California". Journal of Public Economics 74 (3), 327–350.

Fernandez, R., Rogerson, R. (2003). "Equity and resources: An analysis of education finance systems". Journal of Political Economy 111 (4), 858–897.

Ferrayra, M. (2002). "Estimating the effects of private school vouchers in multi-district economies". Working paper. Carnegie Mellon University.

Ferris, J.S., West, E. (2002). "Education vouchers, the peer group problem and the question of dropouts". Southern Economic Journal 68 (4), 774–793.

Figlio, D., Getzler, L. (2002). "Accountability, ability and disability: Gaming the system". Working Paper 9307. NBER.

Figlio, D., Lucas, M. (2000). "What's in a grade? School report cards and house prices". Working Paper 8019. NBER.

Figlio, D., Ludwig, J. (2000). "Sex, drugs and Catholic schools: Private schooling and non-market adolescent behaviors". Working Paper 7990. NBER.

Figlio, D., Winicki, J. (2002). "Food for thought: The effects of school accountability plans on school nutrition". Working Paper 9319. NBER.

Gaviria, A., Raphael, S. (2001). "School-based peer effects and juvenile behavior". Review of Economics and Statistics 83, 257–268.

Gephardt, M. (1997). "Neighborhoods and communities as contexts for development". In: Brooks-Gunn, J., Duncan, G.J., Aber, J.L. (Eds.), Neighborhood Poverty, vol. 1. Russell Sage Foundation, New York, pp. 1–43.

Goldstein, G., Gronberg, T. (1986). "Local public goods and private suppliers: Musical suburbs replayed". Journal of Urban Economics 19 (3), 338–355.

Grogger, J., Neal, D. (2000). "Further evidence on the effect of Catholic secondary schooling". In: Gale, W.G., Pack, J.R. (Eds.), Brookings–Wharton Papers on Urban Affairs. Brookings Institution Press, Washington, DC, pp. 151–201.

Halpern-Felsher, B., Connell, J., Spencer, M., Aber, J., Duncan, G., Clifford, E., Crichlow, W., Usinger, P., Cole, S., Allen, L., Seidman, E. (1997). "Neighborhood and family factors predicting educational risk and attainment in African American and white children and adolescents". In: Brooks-Gunn, J., Duncan, G.J., Aber, J.L. (Eds.), Neighborhood Poverty, vol. 1. Russell Sage Foundation, New York, pp. 146–173.

Hanratty, M., McLanahan, S., Pettit, B. (1998). "The impact of the Los Angeles moving to opportunity program on residential mobility, neighborhood characteristics, and early child and parent outcomes". Working Paper 98-18. Bendheim–Thoman Center for Research on Child Wellbeing.

Hanushek, E. (2001). "Why public schools lose teachers". Working Paper 8599. NBER.

Hanushek, E. (2002). "Publicly provided education". In: Auerbach, A., Feldstein, M. (Eds.), Handbook of Public Economics, vol. 4. North-Holland, Amsterdam, pp. 2046–2141.

Hanushek, E., Kain, J., Markman, J., Rivkin, S. (2001). "Does peer ability affect student achievement?". Working Paper 8502. NBER.

Hanushek, E., Kain, J., Markman, J., Rivkin, S. (2003). "Does peer ability affect student achievment?". Journal of Applied Econometrics 18 (5), 527–544.

Hanushek, E., Rivkin, S. (2003). "Does public school competition affect teacher quality?". In: Hoxby, C. (Ed.), The Economics of School Choice. University of Chicago Press, Chicago, pp. 23–48.

Harris, J. (1998). The Nurture Assumption. The Free Press, New York.

Henderson, V., Mieszkowski, P., Sauvagean, Y. (1978). "Peer group effects and educational production functions". Journal of Public Economics 10, 97–106.

Hoxby, C. (1994). "Do private schools provide competition for public schools". Working Paper 4978. NBER.

Hoxby, C. (1996). "How teachers' unions affect education production". Quarterly Journal of Economics 111 (3), 671–718.

Hoxby, C. (1999). "The productivity of schools and other local public goods producers". Journal of Public Economics 74 (1), 1–30.

Hoxby, C. (2000). "Does competition among public schools benefit students and taxpayers?". American Economic Review 90 (5), 1209–1238.

Hoxby, C. (2001). "All school finance equalizations are not created equal". Quarterly Journal of Economics 116 (4), 1189–1231.

Hoxby, C. (2002). "Would school choice change the teaching profession?". Journal of Human Resources 37 (4), 846–891.

Hoyt, W., Lee, K. (2003). "Subsidies as sorting devices". Journal of Urban Economics 53 (3), 436–457.

Husted, T., Kenny, L. (2002). "The legacy of Serrano: The impact of mandated equal spending on private school enrollment". Southern Economic Journal 68 (3), 566–583.

Jacob, B., Levitt, S. (2003). "Rotten apples: An investigation of the prevalence and predictors of teacher cheating". Working Paper 9413. NBER.

Jencks, C., Mayer, S. (1990). "The social consequences of growing up in a poor neighborhood". In: Lynn, L., McGreary, M. (Eds.), Inner-City Poverty in the United States. National Academy Press, Washington, DC, pp. 111–186.

Katz, L., Kling, J., Liebman, J. (2001). "Moving to opportunity in Boston: Early results of a randomized mobility experiment". Quarterly Journal of Economics 116, 607–654.

Konishi, H. (1996). "Voting with ballots and feet: Existence of equilibrium in a local public goods economy". Journal of Economic Theory 68, 480–509.

Kremer, M. (1997). "How much does sorting increase inequality?". Quarterly Journal of Economics 112 (1), 115–139.

Ladd, H.F., Fiske, E.B. (2001). When Schools Compete. Brookings Institution Press, Washington, DC.

Lankford, H., Wyckoff, J. (1992). "Primary and secondary school choice among public and religious alternatives". Economics of Education Review 11 (4), 317–337.

Lazear, E. (2001). "Education production". Quarterly Journal of Economics 116 (3), 777–803.

Leventhal, T., Brooks-Gunn, J. (2001). "Moving to opportunity: What about the kids?". Working paper. Center for Children and Families, Teacher's College, Columbia University.

Link, C., Mulligan, J. (1991). "Classmates' effects on black student achievement in public school classrooms". Economics of Education Review 10, 297–310.

Loeb, S., Page, M. (2001). "Examining the link between teacher wages and student outcomes: The importance of alternative labor market opportunities and non-pecuniary variation". Review of Economics and Statistics 82 (3), 393–408.

Loeb, S., Strunk, K. (2003). "The contribution of administrative and experimental data to education policy research". National Tax Journal LVI (2), 415–438.

Ludwig, J., Duncan, G., Hirschfield, P. (2001). "Urban poverty and juvenile crime: Evidence from a randomized housing-mobility experiment". Quarterly Journal of Economics 116, 655–680.

Ludwig, J., Duncan, G., Pinkston, J.C. (2000). "Neighborhood effects on economic self-sufficiency: Evidence from a randomized housing-mobility experiment". Working Paper 159. Joint Center for Poverty Research, Northwestern University/University of Chicago.

Ludwig, J., Ladd, H., Duncan, G. (2001). "The effects of urban poverty on educational outcomes". In: Brookings–Wharton Papers on Urban Affairs. Brookings Institution Press, Washington, DC, pp. 147–201.

Manski, C.F. (1993). "Identification of endogenous social effects: The reflection problem". Review of Economic Studies 60, 531–542.

Mayer, S.E. (1991). "How much does a high school's racial and socioeconomic mix affect graduation and teenage fertility rates?". In: Jencks, C., Peterson, P.E. (Eds.), The Urban Underclass. Brookings Institution Press, Washington, DC.

McEwan, P. (2001). "The effectiveness of public, Catholic and non-religious private schools in Chile's voucher system". Education Economics 9 (2), 103–128.

McHugh, C. (2003). "Does competition among public schools benefit students and taxpayers: Comment". Mimeo. Duke University.

McMillan, R. (2000). "Competition, parental involvement, and public school performance". National Tax Association Proceedings 2000, 150–155.

McMillan, R. (2004). "Competition, incentives and public school productivity". Journal of Public Economics 88, 1871–1892.

Moffitt, R. (1998). "Policy interventions, low-level equilibria and social interactions". In: Durlauf, S., Young, H.P. (Eds.), Social Dynamics. MIT Press, Cambridge, pp. 45–82.

Mora, F. (2003). "Income stratification across public and private education: The multi-community case". Discussion paper in economics. University of York.

Murray, S., Evans, W., Schwab, R. (1998). "Education finance reform and the distribution of education resources". American Economic Review 88, 782–812.

Neal, D. (1997). "The effect of Catholic secondary schooling on education achievement". Journal of Labor Economics 15, 98–123.

Nechyba, T. (1997). "Existence of equilibrium and stratification in local and hierarchical public good economies with property taxes and voting". Economic Theory 10, 277–304.

Nechyba, T. (1999). "School finance induced migration patters: The impact of private school vouchers". Journal of Public Economic Theory 1 (1), 5–50.

Nechyba, T. (2000). "Mobility, targeting and private school vouchers". American Economic Review 90 (1), 130–146.

Nechyba, T. (2002). "Prospects for achieving equity or adequacy in education: The limits of state aid in general equilibrium". Working paper. Duke University.

Nechyba, T. (2003a). "Public school finance and urban school policy: General vs. partial equilibrium results". In: Gale, W.G., Pack, J.R. (Eds.), Brookings–Wharton Papers on Urban Affairs. Brookings Institution Press, Washington, DC, pp. 139–170.

Nechyba, T. (2003b). "Centralization, fiscal federalism and private school attendance". International Economic Review 44 (1), 179–204.

Nechyba, T. (2003c). "Introducing school choice into multi-district public school systems". In: Hoxby, C. (Ed.), The Economics of School Choice. University of Chicago Press, Chicago, pp. 195–226.

Nechyba, T. (2003d). "What can be (and what has been) learned from general equilibrium simulation models of school finance?". National Tax Journal LVI (2), 387–414.

Nechyba, T. (2003e). "School finance, spatial income segregation and the nature of communities". Journal of Urban Economics 54 (1), 61–88.

Nechyba, T., McEwan, P., Older-Aguilar, D. (1999). The Effects of Family and Community Resources on Education Outcomes. Ministry of Education, Wellington, NZ.

Nechyba, T., Strauss, R. (1998). "Community choice and local public services: A discrete choice approach". Regional Science and Urban Economics 28 (1), 51–74.

Oates, W. (1969). "The effects of property taxes and local public spending on property values: An empirical study of tax capitalization and the Tiebout hypothesis". Journal of Political Economy 77 (6), 957–971.

Rangazas, P. (1995). "Vouchers in a community choice model with zoning". Quarterly Review of Economics and Finance 35 (1), 15–39.

Reback, R. (2002). "Capitalization under school choice programs: Are the winners really the losers?". Working paper. University of Michigan.

Rees, D., Argys, L., Brewer, D. (1996). "Tracking in the United States: Descriptive statistics from NELS". Economics of Education Review 15 (1), 83–89.

Robertson, D., Symons, J. (1996). "Do peer groups matter? Peer group versus schooling effects on academic attainment". Unpublished manuscript. London School of Economics Centre for Economic Performance.

Rose-Ackerman, S. (1979). "Market models of local government: Exit, voting and the land market". Journal of Urban Economics 6, 319–337.

Rosenbaum, E., Harris, L. (2000). "Short-term impacts of moving for children: Evidence from the Chicago MTO program". Working paper. Department of Sociology and Anthropology, Fordham University.

Rosenbaum, J. (1991). "Black pioneers – do their moves to the suburbs increase economic opportunity for mothers and children?". Housing Policy Debate 2, 1179–1213.

Rouse, C. (1998). "Private school vouchers and student achievement: An evaluation of the Milwaukee parental choice program". Quarterly Journal of Economics 113 (2), 553–602.

Sacerdote, B. (2001). "Peer effects with random assignment: Results for Dartmouth roommates". Quarterly Journal of Economics 116, 681–704.

Sander, W. (1999). "Private schools and public school achievement". Journal of Human Resources 34 (4), 697–709.

Slavin, R. (1987). "Ability grouping and student achievement in elementary schools: A best-evidence synthesis". Review of Educational Research 57, 293–336.

Slavin, R. (1990). "Achievement effects of ability grouping in secondary schools: A best-evidence synthesis". Review of Educational Research 60, 471–499.

Solon, G., Page, M., Duncan, G. (2000). "Correlations between neighboring children in their subsequent educational attainment". Review of Economics and Statistics 82, 383–392.

Summers, A., Wolfe, B. (1977). "Do schools make a difference?". American Economic Review 67, 639–652.

Toma, E. (1996). "Public funding and private schooling across countries". Journal of Law and Economics 39 (1), 121–148.

Vigdor, J., Nechyba, T. (2006). "Peer effects in North Carolina public schools". In: Peterson, P., Wössmann, L. (Eds.), Schools and the Equal Opportunity Problem. MIT Press, Cambridge.

Weimer, D., Wolkoff, M. (2001). "School performance and housing values: Using non-contiguous district and incorporation boundaries to identify school effects". National Tax Journal 54 (2), 231–253.

Westhoff, F. (1977). "Existence of equilibria in economies with a local public good". Journal of Economic Theory 14 (1), 84–112.

Zimmer, R.W., Toma, E.F. (1999). "Peer effects in public schools across countries". Journal of Policy Analysis and Management 19, 75–92.

Chapter 23

PUBLIC INTERVENTION IN POST-SECONDARY EDUCATION

THOMAS J. KANE

Harvard University

Contents

Handbook of the Economics of Education, Volume 2
Edited by Eric A. Hanushek and Finis Welch
© 2006 Elsevier B.V.   All rights reserved
DOI: 10.1016/S1574-0692(06)02023-X

Abstract

This chapter provides an overview of the nature of state and federal subsidies to higher education and the empirical evidence on the impacts on students' college enrollment decisions. The discussion includes a brief discussion of the incentives created by federal and state subsidies for institutions and for students, a summary of trends in enrollment rates by race and income, a survey of the empirical evidence on the impacts of financial aid policies, and a discussion of the possible role supply constraints may have played on the rise in the payoff to schooling over the last two decades.

Keywords

tuition, financial aid, capacity constraints, borrowing constraints, higher education, means-tested grant aid, subsidies-in-kind, faculty salaries, SAT scores, Pell Grant, Stafford Loan, Hope Tax Credit, Lifetime Learning Tax Credit, Expected Family Contribution, implicit tax, enrollment rate, education wage differential, racial gap, National Assessment of Educational Progress, educational attainment, D.C. Tuition Assistance Grant, perfect capital market, Vietnam War, tax credit

JEL classification: I21, I23, J15, J24

1. Introduction

The resurgence of interest in the economics of education is not due to any remarkable technological change or sharp increase in the share of the economy's resources devoted to education – as was the case for the economics of health care a decade ago. Indeed, the technology of education has been remarkably stable and, in higher education, the structure of finance has been largely unchanged for three decades. Rather, the primary reason for the renewed interest in the economics of higher education has been the labor market and the sharp rise in the education wage differential beginning around 1980 [Murphy and Welch (1992) and Levy and Murnane (1992)].

In education policy, there are usually at least two relevant margins, involving both the *quality* and *quantity* of time spent in educational pursuits. The preceding chapters focused on the quality of elementary and secondary education, where economists have traditionally been concerned about the efficiency of public production. Until recently, the quantity margin of most interest to policymakers was high school graduation, and policymakers focused on compulsory schooling laws and programs designed to prevent youth from dropping out of high school. However, given the declines in high school drop-out rates and rise in college entry rates since the mid-Seventies, the quantity margin most relevant to policymakers has shifted to the early childhood and post-secondary years. The proportion of 18–24-year-old adults enrolled in college has increased by more than a third since 1980. This chapter will focus on post-secondary schooling and the state and federal policies intended to influence students' and parents' schooling investments.

In the second section, I discuss the incentive implications of state and federal subsidies to higher education. The structure of higher education finance, and the incentives provided to students and to providers, is at least as misunderstood today as the health care financing system was a decade ago. Yet it is this structure which determines institutions' incentives to keep costs in check and for students to invest optimally.

In the third section, I discuss the evidence on the widening gaps in college enrollment by family income and by race. Although the quality of the data in the federal statistical analysis system is surprisingly weak (at least with regard to differences by family income), the gaps in enrollment seem to have widened as the payoff to college has increased since 1980. Although bachelor's degree completion rates seem to have remained stable despite increases in the proportion of youth entering college, more youth are attending college part time and with periods of leave, leading to an increase in the time required to complete a degree.

In the fourth section, I discuss the literature on the effects of tuition and financial policies on college entry rates. One of the key questions in that literature is whether the state and federal financial aid system has left some families constrained in their borrowing and unable to invest optimally in their education. The empirical evidence thus far, while suggesting that students and families are often quite sensitive to the direct costs of education (at least relative to the magnitude of the enrollment response to rising payoffs to schooling), has not yet resolved the bigger question of the existence of borrowing constraints. This is a large gap in the literature, given that imperfect capital markets are the primary rationale for much state and federal intervention in higher education.

In the fifth and final sections, I discuss the evidence on whether capacity constraints in higher education in the early Seventies may have slowed the growth of educational attainment and contributed to the sharp rise in the payoff to schooling in the early Eighties. In the past decade, the search for explanations of the rising returns to schooling has focused on factors affecting the demand for educated labor – technological change, international trade – rather than the supply of educated labor. However, as argued in Katz and Murphy (1992), the market return reflects both supply and demand. I discuss some provocative evidence suggesting that the capacity constraints in the higher education sector may have played some role in that change.

Throughout the discussion, I endeavor to provide a summary of the empirical evidence currently available while pointing out unresolved issues deserving of future work.

2. The incentive implications of state and federal subsidies

States and the federal government invest large sums each year subsidizing students' college enrollment decisions. The lion's share of such aid comes in the form of direct state appropriations to public post-secondary institutions, which totaled $63 billion in fiscal year 2005 [Palmer (2005)]. In addition to the state commitments, the federal government provided nearly $12.7 billion in means-tested Pell Grants to undergraduates during the 2003–2004 school year and guaranteed $57 billion in student loans (paying the interest on roughly half of that loan volume while students are in school) [College Board (2004)]. In this section, I provide a brief overview of the nature of the incentives introduced by state and federal subsidies to higher education.

2.1. The nature of state subsidies to higher education

Although states do provide a modest amount of means-tested grant aid ($6 billion in 2003–2004), most state support to higher education is provided directly to public institutions. Such funding is used primarily to keep the sticker price of tuition far below the average expenditure per student. In 1996–1997 (the most recent year for which data are available), the average educational expenditure per student in public four-year institutions was $14,329 per full-time equivalent student (or $13,118 after subtracting scholarship and fellowship spending, a transfer from one group of students to another).[1] In contrast, the average tuition at a public four-year institution in that year was $2,975. Therefore, even the students paying full sticker price at these institutions are paying much less than the average cost per full-time equivalent student.

---

[1] This cost estimate excludes the expenditures of auxiliary operations such as hospitals, dormitories, and food service operations. U.S. Department of Education, NCES (2002). *Digest of Education Statistics 2001*, Table 350.

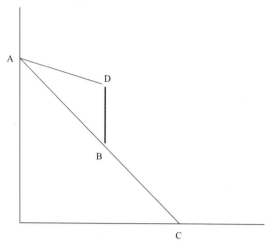

Figure 1. Budget constraint with subsidies in kind.

State legislatures explicitly set tuition at public institutions in only nine states.[2] In the remaining states, university regents or the state higher education coordinating board nominally set their own tuition. However, even in these states where some body other than the legislature has nominal control over tuition decisions, the legislatures' control of state appropriations gives them effective control of just what those prices will be. By determining the revenue that institutions can generate through tuition as well as the revenue they receive in the form of state appropriations, legislatures effectively control both the price and quality of the education provided by public higher education institutions. Therefore, state legislatures do not simply subsidize a family's higher education expenditures, they determine what that subsidized option will be.

Peltzman (1973) discussed the ways in which such "subsidies-in-kind" might differ from general price subsidies for higher education. Figure 1 portrays the budget constraint a typical consumer might face in choosing between spending on higher education and all other goods. (In the figure, the horizontal axis measures dollars' worth of higher education consumed and the vertical axis measures dollars' worth of consumption of all other goods.) In the absence of governmental intervention, a consumer might face a budget constraint represented by the line segment ABC, with a slope of negative one. Suppose that a state opened a public institution, offering a quantity of higher education, D, at that institution at a subsidized price. Because higher education choices are

---

[2] Based on a survey of state higher education executive officers reported in Christal (1997). The states were California, Colorado, Florida, Indiana, New York, North Carolina, Oklahoma, South Dakota, Texas and Washington. Texas subsequently changed its policy.

essentially discrete in nature, it is difficult for the consumer to supplement the public education option, D, with private expenditures. (Of course, this is not strictly true, since someone could purchase textbooks, tutors and a cutting-edge computer to supplement the education provided. The consumer could also presumably spend two years at a public university and then transfer to a private one. However, we are assuming that there are considerable additional costs involved in doing so.) Then, the consumer's budget constraint would become ADBC. If the consumer's tastes are such that a point along the line segment AD offers the best combination of higher education consumption and other consumption, the person will attend a public institution. If some point along the BC segment offers the best choice, the person will forego the subsidies offered at public institutions and attend a private college or university. Given that roughly 80% of higher education enrollment in the U.S. is at public institutions, it seems that the majority of consumers are in the former group.

As argued in Peltzman (1973), the existence of such subsidies in kind could actually lead to lower consumption of the subsidized good than might have happened in the absence of governmental intervention. This would be true if many of those who end up choosing an option along the AD segment and attend a public institution would have chosen an option somewhere along the BC segment in the absence of public involvement. Even if public institutions are operating efficiently, and offering the highest quality output their expenditures would allow, public intervention in this market could actually be reducing human capital investment and the growth that goes along with it.

The possibility of such an outcome is heightened when state governments find it politically painful to raise tuition and when the public has a difficult time evaluating the quality of education being provided at such institutions. Over the last 20 years, most state legislatures have chosen to keep tuition low and restrain expenditure increases, allowing expenditures per student at public institutions to lag behind those at private institutions. Between 1980–1981 and 1994–1995, educational expenditures per student grew less than half as fast at public four-year institutions (where real expenditures per student grew by 28%) as at private four-year institutions (where real expenditures per student grew by 73%) [Kane, Orszag and Apostolov (2005)]. The difference in the rate of growth in expenditures per student is reflected in the differential in faculty salaries at public and private institutions. For example, Zoghi (2003) finds that salaries were roughly two percent lower at public institutions than at private institutions in 1975, but more than 12% lower by 1997.[3] While private institutions have increased the number of faculty per student, public institutions have been moving in the opposite direction [Kane, Orszag and Apostolov (2005)].

---

[3] Hamermesh (2002) reports similar findings. Although the growth in private university salaries is unrelated to the business cycle, public institutions tend to lose ground during recessions and only keep pace with private institutions' salaries during recoveries. Ehrenberg (2003) notes that declining indirect cost recovery rates and rising endowment income at private institutions may also have contributed to the widening gaps in public and private salaries.

Such trends may be having an impact on the quality of education provided in public higher education institutions. Kane, Orszag and Gunter (2003) show that among institutions with similar students in 1986, the measurable quality of incoming students – as reflected in SAT scores and high school class rank – grew more rapidly at private institutions than at public institutions. Moreover, in surveys of faculty in 1993 and 1997, public sector faculty were more likely to lament the declining quality of undergraduate education at their institutions than were faculty at private institutions.

Rising college enrollments, increases in the size of the college-age cohorts (which began in the late Nineties after a decade and a half of decreases) and increases in other state obligations (primarily Medicaid) have all made the traditional state role of providing low-cost public institutions increasingly untenable. One option open to states is to keep a tight rein on both price and expenditures at public institutions and allow the gap in the nature of education provided at public and private institutions to continue to widen. However, a second option, currently being pursued in a few states, is to grant public institutions more control over price, to reduce the subsidies formerly used to operate such institutions, and to convert those subsidies into student financial aid (the so-called "high tuition–high aid" strategy). Two examples of states taking such an approach are Michigan and Virginia, where public subsidies represent a smaller share of the those states' public university budgets and where tuition at the flagship universities has been allowed to rise.

2.2. The nature of federal subsidies

While most of the *state* support is channeled through low-cost public institutions, most of the *federal* subsidies are provided to students rather than institutions, through means-tested grant, loan and work-study programs, as well as tax credits. To reduce their contribution to tuition inflation, all of these programs are subject to maxima that are well below the costs of attendance at the vast majority of institutions – public or private. For example, even after substantial increases in recent years, the maximum Pell Grant for the 2005–2006 academic year is $4,050. The maximum loan for dependent students under the federal Stafford loan program is $2,625 in the first year of college, $3,500 in the second year, and $5,500 in their third through fifth years as an undergraduate.[4] In other words, for the dependent student qualifying for the maximum Pell Grant (generally less than $25,000 in family income), dependent students are eligible for $6,675 in combined federal grant and loan aid in their first year, $7,550 in their second year, and $9,550 in their fourth and fifth years.

The grant and loan limits have become more binding over time as the limits have been eroded by inflation and the average tuition at public and private four-year institutions has increased. Figure 2 reports the trend in the real value of the maximum Pell

---

[4] Independent students – those who are married, have dependents, are veterans, or are over 24 years of age – can qualify to borrow more. Parents may also be eligible to borrow more. However, the largest source of the federal subsidy – the payment of interest while the student is enrolled in school – is not provided on these loans.

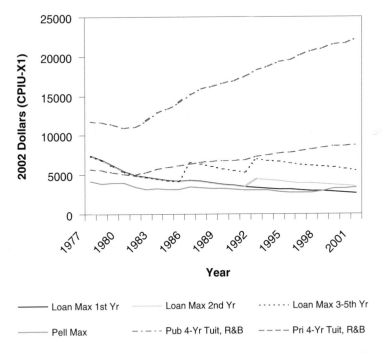

Figure 2. Federal financial aid maxima and four-year college tuition, room and board.

Grant as well as maximum loan amounts for dependent students in their first, second, and third through fifth years of college. There are several aspects of Figure 2 worth noting: First, the loan maxima have declined in real value since the mid Seventies. In 1977, the maximum one could borrow during the first year of college was equivalent to $7,422 in 2002 dollars ($2,500 in nominal dollars). By 2002, the most a dependent student could borrow for the first year of college was $2,625 – roughly one-third as much. The declines were less severe for those in their third through fifth years of undergraduate education – for whom the maximum declined from $7,422 to $5,500 between 1977 and 2002. Between 1977 and 1996, the real value of the maximum Pell Grant for low-income undergraduates had declined by nearly 40%, from $4,156 to $2,683. Since 1996, the real value of the Pell Grant has steadily risen, but the maximum is still below its 1977 value.

Second, while the maxima under the federal programs have declined, the mean tuition, room and board at public and private four-year institutions have been steadily increasing in real value (at least since 1981). For example, the mean tuition at public and private four-year institutions grew by 74% and 101%, respectively, in real value between 1981 and 2002. Part of the increase in sticker price at private institutions has been offset by increasing use of financial aid at these institutions. However, institutional financial aid remains a small share of expenditures at public institutions, where sticker price is a better indicator of actual price students are expected to pay.

Third, since the margins along which institutions and their students are bargaining are typically far above the limits of the federal aid programs, students are typically paying the full marginal cost of attending a more expensive institution. This was not always true. Between 1973 and 1985, a Pell Grant could not exceed 50% of a student's cost of attendance. Between 1986 and 1992, the cap was raised to 60% of the cost of attendance. Because the Pell Grant maxima were higher in real value and the cost of attendance was lower, a significant proportion of students were constrained by the percentage cap and would have been compensated 50% or 60% on the margin if they chose to attend a more expensive institution. Since 1992, the maximum Pell Grant has been 100% of the cost of attendance. But since the Pell Grant maximum has eroded and tuition has increased, very few institutions (public or private, two-year or four-year) have a cost of attendance less than the current maxima. As a result, for most students, the federal grant and loan subsidies are properly thought of as a lump-sum voucher which has the same value regardless of where the student chooses to attend. In so doing, the programs generally preserve students' incentive to shop for the best educational bargain.

In 1997, the federal government created two new tax credits for higher education – the Hope tax credit, which provides a one hundred percent credit on the first thousand dollars of tuition expenditure for a student in the first two years of college and a fifty percent credit on the second thousand dollars in expenditure, and Lifetime Learning Tax Credit, which provides a twenty percent credit on the first five thousand dollars in tuition expenses for those beyond their first two years in college. [For more on the economic impacts of these new tax credits, see Hoxby (1998), Kane (1997) and Long (2004).] Like the grant and loan programs, both tax credits are subject to limits. However, because the limits apply to tuition expenditures (and do not include other costs such as books, room and board) many more institutions in 1997 were posting tuition charges below those limits. As a result, between 20% and 100% of any increase in tuition at these institutions would have been covered by the federal government. Long (2004) reports that a number of institutions raised tuition in response to these new tax credits.

2.3. Implicit taxes in the institutional and federal need analysis[5]

Eligibility for federal grant and loan programs – and for much of the institutional grant aid awarded – depends upon the calculation of a family's "financial need", which is calculated by subtracting a family's "expected family contribution" (EFC) from tuition and other expenses. This calculation imposes an implicit tax on income and savings of students and parents.[6]

---

[5] Much of the discussion in this section is drawn from Kane (1999).

[6] See the discussion in Edlin (1993) and Feldstein (1995) for another description of the implicit taxes in financial aid formula.

In the calculation of parents' expected contribution, parents' "available" income is defined using parents' adjusted gross income from their federal tax form in the most recently completed calendar year. Untaxed income (such as Social Security income and IRA or 401(k) contributions) is added to adjusted gross income and certain allowable expenses (such as employee's social security tax payments, federal, state and local income tax, and an employment allowance of up to $2,800 for two-earner families and single parent families) are subtracted. Depending upon their family size and number of students in college, parents are allowed to protect a certain amount of income. For instance, for the 2005–2006 academic year, a family of four with one student in college was allowed $21,330 in income before being expected to contribute anything toward their children's education.

A portion of a family's assets are also considered available to the student for financing college.[7] However, due to recent changes in the formula, assets are increasingly irrelevant for federal financial aid programs. Future pension benefits, IRA and 401(k) account balances have always been excluded from consideration in the federal formula. Although many private colleges continue to use housing assets in distributing institutional financial aid awards, housing assets were excluded in calculating eligibility for all federal aid programs in 1993. For federal aid, relevant assets include only cash, any business assets, and investments that are not made through retirement accounts. In addition, families are allowed to "protect" any assets below certain limits that vary by age and by the number of adults in the household. For instance, two-parent families with the oldest parent aged 45 could have $37,700 in cash, savings, or other non-retirement, non-housing assets before having them taxed by the federal needs analysis.[8]

Any family income above the "income protection" limit and twelve percent (12%) of any countable assets above the "asset protection" limit is then considered available for the dependent student's education on a progressive schedule. The marginal rates range from 22% for the first $10,000 to 47% of any amounts exceeding $20,000.

The income and assets of students – whether they are dependent or independent – are implicitly taxed even more heavily by the federal financial aid formula. A dependent student is allowed to protect up to $2,440 in income after paying federal, state, and social security taxes. Above that amount, a student loses $0.50 in aid eligibility for every $1 in income. Moreover, 35% of any savings – there is no "asset protection" for the student – is also expected to be available to pay the cost of college.

The federal need analysis system contains a number of other features which may present strong incentives to parents and students. First, under the federal financial aid formula, a family with two members in college is expected to contribute only half as much per member as a family of equal resources with one person currently attending. This is not simply an adjustment for family size. Larger families are allowed to protect

---

[7] Those with family incomes less than $50,000 do not face the asset test.

[8] This limit applies to the 1999–2000 academic year. If a student's parents are divorced, the income and assets only of the custodial parent are considered. If the custodial parent has remarried, the income and assets of the step-parent are also considered in the federal formula.

more income from the "taxation" implied by the formula. Rather, the effect of such a rule is to distribute aid on the basis of the timing of college attendance. Families with children closer in age, or in which a secondary worker has returned to school part time, or in which youth stay in school longer and are therefore more likely to overlap, are eligible for considerably more aid than other families of equal size.

Second, a parent's and an applicant's income in the most recent completed calendar year is the only income that matters in determining eligibility for financial aid. This necessarily implies very high tax rates on a single year's income for those who are eligible for aid. Because such tax rates apply to income only during the years in which one's children are in college, families have a strong incentive to shift income into the years before and after college. Job bonuses and capital gains are likely candidates for shifting. In addition, because aid is based upon "adjusted gross income", above-the-line deductions to income produce higher eligibility.

Third, the tax on assets is imposed every year in which a child is in school, implying high cumulative tax rates on savings. Parental assets above a threshold are included in a family's ability to pay for school. For instance, as noted above, a two-parent family with a head aged 45 is allowed to protect $37,700. However, any savings above this amount is subject to a maximum "tax rate" of 5.6%. The magnitude of the tax rate on savings is one issue on which the guidebooks for parents often miss the mark by downplaying the savings tax. This rate does not sound very high until one recognizes that the same rate is applied for each year that one has a child in college. If one has a child in school for four years, the marginal dollar in savings results in 23 cents in reduced financial need over the years one has a child in college. Similarly, if one has two children attending college consecutively for eight years, the tax rate is nearly 50%. In other words, every dollar that one puts away for college may be offset by nearly a $0.50 decline in estimated need over the course of eight years of college education [Feldstein (1995)].

However, the actual impact of student financial aid rules on family savings is tempered for at least three reasons. First, only parental savings above the asset protection allowance are subject to the financial aid tax. Second, high-income or high-asset families face a zero marginal tax from the federal financial aid system – that is, if their income or assets are sufficiently high to be ineligible for financial aid.

Third, all of the above inferences regarding implicit tax rates assumed that any gap between expected family contribution and the cost of attendance – in financial aid jargon, the student's "financial need" – is being met. However, as Dick and Edlin (1997) note, not all financial need is met, and the marginal tax rates are often substantially less than the rates implied by the expected family contribution formula. For instance, Dick and Edlin estimate that families faced marginal income tax rates between 2% and 16% and marginal savings tax rates between 8% and 26% as a result of the student financial aid system.

For most families, the implicit tax rates in the financial aid formula are difficult to observe. Nowhere on the Free Application for Federal Student Aid (FAFSA) is the expected family contribution formula explained. Rather, families are simply asked to report family income, family size, financial assets, and the other data items required for calculating financial aid. Unlike a tax form, there is no bottom line. Therefore, there is no way to evaluate the impact of changes in income, savings, family size, or other items on the bottom line calculation. The information on the FAFSA is transferred to one of several federal contractors who then run each family's data through the federal formula. Families are then informed of their Expected Family Contribution by mail. Although the many privately-published financial aid guidebooks attempt to lift the veil of mystery surrounding the Expected Family Contribution, many families are likely to be ignorant of the formula. (Moreover, even if they learned about the implicit tax rates after seeing their financial aid package change from year to year while their children were in college, it would have been too late to have an effect on savings behavior.)

One way to judge the behavioral impacts of the financial aid formula on private savings would be to look for evidence of families "stacking up" at the asset protection limits in the financial aid formulae. Kane (1999) studied the distribution of financial assets above and below the relevant asset protection limits. Only a quarter of the sample of dependent undergraduates had parents with assets above the asset protection allowance (although, since high-asset households were probably less likely to apply for aid, this estimate probably understates the proportion of households affected). Most importantly, the distribution offers very little evidence that parents are reporting assets close to the asset protection allowances. As an informal test of the impact of the tax incentive on the amount of assets reported on the financial aid form, the distribution of savings does not provide strong evidence of a behavioral response to the asset test.[9]

Moreover, beginning in 1993, housing equity was excluded from the federal formula for calculating financial aid, thereby boosting the number of families qualifying for Pell Grants and subsidized Stafford loans. Families with college-age children now have a strong incentive to move their equity into housing. For instance, a family with financial assets above the protected amount could use those resources to prepay a portion of their mortgage and, when their children emerge from college, refinance their home and reinvest their savings in some other financial instrument such as a mutual fund.

On one hand, the impact of financial aid rules on savings behavior is likely to be smaller as a result of the exclusion of home equity, since the most alert parents, who would have been willing to adjust their savings behavior, can now avoid the tax by shifting resources into home equity. On the other hand, the asset test has now become a tax on naive, nonstrategic behavior. From the point of view of economic efficiency, taxing the myopic or the nonstrategic may be desirable, since those families who are caught by the tax are those whose savings behavior is the most inflexible. One may question the fairness of such a policy, however.

---

[9] Admittedly, this may not be a test of the full savings impact of the financial aid rules. Even if families do not know exactly where the marginal tax rates become zero, they may understand – however vaguely – that a dollar in savings could hurt them when it comes time to apply for college and adjust their behavior accordingly. However, given that marginal tax rates are a function of income and assets, it is difficult to do much better.

3. Gaps in college-going by family income and race

Enrollment rates among 18- to 24-year-olds began rising at the same time that the education wage differential for young adults began expanding around 1980. For both men and women, the mean annual earnings of both educational groups grew relative to high school graduates, beginning in 1979. The top left panel of Figure 3 portrays the percentage of 18–24 year olds enrolled in college. In the early Seventies, the trends were quite different for men and women, with declining enrollment rates for men and increases for women. (The difference may have been partially due to the end of the Vietnam draft deferment for men and the opening up of job markets for women.) However, since the mid-Seventies, enrollment rates were rising for both men and women, although the magnitude of the increase was larger for women than for men. Between 1980 and 2000, the proportion of 18–24 year olds enrolled in college rose from 0.25 to 0.40 for women (a 60% increase) and from 0.26 to 0.34 for men (a 31% increase). The top right panel reports college enrollment rates for high school graduates. The trend in college enrollment among high school graduates is similar to the trend in college enrollment for the civilian population of 18- to 24-year-olds.

The bottom panel reports the number of 18- to 24-year-olds by year. Growth in enrollment rates accelerated as the size of the college-age population began shrinking in the Eighties. (The discontinuities in 1982 and 1994 reflect changes in the census weights.)

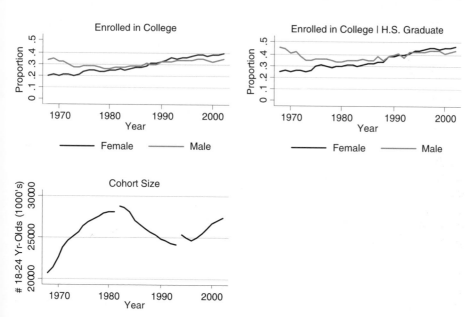

Note. Based on author's tabulation of October CPS.

Figure 3. College enrollment rates, high school graduation rates and cohort sizes.

As will be discussed below, the slower growth in enrollment rates during the Seventies when cohort sizes were growing and the rapid rise in enrollment rates as cohort sizes were shrinking during the Eighties points to the potential importance of capacity constraints in higher education. Moreover, the decline in cohort sizes during the Eighties was certainly fortuitous for state budgets, since cohort sizes began shrinking about the same time that enrollment rates began rising. As reported in the bottom panel, the trend in cohort sizes reversed in the mid-Nineties, increasing the pressure on state budgets from historically high college enrollment rates.

There are large gaps in college-going by family income. The top panel of Table 1 reports differences in college-going among seniors from the high school classes of 1980–1982, as reported in Ellwood and Kane (2000).[10] 80% of the students from the top income quartile attended some type of post-secondary institution within 20 months of their high school graduation, as compared with 57% of those from the lowest income quartiles. The gaps by family income were particularly large in four-year college entrance, with 55% of the highest-income youth attending a four-year college at some point and only 29% of the lowest income youth.

For the class of 1992, Ellwood and Kane (2000) report that 40% of the gap in post-secondary enrollment between the highest and lowest income quartile is attributable to differences in test scores administered in 12th grade (and 60% of the gap in four-year college entry).[11] As Kane (1999) reports, the gaps associated with family income are wider among those with test scores in the bottom quartile. However, there are gaps in college enrollment associated with family income even among those with test scores in the top quartile.

The gaps in college enrollment by family income appear to be widening over time. It is surprisingly difficult to keep track of differences in college-going by family income with the data available in the federal statistical system. The annual October Current Population Survey, for instance, collects data on college enrollment of youth, but only collects income information for their current household (not their parents' household).[12] One observes parental income only when the child is still a member of the parents' household. Moreover, the major longitudinal surveys collected by the National Center for Education Statistics (the High School and Beyond and National Education Longitudinal Study of 1988) which do contain information on the income of parents while their youth were in high school, asked about parental family income in slightly different ways for different cohorts. The results in the bottom panel of Table 1 represent an attempt by Ellwood and Kane (2000) to define parental family income quartiles in consistent ways using the NELS and High School and Beyond.[13]

---

[10] These data rely upon the parent-reported family income data, rather than the less reliable student responses. If students attended more than one type of post-secondary institution, they were categorized as four-year college entrants if they ever attended a four-year college and, if not, as two-year college entrants if they ever attended a two-year college.

[11] Ellwood and Kane (2000, Table 10-4, p. 298).

[12] For an analysis using the October CPS, see Hauser (1993).

[13] Both sets of estimates are based upon parent-reported, not student-reported, family income.

Table 1
Proportion of students from families in each income quartile who enroll in post-secondary schools within 20 months of high school graduation

Parental income quartile	Any post-secondary schooling			
	Total	Vocational, technical	Two-year college	Four-year college
Class of 1980–1982				
Bottom	0.57	0.12	0.16	0.29
3rd	0.63	0.11	0.19	0.33
2nd	0.71	0.10	0.22	0.39
Top	0.80	0.06	0.19	0.55
Total	0.68	0.10	0.19	0.39
Class of 1992				
Bottom	0.60	0.10	0.22	0.28
3rd	0.70	0.07	0.25	0.38
2nd	0.79	0.06	0.25	0.48
Top	0.90	0.05	0.19	0.66
Total	0.75	0.07	0.23	0.45

Note. Based upon tabulations of the High School and Beyond Survey and National Education Longitudinal Study of 1992. Parental income was reported by parents. Figures were reported in Ellwood and Kane (2000).

Although college entry rates grew for all groups between the high school classes of 1980–1982 and 1992, the increases were larger for middle and higher income families. For example, there was a 10 percentage point increase in the proportion of the highest income youth attending some post-secondary institution between 1980–1992 and 1992. Moreover, the increase in post-secondary schooling was largest for high-income youth attending four-year colleges, rising from 55% to 66%. In contrast, we estimate that there was only a 3 percentage point rise in post-secondary entry for youth from the lowest income quartile and a 1 percentage point decline (albeit statistically insignificant) in the proportion of low-income youth attending a four-year college.[14]

3.1. Widening gaps in college enrollment by race

While the Current Population Survey makes it difficult to track college-going rates by parental income level, it is possible to track college-going rates by race. Given the correlation between race and income, any increase in gaps by income ought to be reflected in a widening of the racial gap. Figure 4 reports the trend in the percentage of 18- to

[14] Kane (1994) also report that the gap in college enrollment by income seems to have widened, using data for dependent students in the October *Current Population Survey* (CPS).

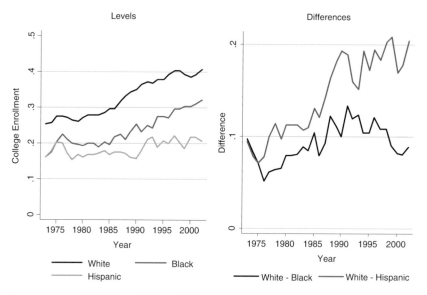

Note. Based on author's tabulation of October CPS.

Figure 4. College enrollment rates by race, 1973–2002.

24-year-olds enrolled in college by race/ethnicity between 1973 and 2002.[15] The panel
on the left reports enrollment rates by race/ethnicity, while the panel on the right reports
the difference in enrollment rates relative to white, non-Hispanic youth. After remaining flat for most of the Seventies, enrollment rates began to rise during the Eighties
for all groups. The proportion of white, non-Hispanic 18- to 24-year-olds enrolled in
college began increasing as the earnings gap began to widen, increasing from 27% to
41% between 1980 and 1998. Enrollment rates for African American youth also increased over that period – from 19% to 29%. However, the magnitude of the increase
was larger for whites (14 percentage points) than for African American youth (10 percentage points). As a result, as reported in the right panel, the gaps in college enrollment
by race/ethnicity also increased.

The widening racial gaps in college enrollment rates are particularly striking when
contrasted with the gradual closing of the racial gaps in high school graduation and test
performance over the same period. Throughout much of the period, high school dropout
rates were gradually falling for all three groups. However, the decline among African
Americans accelerated between the mid-Seventies and the mid-Eighties, closing somewhat the black–white gap in high school graduation rates. Between 1975 and 1988, the
status dropout rate fell from 11.4% to 9.6% for white non-Hispanics (a 1.8 percentage
point drop) and from 22.9% to 14.5% for black non-Hispanics (a 8.4 percentage point
drop).

[15] The data in Figures 3 and 4 are based on author's tabulation of the October CPS, 1968–2002.

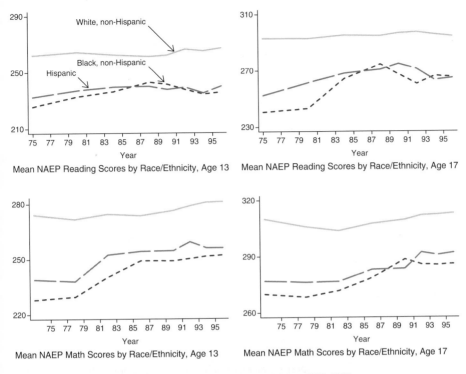

Figure 5. NAEP test scores by race and age, 1972–1999.

Figure 5 reports the trend in math and reading test scores on the National Assessment of Educational Progress exams by race/ethnicity for 13- and 17-year-olds since 1975.[16] For both age groups, in both reading and math, blacks and Hispanics were closing the gap in achievement relative to white non-Hispanics. A student-level standard deviation on the NAEP reading test was approximately 40 points over this time period. Between 1975 and 1988, the black–white gap in reading test scores at age 17 closed from approximately 1.25 standard deviations to 0.5 standard deviations. Since 1988, it seems that the gap has opened up again slightly, but the gap remains considerably smaller than it was in 1975.

3.2. Trends in educational attainment

Figure 6 reports trends in the proportion of 27- to 29-year-olds reporting any post-secondary enrollment and BA completion by gender.[17] Three facts are worth not-

---

[16] For a more detailed discussion of the closing gaps in test performance between blacks and whites, see Jencks and Phillips (1998), particularly chapters 5 and 6.

[17] Prior to 1992, we measure BA degree completion as the proportion completing 16 years of schooling or attending more than 16 years of schooling. Beginning in 1992, the format of the educational attainment

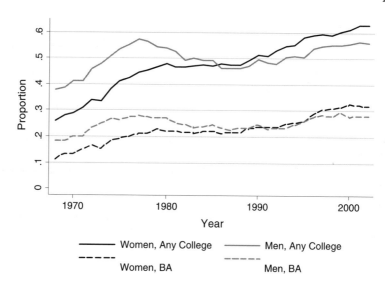

Figure 6. Attainment at age 27–29 by gender 1968–2002.

ing.[18] First, the timing of the rise in the proportion of 27- to 29-year-olds reporting ever having entered college matches the timing of the rise in college enrollment rates of 18- to 24-year-olds. The rise for 27- to 29-year-old white non-Hispanic began in approximately 1990, meaning that the increase began with the cohort turning 18 in 1979 – the same year in which college enrollment rates began to rise. Second, because it reflects the "stock" of students enrolled in college and not the "flow" of new entrants, the magnitude of the rise in college enrollment of 18- to 24-year-olds somewhat overstates the rise in college entry. As we saw in Figure 3, the proportion of 18- to 24-year-olds enrolled in college grew by 31% between 1983 and 1994. (These cohorts should roughly correspond to the cohorts of 27- to 29-year-olds in 1990 and 2001.) The proportion of these cohorts *ever* entering college also rose (from 50% to 59%), but only by two-thirds as much on a proportionate basis (18%). Third, the proportion of 27- to 29-year-olds

question changed. Rather than asking about highest grade attended or completed, the survey focused on the type of degree completed. As a result, we have to be careful in comparing rates of degree completion before and after 1992. However, there does not seem to be a discontinuity in either trend in 1992.

[18] As reported in Figures 3 and 6, the rise in college entry since 1980 was larger for women than for men. Administrative data published by the U.S. Department of Education confirms that women now account for a disproportionate share of enrollment, and more than half of the associate, bachelor's and master's degrees conferred. As argued in Kane (1994) and Charles and Luoh (2003), it is difficult to attribute the widening gap by gender to any differences in the rise in the education wage premium since 1980, since the apparent rise in the payoff to schooling was quite similar for men and women through the early Nineties. There may be other explanations, such as advantages in non-wage characteristics of jobs for college graduates (e.g., flexibility in hours), that could account for the large increases in enrollment by women. However, this important trend is currently not very well understood.

reporting any college rose by a similar proportion between 1990 and 2002 (from 0.50 to 0.59 or 18%) as the rise in the proportion of the population reporting a BA (from 0.24 to 0.30, or 24%), implying little change in the proportion of college entrants finishing college. In other words, the proportion of entrants completing college did not decline despite rapidly rising college entry rates.[19]

As noted above, the percentage increase in the "stock" of college enrollees was larger than the rise in the "flow" of college entrants or college completers. This reflects an increase in part-time enrollment and a lengthening time-to-degree. Over this time period, there was rapid growth in the proportion of college students enrolled part time. In 1970, part-time students accounted for less than half of post-secondary enrollment. However, by 1992, 77% of post-secondary enrollment was part-time.

Figure 7 reports the proportion of 27- to 29-year-olds reporting any college and reporting BA degree completion by race/ethnicity. Relative to white, non-Hispanics, the trends in enrollment at age 18–24 are reflected in the trends in educational attainment at age 27–29. Between 1973 and 1987, the black–white difference in BA degree completion rates at age 27–29 declined from 13 percentage points to 9 percentage points.

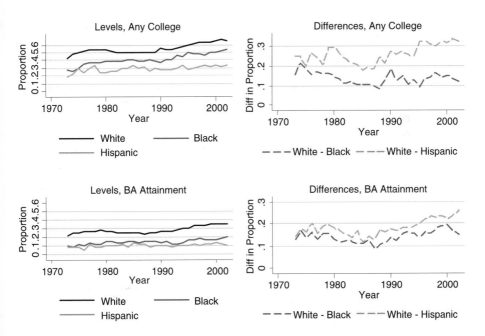

Figure 7. Attainment at age 27–29 by race, 1973–2002.

[19] Turner (2004) finds that, if one focused on completions by age 23, one would have concluded that completion was lagging behind the rise in entry. However, much of that gap appears to have been closed by age 27. In other words, students are taking longer to complete, perhaps because of the rise in part-time enrollment.

This reflects the convergence in college enrollment rates among 18- to 24-year-olds in the Seventies. As reported in Figure 4, the black–white gap in college enrollment rates among 18- to 24-year-olds was closing rapidly up through 1976. However, the black–white gap in enrollment rates among 18- to 24-year-olds began to widen again. This fact is also reflected in the black–white gap in educational attainment of 27- to 29-year-olds. The black–white difference in BA degree completion at age 27–29, which had closed to 9 percentage points in 1987, had more than doubled to 19 percentage points in 1999.

4. Estimates of the impact of price subsidies on enrollment decisions

Over the years, a large literature has developed studying the impact of tuition and financial aid policies on college-going. In their review of the literature on student responsiveness to changes in college cost, Leslie and Brinkman (1987, 1988) report a consensus estimate that a $1,000 change in college costs (1990 dollars) is associated with an approximately 5 percentage point difference in college enrollment rates.

A number of papers, such as those by Kane (1994) and Cameron and Heckman (1998), use between-state differences in state tuition policy and essentially compare the college entry rates of otherwise similar youth in high- and low-tuition states. The empirical strategy in this literature uses the assumption that the price that is relevant for the marginal student is the tuition at public institutions in the home state and evaluate the effect of tuition and college-going by comparing college-going rates in high- and low-tuition states. Such studies also assume that the supply of college slots is perfectly elastic: Given a change in price, it is solely student demand which determines enrollment and not the supply of college slots.

Two characteristics of these studies deserve comment: First, papers using different data sets – the October Current Population Survey, the National Longitudinal Survey of Youth and the High School and Beyond – generate similar results. A $1,000 difference in tuition is associated with a 6 percentage point difference in college-going. Indeed, these estimates are quite consistent with the older literature summarized by Leslie and Brinkman (1988).

Second, a weakness of these studies is that they rely on relatively fixed differences in tuition levels between states. For instance, California has been a relatively low-tuition state for the past forty years. California has also built a number of community colleges around the state. One may be attributing to tuition policy the effect of these other policy differences, such as the construction of community colleges.

Kane (1994) and Card and Lemieux (2001) include state fixed effects in an analysis using Current Population Survey data and find that the effect of public tuition levels is often not statistically significant. Kane (1994) finds a negative and statistically significant effect of tuition on African American youth after including state fixed effects, but the coefficient on tuition is no longer significant for whites with the inclusion of state fixed effects. Card and Lemieux (2001) report small (1 to 2 percentage point difference in college enrollment per $1,000 difference in tuition) and occasionally statistically insignificant effects of tuition on college-going. However, the CPS might not provide the ideal data for testing the effect of tuition, particularly when looking within states. The CPS classifies youth who are temporarily away from home by the state of residence of their parents. College-age youth who have set up their own households will be categorized according to their current state of residence. About twenty percent of college students in the United States attend a college outside of their parents' state of residence. Therefore, the public tuition level in one's current state of residence in the CPS will be an imperfect measure of the price one actually faces, and the bias due to this measurement error would be exacerbated by the inclusion of state fixed effects. Rather than using the CPS, Kane (1999) used administrative data on enrollments in public institutions to study the impact of tuition increases and declines within states. Interestingly, one sees comparable effects of tuition changes within states over time as one would estimate looking across states.

Despite strong evidence of student and parent responsiveness to tuition costs, the evidence for the impact of the Pell Grant program is much weaker. Hansen (1983) first noted that there had been little evidence of a disproportionate rise in college enrollment by low-income youth during the Seventies, when the Pell Grant program was established. Although that paper was criticized for relying too heavily on two years of data and for including males, whose decisions may also have been affected by the end of the Vietnam War, later work [Kane (1994)] confirmed that the result was not sensitive to the choice of annual end-points or to the inclusion of males. Manski (1992–1993) also reported little evidence of a disproportionate growth in BA completion by low-income youth graduating from high school between 1972 and 1980. [Despite little evidence of impacts on enrollment of college-age youth, Seftor and Turner (2002) report evidence of enrollment impacts on older adults.]

One hypothesis to reconcile the estimates of tuition impacts with the failure to find an increase in enrollment by low-income youth following the establishment of the Pell Grant program is that students are expected to make a significant up-front investment to apply to college and to apply for financial aid before they learn anything about the amount of aid available. In contrast, they can read about a tuition increase in the newspaper or see it in a college's application materials.

Dynarski has estimated the impact of two other programs which operated outside of the federal need-analysis framework: one looking at the impact of the cessation of tuition benefits for Social Security survivors and the other evaluating the effect of the Hope Scholarship program in Georgia. Dynarski (2003) found that after the discontinuation of the Social Security Student Benefit program, college entry by students with deceased parents declined by 19.4 to 25.6 percentage points relative to other youth. To convert this estimate to a similar scale reported above, Dynarski calculated that the value of the benefit program had been roughly $5,300 (1990 dollars). This implies an impact of 3.7 to 4.8 percentage points per thousand dollar change in price. Although the change in policy was plausibly exogenous, it is difficult to know whether the responsiveness of such a narrow subgroup – youth with deceased parents – can be generalized to other groups. Moreover, the estimate is based upon an exceedingly small sample of 107 children of deceased parents before the change in policy and 49 after the change.

In a second paper, Dynarski (2000) studied enrollment rates for youth in Georgia relative to other southern states, before and after the Hope Scholarship program was initiated in that state. She estimates that the program increased college enrollment rates of 18- to 19-year-olds by 7.0 to 7.9 percentage- points. Given the value of the Hope Scholarship, this estimate converts to an estimate of 3.1 to 3.5 percentage points per $1,000 difference in cost.

Dynarski (2000) also found that the impact of the Hope Scholarship in Georgia was concentrated among whites and among those from families with income above $50,000. This may have been due to the fact that, in the early years of the program, any federal Pell Grant aid was subtracted from one's Hope Scholarship – meaning that low-income youth would qualify for much less of a net increase in aid than higher income youth.

Interestingly, because both programs operate outside the typical need analysis system, eligibility was known *a priori*, and did not require one to submit a FAFSA form and wait for an award letter to know whether or not one qualified for the aid. As such, both financial aid programs operated similarly to a tuition increase, which is relatively costless to anticipate. In contrast, the Pell Grant program requires remarkable foresight. One has to fill out a FAFSA, be assigned an expected family contribution, and receive an award letter from a school simply to learn how much federal aid is on offer. It may not be a coincidence that the estimated impacts of such nontraditional forms of aid and tuition increases are so similar, and are larger than the apparent impact of the establishment of the Pell Grant program.

Kane (2003) found large impacts of grant aid on student college enrollment decisions for California residents submitting financial aid applications with GPAs in the range of eligibility for the Cal Grant program. The Cal Grant program provides California residents with grants to attend college if their high school grade point average (GPA) exceeded a specific threshold – and if their family income and assets fell below program maxima. Before 2001, the GPA threshold was unknown to parents or to program administrators until after the application deadline had passed. The reason was that the legislature funded a fixed number of grant awards, and the minimum GPA was set where the maximum number of grants were awarded. When many students were applying to college the threshold was set high; when fewer students were applying the threshold would be lower. This may have made it difficult for parents to make their financial plans, but it was certainly fortuitous for the purpose of evaluation, since those immediately above or immediately below the threshold might plausibly be considered similar.[20] There was a 3–4 percentage point difference in college enrollment rates for

---

[20] Under an entitlement program where the threshold is known beforehand, the group with GPAs immediately above the threshold is likely to disproportionately include the college-bound, while the group immediately below the threshold would disproportionately contain those who did not need the funding.

eligible youth with GPA immediately above and immediately below the threshold. However, there was no corresponding discontinuity for those with incomes too high or too low to be affected.

The introduction of a new subsidy for residents of the District of Columbia (DC) in the 2000–2001 academic year provides another opportunity to learn about families' responsiveness to public subsidies. Historically, there has been only one low-tuition public institution available to the residents of the District of Columbia – the University of the District of Columbia. However, for the first time, in the fall of 2000, young high school graduates from the District of Columbia were provided with the same menu of subsidized public institutions available to other students around the country. Under the federally funded DC Tuition Assistance Grant program, residents of DC are eligible to receive the difference between in-state tuition and out-of-state tuition (up to $10,000) to attend any public institution in the country, or $2,500 to attend private colleges in DC or historically black institutions in Maryland or Virginia. (Historically black institutions outside of DC, Maryland, and Virginia were made eligible in the fall of 2003.) Using data on freshman enrollments by state of residence, Kane (2004) and Abraham and Clark (2003) found that between 1998 and 2000, the number of DC residents attending public institutions in Virginia and Maryland more than doubled. When public institutions in other states were added in 2001, the number of DC residents attending these institutions also nearly doubled. The impact was largest at nonselective public four-year colleges, particularly predominantly black institutions. The total number of financial aid applicants, Pell Grant recipients, and college entrants from DC also increased by 15% or more.

While there is strong evidence that financial aid can increase college attendance, there is less evidence that financial aid leads to higher degree completion (as opposed to initial entry). Dynarski (2005) used the 2000 census to study the relative growth in BA degree completion in two states – Georgia and Arkansas – which created large merit-based financial aid programs in the early Nineties. She finds that the aid programs do increase the share of the population that completes a college degree by three percentage points.

4.1. Interaction between tuition and family income

Manski and Wise (1983), Radner and Miller (1970), Bishop (1977) and Kohn, Manski and Mundel (1976) all report greater responsiveness to tuition differences among those from lower income quartiles. More recently, McPherson and Schapiro (1991) and Kane (1994) also find greater impacts of tuition on the enrollment decisions of low-income youth. Ellwood and Kane (2000) reported findings with the NELS data that are somewhat sensitive to specification. In some specifications they find an interaction effect, but not in others. Cameron and Heckman (1998) fail to find evidence of an income interaction effect. Although their point estimates show decreasing effects of tuition as parental income rises (estimated separately for blacks, whites, and Latinos, the point estimate of the effect of a $1,000 difference in tuition was roughly twice as large as the impact for the lowest income quartile), they could not reject the hypothesis that tuition has similar effects at varying income levels.

4.2. Response to rising returns to college

As noted above, the timing of the rise in college entry by cohorts of high school graduates in the early 1980s coincided with a rise in the educational wage differential among 25- to 34-year-olds. As portrayed in Figures 3 and 4, enrollment rates of 18- to 24-year-olds began rising about the same time that educational wage differential began rising.

Based primarily on the coincidence in the timing of the rise in payoff with the rise in enrollment, families would seem to be responding to the rising payoffs to college. Yet the above estimates would suggest that parents and students are more sensitive to tuition and financial aid policies than they have been to the rise in the payoff to schooling. As reported in Table 1, there was a 7 percentage point increase in college entry by high school graduates between 1980–1982 and 1992, from 68% to 75%. This seems large, until one realizes that the rise in college enrollment witnessed during the Eighties was roughly as large as we might have expected to see in response to a $1,000 to $1,500 increase in annual tuition, based upon the empirical estimates cited above. For someone who was considering being in school over a period of four years, this would have amounted to a $3,700 to $5,500 increase in anticipated expense (using a discount rate of 6%).

Obviously, the actual payoff of a college degree for the cohort of youth graduating from high school in 1992 remains to be seen, since they have yet to enjoy the benefit of a full career. However, such an estimate would likely suggest that the payoffs to college have risen much more than $5,500 in present value. Among 25- to 34-year-old males, high school graduates working full-year, full-time earned $26,984[21] in 1980 while college graduates earned $34,096. The differential in annual earnings between the two educational groups had grown from $7,112 in 1980 to $14,579 by 1992. Therefore, the differential in annual earnings for one year grew by more than $5,500.

Recent attempts to estimate the response of students to rising payoffs to schooling [Card and Lemieux (2001)] typically focus on the widening gap in mean earnings between high school and college graduates. However, there are at least two reasons why the above calculations could be misstating the rise in the payoffs to schooling for those on the margin of college entry. First, the payoffs for those on the margin may be very different from the average. Recent work by Carneiro (2002) and Carneiro, Heckman and Vytlacil (2001) suggest that the payoff to schooling for the marginal student is much lower than the comparison of averages would imply. (However, neither paper addresses the question of whether *changes* in marginal returns may have been larger or smaller than the changes in average returns.) Second, although the gap in mean earnings between high school and college graduates widened, the variance in earnings also grew

---

[21] All figures in this paragraph have been converted to 1990 dollars using the GDP deflator.

within each educational group. Therefore, students' uncertainty regarding future returns may also have grown. Although the average payoff may have increased, the variance in expected returns may also have increased. However, to the extent that the increase in the within-group variances reflected a rise in the price of some unmeasured trait – such as unmeasured ability – then variance in expected returns for any individual may not have grown at all, since the covariance in one's expected earnings as a high school and college graduate would also have been growing. Since we rarely observe one's earnings at different educational attainment levels, this covariance is difficult to estimate empirically.

4.3. Borrowing constraints

As pointed out by Becker (1993) in his classic volume, *Human Capital*, the capital market for college investments is likely to be imperfect. Potential college entrants have little collateral to provide to investors. And, as a result, without contracts allowing for indentured labor, there is no way for lenders to force college graduates to earn up to their potential. Families are likely to be in the best position to do so (although as any parent would testify, even their points of leverage are limited). Those with greater family resources are likely to have the greatest access to such capital.

The federal government has attempted to create such a market, by providing a federal guarantee on student loans. However, the solution is incomplete. As noted above, the most a student can borrow under the federally guaranteed student loan programs is $2,625 the first year in college, $3,500 the second year and $5,500 for subsequent undergraduate years. With the average tuition at public two-year and four-year institutions and at private four-year institutions being $1,600, $3,200 and $14,500 respectively in 1998–1999, the loan limits are insufficient to cover expected expenses. Beginning in 1993, a student's parents could borrow to cover the combined cost of tuition and room and board costs for a student – but payments on such parental loans begin immediately, limiting their usefulness to those parents with insufficient cash flow. Although parental loans have accounted for much of the growth in loan volume over time, a small share of parents have taken advantage of such loans.

The loan limits may be sufficient to pay tuition expenses at some institutions, but are likely to fall short of the sum of tuition expenses and the level of consumption one would choose if one could borrow against future earnings. As such, the loan guarantees are an incomplete solution to the capital market imperfection noted by Becker (1993). Moreover, given the moral hazard problems in allowing students to borrow to cover their foregone earnings, it is difficult to imagine any government guarantee which would allow students to borrow up to the full cost of a year in college.

The large differences in college-going by family income among those with similar test scores would be consistent with borrowing constraints. Moreover, there is evidence that higher income parents provide more college financing to their children than low-income parents do. Among students attending the same public four-year institutions, Ellwood and Kane (2000) report that parents from the top income quartile provide $4,083 more per year to their children than parents from the bottom income quartile. Part of that difference is made up by federal, state, and institutional grant funding, which is targeted toward low-income students. However, the net price facing dependent students from families in the top income quartile is still $2,210 lower than the price faced by dependent students from the lowest income quartile attending the same institutions. If we were to multiply the difference in the net cost of college for dependent high- and low-income youth ($2,210) by the 5 percentage point difference in college-going per $1,000 difference often found in empirical studies, we "explain" virtually all of the difference in college-going between high- and low-income youth.

However, the differences in college-going associated with family income would be consistent with other explanations as well. First, to some extent, education is not only an investment, it is a consumption good for parents. One might expect higher income parents to want to consume more education. This might be true even if low-income students could borrow against their future earnings. Second, a single test score is likely to be an imperfect measure of a student's academic preparation. Observed differences in college-going by family income among students with similar test scores may simply reflect unmeasured differences in academic preparation between high- and low-income youth.

When testing for differences in college-going by family income, the differences are diminished when one controls for variables that reflect differences in family wealth, such as parental education. Carneiro and Heckman (2002) distinguish between short-term borrowing constraints – created by short-term cash-flow problems when a child is on the threshold of college enrollment – and long-term borrowing constraints related to a family's ability to finance a high quality education through a youth's lifetime. They argue that one would want to control for indirect measures of family assets – such as parental education – when weighing the effect of income immediately before enrollment. They argue that when one does so, a large share of the difference in enrollment between high- and low-income youth is accounted for by "longer-term" factors such as wealth and higher test performance of youth. However, to the extent that parents can help finance their children's education with current income or accumulated assets, the distinction between short-term constraints and long-term constraints is unclear. Indeed, we may be understating the effect of borrowing constraints by first conditioning on test performance, to the extent that these factors, too, are related to long-term family wealth.

The greater sensitivity of low-income youth to tuition policies (which, as noted above, has been reported in a number of empirical papers) has sometimes been cited as evidence consistent with borrowing constraints. However, Keane and Wolpin (2001) point out that borrowing constraints do not necessarily imply an interaction between tuition sensitivity and parental income. As a result, such an interaction does not provide much evidence either way on the existence of borrowing constraints.

Recent instrumental variable estimates of the payoff to schooling have suggested that those on the margin, whose decisions about entering college are influenced by such things as proximity to college and college costs, may have higher than average payoffs to college. Such results would also be consistent with borrowing constraints, since only those with higher-than-average returns to college would have surmounted the barriers presented by borrowing constraints to attend. In the presence of borrowing constraints, Lang (1993) and Card (1995a) point out that the estimated payoff to college should be higher for those on the margin, since their cost of borrowing funds would be higher. Recent instrumental variable estimates using geographic distance to college to estimate payoff to college [Kane and Rouse (1994) and Card (1995b)] have found that those on the margin, whose decisions about college are influenced by such factors, do tend to exhibit higher marginal returns. However, recent papers by Carneiro (2002) and Carneiro, Heckman and Vytlacil (2001) question the validity of the instruments used in those studies, and using an alternative identification strategy find lower returns for those on the margin.

A recent paper by Cameron and Taber (2000) takes issue with such an interpretation of the instrumental variable results. They argue that borrowing constraints are more likely to be binding with respect to direct costs of college – such as tuition and transportation costs – than with respect to foregone earnings. They proceed by comparing the instrumental variable estimates one finds using proximity to college and the average earnings of high school graduates in one's county as two different sources of variation in college costs. In fact, they do not find higher payoffs to college when using college proximity as an instrument than when they use foregone earnings as an instrument.[22] They cite this as evidence against the presence of borrowing constraints.

A final piece of evidence that may be useful in identifying the potential importance of borrowing constraints is the difference in timing of college entry in high and low tuition states. Kane (1996) finds that youth graduating from high school in states with higher levels of tuition for state residents at public colleges in the state (presumably the least cost alternative for most students) tend to enter college later. This, too, would be consistent with borrowing constraints, because in the absence of borrowing constraints, students would want to complete their educational investments as early in life as possible. Kane (1996) shows that in a simple version of the Ben-Porath (1967) model of life-cycle human capital investment, part-time schooling and delayed entry are difficult to explain in the presence of constant returns to time spent in school and perfect capital markets. As long as the human capital production function is constant returns to scale, one would be expected to invest full time when in school.[23] The intuition is simple: when delaying school an extra period, one must discount the future benefits further and forfeit a period of returns later in life. (One is also pushing off the costs but, as long as the subsequent earnings gains exceed the costs, the net change in present value is negative as long as the present value of a year in college is positive.) In other words, since there are costs to delaying, it is worthwhile getting out of school as soon as possible. But because the production function is constant returns to scale, there is no decline

---

[22] They also report the results from a structural model which also uses the same assumption for identification, that is, that borrowing constraints should apply to direct costs and not to indirect costs.

[23] For an illustration of how full-time enrollment is implied by the necessary conditions of the optimum, see Jacoby (1994) and Glewwe and Jacoby (1995).

in the marginal productivity of investment from investing full time. Unless one makes more stringent assumptions – such as decreasing returns to scale in the human capital production function – one would not expect part-time schooling within such a model. The growing incidence of delayed entry and part-time enrollment during the Eighties may be related to the declining real value of borrowing limits during that period.

In summary, even though there are some pieces of evidence that would be consistent with borrowing constraints, it is difficult to find a definitive test of the existence of borrowing constraints in the literature. In each case, there are alternative explanations for the same facts, which would not require borrowing constraints to be part of the story. In this regard, the debate over borrowing constraints is similar to the debate over whether the payoff to educational attainment is a payoff to concrete skill or a payoff to the signal provided by that skill. Although the answer is fundamental to any consideration of the social benefits of further investments in training, many pieces of evidence would be consistent with either interpretation.[24]

5. Role of supply constraints in rising payoff to schooling

Most analyses of the students' college enrollment decisions have focused on the decisions of individual students, taking the market value of a college education as given. Yet fluctuations in the aggregate supply of college graduates – either due to shifts in enrollment rates or changes in cohort sizes – may well have a direct effect on that market price. Thirty years ago, Freeman (1975a, 1976a) noted that the rapid rises in college enrollment and the growth in college-age cohorts as the baby boom attended college had coincided with a decline in the value of a college degree. Freeman (1975b, 1976b) used "cob-web" models to describe the market for lawyers and engineers. In such models, the investment decisions made by entering students while the returns are high lead to declines in the payoffs when the bumper crop of new graduates arrives on the market several years later. More recently, Katz and Murphy (1992), Autor, Katz and Krueger (1998) and Card and Lemieux (2001) have concluded that fluctuations in the rate of growth in the aggregate supply of college graduates played a direct role in the fluctuations in the value of a college degree in the Seventies and Eighties.

Autor, Katz and Krueger (1998, Table 2) show that one could explain much of the variation in the payoff to a college degree between 1950 and 1990 with a relatively constant growth in demand for college-educated labor and an elasticity of substitution of 1.4. Relative supply changes could account for most of the changes in the payoff to college. In the postwar period, from 1950 through 1970, the relative supply of college graduates grew at a steady pace and the relative wage of college educated labor remained stable. Then, the rate of growth in the supply of college educated labor accelerated between 1970 and 1980, and the college wage differential rose. After 1980, the

---

[24] Weiss (1995) provides explanations for the same set of empirical findings that would involve either education as a skill or education as a job market signal.

rate of growth in the relative supply of college-educated labor slowed and the college wage differential rose. (As we saw in Figure 6, the relative supply of college-educated 27–29-year-old men actually fell between 1980 and 1990.)

The causes of the slowdown in the growth in educational attainment for youth entering college in the early Seventies (who would have been 25–34 in 1979) are a critical part of the story behind the rising payoff to education – but are currently not well understood. One hypothesis is that the end of the Vietnam draft deferment for college graduates may have contributed to both the acceleration and the slowdown. However, such an explanation could not account for all of the decline, since a similar acceleration and deceleration occurred for females as well. A recent paper by Bound and Turner (2003) suggests that a retrenchment in state and federal support for colleges and universities in the late Sixties, combined with expansions in cohort size for those reaching college age in the Seventies, may have contributed to the slowdown. Card and Lemieux (2000) also suggest that cohort sizes and capacity constraints at colleges and universities in the early 1990s may have played some role in the slowdown in educational attainment.

Most of the papers evaluating the role of supply factors in affecting the college/high school wage differential [Katz and Murphy (1992) and Autor, Katz and Krueger (1998)] assume that young and old college graduates are perfect substitutes. Card and Lemieux (2001) argue that a model in which young and old college graduates are imperfect substitutes fit the data more closely. For instance, the model with perfect substitutability has a difficult time accounting for the leveling off in the returns to college which began in the early Nineties. There was little evidence of an acceleration in the supply of college equivalents in the Nineties. Indeed, the model used by Autor, Katz and Krueger (1998) would lead one to infer a rapid *deceleration* in the demand for college-educated labor in the 1990s. Although we do not measure demand directly, this hardly seems plausible given the Internet boom of the late Nineties. A model allowing imperfect substitutability between younger and older college-educated workers would seem more consistent with deceleration in the payoff to a college degree, given the apparent acceleration in the supply of college equivalents among those aged 25–34 in the Nineties.

The degree of substitutability between young and old college graduates is critical not only in setting the historical record straight, but it is also critical in anticipating the future trend in the college/high school wage differential. It is much more plausible to expect continued growth in educational attainment for entering cohorts than to expect a return to the pre-1970 rate of growth in educational attainment of the labor force as a whole. The reason is that much of the growth in educational attainment among the pool of prime-age males before 1970 was due to the large differential in educational attainment between entering cohorts and exiting cohorts. However, after a period of decelerating or, in the case of males, declining educational attainment, the differential between entering and exiting cohorts is much less pronounced than before. Moreover, the current college-age cohorts are small relative to the baby-boom cohorts that preceded them. Between 1980 and 2000, the share of the labor force with a college degree rose by 8 percentage points, from 22% to 30%. Even under very optimistic assumptions, Ellwood (2001) projects that the percentage of the labor force with a college degree will grow by only 5 percentage points over the next 20 years.

6. Conclusion

Given the rising wage differential for college graduates, the proportion of high school graduates going on to college is an increasingly important determinant of economic growth and wage inequality. We have made progress over the last decade on a number of issues. For instance, the evidence on the impact of tuition and grant subsidies on students' college enrollment decisions has been accumulating. The evidence on the impact of tuition policies and well-publicized sources of grants (such as the Hope Scholarship program in Georgia, tuition benefits for Social Security Survivors, and the Cal Grant program in California) are quite large. Moreover, although there seems to have been a response to the rising educational wage differentials since 1980, the magnitude of the response per dollar of present value has been smaller than the tuition impacts. We have also made some progress in thinking about the incentive effects of state and federal financial aid policies – in taxing income and savings and in encouraging tuition inflation.

Yet, many fundamental questions on the impact of state and federal subsidies on college enrollment decisions remain unresolved. For instance, it remains unclear to what extent the existing federal loan guarantees have loosened the borrowing constraints on students and families. Moreover, we know little about the bang-for-the-buck achieved by different forms of financial aid subsidies – the effect of a dollar in loan subsidies or better student counseling may be larger than the effect of an additional dollar in Pell Grants.

However, a number of factors are converging to raise the stakes for public policy toward higher education. First, between 1995 and 2015, the number of college-age youth is expected to grow by 22% (with much larger increases in some states, such as California). Between 1980 and 1995, demographic trends had actually been offsetting the impact of rising college enrollment rates on state budgets (with an 18% decline in the number of college-age youth). That trend has now begun to reverse and states are faced with the combination of high college enrollment rates and growing numbers of college-age youth. Second, although state finances are likely to recover from the current recession, the pressure on state budgets from increasing Medicaid obligations will continue. Kane, Orszag and Apostolov (2005) estimate that the declines in state support for higher education during the Nineties were concentrated in states with large Medicaid obligations at the beginning of the Nineties. The Congressional Budget Office estimates that Federal Medicaid costs will rise from 1.2% of GDP today to 2.8% of GDP by 2030. Given the cost-sharing between the Federal government and state governments inherent in the Medicaid program, this projection also implies a substantial increase in state Medicaid costs. (Federal financial aid subsidies mean that an additional dollar in state spending to reduce tuition requires states to forfeit some federal subsidies. Just the opposite is true for state Medicaid spending for which the federal government matches state spending.) The declining state support to public institutions of higher education seems to be contributing to an increasing differential in faculty salaries, faculty/student ratios and student characteristics at public and private institutions.

The rise in college costs over the last two decades and the resulting parental anxiety have created a hunger among politicians for policy proposals to assuage that anxiety. The introduction of federal tax credits for higher education and the growth in state grant programs, such as the Hope scholarship program in Georgia and the Cal Grant program in California, reflect the political urge to offer a response to rising tuition costs. However, the policy community has not been forthcoming with many new ideas in this field. The growing demand in the political arena and the lack of well-thought-out proposals for state and federal action present a dangerous combination.

References

Abraham, K.G., Clark, M. (2003). "Financial aid and students' college decisions: Evidence from the District of Columbia's tuition assistance grant program". Working Paper 2 (August), Princeton University Education Research Section.

Autor, D., Katz, L., Krueger, A. (1998). "Computing inequality: Have computers changed the labor market?". Quarterly Journal of Economics 113 (4), 1169–1213.

Becker, G.S. (1993). Human Capital: A Theoretical and Empirical Analysis, with Special Reference to Education, third ed. University of Chicago Press, Chicago.

Ben-Porath, Y. (1967). "The production of human capital and the life cycle of earnings". Journal of Political Economy 75, 352–365.

Bishop, J. (1977). "The effect of public policies on the demand for higher education". Journal of Human Resources 12 (3), 285–307.

Bound, J., Turner, S. (2003). "Cohort crowding: How resources affect collegiate attainment". Unpublished paper. University of Virginia (March).

Cameron, S.V., Heckman, J.J. (1998). "Life cycle schooling and dynamic selection bias: Models and evidence for five cohorts of American males". Journal of Political Economy 106 (2), 262–333.

Cameron, S.V., Taber, J.J. (2000). "Estimation of educational borrowing constraints using returns to schooling". Journal of Political Economy 112 (1), 132–182.

Card, D. (1995a). "Earnings, schooling and ability revisited". Research in Labor Economics 14, 23–48.

Card, D. (1995b). "Using geographic variation in college proximity to estimate the return to schooling". In: Christofides, L., Grant, E.K., Swidinsky, R. (Eds.), Aspects of Labor Market Behavior: Essays in Honor of John Vanderkamp. University of Toronto Press, Toronto, pp. 201–222.

Card, D., Lemieux, T. (2000). "Dropout and enrollment trends in the post-war period: What went wrong in the 1970's". Working Paper 7658, NBER.

Card, D., Lemieux, T. (2001). "Can falling supply explain the rising return to college for younger men? A cohort-based analysis". Quarterly Journal of Economics 116 (2), 705–746.

Carneiro, P. (2002). "Hetergeneity in the returns to schooling: Implications for policy evaluation". Working paper. University of Chicago (November).

Carneiro, P., Heckman, J. (2002). "The evidence on credit constraints in post-secondary schooling". Economic Journal 112, 705–734.

Carneiro, P., Heckman, J., Vytlacil, E. (2001). "Estimating the rate of return to education when it varies among individuals." Working paper. University of Chicago.

Charles, K.K., Luoh, M.-C. (2003). "Gender differences in completed schooling". Review of Economics and Statistics 85 (3), 559–577.

Christal, M. (1997). State Tuition and Fee Policies: 1996–97. State Higher Education Executive Officers, Denver.

College Board (2004). Trends in Student Aid, 2004. College Board, Washington, DC.

Dick, A.W., Edlin, A.S. (1997). "The implicit taxes from college financial aid". The Journal of Public Economics 65 (3), 295–322.

Dynarski, S. (2000). "Hope for whom? Financial aid for the middle class and its impact on college attendance". National Tax Journal 53 (3), 629–661.

Dynarski, S. (2003). "Does aid matter? Measuring the effect of student aid on college attendance and completion". American Economic Review 93 (1), 279–288.

Dynarski, S. (2005). "Finishing college: The role of state policy in degree attainment". Working paper. Kennedy School of Government (April).

Edlin, A.S. (1993). "Is college financial aid equitable and efficient?". Journal of Economic Perspectives 7 (2), 143–158.

Ehrenberg, R.G. (2003). "Studying ourselves: The academic labor market". Journal of Labor Economics 21 (2), 267–287.

Ellwood, D.T. (2001). "The sputtering labor force of the 21st century: Can social policy help?". In: Krueger, A.B., Solow, R.M. (Eds.), The Roaring Nineties: Can Full Employment Be Sustained? Russell Sage Foundation, New York, pp. 421–489.

Ellwood, D., Kane, T.J. (2000). "Who is getting a college education: Family background and the growing gaps in enrollment". In: Danziger, S., Waldfogel, J. (Eds.), Securing the Future. Russell Sage Foundation, New York, pp. 283–324.

Feldstein, M. (1995). "College scholarship rules and private saving". American Economic Review 73, 398–410.

Freeman, R.B. (1975a). "Overinvestment in college training?". Journal of Human Resources 10 (3), 287–311.

Freeman, R.B. (1975b). "Legal cobwebs: A recursive model of the labor market demand for new lawyers". Review of Economics and Statistics 57 (2), 171–179.

Freeman, R.B. (1976a). The Overeducated American. Academic Press, New York.

Freeman, R.B. (1976b). "A cobweb model of the supply and starting salary of new engineers". Industrial Labor Relations Review 29 (2), 236–248.

Glewwe, P., Jacoby, H.G. (1995). "An economic analysis of delayed primary school enrollment in a low income country: The role of early childhood nutrition". Review of Economics and Statistics 77 (1), 156–169.

Hamermesh, D. (2002). "Quite good news – for now". The Annual Report on the Economic Status of the Profession 2001–02. American Association of University Professors, Washington, DC.

Hansen, W.L. (1983). "Impact of student financial aid on access". In: Froomkin, J. (Ed.), The Crisis in Higher Education. Academy of Political Science, New York, pp. 84–96.

Hauser, R. (1993). "Trends in college entry among whites, blacks, and Hispanics". In: Clotfelter, C., Rothschild, M. (Eds.), Studies of Supply and Demand in Higher Education. National Bureau of Economic Research and University of Chicago Press, Chicago, pp. 61–119.

Hoxby, C. (1998). "Tax incentives for higher education". In: Poterba, J. (Ed.), In: Tax Policy and the Economy, vol. 12. National Bureau of Economic Research and Massachusetts Institute of Technology, Cambridge, MA, pp. 49–81.

Jacoby, H.G. (1994). "Borrowing constraints and progress through school: Evidence from Peru". Review of Economics and Statistics 76 (1), 151–160.

Jencks, C.S., Phillips, M. (1998). The Black–White Test Score Gap. Brookings Institution Press, Washington, DC.

Kane, T.J. (1994). "College attendance by blacks since 1970: The role of college cost, family background and the returns to education". Journal of Political Economy 102 (5), 878–911.

Kane, T.J. (1996). "College cost, borrowing constraints and the timing of college entry". Eastern Economic Journal 22 (2), 181–194.

Kane, T.J. (1997). "Beyond tax relief: Long-term challenges in financing higher education". National Tax Journal 50 (2), 335–349.

Kane, T.J. (1999). The Price of Admission: Rethinking How Americans Pay for College. Brookings Institution Press (with Russell Sage Foundation), Washington, DC.

Kane, T.J. (2003). "A quasi-experimental estimate of the impact of financial aid on college-going". Working Paper 9703. NBER (May).

Kane, T.J. (2004). "Evaluating the impact of the D.C. tuition assistance grant program". Working Paper 10658. NBER (July).

Kane, T.J., Orszag, P.R., Apostolov, E. (2005). "Higher education appropriations and public universities: The role of Medicaid and the business cycle". In: Brookings–Wharton Papers on Urban Affairs. Brookings Institution Press, Washington, DC, pp. 99–146.

Kane, T.J., Orszag, P.R., Gunter, D.L. (2003). "State fiscal constraints and higher education spending: The role of Medicaid and the business cycle". Urban Institute Brookings Institution Tax Policy Center Discussion Paper No. 11 (May).

Kane, T.J., Rouse, C. (1994). "Labor market returns to two-year and four-year colleges". Working paper, Princeton University Industrial Relations Section.

Katz, L.F., Murphy, K. (1992). "Changes in relative wages, 1963–1987: Supply and demand factors". The Quarterly Journal of Economics 107, 35–78.

Keane, M., Wolpin, K. (2001). "The effect of parental transfers and borrowing constraints on educational attainment". International Economic Review 42 (4), 1051–1103.

Kohn, M., Manski, C., Mundel, D. (1976). "An empirical investigation of factors which influence college-going behavior". Annals of Economic and Social Measures 5, 391–419.

Lang, K. (1993). "Ability bias, discount rate bias and the return to education". Discussion paper. Boston University, Department of Economics (May).

Leslie, L., Brinkman, P.T. (1987). "Student price response in higher education: The student demand studies". Journal of Higher Education 58 (2), 181–204.

Leslie, L., Brinkman, P. (1988). Economic Value of Higher Education. MacMillan, New York.

Levy, F., Murnane, R. (1992). "U.S. earnings levels and earnings inequality: A review of recent trends and proposed explanations". Journal of Economic Literature 30, 1333–1381.

Long, B.T. (2004). "The impact of federal tax credits for higher education expenses". In: Hoxby, C. (Ed.), College Choices: The Economics of Where to Go, When to Go, and How to Pay for It. University of Chicago Press, Chicago, pp. 101–165.

Manski, C.F. (1992–1993). "Income and higher education". Focus 14 (3), 14–19 (University of Wisconsin–Madison, Institute for Research on Poverty).

Manski, C.F., Wise, D.A. (1983). College Choice in America. Harvard University Press, Cambridge, MA.

McPherson, M.S., Schapiro, M.O. (1991). "Does student aid affect college enrollment? New evidence on a persistent controversy". American Economic Review 81, 309–318.

Murphy, K.M., Welch, F. (1992). "The structure of wages". Quarterly Journal of Economics 107 (1), 285–326.

Palmer, J.C. (Ed.) (2005). Grapevine: A National Database of Tax Support for Higher Education. Illinois State Univ. Available at http://www.coe.ilstu.edu/grapevine/50state.htm.

Peltzman, S. (1973). "The effect of government subsidies-in-kind on private expenditures: The case of higher education". The Journal of Political Economy 81 (1), 1–27.

Radner, R., Miller, L.S. (1970). "Demand and supply in U.S. higher education: A progress report". American Economic Review 60, 326–334.

Seftor, N.S., Turner, S.E. (2002). "Back to school: Federal student aid policy and adult college enrollment". Journal of Human Resources 37 (2), 336–352.

Turner, S.E. (2004). "Going to college and finishing college: Explaining different educational outcomes". In: Hoxby, C. (Ed.), College Choices: The Economics of Where to Go, When to Go, and How to Pay for It. University of Chicago Press, Chicago, pp. 13–56.

U.S. Department of Education, NCES (2002). Digest of Education Statictics 2001 (NCES 2002-130), by T.D. Snyder, Project Director, and C.M. Hoffman, Production Manager. Washington, DC, Table 350.

Weiss, A. (1995). "Human capital vs. signaling explanations of wages". Journal of Economic Perspectives 9 (4), 133–154.

Zoghi, C. (2003). "Why have public university professors done so badly?". Economics of Education Review 22 (1), 45–57.

Chapter 24

US HIGHER EDUCATION FINANCE

MICHAEL S. McPHERSON

MORTON OWEN SCHAPIRO

Contents

Handbook of the Economics of Education, Volume 2
Edited by Eric A. Hanushek and Finis Welch
© 2006 Elsevier B.V.   All rights reserved
DOI: 10.1016/S1574-0692(06)02024-1

Abstract

We review basic facts about higher education finance in the United States and analytical, empirical and policy issues in that realm. Examining trends in higher education finance, we demonstrate growth in the share of revenues provided by government up to about 1980, with a steady decline thereafter. Student financial aid, a feature of growing importance, is awarded to students on the basis both of financial need and academic (and other) merit, with merit influencing not only total amounts of aid received but also the "quality" of aid packages, as indexed by the fraction of aid in the form of grants rather than loans or work.

Although nearly two-thirds of American high school graduates now attend some form of post-secondary education, both whether and where they attend are importantly influenced by family background. Among students who score well on aptitude tests in high school, 95% of those from affluent family backgrounds attend college immediately following graduation, while only about 75% of those from low SES backgrounds do. High-income students are also more likely to attend private universities and colleges than are lower-income students, who are particularly likely to attend community colleges.

Much more attention has been devoted to examining the demand for higher education than to explaining its supply. We review a number of topics on the supply side, including the state of evidence concerning the pricing and output levels of government financed and of nonprofit institutions as well as concerning the impact of government financial aid policies on institutional pricing and aid decisions. An important analytical and empirical challenge in studying higher education supply is the fact that institutional enrollment levels are regulated by selective admissions as well as by price.

Keywords

higher education, finance, student aid, college, university

JEL classification: I22

1. Introduction

The American system of finance for higher education (if indeed such a tangled and decentralized set of arrangements warrants the label "system") has a number of characteristics that make it unique in the world. Perhaps most obvious is the stable coexistence of large numbers of private, not-for-profit colleges and universities with a substantial set of government-owned institutions – the latter themselves decentralized through ownership by states and (in the case of community colleges) sometimes localities. Interestingly, while the share of public colleges in total enrollments grew more or less continuously through the first three quarters of the twentieth century, since then it has stabilized at approximately 80% of total enrollment [Goldin and Katz (1999)].

Also distinctive is the enormous range of institutional types offered in US postsecondary education. The system includes large public and private research universities that combine substantial, largely federally funded research enterprises with extensive graduate and professional educational programs and undergraduate education in one complex. This arrangement contrasts strikingly with that in many other countries, where there is often more separation of advanced research from teaching and of professional schools from undergraduate education. Moreover, the United States was the progenitor and is still the principal home of the traditional "liberal arts college", providing general undergraduate education, usually in a residential setting, and often to a selected group of students. Finally, there is a small but growing segment of for-profit institutions, focused mostly on the large market for adult, vocationally oriented students (in 1999–2000, only about 5.5% of first-time, full-time undergraduates attended for-profit colleges that were eligible for federal student aid [U.S. Department of Education (2002b)].

It is generally accepted in the United States, unlike many countries, that the cost of higher education will be shared among a group of payers, including the student, his or her family (at least for traditional-aged students), government and philanthropists. Subsidies come in a variety of forms, including direct appropriations by governments to public colleges and universities to defray expenses, analogous subsidies through endowment earnings and gifts at private nonprofit institutions, and financial assistance to students in the form of loans and gifts. Most recently, the federal government has introduced significant tax credits for college tuition.

Student aid has become a strikingly important institutional feature of American higher education finance. In addition to federal loans and grants, aid comes from state governments, philanthropic organizations and the colleges and universities themselves. In 1999–2000, more than 64% of public college students and more than 81% of private not-for-private college students received some form of financial aid (beyond support from their families) in paying for college [U.S. Department of Education (2002b)]. Not unlike airlines, different students at the same college often pay very different prices for their education.

The various subsidies to higher education presumably reflect some broad collective judgment that higher education provides both private benefits to individual students and broader social benefits, so that both fairness and efficiency argue for sharing the costs between students and larger social groups.[1] In addition, some subsidies are shaped by the widely-held view that equality of educational opportunity is a valid social aim, leading to a further case for subsidizing the college costs of disadvantaged students.

An important efficiency consideration in helping students pay for college is that there is reason to expect capital market failure in the case of human capital investments. As classically argued by Milton Friedman (1955), unlike investments in physical capital, investments in human capital cannot be secured by the asset that is acquired without running afoul of laws against involuntary servitude. The aim to overcome this capital market imperfection helps to rationalize the extensive federal programs of loan guarantees and in recent years direct loans by the federal government to help finance education. Economists have long seen the attraction of "income-contingent" loans, which would come closer to equity finance of human capital, by allowing lenders to share in the income gains that result from education. Although such loans have become an important feature of college finance in some countries, they have not to date figured importantly in US college finance [Johnstone (2001)].

The complex pattern of subsidies in American higher education reflects not only judgments about the social good, but also the presence of large numbers of competing institutions (both public and private) for whom student aid provides opportunities to advance institutional goals. From an economic perspective, institutional awards of student aid can be viewed as a form of price discrimination, with lower prices offered to those "customers" whose demand is more price-elastic and those who, for one reason or another, are more desirable to the institution [see, for example, Ehrenberg and Sherman (1984)]. Presumably student aid policies at both private and not-for-profit institutions reflect a mixture of principled and self-interested motivations.

Although American colleges and universities undertake significant amounts of research and graduate and professional education, by far their main business is educating undergraduates. (Only about 14% of total enrollment in degree-granting colleges and universities is at the graduate or professional level [U.S. Department of Education (2002b)]. According to Table 8 (see Section 5), only about 13% of total revenues in higher education come from externally supported research.) While not altogether neglecting issues about graduate education and research, this essay is organized mainly around that principal business of undergraduate education. In what follows, we first provide a broad overview of time trends in American higher education finance, and then focus on the important issue of student aid, both "need" and "merit" based, in student finance. The implications of student finance trends for access to college and choice of colleges are our next topic. We then examine evidence on the sources and uses of revenues and expenditures in the various types of American colleges and universities. We devote a further section to analysis of the supply behavior of colleges and universities, a difficult but important subject for research. After a brief overview of other areas of research, we offer conclusions.

---

[1] A classic statement of the public benefits of higher education (as well as nonpecuniary private benefits) is Bowen (1977).

2. Financing higher education: Changes over time

Tables 1 and 2 present a long-run view on college finance, containing data from selected years between 1939 and 2000. Table 1 shows how colleges' principal sources of revenue have changed over the past half century.[2] For public institutions, state and local government spending has been the primary revenue source (accounting for more than half of revenues), with tuition providing a much smaller share (no more than a quarter of revenues). On the other hand, for private institutions, tuition has by far been the principal source of revenue (accounting for between 43% and 57% of revenues).

This long view allows us to put recent changes in historical perspective. For public institutions, the contribution of state and local government spending has been declining for more than a decade, reaching its lowest post-war level (51%) in the two most recent academic years for which we report data. While there has been an increase in the contribution of gifts and endowment earnings (from 3% to 7%), a much more important change has been the increased role of tuition (from 13% to 24%). Tuition at private institutions has also taken its largest role in forty years (going from 45% in 1955–1956 to 55% in 1995–1996) as the contribution of federal funding has declined to its lowest level since the late 1950s (falling from a peak of 30% in 1965–1966 to 17% in 1995–1996).

The pattern here is clear: tuition has been replacing government spending at both public and private institutions. Indeed, the pattern of revenue shares in the 1990s looks more like that of the late 1940s than of any intervening decade.

Table 2 reports revenue shares for the major categories given in Table 1, averaged over public and private institutions, and also breaks down gross tuition by its sources – showing the share paid by families directly and the shares paid by various forms of student aid.

The most striking trend is the steady decline through 1980 in the overall share of tuition paid by families, the result of an increase in the enrollment share of public institutions, the growth of federal grants and contracts, and the rise in financial aid. However, the decline in the share of higher education revenues provided by families came to an abrupt halt in the 1980s, with the family share increasing by 10 percentage points in the 1979–1980 to 1995–1996 period [reaching the highest level (24%) since before 1959–1960].

Table 2 also underscores that it is the states rather than the federal government whose role is changing most dramatically. As late as 1979–1980, state governments contributed 45% of higher education revenues, almost all of it through direct (nontuition) support of state-run institutions. By 1995–1996 that share had fallen to 33%. The efficiency and equity of the across-the-board subsidies states provide to higher education institutions have long been questions of controversy among economists. In a famous and influential

---

[2] Revenues from dormitories, hospitals and other "auxiliary enterprises" are excluded, as well as several minor revenue sources. Changes in accounting rules for private institutions make data for 1996–1997 and later not comparable with earlier years or across sectors.

Table 1
Shares of higher education revenue, by source, by sector, selected academic years, 1939–2000 (%)

| Year | Gross tuition | Government | | Gifts and endowment earnings | Other |
		Federal	State and local		
Public institutions					
1939–1940	0.20	0.13	0.61	0.04	0.01
1949–1950	0.25	0.13	0.56	0.03	0.03
1955–1956	0.13	0.17	0.62	0.04	0.04
1959–1960	0.13	0.21	0.59	0.04	0.03
1965–1966	0.14	0.23	0.54	0.03	0.05
1969–1970	0.15	0.19	0.57	0.03	0.05
1975–1976	0.16	0.18	0.61	0.03	0.02
1979–1980	0.15	0.16	0.62	0.04	0.03
1985–1986	0.18	0.13	0.61	0.05	0.03
1989–1990	0.20	0.13	0.58	0.05	0.04
1991–1992	0.22	0.14	0.55	0.06	0.03
1992–1993	0.24	0.14	0.53	0.06	0.04
1993–1994	0.24	0.14	0.52	0.06	0.04
1994–1995	0.24	0.14	0.52	0.06	0.04
1995–1996	0.24	0.14	0.51	0.06	0.04
1999–2000	0.24	0.13	0.51	0.07	0.05
Private institutions					
1939–1940	0.55	0.01	0.03	0.38	0.03
1949–1950	0.57	0.12	0.04	0.23	0.05
1955–1956	0.45	0.18	0.02	0.28	0.06
1959–1960	0.43	0.25	0.02	0.25	0.05
1965–1966	0.43	0.30	0.02	0.18	0.06
1969–1970	0.44	0.26	0.03	0.19	0.08
1975–1976	0.48	0.25	0.04	0.19	0.04
1979–1980	0.47	0.25	0.04	0.19	0.05
1985–1986	0.50	0.22	0.03	0.19	0.06
1989–1990	0.51	0.21	0.04	0.18	0.06
1991–1992	0.53	0.20	0.04	0.17	0.06
1992–1993	0.54	0.19	0.04	0.17	0.06
1993–1994	0.55	0.19	0.04	0.17	0.06
1994–1995	0.55	0.19	0.03	0.17	0.06
1995–1996	0.55	0.17	0.03	0.18	0.07

Notes. Figures do not include revenue from auxiliary enterprises or from sales and services. Government figures do not include student aid (which is included under gross tuition). The federal government changed the reporting scheme for private colleges and universities for financial data in the IPEDS system in 1996–1997, in response to changes in accounting standards. These changes do not permit comparisons of data from that date forward with earlier data.

Sources: See McPherson and Schapiro (1991a, p. 21), plus, for data after 1986, Table 328 (p. 359) and Table 329 (p. 360) of the *Digest of Education Statistics, 2001*, National Center for Education Statistics (2002b) (online version, January 2001) and U.S. Department of Education (2002a).

Table 2

Shares of higher education revenue, by source, selected academic years, 1939–1996 (%)

Year	Gross tuition	Tuition paid by				Nontuition revenue		
		Families	Institutions	Government		Federal	State and local	Gifts and endowment earnings
				Federal	State			
1939–1940	0.37	0.35	0.02	0.00	0.00	0.07	0.33	0.21
1949–1950	0.40	0.37	0.03	0.00	0.00	0.12	0.32	0.12
1959–1960	0.26	0.22	0.03	0.00	0.01	0.23	0.34	0.13
1965–1966	0.26	0.21	0.04	0.00	0.01	0.26	0.33	0.09
1969–1970	0.25	0.20	0.04	0.00	0.01	0.22	0.38	0.08
1975–1976	0.26	0.16	0.04	0.04	0.02	0.20	0.43	0.08
1979–1980	0.26	0.14	0.04	0.06	0.02	0.19	0.43	0.09
1985–1986	0.29	0.17	0.05	0.05	0.02	0.16	0.41	0.10
1989–1990	0.31	0.19	0.05	0.05	0.02	0.16	0.37	0.10
1991–1992	0.34	0.22	0.05	0.05	0.02	0.16	0.35	0.10
1992–1993	0.35	0.23	0.05	0.05	0.02	0.16	0.33	0.10
1993–1994	0.35	0.22	0.06	0.05	0.02	0.16	0.32	0.10
1994–1995	0.35	0.23	0.06	0.04	0.02	0.16	0.32	0.10
1995–1996	0.36	0.24	0.06	0.04	0.02	0.15	0.31	0.11

Notes. Figures do not include revenue from auxiliary enterprises or from sales and services. Both veteran's educational benefits and social security benefits paid to qualified college students are excluded from federal tuition payments.

Sources: See McPherson and Schapiro (1991a, p. 23), plus, for data after 1986, Table 327 (p. 358) of the *Digest of Education Statistics, 2001*, National Center for Education Statistics (2002b) (online version, January 2001) and Table 1 (p. 6) of *Trends in Student Aid: 2000*, the College Board (2002).

paper, Hansen and Weisbrod (1969) argued that such subsidies were regressive, in that benefits flowed disproportionately to more affluent families who received benefits that far exceeded the costs they paid through the tax system. Pechman (1970) countered by arguing that, aggregating over all taxpayers, whether they had children in college or not, the affluent paid taxes far exceeding the costs of their participation in the higher education system, while less affluent groups of taxpayers wound up with benefits from higher education that exceeded the taxes they paid to support the system. In a lucid comment on the controversy, Hartman (1970) contended that neither of these simple calculations is adequate to judge the relative effectiveness of different schemes for financing higher education, from the standpoints either of equity or efficiency.

It is noteworthy that, even though states' economic fortunes improved considerably during the years between the recession of the early 1990s and the recession ten years later, the downward trend in the share of higher education revenues provided by the states continued during the entire period for which we have data. Several analyses suggest that this secular decline in state support for higher education relative to other state-financed activities will prove persistent [Hovey (1999)]. The reliance on state operating subsidies leaves public colleges and universities extremely vulnerable to the business cycle. The current devastation regarding state budgets implies very difficult times ahead. Arnone, Hebel and Schmidt (2003) report that institutions are seeking to aggressively raise tuition while bracing themselves for layoffs and program cuts. It is expected that about half of the states will cut higher education appropriations for the current fiscal year (2002–2003), and that 2003–2004 will be even worse.

The share of revenues supplied by federal student aid has remained roughly constant since the mid-1970s, but the share provided by federal research support has declined substantially (from 26% to 15%) from its high in the mid-1960s. Since research support is concentrated in a fairly small number of institutions, this decline is of major importance for that subgroup.

We turn now to a detailed look at changes in the sources of financial aid. Table 3 shows the overall magnitudes of federal and other forms of student aid, expressed in constant 2001–2002 academic year dollars, for selected years since 1963. With respect to how federal funding has developed, the period from 1963 to the present can be usefully divided into four subperiods. For most of its history, the federal government, as a matter of policy, did not help fund undergraduate education on a regular basis, viewing it as the province of the states and of private philanthropy. The federal government purchased services in the form of research contracts and provided aid to veterans in recognition of their service, but had no sustained programs of aid until the National Defense Education Act introduced loans (now called Perkins loans) in 1957. Guaranteed loans and grants to colleges to be awarded to needy students were introduced in 1965. Thus, before 1975, a fairly modest total of "generally available" aid was divided between guaranteed loans and the so-called "campus-based" programs, which provide funds for institutions to use for student aid in the form of grants, loans and work. From 1975 to 1980, the generally available federal aid budget grew rapidly (doubling in real dollars between 1975–1976 and 1980–1981), with substantial expenditures on the newly introduced Pell program, the means-tested grant program put in place under the Nixon administration in 1974 (under the name Basic Educational Opportunity Grants). From 1980 to the early 1990s, both the Pell program and guaranteed loans increased at a slower rate (with a real increase of about one third in each). Since that time, growth in guaranteed and direct loans has been enormous (having more than doubled in real dollars between 1990–1991 and 2001–2002), while expenditures on the Pell program have risen by a significant but more modest 52% in real dollars. Thus, while total federal aid in 2001–2002 totaled $62.0 billion, up from only $28.1 billion in 1990–1991 (in 2001–2002 dollars), the vast majority of this increase was in the form of loans. Moreover, most of the increase in federal spending unrelated to loans was not in the form of grants aimed at students from low-income families, but rather was attributed to the introduction in 2000 of education tax credits that have disproportionately benefited more affluent families.[3]

---

[3] A GAO study released in September of 2002 [U.S. Department of Education (2002b)] examined the distribution of benefits from the Hope and Lifelong Learning credits enacted in 1997. The Hope credit is aimed at

Table 3

Aid awarded to students, by source of aid, selected academic years, 1963–2002, in millions of 2001–2002 academic year dollars

Federal programs	1963–1964	1970–1971	1975–1976	1980–1981	1985–1986	1990–1991	1995–1996	2000–2001	2001–2002
Generally available aid									
Pell grants	0	0	2,964	4,892	5,869	6,542	6,287	8,066	9,950
Supplemental educational opportunity grants	0	736	769	756	671	607	670	630	691
State student incentive grants	0	0	63	148	124	78	74	38	50
Work–study	0	895	944	1,353	1,070	965	877	1,139	1,215
Perkins loans	654	1,075	1,472	1,421	1,147	1,154	1,182	1,073	1,113
Guaranteed and direct loans	0	4,536	4,056	12,710	14,419	16,794	31,742	38,533	41,275
Subtotal	654	7,241	10,268	21,280	23,300	26,147	40,832	49,478	54,295
Specially directed aid									
Social security	0	2,230	3,499	3,859	0	0	0	0	0
Veterans	386	5,009	13,380	3,513	1,409	900	1,497	1,667	1,714
Military	240	288	310	411	559	489	503	567	619
Other grants	52	71	202	250	110	156	264	256	270
Other loans	0	187	144	127	608	457	374	110	110
Subtotal	678	7,786	17,534	8,160	2,685	2,002	2,637	2,599	2,714
Education tax credits	0	0	0	0	0	0	0	4,953	5,001
Total federal aid	1,332	15,027	27,802	29,440	25,985	28,149	43,470	57,030	62,010
State grant programs	322	1,055	1,568	1,641	2,138	2,465	3,447	4,835	5,048
Institutional and other grants	1,552	3,739	3,741	3,329	4,832	7,637	10,301	15,475	16,978
Nonfederal loans	0	0	0	0	0	0	1,532	4,165	5,588
Total federal, state and institutional aid	3,206	19,821	33,111	34,411	32,955	38,251	58,749	81,506	89,624

Note. 2000–2001 data are estimated and 2001–2002 data are preliminary.

Source: Trends in Student Aid: 2002, The College Board (2002), Tables 2 (p. 7) and B (p. 19).

The real value of state grants has followed a positive trend throughout the entire period. The College Board (2002, p. 16), reports that the percent of total state aid not based on need was flat at 10% between 1981 and 1993, at which time it began its steep rise to almost 25% in 2000. Thus, the surge in need-based aid has been dwarfed in percentage terms by the increase in merit aid, although in absolute terms need-based state grants still exceed merit-based grants substantially.

The absolute increase in state-funded grants has been dwarfed by the growth in institutional grants. The real value of institutional grants has gone up by more than five-fold over the past few decades, rising from $3.3 billion in 1980–1981 (in 2001–2002 dollars) to $17.0 billion in 2001–2002. These institutional grants are, in effect, discounts from posted tuition. Their changing role has received much attention, and will be further discussed in the next section. In total, financial aid has grown at a staggering rate, especially after 1990. But that does not necessarily imply that needy students have been "held harmless" from tuition increases. The combination of tax credits, guaranteed and direct loans from the federal government, and non-federal loans account for most of the increase, while both state and institutional grants have increasingly been allocated on the basis of "merit" as opposed to need. With almost $90 billion in total aid, rather little of it is in the form of grants to students from low-income families.

3. Merit versus need-based financial aid

The phenomenon of "merit aid" or "nonneed-based" aid has come in for increasing commentary in American higher education. A number of observers (including the authors) have argued that the growing significance of merit aid is an indicator of the rising competitive pressures on colleges and universities, and is one factor undermining the commitment to the principle of pricing a college education according to family ability to pay.

The distinction between "need-based" and "nonneed-based" student aid grants is, however, a slippery one. Normal practice at American colleges is to present a prospective student with a "package" of aid, generally including some combination of federal, state and institutional grant, a recommended loan, and a work–study job. Many students who receive need-based assistance from a college will also receive a "merit award" which is included in the student's overall aid package. Sometimes such a merit award will boost that student's total grant dollars above those of another student with similar means who did not get any "merit" award, but in other cases the school may simply be putting a different "merit" label on dollars the student would have gotten anyway.

---

freshman and sophomores and is worth a maximum of $1,500 per year. The Lifelong Learning credit is aimed at juniors and seniors as well as graduate students and part-time undergraduates, and provides a maximum of $1,000 per year. The GAO found that in 1999–2000, around two thirds of students awarded Hope credits, and around 70% of those receiving Lifelong Learning credits, were from families earning $60,000 or more. See also Long (2004).

Avery and Hoxby (2004) present evidence that student choices are in fact influenced by the labels attached to aid dollars. By the same token, two students at the same college, both receiving only need-based aid, may receive quite different aid packages. The more desirable student may receive either a larger total aid package or a similar total aid package with a larger component of grant aid and lower amounts of loan and work. And this can happen without any of the dollars being labeled "merit" dollars.

In other work [McPherson and Schapiro (2002)], we have attempted to look beyond the "merit" and "need" labels to provide empirical evidence on the sensitivity of aid awards to both "need" and "merit", understood as evidence of academic achievement or potential. Our results indicate that a focus simply on dollars labeled as "merit" scholarships misses a good deal of the action regarding the responsiveness of grant awards to indicators of merit. Relatively few students receive awards that are explicitly labeled as "nonneed-based" or "merit" awards (in the data set we examined, for example, only 4% of undergraduates at public colleges and 15% at private colleges receive such awards from institutional funds – these figures exclude athletic scholarships), while many more receive "need-based" awards (22% at public colleges and 52% at private colleges).

Yet in an analysis seeking to explain the size of aid grants that students receive, we find that the size of a student's *need*-based grants varies significantly with the student's score on standardized tests, after controlling for such factors as the type of school attended, parental resources and cost of attendance. Moreover, the size of these need-based grants is less sensitive to family financial resources than standard need analysis formulas would imply. Thus, a focus solely on so-called "nonneed" or "merit" aid significantly understates the role that academic promise and achievement play in the distribution of institutional grant aid.

Even apart from this sensitivity of need-based awards to indicators of merit, there is ample evidence that merit awards have grown in importance in student finance of higher education. Growth in merit awards relative to need-based awards has been observed in public and in private institutions, as well as in state grant programs [U.S. Department of Education (2002b), Heller (2003)]. A variety of factors probably help explain this trend. For both public and private institutions, enrolling more talented students offers potential benefits of at least two kinds. First, peer effects may imply that the education of all students at an institution is improved by the presence of more talented students [see Winston and Zimmerman (2004)]. Second, the measured quality of entering students is a major factor in assessing an institution's reputation, for example in US News' influential college rankings, whether because of true peer effects or for other reasons. Schools may value these reputational effects because they increase demand for their education [Ehrenberg and Monks (1999)] or because they please trustees and institutional leaders or, for public institutions, legislators. Ehrenberg and Sherman (1984) provide a systematic analysis of optimal aid award policies for an institution facing a set of potential applicants who differ in desirability to the school and in price elasticity of demand for enrollment.

Competition among institutions for "meritorious" students obviously amplifies these forces. [For a journalistic account of competitive discounting among colleges, see

Crenshaw (2002).] Particularly in light of the fact that reputational competition is inherently relative, the competitive environment has some of the characteristics of a tournament. Frank and Cook (1995) and Frank (1999) have argued that merit aid competition helps encourage the concentration of top students at a small set of institutions, and has the qualities of a "winner-take-all" competition.

Growing use of merit aid raises interesting questions of public policy.[4] First, there is a persistent tendency in state and to some extent in federal policy discussions to argue for introduction of more "merit-based" aid programs on the grounds that existing programs do not give students significant incentives to perform well in high school. The results from our study mentioned above suggest that there already are considerable financial awards to achievement – for those students who receive financial aid at public institutions, a 100 point difference in SAT scores translates into an increase in grant aid equal to nearly $500 over the course of an undergraduate career. At private institutions, a 100 point SAT increase translates into more than $2,300 in added grants over the course of a college career. These appear to be significant incentives. When one recognizes the additional benefits of improving one's probability of attending a more selective college through performing better in high school, the fact that our admissions and aid system as it exists does indeed reward high school achievement is clear.

A second question is whether efforts by institutions to limit or regulate merit competition are socially desirable and/or legally permissible. In the early 1990s, the Justice Department investigated a group of Northeastern private colleges and universities whose financial aid officers met to agree on the size of aid awards to be offered to individual students. All but one of the schools involved agreed to a consent decree ending the practice. MIT however declined to settle and was sued. The Justice Department alleged that these so-called "overlap" agreements were a conspiracy in restraint of trade and harmed students who might have received larger aid awards in a competitive setting. MIT argued, among other things, that the practice of constraining aid awards helped the colleges involved to achieve the desirable public purpose of allocating their limited aid resources to those most in need of them. The case was ultimately settled out of court without a definitive ruling on the merits [see Carlton, Bamberger and Epstein (1995)]. Hoxby (2000) presents evidence that the ending of the agreements among colleges brought about by the Justice Department action resulted in a partial breakdown of the need-based aid system at several of the colleges.

A broader question raised by the "merit vs. need" controversy relates to the consequences for educational productivity of stratifying students by "aptitude" or "ability". It seems plausible that a given student will learn more if he or she is paired with more able rather than less able peers, although it is only recently that researchers have begun to aim at establishing such effects [see, for example, Winston and Zimmerman (2004)].

---

[4] For recent discussions of policy issues regarding merit scholarships, see a dialogue between Gary Orfield and David Longanecker [Longanecker and Orfield (2003)]. See also Selingo (2001, 2002) and two *New York Times* pieces, Winter (2002) and a *New York Times* (2002) editorial on November 4.

If peer effects exist and take this form, any one school can raise its educational output by attracting more able students. But is the learning output of the group of colleges taken together higher or lower if students are stratified by ability or if students of differing abilities are mixed together? The answer to this question depends on the shape of the function relating the performance of a student to the quality of his or her peers. We are far from having any empirically satisfactory answer to this question, nor is it at all clear whether market competition for students of differing ability will lead to an optimal result [see also Rothschild and White (1995) and McPherson and Schapiro (1998, 2002)].

4. College access and choice

Many worry about a run-up in the real costs to students of attending college, even after allowing for the effects of financial aid. The access consequences of substantial increases in college costs are well known – one simple indicator is that gaps in enrollment rates by race and by income are larger now than they were in the late 1970s. This is not surprising given empirical estimates of the enrollment responsiveness of low-income students to changes in price [see, for example, McPherson, Schapiro and Winston (1993, Chapter 8), McPherson and Schapiro (1991a, Chapter 3), McPherson and Schapiro (1991b) and Kane (1999)].

Another aspect to the access story considers student ability along with income background. Low-income students on average are less likely to participate in American higher education, but what about the most talented low-income students? It has long been a goal of federal policy to break the link between family background and college enrollment, especially for students with the motivation and ability to succeed in college.

Table 4 examines enrollment data from four different dates, with students broken down into three family income groups and, except for the most recent year, into four ability groups. For 1994, only three ability groups were distinguished.

In 1994, 38% of students from the bottom ability group attended higher education compared with 63% of students from the middle ability group and 87% from the upper ability group. That finding seems reasonable – most people would agree that students with the highest demonstrated ability should have the greatest propensity to participate in further education. But it is striking that 64% of the low ability students from high-income families proceed to colleges and universities versus only 29% of their low-income counterparts. Further evidence of unequal opportunity is provided by the finding that only 49% of middle-ability students from low-income families and 75% of high-ability students from low-income families advance to postsecondary training – compared with 81% and 95% of students from the high-income group. The fact that one out of four high-ability students from low-income backgrounds find no place among our roughly 3,500 colleges and universities seems undesirable from the standpoint of economic efficiency as well as equality of opportunity.

Table 4
College enrollment rates by family background and student ability, selected years

Year	Test score group	Family income (%)			
		Low	Middle	High	All
1961–1963	1	14	24	42	
	2	24	36	55	
	3	38	51	77	
	4	60	77	91	
1972	1	18	21	35	
	2	25	35	53	
	3	38	51	72	
	4	58	68	84	
1980	1	21	26	40	
	2	31	39	68	
	3	47	59	77	
	4	58	76	86	
1994	1	29	47	64	38
	2	49	68	81	63
	3	75	86	95	87
	All	44	69	86	

Notes. Data for 1961–1963, 1972 and 1980 are from Project Talent, National Longitudinal Study, and High School and Beyond, as compiled in the Eureka Project (1988, p. 35). Data for 1994 are from the National Education Longitudinal Study, as reported in Akerhielm et al. (1998, p. 19).

Even when entry into one of America's higher education institutions does in fact take place, it is important to recognize that these institutions provide widely differing experiences. While the emphasis on access is well founded, many analyses neglect key questions regarding college choice.

When we consider the topic of educational opportunity, we should instead take into account both the issue of the accessibility of higher education to lower-income students and the overall distribution of students across institutional types. Despite the concerns we have about the impact on access of the recent rise in net college costs facing low-income students, the high overall rates of college attendance in recent years point to considerable success in making *some* form of post-secondary education financially accessible to a very wide range of Americans. Yet the existing financing system may be much less successful in providing a *suitable* post-secondary experience for many disadvantaged students. The range of alternatives available to students appears to be quite sharply constrained by their incomes under existing arrangements. In most states community colleges are the cheapest and most accessible alternative for low-income students, a fact which is reflected in their disproportionate representation in these institutions. Although the issue of "choice" is often expressed in terms of public versus private alternatives, opportunity to attend a flagship public university or indeed any four year public institution is importantly constrained by income in many states.

It is interesting to note that much of the popular discussion regarding where students go involves middle-income students, not lower-income students. It is often suspected that students from middle-income backgrounds have been most affected by the considerable real increases in tuition at private colleges and universities. Students from lower-income backgrounds qualify for need-based financial aid, lessening the chance that these students experience an affordability problem. Students from upper income backgrounds receive a different but analogous form of financial aid – parental contributions that do not require major proportions of available annual incomes. But, the story goes, when tuitions rise faster than other economic indicators, students from middle-income backgrounds are forced to switch to less costly educational alternatives. In fact, for more than a decade the view that middle-income students – too rich for financial aid but too poor to afford private school tuitions – are increasingly showing up at public institutions has been stated as truth in the national media [see, for example, Kuttner (1989)].

We now examine changes over time in the higher education destinations for students from different economic backgrounds. This allows us to consider not only the "middle-income melt" topic, but also to examine the broader question of who goes where and how that compares with more than a decade ago.

Table 5 presents data on the distribution of students from different income backgrounds across institutional types. The institutional types are private universities (typically large institutions with substantial graduate and research programs), private four-year colleges (typically small, liberal arts colleges), private two-year colleges (a collection of mainly religious, business, and art colleges), public universities (again, large graduate universities), public four-year colleges (typically branches of public universities other than the "flagship" campus – for example, the branches of the California State University system, the University of Michigan at Dearborn, the University of Wisconsin at Stout) and public two-year colleges (community colleges). In addition, categories are subdivided based on institutional selectivity.

In 1999, 25.9% of students in our sample attended private institutions, roughly the same as in 1981. But it is clear that the percentage of students attending private schools in 1999 varied considerably with income: 21.0% of lower-income students attended private colleges and universities, a figure that rises to 22.8% for middle-income students, and all the way to 51.7% for the richest students. Only 2.8% of all lower-income students enrolled in higher education were at private universities, with 14.5% at private four-year colleges. On the other hand, 21.7% of the richest students enrolled in higher education were at private universities and 26.5% were at private four-year colleges. Middle-income students had intermediate enrollment percentages of 3.8% and 16.6%. While the chances that a student attended a public university were generally positively related to parent's income there was not a clear relationship between income and attendance at a public four-year college.

Perhaps the most striking finding is that 38.7% of upper income and 47.0% of students from the most affluent backgrounds attended a university (private or public), compared with only 16.6% of lower-income students. Where did lower-income students disproportionately enroll? 39.0% of lower-income students were at public two-year colleges, more than twice the percentage of upper-income students (16.8%) and almost four times the percentage of the richest students (10.1%).

How have these proportions changed over time? Comparing 1999 to 1981, the percentage of upper-income students who attended either private or public universities rose a bit from 37.2% to 38.7% while the percentage of the richest students who attended a university rose from 41.4% to 47.0%. While private universities more than held their own in their ability to attract affluent students, the increased attractiveness of public universities to affluent students is particularly noteworthy: their share of upper-income students rose from 25.9% to 27.5% and their share of the richest students rose from 22.8% to 25.3%.

It was private four-year colleges that have suffered the loss of affluent students in recent years – the proportion of upper-income students who enrolled at these schools fell slightly from 21.9% to 21.1% while the proportion of the richest students fell much more dramatically from 32.4% to 26.5%. On the other hand, there is no evidence from these data supporting the notion of "middle-income melt" from either private universities or private four-year colleges. In 1981, 14.9% of middle-income students and 16.3%

Table 5

Distribution of freshman enrollment by income background across institutional types, fall of 1981 versus fall of 1999 (%)

	Lower	Lower-middle	Middle	Upper-middle	Upper	Richest	All groups
1999	<$20	$20–$30	$30–$60	$60–$100	$100–$200	>$200	
Private university	2.8	3.1	3.8	5.4	11.2	21.7	5.9
Low select	(1.4)	(1.5)	(1.7)	(2.1)	(3.3)	(4.6)	(2.1)
Medium select	(0.6)	(0.6)	(0.8)	(1.3)	(2.9)	(5.9)	(1.4)
High select	(0.9)	(1.0)	(1.2)	(2.0)	(5.0)	(11.2)	(2.4)
4-year colleges	14.5	14.9	16.6	17.6	21.1	26.5	17.6
Low select	(11.4)	(11.7)	(12.5)	(12.3)	(12.5)	(12.9)	(12.3)
Medium select	(2.3)	(2.5)	(3.2)	(4.1)	(5.8)	(7.9)	(3.8)
High select	(0.8)	(0.7)	(0.9)	(1.3)	(2.8)	(5.7)	(1.4)
2-year colleges	3.7	2.7	2.4	1.8	2.2	3.5	2.4
All private	21.0	20.7	22.8	24.9	34.5	51.7	25.9
Public university	13.8	16.2	17.3	22.1	27.5	25.3	19.9
Low select	(4.9)	(6.3)	(6.8)	(8.4)	(9.2)	(7.9)	(7.3)
Medium select	(4.9)	(6.4)	(7.3)	(9.0)	(10.1)	(8.8)	(7.9)
High select	(4.1)	(3.4)	(3.3)	(4.8)	(8.2)	(8.6)	(4.7)
4-year colleges	26.2	24.3	24.4	23.3	21.2	12.9	23.3
Low select	(24.2)	(22.4)	(20.8)	(19.6)	(16.9)	(10.1)	(20.0)
Medium select	(2.0)	(2.0)	(3.6)	(3.7)	(4.3)	(2.9)	(3.3)
2-year colleges	39.0	38.8	35.5	29.8	16.8	10.1	30.9
All public	79.0	79.3	77.2	75.1	65.5	48.3	74.1
	100.0	100.0	100.0	100.0	100.0	100.0	100.0

Table 5
(*Continued*)

	Lower	Lower-middle	Middle	Upper-middle	Upper	Richest	All groups
1981	<$10	$10–$15	$15–$30	$30–$50	$50–$100	>$100	
Private university	2.2	2.7	3.2	5.4	11.3	18.6	4.8
Low select	(1.3)	(1.4)	(1.5)	(1.8)	(3.0)	(4.6)	(1.7)
Medium select	(0.5)	(0.7)	(0.9)	(1.6)	(3.1)	(4.4)	(1.3)
High select	(0.4)	(0.6)	(0.9)	(2.0)	(5.1)	(9.6)	(1.7)
4-year colleges	13.6	15.0	14.9	16.3	21.9	32.4	16.2
Low select	(11.6)	(12.2)	(11.3)	(10.8)	(12.6)	(17.1)	(11.7)
Medium select	(1.6)	(2.3)	(3.0)	(4.2)	(5.8)	(9.5)	(3.5)
High select	(0.4)	(0.5)	(0.6)	(1.3)	(3.4)	(5.8)	(1.1)
2-year colleges	6.2	5.5	4.2	3.6	3.5	3.0	4.3
All private	22.0	23.2	22.3	25.3	36.7	54.0	25.3
Public university	10.1	12.9	16.1	22.0	25.9	22.8	17.7
Low select	(4.2)	(5.0)	(6.2)	(8.2)	(9.7)	(9.2)	(6.8)
Medium select	(3.7)	(5.4)	(6.5)	(8.9)	(10.0)	(8.4)	(7.1)
High select	(2.2)	(2.6)	(3.3)	(4.8)	(6.3)	(5.1)	(3.8)
4-year colleges	23.4	22.5	22.2	21.6	16.9	10.0	21.4
Low select	(22.2)	(20.8)	(18.9)	(17.9)	(13.7)	(8.5)	(18.5)
Medium select	(1.2)	(1.7)	(3.3)	(3.7)	(3.2)	(1.5)	(2.9)
2-year colleges	44.6	41.4	39.3	31.2	20.4	13.2	35.6
All public	78.0	76.8	77.7	74.7	63.3	46.0	74.7
	100.0	100.0	100.0	100.0	100.0	100.0	100.0

Notes. The survey of freshmen in 1999 reflected family income in the 1998 calendar year while the survey of freshmen in 1981 reflected family income in the 1980 calendar year. Inflation between 1980 and 1998 equaled 97.9%. Inflation-adjusted income brackets for the 1981 survey would be as follows: less than $10.1, $10.1–$15.2, $15.2–$30.3, $30.3–$50.5, $50.5–$101.1 and more than $101.1. The selectivity definitions vary somewhat across institutional categories. We define low selectivity as having the following SAT ranges: less than 1050 for private universities, less than 1025 for private nonsectarian 4-year colleges, less than 1050 for protestant 4-year colleges, less than 1025 for Catholic 4-year colleges, less than 1000 for public universities, and less than 1025 for public 4-year colleges. We define medium selectivity as having the following SAT ranges: 1050–1174 for private universities, 1025–1174 for private nonsectarian 4-year colleges, more than 1049 for protestant 4-year colleges, more than 1024 for Catholic 4-year colleges, 1000–1099 for public universities and more than 1024 for public 4-year colleges. We define high selectivity as having the following SAT ranges: more than 1174 for private universities, more than 1174 for private nonsectarian 4-year colleges and more than 1099 for public universities.
Source: Calculated from results from *The American Freshman Survey*.

of upper-middle-income students were enrolled at private four-year colleges and universities; in 1999, 16.6% of middle-income students and 17.6% of upper-middle-income students were in those institutions. Although leaders at private liberal arts colleges have been vocal in talking about middle-income melt, it appears that what they have experienced is in fact upper income melt. It seems likely that this loss of full-pay students is a significant part of the explanation for the growing interest of these schools in reviewing their student aid policies and entering into merit aid competition.

Why has this generation of affluent students found private liberal arts colleges to be a less attractive option that it was in the past? Some argue that the phenomenon of "brand-name" identification that became such an important part of American consumerism in recent decades has also taken hold in higher education, with students leaving small, usually regional private colleges for larger and better known universities. In fact, it is interesting to note that the breakdowns by selectivity show that it was the low selectivity private four-year colleges that absorbed the largest loss of the richest students – their percentage fell from 17.1% to 12.9% while the share of the richest students attending high selectivity private four-year colleges stayed about the same. Even for private universities, which did better in attracting the richest students in 1999 than in 1981, the increases were all at medium and high selectivity schools rather than at low selectivity universities.

While this analysis may be of interest from the perspective of individual institutions looking to generate sufficient net tuition revenues, from the point of view of society, these numbers point to a degree of stratification that is worrying. Table 6 depicts the relationship between the income background of students and the selectivity of the colleges or universities (regardless of whether it is private or public) they attend. In 1981, only 10.0% of all lower income and 13.7% of lower-middle income first-time, full-time freshmen were enrolled at medium or highly selective four-year institutions. Compara-

Table 6

Distribution of freshman enrollment by income background by institutional selectivity, fall of 1981 versus fall of 1999 (%)

	Lower	Lower-middle	Middle	Upper-middle	Upper	Richest	All groups
1999	<$20	$20–$30	$30–$60	$60–$100	$100–$200	>$200	
2-year public	39.0	38.8	35.5	29.8	16.8	10.1	30.9
2-year private	3.7	2.7	2.4	1.8	2.2	3.5	2.4
Low select 4-year	41.9	41.8	41.8	42.4	42.0	35.4	41.7
Medium select 4-year	9.7	11.5	14.9	18.0	23.1	25.6	16.5
High select 4-year	5.8	5.2	5.4	8.0	16.0	25.5	8.5
	100.0	100.0	100.0	100.0	100.0	100.0	100.0
1981	<$10	$10–$15	$15–$30	$30–$50	$50–$100	>$100	
2-year public	44.6	41.4	39.3	31.2	20.4	13.2	35.6
2-year private	6.2	5.5	4.2	3.6	3.5	3.0	4.3
Low select 4-year	39.3	39.3	38.0	38.7	39.1	39.4	38.6
Medium select 4-year	7.0	10.1	13.7	18.4	22.1	23.9	14.8
High select 4-year	3.0	3.6	4.9	8.1	14.8	20.5	6.7
	100.0	100.0	100.0	100.0	100.0	100.0	100.0

See notes to Table 5 for a discussion of income brackets and selectivity categories.

ble figures for upper-income and the richest students were 36.9% and 44.4%. By 1999, the proportion of students from the low-income groups that were enrolled at medium or highly selective schools rose to 15.5% and 16.7%, an encouraging sign. Still, those percentages pale besides the comparable numbers for their affluent counterparts whose percentages ended up at 39.1% and 51.1%. Thus, we are now in the situation where fewer than one of six lower-income students enrolled anywhere in American higher education is at a medium or highly selective four-year institution as opposed to more than one out of two of the richest students.

Should we care? There is a good deal of evidence that attendance at a selective (prestigious) college or university carries with it a number of advantages. Gordon Winston (1999) has been monitoring costs, prices and subsidies in American higher education for some time. He has shown that subsidies (the difference between educational expenditures and the cost to students) vary much more within sectors than across them. While the average subsidy at a private institution is only modestly higher than in the public sector, in each sector the amount of subsidy varies widely. The pattern is clear: more selective colleges and universities – which disproportionately attract affluent students – provide much larger subsidies than their less selective counterparts.

5. Breakdown of revenues and expenditures by institutional type and control: Where does the money come from? Where does it go?

Our earlier discussion included an examination of the changing revenue patterns at both public institutions and at private ones. But the heterogeneity of American higher education suggests that a breakdown by institutional type would be illuminating. Table 7 presents the most recent data available on revenue sources for public colleges and universities (from 1996–1997) and from private colleges and universities (from 1995–1996). We break down revenues into four principal groups: net tuition revenue (gross tuition less institutional aid), federal expenditures (other than for financial aid which shows up in net tuition revenue), state and local expenditures, and gifts and endowment earnings. Institutions are divided into four categories: research/doctoral universities, master's (comprehensive) universities, baccalaureate colleges and two year colleges.

The large role that net tuition revenue plays at private institutions is very clear. Even at private research universities, this is the largest single revenue source (providing 37% of all revenues), slightly surpassing the contribution made by the federal government (35%, mainly grants and contracts supporting research efforts). While state appropriations provide relatively little, gifts and endowment earnings are responsible for almost one of four revenue dollars. Not surprisingly, less research intensive private master's universities get a much lower percentage of revenues from the federal government (only 7%), and their relatively small endowments explain the more modest role played by gifts and endowment earnings (13%). The tuition dependency of these schools (more than three of four revenue dollars come from tuition) is even greater than at private

Table 7
Percent distribution of revenues in colleges and universities by type and control

	Research/Doctoral	Master's	Baccalaureate	Associate of arts
Public – 1996–1997				
Net tuition revenue	20.4	28.4	32.5	20.3
Federal government	19.8	7.6	8.9	6.1
State and local government	49.3	61.0	55.1	72.3
Gifts and endowment earnings	10.5	3.1	3.5	1.3
	100.0	100.0	100.0	100.0
Private – 1995–1996				
Net tuition revenue	37.2	76.0	64.4	80.6
Federal government	35.2	6.7	5.0	5.0
State and local government	3.1	3.8	4.2	7.4
Gifts and endowment earnings	24.4	13.4	26.5	7.0
	100.0	100.0	100.0	100.0

Notes. Changes in accounting rules for private institutions make data for 1996–1997 and later not comparable with earlier years or across sectors. We therefore use 1995–1996 data for private institutions.
Source: National Center for Education Statistics (2002b), *Digest of Education Statistics, 1999 and 2001.*

baccalaureate colleges (which get a bit less than two of three revenue dollars from tuition). Private colleges, a number of which have sizable endowments, generate an even larger percentage of revenues (27%) from gifts and endowment earnings than do private research universities. Private two-year colleges (a group comprised mostly of small specialty schools) are the most tuition dependent of all.

State and local governments provide the overwhelming amount of support at all types of public colleges and universities. The contribution of these expenditures (which are mainly state operating subsidies) ranges from 49% of all revenues at public research universities, to 55% at public colleges, 61% at master's universities and 72% at community colleges. Net tuition revenues comprise the next largest revenue source, even at public research universities where tuition only slightly exceeds federal research support as a revenue item (contributing 20.4% of all revenues versus 19.8% from federal expenditures). Tuition provides 20% of revenues at community colleges, rising to 28% at master's universities and 33% at public colleges. Finally, gifts and endowment earnings contribute a nontrivial amount of revenue (11%) at public research universities.

Now that we know where the money comes from, we turn our attention to where it goes. We begin in Table 8 reviewing changes over time in expenditures for public colleges and universities and for their private counterparts. Expenditures are broken down into eight categories: instruction (institutional funding of faculty salaries for teaching and self-supported research), research (externally supported research), public service, academic support other than libraries (administration, academic computing, etc.), library expenditures, student services (career and health services, etc.), institutional support (legal and business operations, etc.) and operation and maintenance.

Table 8
Percent distribution of college and university expenditures, by control over time

	1980–1981	1985–1986	1990–1991	1995–1996	1996–1997*
Public					
Instruction	45.5	45.1	44.3	43.1	42.9
Research	11.7	11.7	13.2	13.5	13.5
Public service	5.3	5.2	5.6	5.9	6.1
Academic support other than libraries	5.6	6.2	6.7	7.0	7.2
Libraries	3.6	3.5	3.1	3.0	3.0
Student services	6.0	6.0	6.2	6.5	6.6
Institutional support	10.9	11.7	11.4	12.0	11.9
Operation and maintenance of plant	11.3	10.7	9.4	8.9	8.8
	100.0	100.0	100.0	100.0	100.0
Private					
Instruction	41.6	41.2	41.4	41.4	
Research	13.0	12.3	12.0	11.8	
Public service	2.4	2.7	3.2	3.6	
Academic support other than libraries	4.7	5.0	5.7	5.8	
Libraries	4.0	3.9	3.4	3.5	
Student services	6.8	7.4	7.7	8.3	
Institutional support	15.6	16.6	16.7	16.3	
Operation and maintenance of plant	11.8	10.9	10.0	9.3	
	100.0	100.0	100.0	100.0	

Note. Minor categories excluded.
Source: U.S. Department of Education (2002b), *Digest of Education Statistics, 2001*.
*Preliminary data.

There is a good amount of stability in expenditures over time. One systematic change, however, appears to be a steady decline in the share of spending going to operation and maintenance, which went from 11% to 9% at public institutions and from 12% to 9% at privates. Library funding declined slightly in each sector, perhaps suggesting that over the past two decades institutional leaders have been more willing to trade off the interests of future generations to support the current group of faculty and students. Or perhaps this reflects an increase in the bureaucratic infrastructure as the combination of academic support, student services and institutional support went from 22.5% to 25.7% at publics and from 27.1% to 30.4% at privates. Comparing the two sectors, it is not surprising to observe that one of the larger differences is that public institutions allocate more to public service.

Do different types of institutions allocate their spending differently? Table 9 examines the latest available data on expenditure patterns across school types. At public and private research universities, spending the money generated by research accounts for a sizable percentage of all expenditures (22% at publics and 20% at privates). The pattern of spending at research universities does not vary much by control, except for the

Table 9
Percent distribution of expenditures in colleges and universities by type and control

	Research/Doctoral	Master's	Baccalaureate	Associate of arts
Public – 1996–1997				
Instruction	37.8	48.8	44.5	49.8
Research	22.4	3.7	1.7	0.1
Public service	8.1	4.0	4.1	2.6
Academic support less libraries	7.6	6.8	7.6	6.8
Libraries	3.2	3.9	4.0	2.3
Student services	4.4	8.8	10.9	11.0
Institutional support	9.1	13.6	15.7	16.7
Operation and maintenance of plant	7.3	10.4	11.5	10.6
	100.0	100.0	100.0	100.0
Private – 1995–1996				
Instruction	42.3	44.5	40.9	35.3
Research	20.0	2.3	1.2	0.1
Public service	3.5	1.7	0.9	0.2
Academic support less libraries	5.9	6.2	5.3	6.1
Libraries	3.6	3.7	3.9	1.5
Student services	4.6	12.5	14.1	17.5
Institutional support	12.1	19.6	22.2	25.1
Operation and maintenance of plant	8.1	9.6	11.5	14.2
	100.0	100.0	100.0	100.0

Source: National Center for Education Statistics (2002b), *Digest of Education Statistics, 1999 and 2001*.

larger role played by public service at public research universities. Looking at other types of institutions, the largest differences between publics and privates is in the allocation toward student services and institutional support, which is substantially larger at private institutions than at their public counterparts (16.7% versus 13.5% at private and public research universities, 32.1% versus 22.4% at master's universities, 36.3% versus 26.6% at baccalaureate colleges and 42.6% versus 27.7% at two-year schools). Whether this reflects enhanced services to students paying higher fees or greater inefficiency is impossible to tell from these data.

6. The supply side

Having described the patterns of financing in American colleges and universities, we turn to examining research that aims to explain their pricing, discounting and resource allocation decisions. The higher education industry in the United States is dominated by not-for-profit and governmental suppliers. This is notably true among institutions that award degrees, where as noted above only about 5.5% of full-time enrollees are in proprietary institutions. There is a substantial postsecondary vocational education sector, offering nondegree programs, which competes with government-owned community colleges.

The predominance of governmental and private not-for-private suppliers creates difficulties in explaining the supply side of the higher education market, since theory for the behavior of such suppliers is not well developed [see generally, Weisbrod (1988)]. The limited role of efficiency considerations in the management of nonprofit universities is a major theme in Ehrenberg (2000). Issues of cost escalation at "elite" institutions are also examined in Clotfelter (1996). Ehrenberg (2001) provides an excellent overview of the supply of American higher education. A further complication is that a number of higher education producers, especially on the private side, practice "selective admissions", rationing the number of purchasers not only by price but by various characteristics, notably academic and athletic ability.[5] During the rapid expansion of demand for higher education during the baby boom years of the 1960s, for example, most of the increase in supply of higher education came from government suppliers, through expansion of existing campuses and the creation of many new ones, especially community colleges. Selective private institutions responded in large measure by raising their admission standards more than by expanding their operations [Duffy and Goldberg (1997)]. One motivation for curtailing expansion is the role of endowments, whose per-student value is diluted by expanded enrollments [Winston (1999)]. A partial exception to the generalization that private colleges do not want to expand was the decision by leading Northeastern private colleges and universities at the end of the 1960s to expand their size in the course of admitting women. This was probably influenced more by male demand for coeducational education and by educational considerations than by a desire to expand output.

The American higher education marketplace has become much more national in character over the last 50 years. Increasing consumer sophistication, erosion of local and religious ties to colleges, improved communications and declines in transportation costs have led to greater product differentiation, increasing concentration of the "best" students at the most prestigious universities [Cook and Frank (1993)], and much greater student mobility. These phenomena were first systematically discussed in Jencks and Reisman (1968) and have received systematic analysis in a series of important papers by Caroline Hoxby (1997, 2000a).

Relatively little is known about the economic factors governing entry and exit of "firms" from the industry [for a historical treatment, see Goldin and Katz (1999)]. In private higher education, churches have historically been the leading founders of colleges and universities. On the public side, most "flagship" public universities were founded in the decades following the Morill "land grant" act of 1867. Since then, demand growth from demographics and from the rising economic value of higher education have been significant sources of pressure to add campuses. In many states, there is also a strong

---

[5] Economic rationales for this behavior are discussed in Rothschild and White (1995) and in McPherson and Schapiro (1990).

desire to have campuses, which are significant sources of employment and of consumers for local merchants, widely dispersed geographically. Despite the continued founding of new colleges in both public and private sectors, it is striking, as Goldin and Katz (1999) note, that very few of the currently highly ranked colleges and universities have been founded since 1900. Barriers to entry, especially to the more prestigious end of the market, appear to be strong. Nonetheless, once in place, both private and public campuses are notoriously hard to close. Local legislators have a strong interest in preserving local campuses, public or private. In addition, on the private side, the fact that the "owners" of a private college or university – its trustees – are legally precluded from benefiting economically from its sale or liquidation eliminates a main motive for exit in for-profit businesses. Between 1975 and 2000, campuses closed at the rate of about 15 per year, 90% of them private, and most of them very small [Ehrenberg (2001), p. 17]. Some observers have suggested that this combination of forces results in chronic excess supply of places in the less prestigious and less selective elements of the industry.

The behavior of public institutions and public funders

States differ widely in the organization, pricing and access conditions for higher education. California, for example, lays down firm ground rules, based on high school performance, that determine who may enter the University of California, the California State Universities and the community college system. Access to the California system, especially its prestigious University of California schools, is sharply restricted for out-of-state students. Other states, including Michigan, sustain a much higher share of out-of-state enrollment while still others, including Minnesota, make the flagship university accessible to a broader share of the state's high school graduates. As Ehrenberg (2001) notes, we lack systematic explanations for these and other differences.

The fact that families are both consumers of higher education services and voters raises analytic and econometric challenges in sorting out the role of supply and demand forces in explaining prices and output in public higher education. Peltzman (1973), Quigley and Rubinfeld (1993) and Lowry (2001) use state cross-section data to analyze these relationships. Hoenack and Pierro (1990) use time series data for a single university for the same purpose.

In addition to direct support of government owned institutions, some states also run student aid programs that supply funding directly to students. Typically such funds are restricted to students from the state attending college in that state. Traditionally such programs have been geared to student ability to pay and cost of attendance; the creation of such programs has been encouraged by federal matching funds through the LEAP program. In recent years, there has been growing interest in state merit aid programs, typically conditioned on high school and college grade performance and sometimes (but not always) restricted to families below specified income levels. Heller (2003) tracks the shift toward merit aid in state student aid. Obviously, this shift raises a set of questions about who benefits from the different approaches to state aid and what the implications are for enrollment of students from different income groups [see Dee, Dynarski and

Jackson (1999)]. Similar questions arise regarding the federal HOPE Scholarship and Lifelong Learning Tax Credits [see Long (2004)]. These programs are sometimes defended on the grounds that the state gains economically by keeping more of its most talented students at home; the validity of this argument depends in part on how likely students are to remain in the state where they attended college [Bound et al. (2004)].

A different set of questions arises concerning the implications of this change in program targeting on the total supply of student aid funds from state governments. As Baum (2003) has argued, Georgia and other states have substantially increased the total resources they devote to student aid as they have shifted focus. At the same time, expanded funding for student aid may lead to declines in direct appropriations for public institutions. Parallel questions can be asked about the federal HOPE and Lifelong Learning Credits. Do they in effect substitute for traditional federal student aid programs, or are they, in a political sense, complements? What, in effect, is the elasticity of supply of federal support with respect to the income levels of recipients? These questions bear an analogy, broadly, to familiar political trade-offs between target efficiency and broad political support for public programs such as housing assistance, welfare, health care and Social Security. We are not aware of systematic empirical work on these political economy questions in the context of higher education.

Resource allocation and financing choices within institutions

A variety of questions arise about how colleges and universities determine where to put their resources and how they respond to the external environment in making those choices. Models have been put forward which conceive the university as maximizing a complex objective function relative to a set of constraints [see, for example, Hopkins and Massy (1981)]. A particular version of such a model characterizes universities (and other not-for-profits) as engaging in certain activities to produce revenue that is used to enhance the production of other "mission" goods that are valued intrinsically [see Weisbrod (1998) and James (1978)]. Another line of analysis models the university as a faculty cooperative [James (1981)].

Some issues apply to broad strategic choices about how universities allocate resources, for example between research and teaching [Nerlove (1972)] or between undergraduate and graduate education. But there are also more specific questions relating to finance. There is considerable evidence that colleges give substantial and growing attention to strategic uses of student aid, as discussed above. Empirical evidence about how colleges manage the resulting trade-offs is difficult to come by. Do colleges, for example, "pay for" increasing investments in merit aid by reducing need-based aid, by withdrawing resources from other parts of college operation, by raising prices, or in other ways? Given the interdependencies among these decisions, determining causal linkages is difficult, and much work remains to be done in this area.

A different but closely related question is how colleges adjust their own pricing and aid decisions in response to changes in the external funding environment. In the mid-1980s, Secretary of Education William Bennett made headlines with the assertion that colleges captured the benefits of increases in federal student aid by a combination of raising their tuition and reducing their own aid awards. Similar concerns have been raised about the possibility of colleges capturing the benefits of tuition tax credits [McPherson and Schapiro (1997), Kane (1997)].

Plausible answers to these questions are highly sensitive to institutional details. For example, it might appear that colleges can readily capture increases in the size of the Pell grant simply by raising tuition. In fact, however, at current award levels, the maximum Pell award most students can receive is constrained by their income level and not by the price of the college they attend. If the Pell grant were to increase dramatically, this situation could change and the behavioral effects might be very different. It is, however, true that in a need-based aid system, an increase in the Pell award to a student will reduce the amount of aid a college must provide to meet the student's full need. Such a reduction in the college's investment in aid could, however, be offset to a greater or less extent by the greater incentive to enroll highly needy Pell students that would be occasioned by larger grants.

Ultimately, the response of colleges to changes in federal student aid grants in terms of both price and use of the institutions' own aid is an empirical question. At least two considerations make the question hard to answer. First, in the case of a national formula-driven program like Pell, exogenous variation in the amount of grants awarded to an institution is hard to come by. Second, the interdependencies among the different variables under the institution's control, including price, aid awards, spending levels, admissions policies, etc. make it difficult to isolate specific effects. What's really called for is a convincing empirical model of the whole set of university financial and allocation decisions – a tall order.

McPherson and Schapiro [Chapter 10 in McPherson, Schapiro and Winston (1993), updated in McPherson and Schapiro (1998, Chapter 8)], was an early attempt to address this problem empirically. We estimated relations between changes in the levels of funding from various sources and changes in universities' and colleges' financial behavior. The analysis focused on explaining three financial variables over which institutions have control: their spending per student on institutional aid, their level of gross tuition and fees per student, and their level of instructional expenditures per student. The external financing variables fell into three categories: revenue from government, revenue derived from private gifts and endowment income, and revenue generated by the institutions' pricing and aid policies.

We found no evidence of the "Bennett hypothesis", that private institutions increased their tuitions when they received more federal student aid, nor was there a significant impact of changes in federal student aid on changes in instructional spending at private institutions. For public institutions, the effects of federal student aid differed in important ways from what we found at private institutions. We did not find any significant relationship between federal aid and instructional expenditures. We did, however, find that public four-year institutions tended to raise tuition by $50 for every $100 increase in federal student aid. As noted earlier, the institutional details make it more plausible for public rather than for much higher priced private institutions to respond to increases in federal aid by raising tuition.

We also investigated whether federal student aid increases led to reductions in institutional student aid commitments, which would be the case if federal aid substituted for need-based student aid provided by colleges and universities. Although no significant relationship between institution-based aid and federal student aid emerged at public institutions, we found that private institutions tended to increase their spending on institution-based aid when federal student aid increased. Specifically, private colleges and universities increased institutional financial aid by \$20 for every \$100 increase in federal student aid. This is consistent with the notion that the availability of federal aid encourages students of lesser means to go to college and encourages colleges to admit them, with the result that schools wind up admitting a needier clientele, which in turn draws more heavily on the institution's own aid resources. More recently, Turner (1997, 1998) found that increases in federal aid induced colleges to rearrange their own aid funding in a way that led some of the additional resources provided to (generally low-income) Pell recipients to be redistributed toward middle-income students.

7. Other areas for research

A number of other aspects of university financing behavior can benefit from theoretical and empirical investigation. Research universities obtain a significant share of their funding from federal research grants. Indirect cost recovery formulas and policies may create significant incentives for universities, influencing the economics of university building construction, the balance of investments in research and teaching, and other matters [see Noll and Rogerson (1998)]. Colleges and universities, both private and increasingly public, depend significantly on fundraising as a revenue source and invest systematically in their fundraising operations. Important questions arise about the influence of taxes and other incentives in shaping the behavior of individual donors [see Clotfelter (2001)]. As Ehrenberg (2004) notes, there has been little attention to the question of how to invest optimally in this activity and only limited attention empirically to the impact of investments in fundraising. A further set of questions concerns the influence of donor preferences on institutional behavior. Questions of optimal policies toward endowment received systematic study in the 1960s and 1970s [Tobin (1974)] but such analyses have not taken into account the implications of uncertainty in other income streams [Ehrenberg (2004) and Nordhaus (1990)].

Measurement issues

Much popular – and some professional – discussion of college "costs" and "prices" suffers from conceptual unclarity about the meaning of these terms. To an economist, of course, the private cost of an investment in higher education includes tuition and fee payments to the institution and the opportunity cost of the student's time. Expenditures for room and board only count as economic costs of higher education to the extent that they are different from what they would be in the absence of the college investment. The social cost of an investment in higher education includes both the opportunity cost to the student and whatever resources are consumed in the provision of the education, whether or not these are billed to the student.

In popular discussion, "cost" of higher education often refers to the bills paid by the family, which typically include room and board costs, omit opportunity costs to the student and overlook those costs incurred in producing the education which are not billed to the student. A recent Congressional Commission on College Costs, chaired by William Troutt, President of Rhodes College, urged that for public policy purposes, clear distinctions should be drawn among three concepts [National Commission on the Cost of Higher Education (1998)]. "Cost" should refer to the cost incurred by colleges and universities in providing educational services. "Price" should refer to the payments families make to colleges. "Subsidy" should refer to the difference between cost and price.[6] A further refinement is to note that the price paid by a student may be less than the posted price owing to student aid. In such a case the student may be described as receiving both a "general" subsidy (difference between cost and posted price) and a student-specific subsidy (difference between posted price and what s/he actually pays).

Identifying the costs involved in providing educational services can itself be problematic. As Gordon Winston has long argued [see, for example, Winston (1993)], the conventions of traditional fund accounting lead colleges to employ revenue and cost measures that differ from those implied in economic analysis. In particular, the value of the services of college-owned land and capital goods is often neglected in traditional accounting of college costs, and can be a quite significant part of the total.

A further complication is that of allocating the costs of a university's operations among its different outputs – the classical "joint costs" problem. The problem is most acute in allocating costs between research and teaching and between graduate and undergraduate teaching. These problems arise both in accounting for research costs for federal cost recovery purposes and in reporting to the public on costs of education. It is generally believed that graduate education is more resource-intensive than undergraduate education, although the degree of difference is hard to quantify. Further, it is conventional to allocate all of a faculty member's time that is not explicitly accounted for through externally funded research to teaching, even though it is clear that at many universities faculty are expected to allocate a significant share of their unfunded time to so-called "intramural" research. All these considerations make the problem of comparing costs among programs within a university, and of comparing costs for similar programs across universities, difficult.

A final measurement dilemma is that of how to regard a university's "expenditure" on student aid. Until recently, discounts universities offer from the posted price have been accounted as costs – a markedly different practice from the familiar practice at retail

---

[6] Winston (1999) shows that virtually all college students receive subsidies.

stores and airlines.[7] As Bowen and Breneman (1993) have argued, the economically proper treatment of these discounts varies depending on an institution's circumstances. Consider University A that has sufficient demand that it can enroll a fully qualified class of students, all of whom will pay the posted price.[8] The university, if it is rational, will then only offer discounts to students for specific purposes – for example, to enroll able students who will enhance others' education or promote the school's reputation or to enroll needy students in furtherance of a mission of social justice. In this circumstance, the discount is best understood as a cost of education, incurred in order to improve the "product" (relative to the institution's goals). At the other extreme, consider University B, which lacks sufficient demand to enroll a qualified class at the posted price. It will discount tuition in order to attract students who will pay more at the margin than their marginal cost. In this case, the discount is best understood as simply a reduced price and not an opportunity cost. University A is forgoing revenue in order to achieve non-revenue objectives; University B is not. Bowen and Breneman (1993) assert, and we agree, that in the higher education market as a whole, most colleges and universities are more like University B than University A, and therefore treating institutionally-based student aid as a price discount in working with national data makes sense.

8. Conclusion

American higher education is a significant industry with revenues of almost 3% of GDP. Arguably the social significance of higher education exceeds even its economic cost, owing to its strategic role in public life, in research, and in influencing the distribution of educational and economic opportunity. For all that, it is probably fair to say that the finance of higher education is under-researched by economists relative to such other industries as health care, energy and transportation. No doubt this phenomenon can be explained in part by the fact that economists, true to their profession, respond to incentives, and research funding has been relatively less available in the field of higher education than for some other industries. It is also, however, a difficult area analytically, owing to several distinctive features of the industry. These include the prevalence of nonprofit and governmental suppliers, whose behavior economists find difficult to model, the great difficulty in measuring output, which involves transformation of the capacities of human beings, and the peculiarity that the "consumers" of higher education are also its producers – in the sense that the quality of the education achieved by any one student is a function both of her own effort and of the quality of her fellows. These difficulties, however, also present extremely interesting challenges to able researchers.

We are heartened to see that a number of very talented younger economists have put higher education near the center of their work, and their efforts are already bearing fruit, as many of the references in this essay show.

---

[7] We do not assume that American Airlines treats all those discounts from full coach fare as "passenger aid".

[8] There are fewer than 25 private institutions in the United States for which this is true, and most readers of this essay can name them.

References

Akerhielm, K. et al. (1998). "Factors related to college enrollment: Final report". Mathtech, Inc.

Arnone, M., Hebel, S., Schmidt, P. (2003). "Another bleak budget year: As state legislatures convene, concerns over money dominate the agenda". The Chronicle of Higher Education (January 3), A21–A22.

Avery, C., Hoxby, C.M. (2004). "Do and should financial aid packages affect students' college choices?". In: Hoxby, C.M. (Ed.), College Choices: The Economics of Where to Go, When to Go, and How to Pay for It. National Bureau of Economic Research Conference Report. The University of Chicago Press, Chicago, IL, pp. 239–301.

Baum, S. (2003). "The financial aid partnership: Strengthening the Federal Government's leadership role". National Dialogue on Student Financial Aid. The College Board, New York.

Bound, J., Groen, J., Kezdi, G., Turner, S. (2004). "Trade in university training: Cross state variation in the production and use of college educated labor". Journal of Econometrics 121 (1/2, July–August), 143–173.

Bowen, H.R. (1977). Investment in Learning: The Individual and Social Value of American Higher Education. Jossey-Bass, San Francisco, CA.

Bowen, W.G., Breneman, D.W. (1993). "Student aid: Price discount or educational investment?". Brookings Review 11 (Winter), 28–31.

Carlton, D.W., Bamberger, G.E., Epstein, R.J. (1995). "Antitrust and higher education: Was there a conspiracy to restrict financial aid?". The RAND Journal of Economics 26 (1, Spring), 131–147.

Clotfelter, C. (1996). Buying the Best: Cost Escalation in Elite Higher Education. Princeton University Press, Princeton, NJ.

Clotfelter, C. (2001). "Alumni giving to elite private colleges and universities". Working paper. Stanford Institute, April.

College Board (2002). Trends in Student Aid, 2002. College Board Washington Office, Washington, DC.

Cook, P.J., Frank, R.H. (1993). "The growing concentration of top students at elite institutions". In: Clotfelter, C.T., Rothschild, M. (Eds.), Studies of Supply and Demand in Higher Education. The University of Chicago Press, Chicago, IL, pp. 121–140.

Crenshaw, A.B. (2002). "Price wars on campus: Colleges use discounts to draw best mix of top students, paying customers". Washington Post (October 15), A01.

Dee, T.S., Dynarski, S., Jackson, L.A. (1999). "Who loses HOPE? Attrition from Georgia's college scholarship program". Southern Economic Journal 66, 379–390.

Duffy, E.A., Goldberg, I. (1997). Crafting a Class. Princeton University Press, Princeton.

Ehrenberg, R.G. (2000). Tuition Rising: Why College Costs So Much. Harvard University Press, Cambridge, MA.

Ehrenberg, R.G. (2001). "The supply of American higher education institutions". In: McPherson, M.S., Schapiro, M.O. (Eds.), Ford Policy Forum 2001. Forum for the Future of Higher Education, Cambridge, MA.

Ehrenberg, R.G. (2004). "Econometric studies of higher education". Journal of Econometrics 121 (1/2, July–August), 19–37.

Ehrenberg, R.G., Monks, J. (1999). "U.S. News & World Report college rankings: Why do they matter?". Change (November/December).

Ehrenberg, R.G., Sherman, D. (1984). "Optimal financial aid policies for a selective university". Journal of Human Resources (Spring), 202–230.

Eureka Project (1988). "The critical difference: Student financial aid and educational opportunities in California". Sacramento, CA.

Frank, R.H. (1999). "Winner-take-all markets and need-based financial aid". In: Is This What It's Come To – Winner-Take-All? The College Board, New York. Report on a College Board Colloquium, pp. 50–58.

Frank, R.H., Cook, P.J. (1995). The Winner-Take-All Society: How More and More Americans Compete for Ever Fewer and Bigger Prizes, Encouraging Economic Waste, Income Inequality, and an Impoverished Cultural Life. Free Press, New York.

Friedman, M. (1955). "The role of government in education". In: Solow, R.A. (Ed.), Economics and the Public Interest. Rutgers University Press, Piscataway, NJ, pp. 123–144.

Goldin, C., Katz, L.F. (1999). "The shaping of higher education: The formative years in the United States, 1890–1940". Journal of Economic Perspectives 13, 37–62.

Hansen, W.L., Weisbrod, B.A. (1969). "The distribution of costs and benefits of public higher education: The case of California". Journal of Human Resources 4 (Spring), 176–191.

Hartman, R.W. (1970). "A comment on the Pechman–Hansen–Weisbrod controversy". The Journal of Human Resources 5 (Autumn), 519–523.

Heller, D.E. (2003). "State financial aid and college access". National Dialogue on Student Financial Aid. The College Board, New York.

Hoenack, S.A., Pierro, D.J. (1990). "An econometric model of a public university's income and enrollments". Journal of Economic Behavior and Organization 14, 403–423.

Hopkins, D.S.P., Massy, W.F. (1981). Planning Models for Universities and Colleges. Stanford University Press, Stanford, CA.

Hovey, H. (1999). "State spending for higher education in the next decade: The battle to sustain current support". Prepared by State Policy Research, Inc. for The National Center for Public Policy and Higher Education, July.

Hoxby, C.M. (1997). "The changing market structure of U.S. higher education". Harvard University. Unpublished manuscript.

Hoxby, C.M. (2000). "Benevolent colluders? The effects of antitrust action on college financial aid and tuition". Working Paper 7754. NBER (June).

Hoxby, C.M. (2000a). "The effects of geographic integration and increasing competition in the market for college education". Revision of NBER Working Paper 6323, May.

James, E. (1978). "Product mix and cost disaggregation: A reinterpretation of the economics of higher education". The Journal of Human Resources 13 (2, Spring), 157–186.

James, E., Neuberger, E. (1981). "The academic department as a non-profit labor cooperative". Public Choice 36 (January), 585–612.

Jencks, C., Reisman, D. (1968). The Academic Revolution. Doubleday, New York.

Johnstone, D.B. (2001). "The economics and politics of income contingent repayment plans". The International Higher Education Finance and Accessibility Project. State University of New York, Buffalo.

Kane, T.J. (1997). "Beyond tax relief: Long-term challenges in financing higher education". National Tax Journal 50 (2), 335–349.

Kane, T.J. (1999). The Price of Admission: Rethinking How Americans Pay for College. Brookings Institution Press, Washington, DC.

Kuttner, R. (1989). "The squeeze on young families". Washington Post (September 8), A23.

Long, B.T. (2004). "The impact of federal tax credits for higher education expenses". In: Hoxby, C.M. (Ed.), College Choices: The Economics of Where to Go, When to Go, and How to Pay for It. National Bureau of Economic Research Conference Report. The University of Chicago Press, Chicago, IL, pp. 101–165.

Longanecker, D., Orfield, G. (2003). "Merit vs. need: Where is the balance?". Trusteeship (January/February), 14–19.

Lowry, R.C. (2001). "The effects of state political interests and campus outputs on public university revenues". Economics of Education Review 20, 105–120.

McPherson, M.S., Schapiro, M.O. (1990). Selective Admission and the Public Interest. The College Board, New York.

McPherson, M.S., Schapiro, M.O. (1991a). Keeping College Affordable: Government and Educational Opportunity. Brookings Institution Press, Washington, DC.

McPherson, M.S., Schapiro, M.O. (1991b). "Does student aid affect college enrollment? New evidence on a persistent controversy". American Economic Review 81 (1, March), 309–318.

McPherson, M.S., Schapiro, M.O. (1997). "Financing undergraduate education: Designing national policies". National Tax Journal L (3, September), 557–571.

McPherson, M.S., Schapiro, M.O. (1998). The Student Aid Game: Meeting Need and Rewarding Talent in American Higher Education. Princeton University Press, Princeton, NJ.

McPherson, M.S., Schapiro, M.O. (2002). "The blurring line between merit and need in financial aid". Change 34 (2, March/April), 38–46.

McPherson, M.S., Schapiro, M.O., Winston, G.C. (1993). Paying the Piper: Productivity, Incentives, and Financing in U.S. Higher Education. The University of Michigan Press, Ann Arbor, MI.

National Commission on the Cost of Higher Education (1998). Straight Talk About College Costs and Prices. Oryx Press, Phoenix, AZ.

Nerlove, M. (1972). "On tuition and the costs of higher education: Prolegomena to a conceptual framework". The Journal of Political Economy 80 (3), S178–S218. Part II, May/June.

New York Times (2002). "When a college scholarship buys a car". New York Times (November 4) (editorial).

Noll, R., Rogerson, W.P. (1998). "The economics of university indirect cost reimbursement in Federal Research Grants". In: Noll, R.G. (Ed.), Challenges to Research Universities. Brookings Institution Press, Washington, DC, pp. 105–146.

Nordhaus, W. (1990). "Risk analysis: Applications to university finances". In: Anderson, R. (Ed.), The Financing of Higher Education. Joffrey, pp. 142–167.

Pechman, J.A. (1970). "The distributional effects of public higher education in California". Journal of Human Resources 5 (Summer), 361–370.

Peltzman, S. (1973). "The Effect of Government Subsidies-in-Kind on Private Expenditures: The Case of Higher Education". The Journal of Political Economy 81 (1, January–February), 1–27.

Quigley, J.M., Rubinfeld, D.L. (1993). "Public choice in public higher education". In: Clotfelter, C.T., Rothschild, M. (Eds.), Studies of Supply and Demand in Higher Education. The University of Chicago Press, Chicago, IL.

Rothschild, M., White, L.J. (1995). "The analytics of the pricing of higher education and other services in which the customers are inputs". The Journal of Political Economy 103 (3, June), 573–586.

Selingo, J. (2001). "Questioning the merit of merit scholarships". Chronicle of Higher Education (January 19), A20–A22.

Selingo, J. (2002). "Speakers rebut criticism of state-based merit aid, saying plans help needy students". Chronicle of Higher Education (August 29). On-line version.

Tobin, J. (1974). "What is permanent endowment income?". The American Economic Review 64 (2), 427–432. Papers and Proceedings of the Eighty-Sixth Annual Meeting of the American Economic Association, May, 1974.

Turner, S.E. (1997). "Does federal aid affect college costs? Evidence from the Pell Program". Unpublished paper.

Turner, S.E. (1998). "The vision and reality of Pell Grants: Unforeseen consequences for students and institutions". In: Gladieux, L.E. et al. (Eds.), Memory, Reason, Imagination: A Quarter Century of Pell Grants. The College Board, New York, pp. 49–65.

U.S. Department of Education, National Center for Education Statistics [ED Tabs] (2002a). Enrollment in Postsecondary Institutions, Fall 2000 and Financial Statistics, Fiscal Year 2000. NCES 2002-212. Washington, DC. By L.G. Knapp et al. Project Officer: S.G. Broyles.

U.S. Department of Education, National Center for Education Statistics (2002b). Digest of Educational Statistics, 2001. U.S. Government Printing Office, Washington, DC.

Weisbrod, B.A. (1988). The Non-Profit Economy. Harvard University Press, Cambridge, MA.

Weisbrod, B.A. (Ed.) (1998). To Profit or Not to Profit: The Commercial Transformation of the Nonprofit Sector. Cambridge University Press, New York.

Winston, G.C. (1993). "The necessary revolution in financial accounting". In: McPherson, M.S., Schapiro, M.O., Winston, G.C. (Eds.), Paying the Piper: Productivity, Incentives, and Financing in U.S. Higher Education. The University of Michigan Press, pp. 279–304. Chapter 12.

Winston, G.C. (1999). "Subsidies, hierarchy, and peers: The awkward economics of higher education". Journal of Economic Perspectives 13 (1, Winter), 113–136.

Winston, G.C., Zimmerman, D.J. (2004). "Peer effects in higher education". In: Hoxby, C.M. (Ed.), College Choices: The Economics of Where to Go, When to Go, and How to Pay for It. National Bureau of Economic Research Conference Report. The University of Chicago Press, Chicago, IL, pp. 395–421.

Winter, G. (2002). "B's, not need, are enough for some state scholarships". New York Times (October 31), A1.

Chapter 25

INCOME CONTINGENT LOANS FOR HIGHER EDUCATION: INTERNATIONAL REFORMS

BRUCE CHAPMAN

Research School of Social Sciences, Australian National University

Contents

Handbook of the Economics of Education, Volume 2
Edited by Eric A. Hanushek and Finis Welch
© *2006 Elsevier B.V. All rights reserved*
DOI: 10.1016/S1574-0692(06)02025-3

Abstract

It is well known that higher education financing involves uncertainty and risk with respect to students' future economic fortunes, and an unwillingness of banks to provide loans because of the absence of collateral. It follows that without government intervention there will be both socially sub-optimal and regressive outcomes with respect to the provision of higher education. The historically most common response to this market failure – a government guarantee to repay student loans to banks in the event of default – is associated with significant problems.

Income contingent loans offer a possible solution. Since the late 1980s ICLs have been adopted in, or recommended for, a significant and growing number of countries, and it is this important international policy reform that has motivated the chapter.

An ICL provides students with finance for tuition and/or income support, its critical and defining characteristic being that the collection of the debt depends on the borrowers' future capacity to pay. ICL have two major insurance advantages for borrowers over more typical arrangements: default protection and consumption smoothing.

With reference to countries with both successful and unsuccessful ICL, the chapter illustrates that the operational and design features of such schemes are of fundamental importance with respect to their potential efficacy. It also seems to be the case that in many institutional and political environments there is not yet the administrative sophistication to make ICLs viable, although for reasons documented this is unlikely to be the case for the vast majority of OECD countries.

For one country, Australia, there is now a significant amount of research into the consequences of an ICL, and the evidence is explored in some detail. The investigation into the Australian experience helps in the development of a research agenda.

Keywords

income contingent loans, student loans, higher education financing, HECS

JEL classification: I00, I2, I20, I21, I22, I28, J2, J24

1. Introduction

What follows is an examination and analysis of what is, by historical policy standards, a new phenomenon in the financing of higher education: income contingent loans. The broad concept of income contingent loans (ICL) can be traced to the pioneering work of Friedman (1955), in which a particular form of the instrument, a graduate tax, was promoted as a possible response to the capital market problem associated with higher education financing. But it was not until the 1980s that arrangements of this form began to be adopted.

An ICL for higher education funding takes the following form. Borrowers, students, are provided with finance for tuition and/or income support, usually with the resources being provided by the public sector, although there is no reason why funding could not come from commercial banks. The critical and defining characteristic of an ICL is that the collection of the debt depends on the borrowers' future levels of income. Capacity to pay, and not time, defines the repayment obligation.

Yale University offered a particular type of ICL in the 1970s, but in national terms it happened first in a very blunt way in Sweden, with respect to a limited form of student income support in the early 1980s. This was followed by the adoption in Australia in 1989 of a national income contingent charging mechanism where, for the first time, repayments were collected through the tax system. New Zealand implemented an ICL in 1991 with a similar, although more market oriented, scheme which covered living costs as well as tuition.

An unusual form of an ICL was put in place in the US in 1993, but its take-up has been very low, for reasons explained below. The concept was also introduced in Chile in 1994, with the conversion of its existing conventional bank loan scheme to an income contingent form. South Africa followed in 1996 with arrangements designed mainly for tuition, as was the case in Australia, but with a small proportion of students being allowed additional funds for living expenses.

The UK government instituted an ICL for the recovery of student loans in 1997, and this was a complicated version of the original Australian system for tuition. This has been changed in 2006 to more closely resemble the form of the New Zealand initiative. Ethiopia changed its higher education financing arrangements with an unusual variant of ICL in 2003, and Thailand is on track to introduce a close variant of the Australian system in late 2006.

It is clear that over the last decade or so governments, researchers and policymakers of many countries have been engaged in public debate concerning the potential of ICL to replace existing higher education financing arrangements. They include Canada, Hungary and a host of developing countries, with a significant number in the last group exploring ways in which an ICL scheme for higher education could be implemented. With the encouragement of the World Bank and other international aid agencies, these ideas became a major part of active debate for developing countries in the late 1990s and early to mid-2000s, including in: Indonesia, Namibia, Nepal, Mexico, Rwanda and the Republic of South Korea.[1] As well, in March 2003 the World Bank sent a mission to the Philippines to explore tertiary education financing, including the viability of ICL. Further, international aid agencies and national governments are (at least in informal ways) in the process of examining possible similar avenues for higher education financing reform in Slovakia, Bulgaria, Bosnia, Germany and Colombia.

This chapter is an attempt to describe and explain the background to, and provide the analytical basis of, these policy debates and international reforms. It begins with an exploration of the case for both public sector university charges for students and taxpayer subsidies. A critical issue relates to the role of government beyond just the provision of a subsidy, which can be traced to market failure in the provision of private sector finance for higher education.

The essential issues for policy can be understood to be the result of uncertainty and risk with respect to students' future economic fortunes, and the understandable lack of willingness of banks to provide loans in the absence of collateral in the event of former students' defaulting. It is clear that without government intervention of some kind there will be both socially sub-optimal and regressive outcomes with respect to the provision and outcomes of higher education.

A key point in the discussion is that the historically most common response to this market failure – a government guarantee to repay student loans to banks in the event of default – is associated with significant problems. Alternative approaches to the problem, such as the provision of means-tested scholarships to individuals from poor backgrounds, are also flawed for several reasons, and these are explained. Something different is needed as a response to the traditional policy mechanisms.

The conceptual basis of income contingent loans as an alternative approach to higher education is explained in detail. ICL have two major advantages over more typical borrowing arrangements involving bank loans with government guarantees. Both benefits involve the provision of insurance, and can be traced to the fact that ICL repayments are defined by the borrower's capacity to repay debt.

The first insurance benefit of ICL concerns default. That is, because repayments are not required in periods of low income, borrowers are never in a financial situation in which they are unable to meet their loan repayment obligation. This will not be the case with respect to normal bank loans.

The second insurance benefit of ICL for borrowers is that they can eliminate expected future hardships associated with repayment. Compared to bank loans ICL provide consumption smoothing, which is again the result of repayments being determined by capacity to pay. When incomes are low ICL payments are not required, the tradeoff being that when incomes are high repayment obligations are greater.

---

[1] In Rwanda there have been active steps toward this type of policy initiative but it seems to be the case that in many countries implementation and administrative challenges are considerable, and this issue is examined in detail in Section 5.

It is argued that so long as they are designed sensibly, and can be made operationally efficient, ICL schemes have significant potential as a solution to higher education financing challenges. The chapter illustrates that the operational and design features of such schemes are of fundamental importance with respect to the potential efficacy of funding reforms.

There are many forms of income contingent financing instruments, and in what follows the different variants are compared and contrasted with respect to a host of economic issues, such as adverse selection, moral hazard, allocative efficiency, equity and administrative feasibility. It seems to be the case that a particular form of ICL, using the public sector as the insurer (a 'risk-sharing' ICL), has more attractive properties than other types of ICL. For reasons that are easy to understand, this particular variant is the form now emerging as the preferred type of ICL in many countries. There is also a growing interest, and expanding practice, in the use of income related instruments for higher education financed through the private sector, so-called human capital contracts.

The nature of schemes that have been tried in different countries is documented, and the essential characteristics of the various approaches are compared and contrasted. However, the available data and evidence on the effects of ICL are limited, the reason being that in most countries ICL have been adopted only recently. Even so, for one country, Australia, there has now been a significant amount of research into the consequences of a risk-sharing ICL, and the evidence is explored in some detail. The nature of the investigation into the Australian experience helps in the development of a research agenda for other national environments.

The essential policy challenges of administration and collection are raised through an examination of the nature of the issues concerning the adoption of ICL in developing countries. The bottom line in this context is that efficient collection lies at the heart of this type of policy reform. It also seems to be the case that in many institutional and political environments there is not yet the administrative sophistication to make ICLs administratively viable, although for reasons documented this is unlikely to be the case for the vast majority of OECD countries.

For a chapter in the Handbook of Economics series, the discussion following has a strong policy focus, and this can be traced in part to the absence of a major theoretical and empirical literature in the area of ICL. This is good news for research, since it implies that there is considerable potential with respect to ICL in all areas: theory, evidence and policy implementation. Promising avenues of research are documented in a final section.

2. Charging students for higher education: Conceptual issues

2.1. Introduction

What now follows presents the basic cases for some fundamental aspects of higher education financing. These include the division of payment between individual beneficiaries and society, and the justification for government intervention.

2.2. *Who should pay in theory: efficiency*

The conventional way of analyzing efficiency issues with respect to public expenditure uses a proposition well known in welfare economics concerning allocative efficiency. This is that, if there are no market distortions, goods and service should be priced at: $P_x = M_x - E_x$, where P_x is the price of good or service x; M_x is the marginal cost of producing x; and E_x is the marginal value of the externalities associated with the production or consumption of x.

Figure 1 helps explain the basis of this pricing rule for higher education [Chia (1990)]. The curves are all given in present value terms, and an understanding of their bases is as follows. The marginal benefit curves slope downward since the higher is the number of tertiary students the greater will be the supply of graduates and thus the lower are graduate wages. The distance between the social and private benefit curves reflects the value of the externalities, a topic considered below. It is assumed in the diagram that the marginal value of the externalities is invariant to the number of students, meaning that the social benefit curve is drawn parallel to the marginal private benefit curve. However, it is arguable that as the number of graduates increases, so too will the value of the externalities fall, a point used in Barr and Crawford (1998) to justify fee increases as enrollments increase.

In the figure the marginal private cost curve is shown for a zero-fee regime, and slopes upward since there will be increasing opportunity costs to enrolling the more

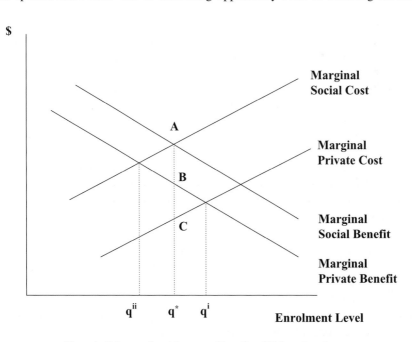

Figure 1. Private and social costs and benefits of higher education.

enrollments there are, given that additional enrollments decrease the supply and thus the wages of nongraduates. The difference between the marginal private and marginal social cost curves reflects the extent of the subsidy implicit in a no-fee regime.

As drawn the figure shows a situation characterized by over-investment in higher education ($q^i > q^*$), since it is assumed that there is no tuition fee. However, if all the direct costs are paid for by students (a full-fee regime), then the marginal social costs and marginal private benefits would be identical, but this then leads to an under-investment of higher education ($q^{ii} < q^*$). Thus the optimal fee is given by the distance BC which is derived from AB, the value accorded the marginal value of the externalities and thus the level of government subsidy.

Of some interest for policy issues considered below, the marginal cost pricing rule explained here suggests that financing arrangements that do not reflect the interaction of marginal benefits and marginal course costs will not deliver allocative efficiency. It is explained below that several variants of student charging are of this genre.

It should be noted that while the issues raised from analysis of Figure 1 sit comfortably with mainstream economics, this does not necessarily mean that the conclusions drawn with respect to allocative efficiency and taxpayer subsidies are obvious and easily analyzed. Instead it might well be the case that, at least with respect to public sector institutions, the higher education market is supply-constrained and is thus characterized by excess demand at given tuition and income support levels.

In the above context, Finnie and Usher (2006) argue that the framework presented above misses an important part of adjustment processes in public sector higher education. That is, if governments typically do not provide sufficient resources to allow all 'qualified' prospective students to enter higher education, the role of admission scores as an adjustment mechanism to changes in funding and demand is paramount. If this is the case the strength of the allocative efficiency issues concerning price adjustments raised above are necessarily weakened.

2.3. Externalities

Critical issues for policy concern the nature of social benefits and their likely size, given that economic theory suggests that answers to the latter should form the basis of the level of government subsidy. With respect to policy, significant issues are: what, and how valuable, are higher education externalities?

The externalities have been argued traditionally to include, among other things: reduced criminal activity, more informed public debate, better informed judgments with respect to health, and more sophisticated voting behavior.

However, the value of these particular externalities is likely to be small and debatable relative to the externality effect of education on economic growth. Since the early 1960s it has been argued that in a world of rapidly changing information more highly-educated workers have an advantage in adapting to different environments, in 'dealing with disequilibria' – the capacity to adjust to unanticipated shocks [Schultz (1975), Huffman (1974), Fane (1975), Wozniak (1987)].[2]

Related issues have emerged in new growth theory, which stresses the role of endogenous technical change, and the connections between and interdependencies of knowledge, innovation and human capital investments. The role of higher education with respect to productivity growth is highly complex with educational improvements seen to facilitate technological progress, which is the engine of growth.

There are several (highly-related) ways education is seen to impact on technological change:

- high levels of formal education are necessary for the successful introduction of capital equipment [Bartel and Lichtenberg (1987)];
- the above connection encourages physical capital investments [McMahon (1999)];
- during periods in which a population is undergoing increases in education there will be an effective increase in the size of the labor force, so long as education raises productivity [Barro (1991)]; and
- education disseminates information and through this adds to growth because death does not result in knowledge loss [Lucas (1988)].

These notions have received wide acceptance in the economic research community. However, the increasing consensus with respect to the conceptual importance of these factors, and the likely role of education in them, has not been matched with an emerging agreement concerning the empirical evidence.

Measuring the impact of higher education on economic growth is not straightforward. An important reason is that the growth impact of education on the skills of the labor force will be determined by both its quantity (that is, higher participation rates) and its quality (that is, the amount of knowledge imparted at any given schooling level). Understandably, given data availability, most analyses focus on the former.

The role in economic growth of both the quality and quantity of education internationally are compared in Hanushek and Kimko (2000). They test the extent to which educational quality as measured by standardized scores for mathematical and scientific literacy has contributed to economic growth differences averaged over thirty years across 139 countries. The test results are compared with the effect of changes in schooling quantities (as measured by the number of years of schooling).

They find that increases in workforce quality have a profound influence on economic growth. For example, on average a one standard deviation increase in test scores adds about 1.0 percent to a country's GDP per capita annual growth rate, which is arguably a very high impact. By contrast, increases in the quantity of schooling required to match this growth rate change seem to be very much higher: that is, to achieve a one per cent increase in the annual growth rate of a country's GDP per capita requires on average that workers had nine additional years of education.

---

[2] For education to result in social as well as private gains requires that the rents from the process are not captured completely by the educated individuals or the firms employing them. However, this will be the case if technological change flows easily from one workplace to the next [Romer (1994)].

The Hanushek and Kimko analysis does not address the sources of labor force quality, that is, in their context, the determinants of test scores. And it is very possible that these have been correlated over time with rising school participation rates. As well, there is little direct role played here with respect to higher education. To argue that the Hanushek and Kimko result supports the role of higher education as a direct growth determinant requires a link between higher education and labor quality, an issue not tested.

Barro and Sala-I-Martin (1995), Gemmel (1996) and McMahon (1999) attempt to measure the direct role of education on economic growth. The former finds that a one standard deviation increase in the ratio of public education outlays to GDP of the order of 0.3 percentage points, with relatively high effects from the tertiary education sector. For the UK, Gemmel finds that a 15 percentage point increase in educational enrollments leads to just over half a percentage point higher rate of productivity growth. These broad results are supported in Englebrecht (2003), which emphasizes in particular the positive role of human capital as a catalyst to technological diffusion.

An essential problem with these types of studies is capturing the obvious complexities in the relationships between human capital investments, innovation, knowledge and technical change. Issues of measurement and of timing loom large, with most empirical exercises being constrained to use annual data; however, there are no apparent statistical guides as to the length and nature of these dynamic processes.

While the case in theory for the importance of links between economic growth and higher education investments is strong, its statistical basis is not as yet compelling. The bottom line is that there is an argument for government subsidy of higher education, but with respect to its size there is no agreement.

2.4. Who should pay: equity

There is a commonly expressed lifetime income distribution argument for charging for higher education. The appropriate way of analyzing this issue is with respect to after-tax rates of return to higher education. There have always been a host of interpretation problems in this literature, including: the role of unmeasured ability and motivation; the significance of measurement error; and the seemingly strong assumptions associated with the use of cross-sectional data to predict the true future return to an educational investment.

However, through possibly the most pervasively used tool in applied microeconomics, the earnings function [Mincer (1974)] it is by now fairly clear that these rates of return are high [Krueger (1999)], and arguably as high as are the returns found for a host of other investment processes. This commonly found result is able to be juxtaposed with data on students' parents, which invariably find that those enrolled in higher education are much more likely on average to come from relatively advantaged families.[3] This suggests that, on average, government subsidies to higher education re-

---

[3] The evidence is compelling in all countries for which data exists. As examples, see Greenaway and Haynes (2003) for the UK, Carneiro and Heckman (2002) for the US, Chapman (1997) for Australia and Finnie and Schwartz (1997) for Canada.

distribute tax resources to individuals who as children are from privileged backgrounds and who as adults receive high individual economic returns from the higher education investment process. Barr (2001), Chapman (1997), Belfield (2000) and many others argue this proposition generally, and with respect to a host of countries. That is, a social implication of a large public sector financial support of the beneficiaries of higher education is that such approaches are regressive and undesirable.

Such a judgment is underwritten by the view that a role for government is to redistribute toward and not away from the lifetime poor. It is also based on the judgment that it is desirable to diminish the strength of the already strong nexus between childrens' lifetime economic opportunities and the socio economic standing of their parents. In these contexts the equity case for a charge is clear.

2.5. Efficiency and equity: a false distinction?

In general, analyses of public sector involvement in particular areas of economic activity treat efficiency (usually interpreted to mean the optimal use of scarce resources) and equity (which concerns fairness and income distribution) as if they are conceptually distinct. That is, it is often the case that efficiency and equity are characterized as trade-offs, with a role for government being to find an acceptable position between these goals.

However, with respect to higher education the distinction between efficiency and equity is not clear-cut. This point is clarified through consideration of the notion of equality of opportunity, which is usually seen to be a major goal for higher education policy. What the expression means is not always clear, but in the higher education context it can be interpreted as highlighting the value of policy ensuring the absence of barriers to the participation of disadvantaged prospective students in higher education. In an economic policy context, the notion of equality of opportunity underscores the point that the distinction between efficiency and equity is in many senses artificial.

That is, there are both economic and social reasons for governments to act in ways that ensure that the higher education system does not exclude talented but poor students. The reasons are as follows.

Poor prospective students can deliver important social benefits given access to higher education. That is, if able and motivated people cannot participate in higher education for financial reasons the whole economy is worse off, because talent is being wasted; there will be a less than optimal delivery of spill-overs, as well as foregone private opportunities for the excluded poor. Both Barr (2001) and Palacios (2004) emphasize these issues.

In terms of equity and distributive justice, it needs to be recognized that there is already a strong nexus between the family circumstances of children and their lifetime income prospects. Thus, if a society values equality of opportunity it should ensure that the strength of this nexus is not reinforced by education policy.

With this as background it is now useful to explore the shortcoming of the market that constitutes an overwhelming case for some sort of government intervention.

2.6. The need for government intervention: capital market 'failure'

Given that a critical aim of a higher education financing system is to not erect barriers to the participation of talented but poor students, what problems would arise in the absence of government intervention? That is, is the right approach for the government to decide the size of the per student subsidy, pay this to higher education institutions which would then require students to pay fees on enrollment?

There are major problems with this arrangement, traceable in most instances to issues of uncertainty and risk, an issue first raised by Friedman (1955). The argument can be best understood with reference to the nexus between labor markets and human capital investments. The essential point is that educational investments are risky, with the main areas of uncertainty being as follows [Barr (2001)] and [Palacios (2004)].

- Enrolling students do not know fully their capacities for (and perhaps even true interest in) the higher education discipline of their choice. This means in an extreme they cannot be sure that they will graduate and, in Australia for example, around 25 percent of those enrolling end up without a qualification.
- Even given that course completion is expected, students will not be aware of their likely relative success in the area of study. This will depend not just on their own abilities, but also on the skills of others competing for jobs in the area.
- There is uncertainty concerning the future value of the investment. For example, the labor market – including the labor market for graduates in specific skill areas – undergoes constant change. What might have looked like a good investment at the time it began might turn out to be a poor choice when the process is finished,[4] and
- Many prospective students, particularly those from disadvantaged backgrounds, may not have much information concerning graduate incomes, due in part to a lack of contact with graduates.

These uncertainties are associated with important risks since if future incomes turn out to be lower than expected, the individual is unable to sell part of the investment to refinance a different educational path, for example. This is critical in an understanding of capital market failure, and explains why banks will not be interested in unsecured loans for higher education investments: in a nonslavery world there is no collateral to be sold in the event of default. And even if it was possible for a third party to own and sell human capital, its future value might turn out to be quite low taking into account the above possibilities. The point is taken up further below.

Thus, given these uncertainties, very risk-averse potential students will be reluctant to finance higher educational investments. It is likely that those with relatively low access to finances – that is, prospective students from poor backgrounds – are particularly influenced by these realities, given a relative lack of financial resources, an underlying assumption being that there are binding credit constraints for some potential borrowers. It is instructive to examine briefly the related empirical literature.

---

[4] Freeman's (1971) 'cobweb' model of college training is apposite in this context.

2.7. Are credit constraints an issue?

The borrowing problem described above takes on a very serious form if it is actually the case that there are in reality constraints on the borrowing for individuals interested in bank financing of higher education investments. The evidence with respect to the extent to which access to credit limits human capital investment takes several forms.

The first area of research seeks to establish the strength of the relationship between family income and educational outcomes. The argument is that if there are no borrowing constraints to finance skill investments, there should also be no relationship between family income and an individual's level of education. This turns out to be a difficult research assignment because of the complicated relationships between family income and its likely association with the plethora of factors associated with educational choice. These include the quality of compulsory schooling, inherent ability, educational motivation and the transfer of values between parents and children associated with education. Recent important attempts to disentangle these relationships are found in Cameron and Taber (2001) and Carneiro and Heckman (2002).

Carneiro and Heckman make the valid point that long-run environmental and family factors are likely to be critical determinants of a young person's interest in and capacity for college education. In other words, credit constraints will not be the only determinant of access to college. They provide evidence suggesting strongly that family income is not correlated with college attendance given proper control for individuals' educational abilities (as proxied by test scores). They suggest that the main factor behind the family income-schooling relationship is ability, although they identify about 8 percent of the population "who seem to be facing short run credit constraints" [Carneiro and Heckman (2002), p. 732]. That is, credit constraints might matter, but it is important not to overstate their role in an understanding of the nexus between family income and enrollments.

Cameron and Taber provide similar evidence for the above result. With the use of instrumental variables and structural equations estimations, they explore the issue of whether or not estimates of the foregone earnings faced by groups differing with respect to family income have different effects on educational outcomes. Their range of different approaches comes to the same conclusion: there is no relationship between family background and educational outcomes.

There are empirical issues associated with interpreting the weakness of the relationship between family income and enrollments as strong evidence that there are in general low or even no credit constraints. The first, recognized by Cameron and Taber, is that empirical tests of the role of family income with respect to college choice are typically undertaken in a policy environment with programs designed to mitigate the effects of credit constraints.

Cameron and Taber (2001) write: "... it is important to keep in mind that [the results do] not necessarily mean that credit market constraints would not exist in the absence of the programs currently available" (p. 32). That is, if programs in operation are an effective solution to the lack of borrowing opportunities for poor prospective students no systematic credit constraint evidence will emerge with the use of data including program participants. Carneiro and Heckman acknowledge that the credit constraint results apply in the context of the existing policy environment, it following that their analysis should not be interpreted as evidence that credit constraints are not generally an issue for access to higher education.

This point matters for policy assessment, now explained. Suppose there is no significant evidence for the existence of credit constraints conducted in an environment in which there is policy intervention targeted on those from low family incomes. Such analyses might well reveal no, or at least low, levels of credit constraints (as do the above reported exercises).

However, the policy issue concerns the effective use of public sector resources to break down barriers to participation, and it might be that current arrangements could be improved in this context. For example, grants or loan subsidies to children from poor families, while mitigating the impact of credit constraints, may not be the best forms of intervention, a matter explored further later.

The second issue is also recognized by Carneiro and Heckman (2002). They observe that: "...children from higher income families still depend on the goodwill of their parents to gain access to funds" (p. 708). This point is critical to an interpretation of the relationship between family income and educational outcomes, because it raises the possibility that some prospective students from high income backgrounds are unable to gain access to college if their parents are unwilling to finance the investment. Under the assumption that a lack of parental support from some higher income families has the effect of precluding the participation of educationally qualified children there is a potential for underestimation of the true size of the relationship between family income and participation.

The different type of approach provided in analyses of credit constraints asks whether or not there is a relationship between family income and individuals' investment strategies. Kane and Rouse (1999) explore these issues with respect to both rates of return to education and the relative role of increases in tuition. With respect to the first, the idea is that credit constrained individuals will under-invest in college and this will result in relatively high rates of return for members of these groups. In support of this proposition they cite the evidence from Card (2000), which suggests that those from poor backgrounds receive relatively high returns to college.

Kane and Rouse also provide evidence that increases in tuition costs, compared to increases in relative graduate wages, impact relatively highly on the educational choices of the poor. They interpret these findings as evidence for the existence of credit constraints.

There might be an issue here with their conclusions suggesting the existence of credit constraints from these data. With respect to rates of return, the fact that average rates of return to higher education for members of disadvantaged groups are high does not necessarily mean that marginal returns are also high, although this potential seems likely. Unfortunately marginal returns are unable to be measured from the data.

Second, as with the Cameron and Taber, and Carneiro and Heckman, exercises, it is important to interpret relationships concerning the role of tuition in the context of the policy environment. That is, at the same time as tuition increased it might be the case that access to, and the generosity of, PELS grants for the disadvantaged also changed. In other words, analysis of college choices with respect to family income and costs of attendance needs to condition on the policy environment. Even so, the Kane and Rouse work casts doubt on a view that credit constraints are insignificant.

In a different approach to the issue using the National Longitudinal Study of Youth, Hazarika (2002) finds that the proportion of youth from wealthier families increases in a recession, as measured by local unemployment rates. This is attributed to poorer families having lower incomes, from lower employment probabilities, in recessions, implying that in hard times they are less able to afford the college enrollment of their children.

The size of the above effect is reported as follows: "...among teens with family permanent incomes below the median, a one percentage increase in the county unemployment rate is associated with a 5.8 percent decrease in the relative probability of two-year college attendance as opposed to a 3.8 percent decrease in the relative probability of four-year college attendance" (p. 141). However, another interpretation is that there is an added worker effect, such that families require their youth to take employment to supplement family incomes in recessions. But even this latter interpretation might be consistent with a credit constraint story.

Chapman, Crossley and Kim (2003) report direct tests of the role of credit constraints for an unusual sample of unemployed Canadians, surveyed in the mid-1990s. Respondents who had not undertaken training after job loss were asked the reasons. Around 12 percent replied that they wanted to participate in formal training but could not afford to, and (implicitly) were unable to borrow the financial resources to do so. The authors argue that this implies credit constraints influence human capital investments for a small, but significant, minority of disadvantaged people.

Overall, it would appear that there are many factors behind the fact that children from poorer families are less likely to attend higher education, which means that this stylized fact alone is not sufficient evidence for the existence of credit constraints. However, there is now considerable research taking into account the influence of nonfamily background factors related to access to higher education. A reasonable conclusion is that, at some points in time, it is very likely that the existence of credit constraints constitutes a financial barrier for a minority of the potential student population. In the absence of existing targeted policy aimed at decreasing the role of credit constraints there is little doubt that the problem would be measured larger.

3. The case for income contingent loans

3.1. Introduction

This section examines the case for income contingent loans for higher education. It begins with an analysis of why conventional approaches to the credit market failure explained above have important limitations. Income contingent loans take many different forms, and these differences are explored. An important part of this analysis considers the costs and benefits of different types of ICL.

3.2. Are ICLs necessary?: the problems with (government guaranteed) bank loans

A possible solution to the capital market problem described above is used in many countries, such as the US and Canada [Finnie and Schwartz (1997)]. It involves higher education institutions charging up-front fees but with government-assisted bank loans being made available to students on the basis of means testing of family incomes. Public sector support usually (for example, in Canada) takes two forms: the payment of interest on the debt before a student graduates; and the guarantee of repayment of the debt to the bank in the event of default. Arrangements such as these are designed to facilitate the involvement of commercial lenders, and the fact that they are internationally a common form of government financial assistance would seem to validate their use.

This form of assistance seems to address the capital market failure problem. With this approach banks do not need borrowers to have collateral because the public sector assumes the risks and costs of default. However, solving the problem of the provision of finance from the perspective of the banks is not the end of the story. Government assistance of this type is associated with significant other problems, now considered.

The first inadequacy of government guaranteed bank loans relates to the fact that the loans are typically not universally available.[5] That is, usually loan provision is means-tested on the basis of family income, although for many countries there are also complex sets of rules associated with age and the presumed independence of students from parental circumstances. This raises the important issue explained above and noted by Carneiro and Heckman (2002), concerning the role of the sharing of financial resources within families. If students are in families not qualifying for a subsidized loan from a bank, and yet are still unable to access household financial resources to pay an up-front fee, they face the same credit market failure as they would in the absence of a government guarantee of a bank loan. Means-testing the availability of loans must mean that some prospective students will be unable to access the system because they do not have sufficient finances to enable them to pay up-front tuition.

This problem could be addressed by making the loans available to all prospective students, since in this situation the sharing of financial resources within families becomes

---

[5] Canada Student Loans, for example, are offered to less than half of the student population [Finnie and Schwartz (1997)].

irrelevant to a student's capacity to pay fees. However, universality in the provision of loans of this type would be very expensive, given the high public costs associated with governments paying the remaining debts of those in default[6] [Barr and Crawford (1998)].

The issue of default lies at the heart of higher education financing policy. The default problem has different dimensions depending on the perspective of those involved in the process: banks, government and students.

The problem of default risk for banks is the reason that government guarantees are necessary to make commercial bank loans practical for higher education financing. But, perhaps ironically, government guarantees increase the probability of default, since with this type of insurance there is little incentive for a bank to ensure and chase repayments. And since the repayments are guaranteed by the public sector this aspect of such schemes potentially imply relatively high subsidies from taxpayers.

A critical set of related issues concerns the potential costs for prospective students with loan repayments required in regular installments, and not sensitive to a person's future capacity to repay. There are two significant problems.

The first is that some borrowers faced with obligations to repay loans that are not sensitive to their financial ability to meet these obligations might be concerned with the prospect of default. Defaulting on a student loan has the major cost of damage to a borrower's credit reputation, and thus her or his concomitant lack of eligibility for (or higher costs associated with) other prospective loans, such as for a home mortgage [Chapman (1997)].[7] It follows that particularly risk-averse prospective students may prefer not to take the default risk of borrowing. Moreover, there is important empirical evidence to suggest that those borrowers experiencing the costs of default are disadvantaged in a lifetime context, and this is now considered.

Dynarski (1994) used the National Post-Secondary Student Aid Study to explore the characteristics of debtors and finds strong evidence that earnings after leaving formal education is a strong determinant of default; those in financial difficulties are found to be much more likely to be unable to meet their loan repayment requirements. Importantly, Dynarski found that borrowers from low-income households, and minorities, were more likely to default, as were those who did not complete their studies. Her evidence offers important support for the use of ICL instead of bank loans, since the latter could discourage the participation in higher education of the relatively disadvantaged, and has the potential to punish those students who eventually become disadvantaged.

Compared to bank loans, a major advantage of ICL is that they diminish the prospect of borrowers defaulting. A properly designed ICL has as its major characteristic complete default-protection for borrowers and thus the capacity to solve an important part of the essential capital market failure for human capital investments.

---

[6] Harrison (1995) notes that in US Propriety Colleges the default rate is as high as 50 percent. The average default rate for student loans is around 15–30 percent [Wran Committee Report (1988)].

[7] This prospect is made very clear in the poster designed to encourage loan repayments for students borrowing in the Canada Student Loan scheme. It is stated that a major reason for students to meet repayments is that in the event of nonpayment they will 'risk damage to their credit reputations'.

The second problem with bank loans as a solution to the capital market financing problem is also related to their time nature of repayments. It is that, faced with the prospect of repaying a loan with a fixed level of obligations, prospective borrowers might well be concerned with future hardships in the event that their income circumstances turn out to be poor. ICL solves this problem because repayment obligations are minimized or eliminated in periods of future financial adversity. That is, ICL can deliver the important benefit of consumption smoothing, a point explained further below in a theoretical context provided by both Grout (1983) and Quiggin (2003).[8]

A final possible advantage of ICL compared to bank loans is particularly pertinent to US higher education financing policy debate over the 1990s, and is not directly related to issues of risk and uncertainty. It is instead the concern that graduates with very high levels of bank debt will be forced to undertake employment associated with relatively high earnings in order to be able to repay comfortably their college debts. A concern that this would adversely affect the supply of graduates for low pay public interest employment encouraged the Clinton administration to introduce an ICL option in the US in 1993.[9]

In summary, it seems clear that government intervention is required for optimal and equitable outcomes with respect to higher education financing. A government guarantee to cover losses for banks in the event of default solves the financing problem for the lender, but there are important problems with this approach. The costs and benefits of the alternatives are as follows:

  (i) Restricting the availability of bank loans on the basis of means-testing on household income (which is the usual form taken with such assistance) has the potential to exclude some prospective students because of their lack of access to family resources.

 (ii) Unlike bank loans ICL repayments are defined by the borrower's capacity to repay and this feature has the potential to deliver two critical benefits to borrowers: insurance against default, and consumption smoothing.

(iii) Of particular importance in the US is that commercial debt repayments unrelated to a capacity to pay have the strong prospect of influencing career choices in ways that might be seen to be socially undesirable.

However, it is important to recognize that there are different forms of income contingent financial instruments, and, even within genres, there are very distinct ways in which they can be made operational. The nature of these differences and their effects are now examined.

3.3. The various types of income contingent instruments: costs and benefits

It is important to understand that there are quite different forms of ICL, and that they have the potential for considerably different economic and social outcomes. Broadly,

---

[8] Chapman (2006b) illustrates the extent to which an ICL can deliver consumption smoothing benefits and this is discussed further below.

[9] The Clinton ICL policy initiative is analyzed in detail in Section 4.

the different forms are known as: income contingency with risk-pooling; income contingency with risk-sharing; graduate taxes; and human capital contracts. Within these broad categories there are myriad designs differentiated by parameters such as: the level of the charge; the percentage of income to be repaid; interest rates; forgiveness of the debt; and income thresholds. Even so, the broad categories are open to meaningful comparisons and analysis, and this now follows.

3.3.1. Income contingency with risk-pooling

An ICL with so-called 'risk-pooling' is one with a fixed total debt for members of cohorts involved, usually defined by students' year of enrollment. With this approach students are obligated to take some financial responsibility for debts that are not paid by others in their cohort.

Like all ICL, the risk-pooling variety offers default protection and consumption smoothing but repayment obligations are adjusted ex post to take into account the repayment experience of others in the borrowing cohort. This means that borrowers with high future incomes, the 'winners', will repay more than is repaid by those with low future incomes, the 'losers', and that the former pay more the less is repaid by members of the latter group.

Thus a risk-pooling ICL transfers some part of the default risks and costs to nondefaulters and thus has the potential to increase the repayment obligations of members of the latter group. This apparently is what happened with respect to the Yale Plan, considered in some detail below.

Nerlove (1975) analyzed risk-pooling ICLs with particular reference to the Yale Plan, and explored the behavioral consequences of such schemes with particular reference to two major micro-economic issues: adverse selection and moral hazard.

With respect to adverse selection Nerlove suggested that risk-pooling ICL are designed to be revenue-neutral; this means that individuals expecting to be winners (future high-income earners) have incentives to avoid being involved, and those potential borrowers with expectations of poor future prospects have an incentive to take such loans, because their repayments will be subsidized by the winners. This implies that the cohort of students willing to borrow from a risk-pooling ICL will on average be made up of individuals expecting their future earnings to be low; for a university such as Yale, hoping to attract the highest-quality students, the scheme has the perverse effect of encouraging those students who expect to be successful in the labor market to seek enrollment at universities offering non-ICL financial assistance.

The effects of risk-pooling ICLs have also been analyzed by Hanushek, Leung and Yilmaz (2004). They use a general equilibrium approach to examine the implications of different types of college aid, including risk-pooling ICL, on the efficiency of the economy, intergenerational mobility and income inequality. They find that, compared to both needs-based and merit-based aid, a risk-pooling ICL potentially can result in more equal distributions of income, but similarly to the conclusions of Nerlove, such schemes are likely to result in adverse selection. They raise the possibility that this form of ICL might mean that: "...the smart poor end up subsidizing the other participants, including the lower ability rich kids" (p. 26).

The above conclusion from the Hanushek, Leung and Yilmaz (2004) analysis leads the authors to promote an ability cut-off for ICL eligibility. This idea relies on the assumption that prospective students with relatively low measured ability at the point of entry have higher chances of relatively low lifetime incomes, but no evidence is offered for this proposition. An alternative policy response to the problem of adverse selection would be to make ICL borrowing mandatory, which is obviously not possible if loans of this type are available only in some universities.[10]

The second problem for risk-pooling ICL, also identified by Nerlove, involves moral hazard, and relates to repayment behavior. The issue is that since risk-pooling ICL in effect taxes the successful on the basis of declared income, the incentive is for debtors to arrange their incomes, or make job choices, to minimize repayment obligations. This could take the form of graduates choosing jobs with nonincome benefits.

The implication of this form of moral hazard behavior is that, if successful, it has the effect of requiring those debtors who have done relatively poorly in the labor market paying more than would have been expected on the level of incomes they earn. That is, there is a built-in incentive for risk-pooling ICLs not to achieve the promised levels of protection for unsuccessful debtors.

In relation to these conceptual points Raymond and Sesnowitz (1976) explores the extent to which repayment obligations from those involved in risk-pooling ICLs might be considered burdensome. Through a series of simulation exercises they found that under most sensible parameters of potential repayment, ICLs of these types would still leave most borrowers better off in terms of the effect of the repayments on rates of return to higher education.

However, even if graduates are 'better off' than not undertaking higher education in terms of retaining average high rates of return, the moral hazard point with respect to the labor/leisure choice remains. Responding to Nerlove's lament concerning the paucity of empirical evidence on the potential size of the behavioral effects from risk-pooling ICLs, Feldman (1976) conducted a series of simulations of the effects of ICL financing arrangements with respect to different medical specialty incomes. Under a range of plausible assumptions concerning labor supply, his major finding is that there would be a 6.6 percent fall in weeks worked, equivalent to an effective overall loss of about 725 new physicians in the US per year (in the mid-1970s).

The issues of adverse selection and moral hazard raised by Nerlove constitute serious challenges for those advocating risk-pooling ICLs as a solution to capital market failure and as an answer to the problems associated with government guaranteed bank loans. This seems to be particularly likely with respect to the ex post implications of risk-pooling ICL. Once graduates begin to earn relatively high incomes it should be expected

---

[10] Interestingly, risk-sharing ICLs successfully operating in some countries, and considered conceptually in the next section, are able to avoid the adverse selection essentially because they are mandatory.

that there would be some behavioral responses to what are effectively high levels of marginal tax rates.

There is an additional issue concerning the efficacy of risk-pooling ICLs not raised by Nerlove or more generally in the academic literature. It concerns transaction costs concerning how the debt is to be repaid.

As noted above, a critical aspect of ICL schemes is that of collection. Barr (2001), Palacios (2004) and Chapman (2006b), point out that there are several important conditions that have to be met in order for an ICL to be workable. While this is considered in detail below, basic points are that the collection agency has to have the capacity to accurately assess a former student's lifetime income, and to be then able to deduct debts in accordance with these incomes in a low cost way. This suggests that private institutions – such as Yale University – are likely to face major difficulties, and these may be significant enough to render nongovernment schemes unworkable.

That is, in principle, while an ICL with risk-pooling could be operated within or outside the public sector, the public sector has the distinct advantage of administrative efficient collection of debt using the internal revenue service (or tax office). This is likely to be critical for the operation of such schemes, since the probability of default of a risk-pooled ICL will determine in part how much winners compensate losers and thus reflects the extent of unequal distributions of repayments between different borrowers. Collection of ICL, and more generally ICL design, is an important matter considered further below.

3.3.2. Income contingency with risk-sharing

A different form of ICL, and one typically associated with public sector financing,[11] is known as 'risk-sharing'. With risk-sharing ICLs borrowers are obligated to repay a maximum amount in present value terms but the extent of the obligation is unrelated to the actual incomes received, and thus the repayment levels, of others contemporaneously involved in the scheme. That is, the risks of nonrepayment – the costs of income contingency – can be shared with taxpayers; consequently they will necessarily differ between loan cohorts, defined at different points in time, because of time dependent labor market exigencies.

This is a critical difference to risk-pooling ICL, particularly with respect to the implications for both adverse selection and moral hazard. That is, it is less likely for a risk-sharing ICL to repel relatively more students expecting to do very well in the labor market, and less important for those eventually repaying to attempt to avoid the obligation if the number in the cohort 'defaulting' turns out to be higher than expected.

To understand how a risk-sharing ICL might work, and in so doing clarify some of the behavioral implications of these approaches (particularly why adverse selection and

---

[11] There is no reason that risk-sharing ICL could not be provided by the private sector, however, an issue explored below with respect to human capital contracts.

moral hazard are likely to be less important problems), consider the following hypothetical example, of how a scheme might work. All the discussion is in present value terms.

The government puts a marginal value on the externalities of x, and for reasons of economic efficiency (see Section 2 above) sets tuition for a public sector university at t, where $t = MC - x$ (with MC being the marginal cost of the course). Let us assume that the government knows that with respect to all students undertaking an ICL, some proportion, d, of total loan outlays, has not been repaid in the past. So, in order to cover this exigency, on average the government requires a student undertaking a tuition ICL to commit ex ante to repaying $(1+d)t$. Ex post, if the parameters have been set accurately, the government receives in total the full tuition payment t.

With this arrangement some former students (the successful ones) will pay more than t, and some former students (the unsuccessful ones) will obviously pay less than this (including a small number who repay nothing).[12] If the parameters have been set incorrectly, and total repayments lost through default turn out to be higher than dt, taxpayers cover this additional cost. This is the sense in which taxpayers are 'sharing' the risk and, in this circumstance, taxpayers in aggregate will lose. If the parameters have been set incorrectly in the other direction, and repayments lost through default turn out to be lower than dt, taxpayers receive this windfall. In this circumstance taxpayers in aggregate will win.

The critical point is that, unlike with respect to a risk-pooling ICL, with risk-sharing ICL there are no down side risks for any of the borrowers. That is, if the government receives lower than expected repayments there are no associated penalties for borrowers.[13] Nor are there any rewards to borrowers if the opposite turns out to be the case.

The advantage of this type of ICL is that some part of the adverse selection and moral hazard associated with risk-pooling ICL can be avoided. However, even with risk-sharing ICL there is an element of adverse selection, since some prospective borrowers, those who expect with confidence to be high earners, may prefer to undertake different financing strategies to avoid paying the additional impost, dt. Because of this it is in the interest of the policymaker to have in place mechanisms and collection parameters resulting in a small d. The importance of adverse selection issue can also be minimized through the mandatory ICL collection of tuition, such as happens in Australia.

The examples of risk-shared ICLs best known are those initiated in Australia in 1989, New Zealand (1991) and the UK in 1997 (extended in 2006). But even within this category, it is clear that the forms of ICLs in these countries differ in important dimensions and thus with respect to their likely economic and educational consequences. With this important caveat in mind, there are still significant broadly based theoretical insights available with respect to risk-sharing ICLs.

---

[12] Note that the arrangement can still be attractive to all potential students because ICL offer default-protection and consumption-smoothing.

[13] The point is made in different terms by Johnstone (1972).

Conceptual issues are important to this discussion. As background, it is useful to understand that before the 1990s research on the return to education or human capital investments had proceeded in two directions. Labor economists were building increasingly sophisticated models based on expected utility maximization [e.g., Levhari and Weiss (1974), Eaton and Rosen (1980), and Paroush (1976)]. Most researchers, however, continued to use rates of return calculations [e.g., Psacharopoulos (1973, 1985)] with scant attention being paid to the private and social risks associated with the investment.

Chia (1990) attempted to combine these two strands of research by developing a simple framework whereby the risks associated with investment in higher education can be readily incorporated into conventional measures of profitability, such as the net present value. Coming at the issue of rates of return in this way allowed Chia to develop a framework robust enough to calculate the benefits to the borrower of risk-sharing ICLs, now explained.

The essence of Chia's work was to use an expected utility framework to estimate an uncertainty premium, which was then used to adjust the net present value resulting from investment in higher education. This allowed him to quantify the 'insurance content' of an ex post income-contingent fee scheme (of the risk-sharing variety) and to compare this calculation with the payment of fees with no insurance for both given levels of uncertainty and with respect to a range of risk aversion.

Chia found that if individuals are uncertain of their ability (and thus face greater uncertainty in potential income streams as a result) they would prefer an income-contingent fee scheme to paying up-front fees. The 'insurance content' of the income-contingent scheme could, in some instances, amount to more than the equivalent of a year's fees. On the other hand, if individuals are fully aware of their abilities, then those with high abilities would prefer to pay their fees up-front while the less able would opt for the income-contingent scheme. It should be recognized that there are, of course, forms of uncertainty unrelated to an individual's ability, such as the future state of the labor market, meaning that even those fully aware of their individual capacities will not be able to predict their lifetime incomes.

Grout (1983) presented a version of the Arrow (1973a, 1973b) discrimination model with imperfect information and showed that "... an element of income contingency will offset to some extent the misallocation of educational resources resulting from imperfect expectations". Similar to Chia's result concerning ability, he showed that the benefits of risk-sharing ICLs are greater the less certain individuals are of their future incomes and the greater is risk aversion. From Grout's simulation exercises ICLs seem to have the most propitious leverage in terms of the reduction of the costs of uncertainty. That is, the effects of ICLs on welfare even given a significant range of risk aversion are relatively small compared to their benefits in terms of minimizing the effects of uncertainty.

Quiggin (2003) extends these results, showing that educational financing schemes with income-contingent repayments provide a mixture of consumption-smoothing benefits and insurance against the uncertain outcomes of risky educational investments. Using a conventional two period modeling approach with risk aversion and imperfect information, Quiggin establishes that educational financing schemes with income-contingent repayment will enhance welfare relative to the alternative of up-front fees yielding the same revenue in present value terms.

Quiggin also demonstrates that the form of ICL with the best welfare properties has a threshold below which no repayments are required, since the threshold delivers the highest level of consumption smoothing. However, there is a critical trade-off with respect to the design of an ICL, at least with respect to risk-neutral individuals: there is an insurance effect, which is welfare improving, and there is a subsidy effect, which is welfare reducing. This promotes for policy consideration the critical role played by the choice of collection parameters: if they are insufficiently generous there will be inadequate insurance provision; but if they offer considerable protection the associated subsidies will be too high. This is a critical trade-off for the design of such schemes.

Moen (1998) analyzes variants of risk-sharing ICLs using an equilibrium search model of the Diamond–Mortensen–Pissarides variety. His analysis begins with the familiar point that human capital investments are irreversible, and he shows that given this irreversibility, investments will be less than optimal unless ex post those investing are able to share the costs of job search.

He illustrates that this is possible with an ICL in which the interest rate on the debt is zero in periods of unemployment. In this model the costs of job search are shared and the essential financing problem is addressed. The question of whether or not this is a large or small issue for policy should be addressed by noting that graduates in fact spend very little time over their lifetimes in unemployment, even though they may be involved in extensive periods of search for preferred employment. It is arguable that the Moen result could be generalized to other periods of graduate job search characterized by the receipt of relatively low wages.

The overall conclusion from these somewhat different modeling approaches is the same: an ICL risk-sharing system is in general welfare increasing compared to either bank loans or up-front fees. The greater are both risk-aversion and uncertainty, the stronger are these results. Moreover, these analyses focus on economic efficiency with the conclusions implicitly giving no weight to the potential for ICLs of this type to contribute propitiously in equity terms. This suggests that the relatively high welfare properties of risk-sharing ICLs implied understate the overall social benefits of these types of approaches to higher education financing.

There is a caveat to the general thrust of the analytical results. This is that the greater is the insurance protection offered (through, for example, having a very high first income-threshold of repayment, or a very low nominal rate of interest on the debt), the less likely is an ICL to achieve a social optimum. This is the result of risk-sharing arrangements offering relatively higher taxpayer subsidies as a trade-off to the provision of default-protection for borrowers.

3.3.3. Graduate taxes

A very different form of an income contingent instrument, and one that has yet to be implemented, is known as a graduate tax. A GT takes the following broad form.

Graduates (or former students, more generally) agree to repay a proportion of their incomes, say 2 percent per year, for a given length of time (which could be as long as a lifetime). Thus they share the essential ingredients of both risk-pooling and risk-sharing ICLs, which is that 'loan' payments are made in such a way as to ensure default-protection. They can be designed to raise considerable revenue, even at the same time as their influence on returns to higher education are not affected significantly, a point made by Lincoln and Walker (1995) through some plausible simulations.

However, there are significant differences between GTs and ICLs. The most obvious is that the former are in no sense based on cost-recovery. This can lead to the so-called 'Mick Jagger' problem, as explained in Barr (2001). The lead singer of the Rolling Stones rock band studied for a short time at the London School of Economics. If a GT was applied to his income for life (and if it could be collected), Mr Jagger's payments would massively exceed the direct costs of his higher education, even by several hundred fold. The example is very extreme, but serves to illustrate that the revenue collected can be seen to be excessive in many cases, and also unrelated to the benefits accruing from higher education.

A second and related difference is that for very high earners the fact that the GT is on-going, that is, an addition to income tax, suggests that there are much higher work disincentives from this form of payment than there would be for a risk-sharing ICL [Barr (2001)]. This is a variant of the moral hazard problem associated with risk-pooling ICLs raised by Nerlove (1975) and given empirical content by Feldman (1976).

Third, the revenue from GTs will not reflect marginal cost pricing rules, and nor do the resources received have the any allocative implications – instead they are essentially a device designed to raise money from the direct beneficiaries of higher education. The incapacity of GTs to influence economic efficiency is highlighted in both Barr (2001) and Greenaway and Haynes (2003) as a major reason to prefer different forms of income contingent instruments, such as a risk-sharing ICL.

The major possible benefit of a GT is that the arrangement has the potential to deliver considerable resources to the public sector, much more than is the case with respect to ICLs. As well, and associated with this, if collected efficiently and fairly, GTs will generally provide the highest level of progressivity in a lifetime sense since graduates with the highest incomes will pay more than they would under alternative financing arrangements. On the other hand, the fact that GT payments will exceed public sector outlays for many graduates suggests that they are unlikely to have propitious resource allocation implications.

A final point concerning the efficacy of a GT is also related to the pricing rules, and has a critical administration challenge as well. That is, should there be any attempt to have repayments reflect the time and other higher education resources absorbed by the student? While this is a general issue for courses of markedly different length, the point applies also to the issue of whether or not identical repayment rates should apply for students enrolling in one course only, or not graduating, compared to those completing a degree (or several degrees). In one sense this is a similar issue to that raised above concerning marginal cost pricing.

3.3.4. Human capital contracts

There has been recent interest in whether private firms could be involved in financial arrangements in which payments are tied to the borrower's income. Proponents of these arrangements question the notion that it should only be the public sector, and not the private sector, sharing in the risk involved with ICL schemes. That is, some analysts argue that there are circumstances in which governments could let the investment and risk-taking of investments in education be placed solely in private hands. Moreover, private involvement could take place with or without a framework of national higher education financing assistance.

The most common incarnation of the above idea is a contract that specifies a percentage of income to be paid over a predetermined time period. With such an arrangement the instrument takes a form similar to a GT (with the additional twist that the percentage is determined by the amount paid in the 'borrowing' period). This way, a high earner would pay more than was borrowed and a low earner would pay less. From the investor's perspective, the loan resembles a significant investment in the borrower's earning power. In the spirit of recognizing the nature of the lender's investment, arrangements of this type have been called human capital contracts (HCC) by those interested in private investments in education.

Palacios (2004) argues that these instruments would promote efficiency in the higher education market by increasing the information available about future earnings with respect to different universities and fields of study. The contracts would therefore reflect market expectations of students' future earnings, thereby creating an observable 'market value' for different types of education or different cohorts of individuals. He adds that this information would also create a market instrument for measuring the value of the insurance implicit in ICLs, thereby introducing a market measure of the extra d that governments should ask students to pay to compensate the repayment losses on an ICL.

Recognizing the possibility that using loans whose payments are tied to income may mitigate income risk, there have been a few attempts to understand the personal financial impacts from the borrower's perspective. Rather than using aggregate data to infer the needs of borrowers, these studies have applied financial decision theory to the market for loans.

Carver (2004) creates a model of individual choice for loans to explore preferences among different loan alternatives. In the model utility maximizing borrowers with uncertain income prospects consider the effect of both standard debt and percentage of income loans (HCC) on the probability distribution of the NPV of future income. The borrower receives funding from a risk neutral lender who offers prices for debt and HCC funding. The model shows that according to Pareto criteria, optimal contracts can consist of: (i) all standard debt; (ii) all HCC funding; or (iii) some combination of debt and HCC.

The type of contract that is optimal depends on the lender's beliefs about the borrower's income prospects, the borrower's beliefs about his own income prospects and also the borrower's degree of risk aversion. Carver then goes on to suggest that the individual borrowing decision can be made in a manner similar to the corporate borrowing decision. The results indicate that borrowers who are more uncertain about future income or who are risk averse about future income prospects will choose to raise money by pledging percentages of income rather than taking on standard debt. Carver's model can be adapted to arrive at the same conclusions for HCCs as Chia reaches with respect to risk-sharing ICLs.

HCC are now in operation, with the first business formed known as MyRichUncle, founded by Vishal Garg and Raza Khan, in the US in 2002. MyRichUncle began with a subset of engineering students at the University of California, San Diego. To minimize problems of adverse selection, eligibility for the contract is determined in part through academic merit. Repayments of the obligation are remitted directly to the company, with amounts validated through the provision of income information made available to the IRS. This is bound to be less efficient than would be a direct deduction, as operates in Australia, New Zealand and other countries, but the principle of default protection remains intact.

3.4. Summary

Market failure in the provision of resources for human capital investments is a critical issue for higher education financing policy. Given the presence of credit constraints associated with a lack of collateral to underwrite human capital investment borrowing, there is a case for government intervention. One typical way in which this issue is addressed takes the form of guarantees for bank loans.

However, there are important shortcomings with this approach. One, loans will not be universally available, suggesting that some students with unwilling families will not be able to borrow, and will thus face the inequities and difficulties associated with the payment of up-front tuition. Two, the costs for the public sector can be high, due to student default. Three, some risk averse potential students will not be prepared to undertake loans with repayment burdens which are insensitive to a student's future capacity to pay. And four, there might well be socially unproductive career choices made by graduates facing very high loan repayments that are not sensitive to capacity to pay. These shortcomings imply strongly that some other approach to the capital market problem is required.

Income contingent loans offer a potential solution. An ICL requires a student to repay a debt depending on the level of their future incomes. Their essential benefit is that, if properly designed, they can eliminate the prospect of default and in so doing address the basic capital market failure.

It has been explained that here are several forms of income contingent financing instruments: risk-pooling, risk-sharing, graduate taxes and human capital contracts. The discussion has illustrated major differences between, and complexities within, all genres.

ICL with risk-pooling are characterized by adverse selection in terms of who chooses to be involved in such schemes, and moral hazard with respect to the labor/leisure choice once the repayment period begins. ICLs with risk-sharing can avoid these problems, but are associated with trade-offs between offering insurance against risk for the student: the greater is the insurance provided, the higher necessarily is the degree of public sector subsidy.

GTs have little prospect of allocative efficiency because there are no economic benefits delivered to institutions from price competition. However, GTs offer what is arguably the most progressive basis of the collection of charges. GTs do not yet exist.

A recent innovative instrument involving only the private sector is known as human capital contracts. These arrangements are between students and a financing company, in which the former is given a sum of money for tuition and living expenses in return for a contractual obligation to pay the lender a percentage of income for a pre-determined period after graduation. HCC thus involve risk-sharing – with the risk burden being assumed by the lender – and are more a form of equity than they are debt. There are now several examples of operating HCC, and a burgeoning research literature [see particularly Palacios (2004) and Carver (2004)].

4. Income contingent loans: International applications

4.1. Background

A typical chapter in the Handbook of Economics series takes the form of offering a description, synthesis and critical analysis of a well-defined body of academic research. While this has been possible with respect to higher education financing theory and the role of income contingent loans, there is a relative paucity of research into the effects of these types of financing policies.

In part this is traceable to the fact that national governments' experience with ICL is both recent and limited, even though it is clear that policy models of this type are increasingly becoming a favored way for higher education financing policy. It is also due in part to the fact that there is often only poor data available, for example with respect to the access of the disadvantaged to higher education.

As well as the relative paucity of both evidence and analysis concerning ICL, there are also research limitations with respect to the effects of particular variants of ICLs. For example, there is only one well-reported example of a risk-pooling ICL, which is the Yale Plan. As well, a graduate tax has not been instituted anywhere at this stage.

Finally, for only one country, Australia, is there a substantial body of research on the operation and effects of the most common ICL, the risk-sharing form.[14]

An implication is that the discussion following is uneven in terms of the coverage of recent experience with ICLs. However, significant space is given in Section 6 to the reporting and analysis of Australia's risk-sharing ICL. It is the only example in which there has been considerable research with respect to the many empirical and administrative policy issues raised concerning ICL schemes.

4.2. The international experience with ICLs in brief

4.2.1. The Yale Plan

Yale University introduced an ICL in 1972, extended in 1976 but discontinued several years later. Apart from loans being repaid depending on income, the scheme had the feature of borrowing being of a 'group loans' form, in which there was mutual responsibility between members with respect to the repayment of the total debt. That is, the Yale scheme was a risk-pooling ICL.

Individual repayments were not unlimited, however, with a cap being defined at 150 percent of the borrower's loan. This then became a 'buy-out' option for former students wishing to discontinue in the program [Palacios (2004)]. Even so, risk-pooling necessarily meant that high-income earners covered the unpaid debts of low-income earners and those who defaulted for other reasons.

Initial default rates of 15 percent exceeded expectations, and this had an unfortunate behavioral implication. This was to encourage those remaining in the scheme to avoid repayments as well, increasing the burden further for those not so doing. These effects are close to what would be expected with the moral hazard issue raised by Nerlove (1975).

One of the major problems with the Yale scheme was that the university acted as the collection agency. However, an educational institution is poorly equipped to efficiently enforce the payment of income contingent loans, and this lack of expertise effectively encouraged and reinforced the sense of inequity of those Yale debtors remaining in the scheme. The critical role of administration and collection is taken up further below.

4.2.2. Sweden

In Sweden in 1988 the government's student assistance scheme had both a grant and a loans component [Morris (1989)]. The repayment arrangements were of the conventional type except that at low levels of income former students were allowed to defer repayments. There was evidence of student concerns about repayments at the time [Morris (1989)].

---

[14] The New Zealand experience is becoming more studied, but is still relatively unknown with respect to questions of access.

The scheme was changed in 1989 to allow a fuller embrace of the notion of income contingent repayment. The arrangement is that former students now repay 4 percent of their average incomes over the previous two years. The collection is done through an education loans office. There is little available evidence of the effect of the scheme.

4.2.3. Australia (in summary)

In 1989 Australia instituted the world's first broadly based income contingent charging system for higher education, known as the Higher Education Contribution Scheme. HECS seeks to recover a part of tuition costs, and is not concerned with student income support.[15] It is a risk-sharing ICL and is analyzed in detail in Section 6.

4.2.4. New Zealand

The second country to adopt a broadly based ICL was New Zealand, with this happening in 1991. The New Zealand system shares several features of HECS. Specifically:
- loan repayments depend on an individual's income, and are collected through the tax system which made this simple in operational terms; and
- there is a first income threshold of repayment, after which there is a progressive percentage rate of collection.

The New Zealand arrangements differ importantly to those introduced in Australia. In particular:
- the loans are designed to cover both university fees and some living expenses, although there is also a system of means-tested grants for students from poor backgrounds;
- initially the loans carried a market rate of interest, but now interest charges are subsidized and depend on the financial circumstances of debtors; and
- universities were originally free to set their own fees, with a maximum level being introduced in 2003.

There have been more changes to the New Zealand loan arrangements than has occurred with HECS, and most of this has been with respect to the interest rate regimes. While starting with an approximate real rate reflecting market conditions, in 2000 the scheme was changed to incorporate a zero nominal interest rate for the period a student is enrolled, and variations to the application of real rates of interest were determined by graduates' employment circumstances [Warner (1999)].

The administrative sophistication associated with the now complex interest rate regime might have been expected to add to the costs of the scheme, but it still appears to be the case that collection costs are low;[16] LaRocque (2005) reports that in 2004 the annual costs of collection were around (NZ) $23 million per year, which is even lower than estimates for the collection of HECS.

---

[15] In Australia income support takes the form of means-tested grants.
[16] LaRocque (2005).

A potential advantage of the New Zealand scheme is that universities receive the tuition revenues directly. This implies that in New Zealand there is the prospect of resource allocation effects within the higher education system. For this reason some commentators, for example Barr (2001), have compared the New Zealand approach favorably with the pre-2005 Australian arrangements, in which ICL revenues accrued to the Treasury with no implications for resource allocation. In the 2005 the Australian system was changed along New Zealand lines in this regard.

There is little direct evidence of the effects of the New Zealand ICL on the access of disadvantaged prospective students. However, both Maani and Warner (2000) and LaRocque (2005) report data on changes in participation with respect to ethnicity at the University of Auckland over the 1990s. The former suggest that there has been a marked relative decrease in Maori enrollments, but the latter points nevertheless to a substantial increase in the proportions of Maoris enrolling over the post-ICL reform period.

4.2.5. The Republic of South Africa

The Republic of South African introduced an ICL in 1991, known as the National Student Financial Aid Scheme. NSFAS was motivated essentially by a concern that without assistance the marked racial skewing of the higher education system away from nonwhite students would remain [Jackson (2002), Ishengoma (2002)]. While bursaries could have been used instead of ICL, it was considered that the costs involved "... would not be financially sustainable" [Jackson (2002), p. 83]. The scheme initially provided resources to about 7,500 students, but by 2002 this number had risen to over 100,000, or more than 20 percent of South Africa's higher education students.

Resources are distributed via the universities, with preference going to prospective students who are both poor and academically able. That is, unlike other national schemes, the South African ICL involves means testing on the basis of family income at the point of entry to higher education.

Collection takes the form of former students repaying directly to NSFAS when their income reaches R26,000 per annum, at a rate of 3 percent of income, and this proportion rises to reach a maximum of 8 percent of income per year when income exceeds R59,000. In this sense the collection parameters are similar to HECS in that they are progressive, but there are two major differences between the South African approach and those used in both Australia and New Zealand.

The first concerns the first income level of repayment, which at about $US5,000 is very much lower than the thresholds used in other countries' ICLs.[17] Second, in the first instance the student repays directly to the lending institution. That is, the taxation system is not the first port of call, but is instead a last resort. Employers are required to be involved only when a student is apparently not maintaining expected debt repayments. It is unclear how much this adds to administrative costs, but it would seem to suggest that

---

[17] See Jackson (2002).

collection would necessarily be relatively expensive with such an approach.[18] NSFAS loan repayments are ploughed back into the system, so to some extent the arrangements are self-financing.

4.2.6. The UK

Higher education financing policy over the last 15 years or so in the UK has been characterized by considerable instability. Until very recently there were no tuition charges, but such charges were introduced in 1997 with the adoption of (a highly modified) version of HECS.

As well, there have been notable changes over time in the value and institutional nature of student income support. In the 1980s grants were offered on the basis of parental income, but the real value of this support eroded significantly and Barr argues that "by the late 1980s [it] was no longer adequate fully to support a student's living costs".[19]

In 1990 a loan scheme was introduced, but collection was not based on a former student's income. The loans were designed to replace half of the support previously covered by the grant, but in effect their impact was likely to be smaller than this given that they attracted a zero rate of interest. Barr (2001) notes critically that "It would have been cheaper to give the money away".[20]

In 1995 the Conservative Government set up a higher education funding committee, due to report after the election of 1997. Chaired by Sir Ron Dearing, the report[21] recommended strongly the adoption of a scheme based on HECS. It had the following features:

- a uniform charge of about 25 percent of average course costs;
- the charge to take the form of a debt, with loan recovery to be contingent on income and collected through the tax system;
- the debt to be adjusted over time, but by less than the market rate of interest; and
- revenue from the scheme to flow to the Internal Revenue Service.

The Labour Government, elected in 1997, adopted a heavily modified version of the Dearing Committee's recommendation. In particular an income test was introduced, and this takes the following form: students from poor backgrounds are excused from paying any tuition, while students from rich families incur the entire debt. In between the debt obligation is determined by means of a sliding scale.[22] This decision seemed to reflect a concern by the government that relatively disadvantaged students would be

---

[18] Jackson (2002) argues that the annual administrative costs are less than 2 percent of the total value of loans distributed. The more important figure however would be costs as a proportion of revenues collected, data not reported.

[19] Barr (2001), p. 202.

[20] Barr (2001), p. 202.

[21] Dearing (1997).

[22] Barr (2001).

more likely than others to find an ICL a deterrent to higher education participation, a view at variance with the evidence from the HECS experience documented in Section 6. The important point for ensuing policy development, however, is that the 1997 changes introduced ICL to the UK.

In 2006, the UK Government is implementing further reforms to higher education financing. The major changes are:

- the introduction of price discretion for universities, but with a cap of 3,000 pounds per full-time student year; and
- the introduction of tuition for all students, but with the poorest being provided with subsidies.

An arguable advantage of the 2006 UK system over that of Australia and more consistent with the New Zealand approach is the introduction of some price discretion; universities are able to charge what they want up to a maximum level of about (US)$5,000 per full-time course, with the resources going directly to the universities. However, it appears that practically all universities have opted for the maximum charge, implying no real consequences for allocative efficiency.

As with the Australian and New Zealand schemes, the UK ICL policy is likely to be relatively inexpensive to administer: that is, income tax collection arrangements greatly facilitate an ICL's operation.

The last is a major conclusion from the adoption of such arrangements in countries with efficient, comprehensive and settled income tax collection mechanisms. As explained in Section 5, this is far from the case with respect to developing countries, where public administrative challenges related to the collection of ICL loom large.

4.2.7. The US

In 1993 the Clinton Administration introduced broadly based reforms to student loan programs [Brody (1994), Schrag (2001)]. One noteworthy aspect of the reforms adopted at this time included an option for students to adopt income contingent repayments for some part of their loan obligations, with the ICL obligation being up to 20 percent of an agreed income basis. Given the focus of earlier discussion concerning the advantages of ICL over other loan mechanisms, it is of interest to explain the motivation for the introduction of the US approach. In short, the justification for an ICL option in the US reform can be traced not to risk or uncertainty with respect to the future graduate incomes.

Instead the background to the introduction of an ICL option in the US seems to be the Clinton administration's concern for the job choice of graduates. Specifically the perceived problem was that the very high loan repayment burdens of graduates were such as to make job choices in relatively low paid, but presumably socially productive employment, close to impossible. Brody argues that this was the foundation of the proposal, and quotes President Clinton (who participated in the Yale Plan):

A student torn between pursuing a career in teaching or corporate law, for example, will be able to make a career choice based on what he or she wants to do, not how much he or she can earn to pay off the college debt.[23]

This perspective is supported by Schrag (2001), who reports Kramer (1987) suggesting that the effect of escalating costs and debts for law schools is that they would

... be filled with many more students who, as they become lawyers, do so with the single-minded objective of milking the profession for all it is worth in order to be able to pay retrospectively for their legal education.[24]

Schrag suggests that law graduates in public sector jobs would typically face repayments of conventional loans that were around 40 percent of after-tax earnings.[25]

In support of the above, a survey[26] of Georgetown and Catholic University law students, conducted by Schrag (2001), suggested that up to 70 percent of students who responded that they were interested in public sector law employment said that they would have to choose jobs in more highly paid private practice because of their loan obligations. US Senate hearings at the time, consistent with President Clinton's view, documented that this was the major motivation for the income contingent loan scheme [Schrag (2001)].

That is, ICL was promoted in the US as a result of the perceived problems associated with the very high level of conventional loan repayments, which is certainly not the case with respect to the background to ICL introduction in Australia, New Zealand and the UK. In these countries, the regressivity of having a no-charge system, the importance of default protection in the repayment of loans, and the need for resources to allow expansion of higher education were the principal motivations for the introduction of ICL schemes.

The ICL reforms introduced in the US have not worked. With respect to take-up, for example, in 1999 only 7 percent of the eligible student population had chosen to convert their loan obligations to the ICL option [Schrag (2001)]. The reasons for this are now explored.

The basis for low take-up of ICL in the US seems to have two, arguably closely related, explanations. In broad terms these are: the poor design characteristics of the scheme; and the government's ineptitude in explaining and publicizing accurately the scheme's implications for student debt and repayment obligations. It is possible that both weaknesses reflect a lack of ICL policy experience on the part of those with US policy influence.

---

[23] President William J. Clinton, Radio Address to the Nation (1 May 1993).

[24] Kramer (1987), pp. 240–241.

[25] This is very much higher that the repayment proportions of taxable income required in the ICL schemes of Australia and New Zealand, for example, of around 3–6 percent of taxable incomes.

[26] It should be noted that the response rate of the survey of around 30 percent was very low, raising the possibility that the data are an inaccurate reflection of general views concerning the scheme.

With respect to design, the US ICL scheme has several anomalies. The first is that the option for students to convert their loans into an ICL did not cover borrowing obligations that could be sourced to their college. This meant that a graduate with other loan repayments would have to repay 20 percent of their income at the same time that they faced high additional loan obligations. That is, for some students choosing the part-ICL option would result in lower future disposable incomes than would have been the case with alternative borrowing choices.

Second, the ICL scheme incorporated an adjustment of a debtor's income to take into account expenditure for necessities, and this was related to legislative assessments of poverty levels. Unfortunately, the adjustment to incomes was insensitive to household composition, the implication being that married debtors in some circumstances faced a far higher burden than would be the case for the unmarried. That is, the scheme implicitly taxed marriage and thus was likely to place particular loan obligations on spouses who have no responsibility for the debt.

Third, the scheme had an unusual arrangement with respect to what is known as 'forgiveness'. That is, debtors who had not repaid their loans after 25 years were not obliged to repay their remaining obligations, a feature of other loan systems (such as Canada Student Loans), known as forgiveness. However, for the US scheme the slate is not wiped clean, with the amount still owed after 25 years being treated as income to be taxed accordingly. This could mean for some ICL debtors that they would face loan repayments in the final year that were a very high proportion of (or in an extreme, even exceeding) actual income. This suggests that the US ICL scheme was not a repayment arrangement completely sensitive to future capacity to repay.

The other reasons behind the poor take-up of the US ICL scheme are related to government information processes. Two points are worth noting.

The first is that, according to the Schrag survey, only a small proportion of students who might have converted into ICL were informed of its existence, with more than two-thirds of respondents saying that they had never heard of it. Further, in a related survey only 14 percent of student Financial Aid Advisers said that they 'Understood the (income contingent loan) option well'.[27]

Second, while the US government disseminated information about the relative merits of different loan options for students, some of the data were misleading. For example, comparisons of the expected total repayments of alternative loan repayment streams were presented with an implicit discount rate of zero. This error implied that the ICL option was much more expensive than it was and, because the ICL repayment process would usually take more time than other options, it also suggested that it would cost more in total. As well, relative loan repayment comparisons of amounts to be repaid only give no weight to the value of the default protection inherent in ICL, which is arguably a very important feature of an ICL.

In short, it should be no surprise that the US government ICL reforms have not been productive. The basic point from the experiment is that policy design and information

---

[27] Schrag (2001), p. 795.

processes are critical to the success of public sector initiatives. That is, the US scheme does not adequately address the issue of default protection, and has been inaccurately and insufficiently promoted to its potential users.

In the US over the last decade or so, there has also been a move by private universities toward a form of income contingent repayment of the debt of law students. These schemes are known as 'loan repayment assistance programs' (LRAP). The arrangement, now with 56 law schools [American Bar Association (2003)], entitles law graduates to some forgiveness of loan obligations who choose employment in '... lower-paying public service jobs – such as legal services programs or some government agencies ... '.[28] The motivation behind universities' subsidies of LRAP is clear, which is to facilitate the role for private colleges of enabling more lawyers than otherwise to undertake periods of relatively socially productive employment, the same basis as that which encouraged the Clinton reforms. The effects of these programs are not so far well documented.

4.2.8. Chile

In 1994 Chile introduced an income-contingent loan scheme to replace the previous fixed-payment loan system [Leiva (2002)]. The loan carries a real interest rate of 2 percent, and requires from the student annual payments of the lesser between 5 percent of income and a fixed amount [Palacios (2004)].

Importantly, each university is responsible for collecting the payments from the University Credit resulting in widely varied collection results from institution to institution, with average country-wide cost-recovery levels at around 60 percent, as reported in Palacios (2004).[29] Palacios also notes that the system is not widely considered to be successful, for the following reasons: cost-recovery levels are low, and the amounts available for lending are far from satisfying student demand.

According to Palacios, Chile's example reinforces the notion that universities are poorly suited to debt collecting, a point which seems to follow from the Yale ICL experience. That is, for an ICL scheme to work it is critical that repayment collections use a national tax or social security agency. This issue is taken up in Section 5 following.

4.3. Common factors in the successful adoption of ICLs[30]

It is interesting to examine some of the circumstances behind the apparent successful adoption of ICL in Australia, New Zealand, the Republic of South Africa and the UK. Chapman and Greenaway (2006) record there are several factors shared by these four countries which might help in an understanding of their adoption of ICL schemes

---

[28] American Bar Association (2003), Appendix.

[29] This number reflects collection for other types of loans as well, so the collection amount for only the income-contingent ones could be different.

[30] The discussion of Section 4.3 follows closely Chapman and Greenaway (2006).

within a similar time frame. Two critical aspects of this relate to shared institutional background.

The first is that the above four countries all have in place taxation systems that could be used to collect efficiently student charges on the basis of future incomes. This is a critical administrative issue, and is fundamental to the prospects of the adoption of ICLs in other countries. It is interesting that in the South African case authorities chose to use the tax system as a back-up rather than the port of first call for loan collection, but it still remains the case that the tax system is available for collection.

Second, in all four countries there is a similar higher education system, essentially inherited from the UK. An important characteristic is that the vast majority of universities are public sector institutions, which has meant that the recovery of a loan designed to pay a charge is uncomplicated if the collection authority is also part of the public sector (the internal revenue service or equivalent). Indeed in the Australian and UK cases the revenue from ICLs were centralized and accrued to the Treasury without reference to, and with no implications for, the direct financing of universities. This has meant that the more complicated problems associated with delivery of a direct revenue base to specific universities are avoided.[31]

It is also worth stressing that in all of these countries there was a clear recognition that the time for 'free' higher education was over (a position not shared for example in the US, since charges were the norm in that country). The expansion of the number of university places, or improvements in the quality of the service, were seen to be desirable, and none of the governments was prepared to finance the required outlays from additional taxation or reduced public services. Chapman and Greenaway argue that this can be traced to a world wide move toward more parsimonious government after about the mid-1980s and, perhaps more importantly, to the recognition that university education financed without direct contributions from the private beneficiaries is in essence regressive and inequitable.[32]

It is possible that the apparent successful implementation of the Australian ICL helped motivate administrative change in these directions in some of the other countries. That is, New Zealand policy advisers were aware of developments in Australia, and there is little doubt that direct contact between analysts from Australia and the UK influenced the nature and form of debate in the latter country. Perhaps the policy point is, as Kenneth Boulding once observed: 'If it exists, then it is possible'.[33]

While there have been significant reforms in the direction of the adoption of ICLs in the above countries, this has not so far been a shared experience in developing countries. This is the case even though there has been a significant amount of attention with respect to ICL reforms from the World Bank, the UK Department of International Development

---

[31] As Chapman (1997), Barr (2001) and others note, this characteristic of ICLs has the important cost of not delivering any resource allocation benefits from price competition.

[32] These arguments were part of the explicit policy debate in Australia [Chapman (1997)], New Zealand [Warner (1999)] and the UK [Barr (2001)].

[33] Kenneth Boulding, unpublished lecture, Harvard University, 1972 (as recalled by Glenn Withers).

and other international aid agencies. The following section examines the experience of these countries, and derives conclusions as to the relative lack of successful implementation of ICLs in developing countries.

4.4. Summary

There are several recent applications of the concept of ICL for higher education, and just about all of are of the risk-sharing form, meaning that the public sector bears the costs of uncertainty. There are no national risk-pooling loans, nor is there yet an example of a GT. HCC are just being implemented, but the numbers thus far are small.

There is not a great deal of information or analyses of income contingent financial instruments. This is due in part to the fact that ICL policy initiatives are still new, and also that the data requirements of important aspects of ICL schemes are significant. To address this paucity of information the Section 6 considers in detail the experience of an ICL in which there has already been considerable research and analysis, that of Australia.

Some lessons are already clear. One is that ICL of the risk-pooling variety seem destined to fail, and this can be traced to the adverse selection and moral hazard issues raised by Nerlove (1975) and others. As well, an essential lesson for public policy is that collection, design and information issues seem to be critical to the acceptance and success of loan schemes, a point emphasized in a different form in Section 5.

5. Application issues for income contingent loans in developing countries: The importance of institutional context and administration

5.1. Application issues for income contingent loans in developing countries: background

There have been many missions to developing countries exploring higher education financing reform, with a particular focus on the possibility of introducing ICLs. Specifically and among others, these have been to: Indonesia (1995 and 1998), Papua New Guinea (1996), Namibia (1996), Malaysia (1999), Ethiopia (2000), Rwanda (2001), the Philippines (2002 and 2003)[34] and Mexico (in 2003). A major problem seems to be that of implementation and administration.

This section explores the policy debate and intervention with respect to the developing countries noted above. An attempt is made to draw some lessons from what are obviously disparate experiences and different challenges; it does become clear, however, that there are broad points of commonality and shared problems to be addressed in the reform of higher education financing in developing countries. As a practical guide

---

[34] For a fuller description and analyses of these experiences, see Chapman (2006b).

concerning how to go about such reform in a generic sense, a primer is offered to provide a checklist for productive change in a hypothetical developing country, the essence of which is based on the case studies.

Chapman (2006b) argues that developing countries, with some notable exceptions, typically do not enjoy the soundly based, efficient and comprehensive income tax arrangements that characterize the policy environments of Australia, New Zealand and the UK, for example. Most often, alternative potential systems of collection – such as those associated with universal delivery of social security – are also not to be found. As well, many countries are beset by problems of corruption in public administration, and their informal economies are comparatively large. There is intense competition between various priorities for public finances and, due in part to weaknesses in the taxation system, there is little revenue to ensure propitious public administration.

Where government-subsidized student loan schemes, of any description, exist or have been tried, failures and extremely high default rates have induced scepticism about the potential for success of any future programs in this area. The legislative frameworks surrounding the financial sector are often weak, archaic and/or undeveloped, with the practical effect that there is little legal recourse where borrowers default on loans. Furthermore, in some countries a culture has developed among students and former students that relates specifically to student loans: namely, an atmosphere of disregard for the integrity of student loans as legitimate policies.

Much of the contribution of this chapter is far from unique, and there is an emerging literature focusing on administrative and institutional constraints related to education reforms in developing countries. For example, Ziderman and Albrecht (1995), Johnstone and Aemero (2001), Salmi (1999) and others analyze the problems associated with the institution of student loan programs in developing countries. While there has been an increasing emphasis on imposing charges, and moving student income support away from grants and toward loans, the significant problems of administration and collection are an important theme of this literature.

5.2. *The ICL adoption debate in developing countries: case studies*

5.2.1. *Ethiopia*

In Ethiopia only 30 percent of children commence primary school. Student numbers fall sharply at upper secondary level, where substantial up-front tuition fees are charged. Until only five years ago, higher education had been located exclusively in the public sector. Ethiopia, however, educates at this level only a minute proportion: 30,000 students are enrolled in subsidized or 'regular' places. A similar number is enrolled on a full-fee basis in evening courses and the rapidly burgeoning private sector, however, enrolled 9,000 students in 2001. At that point most students paid no tuition fees and were provided with accommodation, meals and other benefits free of charge.

In 1990 the national government, assisted by the World Bank, began exploring cost-sharing for public higher education students. As was the case for Australia, New

Zealand and the UK, a major justification for reform was the inequity of a no-charge system, it being estimated in the 1990s that private rates of return to tertiary education were very high, possibly as much as 27 percent per annum.[35]

The necessary support of various government agencies was initially difficult to secure. Furthermore, while Ethiopia has a robust system of public administration, the relationships between levels of government – central and regional – are complex, with taxation arrangements being somewhat convoluted.

Therefore an alternative plan was considered, involving the application of a flat graduate tax collected as a percentage of salary over a set period of years (for discussion of the conceptual characteristics of a graduate tax, see Section 3.3.3). This is the simplest possible version of an income related system of deferred payments, and was introduced in the 2003/04 academic year.

The Ethiopian graduate tax has the following repayment characteristics:[36]

- payments to be collected from ex-students on the basis of a formula calculated as a percentage (proposed as 10 percent) of annual income, automatically deducted from salaries;
- the exemption of around 35 percent of students from payment of the tax, including teachers and other professionals deemed to be of public interest; and
- there is a discount for an up-front payment for those paying on an on-going basis, which is apparently 5 percent of expected future average payments.[37]

The World Bank has broadly applauded the new graduate tax scheme, but offers some telling criticisms,[38] including that:

- the minimum repayment rate of 10 percent looks to be very high for Ethiopian graduates given their levels of income;
- excusing a large number of graduates from any repayment obligations is questionable, and if they were also subjected to payments the high rate of 10 percent could be reduced; and
- the 5 percent discount for up-front payments seem to be too low to encourage any take-up.

This last point is undoubtedly true, particularly for a scheme in which the collection mechanism is untested and has a high probability of allowing many debtors to escape payments. To help ensure efficient and widespread repayments the following institutional reforms are being initiated:

- a proposed collection mechanism to be established within the Social Security Authority (SSA), whose core purpose until now has been the collection of contributions from provincial and Central Government employing agencies to fund

---

[35] See Project Appraisal Document, Ethiopia Education Sector Development Project, 1998.

[36] As described in World Bank Sector Study (2003).

[37] It is difficult to understand how this figure was arrived at, or what it means. This is because, unlike a normal ICL in which the debt is obvious, graduate tax obligation levels are not transparent since they depend on future income streams. The documents describing the scheme do not clarify this issue.

[38] See the World Bank Sector Study, pp. 23–24.

the retirement incomes of civil servants, utilizing the unique numerical identifiers assigned to public-sector employees by the Authority;

- extension of licensing provisions regulating foreign private companies to require them to register with the SSA for the purposes of collecting repayments from Ethiopian graduates;
- formalization and active encouragement of the extension of the reach of the SSA to privatized former Government enterprises and assets, and, on a voluntary but strongly encouraged basis, into other parts of the private sector including foreign NGOs; and
- restrictions on the issuing of exit visas to graduates to require them to repay their student loans prior to leaving the country.

Even so, there remains uncertainty that a sufficiently accurate record-keeping system can be developed which maintains the records of each former student's repayments and progressive level of indebtedness. On the positive side it is worth noting that most graduates are employed in the public sector and, since their incomes are known with some accuracy, the income stream generated from the measure can be predicted. A virtue of the plan is that, while the amount collected from each graduate will be related to actual income, ensuring the benefits of default insurance and consumption smoothing,[39] there is no need to calculate and track the payments and remaining debts of each graduate.

However, implementation remains the big issue, and the Ethiopia case highlights the need for administrative simplicity and promotes to center stage the importance of collection. Johnstone and Aemero (2001) argue that the Ethiopian collection difficulties are serious enough to mean that any ICL is unlikely to be workable. To date there is no direct evidence on the success or otherwise of the graduate tax reform.

5.2.2. Namibia

A country of two million people, Namibia has been independent from its colonizers, South Africa, since only 1990. The legacy of *apartheid*-based policies is an education system characterized by racial inequality. Namibia has inherited, however, a relatively strong legal and administrative framework.

Namibia achieved independence from South African rule in the early nineties. The country's student financing arrangements were a legacy of the former colonial regime. In 1996, following sustained and widespread student unrest surrounding the nation's selective bursary scheme, the Namibian Government, in conjunction with a wealthy international philanthropic organization, approached the World Bank for assistance. A steering committee, composed of government and nongovernment representatives, was established. This committee selected an Australian consultant (Jane Nicholls), whose visit to Namibia was funded by the Bank. The consultancy resulted in a proposal for a universally-applicable program of financial assistance which was subsequently implemented on a national basis.

---

[39] These are considered in detail in Section 3.

At this time Namibia's higher education system was compromised by a fundamental breakdown of the country's system of student financial assistance. This had consisted of a bursary scheme designed to provide bonded scholarships and grants for students willing to commit to work in the civil service following graduation. Bursaries were allocated on the basis of academic merit rather than need, a consequence being that the system was unpopular with students. Since severe cutbacks in public sector recruitment meant that many bonded graduates could not find work a consequence was that many were required to repay the government an amount equal to their bursary assistance.

The replacement developed for the bursary scheme was based on cost recovery, and represented a radical change in policy. It is universal, rather than selective, and requires those students choosing to take advantage of the assistance to repay the government on an income contingent basis following graduation. The scheme replaces grants with loans.

The policy reform is designed to provide a leverage point, through financial incentives, to encourage students into courses where labor market needs are seen to be greatest. Two types of financial assistance are provided – scholarships, for students in greatest financial need and also for those prepared to undertake courses in areas of high economic priority, and loans for other students. These are in two categories: smaller loans covering tuition fees only, and larger ones that go to living costs. Thus there is considerable flexibility both for students and for the government, and this presumably matters with respect to influencing student choice.

The plan involves establishing the scheme legally as a Fund, with powers to invest and borrow money, but required under its legislation to take the advice of the government on certain policy matters. Namibia does not have a taxation system of sufficient reach to render it suitable for collection purposes as part of the scheme. Instead, the Social Security Commission was identified as a suitable collection agency, because of its potential to track graduates through unique numerical identifiers and a computerized record-keeping system. Repayments will be pegged to graduates' salaries and are payable only when a specified salary threshold is reached.

The scheme is designed to enable students to select the level of financial assistance they need, and the government to adjust financial incentives and assistance levels as necessary. The new program is seen by Chapman (2006b) to be a potentially more effective means of assisting students than the former bursary regime. What is not yet clear is the extent to which the proposed collections system can operate efficiently, but inevitably there will be problems. Again, collection difficulties loom large.

5.2.3. Indonesia

In 1995 as a component of its Engineering Education Development Project designed to assist public-sector tertiary education institutions, the Asian Development Bank piloted a small income contingent student loan scheme as part of a student financial assistance package. Design commenced during the project's planning phase in 1995. Due to the

1997 onset of the Asian economic crisis, however, project implementation was delayed until 1998, when an Australian team, including a student financing consultant, Jane Nicholls, commenced work in Jakarta.

Indonesia lacks a sound public administrative infrastructure that might underpin a collection system for an income related student loan program. In Chapman (2006b) it is argued that the country is apparently beset by ongoing economic and political difficulties, its legislative system is weak, and the legal framework surrounding the financial system is particularly so. Thus Indonesia might seem to be a poor candidate for a program of student loans.

In this, as in many developing countries, the history of government-subsidized student financial assistance schemes has been vexed. A previous loan scheme had collapsed, and this was run through a commercial bank with default rates being over 90 percent. Attempts to design and establish an ICL scheme for Indonesia have been associated with an Asian Development Bank (ADB) project concentrating on engineering education in twelve selected public-sector universities and polytechnics. The initial design phase for the program took place in 1995: implementation, originally scheduled for 1997, was delayed until 1998 following onset of the Asian financial crisis in that year.

The central feature of the Indonesian scheme as proposed at the time involves an advance of a lump sum [originally (US)$3 million] to (BNI) the national bank, which, as the largest public-sector bank, has branches on every university campus. This bank also serves as the vehicle for financial transactions between the government on the one hand and public universities and polytechnics on the other. The funds are advanced subject to a detailed agreement between BNI and the government (established according to a Heads of Agreement signed between BNI and the ADB in late 1995). The essential agreement entails the commercial bank having full access to the funds in return for administering and financing the loan scheme.

Following the financial crisis of 1997–1998 the proposed scheme was replaced by a much less ambitious, small-scale, locally based grant and emergency loan program. Funding for the financial assistance scheme was also reduced. While the government has promoted the intention to implement such a program when economic circumstances permit, it seems unlikely in 2006 that ICLreform will transpire over the next few years.

5.2.4. Rwanda

Like many African countries, Rwanda's 7,000 higher education students receive free tuition and grants to cover the cost of board and lodging. Secondary school students, on the other hand, pay tuition fees: therefore those eligible to enter university come from relatively privileged backgrounds. University students receive substantial public subsidies, and as graduates they also enjoy significantly higher average lifetime earnings than do nongraduates [see Chapman and Fraser (2000)].

The UK Department of International Development financed a consultancy to examine proposals for higher education reforms in 1999, involving Bruce Chapman and William

Fraser. It was recognized at the time that there was an apparent need to expand the country's higher education system and sources of finance other than government funding needed to be found. Resources could then be used to eliminate the up-front fees in secondary schooling, seen to be responsible in part for the very low participation of poor young people in any form of post-primary education. Ideally, this would mean the introduction of deferred payment, not only for a share of tuition costs (for example, 20 percent), but also for the grant provided for students' board and lodging. This latter amount represents a sum almost equivalent to the full average course costs per capita.

A UK Department of International Development study [Chapman and Fraser (2000)] suggested that, initially, tuition charges should be imposed, along with a deferred-payment scheme, with the proceeds being used to help move secondary schooling arrangements away from up-front fees. The case has been made that the higher education grants scheme is also in need of reform, and that savings in this area could similarly be used to decrease up-front secondary schooling costs. A movement from grants to loans would seem to be justified if the imposition of an income related repayment system could be established and found to be workable.

Chapman and Fraser (2000) note that the country has a system of unique numerical identifiers available to all from the age of 16, and that this arrangement is mandatory from age 18 years. Their plan suggested that upon enrollment, students would be given the option of paying their tuition charge up front, at a lower rate, or otherwise of deferring payment until following graduation when they would repay on an income-contingent basis. The higher education institution would be required to establish a new record for each enrolling student who has chosen to defer payment, along with the year of study and the course charge applying.

Rwanda has an income tax collection system that could be used to collect repayments from graduates, via deductions from salary made by employers. Graduates could be asked to produce evidence that they have paid their university charge in full. Where they have not done so, the employer would be required to keep a record of the graduate's unique personal ID number and to remit payments monthly, along with income tax, at the rates suggested under the scheme; for example, of 2, 3 or 4 percent of salary, dependent upon taxable annual income.

It was suggested that the tax authority (Rwanda Revenue Authority) could adjust the individual records of graduates and remit the payments in turn to the Government of Rwanda Treasury. A variant on this scheme would involve the establishment of a separate administrative body, which would manage the scheme. The Commissioner General of the Rwanda Revenue Authority has suggested that the organization is administratively able to carry out the functions as specified under the suggested structures. However, by 2006 no concrete advances had been made toward the implementation of a Rwandan ICL and, as with similar cases, there is the real potential that collection difficulties as well as a lack of strong political commitment to change loom sufficiently large to make its successful implementation unlikely.

5.2.5. The Philippines

The Asian Development Bank (ADB) has had long-standing concerns about the failure of publicly financed student loan schemes in the Philippines. In connection with a proposed higher education financing reform project, a Filipino consultant produced a design for a program for the public higher education sector in 2001, but this relied exclusively on private-sector funding and was considered unworkable. A subsequent ADB project, aimed at the technical-vocational education and training sector, was implemented on contract by an Australian consultancy company in 2003–2004. The project included a small student loan component, intended as a pilot for a more broadly based scheme. Project design specified that this should, if possible, be based on an income contingent repayment principle.

Like many other developing countries, the Philippines has experienced severe problems in the implementation of student loan schemes. The government's 'Study Now, Pay Later' (SNPL) program in higher education, a conventional loan in which repayments are made on the basis of time, is offered right across the sector (including the extensive private college and university system) but the take-up rate is very low. This is due largely to the modest level of funds available to borrowers, and these have not increased since the program was initially established in 1975.

Since its introduction repayment rates have dropped to around two percent. A feature of the climate surrounding loan schemes in the Philippines is that students, their families and even their teachers and lecturers often seem to regard loans simply as handouts. This creates an obvious difficulty for those responsible for policy credibility in this area.

Small-scale loan schemes have been more successful than the SNPL program, especially in private higher education, where institutionally based arrangements have enabled students effectively to stagger the payment of tuition fees over the academic year. Notably more successful – achieving repayment rates of up to 98 percent – have been micro-credit programs in both higher education and the technical/vocational education and training (TVET) sector, where students and trainees have been able to borrow to meet costs associated with practical work and projects.

In 2001–2002 an attempt was made to design a higher education student loan scheme as part of an Asian Development Bank project – the Education Sector Development Project. Design parameters required the program to be financed entirely from the private sector: this factor created severe difficulties and so far no credible, potentially sound model has emerged, although in the longer term it may be possible to establish a program that utilizes the administrative structures and the financial resources of the country's two major pension funds. These organizations, however, were initially involved in the failed SNPL program, a central reason for the failure being that the government provided a 100 percent guarantee to administering institutions against default, thus providing no financial incentive to collect repayments.

In 2003 a small-scale program was proposed for the public TVET sector in the Philippines. Again, this was associated with an ADB project, this time the Technical

Education and Skills Development Project (TESDP). Thus far little progress has been made in its implementation.

5.2.6. Mexico

The current Mexican public higher education system is one in which there are no tuition charges for students, and is characterized by excess demand (a large number of prospective and qualified students are unable to gain public sector places). Moreover, it is very likely to be the case that individuals from the least advantaged backgrounds have less access to the system than do others. There is a compelling case for increasing the financial resources available to allow increased enrollments and improvements in service, and that this should be financed in part by tuition charges.

However, a challenge is how to redress current inequities and facilitate an expansion without diminishing access to the system of talented prospective students. Analysts have argued that a possibly fruitful approach would be through the use of an income contingent loan scheme.

The fact that there is no charge for higher education students in Mexico implies that the system is regressive. There are two aspects.

The first relates to the socio-economic background of students. Data supplied by the SOFES group from the Census suggests strongly that higher education students come disproportionately from the most advantaged parts of Mexican society. For example, as measured by household income, it was suggested that less than 7 percent of the bottom two deciles of youth attend university, but that this figure is around 90 percent of the top two deciles.

The second concerns the private benefits associated with being a university graduate. This has been addressed in the typical human capital approach concerning estimations of Mexican private rates of return to higher education, and the data show that these are apparently very high, upward of around 25 percent.[40]

According to Mexican higher education officials currently there is considerable excess demand by prospective student for public university places. It is apparently the case that up to 80 percent of new prospective students each year are not offered enrollment, and it is considered that around half of this group are qualified for entry and would likely benefit from the investment. Many of those rejected consequently enroll in the private university system where, although there is a small student loan scheme (SOFES) available, a majority pay up-front tuition without student loan assistance.

Together with the data concerning socio-economic background there seems to be little doubt that in a lifetime income sense Mexican university graduates are relatively

---

[40] These findings are reinforced in Roman (2003) for Mexico City, using the National Survey of Urban Employment, where it is suggested that in 2002 degree holders earn around 60 percent more than those without.

advantaged, arguably significantly so. Having the public sector cover the vast majority of the direct costs is unquestionably regressive. Thus the basic equity point for charging higher education students for part of the costs is easy to establish in Mexico, as it is in other countries.

It is unclear at this stage if the pre-conditions outlined above can be met in Mexico. The most important of these, the capacity to determine with accuracy students' future incomes, has been explored in discussions with tax officials who have suggested that the potential is there. For example, there is a unique identifier system, with photo ID, which is required for employment and which is used in the collection of income tax. This is an essential pre-requisite, but additional exploration of the possible successful operation of the collection system would be of great value. The reform debate, initiated in 2003 with the assistance of the World Bank, is currently in abeyance, in part because of political concerns with respect to the likely unpopularity of the introduction of a charge even in the context of an ICL system.

5.3. ICL implementation requirements

5.3.1. Introduction

The countries under discussion above are very different. While the differences matter, there are several essential policy anchors that remain central to the successful development of any higher education financing arrangement based on the principle of income contingency. In this section these general points are now considered.[41]

5.3.2. Administrative and legal preconditions

In Australia and other countries in which an ICL system has been introduced, this has been a relatively simple matter from an administrative point of view. The reasons for this are that the public administration systems of these countries feature a strong legal framework, a universal and transparent regime of personal taxation and/or social security collection, and an efficient payment mechanism. The last involves computerized record keeping of residents' vital financial particulars and, very importantly, a universal system of unique identifiers (usually numbers, often accompanied by an identity card).

Under these circumstances it is not complicated to identify and track individual citizens over time and space. It is not expensive, moreover, to tack onto some existing tax collection mechanism an additional function: the collection of payments from ex-students, on the basis of a fixed proportion of income.

---

[41] A useful addition to this discussion is the checklist for deferred repayment schemes offered in Ziderman and Albrecht (1995), pp. 164–167.

In the developing world, however, as we have seen, these preconditions are often lacking. Administrative systems are likely to be weak, and often rely on intensive and inefficient manual record keeping. Taxation regimes may be shaky or even corrupt, and usually no reliable system of unique identifiers exists. Financial regulation, bankruptcy laws and contract laws are often ineffectual. Nevertheless, it is in these countries, where social and economic inequalities are usually profound, that even a modest up-front charge for higher education constitutes a significant barrier to participation for citizens other than the very privileged.

The economic and political rationale, however, for the imposition of at least a low level charge for higher education is compelling: in countries characterized by serious inequality the comparative economic benefit accruing to graduates, compared to other citizens, is clear. And if it can be done efficiently on the basis of income contingency this is preferable in economic terms, as explained in Sections 2 and 3. The major challenge is how to achieve these positive policy goals in the face of the difficulties described.

5.3.3. Minimum requirements in summary

The minimum conditions ideally required in order to implement a successful system are:
- a reliable, preferably universal, system of unique identifiers;
- accurate record-keeping of the accruing liabilities of students (while studying);
- a collection mechanism with a sound, and if possible, a computerized record-keeping system; and
- an efficient way of determining with accuracy, over time, the actual incomes of former students.

Some would argue that a further basic requirement for the introduction of ICL is a strong legal framework and functional judicial system. Indeed, it is hard, from a developed-world perspective, to imagine implementing a workable scheme outside this context.

While the above noted four conditions for the implementation of an ICL are hard to achieve, it is worth noting that three apply also to the collection of any kind of loan. The exception involves determining with accuracy, over time, the actual incomes of former students. This particular criterion is likely to be the most difficult institutional barrier to ICL loan and tuition reform in developing countries.

It should also be recorded that political commitment to change is a necessary, albeit not sufficient, condition for change. In Australia, New Zealand and the UK, it was clear, or became clear over time, that the higher education systems would inexorably deteriorate without funding reform, and that the main players were prepared to live with short-term political costs to achieve longer-term social and economic benefits. In some of the countries considered above it is not obvious that this is the case; in the absence of a different political landscape there is little doubt that required funding reforms will not eventuate.

5.4. Necessary steps for implementing an ICL

The discussion of different countries' schemes or proposals clarifies what steps might be necessary in a generic sense in setting up an income contingent loan scheme. In theory and in summary the system might work as follows:

(i) upon enrollment students choose between an up-front payment, or incurring a debt reflecting course costs and living expenses;

(ii) those paying up-front do not have to be followed further, but might be later if they choose to incur debt in following years of study;

(iii) those incurring the debt are issued with a social security number by the university (which has access to blocks of unused numbers);

(iv) the number a student receives is unique and will apply also to that student's future pension arrangement (if applicable);

(v) the size of the debt is recorded and the information is communicated to the (new) higher education unit in the Ministry of Finance;

(vi) a higher education debt record is set up, which will be unique for each student;

(vii) at the time of employment the former student is required to let the employer know what their number is, and the employer is required by law to remit debt repayments (contingent on the employees' annual income and the repayment parameters) to the relevant tax authority (this remittance could take the form of with-holding, as is currently the case with respect to income tax);

(viii) the relevant tax authority is required to remit the debt repayment to the higher education unit in the Ministry of Finance, where the unique identifier allows a former students' debt to be adjusted accordingly; and

(ix) after the debt is repaid in full the Ministry of Finance lets the employer know that no further obligations exist, and the employer ceases collection from that former student.

5.5. Summary

The systems and structures most resembling those prevailing in the 'template' countries, such as Australia, New Zealand and the UK, will not generally be available. It should be clear that if the right administrative arrangements are not available the institution of an ICL is not viable.

In many countries there are severe difficulties associated with the establishment of ICL policy integrity, credibility and collection. Even so, at the same time there seems to be an important economic and social case for charging tuition. Given this policy context, both Johnstone and Aemero (2001) and Chapman (2006b) suggests that it may be desirable to proceed with the imposition of up-front fees and scholarships instead of ICL. Johnstone and Aemero (2001) offer considerable scepticism with respect to the possibility of applying ICL in developing countries, and the evidence seems so far to be consistent with their perspective.

The case for and against the promotion of ICL policy for higher education financing in developing countries can be expressed with reference to the discussion of both the theoretical issues and the problems of administration examined above. The issues for the policymaker are as follows.

A workable risk-sharing ICL higher education financing policy is the approach most likely to deliver outcomes consistent with economic theory. That is, unlike alternatives such as government guarantees to banks for commercial loans, ICL offer default protection for both lenders and debtors. As well, because a student's loan repayments can be designed to be a relatively low proportion of expected future taxable income, ICL offer the prospect of agents making career choices which are insensitive to debt obligations. An implication would seem to be that this type of debt promotes relatively effective job matching and thus arguably results in higher levels of allocative efficiency.[42]

These arguments rest on the assumption that an ICL can be instituted in an operational efficient way. However, if this is unlikely to be the case, as still seems to be the case presently in most of the developing countries examined above, policymakers have an inferior set of choices: to charge tuition without adequate default protection for borrowers; or to have highly regressive systems with no tuition. Currently for most developing countries the preferred policy appears to be the latter.

6. A detailed case study of a risk-sharing ICL: Australia, 1989–2003[43]

6.1. Introduction

The analysis and discussion presented above suggest that, if it can be made operational, a risk-sharing ICL is the higher education financing approach most likely to be consistent with economic (and social) principles. This raises the critical empirical question for policy: what are the effects of such schemes? Addressing this is problematic.

The difficulty relates to the fact that ICLs of this genre are both unusual and historically quite recent. As noted, the first national scheme was introduced in Australia in 1989, and while New Zealand, South Africa, Chile and the UK have adopted broadly-based ICLs of this type, preceding discussion has suggested that there is a paucity of information on the implications of ICL in these countries. With respect to Australia, however, there has been considerable research on the topic. Consequently, this section focuses on the Australian experience.

---

[42] To be valid, this assertion would seem to rely on the notion that 'normal' (non-ICL) loans are a nonoptimal financing mechanism. This case has been argued in Section 2.

[43] Much of the discussion in this section relies on Chapman and Ryan (2002). Chris Ryan is not responsible for errors and omissions.

6.2. HECS described

6.2.1. Background

In 1989, faced with a burgeoning demand for higher education services, and a reluctance to finance the required expansion from tax revenue, the Australian government introduced a radical scheme of education charges [described in Chapman (1997)]. The Australian experience with a risk-sharing ICL, the Higher Education Contribution Scheme (HECS), is relatively long-lived in policy terms, in 2006 aged 17. While many other countries introduced ICL after the beginning of the 1990s, HECS is the most studied in all dimensions. These are the reasons that the Australian policy is now reported in detail.

In 1989 HECS was characterized by the following:

- a charge of A$1,800 (1989), pro-rated by course load, but with no variation by discipline;
- on enrollment students could choose to incur the debt, to be repaid through the tax system depending on personal income; or
- students could avoid the debt by paying up-front, which was associated with a discount of 15 percent (later increased to 25 percent);
- those students choosing to pay later faced no repayment obligation unless their personal taxable income exceeded the average income of Australians working for pay [about A$22,000 (1989) per annum];
- at the first income threshold of repayment a former student's obligation was 2 percent of income, with repayments increasing in percentage terms above the threshold; and
- apart from the fact that HECS could be paid up-front with a discount, there was no additional interest rate on the debt, although the debt and the repayment thresholds were indexed to the CPI.

While in 2006 its essence remains, HECS has changed significantly from 1989, most importantly in 1997. At this time there were three significant reforms. One, all the charges increased significantly, by about 40 percent on average. Two, differential charges were introduced according to a student's course of study, with the new charges essentially reflecting cost differences. And three, the income thresholds for repayment were reduced significantly.[44]

6.2.2. HECS tuition charges described

Students intending to enroll in Australian universities in 2001 faced tuition charges that varied by course. The bands are now shown in Table 1.

---

[44] Chapman and Salvage (1998) argue that the last of these changes was the most likely policy variation to affect access.

Table 1
HECS costs by band, 2001

HECS band	HECS cost for each full-time year (A$)	Disciplines
Band 1	3,521	Arts, Humanities, Social Studies/Behavioural Sciences, Education, Visual/Performing Arts, Nursing, Justice and Legal Studies
Band 2	5,015	Mathematics, Computing, other Health Sciences, Agriculture/Renewable Resources, Built Environment/Architecture, Sciences, Engineering/Processing, Administration, Business and Economics
Band 3	5,870	Law, Medicine, Medical Science, Dentistry, Dental Services and Veterinary Science

Source: Commonwealth Department of Education, Training and Youth Affairs (2001). HECS: Your Questions Answered.

These charges meant that Arts graduates at the time who completed their course in three years would incur a HECS debt of between A$10,000 and A$11,000, a Science graduate would have had a debt of just over A$15,000, and a Law graduate (typically a four-year course) would have incurred of debt of around A$20,000. Debts are indexed to inflation (the Consumer Price Index), and thus there is a zero real interest rate for those choosing the pay later option, but initially there was a 15 percent discount for those paying up-front.

6.2.3. HECS repayment parameters

Students can choose either to pay their HECS charges at the time of enrollment or defer payment, in which case repayments are collected through the tax system. Those who choose to pay their HECS charges up-front now receive a discount of 25 percent, but the implications of this are not necessarily what they seem. Those opting to defer payment and repay the debt after graduation receive interest rate subsidies equal to the real rate of interest for each year the debt remains unpaid. A consequence is that students who take the pay-later option will receive greater subsidies the longer it takes to repay the debt (that is, the lower their future income).[45] The 'discount' effectively introduces a blunt form of a real rate of interest.

The majority of students choose to defer payment of the HECS charge, and for them repayments commence when individual annual income exceeds a minimum threshold level. In the 2000–2001 taxation year, this minimum threshold was A$22,346 per annum, or about 65 percent of Australian average earnings. The repayment conditions are shown in Table 2.

What these parameters mean for typical graduates is now described.

[45] For analysis of the extent of the subsidy see Chia (1990) and Chapman and Salvage (1998).

Table 2
HECS income thresholds and repayment rates, 2001–2002

HECS repayment incomes in the range (A$)	Percent of income applied to repayment
Below $23,242	Nil
$23,242–$24,510	3
$24,511–$26,412	3.5
$26,413–$30,638	4
$30,639–$36,977	4.5
$36,978–$38,921	5
$38,922–$41,837	5.5
$41,838 and above	6

Source: Australian Taxation Office, Repaying your HECS debt 2000–2002.

6.2.4. HECS repayments by age for typical graduates working full-time

It is instructive to illustrate the effect of these charge levels and repayment parameters on the after-tax incomes of graduates working full-time, by age. In what follows the 2001 HECS repayment parameters have been applied for male and female students, assuming: they begin a four year Science degree at age 18, graduating at age 22; and, after graduation take a full-time job earning the average income by age of graduates of their sex. The earnings function data have been derived from the Australian Bureau of Statistics 1995 Income and Household Survey, updated to 2002 Australian dollars.[46]

The results for males and females respectively are shown in Figures 2 and 3.

The data of Figures 2 and 3 illustrate the following: male science graduates earning average graduate incomes for those working full-time will repay HECS in about 8 or 9 years; equivalent females will repay HECS after about 12 years. The above data are offered to illustrate typical HECS repayments. Of course, there will be a large variation in repayment profiles given that annual contributions depend on individual graduates' incomes. Micro-simulation analysis of repayment profiles of HECS illustrates this point [see Harding (1995)].

The main conclusion from the figures is that a male graduate working full-time takes on average around 9, and a similarly employed female graduate around 12, years to repay typical HECS debts. There will necessarily be a large variance with respect to the time taken to repay, a natural consequence of an ICL; this issue is now considered in the context of earlier conceptual discussion concerning the consumption smoothing benefits of an ICL.

---

[46] In 2002 the US:Australian exchange rate was about 0.65:1.

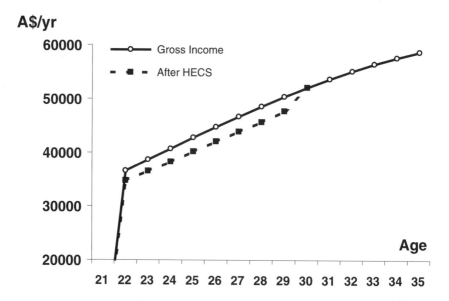

Figure 2. Earnings before and after HECS: graduate males working full-time, 2002 (A$). *Source*: Chapman and Ryan (2002).

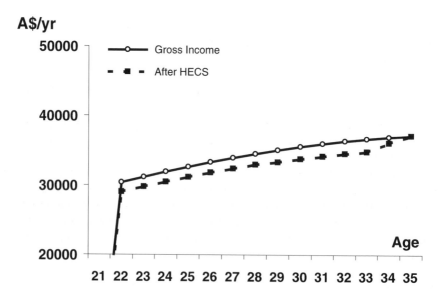

Figure 3. Earnings before and after HECS: graduate females working full-time, 2002 (A$). *Source*: Chapman and Ryan (2002).

6.2.5. HECS repayments by age for graduates not working full-time

The illustration of the age related repayments of HECS for full-time workers is of policy interest but does not highlight the consumption smoothing potential benefits of ICL. This is because the consumption smoothing benefits of ICL repayments matter most when a graduate's lifetime income stream has a high variance.

Chapman (2006b) illustrates the point by comparing HECS and bank repayments as a proportion of annual income for a hypothetical graduate who experiences significant variations in income in the 10 year period following graduation. In the example, the hypothetical graduate is full-time employed and earning the income of the average graduate from age 22 to age 25, then receives social security for 4 years. Then at age 29 the graduate is assumed to be employed part-time until age 32, after which income is assumed to be the average of full-time graduates of that age and sex.

The exercise reveals that graduates in the above circumstances face extremely different after-debt incomes if they are repaying HECS compared to if their student loan repayments are for a bank loan (with repayments thus being required at a constant level over time). In the example, the HECS repayment obligation is never greater than around 6 percent of income, and zero when income is relatively low, but the bank loan repayments are up to 25 percent of income in periods of low income. The point is clear: ICL can deliver important levels of consumption smoothing.

6.2.6. HECS revenue

The discussion following relates to the stream of revenue received by the government from HECS. As noted above, students have the choice of paying their HECS charges upon enrollment, or through the tax system. Figure 4 shows the revenue received by the government from 1989 to 1999, and projections of future payments to 2005.

Up-front ('voluntary') payments and repayments through the tax system ('compulsory') are shown separately in the figure. It is of interest that even in the first year of HECS around A$100 million was raised from up-front payments encouraged by the (then) 15 percent discount. The policy implications of this are significant: it shows that the introduction of an ICL can provide substantial revenue quite quickly.

Not surprisingly, repayments through the tax system were modest in the early years of the operation of HECS. This is because very few graduates earned incomes high enough to require repayment. However, income contingent repayments increased substantially as more graduates became eligible for repayment, thresholds were lowered and a higher proportion and number of graduates faced higher repayment rates.

Taken together, up-front fee and income contingent repayments through the tax system now represent a very significant and growing proportion of the cost of higher education in Australia. In 2001 students provided over A$800 million, which is around 20 percent of the total recurrent costs. In 2006 it is projected that this proportion will rise to over 30 percent.

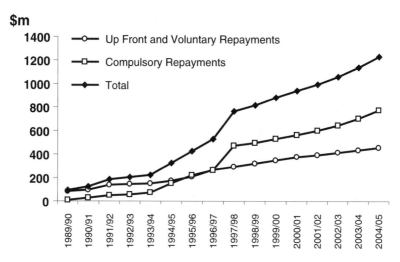

Figure 4. Actual and projected HECS revenue: 1989–2005 (A$). *Source*: Commonwealth Department of Education, Science and Technology, as reported in Chapman and Ryan (2002).

6.3. The effect of HECS on the access of the disadvantaged

6.3.1. Background

HECS was designed, in part, to minimize the extent to which the imposition of a charge would preclude the participation of poor prospective students. This is a critical issue for policy, and dominated political debate at the time. Fortunately there is now considerable evidence on the effects of HECS on the access of the disadvantaged to higher education. Many researchers, including the author of this chapter, have contributed.

6.3.2. The literature

Two approaches have been used to assess the impact of HECS on the participation of the poor. The first has been to ask prospective students about the factors influencing their higher education participation decisions. The second has been to test statistical relations on the question of whether or not higher education participation behavior differed between socio-economic groups after HECS was introduced, and after the radical changes introduced in 1997. Some of these analyses are now described briefly.

Andrews (1999) measured changes in proportions of first-year higher education students from relatively poor backgrounds, as measured by the average income of their local area. His research showed that the share of students from the lowest income quartile did not change after HECS charges and repayment conditions became less generous for students in 1997. Andrews also analyzed attitudes to debt by individuals according to income, and concluded that patterns in Australia tend to reflect an urban/rural dichotomy rather than any variation by income. Andrews concluded that neither higher HECS charges nor the lowering of the income repayment thresholds affected the higher education participation of poor groups.

Other studies concerning the participation of the poor have utilized individually based income measures. Long, Carpenter and Hayden (1999) and Marks, Fleming, Long and McMilan (2000) use panels of longitudinal data from the Youth in Transition Survey conducted by the Australian Council for Educational Research to identify the extent to which education participation changed in Australia from the 1980s to the late 1990s. These studies use an indirect wealth index constructed from responses by individuals to questions about the presence of material possessions in their houses at around age 14.

Not surprisingly, the results of the above studies suggest that wealth is strongly positively related to individuals' higher education participation. While Long et al. (1999) found also that higher education participation differences by wealth widened initially, they suggest that this trend was evident in the earlier cohorts, and not obviously related to HECS. The Marks et al. (2000) research added a new cohort to the same panels employed by Long et al. Their research suggests that socio-economic status became less important in determining higher education participation in the late 1990s than was the case for earlier cohorts. That is, HECS did not seem to be associated with lower higher educational participation of relatively poor prospective students.

There are a number of methodological and measurement questions in both the Long et al. and Marks et al. exercises. These issues are considered in Chapman and Ryan (2002) in exercises using the same data sets, and this research is described below.[47]

As well as the analysis of Andrews (1999), the Australian government has undertaken recent research focusing in particular on the potential effects on applications and commencements as a result of the 1997 HECS changes. Aungles, Buchanan, Karmel and MacLachlan (2002) explore time series relationships concerning university applications, and find a small but significant decrease after 1996, when HECS charges and repayment rules became much less generous for students. However, there are only 14 observations in the data, and very few controls.

The same authors use local area averages concerning education and occupation [the same approach adopted by Andrews (1999)] to explore the possibility of there being an effect on commencements of the relative disadvantaged from the 1997 HECS changes. In general there does not seem to be an issue, except for a small number of males with respect to the courses in which the HECS charge increased the most. Chapman and Ryan (2005) found a similar effect in direction terms, but it was not statistically significant.

With what is arguably an improved approach, Chapman and Ryan (2002, 2005) address the following questions. What was the level of university participation with respect to family wealth of 18 year olds: before the introduction of HECS (as measured in 1988); sometime after this (as measured in 1993); and after the marked changes to the scheme in 1997 (as measured in 1999).

---

[47] Background technical explanations are not apposite here: what matters for the current exercise are the additional insights into the effects of HECS on the access of poor prospective students.

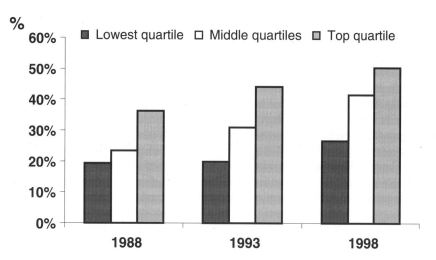

Figure 5. Proportion of 18-year-olds undertaking a degree by family wealth, persons. *Source*: Chapman and Ryan (2002).

For each year Chapman and Ryan (2002) considered only 18 year olds and these groups were classified into three wealth categories: those from the bottom quartile; those from the top quartile; and those from the middle two quartiles. These classifications allowed measurement of the proportion of young people enrolled in higher education from different wealth backgrounds. Figure 5 shows the results.

The data of Figure 5 should be interpreted as follows. For each of the years 1988, 1993 and 1999 the bars show the proportion of those aged 18 who were enrolled in higher education from the three wealth categories. There are three significant results.

First, before the introduction of HECS, there was a clear relationship between enrollment in higher education and measures of family wealth. Specifically, the proportions enrolled from the lowest, middle and highest groups were respectively around 19, 24 and 36 percent. Second, the data show that higher eduction participation rates did not fall for students from any family wealth group after the introduction of HECS. Even so, the increase in the proportion of young people attending university was clearly larger for those from the middle and highest wealth groups. Third, the large changes to HECS introduced in 1997 had no adverse effects on participation for members of any wealth group; indeed, there were large higher education participation increases for those from all family wealth backgrounds.

Chapman and Ryan (2005) report parametric tests of these relationships, differentially by sex, and allowing nonliner effects of policy changes over time. As well, they explored the effects of policy announcements on high school students' intentions to enroll. Their conclusion is essentially that reached by other research: there is no evidence that the introduction of, and changes in, HECS have affected significantly the socio-economic composition of the higher education student body.

Hume (2004) also explores the issue of socio-economic mix changes after the radical changes introduced to the Australian system in 1997. Hume used different data sets – the Australian Longitudinal Survey in 1995, and the Australian Youth Survey in 1998 – to determine if there were changes in the socio-economic mix of (different) students with respect to enrollments in particular types of courses. The important point is that the charges had changed markedly in 1997, so this 'natural experiment' allowed an innovative and indirect tests of the extent to which the changes affected enrollment behaviors. Hume concluded that there were not discernible differences in enrollment patterns between the two survey dates. The result is consistent with all other research on enrollment patterns and the role of HECS.

6.3.3. The research on HECS and access: conclusions

The conclusions from the Australian research with respect to socio economic mix and access are as follows.
  (i) The relatively disadvantaged in Australia were less likely to attend university even when there were no student fees. This provides further support for the view that a no-charge public university system (that is, financed by all taxpayers) is regressive.
 (ii) The introduction of HECS was associated with aggregate increases in higher education participation.
(iii) HECS did not result in decreases in the participation of prospective students from relatively poor families, although the absolute increases were higher for relatively advantaged students.
 (iv) There was a small decrease in the aggregate number of applications after the 1997 changes, but no apparent decreases in commencements of members of low socio economic groups;
  (v) The significant changes to HECS introduced in 1997 were associated generally with increases in the participation of individuals irrespective of their family wealth.
 (vi) There was a small decrease in enrollments in the most expensive courses of relatively poor males after the significant charge increases introduced in 1997, although in one of the exercises reporting this result the effect was not statistically significant.

These conclusions raise some important points. First, with respect to the effects of the scheme on participation, it does not follow that HECS per se resulted in an increase in the demand for higher education. Indeed, if this were the case it would constitute a curiosity for economic theory, since the result would suggest that increasing the price of a service increases also the quantity demanded.

Understanding the positive relationship between the introduction of tuition and higher education participation is assisted through consideration of the theoretical framework of Finnie and Usher (2006). The critical point they make is that typically many public higher education systems are supply-constrained, and this was certainly the case in

Australia at the time of the introduction of HECS. The effect of the introduction of the scheme was to encourage the government to outlay substantially more resources for university places given the promise of higher future revenues.

Second, the apparent finding that neither the introduction of, or changes to, HECS had no apparent effects on the access to the system of poorer students should not be interpreted to mean that risk-sharing ICL schemes have a unique capacity to protect the disadvantaged from any adverse effects of tuition. Indeed, an important finding from the disparate case studies examined in Teixeira, Johnstone, Rosa and Vossensteijn (2006) is that the socio-economic mix of higher education students seems fairly insensitive to funding regimes. That is, marked changes in the levels, incidence and nature of grant and loan support systems (and tax and other fiscal incentives) do not seem to affect significantly the proportion of enrollments of students from different family wealth backgrounds.

It follows from the above that claims suggesting particular financing systems are special because they do not affect the socio-economic composition of higher education should not be taken at face value. This implies that the findings of Carneiro and Heckman (2002) reported above are robust: access to tertiary education is determined in the main by lifetime educational circumstances. If this is so it implies that the relative advantage of ICL lie in their consumption smoothing properties rather than their implications for access only.

6.4. Summary

There are several significant findings from this detailed investigation of the effects of ICL in the only country in which such a scheme has been closely examined with respect to a range of economic and social outcomes, Australia.

First, HECS has turned out to be very inexpensive in administrative terms [Chapman and Ryan (2002)]. That is, while around (2001) A$800 million is currently collected per annum, it costs less than 2–3 percent of this to administer. This is traceable to the facts that students' debts, and their collection, were faICLy straightforward given the mechanisms of the Australian Taxation Office – a point emphasized in ensuing discussion of other countries' administrative arrangements.

Second, HECS has been associated with the delivery of considerable revenue, of the order of (2001) A$8 billion over the 14 years after its introduction. It is projected that the system will provide around (2001) A$1.2 billion per year by 2005, which will be about 20 percent or more of annual recurrent costs.

Third, it appears that from a range of different approaches there have apparently been no consequences for the accessibility to higher education for students from relatively disadvantaged backgrounds. Broadly speaking, the socio-economic make-up of the higher education student body was about the same in the late 1990s as it was before HECS was introduced.[48]

---

[48] See Chapman and Ryan (2002).

Four, higher education enrollments in Australia have increased considerably, by around 50 percent, since the introduction of HECS. This has happened for two reasons: there were no obvious overall deterrent effects from the new system; and in response to the expectation of high future revenue, the government substantially increased higher education expenditure.

Overall, HECS has essentially operated as originally envisaged, implying that risk-sharing ICL can be designed to achieve the basic objectives of higher education financing policy. However, it is critical to note that the findings concerning revenue, access and growth could also be true with respect to other non-ICL changes to higher education financing.[49]

7. Conclusions and suggestions for further research

7.1. Summary

This chapter has critically examined higher education student financing, with a particular emphasis on loans for tuition (and/or student income support) that are repaid in a manner depending on students' future income. Income contingent loans became a reality in the 1970s, but it was not until the late 1980s that their potential was tested in a national context. A rudimentary form was adopted in Sweden and was followed by the institution of a fully-fledged ICL operated through the income tax system in Australia in 1989. Since then New Zealand, Chile, the Republic of South Africa, the UK and the US have all adopted variants of ICL, with differing levels of success with respect to a range of consequences.

In conceptual terms several issues have been explored: the need for government intervention in higher education financing; the case for both a tuition charge and a taxpayer subsidy; and the costs and benefits of different approaches to funding. It is clear that government intervention is necessary, but it has been argued that there are important weaknesses associated with the most common form of government intervention, that of guarantees to repay loans to commercial banks in the event of a former student's default.

The discussion has concentrated on issues of policy, and in this context it is critical to understand that the process of investment in higher education is associated with uncertainty and risk for prospective students. Because of the risk and uncertainty with respect to students' future incomes, an ICL approach is suggested to have the potential for delivering efficacious economic and social outcomes. The essential benefit is that, if designed properly, ICL is the only form of financing that offers both default insurance and consumption smoothing.

It is important to understand that there are several different types of ICL and with associated diverse implications. The approach most likely to deliver desirable outcomes

---

[49] This is an important point made consistently by Bruce Johnstone.

is that known as a risk-sharing ICL, in which the public sector acts as an insurer for default risk. Within that category of ICL there are apparently trade-offs between the extent of insurance offered and the extent of public subsidy.

On the other hand, risk-pooling ICL, in which all members of a cohort are responsible for the total debt of the group, have major problems associated with adverse selection and moral hazard. As well, graduate taxes have little resource allocation potential but could nevertheless be designed to raise significant revenue and to be very progressive. Neither a risk-pooling ICL nor a GT are currently in existence, for reasons analyzed.

The international experience with ICLs has been examined in some detail. Outcomes have been diverse, reflecting the very different design and other policy parameters of countries' arrangements. In Australia and New Zealand, for example, ICL have been successfully instituted, and this is likely to be the outcome in the UK when that country moves comprehensively toward ICL. In the US there is an ICL option, but there has been little take-up, for reasons that can be traced to poor design, and as a result of inadequate public promotion.

The chapter explored several developing countries' experience with ICL. While the World Bank and other agencies have actively pursued this financing option in a number of countries, particularly in Africa, there has so far been little success with respect in terms of implementation. The associated factors are explained, the major point being that the administrative requirements for the institution of ICL are significant, and in many cases unlikely to be met without important reform.

The Australian experience with an ICL is analyzed in depth, since this country has been the most studied in part because of its relative longevity. In administrative terms, and with respect to revenue, access and income distribution, HECS can be seen to have worked, although this does not necessarily mean that different approaches would have delivered inferior outcomes. Even so, it seems that the apparent success of HECS has contributed to the international reforms in higher education financing toward the adoption of ICL.

7.2. Suggested areas for future research

What now follows is a list of potential areas of future research. The approach is to recognize an issue, pose a research question, and offer a suggested method or approach to address the subject. The discussion follows the order of topics examined in the chapter.

(i) One of the alleged externalities from higher education investment is its contribution to economic growth. How should this issue be addressed in the context of the existing empirical growth literature, recognizing that there has been little recognition thus far of the role for economic growth of different levels of educational attainment? Suggested method: a replication of conventional approaches to GDP determinants across both countries and time [following, for example, Hanushek and Kimko (2000), and Dowrick and Nguyen (1987)], with the addition of measures of both levels of and changes in stocks of higher education levels.

(ii) Some commentators argue that graduates pay for the public sector outlays for their education through the extra tax revenue provided from the higher income tax paid by this group. What is an appropriate conceptual framework in which to understand the correct level of taxpayers' subsidies for higher education in this context? Suggested method: a modeling of the returns to both graduates and society (through taxation) of higher education investments.

(iii) Competing, perhaps extreme, interpretations of the relationship between earnings and higher education are: one, that the process simply identifies those with high ability and motivation ('screening'); and two, that higher education endows individuals with greater skills and thus higher incomes (human capital theory). What do these different perspectives imply for the extent to which taxpayers should subsidize the process? Suggested method: an examination of the literature with respect to the conceptual basis and empirical evidence concerning screening versus human capital literature, and an exploration of what the results imply for the role of externalities.

(iv) A conventional argument for government intervention in the process of higher education investment is that there is a 'capital market failure' – banks are alleged to be unprepared to provide loans to prospective students because there is a high risk of default and no collateral insurance for the lender. What is the empirical basis of this claim, and how important is the issue in an overall assessment of the supposed role for government intervention? Why should the argument be based on the unwillingness of banks to lend excluding the possible willingness of capitalists to invest? Suggested method: an examination of the conceptual basis for capital market failure and an investigation of evidence concerning the supposed reluctance of banks to provide unsecured finance (a survey and analysis of banks might be a useful research exercise in this context) and the supposed asymmetry of information between students and lenders (do students really have a better idea about their future earnings than lenders?).

(v) Case studies in political economy. What are the important factors behind a government's willingness and capacity to implement higher education financing reform? Suggested method: an examination of the importance of the institutional and political constraints concerning the adoption of ICL [see Johnstone and Aemero (2001) and Ziderman and Albrecht (1995)].

(vi) In policy design terms it is useful to develop a conceptual framework which allows the costs and benefits for the public sector of alternative approaches to be analyzed. What issues should such a framework take into consideration, and what form should it take? Suggested method: the documentation and justification of alternative government utility functions, paying attention to the rationales behind the weights and forms of their nature in the context of public choice and other theoretical frameworks.

(vii) Comparisons of the relative costs and benefits of alternative approaches for government intervention with respect to higher education financing need to address the consequences of policy design for student behavioral responses; this should canvass, among other issues, adverse selection and moral hazard. What light can economic theory cast on these issues generally, and how should this best be addressed with the use of a conceptual framework? Suggested method: the development of a model allowing analysis of student choices of the effects of different policies on graduate outcomes, taking into consideration different dimensions of risk and uncertainty [perhaps following, or comparing and contrasting, the approaches outlined in Nerlove (1975), Chia (1990), Grout (1983) and Quiggin (2003)].

(viii) The nature and form of government approaches to higher education financing will likely have important consequences for the access of those from disadvantaged backgrounds. What is the empirical evidence concerning the participation of the disadvantaged in higher education with respect to different government approaches concerning conventional financing schemes? Suggested method: an examination of panel data in particular countries with respect to the socioeconomic characteristics of disadvantaged individuals participating in higher education, specifically given the occurrence of a 'natural experiment' involving policy changes [such as adopted by Chapman and Ryan (2002)].

(ix) The reluctance of the private sector to be involved in the financing of education. What are the circumstances under which private investments exist for education? Suggested method: find a place where there is active participation of private financing of education and analyze the circumstances under which it developed.

(x) Hanushek, Leung and Yilmaz (2004) develop a general equilibrium model to analyze the effects of different college aid approaches on economic efficiency, intergenerational mobility and income inequality. However, their modeling of ICL is restricted to risk-pooling schemes, and the only type of uncertainty allowed relates to the probability of a student completing college. What outcomes would result with extensions of their approach to cover risk-sharing ICL, and with additional types of uncertainty, such as with respect to future graduate incomes?

(xi) It is likely that different types of loan schemes affect graduate career outcomes as a result of the different consequences of repayment obligations. What are the conceptual issues, and how can they best be modeled, pertinent to an understanding of job choices given expected variations in future consumption patterns as a result of the timing and nature of student debt repayment? Suggested method: the specification and analysis of different utility functions conditional on both levels and variances of future consumption patterns influenced by alternate paths of loan repayment obligations [see Browning and Crossley (2001)].

(xii) Documentation and analysis of the recent experience of countries implementing, or attempting to implement, ICL (this could be done with respect to a host of economic and policy issues, such as administration, revenue and access). What have been the effects of ICL of different forms? Suggested method: an exploration in detail of the design and (actual and likely) effects of a particular country's ICL policy, perhaps in a comparative context, with the use and improvement of the approaches taken with respect to the best documented example, Australia. There are by now many candidates warranting further research, including New Zealand, Chile, South Africa and the UK.

(xiii) An exploration of the administrative and political economy factors behind the unsuccessful implementation of ICLs in the US. Why is it that ICL policies are seemingly a successful alternative to traditional policy approaches to higher education financing in Australia, New Zealand and the UK, but have not evolved in the similar institutional environment of the US? Suggested method: an examination and documentation of both the influence and nature of US vested interests (specifically the commercial beneficiaries of student loan arrangements), and the design weaknesses of the US ICL approach. If there was to be an informed political economy analysis of the lack of success of the US scheme, it start with the role of commercial vested interests in opposing reform of this type, as implied in Schrag (2001).

(xiv) The lessons for research of the Australian experience with respect to the effects of ICL. What has been the experience of other countries' higher education financing approaches with respect to the major economic variables? Suggested method: a replication of the Australian research in countries experiencing changes to financing policy, including documentation of the consequences for internal rates of return and enrollments, revenue, and access [see Chapman and Ryan (2002)].

Acknowledgements

A version of this paper was presented at a meeting of the Handbook authors in College Station, Texas, on 22 March, 2003. The author is grateful for feedback from participants, Peter Dolton and Eric Hanushek in particular, and for suggestions from Miguel Palacios, Andrew Carver, Bruce Johnstone, Chris Ryan, Deborah Cobb-Clark, Nicholas Barr and participants at seminars given at the World Bank and the Australian Nation University. Some aspects of the discussion have drawn upon material in Chapman (2006a), Chapman (2006b), Chapman and Greenaway (2006) and Chapman and Ryan (2002). All errors remain the author's responsibility.

References

American Bar Association (2003). "Lifting the burden: Law student debt as a barrier to public service". The Final Report of the ABA Commission on Loan Repayment and Forgiveness. ABA, Chicago, IL.

Andrews, L. (1999). "The effect of HECS on access". Research report. Department of Education, Employment, Training and Youth Affairs, Canberra.

Arrow, K.J. (1973a). "Higher education as a filter". Journal of Public Economics 2 (3), 123–132.

Arrow, K. (1973b). "The theory of discrimination". In: Ashenfelter, O., Rees, A. (Eds.), Discrimination in Labor Markets. Princeton University Press, Princeton, NJ, pp. 3–33.

Aungles, P., Buchanan, I., Karmel, T., MacLachlan, M. (2002). "HECS and opportunities in higher education". Research, Analysis and Evaluation Group, Commonwealth Department of Education, Science and Training, Canberra.

Barr, N. (2001). The Welfare State as Piggy Bank. Oxford University Press, Oxford.

Barr, N., Crawford, I. (1998). "Funding higher education in an age of expansion". Education Economics 6 (1), 45–70.

Barro, R.J. (1991). "Economic growth in a cross-section of countries". Quarterly Journal of Economics 106, 407–444.

Barro, R.J., Sala-I-Martin, X. (1995). Economic Growth. McGraw-Hill, New York.

Bartel, A., Lichtenberg, F.J. (1987). "The comparative advantage of educated workers in implementing new technology". Review of Economics and Statistics 69, 1–11.

Belfield, C.R. (2000). Economic Principles for Education. Edward Elgar, UK.

Brody, E. (1994). "Paying back your country through income-contingent student loans". San Diego Law Review 31, 449–518.

Browning, M., Crossley, T.F. (2001). "The life-cycle model of consumption and savings". Journal of Economic Perspectives 80 (1, Summer), 3–22.

Cameron, S., Taber, C. (2001). "Borrowing constraints and the returns to schooling". Working Paper w7761. NBER.

Card, D. (2000). "The causal effect of education on earnings". In: Ashenfelter, O.C., Card, D. (Eds.), Handbook of Labor Economics, vol. 3. Elsevier, Amsterdam, pp. 1801–1863.

Carneiro, P., Heckman, J.J. (2002). "The evidence on credit constraints in post-secondary schooling". The Economic Journal 112 (482), 705–730.

Carver, A. (2004). Income Collateralhed Loons: Market and Policy Explorations, PhD. thesis, Stanford University.

Chapman, B. (1997). "Conceptual issues and the Australian experience with income contingent charging for higher education". The Economic Journal 107 (42), 1178–1193.

Chapman, B. (2006a). "Income related student loans: Concepts, international reforms and administrative challenges". In: Teixeira, P.N., Johnstone, D.B., Rosa, M.J., Vossensteijn, J.J. (Eds.), Cost-Sharing and Accessibility in Higher Education: A Fairer Deal? Springer-Verlag, Dordrecht, The Netherlands, pp. 79–105.

Chapman, B. (2006b). Government Managing Risk: Income Contingent Loans for the Social and Economic Progress. Routledge, London.

Chapman, B., Crossley, T.F., Kim, T. (2003). "Credit constraints and training after job loss". Centre of Economic Policy Research Discussion Paper 466. Australian National University.

Chapman, B., Fraser, B. (2000). "Reforming Rwandan higher education financing". Report to the UK Department of International Development, UK.

Chapman, B., Greenway, D. (2006). "Learning to live with loans? International policy transfer and funding of higher education". The World Economy 29 (1), 1057–1075.

Chapman, B., Ryan, C. (2002). "Income contingent financing of student higher education charges: Assessing the Australian innovation". The Welsh Journal of Education 11 (1), 64–81.

Chapman, B., Ryan, C. (2005). "The access implications of income contingent charges for higher education: Lessons from Australia". Economics of Education Review 24 (5), 491–512.

Chapman, B., Salvage, T. (1998). "Changes to Australian higher education financing from the 1996/97 budget". In: Harman, G. (Ed.), Australia's Future Universities. University of New England Press, Armidale, pp. 49–63.

Chia, T.T. (1990). "Returns to higher education in Australia". PhD. thesis. Economics Program, Research School of Social Sciences, Australian National University, Canberra.

Dearing Sir, Ron (Chairman) (1997). Higher Education in a Learning Society. UK Government, London, UK.

Dowrick, S., Nguyen, T. (1987). "OECD economic growth in the post-war period: Catch-up and convergences". American Economic Review 79 (5, December), 1010–1030.

Dynarski, M. (1994). "Who defaults on student loans? Findings from the national post secondary student aid study". Economics of Education Review 13 (1), 55–68.

Eaton, J., Rosen, H.S. (1980). "Taxation, human capital and uncertainty". American Economic Review 70 (4), 705–715.

Englebrecht, J. (2003). "Human capital and economic growth: Cross-section evidence for OECD countries". The Economic Record 79, S40–S51 (Special Issue).

Fane, G. (1975). "Education and the managerial efficiency of farmers". Review of Economics and Statistics LVII (November), 452–461.

Feldman, R. (1976). "Some more problems with income-contingent loans: The case of medical education". Journal of Political Economy 84 (6), 1305–1311.

Finnie, R., Schwartz, S. (Eds.) (1997). Student Loans in Canada Past Present and Future. C.D. Howe Institute, Toronto.

Finnie, R., Usher, A. (2006). "The Canadian experiment in cost-sharing and its effects on access to higher education, 1990–2002". In: Teixeira, P.N., Johnstone, D.B., Rosa, M.J., Vossensteijn, J.J. (Eds.), Cost-Sharing and Accessibility in Higher Education: A Fairer Deal? Springer-Verlag, Dordrecht, The Netherlands, pp. 159–188.

Freeman, R.B. (1971). The Market for College-Trained Manpower. Harvard University Press, Cambridge, MA.

Friedman, M. (1955). "The role of government in education". In: Capitalism and Freedom. Chicago University Press, Chicago, IL, pp. 123–144.

Gemmel, N. (1996). "Evaluating the impacts of human capital stocks and accumulation on economic growth: Some new evidence". Oxford Bulletin of Economics and Statistics 58, 9–28.

Greenaway, D., Haynes, M. (2003). "Funding high education in the UK: The role of fees and loans". The Economic Journal 113 (485), F150–F166.

Grout, P. (1983). "Education finance and imperfections in information". Economic and Social Review 15 (1), 25–33.

Hanushek, E.A., Kimko, D. (2000). "Schooling, labor force quality, and the growth of nations". American Economic Review 90 (December), 1184–1208.

Hanushek, E., Leung, C.K., Yilmaz, K. (2004). "Borrowing constraints, college aid, and intergenerational mobility". Working Paper 10711, August. NBER.

Harding, A. (1995). "Financing higher education: An assessment of income-contingent loan options and repayment patterns over the life cycle". Education Economics 3, 173–203.

Harrison, M. (1995). "Default in guaranteed student loan programs". Journal of Student Financial Aid 25 (2), 25–42.

Hazarika, G. (2002). "The role of credit constraints in the cyclicality of college enrollments". Education Economics 10 (2, August), 133–144.

Huffman, W.E. (1974). "Decision making: The role of education". The American Journal of Agricultural Economics (56 February), 85–97.

Hume, N. (2004). "What has been the impact of changes in the level of HECS charges on low socio-economic status participation in higher education in Australia?". Term paper. University of Sydney Bachelor of Economics course, the Economics of Education.

Ishengoma, J.M. (2002). "Financing higher education in post-apartheid South Africa: Trends, developments, and challenges ahead". The International Comparative Higher Education Finance and Accessibility Project. University of Buffalo and The State University of New York.

Jackson, R. (2002). "The South African student assistance scheme". The Welsh Journal of Education 12 (1), 63–79.

Johnstone, D.B. (1972). "The role of income-contingent loans in financing higher education". Educational Record (Spring), 161–168.

Johnstone, D.B., Aemero, A. (2001). "The applicability for developing countries of income contingent loans or graduate taxes, with special consideration of an Australian HECS-type income contingent loan program for Ethiopia". The International Comparative Higher Education Finance and Accessibility Project. Buffalo, NY.

Kane, T., Rouse, C. (1999). "The community college: Educating students at the margin between college and work". Journal of Economic Perspectives 13 (1), 63–84.

Kramer, J.R. (1987). "Will legal education remain affordable, by whom, and how?". Duke Law Journal (240), 242–268.

Krueger, N. (1999). Education Matters. Princeton University Press, Princeton, NJ.

LaRocque, N. (2005). "The New Zealand student loan scheme". A Presentation to the KEDU World Bank International Forum Financing Reforms for Tertiary Education in the Knowledge Economy, Seoul, the Republic of Korea, April.

Leiva, A. (2002). "El financiamiento estudiantil para la educacion superior". Cobecion Ideas 3 (2). Santiago: Fundacion Chile 21.

Levhari, D., Weiss, Y. (1974). "The effect of risk on the investment in human capital". American Economic Review 64 (6), 950–963.

Lincoln, I., Walker, A. (1995). "Graduate taxes as an answer to higher education financing". Education Economics 1 (3), 211–226.

Long, M., Carpenter, P., Hayden, M. (1999). "Participation in education and training: 1980–1994". Longitudinal Surveys of Australian Youth Research Report No. 13. Australian Council for Educational Research, Melbourne.

Lucas, R.E. (1988). "On the mechanics of development". Journal of Monetary Economics 22, 3–42.

Maani, S.A., Warner, A. (2000). "The economic implications of tertiary fee rises in relation to student welfare and the policy environment". Report to the University of Auckland Council. Auckland, July.

McMahon, W.W. (1999). Education and Development: Measuring the Social Benefits. Oxford University Press, Oxford.

Marks, G.N., Fleming, N., Long, M., McMillan, J. (2000). "Patterns of participation in year 12 and higher education in Australia: Trends and issues". Longitudinal Surveys of Australian Youth, Research Report No. 17. ACER, Melbourne.

Mincer, J. (1974). Schooling, Experience and Earnings. Columbia University Press, New York.

Moen, E.R. (1998). "Efficient ways to finance human capital investments". Economica 65, 491–505.

Morris, M. (1989). "Student aid in Sweden: Recent experience and reforms". In: Woodhall, M. (Ed.), Financial Support for Students: Grants Loans or Graduate Tax? Kogan Page, London, pp. 85–109.

Nerlove, M. (1975). "Some problems in the use of income-contingent loans for the finance of higher education". Journal of Political Economy 83 (1), 157–183.

Palacios, M. (2004). Investing in Human Capital: A Capital Markets Approach to Higher Education Funding. Cambridge University Press, Cambridge.

Paroush, J. (1976). "The risk effect and investment in human capital". European Economic Review 8, 339–347.

Psacharopoulos, G. (1973). Returns to Education: An International Comparison. Elsevier, Amsterdam.

Psacharopoulos, G. (1985). "Returns to education: A further international update and implications". Journal of Human Resources 20 (4), 583–597.

Quiggin, J. (2003). "The welfare effects of income-contingent financing of higher education". Faculty of Economics Working Paper No. 428. Australian National University, Canberra.

Raymond, R., Sesnowitz, M. (1976). "On the repayment burden of income-contingent student loans". Public Policy 24 (3), 423–436.

Roman, D. (2003). "Higher education and income in Mexico". Mimeo. Universidad Tecnologica de Mexico, MEX.

Romer, P.M. (1994). "The origins of endogenous growth". Journal of Economic Perspectives 8 (1), 3–22.

Salmi, J. (1999). "Student loans in an international perspective: The World Bank experience". The World Bank.

Schrag, P.G. (2001). "The federal income-contingent repayment option for law student loans". Hofstra Law Review 29, 733–862.

Schultz, T.W. (1975). "The value of the ability to deal with disequilibria". Journal of Economic Literature 13 (3, September), 827–843.

Teixeira, P.N., Johnstone, D.B., Rosa, M.J., Vossensteijn, J.J (Eds.) (2006). Cost-Sharing and Accessibility in Higher Education: A Fairer Deal? Springer-Verlag, Dordrecht, The Netherlands.

Warner, A. (1999). "Student loans in New Zealand". Master of Commerce thesis. University of Auckland, Auckland.

World Bank Sector Study (2003). Higher Education Development for Ethiopia: Pursuing the Vision, January.

Wozniak, G.D. (1987). "Human capital, information and the early adoption of new technology". Journal of Human Resources 22, 101–112.

Wran Committee Report (1988). "Report of the Committee on Financing Higher Education (1988)". Australian Government Printing Service, Canberra.

Ziderman, A., Albrecht, D. (1995). Financing Universities in Developing Countries. The Stanford Series on Education and Public Policy, vol. 16. The Falmer Press, Washington.

AUTHOR INDEX

n indicates citation in a footnote.

SUBJECT INDEX